Dedication

To our son Andrew—who keeps us smiling.

Introduction to Epidemiology

Si

M. Merrill,

Professor

ment of Health

Brigham Young University
Provo, Utah

JONES & BARTLETT
LEARNING

World Headquarters
Jones & Bartlett Learning
5 Wall Street
Burlington, MA 01803
978-443-5000
info@jblearning.com
www.jblearning.com

Jones & Bartlett Learning books and products are available through most bookstores and online booksellers. To contact Jones & Bartlett Learning directly, call 800-832-0034, fax 978-443-8000, or visit our website, www.jblearning.com.

Substantial discounts on bulk quantities of Jones & Bartlett Learning publications are available to corporations, professional associations, and other qualified organizations. For details and specific discount information, contact the special sales department at Jones & Bartlett Learning via the above contact information or send an email to specialsales@jblearning.com.

Production Credits
Publisher: Michael Brown
Managing Editor: Maro Gartside
Editorial Assistant: Kayla Dos Santos
Editorial Assistant: Chloe Falivene
Associate Production Editor: Rebekah Linga
Senior Marketing Manager: Sophie Fleck Teague
Manufacturing and Inventory Control Supervisor: Amy Bacus
Composition: Lapiz Online
Cover Design: Michael O'Donnell
Cover Image: © Yalik/ShutterStock, Inc.
Printing and Binding: Edwards Brothers Malloy
Cover Printing: Edwards Brothers Malloy

To order this product, use ISBN: 978-1-4496-6548-7

Library of Congress Cataloging-in-Publication Data
Merrill, Ray M.
 Introduction to epidemiology. — 6th ed. / Ray M. Merrill.
    p. ; cm.
 Includes bibliographical references and index.
 SBN 978-1-4496-4517-5 (paper) -- ISBN 1-4496-4517-8 (paper)
 I. Title.
 [DNLM: 1. Epidemiologic Methods. 2. Epidemiology. WA 950]

 614.4—dc23
                                2012012911
6048

Printed in the United States of America
17 16 15 14 13   10 9 8 7 6 5 4 3 2

Table of Contents

About the Author

Ray M. Merrill, PhD, MPH, MS, is a professor of epidemiology and biostatistics at Brigham Young University. He is also an adjunct professor in the Department of Family and Preventive Medicine and the Department of Health Promotion and Education at the University of Utah. He is a former Cancer Prevention Fellow at the U.S. National Cancer Institute and a visiting scientist in the Unit of Epidemiology for Cancer Prevention at the International Agency for Research on Cancer, Lyon, France. He has won several awards for his research in epidemiology and is currently a Fellow of the American College of Epidemiology and of the American Academy of Health Behavior. He teaches classes in epidemiology and biostatistics and is the author of over 200 peer-reviewed publications and five books.

Preface

The field of epidemiology has come a long way since the days of infectious disease investigations by scientists such as Louis Pasteur, Robert Koch, and John Snow. Historically, the main causes of death were due to a single pathogen, a single cause of disease. Epidemiologists had the challenge of isolating a single bacterium, virus, or parasite. In modern times, advances in nutrition, housing conditions, sanitation, water supply, antibiotics, and immunization programs have resulted in a decrease in various infectious diseases but an increase in many noninfectious diseases and conditions. Consequently, the scope of epidemiology has expanded to include the study of acute and chronic noninfectious diseases and conditions. Advances in biology, medicine, statistics, and social and behavioral sciences have greatly aided epidemiologic study.

This book was written as an introductory epidemiology text for the student who has minimal training in the biomedical sciences and statistics. *Introduction to Epidemiology* is based on the premise that the advanced analyses of empirical research studies, using advanced statistical methods, are more akin to biostatistics than epidemiology and, therefore, receive less attention in this book. Many recent books bearing the title of epidemiology are in fact biostatistics books, with limited information on the basics of epidemiological investigations or the study of epidemics. Epidemiology is unique from biostatistics in that emphasis is placed on completing the causal picture in human populations. Identifying causal factors and modes of transmission, with the assistance of statistical tools and biomedical information, reflect the primary aim of epidemiology. This book maintains that focus.

Chapter 1 presents the foundations of epidemiology, including definitions, concepts, and applications. Chapter 2 covers historical developments in epidemiology. Chapter 3 looks at several important disease concepts in epidemiology. Chapters 4 through 6 focus on descriptive epidemiology. Several design strategies and statistical measures are presented. Chapter 7 presents design strategies and statistical methods used in analytic epidemiology. Chapter 8 covers design strategies and ethical issues relevant to experimental studies. Chapter 9 considers the basics of causal inference. Chapter 10 focuses on basic concepts and approaches used in field epidemiology. Chapter 11 presents chronic disease epidemiology. Chapter 12 presents epidemiology in clinical settings.

New to the Sixth Edition

The sixth edition of this classic text, like its previous editions, continues its mission of providing a comprehensive introduction to the field of epidemiology. Emphasis is placed on the application of the basic principles of epidemiology according to person, place, and time factors in order to solve current, often unexpected, and serious public health problems. Direction is given for how to identify and describe public health problems, formulate research hypotheses, select appropriate research study designs, manage and analyze epidemiologic data, interpret study results, and apply the results in preventing and controlling disease and health-related events. Real-world public health problems involving both infectious and chronic diseases and conditions are presented throughout the book.

Additions to this edition include a greater emphasis on epidemiology in international settings, additional study questions, expanded conclusions, as well as updated tables, figures, and examples throughout the text. Specific additions include a presentation of country-specific leading causes of death by income level; the important contributions to epidemiology by Alice Hamilton, Wade Hampton Frost, and Janet Lane-Claypon; clarification of allergies and inflammatory diseases and a description of *Healthy People* initiatives, with focus on the 12 *Healthy People 2020* topic areas and associated health indicators; a description of how to compute a confidence interval for the standardized morbidity ratio; a revised section on population pyramids; a new section on death-to-case ratios; a new section on misclassification for case-control and cohort studies; descriptions of prophylactic trials and diagnostic and screening studies; a new section on pilot studies, and a presentation of three principles to guide research that involves human subjects (i.e., respect for persons, beneficence, and justice); a new section on statistical inference; a new section on preparing for fieldwork in a field investigation; and new material on mass screening and selective screening.

This sixth edition offers an easy and effective approach to learning epidemiology, including case reports and news files. The case reports and news files represent applications of commonly used research designs in epidemiology. The chapter topics were selected to represent the fundamentals of epidemiology. Learning objectives are presented at the beginning of each chapter, and the chapters are divided into concise sections with several examples. Figures and tables are used to summarize and clarify important concepts and information. Key terms are bolded in the text and defined. Study questions with descriptive answers are provided at the end of each chapter.

Introduction

Epidemiology is a fun and challenging subject to study, as well as an interesting field to pursue as a career. Most undergraduate and graduate degree programs in public health, environmental health, occupational health and industrial hygiene, health education and health promotion, health services administration, nursing, and other health-related disciplines require a basic introductory course in epidemiology. *Introduction to Epidemiology* covers the fundamentals of epidemiology for students and practitioners. It is hoped that this book will be a useful and practical source of information and direction for students of epidemiology in the classroom and for those practicing epidemiology in the field. Readers of this book may be specialists in international projects in developing countries, industrial hygienists within major industrial plants, infectious disease nurses in hospitals and medical centers, chronic disease epidemiologists in government agencies, behavioral scientists conducting health epidemiological investigations, or staff epidemiologists in local public health departments.

1

Foundations of Epidemiology

OBJECTIVES

After completing this chapter, you will be able to:

- Define epidemiology.
- Define descriptive epidemiology.
- Define analytic epidemiology.
- Identify selected activities performed in epidemiology.
- Explain the role of epidemiology in public health practice and individual decision making.
- Define epidemic, endemic, and pandemic.
- Describe common source, propagated, and mixed epidemics.
- Describe why a standard case definition and adequate levels of reporting are important in epidemiologic investigations.
- Describe the epidemiology triangle for infectious disease.
- Describe selected models for chronic diseases and behavioral disorders.
- Define the three levels of prevention used in public health and epidemiology.
- Understand the basic vocabulary used in epidemiology.

Public health is concerned with threats to the population's health. Important subfields of public health include epidemiology, biostatistics, and health services. Epidemiology is commonly referred to as the foundation of public health because it is a study that aids our understanding of the nature, extent, and cause of public health problems, and provides important information for improving the health and social conditions of people. Epidemiology has a population focus in that epidemiologic investigations are concerned with the collective health of the people in a group of individuals who share one or more observable personal or observational characteristic. Geographic, social, family (marriage, divorce), work and labor, and economic factors may characterize populations. In contrast, a clinician is concerned for the health of an individual. The clinician focuses on treating and caring for the patient, whereas the epidemiologist focuses on identifying the source or exposure of disease, disability or death, the number of persons exposed, and the potential for further spread. The clinician treats the patient based on scientific knowledge, experience, and clinical judgment, whereas the epidemiologist uses descriptive and analytical epidemiologic methods to provide information that will ultimately help determine the appropriate public health action to control and prevent the health problem.

Epidemiology is defined as the study of the distribution and determinants of health-related states or events in human populations and the application of this study to the prevention and control of health problems.[1] The word epidemiology is based on the Greek words epi, a prefix meaning "on, upon, or befall"; demos, a root meaning "the people"; and logos, a suffix meaning "the study of." In accordance with medical terminology, the suffix is read first and then the prefix and the root. Thus, the word epidemiology taken literally refers to the study of that which befalls people. As such, epidemiology is commonly referred to as the basic science or foundation of public health.

Epidemiology involves sound methods of scientific investigation. Epidemiologic investigations involve descriptive and analytic methods that draw on statistical techniques for describing data and evaluating hypotheses, biological principles, and causal theory. Descriptive epidemiology involves characterization of the distribution of health-related states or events. **Analytic epidemiology** involves finding and quantifying associations, testing hypotheses, and identifying causes of health-related states or events.[2]

The study of the distribution of health-related states or events involves identifying the frequency and pattern of the public health problem among people in the population. Frequency refers to the number of health-related states or events and their relationship with the size of the population. Typically, the number of cases or deaths is more meaningful when considered in reference to the size of the corresponding population, especially when comparing risks of disease among groups. For example, despite differences in population sizes across time or among regions, meaningful comparisons can be made of the burden of HIV/AIDS by using proportions or percentages. In 2008, HIV prevalence was 7.8% in Kenya, 16.9% in South Africa, and 25% in Botswana.[3]

Pattern refers to describing health-related states or events by who is experiencing the health-related state or event (person), where the occurrence of the state or event is highest or lowest (place), and when the state or event occurs most or least (time). In other words, epidemiologists are interested in identifying the people involved and why these people are affected and not others, where the people are affected and why in this place and not others, and when the state or event occurred and why at this time and not others.

For example, in 1981 the Centers for Disease Control and Prevention (CDC) reported that five young men went to three different hospitals in Los Angeles, California with confirmed *Pneumocystis carinii* pneumonia. These men were all identified as homosexuals.[4] On July 27, 1982, this illness was called AIDS, and in 1983, the Institute Pasteur in France found the human immunodeficiency virus, which causes AIDS.[5]

Identifying the determinants or causes of health-related states or events is a primary function of epidemiology. A cause is a specific event, condition, or characteristic that precedes the health outcome and is necessary for its occurrence. An adverse health outcome can be prevented by eliminating the exposure. If an environmental exposure is required for the health outcome to occur, the causative factor is "necessary." If the health-related state or event always occurs because of the exposure, the causative factor is "sufficient." For example, a mother's exposure to rubella virus (*Rubivirus*) is necessary for rubella to occur; however, exposure to rubella virus is not sufficient to cause rubella because not everyone infected develops the disease.

Identifying causal associations is complex and typically requires making a "judgment" based on the totality of evidence, such as a valid statistical association, time sequence of events, biologic credibility, and consistency among studies. A step towards understanding causation is to identify relevant risk factors. A risk factor is a behavior, environmental exposure, or inherent human characteristic that is associated with an important health condition.[6] In other words, a risk factor is a condition that is associated with the increased probability of a health-related state or event. For example, smoking is a risk factor for chronic diseases such as heart disease, stroke, and several cancers (including cancers of the oral cavity and pharynx, esophagus, pancreas, larynx, lung and bronchus, urinary bladder, kidney and renal pelvis, and cervix).[7-10] A risk factor is typically not sufficient to cause a disease, but other contributing factors, such as personal susceptibility, are also required before a disease occurs.

The term "health-related states or events" is used in the definition of epidemiology to capture the fact that epidemiology involves more than just the study of disease (e.g., cholera, influenza, pneumonia); it also includes the study of events (e.g., injury, drug abuse, and suicide) and of behaviors and conditions associated with health (e.g., physical activity, nutrition, seat belt use, and provision and use of health services).

Epidemiology not only involves the study of the distribution and determinants of health-related states or events in human populations, but it also involves the application of this study to the prevention and control of health problems. Results of epidemiologic investigations can provide public health officials with information related to who is at greatest risk for disease, where the disease is most common, when the disease occurs most frequently, and what public health programs might be most effective. Such information may lead to more efficient resource allocation and to more appropriate application of health programs designed to educate the public and prevent and control disease. Epidemiologic information can also assist individuals in making informed decisions about their health behavior.

ACTIVITIES IN EPIDEMIOLOGY

An epidemiologist studies the occurrence of disease or other health-related events in specified populations, practices epidemiology, and controls disease.[1] Epidemiologists may be involved in a range of activities, such as:

■ Identifying risk factors for disease, injury, and death
■ Describing the natural history of disease
■ Identifying individuals and populations at greatest risk for disease
■ Identifying where the public health problem is greatest
■ Monitoring diseases and other health-related events over time

- Evaluating the efficacy and effectiveness of prevention and treatment programs
- Providing information that is useful in health planning and decision making for establishing health programs with appropriate priorities
- Assisting in carrying out public health programs
- Being a resource person
- Communicating public health information

The interdependence of these activities is evident. For example, carrying out an intervention program requires clearance from an institutional review board and often other organizations and agencies. As is also the case for funding agencies, these groups require quantifiable justification of needs and of the likelihood of success. This presupposes that the risk factors are known, that there is an understanding of the natural history of the disease, and that there are answers to the questions of person, place, and time, as well as some evidence of the probable success of the intervention. Being a resource person in this process requires a good understanding of the health problem as it relates to the individual and community; the rationale and justification for intervention, along with corresponding goals and objectives; and an ability to communicate in a clear and concise manner.[11] All of this implies a good understanding of epidemiologic methods.

In their professional work, the focus of epidemiology may be on the environment, social issues, mental health, infectious disease, cancer, reproductive health, and so on. Epidemiologists are employed by the appropriate health agencies at all levels of local, state, and federal government. They find careers in healthcare organizations, private and voluntary health organizations, hospitals, military organizations, private industry, and in academics.

ROLE OF EPIDEMIOLOGY IN PUBLIC HEALTH PRACTICE

Epidemiologic information plays an important role in meeting public health objectives aimed at promoting physical, mental, and social well-being in the population. Epidemiologic findings contribute to preventing and controlling disease, injury, disability, and death by providing information that leads to informed public health policy and planning as well as individual health decision making. Some useful information provided to health policy officials and individuals through epidemiology is listed in Table 1-1.

Public health assessment identifies if, where, and when health problems occur and serves as a guide to public health planning, policy making, and resource allocation. The state of health of the population should be compared with the availability, effectiveness, and efficiency of current health services. Most areas of the United States have surveillance systems that monitor the morbidity and mortality of the community by person, place, and time. Public health surveillance has been defined as the ongoing systematic collection, analysis, interpretation, and dissemination of health data.[12] Surveillance information about disease epidemics, breakdowns in vaccination or prevention programs, and health disparities among special populations is important for initiating and guiding action.

Accurate assessment requires standard case definitions and adequate levels of reporting. A **case** is a person who has been diagnosed with a health-related state or event. A standard set of criteria, or **case definition**, ensures that cases are consistently diagnosed, regardless of where or when they were identified and who diagnosed the case. Higher levels of reporting ensure accurate representation of the health problem; however, even low levels

TABLE 1-1   Epidemiologic Information Useful for Public Health Policy and Planning and Individual Decision Making

1. Assessment
   - Identify who is at greatest risk for experiencing the public health problem
   - Identify where the public health problem is greatest
   - Identify when the public health problem is greatest
   - Monitor potential exposures over time
   - Monitor intervention-related health outcomes over time

2. Cause
   - Identify the primary agents associated with disease, disorders, or conditions
   - Identify the mode of transmission
   - Combine laboratory evidence with epidemiologic findings

3. Clinical picture
   - Identify who is susceptible to the disease
   - Identify the types of exposures capable of causing the disease
   - Describe the pathologic changes that occur, the stage of subclinical disease, and the expected length of this subclinical phase of the disease
   - Identify the types of symptoms that characterize the disease
   - Identify probable outcomes (recovery, disability, or death) associated with different levels of the disease

4. Evaluate
   - Identify the efficacy of the public health program
   - Measure the effectiveness of the public health program

of reporting can provide important information as to the existence and potential problems of a given health state or event.

When evaluating a prevention or control program, both the efficacy and the effectiveness of the program should be considered. Although these terms are related, they have distinct meanings. **Efficacy** refers to the ability of a program to produce a desired effect among those who participate in the program compared with those who do not.[13] **Effectiveness**, on the other hand, refers to the ability of a program to produce benefits among those who are offered the program.[13] For example, suppose a strict dietary intervention program is designed to aid in the recovery process of heart attack patients. If those who comply with the program have much better recoveries than those who do not, the program is efficacious; however, if compliance is low because of, for example, the amount, cost, and types of foods involved in the program, the program is not effective. Similarly, a physical activity program involving skiing could be efficacious, but the cost of skiing and the technical skills associated with it may make it ineffective in the general public. Finally, it must be taken into account that the administration of some interventions might require the presence of individuals with advanced medical training and technically advanced equipment. In certain communities, a lack of available health resources may limit the availability of such programs, making them ineffective even though they may be efficacious.

EPIDEMICS, ENDEMICS, AND PANDEMICS

Historically, epidemiology was developed in order to investigate epidemics of infectious disease. An **epidemic** is the occurrence of cases of an illness, specific health-related behavior, or other health-related events clearly in excess of normal expectancy in a community or region.[1] Public health officials often use the term outbreak, which is used synonymously with epidemic, but actually refers to an epidemic confined to a localized area.[6] An epidemic may result from exposure to a common source at a point in time or through intermittent or continuous exposure over days, weeks, or years. An epidemic may also result from exposure propagated through gradual spread from host to host. It is possible for an epidemic to originate from a common source and then, by secondary spread, be communicated from person to person.

The word "**endemic**" refers to the ongoing, usual, or constant presence of a disease in a community or among a group of people; a disease is said to be endemic when it continually prevails in a region.[1] For example, although influenza follows a seasonal trend with the highest number of cases in the winter months, it is considered endemic if the pattern is consistent from year to year. A **pandemic** is an epidemic affecting or attacking the population of an extensive region, country, or continent.[1]

Several epidemics of cholera have been reported since the early 1800s. In 1816, an epidemic of cholera occurred in Bengal, India and then became pandemic as it spread across India, extending as far as China and the Caspian Sea before receding in 1826.[14] Other cholera epidemics that also became pandemic involved Europe and North America (1829–1851), Russia (1852–1860), Europe and Africa (1863–1875), Europe and Russia (1899–1923), and Indonesia, El Tor, Bangladesh (India), and the Union of Soviet Socialist Republics (1961–1966).[14] Examples of case reports of cholera, provided by John Snow, along with descriptions of two cholera epidemics investigated by Snow, are presented in Case Study I: Snow on Cholera (**Appendix I**).

In the United States, cholera is now classified as an endemic disease. From 1992 to 1999, the annual numbers of cases reported were 103, 25, 39, 23, 4, 6, 17, and 6, respectively.[15] Other examples of diseases classified now as endemic in the United States include botulism, brucellosis, and plague.

Epidemics are often described by how they spread through the population. Two primary types of infectious-disease epidemics are common-source and propagated epidemics. **Common-source epidemics** arise from a specific source, whereas **propagated epidemics** arise from infections transmitted from one infected person to another. Transmission can occur through direct or indirect routes. Common-source epidemics tend to result in cases occurring more rapidly during the initial phase than do host-to-host epidemics. Identifying the common source of exposure and removing it typically causes the epidemic to abate rapidly. On the other hand, host-to-host epidemics rise and fall more slowly. Some examples of common-source epidemic diseases are anthrax, traced to milk or meat from infected animals; botulism, traced to soil-contaminated food; and cholera, traced to fecal contamination of food and water. Some examples of propagated epidemic diseases are tuberculosis, whooping cough, influenza, and measles.

In some diseases, natural immunity or death can decrease the susceptible population. Resistance to the disease can also occur with treatment or immunization, both of which reduce susceptibility. Disease transmission is usually a result of direct person-to-person contact or of contact with a fomite or vector. Syphilis and other sexually transmitted diseases (STDs) are examples of direct transmission. Hepatitis B and HIV/AIDS in needle-sharing drug users are examples of **vehicle-borne transmission**. Malaria spread by mosquitoes is an example of vector-borne transmission.

Some disease outbreaks may have both common-source and propagated epidemic features. A **mixed epidemic** occurs when victims of a common-source epidemic have person-to-person contact with others and spread the disease, resulting in a propagated outbreak. In some cases, it is difficult to determine which came first. During the mid-1980s, at the beginning of the AIDS epidemic in San Francisco, HIV spread rapidly in bathhouses. Homosexual men had sexual contact before entering the bathhouses, yet the bathhouses would be considered the common source aspect of the epidemic, and the person-to-person spread through sexual intercourse would be the source of direct transmission. Direct disease transmission from person-to-person contact occurred in some individuals before and after entering a bathhouse. The bathhouses (the common source) were clearly a point for public health intervention and control, and thus, the bathhouses were closed in an attempt to slow the epidemic.

CASE CONCEPTS IN EPIDEMIOLOGY

When an epidemic is confirmed and the epidemiology investigation begins, one activity of the epidemiologist is to look for and examine cases of the disease. Any individual in a population group identified as having a particular disease, disorder, injury, or condition is considered a case. A clinical record of an individual, or someone identified in a screening process, or from a survey of the population or general data registry can also be an epidemiologic case. Thus, the epidemiologic definition of a case is broader than the clinical definition because a variety of criteria can be used to identify cases in epidemiology.

In an epidemic, the first disease case in the population is the **primary case**. The first disease case brought to the attention of the epidemiologist is the **index case**. The index case is not always the primary case. Those persons who become infected and ill after a disease has been introduced into a population and who become infected from contact with the primary case are **secondary cases**. A **suspect case** is an individual (or a group of individuals) who has all of the signs and symptoms of a disease or condition yet has not been diagnosed as having the disease, or has the cause of the symptoms connected to a suspected **pathogen** (i.e., any virus, bacteria, fungus, or parasite).[1] For example, a cholera outbreak could be in progress, and a person could have vomiting and diarrhea, symptoms consistent with cholera. This is a suspect case as the presence of cholera bacteria in the person's body has not been confirmed, and the disease has not been definitely identified as cholera because it could be one of the other gastrointestinal diseases, such as salmonella food poisoning.

As indicated previously, since epidemics occur across time and in different places, each case must be described in exactly the same way each time in order to standardize disease investigations. As cases occur in each separate epidemic, they must be described and diagnosed consistently—and with the same diagnostic criteria—from case to case. When standard disease diagnosis criteria are used by all the people assisting in outbreak investigations, the epidemiologist can compare the numbers of cases of a disease that occur in one outbreak (numbers of new cases in a certain place and time) with those in different outbreaks of the same disease (cases from different epidemics in different places and times). Computerized laboratory analysis that is now available, even in remote communities, has enhanced the ability of those involved to arrive at a case-specific definition. With advanced computer-assisted support directly and quickly available from the CDC, case definitions of almost all diseases have become extremely accurate and specific.

Different levels of diagnosis (suspect, probable, or confirmed) are generally used by the physician who is assisting in epidemic investigations. As more information (such as laboratory results) becomes available to the physician, the physician generally upgrades the diagnosis. When all criteria are met for the case definition, the case is classified as a con-firmed case. If the case definition is not matched, then the exposed person is labeled "not a case," and other possible diseases are considered until the case definition fits. Elaborate diagnoses are not always needed in those epidemics in which obvious symptoms can be quickly seen, such as measles and chicken pox.

If people become ill enough to require hospitalization, the severity of the illness is of concern. **Case severity** is found by looking at several variables that are effective measures of it. One such measure is the average length of stay in a hospital. The longer the hospital stay the greater the severity of the illness. Subjectively, severity is also measured by how dis-abling or debilitating the illness is, the chances of recovery, how long the person is ill, and how much care the person needs.[16–19]

THE EPIDEMIOLOGY TRIANGLE

When the colonists settled America, they introduced smallpox to the Native Americans. Epidemics became rampant, and entire tribes died as a result. In the 1500s, the entire native population of the island of Jamaica died when smallpox was introduced. Poor sanitation and basic knowledge of disease, the low levels of immunity, the various modes of transmis-sion, and the environmental conditions all allowed such epidemics to run wild and wipe out entire populations. A multitude of epidemiologic circumstances allowed such epidemics to happen. The interrelatedness of four epidemiologic factors often contributed to an out-break of a disease: (1) the role of the host; (2) the agent or disease-causing organism; (3) the environmental circumstances needed for a disease to thrive, survive, and spread; and (4) time-related issues.

The traditional triangle of epidemiology is shown in Figure 1-1. This triangle is based on the communicable disease model and is useful in showing the interaction and interde-pendence of the agent, host, environment, and time as used in the investigation of diseases and epidemics. The **agent** is the cause of the disease; the **host** is an organism, usually a human or an animal, that harbors the disease; the **environment** includes those surround-ings and conditions external to the human or animal that cause or allow disease transmis-sion; and **time** accounts for incubation periods, life expectancy of the host or the pathogen, and duration of the course of the illness or condition.

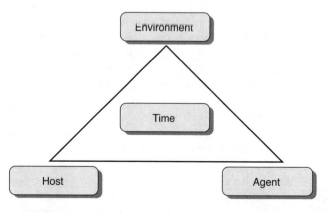

FIGURE 1-1   The triangle of epidemiology.

Agents of infectious disease include bacteria, viruses, parasites, fungi, and molds. With regard to noninfectious disease, disability, injury, or death, agents can include chemicals from dietary foods, tobacco smoke, solvents, radiation or heat, nutritional deficiencies, or other substances, such as rattlesnake poison. One or several agents may contribute to an illness.

A host offers subsistence and lodging for a pathogen and may or may not develop the disease. The level of immunity, genetic makeup, level of exposure, state of health, and overall fitness of the host can determine the effect a disease organism will have on it. The makeup of the host and the ability of the pathogen to accept the new environment can also be a determining factor because some pathogens only thrive under limited ideal conditions. For example, many infectious disease agents can exist only in a limited temperature range.

Environmental factors can include biological aspects as well as physical stresses (excessive heat, cold, and noise; radiation and vehicular collisions; workplace injuries; and so on), chemicals (drugs, acids, alkali, heavy metals, poisons, and some enzymes), and psychosocial milieu (families and households, socioeconomic status, social networks and social support, neighborhoods and communities, formal institutions, and public health policy). The surroundings in which a pathogen lives and the effect the surroundings have on it are a part of the environment. The environment can be within a host or external to it in the community. Finally, time includes severity of illness in relation to how long a person is infected or until the condition causes death or passes the threshold of danger toward recovery. Delays in time from infection to when symptoms develop, duration of illness, and threshold of an epidemic in a population are time elements with which the epidemiologist is concerned.

The primary mission of epidemiology is to provide information that results in breaking one of the legs of the triangle, thereby disrupting the connection among environment, host, and agent, and stopping the outbreak. On the basis of epidemiologic information, public health efforts are able to prevent and control health-related states and events. For example, airplanes are often used to spray the watery breeding places (environment) of mosquitoes in an effort to kill the vector of diseases such as malaria, St. Louis encephalitis, and yellow fever.

SOME DISEASE TRANSMISSION CONCEPTS

Several disease transmission concepts that relate to or influence the epidemiology triangle are fomites, vectors, reservoirs, and carriers.

A **fomite** is an object such as a piece of clothing, a door handle, or utensil that can harbor an infectious agent and is capable of being a means of transmission.[1] Fomites are common routes of infection in hospital settings. Routes in which pathogens are passed between people may include a stethoscope, an IV drip tube, or a catheter. Sterilization of these types of objects can help prevent hospital-acquired infections.

A **vector** is an invertebrate animal (e.g., tick, mite, mosquito, bloodsucking fly) that is capable of transmitting an infectious agent among vertebrates.[1] A vector can spread an infectious agent from an infected animal or human to other susceptible animals or humans through its waste products, bite or body fluids, or indirectly through food contamination. Transmission may be either mechanical (i.e., the agent does not multiply or undergo physiologic changes in the vector) or biological (i.e., the agent undergoes part of its life cycle inside the vector before being transmitted to a new host).

A **reservoir** is the habitat (living or nonliving) in or on which an infectious agent lives, grows, and multiplies, and on which it depends for its survival in nature.[1,2] As infectious organisms reproduce in the reservoir, they do so in a manner that allows disease to be transmitted to a susceptible host. Humans often serve as both reservoir and host. **Zoonosis** is an infectious organism in vertebrate animals (e.g., rabies or anthrax) that can be transmitted to humans through direct contact, a fomite, or a vector. The World Health Organization states that zoonoses are those diseases and infections that are transmitted between vertebrate animals and humans.[20]

A **vehicle** is a nonliving intermediary such as a fomite, food, or water that conveys the infectious agent from its reservoir to a susceptible host.

A **carrier** contains, spreads, or harbors an infectious organism. The infected person (or animal) harboring the disease-producing organism often lacks discernible clinical manifestation of the disease; nevertheless, the person or animal serves as a potential source of infection and disease transmission to other humans (or animals). For example, rodents or coyotes are often carriers of bubonic plague. Fleas serve as vectors in transmitting this disease to humans. The carrier condition can exist throughout the entire course of a disease if it is not treated, and its presence can be unapparent because the carrier may not be sick (healthy carriers). Some people can even be carriers for their entire lives. An example of this is Mary Mallon (Typhoid Mary), who was an asymptomatic carrier of the pathogen typhoid bacilli. Unfortunately, she worked as a cook, thereby contaminating the food she prepared. She was responsible for 51 cases and 3 deaths. Had she lived in modern times, antibiotics would have been effective treatment for Mary Mallon.[21,22] Tuberculosis is another example of a disease that is commonly known to have carriers.

Carriers have been found to have several different conditions or states. Traditionally, five types of carriers have been identified by the public health and medical fields:

1. **Active carrier.** Individual who has been exposed to and harbors a disease-causing organism (pathogen) and who has done so for some time, even though they may have recovered from the disease.

2. **Convalescent carrier.** Individual who harbors a pathogen and who, although in the recovery phase of the course of the disease, is still infectious.

3. **Healthy carrier** (also called **passive carriers**). Individual who has been exposed to and harbors a pathogen but has not become ill or shown any of the symptoms of the disease. This could be referred to as a subclinical case.

4. **Incubatory carrier.** Individual who has been exposed to and harbors a pathogen, is in the beginning stages of the disease, is displaying symptoms, and has the ability to transmit the disease.

5. **Intermittent carrier.** Individual who has been exposed to and harbors a pathogen and who can spread the disease in different places or intervals.[23,24]

MODES OF DISEASE TRANSMISSION

The two general **modes of disease transmission** include direct transmission and indirect transmission.

Direct transmission is the direct and immediate transfer of an agent from a host/reservoir to a susceptible host. Direct transmission can occur through direct physical contact (see Exhibit 1-1 [later in this chapter]), such as exposure to a person or animal or its waste products. Examples of direct transmission include mucous membrane to mucous membrane (STDs), skin-to-skin (herpes type 1, anthrax from direct contact with an infected animal), across placenta (toxoplasmosis), fecal-oral, and ingestion of infected food (trichinosis).

Indirect transmission occurs when an agent is transferred or carried by some intermediate item, organism, means, or process to a susceptible host, resulting in disease. Air currents, dust particles, water, food, oral–fecal contact, and other mechanisms that effectively transfer disease-causing organisms are means of indirect disease transmission. **Airborne transmission** occurs when droplets or dust particles carry the pathogen to the host and cause infection. This may result when a person sneezes, coughs, or talks, spraying microscopic pathogen-carrying droplets into the air that can be breathed in by nearby susceptible hosts. It also occurs when droplets are carried through a building's heating or air conditioning ducts or are spread by fans throughout a building or complex of buildings. **Vector-borne transmission** is when an arthropod (such as a mosquito, flea, or tick) conveys the infections agent. **Vehicle-borne transmission** is related to fomites, food, or water that acts as conveyance. For example, this occurs when a pathogen such as cholera or shigellosis is carried in drinking water, swimming pools, streams, or lakes used for swimming.

Some epidemiologists classify droplet spread as direct transmission because it usually takes place within a few feet of the susceptible host. Logically, however, the droplets from a sneeze or cough use the intermediary mechanism of the droplet to carry the pathogen; thus, it is an indirect transmission. This is also a form of person-to-person transmission, and influenza and the common cold are commonly spread this way. Droplets can also be spread by air-moving equipment and air-circulation processes (heating and air conditioning) within buildings, which carry droplet-borne disease great distances, often to remote locations, causing illness. Such equipment has been implicated in cases of tuberculosis and Legionnaire's disease.

Some vector-borne disease transmission processes are simple mechanical processes, such as when the pathogen, in order to spread, uses a host (e.g., a fly, flea, louse, or rat) as a mechanism for a ride, for nourishment, or as part of a physical transfer process. This is called **mechanical transmission. Biological transmission** is when the pathogen undergoes changes as part of its life cycle while within the host/vector and before being transmitted to the new host. Biological transmission is easily seen in malaria, in which the female Anopheles mosquito's blood meal is required for the *Plasmodium* protozoan parasite to complete its sexual development cycle. This can only occur with the ingested blood nutrients found in the intestine of the Anopheles mosquito.

CHAIN OF INFECTION

There is a close association between the triangle of epidemiology and the **chain of infection** (**Figure 1-2**). Disease transmission occurs when the pathogen leaves the reservoir through a **portal of exit** and is spread by one of several modes of transmission. The pathogen or disease-causing agent enters the body through a **portal of entry** and infects the host if the host is susceptible.

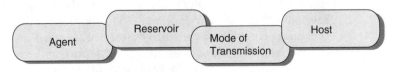

FIGURE 1-2   The chain of infection.

The reservoir is the medium or habitat in which pathogens or infectious agents thrive, propagate, and multiply. Reservoirs are humans, animals, or certain environmental conditions or substances, such as food, feces, or decaying organic matter, that are conducive to the growth of pathogens. Two types of human or animal reservoirs are generally recognized: symptomatic (ill) persons who have a disease and carriers who are asymptomatic and can still transmit the disease.

Once a pathogen leaves its reservoir, it follows its mode of transmission to a susceptible host, either by direct transmission (person-to-person contact) or by indirect transmission (airborne droplets or dust particles, vectors, fomites, and food). The final link in the chain of infection is thus the susceptible individual or host, usually a human or an animal. The host is generally protected from invasion of pathogens by the skin, mucous membranes, and the body's physiological responses (weeping of mucous membranes to cleanse themselves, acidity in the stomach, cilia in the respiratory tract, coughing, and the natural response of the immune system). If the pathogen is able to enter the host, the result will most likely be illness if the host has no immunity to the pathogen.

Susceptibility is based on level of immunity. Natural immunity can come from genetic makeup; that is, some people seem better able to resist disease than others. Active immunity occurs when the body develops antibodies and antigens in response to a pathogen invading the body. Passive immunity comes from antibodies entering a baby through the placenta or from antitoxin or immune globulin injections.[2]

OTHER MODELS OF CAUSATION

The epidemiology triangle as used in a discussion of communicable disease is basic and foundational to all epidemiology; however, infectious diseases are no longer the leading cause of death in industrialized nations, so a more advanced model of the triangle of epidemiology has been proposed. This new model includes all facets of the communicable disease model, and to make it more relevant and useful with regard to today's diseases, conditions, disorders, defects, injuries, and deaths, it also reflects the causes of current illnesses and conditions. Behavior, lifestyle factors, environmental causes, ecologic elements, physical factors, and chronic diseases must be taken into account. Figure 1-3 presents an adapted and advanced model of the triangle of epidemiology, better reflecting the behavior, lifestyle, and chronic disease issues found in modern times.

The advanced model of the triangle of epidemiology, like the traditional epidemiology triangle, is not comprehensive or complete; however, the advanced model recognizes that disease states and conditions affecting a population are complex and that there are many causative factors. The term agent is replaced with causative factors, which implies the need to identify multiple causes or etiologic factors of disease, disability, injury, and death.

Another model that has been developed to capture the multifactorial nature of causation for many health-related states or events is Rothman's causal pies.[25] Assume the factors that cause the adverse health outcome are pieces of a pie, with the whole pie being required to cause the health problem (Figure 1-4). The health-related state or event may have more than one sufficient cause, as illustrated in the figure, with each sufficient cause consisting of multiple contributing factors that are called component causes. The different component causes include the agent, host factors, and environmental factors. Where a given component cause is required in each of the different sufficient causes, it is referred to as a necessary cause. In Figure 1-4, the letter "A" represents a necessary cause because it

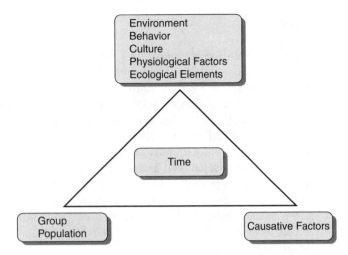

FIGURE 1-3   Advanced model of the triangle of epidemiology.

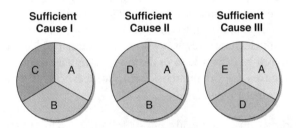

FIGURE 1-4   Three sufficient causes of an adverse health outcome.

is included in each of the three sufficient causes for the adverse health outcome. Exposure to the rubivirus is necessary for rubella-related birth defects to occur but not sufficient to cause birth defects. Component causes that may be required to make a sufficient cause may include a susceptible host who is not immune and illness during the first few months of pregnancy.

Prevention and control measures do not require identifying every component of a sufficient cause because the health problem can be prevented by blocking any single component of a sufficient cause.

The web of causation is an effective method of investigation into chronic disease and behaviorally founded causes of disease, disability, injury, and death. The web of causation shows the importance of looking for many causes or an array of contributing factors to various maladies.

LEVELS OF PREVENTION

Three types of prevention have been established in public health: primary prevention, secondary prevention, and tertiary prevention.

Primary Prevention

Primary prevention is preventing a disease or disorder before it happens. Health promotion, health education, and health protection are three main facets of primary prevention. Lifestyle changes, community health education, school health education, good prenatal care, good behavioral choices, proper nutrition, and safe and healthy conditions at home, school, and the workplace are all primary prevention activities. Fundamental public health measures and activities such as sanitation; infection control; immunizations; protection of food, milk, and water supplies; environmental protection; and protection against occupational hazards and accidents are all basic to primary prevention. Basic personal hygiene and public health measures have had a major impact on halting communicable disease epidemics. Immunizations, infection control (e.g., hand washing), refrigeration of foods, garbage collection, solid and liquid waste management, water supply protection and treatment, and general sanitation have reduced infectious disease threats to populations.

Because of successes in primary prevention efforts directed at infectious diseases, noninfectious diseases are now the main causes of death in the United States and industrialized nations (Table 1-2 and Figure 1-5).[26,27] The leading causes of death today throughout the world vary according to the income level of the country. For example, of the approximately 58 million people that died in 2008 the leading cause of death in low-income countries was lower respiratory infection, accounting for 11.3% of deaths.[28] In contrast, in middle-income countries, lower respiratory infection explained 5.4% of deaths and in high-income countries it explained 3.8% of deaths. The top 10 causes of death in the world are presented in Figure 1-6.[28] Common risk factors for these causes of death are environmental and behavior

TABLE 1-2   Leading Causes of Death in the United States in 1900, 2000, and 2010

1900		*2000*		*2010*	
Pneumonia and influenza	11.8%	Heart diseases	29.6%	Heart diseases	24.1%
Tuberculosis	11.3%	Cancer	23.0%	Cancer	23.3%
Diarrhea, enteritis, ulcerations of the intestines	8.3%	Cerebrovascular diseases	7.0%	Cerebrovascular diseases	5.2%
Heart diseases	8.0%	Chronic lower respiratory diseases	5.1%	Chronic lower respiratory diseases	5.6%
Intracranial lesions of vascular origin	6.2%	Accidents	4.1%	Accidents	4.8%
Nephritis	5.2%	Diabetes mellitus	2.9%	Diabetes mellitus	2.8%
Accidents	4.2%	Pneumonia and influenza	2.7%	Pneumonia and influenza	2.0%
Cancer	3.7%	Alzheimer's disease	2.1%	Alzheimer's disease	3.4%
Senility	2.9%	Nephritis	1.5%	Nephritis	2.0%
Diphtheria	2.3%	Septicemia	1.3%	Intentional self-harm (suicide)	1.5%

Data from Center for Disease Control and Prevention. Leading causes of disease, 1900–1998. Retrieved May 10, 2005, from http://www.cdc.gov/nchs/data/statab/lead1900_98.pdf; and Centers for Disease Control and Prevention. US Mortality Public Use Data Tape, 2000. National Center for Health Statistics; 2002. U.S. Mortality Public Use Data Tape, 2000. National Center for Health Statistics; 2000. Retrieved September 12, 2005, from http://webapp.cdc.gov/sasweb/ncipc/leadcaus10.html. 1. Murphy SL, Xu JQ, Kochanek KD. Deaths: Preliminary Data for 2010. National Vital Statistics Reports; vol 60 no 4. Hyattsville, MD: National Center for Health Statistics. 2012.

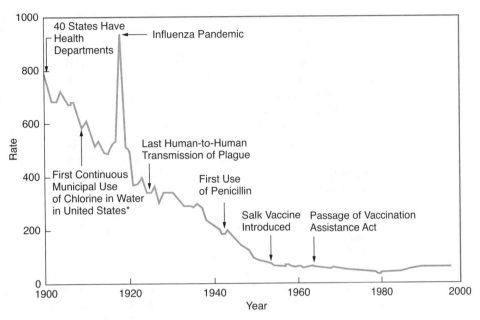

FIGURE 1-5   Crude death rates (per 100,000 person-years) for infectious diseases in the United States, 1900–1996. Reproduced from Achievements in Public Health, 1900–1999: Control of infectious diseases. *MMWR* 1999;48(29);621–629; Adapted from Armstrong GL, Conn LA, Pinner RW. Trends in infectious disease mortality in the United States during the 20th century. *JAMA* 1999;281:61–66.

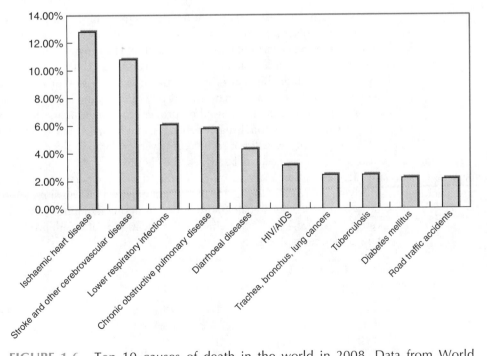

FIGURE 1-6   Top 10 causes of death in the world in 2008. Data from World Health Organization. The top 10 causes of death. http://www.who.int/mediacentre/factsheets/fs310/en/index.html. Accessed January 3, 2012.

related (e.g., fine particulate matter in the air, smoking and tobacco use, alcohol and substance abuse, poor diet, and lack of physical fitness). Prevention at its basic levels now has to be behaviorally directed and lifestyle oriented. Efforts at the primary prevention level have to focus on influencing individual behavior and protecting the environment. In the future, the focus on treatment and health care by physicians should be lessened and replaced with a major effort in the area of primary prevention, including adequate economic support for prevention programs and activities.[16–19]

Two related terms are active primary prevention and passive primary prevention. **Active primary prevention** requires behavior change on the part of the individual (e.g., begin exercising, stop smoking, reduce dietary fat intake). **Passive primary prevention** does not require behavior change on the part of the individual (e.g., eating vitamin-enriched foods, drinking fluoridated water).

Secondary Prevention

Secondary prevention is aimed at the health screening and detection activities used to identify disease. If pathogenicity (the ability to cause disease) is discovered early, diagnosis and early treatment can prevent conditions from progressing and from spreading within the population and can stop or at least slow the progress of disease, disability, disorders, or death.[1] Secondary prevention aims to block the progression of disease or prevent an injury from developing into an impairment or disability.[16,17,20]

Tertiary Prevention

The aim of the third level of prevention is to retard or block the progression of a disability, condition, or disorder in order to keep it from advancing and requiring excessive care. **Tertiary prevention** consists of limiting any disability by providing rehabilitation where a disease, injury, or disorder has already occurred and caused damage. At this level, the goal is to help diseased, disabled, or injured individuals avoid wasteful use of healthcare services and not become dependent on healthcare practitioners and healthcare institutions. Prompt diagnosis and treatment, followed by proper rehabilitation and posttreatment recovery, proper patient education, behavior changes, and lifestyle changes are all necessary so that diseases or disorders will not recur. At the very minimum, the progression of the disease, disorder, or injury needs to be slowed and checked.[29,30]

Rehabilitation is any attempt to restore an afflicted person to a useful, productive, and satisfying lifestyle and to provide the highest quality of life possible, given the extent of the disease and disability. Rehabilitation is one component of tertiary prevention. Patient education, aftercare, health counseling, and some aspects of health promotion can be important components of tertiary prevention.

Pediculosis (Person-to-Person Transmission)

Head Lice: The Epidemic Continues

Some people think of head lice as a nuisance that bothers only the lower class and those with bad personal hygiene. Yet a nationwide epidemic of pediculosis continues to run rampant in both public and private schools.

The bloodsucking lice (Anoplura order) prefer mammal hosts and rarely infest even closely related species, including pets. Head lice limit themselves to the hair of the head near the nape of the neck and the ears. The life cycle of head lice is spent on the host, usually on the same person. The three-stage growth cycle of egg, nymph, and adult takes about 3 weeks. When head lice are not on the host, they die in a day or two. The head louse is very small, about 2 to 3 mm, and can be found grasping the hair shaft near the scalp with its special claws. The adult female louse lives about a month, laying 150 or more eggs called nits, about 10 a day. Nits are not to be confused with solidified globules of hair spray or dandruff. The yellowish-white, oval-shaped nit found glued to the bottom of the hair shaft takes about a week to hatch.

Little disease is transmitted through lice, but they themselves are a problem. They suck blood and inject saliva during the infestation, causing itching and secondary infections from excreta, bites, and scratching.

The louse cannot jump or fly, and thus transmission occurs either directly, from contact with an infested person, or indirectly, through fomites such as shared scarves, hats, coats, brushes, combs, sweaters, and bedding. Schools are particularly vulnerable because children may try on and wear each other's clothing. Because lice like a frequent blood meal and a warm and fuzzy environment, person-to-person transmission is most common. Control comes largely from not sharing combs, brushes, and head clothing, or sleeping with infested persons.

The only way to get rid of nits and lice is to use pesticide treatment, which comes in the form of special shampoos, cream rinses, and topical lotions, with shampoos containing permethrin being most common and effective if used according to directions. Clothing and bedding must be washed in hot soapy water and dried in a hot dryer to destroy lice and nits. Nits must also be removed from the hair with fine-toothed combs. Children should be kept out of school until treatment is complete and successful.

Summarized from California Morbidity, Division of Communicable Disease Control, California Department of Health Services, 1996. http://www.headlice.org/news/classics/camorbidity.htm.

CONCLUSION

Epidemiology is the process of describing and understanding public health problems and the application of this knowledge to the promotion of physical, mental, and social well-being in the population. Epidemiology involves applying scientific models to the description of the frequency and pattern of health-related states or events, the identification of the causes of health-related states or events and modes of transmission, and the guidance of public health planning and decision making. Epidemiologic information is intended to guide health officials and assist individuals in making informed health behavior changes.

EXERCISES

Key Terms

Define the following terms.

Active carrier
Active primary prevention
Agent
Airborne transmission
Analytic epidemiology
Biological transmission
Carrier
Case
Case definition
Case severity
Chain of infection
Common-source epidemic
Convalescent carrier
Direct transmission
Effectiveness
Efficacy
Endemic

Environment
Epidemic
Epidemiology
Fomite
Healthy carrier
Host
Incubatory carrier
Index case
Indirect transmission
Intermittent carrier
Mechanical transmission
Mixed epidemic
Modes of disease transmission
Pandemic
Passive carrier
Passive primary prevention

Pathogen
Portal of entry
Portal of exit
Primary case
Propagated epidemic
Rehabilitation
Reservoir
Secondary case
Secondary prevention
Suspect case
Tertiary prevention
Time
Vector
Vector-borne transmission
Vehicle-borne transmission
Zoonosis

STUDY QUESTIONS

1. The definition of epidemiology includes the terms "distribution" and "determinants." Describe the meaning of these terms.

2. Epidemiology involves the study of more than just infectious diseases. Explain.

3. Describe the chain of infection.

4. List four types of epidemiologic information useful for influencing public health policy and planning and individual health decisions.

5. Define efficacy and effectiveness, and provide examples of both.

Use the following information to answer questions 6 and 7.

Emergency Medical Services (EMS) responses were made to 1,551 nonindustrial injuries resulting from falls. Of total falls, 869 (56%) occurred at home and 682 (44%) occurred elsewhere. The very young (< 4 years old) and the very old (80+ years) were the most vulnerable to falls. Persons over age 60 accounted for 44% of the total emergency calls for nonindustrial falls. On weekends, most injuries from falls occurred in the home. Time pattern analysis revealed that the greatest number of injuries from falls at home occurred in the late afternoon and evening, between 3:00 PM and midnight. Callers from three socioeconomic strata were identified from census tract information. Age and gender were tabulated for the three strata areas based on falls in the home. The greatest use of EMS was by those over 60 years of age in all three strata levels. Those aged 40–59 years in the low socioeconomic group and infants through 9 years of age in the low socioeconomic group were next highest users. The highest socioeconomic group had the lowest rates for each age group.[27] The percentages given are out of total emergency EMS responses. Table 1-3 represents percentages of falls per total population based on the rates per 100,000 people.

- Population for the high socioeconomic group was 143,798.
- Population for the medium socioeconomic group was 249,381.
- Population for the low socioeconomic group was 138,413.

6. With what you have learned from the scenario just described, what can you say about the role age plays in falls? Present statistics and provide a discussion of reasons for the age-related statistics and differences.

7. Explain the effect of socioeconomic status on falls as responded to by EMS, as shown in Table 1-3.

8. Explain the epidemiology triangle and compare and contrast it with the advanced epidemiology triangle.

9. Review Figure 1-6, and explain how the type of disease influences the three levels of prevention that should be considered.

TABLE 1-3   Home Falls and Emergency Medical Service Response in the State of Washington

Age Group	High Socioeconomic Rate/100,000	Percentage of Total Population	Medium Socioeconomic Rate/100,000	Percentage of Total Population	Low Socioeconomic Rate/100,000	Percentage of Total Population
0–9	87.95	3.8	199.88	6.4	260.24	2.9
10–19	35.94	4.8	87.43	6.7	104.81	2.9
20–39	29.69	8.2	60.77	14.9	104.76	9.1
40–59	60.66	6.8	168.42	9.7	288.89	5.1
60+	444.05	3.4	355.18	9.3	420.66	5.9
TOTAL	—	27.05	—	46.91	—	26.04

10. HIV/AIDS can be transmitted from an infected person to another person through blood, semen, vaginal fluids, and breast milk. High-risk behaviors include homosexual practices; unprotected oral, vaginal, or anal sexual intercourse; and needle sharing. Discuss how this information can be used in public health action and individual decision making.

REFERENCES

1. *Stedman's Medical Dictionary for the Health Professions and Nursing*, 5th ed. Baltimore, MD: Lippincott Williams & Wilkins; 2005.
2. Page RM, Cole GE, Timmreck TC. *Basic Epidemiologic Methods and Biostatistics: A Practical Guide Book*. Boston, MA: Jones and Bartlett; 1995.
3. World Health Organization. *Joint United Nations Programme on HIV/AIDS. 09 AIDS epidemic update*. http://www.unaids.org/en/media/unaids/contentassets/dataimport/pub/report/2009/jc1700_epi_update_2009_en.pdf . Accessed January 2, 2012.
4. Centers for Disease Control and Prevention. Pneumocystis pneumonia—Los Angeles. *MMWR*. 1981;30:250–252.
5. Centers for Disease Control and Prevention. Possible transfusion-associated acquired immune deficiency syndrome (AIDS)—California. *MMWR*. 1982;31:652–654.
6. Last JM, ed. *A Dictionary of Epidemiology*. 4th ed. New York, NY: Oxford University Press, 2001.
7. Rigotti NA, Pasternak RC. Cigarette smoking and coronary heart disease: risks and management. *Cardiol Clin*. 1996;14:51–68.
8. Shinton R. Lifelong exposures and the potential for stroke prevention: the contribution of cigarette smoking, exercise, and body fat. *J Epidemiol Community Health*. 1997;51:138–143.
9. U.S. Department of Health and Human Services. *The Health Benefits of Smoking Cessation: A Report of the Surgeon General, 1990*. Rockville, MD: Centers for Disease Control, Center for Chronic Disease Prevention and Health Promotion, Office on Smoking and Health. 1990. (DHHS Publication No. [CDC] 90-8416).
10. U.S. Department of Health and Human Services. *Reducing the Health Consequences of Smoking: 25 Years of Progress. A Report of the Surgeon General, 1989*. Rockville, MD: Centers for Disease Control, Office on Smoking and Health. 1989. (DHHS Publication No. [CDC] 89-8411).
11. Merrill RM, White GL Jr. Why health educators need epidemiology. *Educ Health*. 2002;15:215–221.
12. Thacker SB, Berkelman RL. Public health surveillance in the United States. *Epidemiol Rev*. 1988;10:164–190.
13. Oleckno WA. *Essential Epidemiology: Principles and Application*. Long Grove, IL: Waveland Press, 2002.
14. Merrill RM. Introduction to Epidemiology, 5th ed. Sudbury, MA: Jones and Bartlett Publishers, 2010.
15. Chang M, Glynn MK, Groseclose SL. Endemic, notifiable bioterrorism-related diseases, United States, 1992–1999. *Emerg Infect Dis*. 2003;9:5. http://www.cdc.gov/ncidod/eid/vol9no5/02-0477.htm. Accessed December 10, 2008.
16. Timmreck TC. *Health Services Cyclopedic Dictionary*, 3rd ed. Sudbury, MA: Jones and Bartlett; 1997.
17. Mausner J, Bahn AK. *Epidemiology: An Introductory Text*. Philadelphia, PA: WB Saunders; 1974.
18. Shindell S, Salloway JC, Oberembi CM. *A Coursebook in Health Care Delivery*. New York: Appleton-Century-Crofts; 1976.
19. Lilienfeld AM, Lilienfeld DE. *Foundations of Epidemiology*, 2nd ed. New York, NY: Oxford University Press, 1980.
20. World Health Organization. *Zoonoses: Second report of the Joint WHO/FAO Expert Committee*. Geneva. 1959.

21. 'Typhoid Mary' dies of a stroke at 68. Carrier of disease, blamed for 51 cases and 3 deaths, but she was held immune. *New York Times.* November 12, 1938. http://select.nytimes.com/gst/abstract.html?res=F10D15FE3859117389DDAB0994D9415B888FF1D3. Accessed January 2, 2012.

22. Soper GA. The work of a chronic typhoid germ distributor. *JAMA* 1907;48:2019-22.

23. Thomas CL, ed. *Taber's Cyclopedic Medical Dictionary,* 14th ed. Philadelphia: FA Davis, 1981.

24. Nester EW, McCarthy BJ, Roberts CE, Pearsall NN. *Microbiology.* New York: Holt, Rinehart & Winston, 1973.

25. Rothman KJ. Causes. *Am J Epidemiol.* 1976;104:587–592.

26. Centers for Disease Control. *Leading causes of disease,* 1900–1998. http://www.cdc.gov/nchs/data/statab/lead1900_98.pdf. Accessed April 18, 2012.

27. Centers for Disease Control. *U.S. Mortality Public Use Data Tape, 2000.* National Center for Health Statistics, 2000. http://webapp.cdc.gov/sasweb/ncipc/leadcaus10.html. Accessed April 18, 2012.

28. World Health Organization. *The top 10 causes of death.* http://www.who.int/mediacentre/factsheets/fs310/en/index.html. Accessed January 3, 2012.

29. Picket G, Hanlon JJ. *Public Health: Administration and Practice.* St. Louis: Times Mirror/Mosby, 1990.

30. MacMahon B, Pugh TF. *Epidemiology Principles and Methods.* Boston, MA: Little, Brown and Company, 1970.

Historic Developments in Epidemiology

OBJECTIVES

After completing this chapter, you will be able to:

- Describe important historic events in the field of epidemiology.
- List and describe the contributions made by several key individuals to the field of epidemiology.
- Recognize the development and use of certain study designs in the advancement of epidemiology.

The history of epidemiology has involved many key players who sought to understand and explain illness, injury, and death from an observational scientific perspective. These individuals also sought to provide information for the prevention and control of health-related states and events. They advanced the study of disease from a supernatural viewpoint to a viewpoint based on a scientific foundation; from no approach for assessment to systematic methods for summarizing and describing public health problems; from no clear understanding of the natural course of disease to a knowledge of the probable causes, modes of transmission, and health outcomes; and from no means for preventing and controlling disease to effective approaches for solving public health problems.

Initially, epidemiologic knowledge advanced slowly, with large segments in time where little or no advancement in the field occurred. The time from Hippocrates (460–377 BC), who attempted to explain disease occurrence from a rational viewpoint, to John Graunt (AD 1620–1674), who described disease occurrence and death with the use of systematic methods and who developed and calculated life tables and life expectancy, and Thomas

Sydenham (1624–1689), who approached the study of disease from an observational angle rather than a theoretical one, was 2,000 years. Approximately 200 years later, William Farr (1807–1883) advanced John Graunt's work in order to better describe epidemiologic problems. In the 19th century, John Snow, Ignaz Semmelweis, Louis Pasteur, Robert Koch, Florence Nightingale, and others also made important contributions to the field of epidemiology. Since then, the science of epidemiology has rapidly progressed. Although it is impossible to identify all of the contributors to the field of epidemiology in this chapter, several of these individuals and their contributions are considered here.

HIPPOCRATES, THE FIRST EPIDEMIOLOGIST

Hippocrates was a physician who became known as the father of medicine and the first epidemiologist (Figure 2-1). His three books entitled *Epidemic I, Epidemic III*, and *On Airs, Waters, and Places* attempted to describe disease from a rational perspective, rather than a supernatural basis. He observed that different diseases occurred in different locations. He noted that malaria and yellow fever most commonly occurred in swampy areas. It was not known, however, that the mosquito was responsible for such diseases until in 1900, when Walter Reed, MD, a U.S. Army physician working in the tropics, made the connection. Hippocrates also introduced terms like epidemic and endemic.[1–4]

Hippocrates gave advice to persons wishing to pursue the science of medicine and provided insights on the effects of the seasons of the year and hot and cold winds on health. He believed the properties of water should be examined and advised that the source of water should be considered.[1–4] He asked questions such as, "Is the water from a marshy soft-ground source, or is the water from the rocky heights? Is the water brackish and harsh?" Hippocrates also made some noteworthy observations on the behavior of the populace. He believed the effective physician should be observant of peoples' behavior, such as eating,

FIGURE 2-1   Hippocrates. United States National Library of Medicine, National Institutes of Health, History of Medicine. Available at: http://wwwihm.nlm.nih.gov/ihm/images/B/14/553.jpg. Accessed December 29, 2008.

drinking, and other activities. Did they eat lunch, eat too much, or drink too little? Were they industrious?

For traveling physicians, Hippocrates suggested they become familiar with local diseases and with the nature of those prevailing diseases. He believed that as time passed the physician should be able to tell what epidemic diseases might attack and in what season and that this could be determined by the settings of the stars. Sources of water, smells, and how water sets or flows were always considered in his study of disease states.[1-4]

Hippocrates identified hot and cold diseases and, consequently, hot and cold treatments. Hot diseases were treated with cold treatments, and cold diseases required hot treatments. The process of deciding whether a disease was hot or cold was complex. An example is diarrhea, which was considered a hot disease and was believed to be cured with a cold treatment such as eating fruit.[1-4]

Hippocrates also ascribed to and incorporated into his theory what is now considered the **atomic theory**—that is, the belief that everything is made of tiny particles. He theorized that there were four types of atoms: earth atoms (solid and cold), air atoms (dry), fire atoms (hot), and water atoms (wet). Additionally, Hippocrates believed that the body was composed of four humors: phlegm (earth and water atoms), yellow bile (fire and air atoms), blood (fire and water atoms), and black bile (earth and air atoms). Sickness was thought to be caused by an imbalance of these humors, and fever was thought to be caused by too much blood. The treatment for fever was to reduce the amount of blood in the body through bloodletting or the application of bloodsuckers (leeches). Imbalances were ascribed to a change in the body's "constitution." Climate, moisture, stars, meteorites, winds, vapors, and diet were thought to cause imbalances and contribute to disease. Diet was both a cause and cure of disease. Cures for illness and protection from disease came from maintaining a balance and avoiding imbalance in the constitution.

The essentials of epidemiology noted by Hippocrates included observations on how diseases affected populations and how disease spread. He further addressed issues of diseases in relation to time and seasons, place, environmental conditions, and disease control, especially as it related to water and the seasons. The broader contribution to epidemiology made by Hippocrates was that of epidemiologic observation. His teachings about how to observe any and all contributing or causal factors of a disease are still sound epidemiologic concepts.[1-4]

DISEASE OBSERVATIONS OF SYDENHAM

Thomas Sydenham (1624–1689), although a graduate of Oxford Medical School, did not at first practice medicine but served in the military and as a college administrator. While at All Souls College, Oxford, he became acquainted with Robert Boyle, a colleague who sparked Sydenham's interest in diseases and epidemics. Sydenham went on to get his medical license, and he spoke out for strong empirical approaches to medicine and close observations of disease. Sydenham wrote the details of what he observed about diseases without letting various traditional theories of disease and medical treatment influence his work and observations. From this close observation process, he was able to identify and recognize different diseases. Sydenham published his observations in a book in 1676 titled, *Observationes Medicae.*[4]

One of the major works of Sydenham was the classification of fevers plaguing London in the 1660s and 1670s. Sydenham came up with three levels or classes of fevers: continued fevers, intermittent fevers, and smallpox. Some of Sydenham's theories were embraced, whereas others were criticized, mostly because his ideas and observations went against the usual Hippocratic approaches. He treated smallpox with bed rest and normal bed covers. The treatment of the time, based on the Hippocratic theory, was to use heat and extensive bed coverings. He was met with good results but was erroneous in identifying the cause of the disease.[4]

Sydenham was persecuted by his colleagues, who at one time threatened to take away his medical license for irregular practice that did not follow the theories of the time; however, he gained a good reputation with the public, and some young open-minded physicians agreed with his empirical principles. Sydenham described and distinguished different diseases, including some psychological maladies. He also advanced useful treatments and remedies, including exercise, fresh air, and a healthy diet, which other physicians rejected at the time.[4]

THE EPIDEMIOLOGY OF SCURVY

In the 1700s, it was observed that armies lost more men to disease than to the sword. James Lind (1716–1794), a Scottish naval surgeon, focused on illnesses in these populations. He observed the effect of time, place, weather, and diet on the spread of disease. His 1754 book, *A Treatise on Scurvy*, identified the symptoms of scurvy and the fact that the disease became common in sailors after as little as a month at sea.[3,4]

Lind noticed that while on long ocean voyages, sailors would become sick from **scurvy**, a disease marked by spongy and bleeding gums, bleeding under the skin, and extreme weakness. He saw that scurvy began to occur after 4–6 weeks at sea. Lind noted that even though the water was good and the provisions were not tainted, the sailors still fell sick. Lind pointed out that the months most common to scurvy were April, May, and June. He also observed that cold, rainy, foggy, and thick weather were often present. Influenced by the Hippocratic theory of medicine, Lind kept looking to the air as the source of disease. Dampness of the air, damp living arrangements, and life at sea were the main focus of his observations as he searched for an explanation of the cause of disease and, most of all, the cause of scurvy.[5] Although not correct about the link with weather and climate at sea, Lind looked at all sides of the issue and considered what was happening to the sick. He then compared their experience with the experiences of those who were healthy.

When Lind began to look at the diet of the mariners, he observed that the sea diet was extremely gross and hard on digestion. Concerned with the extent of sickness in large numbers of sailors, Lind set up some experiments with mariners. In 1747, while serving on the *HMS Salisbury*, he conducted an experimental study on scurvy. He took 12 ill patients who had all of the classic symptoms of scurvy. They all seemed to have a similar level of the illness. He described their symptoms as putrid gums, spots, and lassitude, with weakness in their knees. He put the sailors in six groups of two and, in addition to a common diet of foods like water-gruel sweetened with sugar, fresh mutton broth, puddings, boiled biscuit with sugar, barley and raisins, rice and currants, and sago and wine, each of the groups received an additional dietary intervention. Two men received a quart of cider a day on an empty stomach. Two men took two spoonfuls of vinegar three times a day on an empty stomach. Two men were given a half-pint of sea water every day. Two men were given lemons and oranges to eat on an empty stomach. Two men received an elixir recommended by a hospital surgeon, and two men were fed a combination of garlic, mustard seed, and horseradish. Lind says that the men given the lemons and oranges ate them with "greediness." The most sudden and visible good effects were seen in those who ate lemons and oranges. In 6 days, the two men eating citrus were fit for duty. All of the others had putrid gums, spots, lassitude, and weakness of the knees. Free of symptoms, the two citrus-eating sailors were asked to nurse the others who were still sick. Thus, Lind observed that oranges and lemons were the most effective remedies for scurvy at sea.[5] As a consequence of Lind's epidemiologic work, since 1895, the British navy has required that limes or lime juice be included in the diet of seamen, resulting in the nickname of British seamen of "limeys."

The epidemiologic contributions of Lind were many. He was concerned with the occurrence of disease in large groups of people. Lind not only participated in the identification of the effect of diet on disease, but he made clinical observations, used experimental design, asked classic epidemiologic questions, observed population changes and their effect on disease, and considered sources of disease, including place, time, and season.

EPIDEMIOLOGY OF COWPOX AND SMALLPOX

In England, Benjamin Jesty, a farmer/dairyman in the mid-1700s, noticed his milkmaids never got **smallpox**, a disease characterized by chills, fever, headache, and backache, with eruption of pimples that blister and form pockmarks; however, the milkmaids did develop cowpox from the cows. Jesty believed there was a link between acquiring cowpox and not getting smallpox. In 1774, Jesty exposed his wife and children to cowpox to protect them from smallpox. It worked. The exposed family members developed immunity to smallpox. Unfortunately, little was publicized about Jesty's experiment and observations.[4]

The experiment of Jesty and similar reported experiences in Turkey, the Orient, America, and Hungary were known to Edward Jenner (1749–1823), an English rural physician. He personally observed that dairymen's servants and milkmaids got cowpox and did not get smallpox. For many centuries, the Chinese had made observations about weaker and stronger strains of smallpox. They learned that it was wise to catch a weaker strain of the disease. If one had a weak strain of the disease, one would not get the full disease later on. This was termed **variolation**.[3,4]

In the late 1700s, servants were often the ones who milked the cows. Servants were also required to tend to the sores on the heels of horses affected with cowpox. The pus and infectious fluids from these sores were referred to as "the grease" of the disease. Left unwashed because of a lack of concern about sanitation and cleanliness, the servants' grease-covered hands would then spread the disease to the cows during milking. The cowpox in turn was transmitted to the dairymaids. Jenner observed that when a person had cowpox this same person would not get smallpox if exposed to it. Jenner attempted to give a dairymaid, exposed to a mild case of cowpox in her youth, a case of smallpox by cutting her arm and rubbing some of the infectious "grease" into the wound. She did not become ill. Cowpox was thus found to shield against smallpox.[3,4] Jenner invented a vaccination for smallpox with this knowledge. The vaccine was used to protect populations from this disease.[3,4,6]

The Worldwide Global Smallpox Eradication Campaign of the late 1960s and early 1970s encouraged vaccination against smallpox and was effective at eliminating this disease. As part of the effort to eradicate smallpox, a photograph was widely distributed in 1975 of a small child who had been stricken with the disease (Figure 2-2). On October 26, 1977, World Health Organization workers supposedly tracked down the world's last case of naturally occurring smallpox. The patient was 23-year-old Ali Maow Maalin, a hospital cook in Merka, Somalia. Two cases of smallpox occurred in 1978 as a result of a laboratory accident. Because it is believed that smallpox has been eradicated from the earth, vaccinations have been halted; however, some public-health and healthcare professionals are skeptical

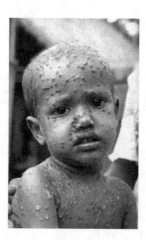

FIGURE 2-2   Picture of a boy with smallpox taken by Dr. Stan Foster, EIS Officer, class of 1962. Pictures courtesy of Centers for Disease Control and Prevention, Atlanta, Georgia.

and fear that such acts may set the stage for an unexpected future epidemic of smallpox because the pathogen still exists in military and government labs. As unvaccinated persons proliferate, so does the risk of future smallpox epidemics.

EPIDEMIOLOGY OF CHILDBED FEVER IN A LYING-IN HOSPITAL

Historically, epidemiology was centered on the study of the great epidemics: cholera, bubonic plague, smallpox, and typhus. As the diseases were identified and differentiated, the focus of epidemiology changed. Such a change in focus came through the work of another physician–epidemiologist, Ignaz Semmelweis, in the early to mid-1800s.[7]

In the 1840s, one of the greatest fears a pregnant mother had was dying of **childbed fever** (a uterine infection, usually of the placental site, after childbirth). Babies were born to mothers with the usual risks that warranted obstetric assistance, and this often resulted in an uneventful birth; however, after the birth of the child, the mother would get an infection and die of childbed fever, a streptococcal disease. Many times the child would become infected and die as well. After many years of observing the course of the disease and the symptoms associated with childbed fever, Semmelweis began a series of investigations.[7]

The Viennese Maternity Hospital (called a lying-in hospital), of which Semmelweis was clinical director, was divided into two clinics. The first clinic consistently had greater numbers of maternal deaths than the second clinic. In 1846, the maternal mortality rate of this clinic was five times greater than that of the second clinic, and over a 6-year period, it was three times as great. Semmelweis observed that the mothers became ill either immediately during birth or within 24–36 hours after delivery. The mothers died quickly of rapidly developing childbed fever. Often the children would soon die as well. This was not the case in the second clinic.[7]

Semmelweis observed it was not the actual labor that was the problem but that the examination of the patients seemed to be connected to the onset of the disease. Through clinical observation, retrospective study, collection and analysis of data on maternal deaths and infant deaths, and clinically controlled experimentation, he was able to ascertain that the communication of childbed fever was through germs passed from patient to patient by the physician in the process of doing pelvic examinations. Semmelweis discovered that, unlike the second clinic, the medical students would come directly from the death house after performing autopsies of infected and decaying dead bodies and then would conduct pelvic exams on the mothers ready to give birth. Hand washing or any form of infection control was not a common practice. Unclean hands with putrefied cadaver material on student doctors' hands were used to conduct the routine daily pelvic exams, and the practice was never questioned. There was no reason to be concerned about clean hands because the theory of medicine that was accepted at the time relied on the Hippocratic theory of medicine and the idea that disease developed spontaneously. Semmelweis observed that a whole row of patients became ill while patients in the adjacent row stayed healthy.[7]

Semmelweis discovered that any infected or putrefied tissue, whether from a living patient or a cadaver, could cause disease to spread. In order to destroy the cadaverous or putrefied matter on the hands, it was necessary that every person, physician or midwife, performing an examination, would wash their hands in chlorinated lime upon entering the labor ward in clinic 1. At first, Semmelweis said it was only necessary to wash during entry to the labor ward; however, a cancerous womb was discovered to also cause the spread of the disease, and thus, Semmelweis required washing with chlorinated lime between each examination. When strict adherence to hand washing was required of all medical personnel who examined patients in the maternity hospital, mortality rates fell at unbelievable rates. In 1842, the percentage of deaths was 12.1% (730 of 6,024) compared with 1.3% (91 of 7,095) in 1848.[7]

At this time in the history of public health, the causes of disease were unknown, yet suspected. It was known that hand washing with chlorinated lime between each examination reduced the illness and deaths from childbed fever, but even with the evidence of this success, Semmelweis's discovery was discounted by most of his colleagues.[7] Today, it is known that hand washing is still one of the best sanitation practices for medical and lay people alike. What Ignaz Semmelweis discovered is still one of the easiest disease- and infection-control methods known.

JOHN SNOW'S EPIDEMIOLOGIC INVESTIGATIONS OF CHOLERA

In the 1850s, John Snow (1813–1858) was a respected physician and the anesthesiologist of Queen Victoria of England (Figure 2-3). He is noted for his medical work with the royal family, including the administration of chloroform to the queen at the birth of her children; however, Snow is most famous for his pioneering work in epidemiology. Among epidemiologists, Snow is considered one of the most important contributors to the field. Many of the approaches, concepts, and methods used by Snow in his epidemiologic work are still useful and valuable in epidemiologic work today.[8–10]

Throughout his medical career, Snow studied cholera. **Cholera** is an acute infectious disease characterized by watery diarrhea, loss of fluid and electrolytes, dehydration, and collapse. From his studies, he established sound and useful epidemiologic methods. He observed and recorded important factors related to the course of disease. In the later part of his career, Snow conducted two major investigative studies of cholera. The first involved a descriptive epidemiologic investigation of a cholera outbreak in the Soho district of London in the Broad Street area. The second involved an analytic epidemiologic investigation

FIGURE 2-3   John Snow. © National Library of Medicine

of a cholera epidemic in which he compared death rates from the disease to where the sufferers got their water, either the Lambeth Water Company or the Southwark and Vauxhall Water Company.[8–10]

In the mid-1840s, in the Soho and Golden Square districts of London, a major outbreak of cholera occurred. Within 250 yards of the intersection of Cambridge Street and Broad Street, about 500 fatal attacks of cholera occurred in 10 days. Many more deaths were averted because of the flight of most of the population. Snow was able to identify incubation times, the length of time from infection until death, modes of transmission of the disease, and the importance of the flight of the population from the dangerous areas. He also plotted statistics based on dates and mortality rates. He studied sources of contamination of the water, causation and infection, and the flow of the water in the underground aquifer by assessing water from wells and pumps. He found that nearly all deaths had taken place within a short distance of the Broad Street pump.

Snow observed that in the Soho district there were two separate populations of persons not so heavily affected by the cholera epidemic, such that death rates were not equal to those of the surrounding populations. A brewery with its own wells and a workhouse, also with its own water source, were the protected populations. Snow used a spot map (sometimes called a dot map) to identify the locations of all deaths. He plotted data on the progress of the course of the epidemic and the occurrence of new cases as well as when the epidemic started, peaked, and subsided. Snow examined the water, movement of people, sources of exposure, transmission of the disease between and among close and distant people, and possible causation. Toward the end of the epidemic, as a control measure, protection from any reoccurrence, and as a political statement to the community, Snow removed the handle from the Broad Street pump.[8–10]

In his early days as a practicing physician before the Broad Street outbreak, Snow recorded detailed scenarios of several cases of cholera, many of which he witnessed firsthand. Many of the details he chose to record were epidemiologic in nature, such as various modes of transmission of cholera, incubation times, cause–effect association, clinical observations and clinical manifestations of the disease, scientific observations on water and the different sources (including observations made with a microscope), temperature, climate, diet, differences between those who got the disease and those who did not, and immigration and emigration differences.[8–10]

In 1853, a larger cholera outbreak occurred in London. London had not had a cholera outbreak for about 5 years. During this period, the Lambeth Water Company moved their intake source of water upriver on the Thames, from opposite Hungerford Market to a source above the city, Thames Ditton. By moving the source of water upriver to a place above the sewage outlets, Lambeth was able to draw water free from London's sewage, contamination, and pollution. The Southwark and Vauxhall Water Company, however, did not relocate its source of water. Throughout the south district of the city, both water companies had pipes down every street. The citizens were free to pick and choose which water company they wanted for their household water. Thus, by mere coincidence, Snow encountered a populace using water randomly selected throughout the south district. Snow could not have arranged better sampling techniques than those which had occurred by chance.[8–10]

The registrar general in London published a "Weekly Return of Births and Deaths." On November 26, 1853, the Registrar General observed from a table of mortality that mortality rates were fairly consistent across the districts supplied with the water from the Hungerford market area. The old supply system of Lambeth and the regular supply of the Southwark and Vauxhall Company were separate systems but drew water from the same area in the river. The registrar general also published a mortality list from cholera. Snow developed comparison tables on death by source of water by subdistricts. Snow was able to conclude that the water drawn upriver solely by Lambeth Water Company caused no deaths. The water drawn downstream, in areas that were below the sewage inlets, mostly by Southwark and Vauxhall Water Company, was associated with very high death rates.[8–10]

Gaining cooperation and permission from the registrar general, Snow was supplied with addresses of persons who had died from cholera. He went into the subdistrict of Kennington One and Kennington Two and found that 38 of 44 deaths in this subdistrict received their water from Southwark and Vauxhall Company. Each house had randomly selected different water companies, and many households did not know from which one they received water. Snow developed a test that used chloride of silver to identify which water source each household had by sampling water from within the houses of those he contacted. Snow was eventually able to tell the source of water by appearance and smell.[8–10]

Vital statistics data and death rates compared according to water supplier presented conclusive evidence as to the source of contamination. A report to Parliament showed that in the 30,046 households that were supplied water by the Southwark and Vauxhall Company, 286 persons died of cholera. Of the 26,107 houses supplied by Lambeth, only 14 died of cholera. The death rate was 71 per 10,000 in Southwark and Vauxhall households and 5 per 10,000 for Lambeth households. The mortality at the height of the epidemic in households supplied with water by Southwark and Vauxhall was eight to nine times greater than in those supplied by Lambeth. Snow was finally able to prove his hypothesis that contaminated water passing down the sewers into the river, then being drawn from the river and distributed through miles of pipes into peoples' homes, produced cholera throughout the community. Snow showed that cholera was a waterborne disease that traveled in both surface and groundwater supplies[8–10] (see Exhibit 2-1).

Snow laid the groundwork for descriptive and analytic epidemiologic approaches found useful in epidemiology today. He identified various modes of transmission and incubation times and, in his second study, employed a comparison group to establish more definitively a cause–effect association. It was not until Koch's work in 1883 in Egypt, when he isolated and cultivated *Vibrio cholerae,* that the accuracy and correctness of Snow's work was proved and accepted.[3,4,8–10] Because of the contributions made by John Snow, he has been referred to by many as the Father of Epidemiology.

EPIDEMIOLOGIC WORK OF PASTEUR AND KOCH

In the 1870s, on journeys into the countryside of Europe, it was not uncommon to see dead sheep lying in the fields. These sheep had died from anthrax, which most commonly occurs in animals (e.g., cattle, sheep, and horses) but can also occur in humans. **Anthrax** is a serious bacterial infection, usually fatal, caused by *Bacillus anthracis*. Anthrax was a major epidemic that plagued the farmers and destroyed them economically.[3,4]

By this time, Louis Pasteur (1822–1895), a French chemist, had been accepted into France's Academy of Medicine for his work in microbiology. Pasteur had distinguished himself as a scientist and a respected contributor to the field of medicine and public health (even though it was not recognized as a separate field at the time). Pasteur had already identified the cause of rabies and many other devastating diseases. Because of his many past successes in microbiology, Pasteur had confidence in his ability to take on the challenge of conquering anthrax.[3,4]

Pasteur was convinced that it was the bacteria identified as anthrax that caused the disease, because anthrax bacteria were always present on necropsy (autopsy) of sheep that died from anthrax. It was unclear, however, why the course of the disease occurred the way it did. The cause–effect association seemed to have some loopholes in it. How did the sheep get anthrax? How were the sheep disposed of? Why did the anthrax occur in some areas and not in others? How was the disease transmitted? How did the disease survive? All were questions that Louis Pasteur sought to answer.

Pasteur observed that the dead sheep were buried. The key and insightful discovery was that anthrax spores and/or bacteria were brought back to the surface by earthworms. Koch had previously shown that the anthrax bacteria existed in silkworms and that anthrax was an intestinal disease. Pasteur made the earthworm connection.

Pasteur and his assistants had worked on a vaccine for anthrax for months, and in 1881, an anthrax vaccine was discovered. After a presentation at the Academy of Sciences in Paris, Pasteur was challenged to prove that his vaccine was effective. He put his career and reputation at stake to prove that his vaccine would work, that disease was caused by microorganisms, and that a cause–effect association exists between a particular microbe and a certain disease.

Pasteur agreed to the challenge with a public demonstration to prove his vaccination process could prevent sheep from getting anthrax. He went to a farm in rural France where 60 sheep were provided for the experiment. He was to vaccinate 25 of the sheep with his new vaccine. After the proper waiting time, Pasteur was then to inoculate 50 of the sheep with a virulent injection of anthrax. Ten sheep were to receive no treatment and were used to compare with the survivors of the experiment (a control group). Pasteur was successful. The inoculated sheep lived. The unvaccinated sheep died, and the control group had no changes. Pasteur successfully demonstrated that his method was sound, that vaccinations were effective approaches in disease control, and that bacteria were indeed causes of disease.

Historically, many scientists have contributed to the method used in epidemiology. Robert Koch (1843–1910) lived in Wollstein, a small town near Breslau, in rural Germany (Prussia). Koch was a private practice physician and district medical officer. Because of his compelling desire to study disease experimentally, he set up a laboratory in his home and purchased equipment, including photography equipment, out of his meager earnings. Robert Koch became a key medical research scientist in Germany in the period of the explosion of knowledge in medicine and public health, and he used photography to take the first pictures of microbes in order to show the world that microorganisms do in fact exist and that they are what cause disease.[3,4,11]

In the 1870s, Koch showed that anthrax was transmissible and reproducible in experimental animals (mice). He identified the spore stage of the growth cycle of microorganisms.

The epidemiologic significance that Koch demonstrated was that the anthrax bacillus was the only organism that caused anthrax in a susceptible animal.

In 1882, Koch discovered the tubercle bacillus with the use of special culturing and staining methods. Koch and his assistant also perfected the concept of steam sterilization. In Egypt and India, he and his assistants discovered the cholera bacterium and proved that it was transmitted by drinking water, food, and clothing. Incidental to the cholera investigations, Koch also found the microorganisms that cause infectious conjunctivitis. One of his major contributions to epidemiology was a paper on waterborne epidemics and how they can be largely prevented by proper water filtration.[3,4,11]

Koch, who began as a country family physician, pioneered the identification of microorganisms and many different bacteria that caused different diseases as well as pure culturing techniques for growing microorganisms in laboratory conditions. Some of the major public health contributions that Koch made were the identification of the tuberculosis and cholera microorganisms and the establishment of the importance of water purification in disease prevention. He was the recipient of many honors throughout his lifetime, including the Nobel Prize in 1905 for his work in microbiology.[3,4,11,12]

Both Pasteur and Koch were successful in putting to rest a major misguided notion of medicine at the time: that the diseases were a result of "spontaneous generation"—that is, organisms would simply appear out of other organisms, and a fly would spontaneously appear out of garbage, and so forth.[8]

THE INVENTION OF THE MICROSCOPE

The important findings of Koch, Pasteur, Snow, and many others in this era of sanitation and microbe discovery would have been impossible without the use of the microscope. Koch's camera would not have been invented if the microscope had not been developed and its lenses adapted to picture taking.

The microscope first found scientific use in the 1600s through the work of Cornelius Drebbel (1572–1633), the Janssen brothers of the Netherlands (1590s), and Antoni Van Leeuwenhoek (1632–1723). The microscope was used for medical and scientific purposes by Athanasius Kircher of Fulda (1602–1680). In 1658 in Rome, he wrote his publication, *Scrutinium Pestis*. He conducted experiments on the nature of putrefaction and showed how microscopic living organisms and maggots develop in decaying matter. He also discovered that the blood of plague patients was filled with countless "worms" not visible to the human eye.

Most of the credit goes to Leeuwenhoek for the advancement, development, and perfection of the use of the microscope. He was the first to effectively apply the microscope in the study of disease and medicine, even though he was not a physician. Because of a driving interest in the microscope, Leeuwenhoek was able to devote much time to microscopy, owning over 247 microscopes and over 400 lenses (many of which he ground himself). He was the first to describe the structure of the crystalline lens.

Leeuwenhoek made contributions to epidemiology. He did a morphologic study of red corpuscles in the blood. He saw the connection of arterial circulation to venous circulation in the human body through the microscopic study of capillary networks. With his microscope, Leeuwenhoek contributed indirectly to epidemiology through microbiology by discovering "animalcules" (microscopic organisms, later called microbes, bacteria, and microorganisms).

In addition to epidemiology and microbiology, chemistry and histology were also developed because of the advent of the microscope, which influenced advances in the study and control of diseases.[4,13]

JOHN GRAUNT AND VITAL STATISTICS

Another major contributor to epidemiology, but in a different manner, was John Graunt (1620–1674). In 1603 in London, a systematic recording of deaths commenced and was called the "bills of mortality." It is summarized in Table 2-1. This was the first major contribution to record-keeping on a population and was the beginning of the vital statistics

TABLE 2-1   Selections from Natural and Political Observations Made Upon the Bills of Mortality by John Graunt

The Diseases and Casualties This Year Being 1632

Abortive and Stillborn	445	Jaundies	43
Afrighted	1	Jawfain	8
Aged	628	Impostume	74
Ague	43	Kil'd by Several Accident	46
Apoplex, and Meagrom	17	King's Evil	38
Bit with a mad dog	1	Lethargie	2
Bloody flux, Scowring, and Flux	348	Lunatique	5
Brused, Issues, Sores, and Ulcers	28	Made away themselves	15
Burnt and Scalded	5	Measles	80
Burst, and Rupture	9	Murthered	7
Cancer, and Wolf	10	Over-laid/starved at nurse	7
Canker	1	Palsie	25
Childbed	171	Piles	8
Chrisomes, and Infants	2,268	Plague	8
Cold and Cough	55	Planet	13
Colick, Stone, and Strangury	56	Pleurisie, and Spleen	36
Consumption	1,797	Purples, and Spotted Fever	38
Convulsion	241	Quinsie	7
Cut of the Stone	5	Rising of the Lights	98
Dead in the street and starved	6	Sciatica	1
Dropsie and Swelling	267	Scurvey, and Itch	9
Drowned	34	Suddenly	62
Executed and Prest to Death	18	Surfet	86
Falling Sickness	7	Swine Pox	6
Fever	1,108	Teeth	470
Fistula	13	Thrush, Sore Mouth	40
Flox and Small Pox	531	Tympany	13
French Pox	12	Tissick	34
Gangrene	5	Vomiting	1
Gowt	4	Worms	27
Grief	11		

Christened	**Buried**
Males 4,994	Males 4,932
Females 4,590	Females 4,603
In All 9,584	In All 9,535

Increased in the Burials in the 122 Parishes, and at the Pesthouse this year—993

Decreased of the Plagues in the 122 Parishes, and at the Pesthouses this year—266

Hull CH. Ed. In *The Economic Writings of Sir William Petty*. New York, NY: Cambridge University Press, 1899.

aspect of epidemiology. When Graunt took over the work, he systematically recorded ages, gender, who died, what killed them, and where and when the deaths occurred. Graunt also recorded how many persons died each year and the cause of death.[4,11]

Through the analysis of the bills of mortality already developed for London, Graunt summarized mortality data and developed a better understanding of diseases as well as sources and causes of death. Using the data and information he collected, Graunt wrote a book, *Natural and Political Observations Made Upon the Bills of Mortality.* From the bills of mortality, Graunt identified variations in death according to gender, residence, season, and age. Graunt was the first to develop and calculate life tables and life expectancy. He divided deaths into two types of causes: acute (struck suddenly) and chronic (lasted over a long period of time).[4,11]

When Graunt died, little was done to continue his good work until 200 years later, when William Farr (1807–1883) was appointed registrar general in England. Farr built on the ideas of Graunt. The concept of "political arithmetic" was replaced by a new term, "statistics." Farr extended the use of vital statistics and organized and developed a modern vital statistics system, much of which is still in use today. Another important contribution of Farr was to promote the idea that some diseases, especially chronic diseases, can have a **multifactorial etiology**.[14]

OCCUPATIONAL HEALTH AND INDUSTRIAL HYGIENE

Bernardino Ramazzini (1633–1714) was born in Carpi near Modena, Italy. He received his medical training at the University of Parma and did postgraduate studies in Rome. Ramazzini eventually returned to the town of Modena, where he became a professor of medicine at the local university. He was interested in the practical problems of medicine and not in the study of ancient theories of medicine, a fact not well received by his colleagues. Through Ramazzini's continuous curiosity and his unwillingness to confine himself to the study of ancient medical theories, he became recognized for his innovative approaches to medical and public health problems. For example, in 1692, at the age of 60, Ramazzini was climbing down into 80-foot wells, and taking temperature and barometric readings in order to discover the origin and rapid flow of Modena's spring water. He tried to associate barometric readings with the cause of disease by taking daily readings during a **typhus** epidemic (infectious disease caused by one of the bacteria in the family rickettsiae characterized by high fever, a transient rash, and severe illness).[3,4,11,13]

Ramazzini came upon a worker in a cesspool. In his conversation with the worker, Ramazzini was told that continued work in this environment would cause the worker to go blind. Ramazzini examined the worker's eyes after he came out of the cesspool and found them bloodshot and dim. After inquiring about other effects of working in cesspools and privies, he was informed that only the eyes were affected.[3,4,11,13]

The event with the cesspool worker turned his mind to a general interest in the relationship of work to health. He began work on a book that would become influential in the area of occupational medicine and provided related epidemiologic implications. The book, titled *The Diseases of Workers*, was completed in 1690 but not published until 1703. It was not acceptable to pity the poor or simple laborers in this period of time, which caused Ramazzini to delay the publication because he thought it would not be accepted.[3,4,11,13]

Ramazzini observed that disease among workers arose from two causes. The first, he believed, was the harmful character of the materials that workers handled because the materials often emitted noxious vapors and very fine particles that could be inhaled. The second cause of disease was ascribed to certain violent and irregular motions and unnatural postures imposed on the body while working.[3,4,11,13]

Ramazzini described the dangers of poisoning from lead used by potters in their glaze. He also identified the danger posed by the use of mercury as used by mirror makers, goldsmiths, and others. He observed that very few of these workers reached old age. If they did not die young, their health was so undermined that they prayed for death. He observed that many had palsy of the neck and hands, loss of teeth, vertigo, asthma, and paralysis. Ramazzini also studied those who used or processed organic materials such as mill workers, bakers, starch makers, tobacco workers, and those who processed wool, flax, hemp, cotton, and silk—all of whom suffered from inhaling the fine dust particles in the processing of the materials.[3,4,11,13]

Ramazzini further examined the harmful effects of the physical and mechanical aspects of work, such as varicose veins from standing, sciatica caused by turning the potter's wheel, and ophthalmia found in glassworkers and blacksmiths. Kidney damage was seen to be suffered by couriers and those who rode for long periods, and hernias appeared among bearers of heavy loads.[3,4,11,13]

Major epidemiologic contributions made by Ramazzini were not only his investigation into and description of work-related maladies but his great concern for prevention. Ramazzini suggested that the cesspool workers fasten transparent bladders over their eyes to protect them and take long rest periods or, if their eyes were weak, get into a different line of work. In discussing the various trades, he suggested changing posture, exercising, providing adequate ventilation in workplaces, and avoiding extreme temperatures in the workplace.

Ramazzini was an observant epidemiologist. He described the outbreak of lathyrism in Modena in 1690. He also described the malaria epidemics of the region and the Paduan cattle plague in 1712.[3,4,11,13]

FLORENCE NIGHTINGALE

Florence Nightingale (1820–1910) was the daughter of upper-class British parents (Figure 2-4). She pursued a career in nursing, receiving her initial training in Kaiserworth at a hospital run by an order of Protestant Deaconesses. Two years later, she gained further experience as the superintendent at the Hospital for Invalid Gentlewomen in London, England.

After reading a series of correspondence from the London Times in 1854 on the plight of wounded soldiers fighting in the Crimea, Nightingale asked the British secretary of war to let her work in military hospitals at Scutari, Turkey. In addition to granting her permission, he also designated her head of an official delegation of nurses. Nightingale worked for the next 2 years to improve the sanitary conditions of army hospitals and to reorganize their administration. *The Times* immortalized her as the "Lady with the Lamp" because she ministered to the soldiers throughout the night.

When she returned to England, Nightingale carried out an exhaustive study of the health of the British Army. She created a plan for reform, which was compiled into a 500-page report entitled, *Notes on Matters Affecting the Health, Efficiency, and Hospital Administration of the British Army* (1858). In 1859, she published *Notes on Hospitals*, which was followed in 1860 by *Notes on Nursing: What It Is and What It Is Not*. That same year she established a nursing school at St. Thomas's Hospital in London.

Nightingale wanted to make nursing a respectable profession and believed that nurses should be trained in science. She also advocated strict discipline and an attention to

FIGURE 2-4 Bernardino Ramazzini. Picture courtesy of the United States National Library of Medicine, National Institutes of Health, History of Medicine. http://wwwihm.nlm.nih.gov/ihm/images/B/21/633.jpg or http://wwwihm.nlm.nih.gov/ihm/images/B/21/634.jpg. Accessed January 13, 2009.

cleanliness, and felt that nurses should possess an innate empathy for their patients. Although Nightingale became an invalid after her stay in the Crimea, she remained an influential leader in public health policies related to hospital administration until her death on August 13, 1910.

Her outspoken *Notes on Matters Affecting the Health, Efficiency and Hospital Administration of the British Army* (1857) and *Notes on Hospitals* (1859) helped to create changes in hygiene and overall treatment of patients. She also founded the groundbreaking Nightingale Training School for nurses and in later years published dozens of books and pamphlets on public health. Nightingale was awarded the Royal Red Cross by Queen Victoria in 1883 and in 1907 became the first woman to receive the Order of Merit.

With the encouragement of her father, Nightingale received an education, studying Italian, Latin, Greek, and history, and received excellent training in mathematics. During her time at Scutari, she collected data and systematized record-keeping practices. She used the data as a tool for improving city and military hospitals. She collected and generated data and statistics by developing a Model Hospital Statistical Form for hospitals. Nightingale's monitoring of disease mortality rates showed that with improved sanitary methods in hospitals, death rates decreased. Nightingale developed applied statistical methods to display her data, showing that statistics provided an organized way of learning and improving medical and surgical practices. In 1858, she became a Fellow of the Royal Statistical Society, and in 1874 became an honorary member of the American Statistical Association.[15–19]

TYPHOID MARY

In the early 1900s, 350,000 cases of typhoid occurred each year in the United States. **Typhoid fever** is an infectious disease characterized by a continued fever, physical and mental depression, rose-colored spots on the chest and abdomen, diarrhea, and sometimes intestinal hemorrhage or perforation of the bowel. An Irish cook, Mary Mallon, referred to as "Typhoid Mary," was believed to be responsible for 53 cases of typhoid fever in a 15-year period.[12]

George Soper, a sanitary engineer studying several outbreaks of typhoid fever in New York City in the 1900s, found the food and water supply was no longer suspect as the primary means of transmission of typhoid. Soper continued to search for other means of communication of the disease. He began to look to people instead of fomites, food, and water.

He discovered that Mary Mallon had served as a cook in many homes that were stricken with typhoid. The disease always seemed to follow, but never precede, her employment. Bacteriologic examination of Mary Mallon's feces showed that she was a chronic carrier of typhoid. Mary seemed to sense that she was giving people sickness, because when typhoid appeared, she would leave with no forwarding address. Mary Mallon illustrated the importance of concern over the chronic typhoid carrier causing and spreading typhoid fever. Like 20% of all typhoid carriers, Mary suffered no illness from the disease. Epidemiologic investigations have shown that carriers might be overlooked if epidemiologic searches are limited to the water, food, and those with a history of the disease.[12,20]

From 1907 to 1910, Mary was confined by health officials. The New York Supreme Court upheld the community's right to keep her in custody and isolation. Typhoid Mary was released in 1910, through legal action she took, and she disappeared almost immediately. Two years later, typhoid fever occurred in a hospital in New Jersey and a hospital in New York. More than 200 people were affected. It was discovered that Typhoid Mary had worked at both hospitals as a cook but under a different name. This incident taught public health officials and epidemiologists the importance of keeping track of carriers. It also showed that typhoid carriers should never be allowed to handle food or drink intended for public consumption. In later years, Typhoid Mary voluntarily accepted isolation. Typhoid Mary died at age 70 years.[12,20]

The investigating, tracking, and controlling of certain types of diseases that can affect large populations were epidemiologic insights gained from the Typhoid Mary experience. The importance of protecting public food supplies and the importance of the investigative aspects of disease control were again reinforced and further justified as public health measures. Today, antibiotic therapy is the only effective treatment for typhoid fever.

VITAMINS AND NUTRITIONAL DISEASES

Vitamins are organic components in food that are needed in very small amounts for metabolism, growth, and for maintaining good health. The discovery of vitamins and the role they play in life and health has an interesting history. In the mid-to-late 1800s, bacteria were being identified as the major causes of disease; however, the discovery of microorganisms and their connection to disease clouded the discovery of the causes of other life-threatening diseases. Beriberi, rickets, and pellagra were still devastating the populations around the world. It was believed in 1870 that up to one-third of poor children in the inner city areas of major cities in the world suffered from serious rickets. Biochemistry was being advanced, and new lines of investigation were opening up. In the 1880s, it was observed that when young mice were fed purified diets, they died quickly. When fed milk, they flourished. In 1887, a naval surgeon, T. K. Takaki, eradicated beriberi from the Japanese navy by adding vegetables, meat, and fish to their diet, which up until then was mostly rice. In 1889, at the London Zoo, it was demonstrated that rickets in lion cubs could be cured by feeding them crushed bone, milk, and cod liver oil.[11,21,22]

The first major epidemiologic implications of deficiency illnesses came in 1886 when the Dutch commissioned the firm of C. A. Pekelharing and Winkler who sent Christian Eijkman (1858–1930), an army doctor, to the East Indies to investigate the cause of beriberi. Eijkman observed that chickens fed on polished rice developed symptoms of beriberi and recovered promptly when the food was changed to whole rice, but he mistakenly attributed the cause of the disease to a neurotoxin. Eijkman and G. Grijns (1865–1944), a physiologist, suggested that beriberi was a result of the lack of some essential substance in the outer layer of the rice grain. In 1905, Pekelharing conducted a series of experiments based on Eijkman's observations, was more thorough in his work, and came to the same conclusions.

In 1906, Frederick Gowland Hopkins (1861–1947), a British biochemist, did similar studies with a concern for the pathogenesis of rickets and scurvy. Hopkins suggested that other nutritional factors exist beyond the known ones of protein, carbohydrates, fat, and minerals, and these must be present for good health.

In 1911, Casimir Funk (1884–1967), a Polish chemist, isolated a chemical substance that he believed belonged to a class of chemical compounds called amines. Funk added the Latin term for life, vita, and invented the term "vitamine." He authored the book *Vitamines*. In 1916, E. V. McCollum showed that two factors were required for the normal growth of rats, a fat-soluble "A" factor found in butter and fats and a water-soluble "B" factor found in nonfatty foods such as whole grain rice. These discoveries set the stage for labeling vitamins by letters of the alphabet. McCollum in the United States and E. Mellanby in Great Britain showed that the "A" factor was effective in curing rickets. It was also demonstrated that the "A" factor contained two separate factors. A heat-stable factor was identified and found to be the one responsible for curing rickets. A heat-labile factor that was capable of healing xerophthalmia (dryness of the conjunctiva leading to a diseased state of the mucous membrane of the eye resulting from vitamin A deficiency) was also discovered. The heat-stable factor was named vitamin D, and the heat-labile factor was termed vitamin A.[11,21–23]

The discovery of vitamin D connected observations about rickets and cod liver oil. Cod liver oil cured rickets because it contains vitamin D. It was observed that children exposed to sunshine were less likely to get rickets. In Germany in 1919, Kurt Huldschinsky (1883–1940) also showed that exposing children to artificial sunshine cured rickets. It was shown that vitamin D was produced in the body when sunshine acted on its fats. It was later discovered that the antiberiberi substance vitamin B was also effective against pellagra.[11,21,22]

In this era, the role of social and economic factors was observed to contribute much to the causation of disease, especially poverty conditions, which clearly contributed to nutritional deficiencies.[11]

BEGINNING OF EPIDEMIOLOGY IN THE UNITED STATES

In 1850, Lemuel Shattuck published the first report on sanitation and public health problems in the Commonwealth of Massachusetts. Shattuck was a teacher, sociologist, and statistician, and served in the state legislature. He was the chair of a legislative committee to study sanitation and public health. The report set forth many public health programs and needs for the next century. Of the many needs and programs suggested, several of them were epidemiologic in nature. One of the things needed to ensure that epidemiology, its investigations, and the all-important control and prevention aspects of its work be achieved is an organized and structured effort. The organized effort has to come through an organization sponsored by the government.

Shattuck's report set forth the importance of establishing state and local boards of health. It recommended that an organized effort to collect and analyze vital statistics be established. Shattuck also recommended the exchange of health information, sanitary inspections, research on tuberculosis, and the teaching of sanitation and prevention in medical schools. The health of school children was also of major concern. As a result of the report, boards of health were established, with state departments of health and local public health departments soon to follow—organizations through which epidemiologic activities took place.[24,25]

Quarantine conventions were held in the 1850s. The first in the United States was in Philadelphia in 1857. The prevention of typhus, cholera, and yellow fever was discussed. Port quarantine and the hygiene of immigrants were also of concern. Public health educational activities began at this time. In 1879, the first major book on public health, which included epidemiologic topics, was published by A. H. Buck. The book was titled *Hygiene and Public Health*.[24,25]

The infectious nature of yellow fever was established in 1900 (Figure 2-5). In 1902, the United States Public Health Service was founded, and in 1906, the Pure Food and Drug Act passed. Standard methods of water analysis were also adopted in 1906. The pasteurization of milk was shown to be effective in controlling the spread of disease in 1913, and in this same year, the first school of public health, the Harvard School of Public Health, was established.[24,25]

Alice Hamilton (1869–1970) received a doctor of medicine degree from the Medical School at the University of Michigan. She then completed internships at the Minneapolis Hospital for Women and Children and the New England Hospital for Women and Children. She became a leading expert in occupational health and a pioneer in the field of toxicology. In 1919 she became the first woman appointed to the faculty at the Harvard Medical School, joining a new department in Industrial Medicine.[26]

Wade Hampton Frost (1880–1938) received a medical degree from the University of Virginia (Figure 2-6). He later became the first professor of epidemiology at the Johns

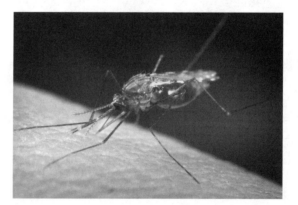

FIGURE 2-5   It has been said that of all the people who ever died, half of them died from the bite of the mosquito. For thousands of years it was not known that the mosquito was responsible for diseases such as yellow fever and malaria. These two diseases are still not fully contained in many parts of the world. In 1900, Walter Reed, MD, a U.S. Army physician working in the tropics, made the epidemiological connection between the mosquito (*Aedes aegypti* species) and yellow fever. Pictures courtesy of Centers for Disease Control and Prevention, Atlanta, Georgia.

FIGURE 2-6   Janet Lane-Clampon. © National Library of Medicine/Photo Researchers, Inc.

Hopkins School of Hygiene and Public Health. Frost created an epidemiology curriculum for the new academic discipline. He also worked closely with Lowell Reed of the Department of Biostatistics, which established the close working relationship between the two disciplines for addressing public health problems. He showed that epidemiology is an analytical science closely integrated with biology and medical science. His work focused on the epidemiology of poliomyelitis, influenza, diphtheria, and tuberculosis. In 1918, Frost, along with Edgar Sydenstriker, investigated the impact of the influenza pandemic on 18 different localities in the United States, providing important insights for public health experts. Because of his contributions to our understanding of the natural history of selected diseases and advances in the methods and scientific discipline of epidemiology, Wade Hampton Frost is often considered to be the father of modern epidemiology.[27]

HISTORICAL DEVELOPMENT OF MORBIDITY IN EPIDEMIOLOGY

An epidemiology professional of the early 1900s who helped advance the study of disease statistics (morbidity) was Edgar Sydenstricker. The development of a morbidity statistics system in the United States was quite slow. One problem was that morbidity statistics cannot be assessed and analyzed in the same manner that death (mortality) statistics are. Sydenstricker struggled with the mere definition of sickness and recognized that to all persons disease is an undeniable and frequent experience. Birth and death come to a person only once but illness comes often. This was especially true in Sydenstricker's era when sanitation, public health, microbiology, and disease control and prevention measures were still being developed.[28]

In the early 1900s, morbidity statistics of any given kind were not regularly collected on a large scale. Interest in disease statistics came only when the demand for them arose from special populations and when the statistics would prove useful socially and economically. Additionally, Sydenstricker noted that there were barriers to collecting homogeneous morbidity data in large amounts: differences in data collection methods and definitions, time elements, and the existence of peculiar factors that affect the accuracy of all records.[28]

Sydenstricker suggested that morbidity statistics be classified into five general groups in order to be of value:

1. Reports of communicable disease. Notification of those diseases for which reasonably effective administrative controls have been devised.

2. Hospital and clinical records. These records were viewed as being of little value in identifying incidence or prevalence of illness in populations (at this time, most people were treated at home unless they were poor and in need of assistance). Such records are only of value for clinical studies.

3. Insurance and industrial establishment and school illness records. The absence of records of illnesses in workers in large industries in the United States was of concern because it added to the difficulty of defining and explaining work-related illness. Criteria for determining disability from illness or injury at work and when sick benefits should be allowed were not well developed. Malingering was also considered, as was its effect on the illness rates of workers. It was suggested that if illness records showing absence from school were kept with a degree of specificity, they could be of value to the understanding of the effect of disease on these populations.

4. Illness surveys. These have been used by major insurance companies to determine the prevalence of illness in a specific population. House-to-house canvass approaches have been used. Incidence of diseases within a given period is not revealed by such methods, whereas chronic-type diseases are found to be of higher incidence (which should be expected and predicted).

5. Records of the incidence of illness in a population continuously or frequently observed. To benefit epidemiologic studies, two study methods have been employed: (1) determination of the annual illness rate in a representative population and (2) development of an epidemiologic method whereby human populations could be observed in order to determine the existence of an incidence of various diseases as they were manifested under normal conditions within the community.[28]

A morbidity study by Sydenstricker and his colleagues under the direction of the United States Public Health Service in Hagerstown, Maryland, was conducted in the years 1921–1924. The study involved 16,517 person-years of observation or an equivalent population of 1,079 individuals who were observed for 28 months beginning in 1921. Illnesses discovered in field investigations, when family members reported being sick or when researchers observed a sick person, were recorded during each family visit. A fairly accurate record of actual illness was obtained by a community interview method. Two findings included were that only 5% of illnesses were of a short duration of 1 day or less and that 40% were not only disabling but caused bed confinement as well. An accurate data-gathering process was developed from the experience.[28]

In the study, 17,847 cases of illness were recorded in a 28-month period. An annual rate of 1,081 per 1,000 person-years was observed, being about one illness per person-year. The illness rate was 100 times the annual death rate in the same population.[28]

The most interesting results of this first morbidity study were the variations of incidence of illness according to age. The incidence of frequent attacks of illness, four or more a year, was highest (45%) in children aged 2–9 years and lowest in those aged 20–24 years (11%).

By 35 years old, the rate rose again to 21%. When severity of illness was looked at, it was found that the greatest resistance to disease was in children between 5 and 14 years. The lowest resistance to disease was in early childhood, 0–4 years, and toward the end of life.[28,29]

THE EPIDEMIOLOGY OF BREAST CANCER

Janet Lane-Claypon (1877–1967) was an English physician who received a doctorate in physiology and an MD at the London School of Medicine for Women. In her early career she applied her skills in the research lab, investigating the biochemistry of milk and reproductive physiology, but later focused her thinking on the epidemiology of breast cancer.[30,31]

In 1912, Lane-Claypon published the results from a novel cohort study showing that babies fed breast milk gained more weight than those fed cow's milk. She used statistical methods to show that the difference in weight between the two groups was unlikely due to chance. She also assessed whether confounding factors could explain the difference. She was a strong advocate for breastfeeding, midwife training, and prenatal services in order to reduce premature births, stillbirths, and maternal mortality.[30,31]

In 1923, Lane-Claypon conducted a case–control study that involved 500 women with a history of breast cancer (cases) and 500 women without history of breast cancer (controls). She then investigated whether the cases differed from the controls with respect to occupation and infant mortality (proxies of social status), nationality, marital status, and age. She also investigated reproductive health histories. Until this study, no large-scale review of this type had been conducted.[30,31]

In 1926, Lane-Claypon conducted another cohort study, which followed a large cohort of surgically treated women with pathologically confirmed breast cancer for up to 10 years. The study showed that disease stage at the time of diagnosis was directly related to survival. She recognized the importance of accurate staging and the potential bias inaccurate staging could have on the results. Further, she showed that breast cancer risk was greater for women who did not have children, who married at a later-than-average age, or who did not breastfeed. She also recognized that genes could influence cancer risk.[30,31]

THE FRAMINGHAM HEART STUDY

In 1948, the Framingham, Massachusetts cardiovascular disease study was launched. The aim of the study was to determine which of the many risk factors contribute most to cardiovascular disease. At the beginning, the study involved 6,000 persons between 30 and 62 years of age. These persons were recruited to participate in a cohort study that spanned 30 years, with 5,100 residents completing the study. In each of the 30 years, medical exams and other related testing activities were conducted with the participants. The study was initially sponsored by the National Health Institute of the United States Public Health Service and the Massachusetts Department of Public Health, along with the local Framingham Health Department.[32–34]

The site for the study was determined by several factors. It was implied that Framingham was a cross-section of America and was a typical small American city. Framingham had a fairly stable population. One major hospital was used by most of the people in the community. An annual updated city population list was kept, and a broad range of occupations, jobs, and industries were represented. The study approach used in the Framingham study was a prospective cohort study.[32–34]

The diseases of most concern in the study were coronary heart disease, rheumatic heart disease, congestive heart failure, angina pectoris, stroke, gout, gallbladder disease, and eye conditions. Several clinical categories of heart disease were distinguished in this study: myocardial infarction, angina pectoris, coronary insufficiency, and death from coronary heart disease, as shown by a specific clinical diagnosis.[32–34]

Many study design methods and approaches were advanced in the investigation, such as cohort tracking, population selection, sampling, issues related to age of the population, mustering population support, community organization, a specific chronic disease focus, and analysis of the study findings.

CIGARETTE SMOKING AND CANCER

After World War II, vital statistics indicated a sharp increase in deaths attributed to lung cancer. The first epidemiologic reports suggesting a link between cigarette smoking and lung cancer appeared in the early 1950s.[35–39] By the time of the 1964 report by the Surgeon General of the United States, there had been 29 case–control studies and 7 prospective cohort studies published, all showing a significantly increased risk of lung cancer among tobacco smokers.[40]

The first case–control studies that assessed the association between smoking and lung cancer were conducted in the late 1940s by Wynder and Graham in the United States (1950) and Doll and Hill in Great Britain (1950).[41,42] These studies first identified cases with lung cancer and controls and then investigated whether people with lung cancer differed from others without the disease with respect to their smoking history. Both studies showed that lung cancer patients were more likely to have been smokers.

The first cohort study assessing the association between smoking and lung cancer was conducted in 1951 by Doll and Hill.[43,44] Physicians in Great Britain were sent a question-naire to determine their smoking habits. They were then followed over a 25-year period with death certificate information collected to determine whether deaths were attributed to lung cancer or some other cause. The study found that smokers were 10 times more likely to die of lung cancer than nonsmokers.

The case–control and cohort study designs used by these researchers remain commonly used in epidemiologic research today.

CONCLUSION

This chapter describes the contributions of many key players to the field of epidemiology. Individuals were presented who helped shape the discipline as we know it today. Pioneers in the area of epidemiology introduced germ theory, the microscope, vaccination, study designs, sources and modes of disease transmission, and the importance of monitoring and evaluating health-related states or events.

Preventing Cholera

A Simple Filtration Procedure Produces a 48% Reduction in Cholera

Cholera continues to plague developing countries and surfaces sporadically throughout the world. In 2001, an estimated 184,311 cases and 2,728 deaths were reported by the World Health Organization. Yet the number of cases and deaths may be much higher because illness and death associated with *Vibrio cholerae* tends to be underreported as a result of surveillance difficulties and threat of economic and social consequences.

Researchers developed a simple filtration procedure involving both nylon filtration and sari cloth (folded four to eight times) filtration for rural villagers in Bangladesh to remove *Vibrio cholerae* attached to plankton in environmental water. The research hypothesis was that removing the copepods (with which *Vibrio cholerae* is associated) from water used for household purposes, including drinking, would significantly reduce the prevalence of cholera. The study was conducted over a 3-year period.

Both the nylon filtration group and the sari filtration group experienced significantly lower cholera rates than the control group. Both filters were comparable in removing copepods as well as particulate matter from the water. The study estimated that the sari cloth filtration reduced the occurrence of cholera by about 48%. Given the low cost of sari cloth filtration, this prevention method has considerable potential in lowering the occurrence of cholera in developing countries.

Data from Colwell RR, Huq A, Islam MS, et al. Reduction of cholera in Bangladeshi villages by simple filtration. Proc Natl Acad Sci. 2003;100(3):1051–1055.

EXERCISES

Key Terms

Define the following terms.

Anthrax

Atomic theory

Childbed fever

Cholera

Multifactorial etiology

Scurvy

Smallpox

Typhoid fever

Typhus

Variolation

Vitamins

Waterborne

STUDY QUESTIONS

1.   Match the individuals in the left-hand column with their contributions.

TABLE 2-2   History of Epidemiology: Names and Contributions II

___ Hippocrates	A. Identified various modes of transmission and incubation times for cholera
___ Thomas Sydenham	B. Prepared a report that set forth the importance of establishing state and local boards of health
___ James Lind	C. Provided classifications of morbidity statistics to improve the value of morbidity information
___ Benjamin Jesty	D. Observed in the 17th century that certain jobs carried a high risk for disease
___ Edward Jenner	E. Eradicated beriberi from the Japanese navy
___ Ignaz Semmelweis	F. Introduced the words "epidemic" and "endemic"
___ John Snow	G. Advanced useful treatments and remedies including exercise, fresh air, and a healthy diet, which other physicians rejected at the time
___ Louis Pasteur	H. Through an experimental study, showed that lemons and oranges were protective against scurvy
___ Robert Koch	I. Identified as the first person in the United States to be a healthy carrier of typhoid fever
___ John Graunt	J. Invented a vaccination for smallpox
___ William Farr	K. The father of modern epidemiology
___ Bernardino Ramazzini	L. Used data as a tool for improving city and military hospitals
___ George Soper	M. Conducted the first cohort study investigating the association between smoking and lung cancer
___ Mary Mallon	N. Promoted the idea that some diseases, especially chronic diseases, can have a multifactorial etiology
___ T. K. Takaki	O. Observed that milkmaids did not get smallpox, but did get cowpox
___ Lemuel Shattuck	P. Developed a vaccine for anthrax
___ Edgar Sydenstricker	Q. Pioneered the use of cohort and case–control studies
___ Doll and Hill	R. A pioneer in the field of toxicology
___ Florence Nightingale	S. Credited as producing the first life table
___ Janet Lane-Claypon	T. Used photography to take the first pictures of microbes in order to show the world that microorganisms in fact existed and that they caused many diseases
___ Alice Hamilton	U. Identified a healthy carrier of typhus
___ Wade Hampton Frost	V. Discovered that the incidence of puerperal fever could be drastically cut by the use of hand washing standards in obstetrical clinics

2. List some of the contributions of the microscope to epidemiology.

3. What two individuals contributed to the birth of vital statistics?

4. What type of epidemiologic study was used by James Lind?

5. What types of epidemiologic studies were used by Doll and Hill?

REFERENCES

1. Hippocrates. Airs, waters, places. In: Buck C, Llopis A, Najera E, Terris M, eds. *The Challenge of Epidemiology: Issues and Selected Readings*. Washington, DC: World Health Organization, 1988: 18–19.

2. Dorland WA, ed. *Dorland's Illustrated Medical Dictionary*, 25th ed. Philadelphia, PA: Saunders; 1974.

3. Cumston CG. *An Introduction to the History of Medicine*. New York, NY: Alfred A. Knopf; 1926.

4. Garrison FH. *History of Medicine*. Philadelphia, PA: Saunders; 1926.

5. Lilienfeld AM, Lilienfeld DE. *Foundations of Epidemiology*, 2nd ed. New York, NY: Oxford University Press; 1980; 30–31.

6. Jenner E. An inquiry into the causes and effects of the variolae vaccine. In: Buck C, Llopis A, Najera E, Terris M, eds. *The Challenge of Epidemiology: Issues and Selected Readings*. Washington, DC: World Health Organization; 1988; 31–32.

7. Semmelweis I. The etiology, concept, and prophylaxis of childbed fever. In: Buck C, Llopis A, Najera E, Terris M, eds. *The Challenge of Epidemiology: Issues and Selected Readings*. Washington, DC: World Health Organization; 1988; 46–59.

8. Benenson AS, ed. *Control of Communicable Diseases in Man*, 15th ed. Washington, DC: American Public Health Association; 1990; 367–373.

9. Snow J. *On the Mode of Communication of Cholera*, 2nd ed.. London: John Churchill, 1855,

10. Snow J. On the mode of communication of cholera. In: Buck C, Llopis A, Najera E, Terris M, eds. *The Challenge of Epidemiology: Issues and Selected Readings*. Washington, DC: World Health Organization; 1988; 42–45.

11. Rosen G. *A History of Public Health*. Baltimore, MD: Johns Hopkins University Press 1958.

12. Nester EW, McCarthy BJ, Roberts CE, Pearsall NN. *Microbiology: Molecules, Microbes and Man*. New York, NY: Holt, Rinehart and Winston; 1973.

13. Seelig MG. *Medicine: An Historical Outline*. Baltimore: Williams and Wilkins; 1925.

14. Fox JP, Hall CE, Elveback LR. *Epidemiology: Man and Disease*. New York, NY: Macmillan Company; 1970.

15. Cohen IB. Florence Nightingale. *Scientific American*. 1984;250:128–137.

16. Cohen IB. *The triumph of numbers: how counting shaped modern life*. New York, NY: W. W. Norton & Company, 2006.

17. Kopf EW. Florence Nightingale as a statistician. *J Am Statist Assoc*. 1916;15:388–404.

18. Nuttal P. The passionate statistician. *Nursing Times*. 1983;28:25–27.

19. Grier MR. Florence Nightingale and statistics. *Res Nurse Health*. 1978;1:91–109.

20. Health News. Medical Milestone: Mary Mallon, Typhoid Mary, November 1968. New York: New York Department of Health; 1968.

21. Krause MV, Hunscher MA. *Food, Nutrition and Diet Therapy*, 5th ed. Philadelphia, PA: Saunders; 1972.

22. Guthrie HA. *Introductory Nutrition*. St. Louis, MO: Mosby, 1975.

23. Clayton T, ed. *Taber's Medical Dictionary*, 14th ed. Philadelphia, PA: Davis; 1981; 762.

24. Green L, Anderson C. *Community Health*, 5th ed. St. Louis, MO: Times Mirror/Mosby; 1986.

25. Picket G, Hanlon J. *Public Health: Administration and Practice*, 9th ed. St. Louis, MO: Times Mirror/Mosby; 1990.

26. Centers for Disease Control and Prevention. The National Institute for Occupational Safety and Health (NIOSH). *History of Alice Hamilton, M.D.* http://www.cdc.gov/niosh/awards/hamilton/HamHist.html. Accessed January 3, 2012.

27. Daniel, TM. *Wade Hampton Frost, Pioneer Epidemiologist 1880–1938: Up to the Mountain.* Rochester, New York: University of Rochester Press; 2004.

28. Sydenstricker E. A study of illness in a general population. *Public Health Rep.* 1926;61:12.

29. Sydenstricker E. Sex difference in the incidence of certain diseases at different ages. *Public Health Rep.* 1928;63:1269–1270.

30. Winkelstein W Jr. Vignettes of the history of epidemiology: three firsts by Janet Elizabeth Lane-Claypon. *Am J Epidemiol.* 2004;160(2):97–101.

31. Morabia A. Janet Lane-Claypon—interphase epitome. *Epidemiology.* 2010;21(4):573–576.

32. Miller DF. *Dimensions of Community Health*, 3rd ed. Dubuque, IA: William C. Brown; 1992.

33. Hennekens CH, Buring JE. *Epidemiology in Medicine.* Boston, MA: Little, Brown and Company; 1987.

34. Dawber TR, Kannel WB, Lyell LP. An approach to longitudinal studies in a community: the Framingham study. *Ann NY Acad Sci.* 1963;107:539–556.

35. Doll R, Hill AB. Smoking and carcinoma of the lung: preliminary report. *BMJ.* 1950;2:739.

36. Norr R. Cancer by the carton. *Read Dig.* December 1952:7–8.

37. Cigarettes. What CU's test showed: the industry and its advertising, and how harmful are they? *Consum Rep.* 1953:58–74.

38. Miller LM, Monahan J. The facts behind the cigarette controversy. *Read Dig.* 1954:1–6.

39. Tobacco smoking and lung cancer. *Consum Rep.* 1954:54, 92.

40. United States Department of Health and Human Services. *Smoking and Health: Report of the Advisory Committee to the Surgeon General of the Public Health Service.* Publication PHS 1103. Washington, DC: U.S. Government Printing Office; 1964.

41. Wynder EL, Graham EA. Tobacco smoking as a possible etiologic factor in bronchiogenic carcinoma: a study of six hundred and eighty-four proved cases. *JAMA.* 1950;143:329–336.

42. Doll R, Hill AB. Smoking and carcinoma of the lung: preliminary report. *BMJ.* 1950;2:739–748.

43. Doll R, Hill AB. Mortality in relation to smoking: ten years' observations of British doctors. *BMJ.* 1964;1:1399–1410.

44. Doll R, Peto R. Mortality in relation to smoking: twenty years' observations on male British doctors. *BMJ.* 1976;2:1525.

3

Practical Disease Concepts in Epidemiology

OBJECTIVES

After completing this chapter, you will be able to:

- Define disease and identify common sources and modes of disease transmission.
- Classify acute and chronic diseases according to infectivity and communicability.
- Understand the major stages in the disease process.
- Know the five major categories of disease.
- Define zoonosis and identify selected zoonotic diseases and potential carriers of infectious organisms that may be zoonotic.
- Describe notifiable disease reporting in the United States.
- Discuss immunity and immunizations against infectious diseases.
- Identify the changing emphasis of epidemiologic study.
- Be familiar with common nutritional deficiency diseases and disorders.
- Be familiar with selected chronic diseases and conditions.

Disease is an interruption, cessation, or disorder of body functions, systems, or organs.[1] Diseases arise from infectious agents, inherent weaknesses, lifestyle, or environmental stresses. Often a combination of these factors influences the onset of disease. The early development of epidemiology was based on the investigation of infectious disease outbreaks. Today, epidemiologic studies also consider diseases that are influenced by noninfectious causes such as genetic susceptibility, lifestyle, and selected environmental factors.

Identifying the causes of disease and the mechanisms by which disease is spread remains a primary focus of epidemiology. The science and study of the causes of disease and their mode of operation is referred to as **etiology**.[1] Disease processes are complex and require an understanding of several factors, which may include anatomy, physiology, histology, biochemistry, microbiology, and related medical sciences. This chapter cannot provide a comprehensive foundation of all these fields of study. Thus, only the basics of diseases, their classification, and processes are presented in this chapter.

COMMUNICABLE AND NONCOMMUNICABLE DISEASES AND CONDITIONS

Infectious diseases are caused by invading organisms called pathogens. Infectious diseases may or may not be contagious. When an infectious disease is contagious, or capable of being communicated or transmitted, it is called a **communicable disease**.[1] Examples of infectious communicable diseases are HIV/AIDS, cholera, and influenza. Although all communicable diseases are infectious diseases, not all infectious diseases are communicable diseases. An example of an infectious noncommunicable disease is tetanus, caused by the bacterium *Clostridium tetani*, which is found in the environment. Spores of the bacterium live in the soil, may remain infectious for over 40 years, and are found throughout the world. Similarly, anthrax exposure may result by breathing spores that have been in the soil for, in some cases, many years. Another example is Legionnaires' disease, which is caused by inhaling *Legionella* bacteria from the environment. Noninfectious diseases may be referred to as noncommunicable diseases and conditions, such as heart disease, most forms of cancer, mental illness, and accidents.

Infectious communicable diseases may be transmitted through vertical or horizontal transmission. **Vertical transmission** refers to transmission from an individual to its offspring through sperm, placenta, milk, or vaginal fluids.[1] **Horizontal transmission** refers to transmission of infectious agents from an infected individual to a susceptible contemporary.[1] Horizontal transmission may involve direct transmission (e.g., sexually transmitted diseases), a common vehicle (e.g., waterborne, food-borne, or blood-borne diseases), an airborne pathogen (e.g., tuberculosis), or a vector-borne pathogen (e.g., malaria).

Pathogens are defined as organisms or substances such as bacteria, protozoa, viruses, fungi, abnormal or infectious prions (proteins produced by mutated genes), or parasites that are capable of producing disease.[1] Infectious diseases are those in which the pathogen is capable of entering, surviving, and multiplying in the host. **Invasiveness** refers to the ability of a pathogen to get into a susceptible host and cause disease. The host plays a major part in the ability of an organism to cause disease by providing nutrients and a life-sustaining environment. The disease-evoking power of a pathogen is called **virulence**.[1]

Antibiotics work against pathogens because of their toxicity—that is, the antibiotic substance contains elements that are more toxic to bacteria than to the human body. **Toxins** are poisons and consequently kill pathogens by poisoning them. For example, arsenic is a toxin once used to treat syphilis.[2] The strength of a substance or chemical is measured by how little of it is required for it to work as a poison and how quickly it acts. The

TABLE 3-1   Examples of Diseases and Conditions According to Selected Classifications

	Communicable		Noncommunicable	
	Acute	**Chronic**	**Acute**	**Chronic**
Infectious	Influenza/pneumonia	Cancer	Tetanus	
	Lyme disease	Leprosy	Legionnaire's	
	Mumps	Polio	Anthrax	
	Measles	Syphilis		
	Cholera	Tuberculosis		
Noninfectious			Accidents	Alcoholism
			Drug abuse	Cancer
			Homicide	Diabetes mellitus
			Stroke	Heart diseases
			Suicide	Paralysistanus

shorter the duration and the less of the substance needed to cause the organism to die, the higher the level of toxicity.

Diseases are classified as acute and chronic.

Acute: relatively severe disorder with sudden onset and short duration of symptoms.[1]

Chronic: less severe but of continuous duration, lasting over long time periods if not a lifetime.[1]

Infectious and noninfectious diseases can be acute or chronic. To help clarify acute and chronic disease classification according to infectivity and communicability, some examples are presented in Table 3-1.

NATURAL HISTORY OF DISEASE

Each disease has a natural history of progression if no medical intervention is taken and the disease is allowed to run its full course. There are four common stages relevant to most diseases.

1. Stage of susceptibility
2. Stage of presymptomatic disease
3. Stage of clinical disease
4. Stage of recovery, disability, or death

The stage of susceptibility precedes the disease and involves the likelihood a host has of developing ill effects from an external agent. The stage of presymptomatic disease begins with exposure and subsequent pathologic changes that occur before the onset of symptoms. This is also typically called the **incubation period**. For chronic diseases, the time from exposure to clinical symptoms is typically called the **latency period**. The stage of clinical disease begins when signs and symptoms are manifest. The final stage reflects the expected prognosis. Several factors may influence these stages including early detection and effective treatment. With regard to prevention, primary prevention may occur during the stage of susceptibility. Secondary prevention may occur during the stage of presymptomatic disease or the stage of clinical disease, and tertiary prevention may occur during the stage of clinical disease or in the final stage.

With an infectious disease, the natural course begins with the susceptible person's exposure to a pathogen. The pathogen propagates itself and then spreads within the host. Factors of each disease, each pathogen, and each individual host vary in the way a disease responds, spreads, and affects the body. The progress of a disease can be halted at any point, either by the strength of the response of the body's natural immune system or through intervention with antibiotics, therapeutics, or other medical interventions (Figure 3-1). Changes in the body are initially undetected and unfelt. As the pathogen continues to propagate, changes are experienced by the host, marked by the onset of such symptoms as fever, headache, weakness, muscle aches, malaise, and upset stomach. The disease reacts in the body in the manner peculiar to that disease. Possible outcomes are recovery, disability, or death. A generalized presentation of the natural history of disease is shown in Figure 3-2.

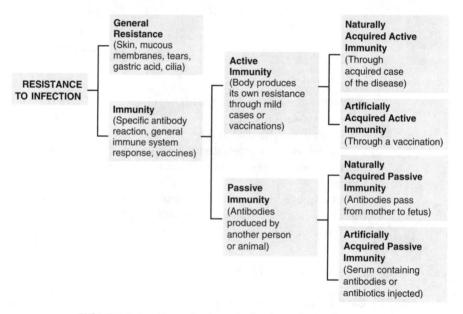

FIGURE 3-1   How the human body resists infections.

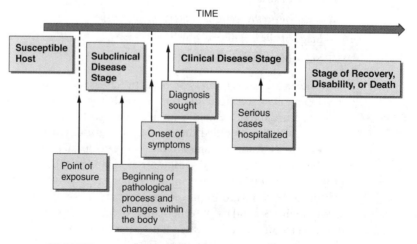

FIGURE 3-2   Natural course of communicable disease.

CLASSIFYING DISEASE

Diseases can be classified into five general categories: congenital and hereditary diseases, allergies and inflammatory diseases, degenerative diseases, metabolic diseases, and cancer. Each of these is defined as follows:

- **Congenital and hereditary diseases** are often caused by genetic and familial tendencies toward certain inborn abnormalities; injury to the embryo or fetus by environmental factors, chemicals, or agents such as drugs, alcohol, or smoking; or innate developmental problems possibly caused by chemicals or agents. They can also be a fluke of nature. Examples are Down syndrome, hemophilia, and heart disease present at birth.[2]

- **Allergies and inflammatory diseases** are caused by the body reacting to an invasion of or injury by a foreign object or substance. An allergen is a substance that can cause an allergic reaction. Animal proteins and animal dander, bacteria and viruses, chemicals, dust, drugs, foods, perfumes, plants, pollen, and smoke are common agents that can cause an inflammatory reaction in the body. Some inflammatory reactions may result in the body forming antibodies. **Antibodies** are formed as a first line of defense. They are protein substances or globulins derived from B and T lymphocytes that originate in the bone marrow.[2]

- **Degenerative diseases** cause a lower level of mental, physical, or moral state than is normal or acceptable. Degenerative diseases are often associated with the aging process but in some cases may not be age related. Arteriosclerosis, arthritis, and gout are examples of degenerative chronic diseases.[2]

- **Metabolic diseases** cause the dysfunction, poor function, or malfunction of certain organs or physiologic processes in the body, leading to disease states. Glands or organs that fail to secrete certain biochemicals to keep the metabolic process functioning in the body cause metabolic disorders. For example, adrenal glands may stop functioning properly causing Addison's disease; the cells may no longer use glucose normally, causing diabetes; or the thyroid gland might fail, resulting in a goiter, hyperthyroidism, or cretinism (hypothyroidism).[2]

- **Cancer** is a collective name that refers to a group of many diseases with one common characteristic: uncontrolled cell growth or the loss of the cell's ability to perform apoptosis (cell suicide). The gradual increase in the number of uncontrolled dividing cells creates a mass of tissue called a tumor (neoplasm). When a tumor is malignant, meaning it is capable of spreading to surrounding tissue or remote places in the body, it is called cancer.[3]

Diseases may also be classified according to their source (Table 3-2) or mode of transmission (Table 3-3).

The ability of a disease to be transmitted from one person to the next or to spread in a population is referred to as the **communicability** of the disease. The communicability of a disease is determined by how likely a pathogen or agent is to be transmitted from a diseased or infected person to another person who is not immune and is susceptible. Five different means of transmission can be used to classify certain infectious diseases. The five classifications are airborne or respiratory transmission, transmission through intestinal (alvine) discharge (which includes water-borne and food-borne diseases), transmission through open lesions, zoonotic or vector-borne transmission, and fomite-borne transmission. The five classifications and some of the major related diseases and modes of transmission are shown in Table 3-3.[4–8]

Diseases can also be classified by the microbe source from which they come. Table 3-4 presents the different classes of microorganisms along with examples.[2,4–6,9–11]

TABLE 3-2   Classification of Sources of Disease or Illness

Classification	Examples of Sources
Allergic	Mold, dust, foods
Chemical	Drugs, acids, alkali, heavy metals (lead, mercury), poisons (arsenic), some enzymes
Congenital	Rubella, cytomegalovirus, syphilis, toxoplasmosis, alcohol abuse
Hereditary	Familial tendency diseases such as alcoholism, genetic or chromosome structure that passes disability, disease, or disorders on to offspring; syndromes
Infectious	Bacteria, viruses, parasites
Inflammatory	Stings, poison ivy, wounds, slivers or impaled objects, arthritis, serum sickness, allergic reactions
Metabolic	Dysfunctional organs within the body producing hypothyroidism, hyperthyroidism, exophthalmic goiter
Nutritional	Vitamin deficiencies such as scurvy or protein deficiencies such as kwashiorkor
Physical agent	Excessive cold or heat, electrical shock, radiation, injury
Psychological	Biochemical imbalances in the brain as in schizophrenia; loss of or destruction of brain tissue such as in Alzheimer's disease
Traumatic	Wounds, bone fractures, contusions, mechanical injury
Tumors	Environmental or behaviorally stimulated tumors, such as cancer of the lung from smoking
Vascular	Smoking, stress, lack of proper diet, lack of exercise, and other behaviorally related implications that contribute to heart and cardiovascular diseases

TABLE 3-3   Classification of Major Infectious Diseases by Mode of Transmission

Airborne Respiratory Diseases	Intestinal Discharge Diseases	Open Sores or Lesion Diseases	Zoonoses or Vector-Borne Diseases	Fomite-Borne Diseases
Chickenpox	Amebic dysentery	AIDS	African sleeping sickness	Anthrax
Common colds	Bacterial dysentery	Anthrax	Encephalitis	Chickenpox
Diphtheria	(shigellosis)	Erysipelas	Lyme disease	Common colds
Influenza	(staphylococcal)	Gonorrhea	Malaria	Diphtheria
Measles	Cholera	Scarlet fever	Rocky mountain spotted fever	Influenza
Meningitis	Giardiasis	Smallpox	Tularemia	Meningitis
Pneumonia	Hookworm	Syphilis	Typhus fever	Poliomyelitis
Poliomyelitis	Poliomyelitis	Tuberculosis	Yellow fever	Rubella
Rubella	Salmonellosis	Tularemia		Scarlet fever
Scarlet fever	Typhoid fever			Streptococcal throat infections
Smallpox	Hepatitis			
Throat infections				Tuberculosis
Tuberculosis				
Whooping cough				

TABLE 3-4   Classification of Microbe Sources of Disease

Organisms	Diseases
Bacteria	
Bacilli	Diphtheria (aerobic—*Corynebacterium diphtheriae*)
	Botulism (anaerobic—*Clostridium botulinum*)
	Brucellosis (*Brucella abortus*)
	Legionellosis (*Legionella pneumophila*)
	Salmonellosis (salmonella)
	Shigellosis (*Shigella dysentariae*)
	Cholera (*Vibrio cholerae*)
Cocci	Impetigo (*Staphylococcus aureus, streptococci*)
	Toxic shock (*staphylococci*)
	Streptococcal sore throat (*streptococci*)
	Scarlet fever (*streptococci*)
	Erysipelas (*streptococci*)
	Pneumonia (*pneumococci*)
	Gonorrhea (*gonococci*)
	Meningitis (*meningococci*)
Spiral organisms	Syphilis (*Treponema pallidum*)
	Rat-bite fever (*Streptobacillusmoniliformis* and *Spirillum minus*)
	Lyme disease (spriochete—*Borrelia burgdorferi*)
Acid-fast organisms	Tuberculosis (*Mycobacterium tuberculosis*)
	Leprosy (*Myocobacterium leprae*)
Rickettsia (very small bacteria)	Rocky mountain spotted fever (*Rickettsia rickettsii*)
	Typhus (*Rickettsia prowazekii*)
Viruses	Chickenpox (*herpes virus*)
	Influenza
	Type A: associated with epidemics and pandemics
	Type B: associated with local epidemics
	Type C: associated with sporadic minor localized outbreaks
	Measles (*Morbillivirus*)
	Mumps (*Paramyxovirus*)
	Poliomyelitis (type 1, most paralytogenic; 2, 3, less common)
	Rabies
	Smallpox (*Variola virus*)
Fungi	Mycosis
Molds	Ringworm
Yeast	Blastomycosis
	Dermatophytosis

Data are from various resources.[2,4–6,9–11]

TABLE 3-5   Classification of Animal Sources of Disease

Organisms	Disease
Protozoa (one celled)	
Amoebae	Dysentery
Plasmodia	Malaria
Worms (metazoa)	
Roundworms	Ascaris (large roundworms)
Pinworms	
Flukes	
Trichinellae	Trichinosis
Arthropods (lice)	Pediculosis
	Scabies (*Sarcoptes scabiei*)

Data are from various resources.[2,4–6,8–11]

In addition, three microscopic animal sources of disease exist. The classifications of the three animal sources are presented in Table 3-5. The organism is presented, along with an example of the disease it causes.[2,4,5,6,8–11]

Pathogens are not the only sources of conditions, disease, or death in humans. Many causes of illness, conditions, and injury exist. Some are of human's own doing; some are naturally occurring, and others are environmentally related. Still other conditions are self-inflicted at work, in industry, at home, or in the process of getting to and from work. Table 3-6 presents the different inanimate sources of illness and disability. The source and an example of illness or disability for each are presented, as is the mode of entry into the body.[12,13]

PORTALS OF ENTRY TO THE HUMAN BODY

Different modes of entry into the body have been identified. They are listed here, with the more common sites of entry listed first.

- Respiratory
- Oral
- Reproductive
- Intravenous
- Urinary
- Skin
- Gastrointestinal
- Conjunctival
- Transplacental

TABLE 3-6   Classification of Inanimate Sources of Illness and Disability

Source	Illness/Disability	Mode of Entry

Dusts
  Silica
  Asbestos
	Silicosis (fibrosis of lung tissue)
	Asbestosis (fibrosis of lung tissue)
	Lung cancer
		Inhalation

Fumes Lead	Lead poisoning	Inhalation, skin
Smoke	Asphyxia from oxygen deficiency Smoke poisoning Asphyxia from carbon monoxide	Inhalation

Gases, mists, aerosols,
  and vapors
	Asphyxia or chemical poisoning
	  (depending on the source)
		Inhalation

Electrical energy	Burns, neurologic damage, death	Skin
Noise	Hearing loss, deafness	Nervous system
Ionizing radiation	Cancer, dermatitis	Skin/tissue
Nonionizing radiation	Burns, cancer	Skin/tissue
Thermal energy	Burns, cancer	Skin/tissue
Ergonomic problems	Muscle, skeletal, tissue problems	Skin/tissue
Stress	Mental, emotional, physiologic, behavioral problems	Nervous system
Bites	Snakebite poisoning, lacerations, tissue damage	Skin/tissue
Stings	Pain, swelling, redness	Skin/tissue
Chemical ingestion	Cancer, liver damage, respiratory damage	Respiratory, digestive, skin/tissue

Data are from various resources.[12,13]

INCUBATION PERIODS FOR SELECTED INFECTIOUS DISEASES

To become ill, an individual has to be inoculated with a disease. This brings to mind a picture of an Anopheles female mosquito biting (inoculation by injection) an unsuspecting susceptible individual on a warm spring evening, infecting the person with a disease such as malaria. The incubation period is the time that elapses between inoculation and the appearance of the first signs or symptoms of the disease. In the case of the victim with the mosquito bite, the incubation for malaria is about 15 days (range, 10–35 days) from the time of the bite until the victim starts having shaking chills, fever, sweats, malaise, and headache. This lasts for about 1 day and then recurs on and off every 48 hours. Difficulty determining when the exposure occurred (inoculation or exposure to illness) makes ascertaining the starting point of the incubation period problematic. Vague prodromal signs of illness make it difficult to determine the end point of the illness, and the signs and symptoms of different diseases are often alike; for example, malaria could initially be mistaken for flu.

Some diseases are transmissible in the last 2 or 3 days of the incubation period, for example, measles and chickenpox. As seen in Table 3-7, incubation periods vary from disease to disease. Incubation periods can also vary with the individual; one who has a more active immune system can retard the pathogen's growth within the body, lengthening the incubation period. It has been observed that diseases with short incubation periods generally produce a more acute and severe illness, whereas long incubation diseases are less severe, although there are, of course, exceptions.

TABLE 3-7   Partial List of Incubation Periods for Major Communicable Diseases (Incomplete List)

Disease	Incubation Period	Communicability Period
Botulism	12–36 hours	When exposed
Chickenpox	2–3 weeks	From 5 days before vesicles appear to 6 days after
Common cold	12–72 hours (usually 24)	From 1 day before onset to 5 days after
Conjunctivitis	1–3 days	As long as infection is present and active
Diphtheria	2–5 days	≤ 2 weeks and not more than 4 weeks
Dysentery (amoebic)	2–4 weeks (wide variation)	During intestinal infection; untreated, for years
Epstein-Barr virus	4–7 weeks	While symptoms are present
Gonorrhea	2–5 days (maybe longer)	Indefinite unless treated
Hepatitis (serum)	45–160 days	Before onset of symptoms
Herpes simplex virus	Up to 2 weeks	As long as 7 weeks after symptoms disappear
Impetigo (contagious)	4–10 days or longer	Until lesions heal
Influenza	1–3 days	Often 3 days from clinical onset
Measles (rubeola)	10 days to onset, rash at 14 days	From prodromal period to 4 days after rash onset
Meningitis	2–10 days	One day after beginning of medication
Mumps	12–26 days (usually 18 days)	From 6 days before symptoms to 9 days after
Pediculosis	Approximately 2 weeks	As long as lice remain alive
Pneumonia, bacterial	1–3 days	Unknown
Pneumonia, viral	1–3 days	Unknown
Poliomyelitis	3–21 days (usually 7–12 days)	7–10 days before and after symptoms
Pinworm (enterobiasis)	2–6 weeks	Up to 2 weeks
Rabies	2–8 weeks or longer	3–5 days before symptoms and during the course of the disease
Respiratory viral infection	A few days to a week or more	Duration of the active disease

TABLE 3-7   Partial List of Incubation Periods for Major Communicable Diseases (Incomplete List) *(continued)*

Disease	Incubation Period	Communicability Period
Ringworm	4–10 days	As long as lesions are present
Rubella (German measles)	8–10 days (usually 14 days)	1 week before and to 4 days after onset of rash
Salmonella food poisoning	6–72 hours (usually 36 hours)	3 days to 3 weeks (wide variation)
Scarlet fever	1–3 days	24–48 hours (treated); 10–21 days (untreated)
Staphylococcal food poisoning	2–4 hours	When exposed
Streptococcal sore throat	1–3 days	24–48 hours (treated); as long as ill (untreated)
Smallpox	7–17 days (usually 10–12)	Primarily within 7–10 days of onset of rash
Syphilis	10 days to 10 weeks (usually 3 weeks)	Variable and indefinite if not treated
Tetanus	4 days to 3 weeks	When exposed
Trichinosis	2–128 days (usually 9 days) after ingestion of infected meat	When exposed
Tuberculosis	4–12 weeks (primary phase)	As long as tubercle bacilli are discharged by patient or carriers
Typhoid fever	1–3 weeks (usually 2 weeks)	As long as typhoid bacilli appear in feces
Whooping cough	7–21 days (usually by 10 days)	From 7 days after exposure to 3 weeks after onset of typical paroxysms

LATER STAGES OF INFECTION

The prodromal period is the second stage of illness and the period in which signs and symptoms of a disease first appear. In most respiratory diseases, this is usually one day. Disease transmission is greatest during the prodromal period because of the high communicability of the disease at this stage and because the symptoms are not clearly evident.

The following terms help to characterize disease further:

■ **Fastigium** is the period when the disease is at its maximum severity or intensity. Diagnosis is easiest at or directly after the differential point. Many respiratory illnesses produce the same symptoms in the prodromal stage, making diagnosis difficult. In the fastigium period, even though the disease is highly communicable, patients do not spread it much. Usually in this phase of the disease, the sick person is home in bed or in the hospital.

- **Defervescence** is the period when the symptoms of the illness are declining. As patients feel that they are recovering from a disease in this period, they may not take care of themselves. If the immune system is weakened and cannot effectively fight off the pathogens, a relapse may occur at this stage. This is also a period when the likelihood of transmission of the disease is quite high because patients may be up and about although not yet recovered and still infectious.

- **Convalescence** is the recovery period. Those affected may still be infectious at this point but are feeling much better. They may be out and about, spreading the disease.

- **Defection** is the period during which the pathogen is killed off or brought into remission by the immune system. In some diseases, defection and convalescence may be the same stage. If isolation is required, it is in the defection stage that isolation is lifted.[6]

A factor that affects not only upper respiratory diseases but many others is the strength or virulence of the disease. Recall that virulence is the strength of the disease agent and its ability to produce a severe case of the disease or cause death. Related to the virulence of a pathogen is the viability of the disease-causing agent. **Viability** is the capacity of the pathogen or disease-causing agent to survive outside the host and to exist or thrive in the environment.

When a disease such as a respiratory disease has not yet manifested itself or produces only a mild case of a disease or condition, it is referred to as being subclinical. The presence of some diseases can be revealed with clinical tests such as blood analysis; however, clinical symptoms may not be apparent. This state is also referred to as a subclinical infection or subclinical case. In the absence of clinical symptoms, such a condition must be confirmed immunologically.

ZOONOSES

It has long been understood that an animal can be the host, vector, or source of certain infections and diseases (Figure 3-3). Historically, it was recognized that certain diseases can be transmitted from animals to humans. A **zoonosis** (plural zoonoses) is an infectious organism in vertebrate animals (e.g., rabies or anthrax) that can be transmitted to humans through direct contact, a fomite, or vector. The word comes from the Greek words zoon (animal) and nosos (ill).

There are numerous potential carriers of infectious organisms that may be zoonotic (Table 3-8).

Zooneses may be classified according to the infectious agent: parasites, fungi, bacteria, viruses, and pria. Another way some diseases are classified and studied is based on the ability of the disease to be transmitted to humans from animals. More than 185 diseases have been shown to be transmitted to humans from animals.[11] Common zoonotic diseases are presented in Table 3-9.

Some animals can be carriers of a disease without showing any signs or symptoms. For example, coyotes can carry plague, never becoming sick from the disease, yet spreading it to rodents and humans via a flea vector. Humans may get bitten by a flea while in the woods or at home, get ill a few days later, and not connect their disease to the inoculation by the insect. Historically, the animal–flea–human set of events was a connection not easily made. For hundreds of years, humans got malaria from mosquito bites and never realized that the disease

Life Cycle of *Taenia solium*

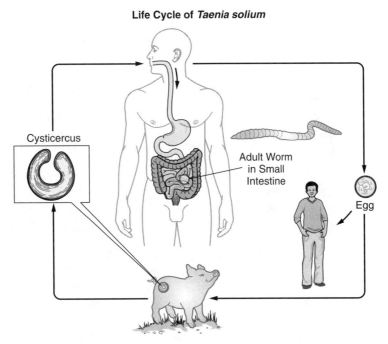

Cysticercus

Adult Worm
in Small
Intestine

Egg

FIGURE 3-3   Example of zoonosis and the disease transmission cycle. The two-host life cycle of *T. solium* involves humans as definitive hosts for the intestinal stage adult tapeworm that is acquired by eating undercooked pork contaminated with cysticerci. Swine, the intermediate host, become infected with the larval stage by ingesting eggs shed in the feces of a human tapeworm carrier. Humans may inadvertently acquire larval-stage infection through the fecal–oral route. From Centers for Disease Control and Prevention, "Locally acquired neurocysticercosis—North Carolina, Massachusetts, and South Carolina, 1989–1991." Morbidity and Mortality Weekly Report, Public Health Services, U.S. Department of Health and Human Services, Vol. 21, No. 1, Jan. 10, 1992, pp. 1–4.

TABLE 3-8   Potential Carriers of Infectious Organisms That Can Be Zoonotic

Assassin bugs	Flies	Possums
Bats	Geese	Pigs
Bank voles	Goats	Rabbits
Birds	Hamsters	Raccoons
Cats	Horses	Rats
Cattle	Humans	Rodents
Chimpanzees	Lice	Sloths
Dogs	Mice	Sheep
Fish	Monkeys	Snails
Fleas	Mosquitoes	Ticks

TABLE 3-9   Partial List of Zoonoses

Acquired immunodeficiency syndrome	Kyasanur forest disease
Amebiasis	Lábrea fever
Anthrax	Lassa fever
Avian influenza (Bird Flu)	Leishmaniasis
Babesiosis	Leptospirosis
Barmah Forest virus	Listeriosis
Bartonellosis	Lyme disease
Bilharzia	Lymphocytic Choriomeningitis virus
Bolivian hemorrhagic fever	Malaria
Bovine popular stomatitis	Marburg fever
Brucellosis	Mediterranean spotted fever
Borna virus infection	Monkey B virus
Bovine tuberculosis	Nipah fever
Campylobacteriosis	Ocular larva migrans
Chagas disease	Omsk hemorrhagic fever
Chlamydophila psittaci	Ornithosis (psittacosis)
Cholera	Orf (animal disease)
Colorado tick fever	Oropouche fever
Cowpox	Plague
Crimean-Congo hemorrhagic fever	Puumala virus
Cryptosporidiosis	Q-Fever
Cutaneous larva migrans	Psittacosis, or "parrot fever"
Dengue fever	Rabies
Ebola	Rift Valley fever
Echinococcosis	Ringworms (*Tinea canis*)
Escherichia coli O157:H7	Salmonellosis
Eastern equine encephalitis virus	Streptococcus suis
Western equine encephalitis virus	Toxoplasmosis
Venezuelan equine encephalitis virus	Trichinosis
Hantavirus	Tularemia, or "rabbit fever"
Hendra virus	Typhus of Rickettsiae
Henipavirus	West Nile virus
Korean hemorrhagic fever	Yellow fever

came from the mosquito. The same was also true for the sequence of events from flea bites to plague.

Humans are most protective of their domestic animals, and any implication that an owner may get a disease from a pet is not well received; nevertheless, the possibility exists and must not be overlooked by the epidemiologist. One of the most common disorders overlooked by pet owners is that of allergies in the family caused by the furry animals in their home. Children or adults may suffer allergies for years and never consider the family pet as the source of the allergic condition until tested by a physician. Tularemia (rabbit fever), cat-scratch fever, worms from dogs, and parrot fever (psittacosis) have long been known to exist and are examples of zoonotic diseases.

INTERNATIONAL CLASSIFICATION OF DISEASES

The World Health Organization (WHO) provides internationally endorsed standard diagnostic classifications for general epidemiologic and health management purposes. These classifications provide a common language of disease for governments, providers of health care, and consumers. In 1990, the 43rd World Health Assembly endorsed International Classification of Diseases 10 (ICD-10). In 1994, it came into use by WHO member states. The first classification of diseases was in the 1850s and was adopted by the International Statistical Institute in 1948. In 1949, the WHO took responsibility for the ICD when the sixth revision was created. For the first time, this revision included causes of morbidity.[14]

The ICD uses death certificates, hospital records, and other sources to classify diseases and health-related problems. The classifications provide a basis for comparing morbidity and mortality statistics among WHO member states. The ICD facilitates the analysis of the general health and well-being of populations. The monitoring of incidence, prevalence, mortality data, and health-related problems is made possible because of standard diagnostic classifications.

NOTIFIABLE DISEASES IN THE UNITED STATES

Beginning in 1961, the Centers for Disease Control and Prevention (CDC) took charge of collecting and publishing data on nationally notifiable diseases. The list of diseases changes from year to year to reflect the emergence of new pathogens or the decline in incidence of certain diseases. Health officials at the state and national levels mutually determine the list of notifiable diseases. Reporting of nationally notifiable diseases to the CDC is no longer required by law but is voluntary; however, reporting of diseases at the state level is required. State regulations specify the diseases that must be reported, who is responsible for reporting, the information required on each case, to whom and how quickly the information is to be reported, and the expected control measures to be taken for specific diseases.[15]

Notifiable diseases are those of considerable public health importance because of their seriousness. As a general rule, a disease is included on a state's list if it (1) causes serious morbidity or death, (2) has the potential to spread, and (3) can be controlled with appropriate intervention. The list of notifiable diseases varies from state to state in order to reflect state-specific public health priorities. Notifiable infectious diseases that are currently reported by most states are presented in Table 3-10.[16] Other reportable diseases or events may include Alzheimer's disease, animal bites, cancer, disorders characterized by lapses of consciousness, and pesticide exposure.

State health departments also expect reporting of diseases experiencing unusually high incidence and the occurrence of any unusual disease that has public health importance.[15] Reporting of notifiable diseases is required of physicians, dentists, nurses, other health practitioners, and medical examiners. It may also be required or requested of laboratory directors and administrators of hospitals, clinics, nursing homes, schools, and nurseries.[15]

TABLE 3-10   Nationally Notifiable Diseases and Conditions in the United States in 2012

Infectious Conditions

Anthrax

Arboviral neuroinvasive and non-neuroinvasive diseases

- California serogroup virus disease
- Eastern equine encephalitis virus disease
- Powassan virus disease
- St. Louis encephalitis virus disease
- West Nile virus disease
- Western equine encephalitis virus disease

Babesiosis

Botulism

- Botulism, foodborne
- Botulism, infant
- Botulism, other (wound & unspecified)

Brucellosis

Campylobacteriosis

Chancroid

Chlamydia trachomatis infection

Cholera

Coccidioidomycosis

Cryptosporidiosis

Cyclosporiasis

Dengue

- Dengue fever
- Dengue hemorrhagic fever
- Dengue shock syndrome

Diphtheria

Ehrlichiosis/Anaplasmosis

- *Ehrlichia chaffeensis*
- *Ehrlichia ewingii*
- *Anaplasma phagocytophilum*
- Undetermined

Free-living Amebae, Infections caused by

Giardiasis

Gonorrhea

Haemophilus influenzae, invasive disease

Hansen disease (leprosy)

Hantavirus pulmonary syndrome

Hemolytic uremic syndrome, post-diarrheal

Hepatitis

- Hepatitis A, acute
- Hepatitis B, acute
- Hepatitis B, chronic
- Hepatitis B virus, perinatal infection
- Hepatitis C, acute
- Hepatitis C, past or present

HIV infection *(AIDS has been reclassified as HIV stage III)*

- HIV infection, adult/adolescent (age > = 13 years)
- HIV infection, child (age >= 18 months and < 13 years)
- HIV infection, pediatric (age < 18 months)

Influenza-associated hospitalizations

Influenza-associated pediatric mortality

Legionellosis

Listeriosis

Lyme disease

Malaria

Measles

Melioidosis

Meningococcal disease

Mumps

Novel influenza A virus infections

Pertussis

Plague

Poliomyelitis, paralytic

Poliovirus infection, nonparalytic

Psittacosis

Q Fever

- Acute
- Chronic

Rabies

- Rabies, animal
- Rabies, human

Rubella (German measles)

Rubella, congenital syndrome

Salmonellosis

TABLE 3-10 Nationally Notifiable Diseases and Conditions in the United States in 2012 *(continued)*

Severe Acute Respiratory Syndrome-associated Coronavirus (SARS-CoV) disease

Shiga toxin-producing *Escherichia coli* (STEC) Shigellosis

Smallpox

Spotted fever Rickettsiosis

Streptococcal toxic-shock syndrome

Streptococcus pneumoniae, invasive disease

Syphilis

- Primary
- Secondary
- Latent
- Early latent
- Late latent
- Latent, unknown duration
- Neurosyphilis
- Late, non-neurological
- Stillbirth
- Congenital

Tetanus

Toxic-shock syndrome (other than Streptococcal) Trichinellosis (Trichinosis)

Tuberculosis

Tularemia

Typhoid fever

Vancomycin-intermediate *Staphylococcus aureus* (VISA) Vancomycin -resistant *Staphylococcus aureus* (VRSA)

Varicella (morbidity)

Varicella (deaths only)

Vibriosis

Viral Hemorrhagic Fevers, due to:

- Ebola virus
- Marburg virus
- Crimean-Congo hemorrhagic fever virus
- Lassa virus
- Lujo virus
- New world arenaviruses (Gunarito, Machupo, Junin, and Sabia viruses)

Yellow fever

Non-Infectious Conditions

Cancer Elevated blood lead levels

- Child (< 16 years)
- Adult (≥ 16 Years)

Foodborne disease outbreak

Pesticide-related illness, acute

Silicosis

Waterborne disease outbreak

2012 Case Definitions: Nationally Notifiable Conditions Infectious and Non-Infectious Case. (2012). Atlanta, GA: Centers for Disease Control and Prevention.

Individual reports are treated as confidential, and the required timing of reporting the disease may be immediately done by telephone, within one day of identification, or within 7 days of identification. For example, anthrax is expected to be reported immediately, whereas AIDS should be reported within a week of identification. Case reports are typically sent to local health departments. The local health department then communicates the information to the state. Where local health departments do not exist or are not in a position to respond to the health problem, or where the state health department has elected to take primary responsibility, case reports are sent directly to the state health department.

The Morbidity and Mortality Weekly Report lists on a regular basis a graphic presentation of the trends of occurrence (decrease and increase) of the top notifiable diseases **(Figure 3-4)**.[17]

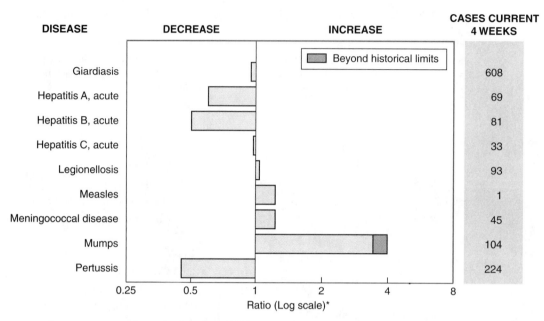

* Ratio of current 4-week total to mean of 15 4-week totals (from previous, comparable, and subsequent 4-week periods for the past 5 years). The point where the hatched area begins is based on the mean and two standard deviations of these 4-week totals.

FIGURE 3-4   Example of selected notifiable disease reports, United States, comparing 4-week totals January 9, 2010, with historical data. From Centers for Disease Control and Prevention. Notifiable diseases/deaths in selected cities weekly information. *MMWR.* 2010;59(44);1208–1219.

PROTECTING PUBLIC HEALTH THROUGH IMMUNIZATION

Before the polio vaccine became available in 1955, a peak of 58,000 cases of polio occurred in 1 year (1952). One of every two cases of symptomatic polio resulted in permanent crippling of the victim. Before the first live virus vaccine for measles was licensed in 1963, the United States had 4 million cases every year. Additionally, there were 4,000 cases of encephalitis, which resulted in 400 deaths and 800 cases with irreparable brain damage. **Immunization** is the introduction of a substance that can cause the immune system to respond and develop antibodies against a disease. The immunization of 60 million children from 1963 to 1972 cost $180 million but saved $1.3 billion by averting 24 million cases of measles. In the end, 2,400 lives were saved, 7,900 cases of retardation were prevented, and 1,352,000 hospital days were saved.[2,4,5,9,18]

The rubella epidemic of 1964–1965 caused 30,000 babies to be born with rubella syndrome, 20,000 of whom lived more than 1 year. Before the rubella vaccine was licensed in 1969, 58,000 cases per year were reported.[2,4,5,9,18]

Mumps was the leading cause of childhood deafness and juvenile diabetes. Of every 300 cases of mumps, one can result in impaired hearing. For those infected with diphtheria, 1 of every 10 dies.[2,4,5,9,18]

The immunization process is very important to all individuals in the United States. According to the CDC, if fewer than 80% of the children in a given area have been inoculated for one of the contagious diseases, the danger of serious outbreaks or localized epidemics remains; every unvaccinated child is at risk.[2,4,5,9,18]

Two classifications of disease immunity are active or passive. With **active immunity**, the body produces its own antibodies against a specific invading substance, called an antigen, thereby providing very selective protection. This can occur through a vaccine or in response to having a specific disease pathogen invade the body. Active immunity is usually permanent, lasting throughout one's lifetime. **Passive immunity** involves the transfer of antibodies to one person produced by another person. Passive immunity may be acquired through transplacental transfer or breastfeeding. Passive immunity can also come from the introduction of already-produced antibodies by another host (e.g., immune globulin). Passive immunity is comparatively short lived, usually lasting a few weeks or months.[2,4,5,9,18]

Table 3-11 is a list of the diseases for which vaccines have been developed and that are in current use in the United States. Many well-known diseases still lack vaccines, many are under study, and others are close to completion. One vaccine that is hoped for is an AIDS vaccine, but the possibilities are still limited at this time. Some vaccines are only partially effective and require booster shots, and others, such as the smallpox vaccine, work very well.

Vaccinia is the live virus used in the smallpox vaccine. This vaccine brought about the supposed global eradication of smallpox. The last naturally occurring case of smallpox was reported in Somalia in 1977. In May of 1980, the World Health Assembly certified that the world was free of naturally occurring smallpox. Even though this report was made worldwide, many public health professionals are skeptical and believe that another epidemic of smallpox is possible. Nonetheless, the vaccine is a good example of the effectiveness of the wide use of immunizations in the eradication of disease.[20]

The introduction of a substance that can cause the immune system to respond and develop antibodies against a disease is what the immunization process is all about. Some substances are given orally (polio for example). Most are given by injection or skin pricks. Specific antigens from inactivated bacteria, viruses, or microbe toxins are introduced into the body in the form of a vaccine. The ability of the antigen system to have the strength, activity, and effectiveness to respond to disease is referred to as **antigenicity**. The antigens stimulate the immune system to make the body think it has the disease. The body's immune system responds by developing antibodies and a natural immunity to the disease. If the pathogen later enters the body, the immune system recognizes it, and the body is protected from the

TABLE 3-11   Diseases for Which Vaccines are Available[19]

Anthrax	Japanese encephalitis	Rabies
Cervical cancer (some forms)	Lyme disease	Smallpox
Cholera	Measles	Rocky mountain spotted fever
Chicken pox	Meningitis	Tetanus
Diphtheria	Mumps	Tuberculosis
German measles (rubella)	Pertussis	Typhoid fever
Hepatitis A	Plague	Typhus
Hepatitis B	Pneumonia	Whooping cough
Influenza	Polio	Yellow fever

From CDC. Summary of notifiable diseases in the US, 1997. *MMWR*. 1998;46(54):27.

disease by the rapid response of the immune system. Some vaccines last a lifetime; others may not. Recent reports indicate that revaccination may be required for some diseases as one gets older. Booster shots keep the immune process active within the body. If antigens and anti-bodies disappear over time, then a booster shot is needed to strengthen or reactivate the immune response. Booster shots are also given at the outset of an immunization program to help build the body's immune defense systems to the fullest extent possible.[2,4,5,9,18]

When the body cannot respond quickly enough or with enough strength, it is then that help is needed. Antibiotics are used to assist the immune system in its fight against pathogens. Antibiotics are substances such as penicillin, tetracycline, streptomycin, or any other substance that destroys or inhibits the growth of pathogenic organisms.[2,5,18]

HERD IMMUNITY

Herd immunity is based on the notion that if the herd (a population or group) is mostly protected from a disease by immunity then the chance that a major epidemic will occur is limited. Jonas Salk, one of the developers of the polio vaccine, suggested that if a herd immunity level of 85% exists in a population, a polio epidemic will not occur. Herd immunity is also viewed as the resistance a population has to the invasion and spread of an infectious disease.

Immunizations or past experience with a disease reduces the number of those who are susceptible in a population. Herd immunity is accomplished when the number of suscep-tibles is reduced and the number of protected or nonsusceptible persons dominates the herd (population). Herd immunity provides barriers to direct transmission of infections through the population. The lack of susceptible individuals halts the spread of a disease through a group (Figure 3-5 and Figure 3-6).

Figure 3-5 graphically shows how a disease can spread through a population when immunity is low and the number of susceptibilities is high. Figure 3-6 shows how barriers to the spread of a disease are developed when susceptible levels are low and how disease transmission in a population is stopped when an 85% level of immunity exists. Both Figures 3-5 and 3-6 demonstrate the effect that just one diseased person can have on the spread of a disease in a population.

One public health immunization goal would be to have close to 100% immunity in a population so that not even one individual would get the disease. This level of immunity is especially important for life-threatening diseases or those diseases that cause extreme dis-ability, such as polio. The goal of any public health immunization program is to reach 100% of the population, even if herd immunity prevents the occurrence of major epidemics.

In the previous chapter, we discussed Edward Jenner's demonstration that immunity to smallpox could occur by inoculating a person with cowpox virus, a virus related to vari-ola but less virulent. Jenner called the infectious material "vaccine." The procedure of administering the vaccine came to be called vaccination. Jenner predicted that his discovery of a smallpox vaccination could lead to the end of smallpox. Up until this time in history, isolation or quarantine was used to control smallpox.

At some time during the 19th century, the virus changed from cowpox to vaccinia (a "pox" type virus related to smallpox) in the smallpox vaccination. By the end of World War I, most of Europe was free of smallpox. By the end of World War II, the transmission of smallpox was interrupted in Europe and North America. In the 1940s, a freeze-dried vaccine was perfected by Collier, which was more stable in high temperatures and in humid climates.[21]

How an Epidemic Spreads in a Population

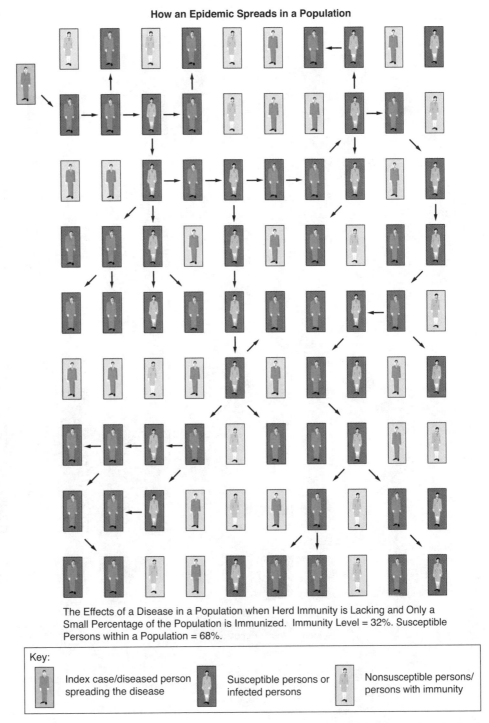

The Effects of a Disease in a Population when Herd Immunity is Lacking and Only a Small Percentage of the Population is Immunized. Immunity Level = 32%. Susceptible Persons within a Population = 68%.

Key:

Index case/diseased person spreading the disease

Susceptible persons or infected persons

Nonsusceptible persons/ persons with immunity

FIGURE 3-5   Diagram of a population, showing a low immunization level which falls short of protecting individuals within the group.

The Protection Given a Population Through Immunizations

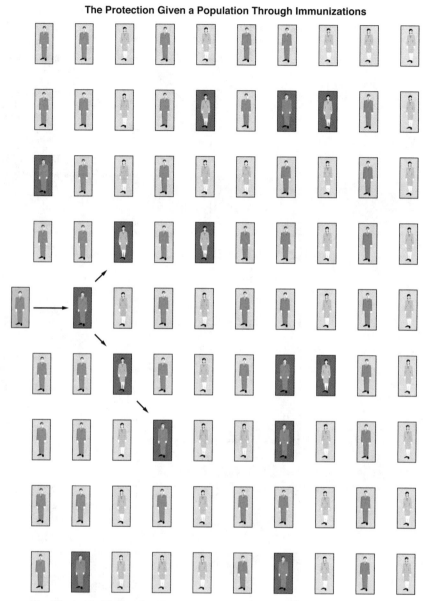

The Effects of a Disease in a Population when Herd Immunity is Complete with a Large Percentage of the Population being Immunized. Immunity Level = 85%. Susceptible Persons within a Population = 15%.

FIGURE 3-6 Diagram of a population showing a high level of immunizations within the group so that it affords a good level of protection to most of the individuals within the group.

In 1945, most of the world had endemic levels of smallpox. In 1950, the Pan American Sanitary Organization (later called the Pan American Health Organization) undertook a global smallpox eradication program. In 1958, a worldwide vaccination program was begun, but not until 1966 when the World Health Assembly intensified the program by providing a budget of $2.4 million per year did the effort show noticeable success. Over 100 million vaccinations occurred over the next 5-year period.

The combination of the development of a stable freeze-dried vaccine and development of the bifurcated needle for vaccination laid the foundation for smallpox eradication. The bifurcated needle resulted in nearly 100% successful vaccine takes, and the dose was about 1/100 the vaccine required using the previous method of vaccination. Thus, availability of the vaccine was much greater.

In addition to the mass vaccination campaign throughout the world intended to reach at least 80% of the population, a surveillance system was used to find cases and outbreaks so that more focused containment methods could be employed. Both methods proved to be necessary for eradicating smallpox. Complications to the effort included lack of organization in national health services; outbreaks among refugees fleeing areas because of war or famine; shortages of funding for the vaccination; difficult terrain, climate, and cultural beliefs; and many other problems.

The eradication program indicated that the spread of smallpox was influenced by temperature and humidity, intensity and duration of contact, length of the contagious period, and coughing or sneezing. Airborne transmission of droplets through close, face-to-face contact and through prolonged contact is the most common form of transmission. Airborne transmission over long distances and fomite transmission was rare. There is no evidence of transmission through food or water. The eradication program also taught us that the vaccine provided protection for several years, but full protection decreased with time; that vaccination soon after exposure can still provide some protection; and that surveillance and targeted vaccination significantly decreased transmission rates during outbreaks.

The estimated herd-immunity thresholds needed to stop transmission for several communicable diseases vary, based on transmissibility. Herd-immunity thresholds for selected vaccine preventable diseases are presented in Table 3-12.[22] As evident, smallpox is actually less "transmissible" than measles and pertussis.

TABLE 3-12   Herd Immunity Thresholds for Selected Vaccine-Preventable Diseases

Disease	Herd Immunity	1999 19–35 Months	1997–1998 Preschool
Diphtheria	85%*	83%*	9%
Measles	83%–94%	92%	96%
Mumps	75%–86%	92%	97%
Pertussis	92%–94%	83%*	97%
Polio	80%–86%	90%	97%
Rubella	83%–85%	92%	97%
Smallpox	80%–85%	—	—

*Four doses.
Modified from *Epi Rev* 1993;15:265–302; *Am J Prev Med* 2001;20(4S):88–153; *MMWR.* 2000;49(SS-9): 27–38.

COMMUNICABLE DISEASE PREVENTION AND CONTROL

Prevention and control of infectious and contagious diseases are the foundation of all public health measures. Several prevention methods, as well as many control measures, have been developed. There are three key factors to the control of communicable diseases.

- Remove, eliminate, or contain the cause or source of infection
- Disrupt and block the chain of disease transmission
- Protect the susceptible population against infection and disease

The methods of prevention and control are used on several fronts. The first front is the environment, the second is the person at risk (host), and the third is the population or community.[4]

ENVIRONMENTAL CONTROL

Environmental control is aimed at providing clean and safe air, water, milk, and food. Also involved in the scope of environmental control is the management of solid waste (trash and garbage), liquid waste (sewage), and control of vectors (insects and rodents) of disease.[4]

Safe air includes the control of infectious pathogens that are airborne. Toxic fumes, ultraviolet light, air pollution, and second-hand smoke are also of concern in air safety control.[4]

Clean and safe water supplies have been key factors in controlling infectious diseases, especially waterborne diseases (enteric or alvine discharge diseases). Maintaining a safe water supply is one of the most basic yet all-important public health activities of the modern age.[4]

Liquid waste carries pathogens, fecal material, chemical pollutants, industrial waste, and many other pollutants and waste. Sewage and dirty water runoff must be safely conveyed without exposure to the human population; thus, underground sewage systems are of keen importance.[4]

Solid-waste management has become one of the greatest public health challenges of modern times. Proper disposal of the massive amounts of garbage and other solid waste, such as hazardous and biohazardous materials, continues to be a challenge. Control of garbage odors, flies, and insect problems, from the garbage at home to the garbage sitting at the street curb and on to the sanitary landfill, help prevent the spread of communicable vector-borne disease.[4]

The protection of water, food, and milk is a hallmark of advanced societies. Milk and the cows it comes from must be tested and proved free of infectious diseases. Milk is constantly tested and is treated by heat (pasteurization) to kill pathogens. Proper storage, distribution, transport, and temperature control of milk must be rigorous and continually ensured.[4]

Food must be protected from adulteration, contamination, and spoilage.[4] Food must also be properly stored and served. Proper temperatures for refrigeration, cooking, storage, and transport must be maintained without fail. Proper food handling, including hand washing during preparation, is extremely important to infection control. Many bacteria, especially staphylococci, salmonella, and shigella, can contaminate food and be transmitted to unwary consumers. Food handlers must also be checked and screened to protect the general public.[4]

Animals and insects are sources of disease and infection. The control of animals (both domestic and wild) and insects in the community, both rural and urban, is essential to disease control and prevention. Proper food storage, refrigeration, water protection, garbage control, and sanitation (including lids on garbage cans as well as screening of windows and doors) all help to control insects and related pathogens.[4]

HOST-RELATED CONTROL AND PREVENTION

The host of a disease can be either human or animal, and both humans and animals are vulnerable to infectious diseases. A goal of public health is to protect the host from contagious diseases and infections by several methods. Protective measures include isolation, quarantine, sanitation, good hygiene, immunizations, and chemoprophylaxis.

The difference between quarantine and isolation has been described by the CDC. **Quarantine** applies to persons who have been exposed to a contagious disease but may or may not become ill. These people may not know whether they have been exposed to a disease or they may have the disease but not manifest clinical symptoms (e.g., Typhoid Mary). Quarantine may also refer to situations where a building, cargo, conveyance, or animal may be believed to be exposed to a dangerous contagious disease and is, therefore, closed or kept apart from others in order to prevent the spread of disease. Quarantine has been used throughout history to stop the spread of disease. Quarantine was probably the first public health measure to show a marked level of effectiveness in controlling the spread of disease. In the late 1800s and early 1900s, quarantine activities became an organized effort by government officials, and this had a major impact on improving the health status of the community, especially with regard to mortality statistics. In modern times, quarantine measures are still in use. Currently, the WHO invokes quarantine measures for three diseases: cholera, plague, and yellow fever.

Isolation applies to persons who are known to be ill with a contagious disease. It is often conducted on an inpatient basis in hospitals or nursing homes. Most state laws as well as accrediting organizations require one or two beds to be kept, designated, and equipped in a hospital or nursing home as isolation beds. The isolation beds are used to segregate and isolate any patient with a communicable disease so that disease will not spread throughout the facility. Isolation is an infection control measure, usually done under the direction and control of the hospital epidemiologist (infection control director) and the infection control committee of a hospital. Isolation measures include the following:

1. One or two private rooms are used as isolation rooms.
2. Separate infection-control gowns are used.
3. Staff must wear masks.
4. All staff must be gloved when interacting, treating, or working with or on the patient.
5. Hand washing is required on entering and leaving the patient's room.
6. All contaminated articles or possibly contaminated articles, including linen, dressings, syringes, instruments, and so forth, must be disposed of properly.

Special isolation concerns arise when it comes to dealing with HIV/AIDS patients. The CDC issued procedures for the control of infections including AIDS. Universal blood and body-fluid precautions, or universal precautions, are to be applied to all patients, from the emergency department to outpatient clinics to the dentist's office to the isolation room in the hospital. Barrier techniques are to be implemented, which include gloves, masks, gowns, protective eyewear, and hand washing when in contact with all patients. Gloves are to be used when touching blood or body fluids. Proper disposal of all articles that could be contaminated must be done with care. Care to avoid accidental self-punctures with contaminated needles must be taken. Patients at high risk for AIDS need to be tested. High-risk hospital and clinic personnel also need to be tested for HIV/AIDS on a regular basis.[4]

INFECTION CONTROL AND PREVENTION MEASURES

Personal hygiene is the process of maintaining high standards of personal body mainte-nance and cleanliness. Cleanliness and health maintenance activities include frequent bathing, regular grooming, teeth cleaning and maintenance, frequent changes of clothes, and hand washing. Family beliefs and practices, food preparation and protection, home environment, and living spaces all contribute to infection control and prevention and are part of hygienic practices (see Exhibit 3-1: News File).

Chemical and antibiotic prophylaxis have shown great success in treating certain infec-tions since 1945 when penicillin was finally mass produced and made available for wide use in the population. In the 1800s, arsenic, a poisonous chemical, was found somewhat effec-tive in treating syphilis, if used in low doses. Sulfa drugs were also found to be effective against many infectious diseases. Use of chemical agents as a means of preventing specific diseases became less common with the development of antibiotic medications.

With the development of both specific antibiotics and broad-spectrum antibiotics, the treatment of individuals and the practice of medicine have greatly changed. The impact of chemical and antibiotic prophylaxis on the health status in the world has been impressive. Infants and mothers no longer die as a result of the childbirth process in the numbers they formerly did. Wounds heal, and surgery is completed without the patient dying later from an infection. Streptococcal infections are quickly halted and no longer turn into rheumatic fever, and now it has been shown through research that antibiotics administered within 2 hours of surgery can help prevent surgical wound infections. Many lives have been saved and much suffering has been avoided because of the development and effective use of chem-ical and antibiotic prophylaxis.[4]

CHANGING EMPHASIS IN EPIDEMIOLOGIC STUDIES

Although epidemiologic studies originated in the investigation of infectious disease out-breaks, increasing life expectancy in modern times and increasing chronic disease have pro-duced a change in the emphasis of epidemiologic studies. See a review of the shift from infectious to chronic disease in the United States in "Leading causes of death in the United States in 1900 and in 2000" (Table 1-2) and "Top 10 causes of death in the World in 2008"(Figure 1-6).[23,24] In 1998, the WHO estimated that chronic diseases contributed to almost 60% of deaths in the world and 43% of the global burden of disease.[25] On the basis of current trends, by 2020 chronic diseases are expected to be responsible for 73% of deaths and 60% of the burden of disease.[25] Long latency periods between exposure and clinical symptoms are characteristic of chronic diseases. Events related to chronic conditions, including smoking, alcohol drinking, substance abuse, environmental/occupational exposure, diet, physical activity level, and sexual behaviors, have also received considerable attention in epidemiologic studies.

Mental and psychiatric disorders and conditions are noninfectious, noncommunicable, chronic diseases. The understanding of psychiatric disorders and behavioral problems has greatly increased over the last 30–40 years. In 1975, a rough draft of the third edition of the *Diagnostic and Statistical Manual of Mental Disorders* (DSM) was presented at a special session of the annual American Psychiatric Association conference. Several additional drafts were subsequently produced, and meetings were held over the next 5 years. Field trials of the suggested new classifications were made. In 1980, the newly developed classifications of psychiatric disorders were published in the third edition (DSM-III). This revision was a major advancement in the structure and classification of mental conditions. The concept of neurosis was removed from the classification, and stress (posttraumatic)-related issues were included. In 1987, a revised addition of the book, DSM-IIIR, was released.[26] Table 3-13 presents diagnostic categories of mental conditions from DSM-IV (published in 1994), and Table 3-14 presents a "V" code section for behavioral conditions and disorders related to mental illness.[27]

TABLE 3-13   Diagnostic Categories of Mental Conditions from DSM-IV

1. Disorders usually first evident in infancy, childhood, or adolescence
2. Delirium, dementia, amnestic, and other cognitive disorders
3. Mental disorders due to a general medical condition not elsewhere classified
4. Substance-related disorders
5. Schizophrenia and other psychotic disorders
6. Mood disorders
7. Anxiety disorders
8. Somatoform disorders
9. Factitious disorders
10. Dissociative disorders
11. Sexual and gender-identity disorders
12. Eating disorders
13. Sleep disorders
14. Impulse-control disorders not elsewhere classified
15. Adjustment disorders
16. Personality disorders
17. Other conditions that may be a focus of clinical attention
18. Medication-induced movement disorders
19. Relational problems
20. Problems related to abuse and neglect
21. Additional conditions that may be a focus of clinical attention
22. Additional codes for unspecified mental disorders (nonpsychotic)

Data are from American Psychiatric Association. *DSM-IV: Diagnostic and Statistical Manual of Mental Disorders*, 4th ed. Washington, DC: American Psychiatric Association, 1994.

TABLE 3-14   V Codes for Behavioral Conditions and Related Disorders

Malingering

Borderline intellectual functioning

Adult antisocial behavior

Childhood or adolescent antisocial behavior

Academic problem

Noncompliance with medical treatment

Phase of life problem or life circumstance problem

Marital problem

Other specified family circumstance

Other interpersonal problem

Additional codes are for unspecified mental disorders (nonpsychotic) and those in which there is a failure to diagnose a condition by the above classification.

Data are from American Psychiatric Association. *DSM-IV: Diagnostic and Statistical Manual of Mental Disorders,* 4th ed. Washington, DC: American Psychiatric Association, 1994.

NUTRITIONAL DEFICIENCY DISEASES AND DISORDERS

Nutritional deficiency diseases and disorders can be classified under chronic diseases. The term **malnutrition** literally refers to a condition that arises when the body does not get the right amount of vitamins, minerals, and other nutrients to maintain healthy tissues and proper organ function. Malnutrition occurs in people experiencing either undernutrition or overnutrition. **Undernutrition** is a consequence of consuming too little essential vitamins, minerals, and other nutrients or excreting them faster than they can be replenished. Inadequate intake may result from excessive dieting, severe injury, and serious illness. Excessive loss may result from diarrhea, heavy sweating, heavy bleeding, or kidney failure. **Overnutrition** is the consumption of too much food, eating too many of the wrong things, too little physical activity and exercise, or taking too many vitamins or dietary supplements.[1] A list of some malnutrition syndromes with their accompanying causes is shown in Table 3-15.

Primary deficiency diseases can contribute to malnutrition and can result directly from the dietary lack of specific essential nutrients. For example, scurvy results from a dietary deficiency of vitamin C. Secondary deficiency diseases result from the inability of the body to use specific nutrients properly—for example, when food cannot be absorbed into the body while in the alimentary tract or when food is not able to be metabolized.

Obesity is influenced by a number of factors: diet, genetics, development, physical activity, metabolic rate (rate that the body uses food as a source of energy), and psychological problems. Some people choose to overeat (binge) in stressful or depressed states. On the other hand, anorexia nervosa and bulimia may also result from psychiatric problems. Some of the health problems associated with obesity in epidemiologic research include diabetes, stroke, coronary artery disease, hypertension, high cholesterol, kidney and gallbladder disorders, and some cancers. Obese individuals are also at increased risk of developing osteoarthritis and sleep apnea.

TABLE 3-15   Malnutrition Syndromes

Kwashiorkor (protein deficiency)

Marasmus (protein and/or calorie malnutrition, chronic undernutrition)

Iron-deficiency anemia

Folic acid-deficiency anemia

Vitamin B_{12}-deficiency anemia

Xerophthalmia (vitamin A deficiency)

Endemic goiter (iodine deficiency)

Beriberi (thiamine deficiency)

Ariboflavinosis (riboflavin deficiency)

Pellagra (niacin and amino acid tryptophan deficiency)

Scurvy (vitamin C deficiency)

Rickets (vitamin D deficiency)

Tetany (mineral deficiency)

Osteomalacia and osteoporosis (impaired calcium and phosphorus metabolism affecting bone formation)

CHRONIC DISEASES AND CONDITIONS

The most prominent chronic diseases in the United States are heart disease, cancer, stroke (cerebrovascular diseases), and chronic lower respiratory diseases. In 2009, these diseases explained roughly 60% of all deaths (25%, 23%, 6%, and 5%, respectively).[28] Chronic diseases are not typically caused by an infectious agent (pathogen) but result from genetic susceptibility, lifestyle, or environmental exposures. Some exceptions are cancers of the cervix, liver, and stomach. Infectious risk factors for cervical cancer, liver cancer, and stomach cancer are human papilloma virus, hepatitis B virus, and the *Helicobacter pylori* bacterium, respectively. Because the human papilloma virus is sexually transmitted and the hepatitis B virus is transmitted via the exchange of body fluids such as blood, semen, breast milk, and in some rare cases, saliva, cancers related to these viruses are classified as chronic infectious communicable diseases.

The latency period for chronic diseases is typically more difficult to identify than is the incubation period for acute infectious diseases. This is because of the multifactorial etiology that characterizes many chronic diseases. In Chapter 5, "Descriptive Epidemiology According to Person, Place, and Time" of this volume, per capita cigarette consumption was compared with lung cancer death rates between 1900 and 2000. See a review of "Reported cases of HIV/AIDS in infants born to HIV-infected mothers, by year, for 25 states in the U.S. (Alabama, Arizona, Arkansas, Colorado, Idaho, Indiana, Louisiana, Michigan, Minnesota, Mississippi, Missouri, Nevada, New Jersey, North Carolina, North Dakota, Ohio, Oklahoma, South Carolina, South Dakota, Tennessee, Utah, Virginia, West Virginia, Wisconsin, and Wyoming)" within Figure 5-15. The comparison suggests that the latency period from smoking to lung cancer death is 20–25 years.

PREVENTION AND CONTROL

The development of many chronic diseases is preventable, and some chronic diseases could also be minimized in their severity by changing behavior and moderating exposure to certain risk factors in life. For example, lung cancer and chronic obstructive pulmonary disease could be greatly reduced if no one smoked. Certain liver diseases could be greatly reduced if alcohol consumption were curtailed. Lifestyle, behavior, and unnecessary exposure to risk factors in life continue to cause many chronic diseases throughout the world. Cardiovascular disease and cancer could be reduced if nutritional and dietary factors were altered. These diseases are also affected by tobacco smoking.

The main lifestyle and behavior changes needed to prevent and control chronic disease include the reduction, and possibly the elimination, of the use of tobacco and smoking (which includes secondhand smoke), the use of alcohol, and drug abuse. Additional changes include dietary changes (a reduction of fat and empty calories in the diet, lowering cholesterol; maintaining proper calcium levels; limiting certain kinds of protein and red meat), increasing fitness and exercise, proper weight maintenance, stress reduction, and increased safety measures.

Prevention measures have made great strides in the area of cancer. Efforts to detect breast cancer at early stages are critical in reducing breast cancer–associated mortality. Early detection programs have been found to be most effective as cancer prevention and control measures. Primary care centers have used early detection programs in order to facilitate cancer screening services. Mammography screening has been done at centers located in shopping centers, and mobile mammography vans have also been used.

Table 3-16 presents the results of a breast cancer screening program in Dade County, Florida in a Hispanic population. From the screening of the 9,434 individuals, 274 biopsies

TABLE 3-16   Characteristics and Results of 9,434 Hispanic Individuals in the Early Detection Program for Breast Cancer in Dade County, Florida, 1987–1990

Patient Characteristic	%	Result	%
Race/Ethnicity		Mammography finding ($n = 11,632$)*	
Hispanic	52.8	Not suspicious for cancer	68.0
Non-Hispanic black	40.8	Additional evaluation	27.7
Non-Hispanic white	6.1	Suspicious for cancer	4.3
Unknown	0.3	Biopsy result ($n = 274$)	
Age (years)		Negative	79.2
< 40	15.2	Positive	20.8
40–49	29.0	Histologic result ($n = 57$)	
50–69	50.1	In situ	17.5
> 70	5.7	Local	36.8
Previous mammogram ($n = 8,397$)†		Regional	35.1
No	74.0	Distant	5.3
Yes	26.0	Unstaged	5.3

*Includes screening, repeat, and followup mammograms.
† This question was not asked of women at the beginning of the program.
From the CDC. Increasing breast cancer screening among the medically underserved—Dade County, Florida, September 1987–March 1991. *MMWR.* 1991;40:16.

were performed, with 57 of the tests being positive for cancer. Late-stage diagnosis of cancer contributes to the 10–15% lower survival rates among women of low socioeconomic status. Early diagnosis and early treatment are the key hallmarks of improving the prognosis of cancer patients.[29]

DISABILITY

Disability is the diminished capacity to perform within a prescribed range.[1] The International Classification of Functioning, Disability and Health defines disability as an umbrella term for impairments, activity limitations, and participation restrictions.[30] **Impairment** is any loss or abnormality of psychological, physiologic, or of the anatomic structure or function.[1] Impairment is often associated with or results from chronic disease because it represents a decrease in or loss of ability to perform various functions, particularly those of the musculoskeletal system and the sense organs. Impairment may also result from a condition, injury, or congenital malformation. **Activity limitation** involves difficulty an individual may have in executing activities. **Participation restriction** is any problem an individual may experience in their involvement in life situations.[30] Some examples of how selected health conditions may be associated with the three levels of functioning is shown in Table 3-17.

Many diseases result in disability. For example, polio can cause a whole range of paralysis, from a mild weakness in a leg or arm to a complete loss of function of legs and arms to

TABLE 3-17   Selected Health Conditions and Disability as Related to Impairment, Activity Limitation, and Participation Restriction

Health Condition	Impairment	Activity Limitation	Participation Restriction
Leprosy	Loss of sensation in extremities	Difficulties in grasping objects	Stigma of leprosy leads to unemployment
Panic disorder	Anxiety	Not capable of going out alone	Leads to lack of social relationships
Spinal injury	Paralysis	Incapable of using public transportation	Lack of accommodations in public transportation leads to no participation in social activities
Type I diabetes	Pancreatic dysfunction	None (impairment controlled by medication)	Does not go to school because of stereotypes about disease
Vitiligo	Facial disfigurement	None	No participation in social relations owing to fears of contagion
Person who formerly had a mental health problem and was treated for a psychotic disorder	None	None	Denied employment because of employer's prejudice

World Health Organization. Toward a common language for functioning, disability and health. The International Classification of Functioning, Disability and Health. Geneva, 2002:17. Available at: http://www3.who.int/icf/beginners/bg.pdf. Accessed May 8, 2005.

loss of the ability to breathe. Reye's syndrome can leave a person with neurologic and muscular deficits and disability. Stroke can leave a person paralyzed. Diabetes can lead to amputation of parts of fingers, hands, and limbs, again causing a disability. Each of these diseases is related to impairment, activity limitation, and participation restriction.

Activity limitation data have been collected annually since 1997 in the National Health Interview Survey. Between 1997 and 2005, the percentage of children with activity limitation averaged roughly 7%. Limitation of activity among children is presented according to selected chronic health conditions in Figure 3-7. Speech problems were the most common limitations in the initial two age groups, but became the least common limitation among children aged 12–17 years. Asthma decreased slightly as a limitation and mental retardation and other developmental problems increased slightly with increasing age. The percentage that experienced limitations because of other mental, emotional, or behavioral problems, attention deficit/hyperactive disorder, and learning disability increased with age. Activity limitation in adults (ages 18–64 years) include limitations in handling personal care needs, routine needs, having a job outside the home, walking, remembering, and other activities. In 2004–2005, the percentage of activity limitations reported by adults in the United States that were caused by chronic health conditions remained stable.[31] The rate of activity limitation among adults in the United States, arranged by selected chronic health conditions, is shown in Figure 3-8. Rates increased with age for each of the selected chronic health conditions. Arthritis or other musculoskeletal conditions were most frequently identified as

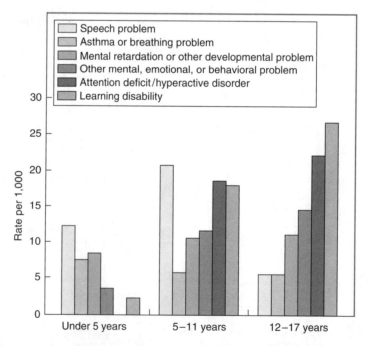

FIGURE 3-7   Activity limitation according to one or more chronic health conditions among children in the United States, 2004–2005. Data from National Center for Health Statistics. *Health, United States, 2007 With Chartbook on Trends in the Health of Americans.* Hyattsville, MD; 2007; 45. Note that data are for the civilian non-institutionalized population. Adults with more than one chronic condition causing activity limitation are counted in each category.

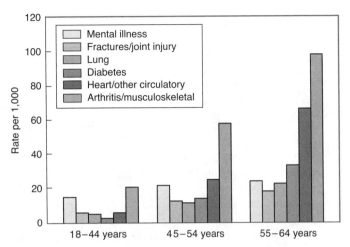

FIGURE 3-8 Activity limitation according to one or more chronic health conditions among adults in the United States, 2004–2005. *Unreliable estimates. From National Center for Health Statistics. *Health, United States, 2007 With Chartbook on Trends in the Health of Americans.* Hyattsville, MD; 2007; 43. Note that children with more than one chronic condition causing activity limitation are counted in each category.

causing activity limitation. The next most frequently mentioned causes of activity limitation were mental illness (for ages 18–44 years) and heart/other circulatory problems (for ages 45–54 years and 55–64 years).

HEALTHY PEOPLE INITIATIVES

Healthy People initiatives are epidemiologic-based, 10-year national sets of objectives for improving the health of all Americans. *Healthy People* initiatives have established benchmarks and have shown progress toward these objectives over the past three decades. In December, 2012, *Healthy People 2020* was launched, which builds on the accomplishments of four earlier *Healthy People* initiatives:

- 1979 Surgeon General's Report, Healthy People: The Surgeon General's Report on Health Promotion and Disease Prevention
- Healthy People 1990: Promoting Health/Preventing Disease–Objectives for the Nation
- Healthy People 2000: National Health Promotion and Disease Prevention Objectives
- Healthy People 2010: Objectives for Improving Health

The *Healthy People 2020* initiative is a comprehensive, nationwide health-promotion and disease-prevention initiative, which includes a set of high-priority health issues facing the United States. Its mission is to identify nationwide health improvement priorities; increase public awareness and understanding of the determinants of health, disease, and disability and the opportunities for progress; provide measurable objectives and goals that are applicable at the national, state, and local levels; engage multiple sectors to take actions to

Disease Transmission and Universal Precautions

Hand Washing Remains Key to Reducing Disease Transmission

Hand washing has long been recognized as one of the most effective ways to reduce the transmission of disease in lay people and professionals alike. Many serious and life-threatening diseases are transmitted because of inadequate hand washing, especially disease transmitted through the fecal–oral route. Feces remaining on the hands after toilet use may then enter the body when the hands are placed in the mouth or when food becomes contaminated during preparation. Escherichia coli 0157:H7, cholera, typhoid fever, salmonella food poisoning, poliomyelitis, and hepatitis A are but some of the diseases transmitted by the fecal–oral route. Dr. Gail Casell, professor and chair of the Department of Microbiology at the University of Alabama, Birmingham, conducted a national survey in Chicago, Atlanta, San Francisco, New Orleans, and New York of 6,333 people, both women and men, directly observed in bathrooms. Although 94% of people asked by telephone say that they always wash their hands after going to the bathroom, direct observation found that only 68% actually did. Generally, women washed their hands more often than men, with women washing 74% of the time and men only 61% of the time (presentation, American Society for Microbiologists, 1996, New Orleans). With the onset of the AIDS/HIV epidemic in the 1980s, universal precautions were developed to protect healthcare professionals, police, and others who come in direct contact with people who could infect them, especially by blood. Universal precautions are aggressive, standardized approaches to infection control in which all human blood and certain body fluids are treated as if they are known to contain HIV, hepatitis B virus, or other blood-borne pathogens. In universal precautions, hand washing is not enough protection, and thus, personal protective equipment, such as gloves, masks, eye protection, and special equipment for mouth-to-mouth resuscitation and CPR, might be needed for exposure to blood or body fluids.

strengthen policies and improve practices that are driven by the best available evidence and knowledge; and identify critical research, evaluation, and data collection needs.[32]

Along with the mission are four overarching goals: attain high-quality, longer lives free of preventable disease, disability, injury, and premature death; achieve health equity, eliminate disparities, and improve the health of all groups; create social and physical environments that promote good health for all; promote quality of life, healthy development, and healthy behaviors across all life stages.[32]

Under 12 topic areas, the document addresses determinants of health that promote quality of life, healthy behaviors, and development across the life span.[33] The 12 topic areas and associated health indicators are:

1. Access to health services
   - Persons with medical insurance
   - Persons with usual primary care provider

2. Clinical preventive services
   - Adults who receive a colorectal cancer screening based on the most recent guidelines
   - Adults with hypertension whose blood pressure is under control
   - Adult diabetic population with an A1c value greater than 9%
   - Children aged 19–35 months who receive the recommended doses of diphtheria, tetanus, and pertussis; polio; measles, mumps and rebella; Haemophilus influenza type b; hepatitis B; varicella; and pneumococcal conjugate vaccines

3. Environmental quality
   - Air Quality Index exceeding 100
   - Children aged 3–11 years exposed to secondhand smoke

4. Injury and violence
   - Fatal injuries
   - Homicides

5. Maternal, infant, and child health
   - Infant deaths
   - Preterm births

6. Mental health
   - Suicides
   - Adolescents who experience major depressive episodes

7. Nutrition, physical activity, and obesity
   - Adults who meet current federal physical activity guidelines for aerobic physical activity and muscle-strengthening activity
   - Adults who are obese
   - Children and adolescents who are obese
   - Total vegetable intake for persons aged 2 years and older

8. Oral health
   - Persons aged 2 years and older who used the oral health care system in the past 12 months

9. Reproductive and sexual health
   - Sexually active females aged 15–44 years who received reproductive health services in the past 12 months
   - Persons living with HIV who know their serostatus

10. Social determinants
    - Students who graduate with a regular diploma four years after starting ninth grade

11. Substance abuse
    - Adolescents using alcohol or any illicit drugs during the past 30 days
    - Adults engaging in binge drinking during the past 30 days

12. Tobacco
    - Adults who are current cigarette smokers
    - Adolescents who smoked cigarettes in the past 30 days

It is intended that organizing these health indicators under the 12 topic areas will facilitate collaboration across diverse sectors, guide individuals toward making informed health decisions, and measure the impact of prevention activities.

CONCLUSION

This chapter covered several disease concepts, primarily as they relate to infectious disease (e.g., disease classification, disease transmission, the natural course of disease, and incubation periods). Infectious disease arises from an infectious agent, referred to as a pathogen. Pathogens include viruses, bacteria, fungi, or parasites capable of producing disease. A pathogen affects a person directly or indirectly by a vector or fomite. Infectious diseases result when pathogens enter, survive, and multiply in the host. Invasiveness refers to the ability of a pathogen to get into a susceptible host and cause disease. Virulence refers to the disease-evoking power of a pathogen. National notifiable diseases are those that have potentially serious public health consequences. The list of national notifiable diseases regularly changes as new pathogens are identified. Several infection control and prevention measures were also developed in this chapter.

The scope of epidemiology has expanded far beyond its original focus on investigating infectious disease outbreaks. This was addressed in this chapter by also covering chronic disease related to malnutrition and other factors, as well as disability. Finally, *Healthy People 2020* was introduced as an initiative to improve the nation's health. The twelve topic areas and associated health indicators address the health issues of our modern society, which are primarily related to access to health care and health promoting, disease preventing lifestyle behaviors.

EXERCISES

Key Terms

Define the following terms.

Active immunity	Defection	Metabolic diseases
Activity limitations	Defervescence	Overnutrition
Acute	Degenerative diseases	Participation restriction
Allergies and inflammatory diseases	Disability	Passive immunity
	Disease	Pathogens
Antibiotics	Etiology	Prodromal period
Antibodies	Fastigium period	Quarantine
Antigen	Herd immunity	Toxin
Antigenicity	Horizontal transmission	Undernutrition
Cancer	Immunization	Vertical transmission
Chronic	Impairment	Viability
Communicability	Incubation period	Virulence
Congenital and hereditary diseases	Invasiveness	Zoonosis
	Isolation	
Convalescence	Malnutrition	

STUDY QUESTIONS

1. Discuss how infectious and noninfectious diseases relate to communicable and noncommunicable diseases and conditions.

2. List and explain the different general classifications of diseases.

3. Classifications were given of major infectious diseases. List the five modes of transmission and provide examples.

4. List the three general sources of infectious diseases and provide examples.

5. How do incubation periods differ from latency periods?

6. Choose five infectious diseases and identify the typical incubation periods for these diseases.

7. Explain the concept of notifiable diseases.

8. Explain and discuss herd immunity.

9. What role does increasing life expectancy over the last century have on the types of diseases and conditions affecting mankind?

10. Describe how activity limitation is associated with age and chronic condition in children (see Figure 3-7).

11. Describe the influence of mental illness and heart disease on activity limitations according to age group in adults (see Figure 3-8).

REFERENCES

1. *Stedman's Medical Dictionary for the Health Professions and Nursing*, 5th ed. Baltimore, MD: Lippincott Williams & Wilkins; 2005.
2. Crowley LV. *Introduction to Human Disease*, 2nd ed. Boston, MA: Jones and Bartlett, 1988.
3. National Cancer Institute at the U.S. National Institutes of Health. Understanding cancer series. http://www.cancer.gov/cancertopics/understandingcancer Accessed April 20, 2012.
4. Evans AS, Brachman PS. *Bacterial Infections of Humans: Epidemiology and Control*, 2nd ed. New York, NY: Plenum Medical Book Company; 1991.
5. Bickley HC. *Practical Concepts in Human Disease*, 2nd ed. Baltimore, MD: Williams & Wilkins, 1977.
6. Green LW, Anderson CL. *Community Health*, 4th ed. St. Louis, MO: CV Mosby; 1982.
7. Wigley R, Cook JR. *Community Health*. New York, NY: D Van Nostrand Company; 1975.
8. Grant M. *Handbook of Community Health*, 4th ed. Philadelphia, PA: Lea and Febiger; 1987.
9. Sheldon SH, ed. Boyd's Introduction to the Study of Disease. Philadelphia, PA: Lea and Febiger; 1984.
10. Berkow R, ed. *The Merck Manual of Diagnosis and Therapy*, 14th ed. Rahway, NJ: Merck and Company; 1982.
11. Acha PN, Szyfres B. *Zoonoses and Communicable Diseases Common to Man and Animals*, 2nd ed. Washington, DC: Pan American Health Organization; 1989.
12. Olishifski JB, McElroy FE. *Fundamentals of Industrial Hygiene*. Chicago, IL: National Safety Council; 1975.
13. Thygerson AL. *Safety*, 2nd ed. Englewood Cliffs, NJ: Prentice Hall; 1986.

14. World Health Organization. Classifications. http://www.who.int/classifications/icd/en/. Accessed May 7, 2005.

15. Centers for Disease Control and Prevention. Epidemiology Program Office. *Principles of Epidemiology: An Introduction to Applied Epidemiology and Biostatistics*, 2nd ed. Atlanta, GA: Centers for Disease Control and Prevention, 1992; 353–355.

16. Centers for Disease Control and Prevention. 2012 Case Definitions: Nationally Notifiable Conditions Infectious and Non-Infectious Case. Atlanta, GA: Centers for Disease Control and Prevention; 2012.

17. Centers for Disease Control and Prevention. Notifiable diseases/deaths in selected cities weekly information. *MMWR*. 2008;57(44):1208–1219. http://www.cdc.gov/mmwr/preview/mmwrhtml/mm5744md.htm. Accessed November 22, 2008.

18. Shulman S, Phair J, Peterson L, Warren J. *The Biologic and Clinical Basis of Infectious Diseases*, 5th ed. New York, NY: Elsevier; 1997.

19. Centers for Disease Control and Prevention. Summary of notifiable diseases in the US, 1997. *MMWR*. 1998;46(54):27.

20. Centers for Disease Control and Prevention. Vaccinia (smallpox) vaccine: recommendations of the immunizations practices advisory committee (ACIP). *MMWR*. 2001;50(RR10):1–25.

21. Henderson DA, Moss M. *Smallpox and Vaccinia in Vaccines*, 3rd ed. Philadelphia, PA: Saunders, 1999.

22. Centers for Disease Control and Prevention. History and epidemiology of global smallpox eradication. From the training course titled Smallpox: Disease, prevention and intervention. http://www.bt.cdc.gov/agent/smallpox/training/overview/pdf/eradicationhistory.pdf. Accessed November 21, 2008.

23. Centers for Disease Control and Prevention. Leading causes of disease, 1900–1998. http://www.cdc.gov/nchs/data/statab/lead1900_98.pdf. Accessed May 10, 2005.

24. U.S. Mortality Public Use Data Tape, 2000. National Center for Health Statistics, Centers for Disease Control and Prevention, 2002. http://webapp.cdc.gov/sasweb/ncipc/leadcaus10.html. Accessed September 12, 2005.

25. World Health Organization. Global strategy for the prevention and control of noncommunicable diseases, 1999. http://ftp.who.int/gb/pdf_files/EB105/ee42.pdf. Accessed May 6, 2005.

26. American Psychiatric Association. *DSM-III: Diagnostic and Statistical Manual of Mental Disorders*, 3rd ed. Washington, DC: American Psychiatric Association; 1987.

27. American Psychiatric Association. *DSM-IV: Diagnostic and Statistical Manual of Mental Disorders*, 4th ed. Washington, DC: American Psychiatric Association; 1994.

28. Kochanek KD, Xu JQ, Murphy SL, et al. Deaths: Preliminary data for 2009. National vital statistics reports; vol. 59 no 4. Hyattsville, MD: National Center for Health Statistics; 2011.

29. Centers for Disease Control and Prevention. Increasing breast cancer screening among the medically underserved—Dade County, Florida, September 1987–March 1991. *MMWR*. 1991;40:16.

30. World Health Organization. Toward a common language for functioning, disability and health. The International Classification of Functioning, Disability and Health. Geneva, Switzerland: World Health Organization; 2002:17. http://www3.who.int/icf/beginners/bg.pdf. Accessed May 8, 2005.

31. National Center for Health Statistics. *Health, United States, 2007 With Chartbook on Trends in the Health of Americans*. Hyattsville, MD: National Center for Health Statistics; 2007.

32. U.S. Department of Health and Human Services. Healthy People 2020. http://www.healthypeople.gov/2020/about/default.aspx. Accessed February 1, 2012.

33. U.S. Department of Health and Human Services. Healthy People 2020. http://healthypeople.gov/2020/TopicsObjectives2020/pdfs/HP2020_brochure_with_LHI_508.pdf. Accessed February 1, 2012.

4

Design Strategies and Statistical Methods in Descriptive Epidemiology

OBJECTIVES

After completing this chapter, you will be able to:

- Define descriptive epidemiology.
- Describe uses, strengths, and limitations of selected descriptive study designs (ecologic study, case report, case series, and cross-sectional survey).
- Define the four general types of data.
- Define ratio, proportion, and rate.
- Identify ways to describe epidemiologic data according to person, place, and time.
- Distinguish between crude and age-adjusted rates and be able to age-adjust rates using either the direct or the indirect method.
- Define the standardized morbidity (or mortality) ratio.
- Be familiar with selected tables, graphs, and numerical methods (measures of central tendency and dispersion) for describing epidemiologic data according to person, place, and time.
- Be familiar with selected measures for evaluating the strength of the association between variables.

A **study design** is the program that directs the researcher along the path of systematically collecting, analyzing, and interpreting data. It is a formal approach of scientific or scholarly investigation. There are both descriptive and analytic study designs. We observe events in descriptive studies as opposed to examining the effects of an applied intervention. In studying a topic we typically begin with an observational study that describes the distribution (frequency and pattern) of health-related states or events. For example, what is the average number of fruit and vegetable servings in the diet of Americans with a history of coronary heart disease? Descriptive studies are usually followed by analytic studies that are used to examine associations to permit inferences about cause-effect relationships. For example, is there an association between fruit and vegetable intake and risk of recurrent myocardial infarction in individuals with a history of coronary heart disease? The final step is an experimental study to evaluate the efficacy of an intervention. For example, does fruit and vegetable consumption reduce total mortality in individuals with coronary heart disease?

Descriptive epidemiology involves observation, definitions, measurements, interpretations, and dissemination of health-related states or events by person, place, and time. A descriptive study assists us in (1) providing information about a disease or condition, (2) providing clues to identify a new disease or adverse health effect, (3) identifying the extent of the public health problem, (4) obtaining a description of the public health problem that can be easily communicated, (5) identifying the population at greatest risk, (6) assisting in planning and resource allocation, and (7) identifying avenues for future research that can provide insights about an etiologic relationship between an exposure and health outcome.

The research problem, question, and hypotheses are supported by descriptive epidemiology. After the public health problem is established, hypotheses are formulated to explain observed and measured associations within the population of interest. Hypotheses are tested using appropriate study designs and statistical methods. Statistical analyses are then followed by interpretation and dissemination of the health findings. An analytic epidemiologic study tests one or more predetermined hypotheses about associations between and among variables; analytic epidemiology is appropriate for addressing why and how diseases, conditions, and deaths occur. See a review of analytic epidemiology in Chapter 7, "Design Strategies and Statistical Methods Used in Analytic Epidemiology" in this volume.

Describing data by person allows identification of the frequency of disease and who is at greatest risk. High-risk populations can be identified by investigating inherent characteristics of people (age, gender, race, and ethnicity), acquired characteristics (immunity, marital status, education), activities (occupation, leisure, medication use), and conditions (access to health care, environmental state). Identifying the influence of beliefs, traditions, cultures, and societal expectations on acquired characteristics, activities, and conditions is important in providing clues to the causes of disease.

Describing data by place (residence, birthplace, place of employment, country, state, county, census tract, etc.) allows the epidemiologist to understand the geographic extent of disease, where the causal agent of disease resides and multiplies, and how the disease is transmitted and spread.

Finally, describing data by time can reveal the extent of the public health problem according to when and whether the disease is predictable. Assessing whether interactions exist among persons, place, and time may also provide insights into the causes of disease.

Descriptive statistics are a means of organizing and summarizing data. Descriptive methods for describing data include tables, graphs, and numerical summary measures. Essentially, descriptive statistics are used to summarize the distribution of data, are a final step in editing, characterize the study participants, and inform the choice of analytic statistics.

DESCRIPTIVE STUDY DESIGNS

Descriptive study designs include case reports and case series, cross-sectional surveys, and exploratory ecologic designs. A description of these study designs, their strengths, and weaknesses is presented in Table 4-1. These designs provide a means for obtaining descriptive statistics, which are used to assess the distribution of data without typically attempting to test particular hypotheses. In an ecologic study, the unit of analysis is the population. On the other hand, in a case report, case series, or cross-sectional survey, the unit of analysis is the individual. Although descriptive studies are often limited in their ability to test hypotheses, they can provide useful information on the extent of the public health problem according to person, place, and time; who is at greatest risk with regard to place and time; possible causal associations; and the need for analytic epidemiologic investigation.

Ecologic Study

An **ecologic study** involves making comparisons between variables where the unit of analysis is aggregated data on the population level rather than on the individual level. For example, suppose that the epidemiologist wanted to study whether there is an association between eating five or more servings of fruit and vegetables per day and obesity. Figure 4-1 shows the percentage of adults who have a body mass index (BMI) of at least 30 (are obese) by the percentage of adults who eat five or more servings of fruit and vegetables per day in the United States and U.S. territories, 2010. Each dot in the graph represents aggregated data for the state or territory. A linear fit to the data shows a negative association between obesity and eating five or more servings of fruit and vegetables per day. A limitation of ecologic data, however, is that they are often unable to control for potential confounding factors that may explain some or all of the association. For example, it is possible that those who fail to eat five or more servings of fruit and vegetables per day are less likely to be physically active and that physical inactivity, not fruit and vegetable intake, leads to obesity.

With ecologic data, when interpreting associations between indices, an error may result if the researcher mistakenly assumes that because the majority of a group has a characteristic, the characteristic is definitively associated with those experiencing a health-related state or event in the group. This is called **ecologic fallacy**.[1] It is possible that although higher levels of fruit and vegetable consumption may occur in states and territories with lower levels of obesity, those eating five or more servings of fruit and vegetables per day may not be the ones with the lower BMI.

Ecologic studies are often appropriate in environmental settings. For example, injuries are often associated with characteristics in the environment and may best be controlled by group-focused interventions (modifications to physical, social, technological, political, economical, and organizational environments) rather than efforts to change individual behaviors.[2]

Case Reports and Case Series

A **case report** is a profile of a single individual. A recent report described a 74-year-old woman who experienced airway obstruction when a piece of meat became lodged in her trachea.[3] A bystander was unsuccessful at practicing the Heimlich maneuver, and the patient became unconscious. While she was in a supine position, the Heimlich maneuver was again

TABLE 4-1   Epidemiologic Descriptive Study Designs

	Description	Strengths	Weaknesses
Ecological	Aggregate data involved (i.e., no information is available for specific individuals). Prevalence of a potential risk factor compared with the rate of an outcome condition.	Takes advantage of pre-existing data Relatively quick and inexpensive Can be used to evaluate programs, policies, or regulations implemented at the ecologic level Allows estimation of effects not easily measurable for individuals	Susceptible to confounding Exposures and disease or injury outcomes not measured on the same individuals
Case study	A snapshot description of a problem or situation for an individual or group; qualitative descriptive research of the facts in chronological order.	In-depth description Provides clues to identify a new disease or adverse health effect resulting from an exposure or experience Identify potential areas of research	Conclusions limited to the individual, group, and/or context under study Cannot be used to establish a cause–effect relationship
Cross-sectional	All of the variables are measured at a point in time. There is no distinction between potential risk factors and outcomes.	Control over study population Control over measurements Several associations between variables can be studied at same time Short time period required Complete data collection Exposure and injury/disease data collected from same individuals Produces prevalence	No data on the time relationship between exposure and injury/disease development Potential bias from low response rate Potential measurement bias Higher proportion of long-term survivors Not feasible with rare exposures or outcomes Does not yield incidence or relative risk

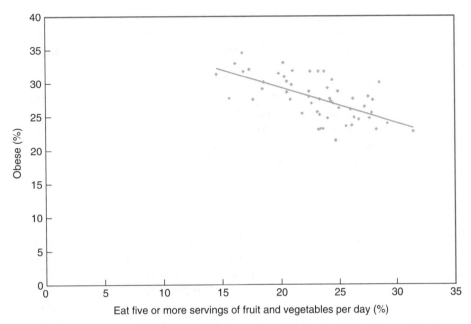

FIGURE 4-1   Correlation between adults eating five or more servings of fruits and vegetables per day and being obese (in the United States and U.S. territories, 2010). From Centers for Disease Control and Prevention. Trends data available at: http://apps.nccd.cdc.gov/brfss/index.asp.

attempted, this time successfully. The woman was then taken to the emergency room, where she was complaining of abdominal pain and distention. Further investigation identified a 2-cm rupture of the lesser curvature of her stomach. Contusions were also identified over the fundus and posterior stomach. Surgery corrected the problem, and she was discharged 6 days after surgery without complications. Hence, gastric perforation and other complications resulting from the Heimlich maneuver may exist, and patients should be evaluated for such problems.

A **case series** involves a small group of patients with a similar diagnosis. For example, from October 4 to November 2, 2001, the first 10 cases of inhalational anthrax were identified in the United States. These cases were intentionally caused by release of *Bacillus anthracis*. Epidemiologic investigation found that the outbreak consisted of cases in the District of Columbia, Florida, New Jersey, and New York. The *B. anthracis* spores were delivered through the mail in letters and packages. The ages of the cases ranged from 43 to 73 years, with 70% being male, and all but one were confirmed to have handled a letter or package containing *B. anthracis* spores. The incubation period ranged from 4 to 6 days. Symptoms at the onset included fever or chills, sweat, fatigue or malaise, minimal or nonproductive cough, dyspnea, and nausea or vomiting. Blood tests and chest radiographs were also used to further characterize symptoms.[4] Identifying the symptoms of these patients may lead to earlier diagnosis of future cases.

These two examples describe a condition and an infectious disease by person. As a result, information was provided that may be useful for identifying potential complications related to the Heimlich procedure and for early detection of anthrax. Case reports and case series may also suggest the emergence of a new disease or epidemic if the disease exceeds what is expected. An example of a case series was presented in Chapter 1; that is, on June 4, 1981, the

Centers for Disease Control (CDC) published a report that described five young men, all active homosexuals, who were treated for biopsy-confirmed *Pneumocystis carinii* pneumonia at three different hospitals in Los Angeles, California during the period from October 1980 to May 1981. This was the first published report of the disease that would become known as AIDS a year later.[5] By the end of 1982, a descriptive epidemiologic study provided strong evidence that the agent causing AIDS was transmitted through homosexual behavior,[6,7] heterosexual behavior,[8,9] blood (needle sharing among drug users), and blood transfusions[10–12] and from mothers with AIDS to their infants.[13] In 2007, 33 million (30–36 million) people were living with HIV worldwide, 2.7 million (2.2–3.2 million) were newly infected with the virus, and 2 million (1.8–2.3 million) people died of HIV-related causes.[14]

Cross-Sectional Surveys

A **cross-sectional survey** is conducted over a short period of time (usually a few days or weeks), and the unit of analysis is the individual. There is no follow-up period. Cross-sectional surveys are useful for examining associations among health-related states or events and personal characteristics such as age, gender, race and ethnicity, marital status, education, occupation, access to health care, and so on. Hence, they reveal who is at greatest risk and provide clues as to the causes of disease. In addition, because cross-sectional surveys are useful for estimating prevalence data, it can also be said that they identify the extent of public health problems.

In 1956, the U.S. Congress passed the National Health Survey Act, which established periodic health surveys to collect information on health-related states or events, use of healthcare resources, and relevant demographic information. Some such studies conducted in the United States now include the Behavior Risk Factor Surveillance System (BRFSS) survey, the National Health Interview Survey, the National Hospital Discharge Survey, and the National Health and Nutrition Examination Survey. Another name for cross-sectional surveys such as these is prevalence surveys. This is because cross-sectional surveys are often effective at obtaining prevalence data. For example, several studies have used cross-sectional surveys to estimate the prevalence of cancer and other chronic diseases.[15–18]

On the basis of a cross-sectional study of 2,531 randomly selected teachers and non-teachers in the public schools from Iowa and Utah, the prevalence of voice disorders (any time when the voice had not worked, performed, or sounded as it normally should) was 57.7% in teachers and 28.8% in nonteachers. Approximately 11.0% of teachers and 6.2% of nonteachers reported that they currently had a voice disorder.[19] Survey results also identified that occupation-related voice dysfunction in teachers may have significant adverse results on job performance, attendance, and future career choices.[20] Thus, the magnitude of a public health problem was determined, and teachers were identified as a high risk group for voice disorders.

Cross-sectional studies are also used to establish the prevalence of knowledge and attitudes about diseases and health-related states or events. A cross-sectional survey of adults in South Australia assessed adult knowledge and attitudes toward a new Human Papillomavirus (HPV) vaccination. Study results found that 2% of respondents knew HPV caused cervical cancer and only 7% identified HPV as a virus. The majority of adults believed that both men and women should receive the new vaccine and 77% of parents claimed they would immunize their children. However, 66% of parents expressed concern about possible side effects from the vaccine. By identifying knowledge and attitudes about the HPV vaccine, public health practitioners can tailor messages to address pervasive health beliefs, like the risk of side effects.[21]

Some of the strengths of cross-sectional surveys are that they can be used to study several associations at once, they can be conducted over a short period of time, they produce prevalence data, they are relatively inexpensive, and they can provide evidence of the need for analytic epidemiologic study. They are limited, however, in being able to establish whether an exposure preceded or followed a health outcome. For example, married men may be healthier than nonmarried men; however, it may not be clear whether married men are healthier because of their marriage or because healthier men self-select marriage. Identifying that an association exists between marriage and health in a cross-sectional study says nothing about the causal direction. Other weaknesses include the fact that this method is not feasible for studying rare conditions and has the potential for response bias.

Response bias is a type of selection bias where those who respond to a questionnaire are systematically different from those who do not respond.[22] They may be more likely to be nonsmokers, concerned about health matters, have a higher level of education, be more likely to be employed in professional positions, be more likely to be married and have children, be more active in the community, and so on. Consequently, the results will not be representative of the population of interest.

Serial Surveys

Many of the national health surveys in the United States are conducted annually. A **serial survey** is a cross-sectional survey that is routinely conducted. These surveys reveal changing patterns of health-related states or events over time. For example, between 1990 and 2007, the BRFSS survey collected national data on the percentage of adults who are overweight or obese, according to BMI. An increasing trend in both overweight and obese individuals is presented in **Figure 4-2**.

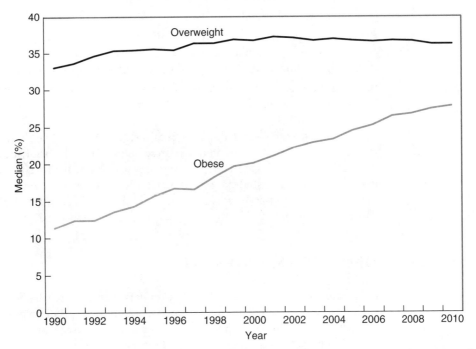

FIGURE 4-2   Percentages of overweight and obese adults in the United States and U.S. territories from 1990 through 2010. From Centers for Disease Control and Prevention. Trends data available at: http://apps.nccd.cdc.gov/brfss/index.asp.

TYPES OF DATA

Appropriate statistical methods for describing epidemiologic data by person, place, and time depend on the type of data used. **Data** may be thought of as observations or measurements of a phenomenon of interest. Data are obtained from observation, measurement, or experiment of variables, where a **variable** is a characteristic that varies from one observation to the next and can be measured or categorized. Before presenting types of methods for describing data, four types of data need defining: nominal, ordinal, discrete, and continuous.

- **Nominal data:** unordered categories or classes (e.g., gender, race/ethnicity, marital status, occupation). Nominal data that take on one of two distinct values are referred to as dichotomous. Nominal data that takes on more than two distinct values are called multichotomous.
- **Ordinal data:** the order among categories provides additional information (e.g., stage or grade of cancer). Ordinal-scale data are commonly used in health behavior research. Suppose health officials want to know if individuals in their area would use an immunization clinic if one was provided in the neighborhood. A cross-sectional survey could be administered with the following 5-point ordinal scale question.

  If an immunization clinic was held in your neighborhood, would you take your children to the clinic for their immunizations? (Check the box that applies most to your intention.)

  ❑ 1. Not likely to attend
  ❑ 2. Will consider attending
  ❑ 3. May attend
  ❑ 4. Most likely will attend
  ❑ 5. Will attend for certain

- **Discrete data:** integers or counts that differ by fixed amounts, with no intermediate values possible (e.g., number of new cases of lung cancer reported in the United States in a given year, number of children, and number of sick days taken in a month).
- **Continuous data:** measurable quantities not restricted to taking on integer values (e.g., age, weight, temperature).

When data are collected, they are typically entered into a spreadsheet in which each row represents a case and each column represents personal characteristics, clinical details, descriptive epidemiologic factors, and so on. A partial **line listing** containing information from the breast cancer study presented previously is shown in Table 4-2. Examples of nominal data are in columns 3, 4, 5, and 8. An example of ordinal data is in column 9. Discrete data are in column 6, and continuous data are in columns 2 and 7.

RATIOS, PROPORTIONS, AND RATES

In epidemiology, it is common to deal with data that indicate whether an individual was exposed to an illness, has an illness, experienced an injury, is disabled, or is dead. Ratios, proportions, and rates are commonly used measures for describing dichotomous data. The general formula for a ratio, proportion, or rate is:

$$\frac{x}{y} \times 10^n$$

TABLE 4-2   Partial Line Listing of Female Breast Cancer Patients

Case (1)	Age (2)	Race (3)	Ever Told You Have Breast Cancer (4)	One or More Blood Relatives Have Developed Cancer (5)	Number of Times Pregnant (6)	How Many Years Have You Breastfed (7)	What Is Your Religious Preference (8)	How Often Do You Attend Church (9)	Etc.
1	59	White	No	Yes	1	0.5	None	Never	
2	39	White	No	No	3	1	Catholic	Weekly	
3	73	White	No	Yes	0	0	LDS	Weekly	
Etc.									

The complete line listing has 927 (848 non-Hispanic white women) rows and 27 columns of data.
Data are from Daniels M, Merrill RM, Lyon JL, Stanford JB, White GL. Associations between breast cancer risk factors and religious practices in Utah. *Prev Med* 2004;38:28–38.

10^n is called the rate base, with typical values of $n = 0, 1, 2, 3, 4, 5$.

In a **ratio** the values of x and y are independent such that the values of x are not contained in y. The rate base for a ratio is $10^0 = 1$. For example, in 2008 there were 36,030 suicides in the United States, of which 28,447 were male and 7,583 were female. The ratio of males to females indicates that males were 3.75 times more likely than females to commit suicide.[23]

In a **proportion**, x is contained in y. A proportion is typically expressed as a percentage, such that the rate base is $10^2 = 100$. Thus, in 2008 the proportion of suicide cases in the United States who were male was 0.79 or 79%.

A **rate** is a type of frequency measure where the numerator involves nominal data that represent the presence or absence of a health-related state or event. It also incorporates the added dimension of time; it may be thought of as a proportion with the addition that it represents the number of disease states, events, behaviors, or conditions in a population over a specified time period. An **incidence rate** is the number of new cases of a specified health-related state or event reported during a given time interval divided by the estimated population at risk of becoming a case. It is calculated as:

$$Incidence\ Rate = \frac{New\ cases\ occurring\ during\ a\ given\ time\ period}{Population\ at\ risk\ during\ the\ same\ time\ period} \times 10^n$$

A mortality rate is the total number of deaths reported during a given time interval divided by the population from which the deaths occurred. It is calculated as:

$$Mortality\ Rate = \frac{Deaths\ occurring\ during\ a\ given\ time\ period}{Population\ from\ which\ deaths\ occurred} \times 10^n$$

For incidence and mortality rates, the time period is typically one year, and the population in the denominator is measured at the midyear. The rate base is typically 1,000, 10,000, or 100,000, depending on how common the health-related state or event is under consideration. The size of the rate base influences the clarity of the rate. For example, the female breast cancer incidence rate in 2008 in the United States was 0.001385.[23] For the sake of presentation, cancer rates are typically multiplied by a rate base of 10^5 or 100,000 such that this rate is 138.5 per 100,000.

Historically, the mortality rate was more readily available and was used to reflect the risk of disease in the population; however, as diagnosis and reporting have improved, incidence rates have become increasingly common for describing the occurrence of a health-related state or event.

If the denominator of the incidence rate is the sum of the time each person was observed, this is called a **person-time rate**. This measure is also referred to as an **incidence density rate**. The denominator is the time each person is observed instead of the number of people. Time can be measured in minutes, days, months, or years. For example, if 100 people were followed for 1 year, there are 100 person years in the denominator.

$$Person\text{-}time\ rate = \frac{New\ cases\ occurring\ during\ an\ observation\ period}{Time\ each\ person\ observed,\ totaled\ for\ all\ persons} \times 10^n$$

The person-time rate is particularly useful when people are at risk for different periods of time. For example, suppose we were interested in the rate of injuries at a worksite in a given month. Some workers may be employed full-time and others part-time. Rather than count each individual equally, we can count up the time (hours) each person worked and total this for all employees. Sometimes the midyear population is used in the denominator of the rate calculation as an estimate of the person-years at risk.

When new cases occur rapidly over a short period of time in a well-defined population, the incidence rate is referred to as an **attack rate**.

$$Attack\ Rate = \frac{New\ cases\ occurring\ during\ a\ short\ time\ period}{Population\ at\ risk\ at\ the\ beginning\ of\ the\ time\ period} \times 100$$

The attack rate is also called the **cumulative incidence rate**. It tends to describe diseases or events that affect a larger proportion of the population than the conventional incidence rate. The denominator includes the population at-risk at the beginning of the time period. By convention the rate base for the attack rate is 100.

On April 19, 1940, the occurrence of an outbreak of acute gastrointestinal illness was reported to the District Health Officer in Syracuse, New York.[24] The illness took place soon after eating contaminated food at a church picnic. The words "**epidemic**" and "**outbreak**" both refer to cases of illness in a place and time above what is normally expected. **Outbreak** refers to more localized situations, whereas epidemic refers to more widespread disease and, possibly, over a longer period of time. The investigation of the outbreak involved first constructing a line listing of those at the picnic. Each line represented an individual, with measurements taken on age, gender, time the meal was eaten, whether illness resulted, date of onset, time of onset, and whether selected foods were eaten. Attack rates were calculated for each of the foods, with the highest attack rate for vanilla ice cream; that is, of those who ate the vanilla ice cream, 43 were ill and 11 were not ill, yielding an attack rate of 80%. That attack rate can be calculated by placing the number of ill individuals who ate vanilla ice cream (43) in the numerator and the total number of individuals who ate vanilla ice cream (54) in the denominator. Of those who did not eat vanilla ice cream, 3 were ill and 18 were not ill, producing an attack rate of 14%. The ratio of these two attack rates is 5.7, indicating that those who ate the vanilla ice cream were 5.7 times more likely to experience acute gastrointestinal illness than those who did not eat the vanilla ice cream. To calculate the rate ratio, place the attack rate of those who ate vanilla ice cream (80%) in the numerator and the attack rate of those who did not eat vanilla ice cream (14%) in the denominator.

Sometimes the epidemiologist is interested in the rate of new cases occurring among contacts of known cases. This incidence rate is known as the **secondary attack rate** (SAR). The formula for SAR is:

$$SAR = \frac{\textit{New cases among contacts of primary cases during a short time period}}{(\textit{Population at beginning of time period}) - (\textit{Primary cases})} \times 100$$

Subtracting primary cases from the total population at the beginning of the time period yields the at-risk population.

Another common measure for describing disease and health-related events is point prevalence proportion (PPP). The numerator contains the number of new and existing cases of a disease or health-related event at a point in time and the denominator contains the total study population at a point in time. The formula for PPP is:

$$PPP = \frac{\textit{All existing cases of the disease or event a point in time}}{\textit{Total study population at a point in time}} \times 100$$

This statistic is useful for measuring diseases where it is difficult to know when an individual became a case, such as with arthritis or diabetes. It is also useful for describing the magnitude of a public health problem (i.e., burden), whereas the incidence rate is more appropriate for describing risk.

It may be informative to think of this statistic as a function of the competing forces of incidence, survival, and cure. High incidence, good survival, and low cure rate reflect high prevalence. Low incidence, poor survival, and high cure rate reflect low prevalence. For example, think of a sink of water, where the water in the sink reflects prevalence, the water coming into the sink through the faucet reflects incidence, the water going through the drain represents death, and the water evaporating reflects cure. If the water flow into the sink is high but little water goes through the drain or evaporates, the water level in the sink will be high (i.e., high incidence and low death or cure equates to high prevalence); if the water flowing into the sink is strong, but goes out through the drain fairly rapidly, the water level in the sink will be low (i.e., high incidence and high death mean low prevalence); and so on. Because it is sometimes difficult to say a patient is "cured," such as with cancer because of physical and mental scars from treatment and the chance of recurrence, prevalence is sometimes defined merely as the proportion of all cases who are still alive. Only at death are they removed from the prevalent pool. In the context of cancer, breast cancer for women and prostate cancer for men have high incidence and relatively good survival. These are the most prevalent cancers in the United States. On the other hand, pancreatic cancer has low incidence and poor survival. Hence, this is among the lowest prevalent cancers in the United States.

Crude and Age-Adjusted Incidence and Mortality Rates

The equations for the incidence and mortality rates discussed above produce crude rates. The **crude rate** of an outcome is calculated without any restrictions, such as by age or gender or who is counted in the numerator or denominator; however, these rates are limited if the epidemiologist is trying to compare them between subgroups of the population or over time because of potential confounding influences, such as differences in the age distribution between groups. For example, suppose the researcher was interested in knowing whether the death rate for whites differed between Florida and Utah. The National Cancer Institute provides a query system where these rates can be easily generated.[23] In 2008, the crude mortality rate in Florida was 927 per 100,000 compared with 515 per 100,000 in Utah. The crude mortality rate ratio is 1.8, meaning the rates in Florida are 1.8 times (or 80%) higher than in Utah; however, the age distribution differs considerably between Florida and Utah. In Florida, 18.3% of the population is under 15 years of age, and 17.0% of the population is 65 years and older.[23] Corresponding percentages in Utah are 26.6% and 8.9%.[29] Because death tends to come at a later age, much of the difference in the crude rates could be explained by different age distributions in the two populations, not greater risk factors and behaviors resulting in death in Florida. To make a more appropriate comparison of the hazard of death between the two populations, it is necessary to adjust for differences in the age distributions. This adjustment allows the researcher to control for the confounding effect of age. An **age-adjusted rate** is a weighted average of the age-specific rates, where the weights are the proportions of persons in the corresponding age groups of a standard population. Two methods are used in practice for adjusting rates called direct and indirect methods.

Direct Method for Age-Adjusting Rates

The direct method of age adjustment, based on the 2000 United States standard population, yielded rates of 686 in Florida and 671 in Utah per 100,000. Thus, after adjusting for differences in the age distribution, the mortality rate in Florida is 1.02 times that in Utah. In this section, application of the direct method to the age adjustment of rates will be illustrated.

The direct method of adjusting for differences in the age distribution between populations at a point in time or within a population over time involves first computing age-specific group rates, such as in 5- or 10-year age intervals. Rates based on data covering age intervals of 5 or 10 years are generally preferred because they are more stable than rates based on single-year age intervals. A standard population is then selected, also divided into corresponding 5- or 10-year age groups. In the previous example, the 2000 U.S. standard population was selected; however, Florida's population, Utah's population, or the sum of both populations could also have been used as the standard. The choice of the standard population is somewhat arbitrary. The key is to select a standard population that is sufficiently large and reflects at least one of the groups being compared, and to apply the standard population consistently between or within groups. The age-specific rates are multiplied by the age-specific standard population to give the expected number of cases had the group experienced the same population distribution as the standard population. The expected numbers of cases are then summed over each age group, with the sum divided by the total size of the standard population. The result is a rate age-adjusted to the standard population; that is, it is a rate that would occur if the population upon which the rate was based had the same age-distribution as the standard population. The age-adjusted rate is what we would expect to see if Utah and Florida had the same age distribution, in this case, the age distribution of the 2000 U.S. population.

Now, consider the cancer data presented in Table 4-3. The data reflect first primary malignant cancers, all sites combined, for the years 2006 through 2008 in the United States.[23] The population values are estimates on July 1 of each year and reflect person-years. Crude and age-group specific rates are presented. Crude cancer rates for males and females were derived by dividing the total counts by the total population values. A rate base of 100,000 was multiplied by the rates to yield 459 for males and 425 for females. In other words, 459 males and 425 females per 100,000 person-years were diagnosed during 2006–2008 with a first primary malignant cancer in the United States.

Age-group specific rates were derived by dividing the age-group specific counts by the corresponding age-group specific population values and multiplying by 100,000. Rates were lower for males through age 49 but higher for males thereafter. Overall, the crude rate ratio for males to females was 1.08 or 8% higher.

Suppose we were interested in comparing the primary malignant cancer rates between males and females, but we did not want differences in the rates to be influenced by differences in the age distributions for the two groups. It is possible to calculate an overall rate for

TABLE 4-3   First Primary Malignant Cancer Incidence Rates, 2006–2008, Among Males and Females According to Age

Age	Male			Female		
	Counts	Population	Rate Per 100,000	Counts	Population	Rate Per 100,000
< 40	25,088	67,565,256	37	35,497	64,234,055	55
40–49	36,315	17,432,372	208	60,476	17,471,794	346
50–59	103,052	14,544,216	709	98,528	15,212,174	648
60–69	149,371	8,627,282	1,731	109,245	9,587,297	1,139
70–79	135,379	5,027,225	2,693	104,824	6,423,527	1,632
80+	82,942	2,811,107	2,951	92,734	5,109,362	1,815
Total	**532,147**	**116,007,458**	**459**	**501,304**	**118,038,209**	**425**

Data from Surveillance Research Program, National Cancer Institute. SEER*Stat software Version 6.4.4. Available at: http:///www.seer.cancer.gov/seerstat. Accessed January 10, 2012.

females, for example, assuming they had the same age distribution as males. Here are the steps to obtain a rate for females, age-adjusted to the male population:

1. Choose a standard population. In this example, we will choose the male population; however, we could have just as easily selected the female population as the standard and calculated an overall age-adjusted rate for males. We could also have chosen another standard population and obtained age-adjusted rates for both males and females.

2. Obtain age-specific rates by dividing age-group specific counts by the corresponding age-group specific population. These are shown in the tables.

3. Multiply the female age-specific rates by the corresponding age-specific male population values to get expected counts of primary malignant cancer cases per age group for females, assuming they had the same age distribution as males (Table 4-4).

4. Sum the expected counts obtained in number 3 and divide by the total male population.

$$Age\text{-}adjusted\ Rate = \frac{37{,}338 + 60{,}340 + 94{,}202 + 98{,}306 + 82{,}038 + 51{,}021}{116{,}007{,}458} \times 100{,}000$$

$$= 365\ per\ 100{,}000\ person\text{-}years$$

TABLE 4-4   Data for Calculating the Age-Adjusted Malignant Cancer Rate for Females Using the Direct Method

Age	Male Population		Female Rate		Expected Counts
< 40	67,565,256	×	0.00055262	=	37,338
40–49	17,432,372	×	0.00346135	=	60,340
50–59	14,544,216	×	0.00647692	=	94,202
60–69	8,627,282	×	0.01139477	=	98,306
70–79	5,027,225	×	0.01631876	=	82,038
80+	2,811,107	×	0.01814982	=	51,021

The rate ratio for males to females is now 1.26, meaning that if females had the same age distribution as males, the first primary malignant cancer incidence rate would be 26% higher for males than females, as opposed to 8% higher found with the crude rates.

The magnitude of an adjusted rate does not represent the actual rate of a health-related state or event in the population but is a hypothetical construct useful for comparison. Once the standard population has been chosen, it must be consistently applied. For example, if rates are being compared over several years, it is important to age adjust the rates for those years using the same standard population. Researchers generally try to select a standard population that lies within the same time period as the data being evaluated as shown in the next example.

As the life expectancy in the United States continues to increase, comparing the risk of health-related states or events over time without the confounding effect of a changing age distribution requires that age-adjusted rates be used. A comparison is made between U.S. crude and age-adjusted rates over time for all-cause mortality and for all malignant cancers shown in **Figure 4-3**. The crude all-cause mortality rates indicate a decrease in mortality between the years 1969–2002; however, when the rates are adjusted for age, the decrease in mortality appears much more pronounced. For all malignant cancers, the crude mortality rate increases more rapidly before the peak in the early 1990s and decreases more slowly after the peak than the age-adjusted all-malignant cancer mortality rates.

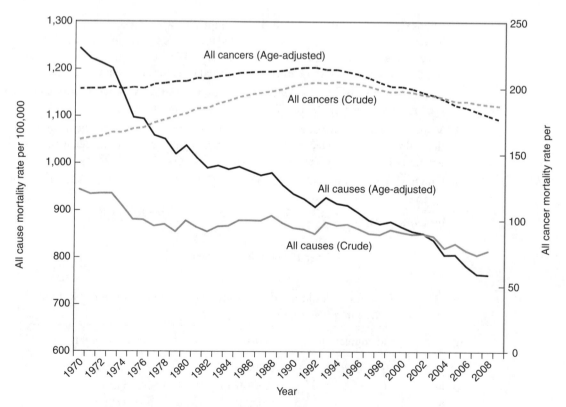

FIGURE 4-3 U.S. crude and age-adjusted (to the 2000 U.S. standard population) rates for all-cause mortality and all cancer deaths according to year. From National Cancer Institute. SEER. Cancer Query System: U.S. Mortality Statistics. Available at: http://seer.cancer.gov/canques/mortality.html.

Indirect Method of Age Adjustment

In situations where age-specific rates are unstable because of small numbers or missing numbers, age adjustment is still possible with the indirect method. As was the case with the direct method, a standard population is selected. This is the larger or more stable and complete of the two populations being compared. Age-specific rates are calculated for the standard population. These rates are then multiplied by the age-specific population values in the comparison population to obtain the expected number of health-related states or events in each age group. The total number of health-related states or events observed in the comparison population is then divided by the total number of expected health-related states or events. This ratio is referred to as the standard morbidity/mortality ratio (SMR).

$$SMR = \frac{Observed}{Expected}$$

Interpretation

- SMR = 1: The health-related states or events observed were the same as expected from the age-specific rates in the standard population.
- SMR > 1: More health-related states or events were observed than expected from the age-specific rates in the standard population.
- SMR < 1: Fewer health-related states or events were observed than expected from the age-specific rates in the standard population.

To illustrate, refer again to the data in Table 4-3; however, suppose that some or all of the female age-specific counts are unavailable but that the total count is available. Further, suppose that the age-specific rates for males can be calculated. Multiply the age-specific rates in the male (standard) population by the age-specific female population values to obtain the expected number of all malignant cancer cases per age-specific group (Table 4-5). Sum the expected counts to obtain the total number of expected malignant cancers in the comparison population. Then the observed count for females divided by the expected count for females if they had the same age-group specific rates as males.

$$SMR = \frac{501,304}{23,851 + 36,397 + 107,785 + 165,993 + 172,980 + 150,752} = 0.762$$

TABLE 4-5   Data for Calculating the Age-Adjusted Malignant Cancer Rate for Females Using the Indirect Method

Age	Male Rate		Female Population		Expected Counts
< 40	0.000371	×	64,234,055	=	23,851
40–49	0.002083	×	17,471,794	=	36,397
50–59	0.007085	×	15,212,174	=	107,785
60–69	0.017314	×	9,587,297	=	165,993
70–79	0.026929	×	6,423,527	=	172,980
80+	0.029505	×	5,109,362	=	150,752

This ratio indicates that fewer malignant cancer cases (approximately 24%) were observed in females than expected had they experienced the same age-specific rates as males.

Category-Specific Rates

Category-specific rates refer to rates computed for select types of disease (e.g., myocardial infarction, stroke, lung cancer) or for select subgroups of the population. Race-, age-, and gender-specific rates are commonly reported in the literature. Category-specific rates allow researchers to compare the risk and burden of disease occurrence, death, and health-related events among subgroups of the population, such as between blacks and whites, between young and old, and between men and women. Rate ratios are commonly used to compare category-specific rates among subgroups of the population. Geographic-specific rates are also common in epidemiology. Identifying the risk of disease according to characteristics related to place may provide clues to the causes of disease (see a review of Chapter 5, "Descriptive Epidemiology According to Person, Place, and Time" in this volume).

Confidence Intervals

When a rate is based on sample data, the sample rate is an estimate of the population rate. Confidence intervals are used to measure the precision of a sample rate. A **confidence interval** is the range of values in which the population rate is likely to fall. By convention, 95% confidence intervals are used to indicate a range in which the investigators are 95% confident the true population rate lies. The formula to calculate a 95% confidence interval for an incidence rate is:

$$Rate \pm 1.96 \sqrt{Rate(1 - Rate) / n}$$

Rate refers to the attack rate (or the cumulative incidence rate) and n equals the population at risk. When computing the confidence interval, make sure the rate is in its decimal form (i.e., not multiplied by a rate base). After the confidence interval is computed, then multiply the lower and upper limits by a relevant rate base. For example, suppose a random sample of 100 workers at a steel plant were selected and monitored over time for respiratory problems. If 25 of these workers complained of respiratory problems after 1 month of follow-up, such that the rate is 25 per 100, the 95% confidence interval for the rate is:

$$0.25 \pm 1.96 \sqrt{0.25(1 - 0.25) / 100} = 0.165, 0.335$$

or

$$16.5 - 33.5 \text{ per } 100$$

Note that the same formula can be applied for calculating a confidence interval for an estimate of the point prevalence proportion.

For a person–time incidence rate, the formula is modified as follows:

$$Rate \pm 1.96 \sqrt{Number\ of\ new\ cases/(person\text{--}time\ at\ risk)^2}$$

To illustrate, let's refer again to the data in Table 4-3. To calculate the 95% confidence interval for the crude male rate of first primary malignant cancer we apply the formula as follows:

$$0.00459 \pm 1.96 \sqrt{532,147/(116,007,458)^2} = 0.00458, 0.00460$$

Thus, we are 95% confident that the true rate of first primary malignant cancer cases per 100,000 person-years in the United States during 2006–2008 is between 458 and 460.

Finally, an approximate 95% confidence interval for the SMR can be calculated if we can appropriately assume a normal distribution.[25] The formula is:

$$SMR \pm 1.96 \sqrt{SMR/Expected}$$

Based on the SMR example presented above,

$$0.762 \pm 1.96 \sqrt{0.762/657,758} = 0.760, 0.764$$

So we are 95% confident that the true SMR reflecting the ratio of female-to-male malignant cancer cases is between 0.760 and 0.764.

TABLES, GRAPHS, AND NUMERICAL MEASURES

Frequency distribution tables, graphs, and numerical measures are common ways to present epidemiologic data.

Tables

The simplest table is the frequency distribution of one variable, such as the number of cases in each age group. A **frequency distribution** is a complete summary of the frequencies or number of times each value appears. The distribution tells either how many or what proportion of the group was found to have each value (or each range of values) out of all possible values that the measure can have. To create a frequency distribution, we list the values or categories that the variable may take and show the number of persons in the group who are at each value or category. **Relative frequency** is derived by dividing the number of people in each group by the total number of people.

A frequency distribution may be used for presenting the frequency of nominal, ordinal, discrete, or continuous data (grouped into class intervals such that each group covers a range of values). For the level of each of these types of data, the numerical counts associated with the levels of the variable are presented. When continuous data are grouped into class intervals, class intervals should not overlap. It is also often useful to present the proportion of counts associated with the level of each variable.

The numbers of individuals (counts) who have experienced a voice disorder (nominal data) are shown in Table 4-6. The prevalence of individuals who have ever had a voice disorder is 43% [(1088 / 2531) × 100]. Table 4-7 is more complex because it shows the frequency of individuals in each category of postnasal drip (ordinal data) for those ever having had a voice disorder compared with those who have not. Comparing the two distributions shows that ever having had a voice disorder is more likely among individuals with seasonal or chronic postnasal drip. Table 4-8 displays the frequency of individuals across age categories (continuous data) according to status of whether they have ever had a voice disorder. Those reporting ever having had a voice problem were more likely to be aged 40–49 or 50–59 years.

TABLE 4-6   Cases Ever Having Had a Voice Disorder: Nominal Data

Ever Had a Voice Disorder	Number of Individuals	Relative Frequency (%)
Yes	1,088	43.0
No	1,443	57.0

Data from Roy N, Merrill RM, Thibeault S, Parsa RA, Gray SD, Smith EM. Prevalence of voice disorders in teachers and the general population. *J Speech Lang Hear Res* 2004;47(2):281–293.

TABLE 4-7   Cases Ever Having Had a Voice Disorder by Classification of Postnasal Drip: Ordinal Data

Postnasal Drip	Number With Voice Disorder	Relative Frequency (%)	Number Without Voice Disorder	Relative Frequency (%)
Not at all	123	11.3	349	24.2
Occasionally	633	58.2	832	57.7
Seasonally	186	17.1	179	12.4
Chronically	146	13.4	83	5.7
Total	**1,088**	**100.0**	**1,443**	**100.0**

Data from Roy N, Merrill RM, Thibeault S, Parsa RA, Gray SD, Smith EM. Prevalence of voice disorders in teachers and the general population. *J Speech Lang Hear Res* 2004;47(2):281–293.

TABLE 4-8   Cases Ever Having Had a Voice Disorder by Classification of Age: Grouped Continuous Data

Postnasal Drip	Number With Voice Disorder	Relative Frequency (%)	Number Without Voice Disorder	Relative Frequency (%)
20–29	79	7.3	193	13.4
30–39	227	20.9	330	22.9
40–49	407	37.4	452	31.3
50–59	306	28.1	328	22.7
60+	69	6.3	140	9.7
Total	**1,088**	**100.0**	**1,443**	**100.0**

Data from Roy N, Merrill RM, Thibeault S, Parsa RA, Gray SD, Smith EM. Prevalence of voice disorders in teachers and the general population. *J Speech Lang Hear Res* 2004;47(2):281–293.

Graphs

Graphs are particularly useful for describing health-related states or events by place and time. Definitions of some common methods for describing data are as follows:

■ **Bar charts** are often used for graphically displaying a frequency distribution that involves nominal or ordinal data. The categories in which the observations fall are shown on the horizontal axis, and the vertical bar is drawn above each category, with the height representing the frequency. In some cases, researchers choose to plot the relative frequency such that the height of the bars then represents the percentage in each category. For example, Figure 4-4 is a bar chart that shows the estimated actual causes of death in the United States. Figure 4-5 is a side-by-side bar chart that shows the data from Table 4-7.

■ A **histogram** shows a frequency distribution for discrete or continuous data. The horizontal axis displays the true limits of the selected intervals. For example, Figure 4-6 displays the frequency of deaths in the United States across the age-span, 2008.

■ A **frequency polygon** is a graphical display of a frequency table. The intervals are shown on the *x*-axis, and the frequency in each interval is represented by the height of a point located above the middle of the interval. The points are connected in that they form a polygon with the *x*-axis.

■ An **epidemic curve** is a histogram that shows the course of an epidemic by plotting the number of cases by time of onset.

■ A **stem-and-leaf plot** is a display that organizes data to show its distribution. Each data value is split into a "stem" and a "leaf." The "leaf" is usually the last digit of the number and the other digits to the left of the "leaf" form the "stem." It provides similar information as a histogram, but the actual data is retained in the plot.

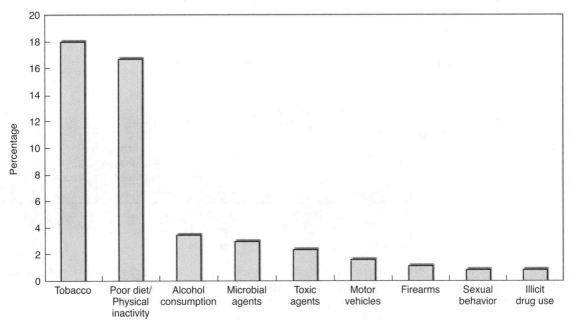

FIGURE 4-4   Actual causes of death in the United States, 2000. Data from Mokdad AH, Marks JS, Stroup DF, Gerberding JL. Actual causes of death in the United States, 2000. *JAMA* 2004;291:1238.

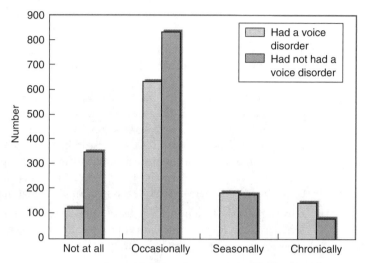

FIGURE 4-5   Frequency of ever having had a disorder or not ever having had a voice disorder, by categories of post-nasal drip. Data from Roy N, Merrill RM, Thibeault S, Parsa RA, Gray SD, Smith EM. Prevalence of voice disorders in teachers and the general population. *J Speech Lang Hear Res* 2004;47(2):281–293.

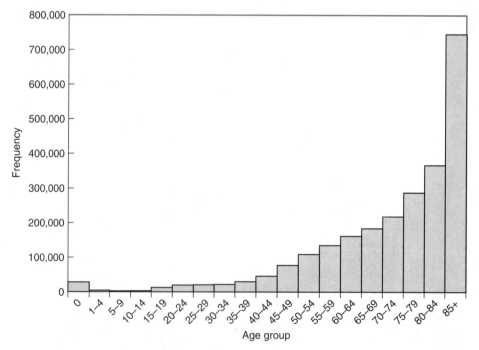

FIGURE 4-6   Frequency of deaths in the United States by age, 2008. Mortality data provided by NCHS (www.cdc.gov/nchs).

■ A **box plot** has a single axis and presents a summary of the data. Figure 4-7 is a box plot showing the distribution of adults in the 50 U.S. states and 4 territories, 2010, who have diabetes or that are obese. The central, vertically depicted box extends from the 25th percentile to the 75th percentile. The 25th percentile represents the first quartile, and 75th percentile represents the third quartile. The line running between the quartiles is the 50th percentile or median (middle). The lines projecting out of the box on either side extend to the maximum and minimum of the data.

■ A **two-way (or bivariate) scatter plot** is used to depict the relationship between two distinct discrete or continuous variables. Points on the graph represent a pair of values; the value of one variable is listed along the horizontal or *x*-axis, and the value of the other variable is listed along the vertical or *y*-axis. Figure 4-1 is an example of a two-way scatter plot.

■ A **spot map** is used to display the location of each health-related state or event that occurs in a defined place and time. With rare diseases or outbreaks, each point on the map represents a case. An example of a spot map of Montgomery, Alabama, showing the place of employment of cases in a typhus epidemic in 1922–1925 is shown in Figure 4-8. An **area map** may also be used, which indicates the number or rate of a health-related state or event by place, using different colors or shadings to represent the various levels of the disease, event, or behavior. For example, Figure 4-9 shows a map of the United States with the shading of each state representing cancer incidence rates of the colon and rectum per 100,000 person-years in 2004–2008.[26]

■ A **line graph** is similar to a two-way scatter plot in that it depicts the relationship between two continuous variables. Each point on the graph represents a pair of values. This graph is distinct from the two-way scatter plot because for each point on the *x*-axis there is only a single point on the *y*-axis. Figure 4-2 is an example of a line graph. The graph shows an increasing trend in the percentage of the U.S. adult population who are obese. Line graphs are useful for describing health-related states or events by time. Line graphs will be developed more fully later in this volume (see Chapter 5).

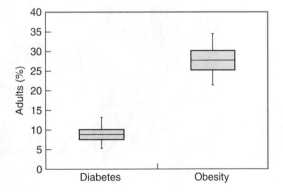

FIGURE 4-7   Box plot showing the distribution of diabetes and obesity among adults in the United States, 2010. Data from Centers for Disease Control and Prevention. Trends data available at: http://apps.nccd.cdc.gov/brfss/index.asp.

FIGURE 4-8   A spot map showing the place of residence of all cases of typhus in Montgomery, Alabama. Adapted from Maxcy, KF, "An Epidemiological Study of Endemic Typhus (Brill's Disease) in the Southeastern United States," Public Health Reports, Vol. 41, pp. 2967–2995, 1926.

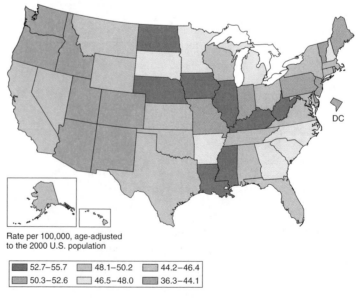

FIGURE 4-9   Incidence rates of cancers of the colon and rectum in the United States, 2004–2008. From Centers for Disease Control. Available at: http://cdc.gov/nccdphp/dnpa/obesity/trend/maps/index.htm.

Numerical Methods

It is often informative to summarize and describe discrete and continuous data with measures of central tendency and measures of dispersion. **Measures of central tendency** refer to ways of designating the center of the data. The most common measures are the arithmetic mean, geometric mean, median, and mode.

■ **Arithmetic mean** is the measure of central location one is most likely familiar with because it has many desirable statistical properties; it is the arithmetic average of a distribution of data. It is an appropriate summary measure for data that are approximately normal. The mean is mathematically responsive to each data value. It is sensitive to extreme values (outliers). Extreme high or low values will cause the mean to not represent the typical values in the frequency distribution because the mean will be pulled in the direction of outliers.

■ If the data are not normally distributed but instead have an exponential pattern (1, 2, 4, 8, 16, etc.) or a logarithmic pattern (1/2, 1/4, 1/8, 1/16, etc.), then the geometric mean is an appropriate measure of central tendency. The **geometric mean** is calculated as the nth root of the product of n observations. It is used when the logarithms of the observations are normally distributed. The geometric mean will always be less than or equal to the arithmetic mean for any given data set.

■ **Median** is the number or value that divides a list of numbers in half; it is the middle observation in the data set. It is less sensitive to outliers than the mean.

■ **Mode** is the number or value that occurs most often; the number with the highest frequency.

   Measures of dispersion, also called the spread or variability, are used to describe how much data values in a frequency distribution vary from each other and from the measures of central tendency. There are several measures of dispersion: range, interquartile range, variance, coefficient of variation, and standard deviation. These are defined as follows:

■ **Range** is the difference between the largest (maximum) and smallest (minimum) values of a frequency distribution.

■ **Interquartile range** is the difference between the third quartile (75th percentile) and first quartile (25th percentile). Note that the distribution of data consists of four quarters. Each quartile represents 25% of the data. Twenty-five percent of the data fall at or below the first quartile. Fifty percent of the data fall below the second quartile (median). Seventy-five percent of the data fall at or below the third quartile, and 100% of the data fall at or below the fourth quartile.

■ **Variance** is the average of the squared differences of the observations from the mean.

■ **Standard deviation** is the square root of the variance. The standard deviation has nice mathematical properties that are used in constructing the confidence interval for the mean and in statistical tests for evaluating research hypotheses.

■ The **coefficient of variation** is a measure of relative spread in the data. It is a normalized measure of dispersion of a probability distribution that adjusts the scales of variables so that meaningful comparisons can be made. It is an appropriate measure for noncategorical data. It is the ratio of the standard deviation to the mean.

   The **empirical rule** states that approximately 68% of the observations are within one standard deviation of the mean, 95% of the observations are within two standard deviations of the mean, and almost all the observations are within three standard deviations of the mean. The empirical rule, however, is an approximation that applies only when the data are symmetric and unimodal.

Alternatively, **Chebychev's inequality** can be used to summarize the distribution of data. It is less specific than the empirical rule but applies for any set of data, no matter what its distribution is. It says that for any number k that is greater than or equal to 1, at least one $[1 - (1 / k)^2]$ of the measurements in the data set lie within k standard deviations of the mean.[27] If $k = 2$, then $[1 - (1/2)^2] = 3/4$, or that 75% of the values lie within two standard deviations of the mean. We can also say that

$$x \pm 2s$$

contains at least 75% of the observations. If $k = 3$, then

$$x \pm 3s$$

contains at least 88.9% of the observations. It is a more conservative statement than the empirical rule. The distribution of adults who are of normal weight in the 50 U.S. states and 4 territories is skewed right; that is, the mean is 36.1 and the median is 35.4 (note that the mean is more sensitive to outliers than the median and is pulled more in the direction of the tail).[28] The standard deviation for the data is 3.2. Based on Chebychev's inequality, the percentage of the adult population in the normal weight classification for 75% of the states and territories is 21.3 to 34.1 and 88.9% is 18.1 to 37.3.

A summary of selected approaches to describe and present nominal, ordinal, discrete, and continuous data is presented in Table 4-9.

TABLE 4-9   Selected Ways to Summarize and Present Data

	Description	Statistics	Graphs
Nominal	Unordered categories		Bar chart
		Frequency distribution	Spot map
		Relative frequency	Area map
Ordinal	Ordered categories with intervals that are not quantifiable		Bar chart
		Frequency distribution	
		Relative frequency	
Discrete	Quantitative—integers	Geometric mean	Bar chart
	Ordering and magnitude important	Arithmetic mean	
		Median	
Continuous	Quantitative—values on a continuum	Mode	Histogram or frequency polygon
		Range	Box plot
		Variance	Stem-and-leaf plot
		Standard deviation	
		Coefficient of variation	
		Chebychev's inequality	

MEASURES OF STATISTICAL ASSOCIATION

Exploratory studies are descriptive and may involve measuring the association between variables. When measuring the association between two nominal or ordinal variables, data are entered into a contingency table, and the frequency distribution of one variable is compared across the levels of the other variable. A **contingency table** is where all entries are classified by each of the variables in the table. That is, a contingency table is a display of data classified according to two variables, with the rows representing one variable and the columns representing the other variable. If two quantitative measures were taken on the same subjects, a scatter plot would be appropriate for displaying the data. Some common measures for assessing the association between quantitative variables are as follows:

- **Correlation coefficient** (denoted by r) measures the strength of the association between two variables (also called the Pearson correlation). The method assumes both variables are normally distributed and that a linear association exists between the variables. When the latter assumption is violated, the investigator may choose to apply the correlation measure over a subsection of the data where linearity holds. The correlation coefficient ranges between -1 and $+1$.

- **Coefficient of determination** (denoted by r^2) is the square of the correlation coefficient, and it represents the proportion of the total variation in the dependent variable that is determined by the independent variable. If a perfect positive or negative association exists, then all of the variation in the dependent variable would be explained by the independent variable. Generally, however, only part of the variation in the dependent variable can be explained by a single independent variable.

- **Spearman's rank correlation coefficient** is an alternative to the Pearson correlation coefficient when outlying data exist such that one or both of the distributions are skewed. This method is robust to outliers.

- **Regression** is a statistical analysis that provides an equation that estimates the change in the dependent variable (y) per unit change in an independent variable (x). This method assumes that for each value of x, y is normally distributed, that the standard deviation of the outcomes y do not change over x, that the outcomes y are independent, and that a linear relationship exists between x and y. Data transformations and other methods are used to respond to violations of these assumptions. In some situations when outliers exist, the model is estimated after the outliers have been dropped. In situations where a linear relationship between variables does not hold, piecewise linear regression or polynomial regression may be employed.

A linear association may be estimated through the use of a procedure called linear regression. This is done by applying the least squares method. This method fits a linear line to the data that minimizes the squared deviations of each point from the straight line. Simple linear regression involves an equation with one independent variable. The equation may be written as

$$y = a + bx$$

The letter a represents the y-intercept of the linear fitted line, and the letter b represents the slope. The slope is a measure of association that indicates how y changes when x changes by one unit.

To illustrate, recall the data shown in Figure 4-1, where we examined the association between eating five or more servings of fruit and vegetables per day and obesity (BMI = 30) in the United States and U.S. territories, 2010. Each dot in the graph represents aggregated data for the state or territory. A linear line fits the data reasonably well. The correlation coefficient is $r = -0.626$. The coefficient of determination is $r^2 = 0.392$. Thus, it can be said that 39.2% of the variation in obesity is associated with the variable fruit and vegetables. The remaining 60.8% is associated with other factors, such as exercise, heredity, and age. In this example, there are no strong outliers. The estimated linear regression line is

$$\text{Obesity} = 43.69 - 0.74 \times \text{Fruit \& Vegetables}$$

For every percent increase in five or more servings of fruit and vegetables per day, the percent obese is expected to decrease by 0.74. Although it could be said that the percent obese is estimated to be 43.69 when percent of five or more servings of fruit and vegetables is zero, zero lies beyond the range of the data on the x-axis. Although y can be estimated for any given value of x, estimating y beyond the range of the x values used to estimate the model may result in misleading and nonsensical results; nevertheless, it is perfectly appropriate to estimate percent obese for the percent of five or more servings of fruit and vegetables per day of 25, for example. This yields an estimated percent of state-level obesity of 25.2%.

The coefficient of determination indicated that most of the variation in obesity among the U.S. states and territories was not explained by fruit and vegetable consumption. Hence, other variables may be included in the model to further explain obesity. In this case, the simple linear regression model could be expanded to include other potential explanatory variables. When more than one independent variable is included in the model, this is called multiple regression.

■ **Multiple regression** is an extension of simple regression analysis in which there are two or more independent variables. In multiple regression, the effects of multiple independent variables on the dependent variable can be simultaneously assessed. This type of model is useful for adjusting for potential confounders. For example, in a regression analysis assessing the relationship between heart disease (y) and exercise (x), age is a potential confounding variable. To control or adjust for this potential confounder, both variables are included as independent variables in the regression model; however, this assumes that data on the suspected confounding factors are available. In many situations there may be confounding factors that are not known to the investigator and, as a result, the data not collected.

If the dependent variable is not quantitative but rather dichotomous (two levels), as is often the case in epidemiology where the outcome of interest reflects the presence of a health-related state or event (e.g., ill vs. not ill, injured vs. not injured, disabled vs. not disabled, dead vs. alive, and so on), then the logistic regression model may be used.

■ **Logistic regression** is a type of regression in which the dependent variable is a dichotomous variable. Logistic regression is commonly used in epidemiology because many of the outcome measures considered involve nominal data.

■ **Multiple logistic regression** is an extension of logistic regression in which two or more independent variables are included in the model. It allows the researcher to look at the simultaneous effect of multiple independent variables on the dependent variable. As in the case of multiple regression, this method is effective in controlling for confounding factors.

The assumptions for these methods (such as linearity and normality) can be evaluated with bivariate scatter plots. It is beyond the scope of this book to explore methods for evaluating model assumptions.

The measures of association presented here assume a sufficiently large sample size. This is because outliers can have large and potentially misleading effects on the statistical measures when the sample size is small. In addition, a measure of association also employs a statistical test to evaluate the role of chance; that is, a statistical test indicates the probability that a result is real or due to chance.

Some of the statistical methods for measuring the strength of associations between variables according to variable type are presented in Table 4-10. The interested reader may refer to statistical texts for corresponding statistical tests for evaluating the measures of association. Explanatory and outcome variables are determined by the investigator. Classifying variables as such is based on observation and logic.

TABLE 4-10   Selected Statistical Techniques for Measuring Association between Two Variables According to Variable Type

| | Outcome Variable | | | |
Exposure Variable	Nominal with 2 categories	Nominal with > 2 categories	Continuous, not normally distributed, or ordinal with > 2 categories	Continuous, normally distributed
Continuous, normally distributed	Logistic regression		Spearman rank correlation	Correlation coefficient Linear regression
Continuous, not normally distributed, or ordinal with > 2 categories	Logistic regression		Spearman rank correlation	Spearman rank correlation
Nominal with > 2 categories	Logistic regression	Contingency table		Analysis of variance
Nominal with 2 categories	Logistic regression Contingency table Risk ratio Rate ratio Odds ratio Prevalence proportion	Contingency table	Polytomous logistic regression Rank analysis of variance	Comparison of means

Along the left column are types of explanatory variables and along the top are types of outcome variables.

CONCLUSION

The purpose of this chapter was to present descriptive study designs in epidemiology and to discuss their functions. Descriptive analysis is the first step in epidemiology to understanding the presence, extent, and nature of a public health problem and is useful for formulating research hypotheses. Descriptive studies are hypothesis generating; they provide the rationale for testing specific hypotheses. The analytic study design, which is the focus of a later chapter, provides better control for evaluating hypotheses about associations between variables. Many of the same measures and statistical tests used in exploratory descriptive studies are also used in analytic studies. After a hypothesis is statistically evaluated for significance and an association between variables is deemed to not be explained by chance, bias, or confounding, then an investigator can use this information as part of the evidence for establishing a cause–effect relationship. Other criteria to consider in making a judgment about causality must also be considered, including temporality, dose–response relationship, biologic credibility, and consistency among studies.[29]

EXERCISES

Key Terms

Define the following terms.

Age-adjusted rate	Ecologic study	Ordinal data
Area map	Empirical rule	Outbreak
Arithmetic mean	Epidemic	Person-time rate
Attack rate	Epidemic curve	Point prevalence
Bar chart	Frequency distribution	Proportion
Box plot	Frequency polygon	Range
Case report	Geometric mean	Rate
Case series	Histogram	Ratio
Chebychev's inequality	Incidence density rate	Relative frequency
Continuous data	Incidence rate	Regression
Coefficient of determination	Interquartile range	Secondary attack rate
Coefficient of variation	Line graph	Serial survey
Contingency table	Line listing	Spearman's rank correlation
Correlation coefficient	Logistic regression	coefficient
Cross-sectional survey	Measures of central tendency	Spot map
Crude rate	Measures of dispersion	Standard deviation
Cumulative incidence rate	Median	Stem-and-leaf plot
Data	Mode	Study design
Descriptive epidemiology	Mortality rate	Two-way scatter plot
Descriptive study design	Multiple regression	Variable
Discrete data	Multiple logistic regression	Variance
Ecologic fallacy	Nominal data	

STUDY QUESTIONS

To answer questions 1 to 3, refer to the data in Table 4-11.

TABLE 4-11   Female Crude Malignant First Primary Breast Cancer Incidence Rates in San Francisco and the Metropolitan Areas of Detroit and Atlanta According to Selected Racial Groups, 2006–2008

Location	White Rate per 100,000	Black Rate per 100,000	Other Rate per 100,000
San Francisco	162.6	128.6	112.0
Detroit (metropolitan)	146.4	116.8	50.2
Atlanta (metropolitan)	124.6	98.2	56.0
Three areas combined	146.8	109.5	94.0

Data from Surveillance Research Program, National Cancer Institute. SEER*Stat software Version 6.4.4. Available at: http:///www.seer.cancer.gov/seerstat.Accessed January 10, 2012.

1. The variables in the table represent what type of data?

2. Describe the extent of the public health problem of female breast cancer according to place.

3. Would age-adjusted rates be more appropriate for comparing the risk of female breast cancer among geographic areas and racial groups? Explain.

For questions 4 to 6, refer to the data in Table 4-12.

TABLE 4-12   Female Age-adjusted (to the 2000 U.S. Standard Population) Malignant First Primary Breast Cancer Incidence Rates in San Francisco and the Metropolitan Areas of Detroit and Atlanta for Whites and Blacks, 2006–2008

Location	White Rate per 100,000	Black Rate per 100,000	Other Rate per 100,000
San Francisco	139.3	122.1	103.2
Detroit (metropolitan)	120.8	120.4	59.2
Atlanta (metropolitan)	120.4	125.9	71.6
Three areas combined	127.6	122.8	95.4

Data from Surveillance Research Program, National Cancer Institute. SEER*Stat software Version 6.4.4. Available at: http:///www.seer.cancer.gov/seerstat.Accessed January 10, 2012.

4. The crude rate ratio between whites and blacks is 1.34. The corresponding rate ratio based on the age-adjusted rates is 1.0 What does this tell you about the age distribution among the geographic populations?

5. Do these data provide any clues as to whether race is a risk factor for female breast cancer?

6. What other descriptive data would be useful for providing clues as to the causes of female breast cancer?

For questions 7 to 12, refer to the data in Table 4-13.

TABLE 4-13   Age-Specific Female Malignant Breast Cancer Incidence in the Combined Areas of San Francisco and the Metropolitan Areas of Detroit and Atlanta According to Selected Racial Groups, 2006–2008

	White		Black		Other	
Years	Cases	Population	Cases	Population	Cases	Population
< 50	3,616	7,420,076	1,415	3,344,874	662	1,586,388
50–54	1,913	830,549	690	293,626	286	148,548
55–59	2,094	736,737	692	244,829	293	131,258
60–64	2,043	567,178	577	162,834	194	89,008
65–69	1,788	400,785	443	111,761	206	69,068
70+	4,940	1,210,138	1,026	266,941	429	177,188

Data from Surveillance Research Program, National Cancer Institute. SEER*Stat software Version 6.4.4. Available at: http:///www.seer.cancer.gov/seerstat. Accessed January 10, 2012.

7. Calculate relative frequencies across age groups for whites, blacks, and other racial groups. How does the age-specific percentage of breast cancer compare among racial groups?

8. Calculate the age-specific rates for each racial group. Graph the age-specific rates for each age group.

9. Calculate the 95% confidence interval for the crude female breast cancer rate for each racial group.

10. Using the white female population as the standard, use the direct method to calculate age-adjusted rates for blacks in the age range 50–69.

11. Using the white female population as the standard, use the indirect method to calculate the SMR for blacks in the age range 50–69.

12. Describe the age distribution for the three racial groups.

13. Compare and contrast the incidence rate with the prevalence proportion.

14. Compare and contrast the person-time incidence rate with the attack rate.

15. If the incidence of disease A is lower than the incidence of disease B, but the prevalence of disease A is higher than the prevalence of disease B, what does that say about the lethality of the two diseases? Assume that the cure rate is similar between both diseases.

16. An accident on the freeway resulted in a chemical leak that exposed several individuals in the nearby community. Many residents complained of respiratory problems. To calculate the probability or risk of illness, describe the statistical measure you would use (including the numerator, denominator, and rate base).

17. There were recently 120 people diagnosed in a certain region with disease A. A total of 440 persons lived in the households where these cases resided. If 50 of these diagnosed patients were primary cases, what is the secondary attack rate?

18. The mean and median ages for a group participating in a clinical trial are 43 and 51, respectively. What can you say about the distribution of ages?

19. Suppose the correlation coefficient measuring the strength of the linear association between exercise (in hours per week) and pulse (per minute) for 1,000 study participants is –0.3. Calculate the coefficient of determination and interpret both these measures.

20. Suppose the estimated slope coefficient in a regression model measuring the association between the independent variable exercise (in hours per week) and dependent variable pulse has a slope of –0.05 (per minute). Interpret this result.

21. If age was a suspected confounder of the relationship between exercise and pulse, how might you adjust for this factor in your analysis?

22. A prospective cohort study showed that 200 new cases of disease X occurred in 2,000 person-years. Calculate the person-time incidence rate and 95% confidence interval.

REFERENCES

1. Page RM, Cole GE, Timmreck TC. *Basic Epidemiological Methods and Biostatistics: A Practical Guidebook*. Boston, MA: Jones and Bartlett; 1995.
2. Stevenson M, McClure R. Use of ecological study designs for injury prevention. *Injury Prev*. 2005;11:2–4.
3. Fearing NM, Harrison PB. Complications of the Heimlich maneuver: case report and literature review. *J Trauma*. 2002;53:978–979.
4. Jernigan JA, Stephens DS, Ashford DA, et al. Bioterrorism-related inhalational anthrax: the first 10 cases reported in the United States. *Emerg Infect Dis*. 2001;7(6):933–944.
5. Centers for Disease Control and Prevention. Pneumocystis pneumonia—Los Angeles. *MMWR*. 1981;30:250.
6. Centers for Disease Control and Prevention. A cluster of Kaposi's sarcoma and Pneumocystis carinii pneumonia among homosexual male residents of Los Angeles and Orange counties, California. *MMWR*. 1982;31:305–307.
7. Jaffe HW, Choi K, Thomas PA, et al. National case-control study of Kaposi's sarcoma and Pneumocystis carinii pneumonia in homosexual men: part 1, epidemiologic results. *Ann Intern Med*. 1983;99:145–151.
8. Centers for Disease Control and Prevention. Immunodeficiency among female sexual partners of males with acquired immune deficiency syndrome (AIDS)—New York. *MMWR*. 1983;31:697–698.
9. Harris C, Small CB, Klein RS, et al. Immunodeficiency in female sexual partners of men with the acquired immunodeficiency syndrome. *N Engl J Med*. 1983;308:1181–1184.
10. Centers for Disease Control and Prevention. Pneumocystis carinii pneumonia among persons with hemophilia A. *MMWR*. 1982;31:365–367.
11. Centers for Disease Control and Prevention. Possible transfusion-associated acquired immune deficiency syndrome (AIDS)—California. *MMWR*. 1982;31:652–654.
12. Centers for Disease Control. Acquired immune deficiency syndrome (AIDS): precautions for clinical and laboratory staffs. *MMWR* 1982;31:577–580.
13. Centers for Disease Controland Prevention. Unexplained immunodeficiency and opportunistic infections in infants—New York, New Jersey, and California. *MMWR*. 1982;31:665–667.

14. Joint United Nations Programme on HIV/AIDS and World Health Organization. 2008 report on the global AIDS epidemic. http://www.unaids.org/en/KnowledgeCenter/HIVData/GlobalReport/2008/2008_global_report.asp. Accessed May 8, 2009.

15. Byrne J, Kessler LG, Devesa SS. The prevalence of cancer among adults in the United States: 1987. *Cancer*. 1992;68:2154–2159.

16. Hewitt M, Breen N, Devesa S. Cancer prevalence and survivorship issues: analyses of the 1992 National Health Interview Survey. *J Natl Cancer Inst*. 1999;91(17):1480–1486.

17. Ahluwalia IB, Mack KA, Murphy W, Mokdad AH, Bales VS. State-specific prevalence of selected chronic disease-related characteristics—Behavioral Risk Factor Surveillance System, 2001. *MMWR*. 2003;52(8):1–80.

18. Harris MI, Flegal KM, Cowie CC, et al. Prevalence of diabetes, impaired fasting glucose, and impaired glucose tolerance in U.S. adults. The Third National Health and Nutrition Examination Survey, 1988–1994. *Diabetes Care*. 1998;21(4):518–524.

19. Roy N, Merrill RM, Thibeault S, Parsa RA, Gray SD, Smith EM. Prevalence of voice disorders in teachers and the general population. *J Speech Lang Hear Res*. 2004;47(2):281–293.

20. Roy N, Merrill RM, Thibeault S, Gray SD, Smith EM. Voice disorders in teachers and the general population: effects on work performance, attendance, and future career choices. *J Speech Lang Hear Res*. 2004;47(3):542–551.

21. Marshall H, Ryan P, Roberton D, Baghurst P. A cross-sectional survey to assess community attitudes to introduction of Human Papillomavirus vaccine. *Australian and New Zealand Journal of Public Health*. 2007;31(3):235-242.

22. Last JM, ed. *A Dictionary of Epidemiology*. New York, NY: Oxford University Press; 1995.

23. Surveillance, Epidemiology, and End Results (SEER) Program (http://www.seer.cancer.gov). SEER*Stat Database: Mortality— All COD, Aggregated with State, Total U.S. (1969–2008) <Katrina/Rita Population Adjustment>, National Cancer Institute, DCCPS, Surveillance Research Program, Cancer Statistics Branch, released September 2011. Underlying mortality data provided by NCHS (http://www.cdc.gov/nchs).

24. Gross M. Oswego revisited. *Public Health Rep*. 1976;91:168–170.

25. Kahn HA, Sempos CT. *Statistical Methods in Epidemiology*. New York, NY: Oxford University Press; 1989.

26. National Cancer Institute. State Cancer Profiles. http://statecancerprofiles.cancer.gov/map/map.withimage.php?00&001&020&00&0&1&0&1&6&0#map. Accessed January 5, 2012.

27. Parzen E. *Modern Probability Theory and Its Applications*. New York, NY: Wiley; 1960.

28. Centers for Disease Control and Prevention. Trends data. http://apps.nccd.cdc.gov/brfss/index.asp. Accessed January 5, 2012.

29. Hennekens CH, Buring JE. *Epidemiology in Medicine*. Boston, MA: Little, Brown and Company; 1985.

5

Descriptive Epidemiology According to Person, Place, and Time

OBJECTIVES

After completing this chapter, you will be able to:

- Describe the extent of a public health problem according to person, place, and time.
- Communicate a public health problem with the use of tables and graphs.
- Identify who is at greatest risk for selected health-related states or events.
- Use surveillance methods to monitor whether unusual health-related states or events exist and to evaluate public health intervention programs.
- Understand how descriptive epidemiology can provide clues as to the causes of disease.

In the previous chapter, many important functions of descriptive epidemiology were presented, which include providing useful information about health-related states or events, providing insights into the presence of new diseases or adverse health effects, identifying the extent of public health problems, obtaining a description of public health problems that can be easily communicated, identifying those at greatest risk, providing information useful for health planning and resource allocation, and identifying avenues for future research that can provide insights about an etiologic relationship between an exposure and health outcome. To this end, descriptive epidemiology describes data according to person, place, and time factors. Implicit in descriptive epidemiology is the notion of public health surveillance, which is the systematic ongoing collection, analysis, interpretation, and dissemination of health data. Surveillance data are a means for evaluating whether changes in health-related states or events occur regularly and can be predicted or are unusual events that are unexpected. Surveillance is also commonly used to monitor the efficacy and effectiveness of public health interventions.

The purpose of this chapter is to describe more fully the person, place, and time elements of descriptive epidemiology.

PERSON, PLACE, AND TIME

Descriptive data on the **person** level characterizes who is getting the disease. Descriptors often include age, gender, race/ethnicity, marital and family status, occupation, and education. Descriptive data by **place** addresses where health-related states or events are occurring most or least frequently. These data often involve comparisons between or among geographic regions, in groups before and after migration, and between twins raised in different settings. Basic to any descriptive epidemiologic study is the analysis and interpretation of the effect of time on the occurrence of health-related states or events. The **time** aspects of epidemiologic investigations range from hours to weeks, years to decades. Short-term disease incubation periods of a few hours can be as important to the epidemiologist as long-term latency periods for chronic diseases that span decades. Another term used occasionally to describe time factors in epidemiology is **temporal**, which means time or refers to time-related elements or issues.

PERSON

Much of the focus of epidemiology is on the "person" aspect of disease, disability, injury, and death. Populations are often characterized according to a number of standard variables and traits, including demographics and the clinical characteristics of disease. From a practical point of view, the traits used to describe the person aspects of epidemiology are limited according to the purpose and resources of concern to a particular study or investigation. Information already available from common sources such as public health departments, government agencies, and information gathered from the investigation should be used.

Epidemiologic studies usually concentrate on several major demographic characteristics of the person: age, gender, race/ethnicity, marital status, occupation, and education. Comparing health-related states or events over time according to these characteristics, and their combinations, can provide clues as to the causes of disease. It is also often insightful to compare health-related states or events among and between classifications of these variables.

Age

Because of the strong influence age often has on the outcomes and findings of studies, it has to be considered and, if necessary, controlled for in the study. One approach to control for the potential confounding effect of age over time is to restrict the study to age-specific categories. For example, malignant female breast cancer rates are presented for ages 50 years and older by selected age groups in Figure 5-1. An alternative approach to controlling for age as a potential confounder is to report age-adjusted rates, as described in Chapter 4,

"Design Strategies and Statistical Methods in Descriptive Epidemiology" in this volume. An important assumption for age adjusting rates over time is that the age-specific rates are approximately parallel, as is the case in Figure 5-1.

Risks of health-related states or events are often related to age. For example, senior adults often face health problems such as high blood pressure, diabetes, joint pains, kidney infections, tuberculosis, Alzheimer's disease, heart problems and heart attack, and cancer. The increasing risk of death in the United States in older ages is largely because of increasing heart disease and cancer (Figure 5-2).[1]

Epidemiologists correlate personal characteristics with health-related states or events in order to provide insights into the determinants and causal mechanisms of disease. For example, the incidence of carcinoma in situ of the uterine cervix increases sharply from about age 15 years, peaks in women aged 25–29, decreases rapidly through ages 50–54, and then gradually decreases thereafter (Figure 5-3).[2] The shape of the age-specific incidence curve suggests that carcinoma in situ of the uterine cervix follows an exposure that affects a substantial number of women close to the same age, and the time from exposure to observable pathologic change is less than 15 years. This pattern is similar to the pattern resulting from an infectious agent. It is now well established that human papillomavirus, transmitted through sexual intercourse, is a primary cause of cancer of the uterine cervix.

Length of life is one of the most basic aspects of a person and one with which epidemiologists are concerned. Longevity or life expectancy continues to be a measure of the health status of specific populations, differing according to demographic and geographic factors. In 2011, the estimated life expectancy was 89.7 (ranked 1) in Monaco, 82.3 (ranked 13) in

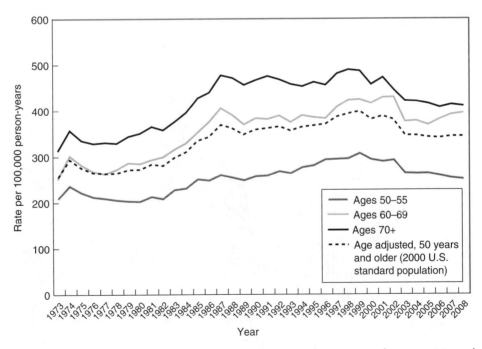

FIGURE 5-1   Female malignant breast cancer incidence rates for ages 50 and older in SEER according to calendar year. Data from Surveillance Research Program National Cancer Institute. SEER*Stat software Version 6.4.4. Available at: http:///www.seer.cancer.gov/seerstat. Accessed January 10, 2012.

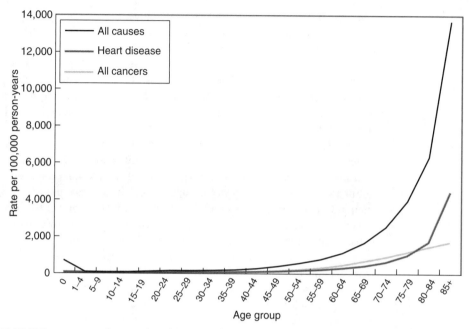

FIGURE 5-2   Death rates for all causes, cancer, and heart disease across the age span in the United States, 2008. Mortality data provided by NCHS (www.cdc.gov/nchs).

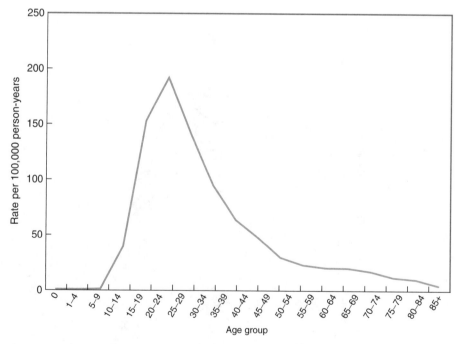

FIGURE 5-3   Age-specific rates of carcinoma in situ of the uterine cervix, 1991–1995. Data from Ries LAG, Kosary CI, Hankey BF, Miller BA, Edwards BK, eds. SEER Cancer Statistics Review, 1973–1996. Bethesda, MD: National Cancer Institute, 1999.

Japan, 80.1 (ranked 28) in the United Kingdom, 78.4 (ranked 50) in the United States, 70.1 (ranked 146) in Iran, 59.5 (ranked 188) in Kenya, and 38.8 (ranked 221) in Angola.[3]

Population Pyramid

The **population** (or **age**) **pyramid** has been used for many years by demographers and epidemiologists to track and compare changes in population age distributions over time. The number of persons in various age groups in a selected population, such as a state or country, is affected by birth rates, fertility levels, wars, death rates, and migration. Thus, the population is dynamic and changes over time. Large or small cohorts of people born in the same year can be seen to move up the life span and the population pyramid over time. Percentages of the population in each age group are represented by the length of the bars on the graph, with the sum of the bars equaling 100% (Figure 5-4). The age distribution of males is shown on the left side of the graph, and the age distribution of females is shown on the right side of the graph. A population pyramid uses two-person characteristics and is an age/gender comparison. The age and gender traits are collected at a specific point in time, usually at the **decennial census** (population census taken by the Census Bureau in years ending in zero).

Social and health-related changes in populations can be seen in birth cohorts when they are plotted on a population pyramid. Some examples of these changes are the effects of wars, famines, droughts, use of birth control measures, fertility levels (number of females between ages 15 and 45 years available to have children), and the rate of marriage. Poor development of public health systems and little control of infectious disease such as sanitation of water supplies and food, control of sewage and garbage, low levels of immunizations, and poor medical care can lead to increased deaths and fewer people entering older age groups. Not only do all of these factors affect the shape of a population pyramid, but the events of society can also be reflected in the pyramid as time passes. As the events affect a population, the events move up through the different age groups in the pyramid.[4-6]

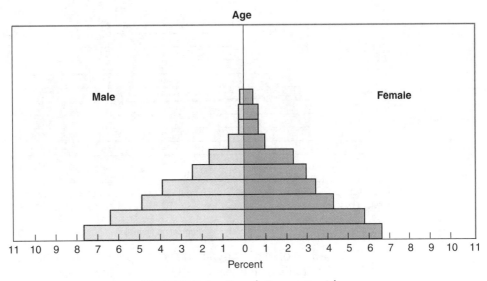

FIGURE 5-4   Population pyramid.

An **expansive pyramid** is a pyramid showing a broad base and has a tall, pointed shape, which represents a rapid rate of population growth and a low proportion of older people (**Figure 5-5**). This pointed top shape also shows that many persons are dying in each birth cohort year so that very few persons are in the older age cohorts at the top of the pyramid. A **stationary pyramid** is more block shaped, with low fertility and low mortality (**Figure 5-6**). This represents a more industrialized society, with effective public health measures in place, good socioeconomic conditions, and good medical care; life expectancy is high with large numbers of age cohorts living into the older age groups. A **constrictive pyramid** is a population pyramid showing a lower number or percentage of younger people (**Figure 5-7**). The people are generally older, with a low death rate but a low birth rate as well. This type of pyramid is occurring more frequently, particularly in European countries.

The ability of a population to support itself economically is of concern to public health and political officials. How dependent certain segments of a population are on others predicts how well these groups or subgroups can contribute to society. The ability to contribute, or the dependency a group has on others, is measured by the dependency ratio. The dependency ratio reflects the amount of potential dependency in a population and the work life span.[4,5] The **dependency ratio** describes the relationship by age between those who have the potential to be self-supporting and the dependent segments of the population—in other words, those segments of the population not in the workforce. The beginning age of economic self-sufficiency ranges from 15 to 20 years. The upper age for being considered part of the workforce has changed in recent times and will probably be reevaluated because of a continued need for workers as the older cohorts of populations increase in size and the numbers of younger persons entering the workforce decline. Retirement at 65 has already

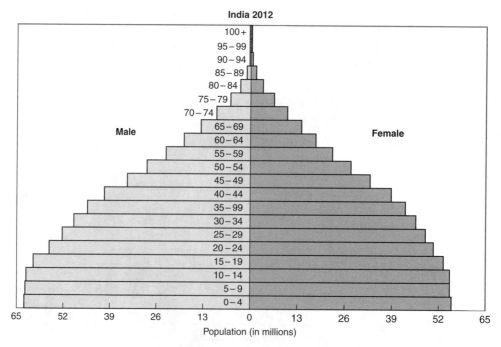

FIGURE 5-5 Population pyramid for the population in India, 2012. Data from U.S. Census Bureau. International Data Base. http://www.census.gov/population/international/data/idb/informationGateway.php

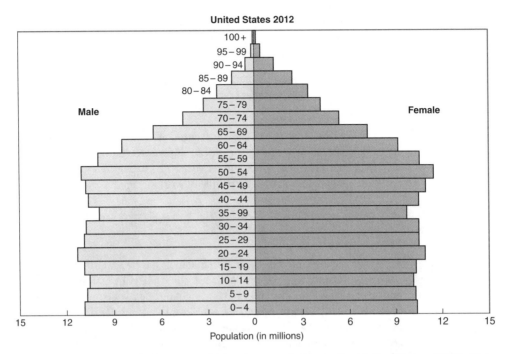

FIGURE 5-6   Population pyramid for the population in the United States, 2012. Data from U.S. Census Bureau. International Data Base. http://www.census.gov /population/international/data/idb/informationGateway.php

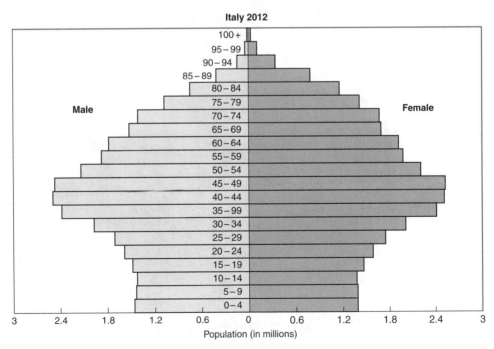

FIGURE 5-7   Population pyramid for the population in Italy, 2012. Data from U.S. Census Bureau. International Data Base. http://www.census.gov/population/international/data/ idb/informationGateway.php

been eliminated in certain work areas of the population. Age 70 years is now viewed as the age of retirement by many and will influence the concept of dependency in society.[4,5]

The formula for the dependency ratio is:

$$Dependency\ ratio = \frac{Population < 15\ and\ 65^+}{Population\ 15 - 64} \times 100$$

For example, suppose in a given region 25% of the population are less than 15 years of age and 5% are 65 years of age or older. This means that 70% [100 − (25 + 5)] of the people are between the ages of 15 and 64 years. The dependency ratio equals 43; that is, there are 43 dependents for every 100 people of working age.

Gender

Sex is biologically founded (i.e., a human female has two X chromosomes, and a human male has one X chromosome and one Y chromosome). In contrast, gender is a socially constructed notion of what is feminine and what is masculine (e.g., a person is not born a man but, instead, becomes a man). Health-related states or events often differ between males and females. For example, the number of females per 100 males in the United States is presented according to age for two time periods in Figure 5-8. About 96 females are born to every 100 males. There are fewer females than males per age group in the younger age groups, but more females than

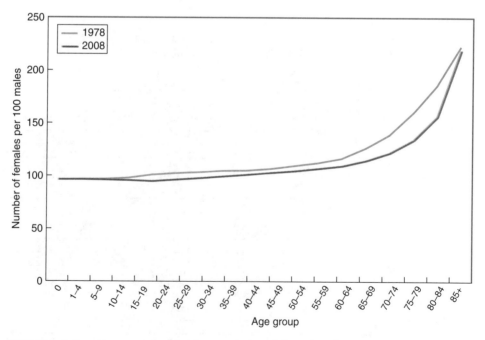

FIGURE 5-8   Age-group specific number of females for every 100 males in the United States, 1978 and 2008. Data from Surveillance Research Program, National Cancer Institute. SEER*Stat software version 6.4.4. Available at: http://www.seer.cancer.gov/seerstat. Accessed January 10, 2012.

males in the older age groups. The number of females to males becomes similar in the age group 20 to 24 in 1978, but in the age group 40 to 44 in 2008. The difference in females to males in the older age groups is less pronounced in 2008 than in 1978. The greater number of females to males in older ages is because of the higher death rates for males. The all-cause death rate is 1.4 times higher for males than females in the United States (Table 5-1).

In 1662, John Graunt also observed a smaller number of female births than male births, but also better life expectancy among females. See a review of "Selections from Natural and Political Observations Made Upon the Bills of Mortality by John Graunt" within Table 2-1. This pattern is observed for countries throughout the world.[7] For example, in 2011 in France, for under 15 years the sex ratio is 0.95 females/males, for 15 to 64 years the sex ratio is 1 females/males, and for 65 years and over is 1.35 females/males.[7]

Race/Ethnicity

It is standard practice in epidemiology to describe individuals by race and ethnicity. For example, the decennial census now classifies individuals into five racial categories (white, black, American Indian or Alaskan Native, Asian, and Native Hawaiian or Pacific Islander) and two ethnic groups (Hispanic origin and not of Hispanic origin). Like gender, these variables may have biological, sociological, and psychological dimensions. Associating risk behaviors and disease outcomes with these variables can provide insights into the causal mechanisms of disease.

Race is a socially constructed variable based on the idea that some human populations are distinct from others according to external physical characteristics or places of origin. Racial or ethnic variations in health-related states or events are explained primarily by exposure or vulnerability to behavioral, psychosocial, material, and environmental risk factors and resources.[8] Historically, biological explanations have played a limited role in explaining

TABLE 5-1   Age-Adjusted (2000 U.S. Standard Population) Cause-Specific Death Rates per 100,000 for Males and Females in 2007 in the United States

	Males	Females	Ratio
All causes	905.6	643.4	1.4
Diseases of the heart	237.7	154.0	1.5
Cerebrovascular diseases	42.5	41.3	1.0
Malignant neoplasms	217.5	151.3	1.4
Chronic lower respiratory diseases	48.0	36.0	1.3
HIV/AIDS	5.4	2.1	2.6
Motor vehicle-related injuries	20.9	8.2	2.5
Homicide	9.6	2.5	3.8
Suicide	18.4	4.7	3.9
Firearm-related injuries	18.2	2.7	6.7
Occupational injury (2008 data)	6.1	0.6	10.2

Source: Modified from National Center for Health Statistics. *Health, United States, 2010 with Chartbook on Trends in the Health of Americans.* Hyattsville, MD: NCHS; 2010, Tables 24, 42.

racial disparities.[9,10] Racial prejudice has been proposed as a social stress that can affect health behaviors such as eating, substance abuse, and access to healthcare services.[11–13] Because of the similarity between race and ethnicity in that both are determined primarily by their group association and distinction, there is an increasing movement toward use of the term race/ethnicity.[14]

A challenge exists in epidemiologic investigations of racial/ethnic disparities in that broad categories of racial/ethnic groups may be inadequate to capture unique cultural differences. For example, about 52 different tribes of Native Americans are registered in the United States today, representing 52 different cultures, backgrounds, and possible genetic makeups. A similar situation is also true for African Americans. African Americans tend to be categorized as blacks. Genetic and genealogic investigations are beginning to show a great deal of diversity among blacks. Like Native Americans, blacks have historically come from different tribes and locations, and all are not the same. Are all whites the same genetically and culturally? Is an Irishman the same as an Italian? Are Swedes the same as Spaniards? Although greater effort to obtain more distinct racial/ethnic groups in research is encouraged, small numbers often limit statistical assessment.

Racial/ethnic population estimates in the United States for 2007 are shown in Table 5-2. Approximately 19% of the male population and 17% of the female population are Hispanic.

The Department of Health and Human Services monitors mortality rates in the United States for several conditions. These mortality rates are presented according to gender, race, and Hispanic ethnicity. Death rates for selected causes in the United States in 2007 are presented according to gender and Hispanic ethnicity in Table 5-3. White, not Hispanic or Latino, males and females have higher death rates for each of the selected conditions with the exception of HIV/AIDS and homicide. We can now try to identify explanations for these differences in rates by identifying unique behaviors or characteristics in each ethnic group.

Marital and Family Status

Studies have related marital status and health for over a century. Married individuals have been shown to experience lower mortality than do nonmarried individuals, regardless of

TABLE 5-2   U.S. Population Estimates for Race and Hispanic or Latino Ethnicity, July 1, 2007

	Male			Female		
	Hispanic	Not Hispanic	% Hispanic	Hispanic	Not Hispanic	% Hispanic
One race	23,199,075	123,064,156	19%	21,653,741	128,848,049	17%
White	21,804,146	97,745,329	22%	20,271,177	101,346,238	20%
Black	845,551	17,641,636	5%	873,697	19,395,568	5%
AIAN	343,775	1,127,654	30%	307,927	1,159,080	27%
Asian	142,439	6,339,413	2%	144,073	6,740,229	2%
NHPI	63,164	210,124	30%	56,867	206,934	27%
Two or more races	324,505	2,071,162	16%	326,990	2,133,479	15%
Total	**23,523,580**	**125,135,318**	**19%**	**21,980,731**	**130,981,528**	**17%**

Black, black or African American; AIAN, American Indian and Alaska Native; NHPI, Native Hawaiian and Other Pacific Islander.

Data are from the U.S. Census Bureau. Available at: http://www.census.gov/popest/national/asrh/NC-EST2007-srh.html. Accessed November 28, 2008.

TABLE 5-3   Age-Adjusted (2000 U.S. Standard Population) Cause-Specific Death Rates per 100,000 in the United States in 2007 According to Sex and Hispanic Ethnicity

	Male			Female		
	White, not Hispanic or Latino	Hispanic or Latino	Ratio	White, not Hispanic or Latino	Hispanic or Latino	Ratio
All causes	906.8	654.5	1.4	647.7	452.7	1.4
Diseases of the heart	239.8	165	1.5	153	111.8	1.4
Cerebrovascular diseases	40.3	34.4	1.2	40.3	30.8	1.3
Malignant neoplasms	220.8	141.4	1.6	155.3	98.6	1.6
Complications of pregnancy				8.1	7.2	1.1
Motor vehicle-related injuries	21.4	19.3	1.1	8.7	6.9	1.3
Homicide	3.7	11.2	0.3	1.8	2.3	0.8
Suicide	21.9	10.1	2.2	5.7	1.9	3.0
Firearm-related injuries	15.4	12.9	1.2	2.8	1.5	1.9

Source: Data from National Center for Health Statistics. *Health, United States, 2010 with Chartbook on Trends in the Health of Americans.* Hyattsville, MD: NCHS; 2010, Tables 29–39.

whether the nonmarried persons were never married, divorced, separated, or widowed.[15,16] Married persons in the United States have also been shown to generally have lower levels of physical, mental, or emotional problems and better health behaviors (more physically active, less smoking, less heavy alcohol drinking);[17] however, married persons, particularly men, were shown to have higher rates of excessive weight or obesity.

Two theories have been proposed to explain better health among married individuals: marriage protection and marriage selection. Marriage protection refers to married people having more economic resources, social and psychological support, and support for healthy lifestyles. On the other hand, marital selection refers to healthier people being more likely to get married and stay married. It is often difficult, if not impossible, to distinguish the specific influence of these two explanations on health.

Family-related factors useful to epidemiologists include family size and placement of members within the family structure. Maternal age is of much concern to the medical and public health community. More Down syndrome babies are born to mothers after age 40. Young teenage births have the highest risk to both the baby and the mother. Considerable healthcare dollars are spent on premature babies, which are often born to unwed mothers.

The absence of one parent in the family has been a major concern in the last several years. Divorce and cohabitation have risen to the highest levels known in the history of the United States. Disrupted families are common, and children of these families suffer the most in terms of psychological and social problems. More research is needed in the study of the effects of the disrupted family on health status and on ways to prevent the destruction of the family. Table 5-4 presents the percentage of first marriage for men and women in the United States according to age and selected years. The median age at first marriage has gotten older from 1970 to 1988 to 2009 for both men and women.

TABLE 5-4   First Marriage for Men and Women in the United States by Age and Year. NCHS: National Center for Health Statistics; ACS: American Community Survey Report.

Age	Men			Women		
	NCHS 1970	NCHS 1988	ACS 2009	NCHS 1970	NCHS 1988	ACS 2009
Under 20	18.4	6.9	3.6	41.8	17.7	6.9
20–24	57.0	38.7	23.5	46.0	43.3	31.5
25–29	16.2	33.9	34.3	7.7	26.1	32.9
30–34	4.1	13.6	19.5	2.0	8.5	15.3
35–39	1.8	4.4	9.0	0.9	2.8	6.3
40–44	1.0	1.4	4.3	0.6	0.8	2.9
45–49	0.6	0.5	2.8	0.4	0.3	1.9
50–54	0.3	0.3	1.4	0.2	0.2	1.0
55–59	0.2	0.2	0.9	0.1	0.1	0.6
60–64	0.1	0.1	0.3	0.1	0.1	0.4
65 and over	0.1	0.1	0.4	0.1	0.1	0.2

Source: Adapted from U.S. Census Bureau, American Community Survey, 2009; National Center for Health Statistics, 1970, 1988. Available at: http://www.census.gov/hhes/socdemo/marriage/data/acs/index.html. Accessed January 7, 2012.

Family Structure and Genealogical Research

Studies have shown that family size and marital status can influence physical and mental health. In addition, health behaviors cluster in families. Parental attitudes and behaviors can directly influence their children's health behaviors. Intervention programs aimed at modifying health behaviors and improving health and well-being should focus on the family as the unit of analysis.

A person inherits many traits, both good and bad, from parents, grandparents, and past family members. Genetically, intelligence levels can be passed down from generation to generation, along with some diseases. For example, some forms of muscular dystrophy are genetically transmitted. Family trees have been used to study the genealogy of both genetically transmitted and communicable diseases. Family trees have been used to confirm hereditary links in many cancers. The Church of Jesus Christ of Latter Day Saints maintains one of the largest genealogy libraries in the world in Salt Lake City, Utah, aiding genealogists and epidemiologists in family history studies.

Occupation

The personal characteristic of occupation can be reflective of income, social status, education, socioeconomic status, risk of injury, or health problems within a population group. Selected diseases, conditions, or disorders occur in certain occupations. Brown lung has been associated with workers in the garment industry, black lung with coal miners, and certain accidents and injuries to limbs with farm workers.

Occupation is requested on many research questionnaires and is used to measure socioeconomic status. It is also a determinant of risk and is a predictor of the health status of and conditions in which certain populations work. Occupations have been divided into five broad classifications:

1. Professional
2. Intermediate
3. Skilled
4. Partly skilled
5. Unskilled

Subclassifications by the five main groups have been used in various epidemiologic reports.

Standard mortality ratios (SMRs) for specific occupations have been developed, based on risks that might be associated with the physical and chemical exposures common to certain occupations. For example, coronary artery disease has been found to be less prevalent in several active occupations than it is in sedentary occupations. Persons who work for larger organizations have medical insurance and access to healthcare providers and medical institutions and thus benefit from better health status.[18,19]

It has also been observed that the health status and mortality of a population can be affected by the levels of employment within the population. The term **healthy worker effect** has been used to describe this observation—that is, employed populations tend to have a lower mortality rate than the general population. Workers tend to be a healthier group to begin with. Persons who are unhealthy or who may have a life-shortening condition are less likely to be employed. As workers go through the life span, the chance of death increases, and the healthy worker effect decreases. Unhealthy workers tend to leave the work environment or retire earlier than healthy employees. Leaving work early in life also reduces exposure to occupational hazards. Instead of exposure to risk factors causing disease, disease causes those at risk to leave work. Absence due to disease produces lower work-related risk exposure levels than would occur if workers remained at their jobs.[19]

Education

Education, like occupation, can be a valuable measure of socioeconomic status. Persons with training, skills, and education make substantially more money per year than persons with no training or skills. Persons with higher education levels are more prevention oriented, know more about health matters, and have greater access to health care. For example, the age-adjusted percentage of current cigarette smoking by those 25 years of age and over in the United States in 2009 was 28.9% for persons with no high school diploma or GED, 28.7% for persons with a high school diploma or GED, 21.4% for persons with some college, and 9.0% for persons with a bachelor's degree or higher.[20] For women aged 40 years and older, the percentage undergoing mammography screening in 2009 was 53.8% for women with no high school diploma or GED, 65.2% for women with a high school diploma or GED, and 73.4% for women with some college or more.[21] Participation in leisure-time aerobic and muscle-strengthening activities that meet the 2008 federal physical activity guidelines for adults 18 years of age and over was also directly related to education level. For the education groups no high school diploma or GED, high school diploma or GED, and some college or more, the percentages of adults meeting aerobic guidelines were 27.7, 37.0, and 54.3, respectively.[22] The percentages of adults who met both the aerobic activity and muscle-strengthening guidelines were 5.9, 10.4, and 24.5, respectively.[22]

Reduced access to medical care, dental care, and prescription drugs during the past 12 months due to cost is presented according to education in Table 5-5. Although cost reduces access to these health services in each education group, it plays a bigger role with lower education. Education has the largest impact on dental care, then prescription drugs, and then medical care.

PLACE

For chronic conditions such as cancer, geographic comparisons of disease frequency among groups, states, and countries can be made to provide insights to the causes of diseases. For example, Utah has the lowest female breast cancer incidence rates in the United States, due in part to low rates among women who are members of the Church of Jesus Christ of Latter Day Saints (LDS or Mormon) who make up a large portion of the population.[23,24] Researchers compared several reproductive and nonreproductive breast cancer risk factors between LDS and non-LDS women in the state. LDS women had a comparatively higher number of births, prevalence of breastfeeding, and lifetime total duration of breastfeeding. These results further support the important role parity and breastfeeding play in reducing breast cancer.

Malignant melanoma of the skin in whites has been associated with low-strength radiation (ultraviolet radiation) because risk of this disease is directly related to annual sunshine. Consider four geographic areas in the United States with different levels of annual sunshine: Iowa, Utah, Metropolitan Atlanta, and Hawaii. Plotting the relationship between malignant melanoma and annual sunshine shows a clear dose–response relationship (Figure 5-9).

Studies of disease among migrants provide insights into the roles of genetics and environment. In one migration study, researchers compared cancer incidence trends among the Japanese in Japan with Japanese and whites in Hawaii between 1960 and 1997.[25] Very strong migrant effects were observed for cancers of the colon and stomach. In general, migration led to lower risks of stomach, esophageal, pancreatic, liver, and cervical cancers, but higher rates for other cancers. The authors concluded that although environment plays

TABLE 5-5   Reduced Access to Medical Care, Dental Care, and Prescription Drugs among Adults 18 Years and Older during the Past 12 Months due to Cost, by Education among: United States, 2009

	No high school diploma or GED	High school diploma or GED	Some college or more
Did not get or delayed medical care due to cost	21.2	17.0	13.7
Did not get prescription drugs due to cost	19.3	14.0	8.8
Did not get dental care due to cost	26.6	19.7	13.7

Modified from National Center for Health Statistics. *Health, United States, 2010 with Chartbook on Trends in the Health of Americans.* Hyattsville, MD: 2010; Table 76.

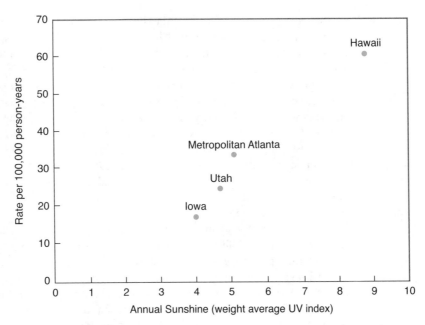

FIGURE 5-9   Malignant melanoma of the skin in whites according to low-strength radiation (UV radiation) and selected geographic areas, 2005. Rates age-adjusted to the U.S. 2000 standard population. Data from Surveillance, Epidemiology, and End Results (SEER) Program, 2007.

an important role in many of these cancers, the persistent differences in incidence found for some cancers, even several generations after migration, support the presence of a genetic component.

Twin studies also provide a powerful means for assessing the roles of genetics and environment on disease. For example, a recent study assessing the effect of sun exposure on nevus density (a primary risk factor for melanoma) in adolescent twins in the United Kingdom showed that 66% of the total variance of nevus count was associated with genetic effects (e.g., eye color, hair color, and skin type).[26]

TIME TRENDS

Time-series designs involve a sequence of measurements of some numerical quantity made at or during two or more successive periods of time. The simple time-series design involves the collection of quantitative observations made at regular intervals through repeated observations. Some examples include air temperature measured at noon each day, number of hospital admissions per day, number of deaths per day, and air pollution levels per day.

Time-series analysis may involve assessment of a group of people who have experienced an event at roughly the same time, such that these individuals may be thought of as a cohort. Time trend analysis of cohort data allows researchers to study the pattern of illness or injury for a group of people who experienced an exposure at roughly the same time. A histogram can be used to depict this, with the horizontal axis representing time and the vertical axis representing frequency. The time begins at the point of exposure and extends over the course of the outbreak. If the duration time of the epidemic is reflected, the histogram is called an **epidemic curve**. Time intervals may reflect hours, days, weeks, or longer. A sufficient lead period should be reflected on the graph between the suspected exposure and clinical manifestations of the disease in order to demonstrate the incubation period. The shape of the epidemic curve is influenced by whether the source of exposure is at a point in time or continuous over time. In a **point source** epidemic, persons are exposed to the same exposure over a limited time period. Because incubation or latency period influences the rate of increase and decrease in the epidemic curve, a point source epidemic tends to show a clustering of cases in time, with a sharp increase and a trailing decline. In a **continuous source** epidemic where exposure is continuous over time but at relatively low levels, the epidemic curve tends to increase more gradually than for a point source exposure, plateau, and then decrease. The rate of decrease depends on the latency period and whether the exposure is removed gradually or suddenly.

If a health event is identified and the source is unknown, the time from a presumed exposure until the manifestation of symptoms of disease can help focus the causal hypothesis. If a causal agent is suspected, then estimating the incubation or latency period can support or dispel a suspicion. For example, if several people attending a picnic become ill, the incubation period can help identify the specific cause of disease. Salmonella has an incubation period of 6–72 hours, botulism has an incubation period of 12 to 36 hours, and E. coli enteritis has an incubation period of 24–72 hours. If several cases occur within 12 hours of eating, then salmonella food poisoning is the likely cause of illness. Another example is lung cancer, where asbestos exposure from a local plant is only a possible cause if cases have been employed for a sufficiently long period of time because of the long latency period that typically accompanies asbestos and lung cancer.

In an outbreak of cholera in the Broad Street–Golden Square area of London in the mid-1800s, the epidemic curve indicates a point-source outbreak (Figure 5-10). The peak of illness occurred during the first week of September. The incubation period for cholera ranges from a few hours to up to 5 days.

Both longitudinal (individual level) data and ecologic (group level) data can be used in time-series analyses. **Longitudinal data** refer to the same sample of respondents being observed over time. Longitudinal data avoid some of the concern regarding confounding in ecologic studies. Factors that change little over time do not confound time-series studies, but confounding could occur from time varying environmental factors (e.g., secular trend, carryover effect-residual influence of the intervention on the outcome).

In studies investigating patterns in time-series data, three potential effects are generally considered: age, period, and cohort. The **age effect** is the change in rate of a condition according to age. This effect is irrespective of birth cohort or calendar time. A **cohort effect** is the change in the rate of a condition according to birth year. This effect is irrespective of age and calendar time. A **period effect** is a change in the rate of a condition affecting an entire population at a given point in time. This effect is irrespective of age and birth cohort. Environmental factors contribute to both cohort and period effects. When researchers observe cohort and/or period effects, this can help in the investigation to determine the causes of health-related states or events.

The birth cohort effect results from lifetime experiences of individuals born at a given time that influence their health. Several studies have demonstrated disease rates to be correlated with the period of birth. For example, in studies conducted in the United States and Canada researchers have observed an increase in testicular cancer with successive birth cohorts.[27,28] William Farr (1807–1883) first described the birth cohort analysis of mortality data in 1870. A birth cohort analysis plots the distribution of age at incidence or death for a

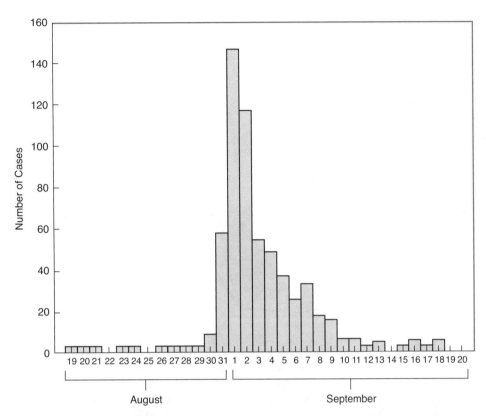

FIGURE 5-10 Example of the time factor in the cholera epidemic in the Broad Street–Golden Square area of London in the 1800s, showing the epidemic curve of the outbreak. From Snow J. *Snow on Cholera*. New York, NY: The Commonwealth Fund; 1936.

selected disease or event by year of birth rather than year of incidence or death. To illustrate, the rate of death from homicide and legal intervention for black males in the United States in four successive cohort groups (1970–1974, 1975–1979, 1980–1984, and 1985–1989) is shown in Figure 5-11. Compared with the cohort 1970–1974, cohort 1975–1979 and cohort 1980–1984 have higher death rates in the age group 15–19 years, but lower death rates in the age group 20–24 years. The most recent cohort has the lowest death rate in the age group 15–19 years.

A period effect involves a shift or change in the trends in rates that affect all birth cohorts and age groups. Period effects are responses to phenomenon that occur at a period of time across the entire population. A period effect may result from the introduction of a new antibiotic, vaccine, or disease-prevention program that affects various age groups and birth cohorts in a similar manner. A period effect may also result from adverse physical stresses or social conditions (e.g., earthquake, flood, terrorism, war, and economic collapse) that impact on the entire population irrespective of age group or birth cohort. For example, the Great Depression started a worldwide economic downturn in 1929. In Australia, for instance, approximately 29% of the workforce was unemployed in 1932, and suicide rates among males rose to unprecedented levels across all age groups.[29]

A period effect is illustrated in the graph showing death rates from homicide and legal intervention among blacks in the United States by calendar year according to selected age

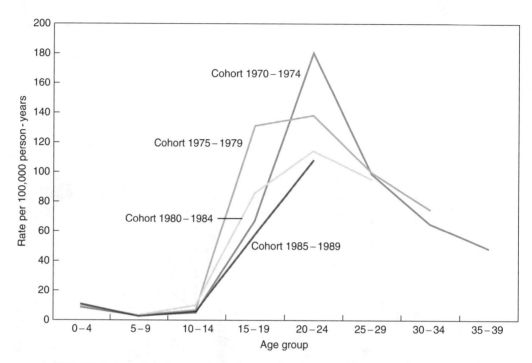

FIGURE 5-11 Death rates from homicide and legal intervention for black males in the United States by selected birth cohorts. Data source: Surveillance Research Program, National Cancer Institute. SEER*Stat software version 6.4.4. Available at: http://www.seer.cancer.gov/seerstat. Accessed January 10, 2012.

groups (Figure 5-12). From 1985 through 1995, a large increase in death rates occurred in each age group. Further investigation explaining this period effect is warranted.

A **time-series design** involves a sequence of measurements of some numerical quantity made at or during two or more successive periods of time. Analysis of time series involves searching for patterns of disease over time and attempting to explain their underlying causes. A simple yet powerful method of identifying whether the data consists of a systematic pattern is to create a visual display of a series. Time-series patterns can be described according to secular trend and seasonality. The **secular trend** is the general systematic linear or nonlinear component that changes over time. It represents the long-term changes in health-related states or events. In the epidemiology literature, another term, temporal variation or trends (also called temporal distribution), has also emerged and is being used interchangeably with secular trends. Increasing changes seen over extended time periods, even several decades in certain diseases, are of concern in epidemiology, especially in terms of prevention and control. Secular trends are usually considered to last longer than 1 year. Figure 5-13 shows that the incidence rate of testicular cancer for males in the United States has steadily increased in recent decades in the United States.

By 1960 in males and the late 1980s in females, lung cancer death rates had outpaced other cancers in the United States.[30] Extensive research has associated cigarette smoking with lung cancer. Increasing, and then decreasing, lung cancer death rates over the century have been associated with cigarette smoking in the United States, allowing for a 20- to 25-year latency period (Figure 5-14).

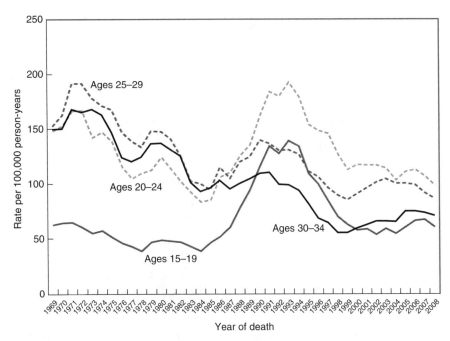

FIGURE 5-12   Death rates from homicide and legal intervention for black males in the United States according to selected birth cohorts. Data source: Surveillance Research Program, National Cancer Institute. SEER*Stat software version 6.4.4. Available at: http://www.seer.cancer.gov/seerstat. Accessed January 10, 2012.

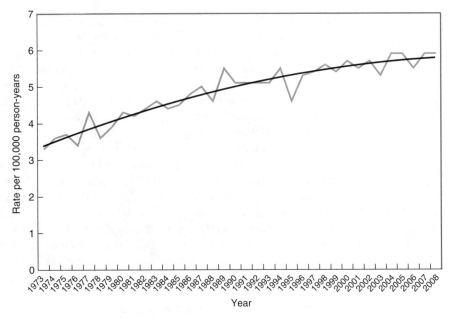

FIGURE 5-13   Age-adjusted (2000 U.S. standard population) incidence rate of testicular cancer for black males in the United States. Data source: Surveillance Research Program, National Cancer Institute. SEER*Stat software version 6.4.4. Available at: http://www.seer.cancer.gov/seerstat. Accessed January 10, 2012.

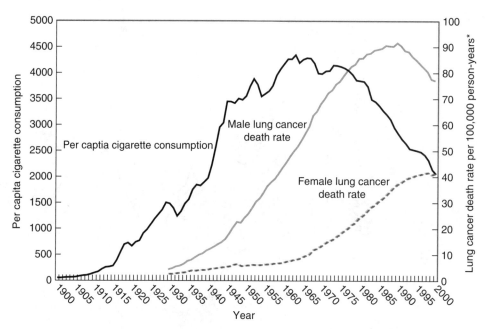

FIGURE 5-14   Lung cancer death rates and per capita cigarette consumption for males and females in the United States during the years 1900 through 2000. From United States Mortality Public Use Data Tapes 1960–2001, U.S. Mortality Volumes 1930–1959, National Center for Health Statistics, Centers for Disease Control and Prevention, 2002 (death rates). U.S. Department of Agriculture, 1900–2000 (cigarette consumption).

On June 5, 1981, the first cases of acquired immunodeficiency syndrome (AIDS) were reported by healthcare providers in California and the Centers for Disease Control and Prevention (CDC). Since then, AIDS has been a disease of concern not only for medical and public health officials but for almost every member of society. AIDS is a condition in humans in which the immune system begins to fail, leading to life-threatening opportunistic infections. In 2006, the estimated rates (per 100,000 people) of human immunodeficiency virus (HIV) in adults and adolescents in the United States were 34.3 for males and 11.9 for females.[31] HIV is a lentivirus (a member of the retrovirus) that can lead to AIDS. AIDS is a diagnosis that depends on a specific list of opportunistic infections or CD4+ cells dropping below 200. HIV is transmitted mostly by the transfer of blood, semen, vaginal fluid, pre-ejaculation fluid, or breast milk. The primary routes of transmission are unprotected sexual intercourse, intravenous drug use (contaminated needles), blood transfusion, breast milk, and vertical transmission from an infected mother to her baby at birth. Epidemiologists have been concerned about the secular trends of persons infected with AIDS, and public health agencies at local, state, and national levels have been following the trends over the years. Figure 5-15 and Figure 5-16 give two examples of the secular trends of AIDS.

In the 1990s, researchers identified an unprecedented change in the secular trend of prostate cancer incidence rates in the United States.[32] A gradually increasing secular trend in prostate cancer incidence rates between 1975–1989 suddenly increased sharply for each racial group, peaking in 1992–1993 (Figure 5-17). The period effect in prostate cancer incidence rates between 1989–1995 has been attributed to rapid and widespread adoption of prostate-specific antigen screening, which began in the late 1980s.[33] A sharp rise in prostate cancer death rates in the 1990s has also been shown to be an artifact of prostate-specific antigen screening.[34]

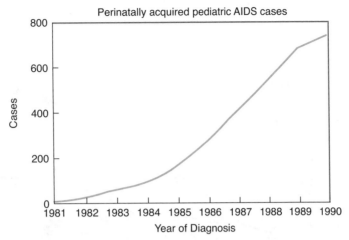

FIGURE 5-15   Reported cases of HIV/AIDS in infants born to HIV-infected mothers, by year, for 25 states in the U.S. (Alabama, Arizona, Arkansas, Colorado, Idaho, Indiana, Louisiana, Michigan, Minnesota, Mississippi, Missouri, Nevada, New Jersey, North Carolina, North Dakota, Ohio, Oklahoma, South Carolina, South Dakota, Tennessee, Utah, Virginia, West Virginia, Wisconsin, and Wyoming). Data source: CDC (http://www.cdc.gov/Hiv/topics/surveillance/resources/reports/2007report/table25.htm).

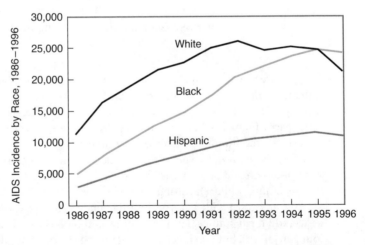

FIGURE 5-16   Human immunodeficiency virus death rates in the U.S. according to calendar year and race. Data source: CDC (http://www.cdc.gov/nchs/products/elec_prods/subject/mortmcd.htm).

A **short-term trend** or **fluctuation** usually reflects a brief, unexpected increase in a health-related state or event. Short-term trends occur over short time intervals or limited time frames. Even though seasonal and cyclic trends occur within short time frames, because of their unique features they are used as separate categories. Most short-term trends are limited to hours, days, weeks, and months. Thus, events of limited duration are included in the short-term trends category. An example of a short-term time frame would be the cholera epidemic studied by John Snow in the mid-1800s, presented in Figure 5-10.

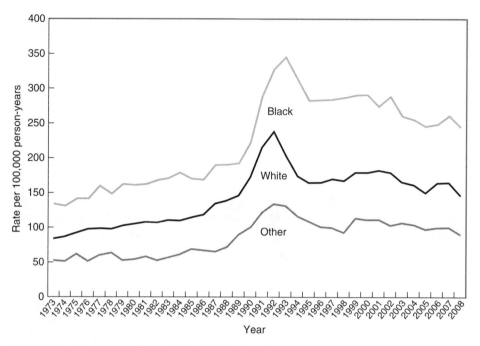

FIGURE 5-17   Age-adjusted (2000 U.S. standard population) prostate cancer incidence rates by racial group and year of diagnosis. Data source: Surveillance Research Program, National Cancer Institute. SEER*Stat software version 6.4.4. Available at: http://www.seer.cancer.gov/seerstat. Accessed January 10, 2012.

A more recent example of an outbreak of gastroenteritis associated with an interactive water fountain occurred in a beachside park in Volusia County, Florida. Since 1989, approximately 170 outbreaks associated with recreational water venues (e.g., swimming pools, water parks, fountains, hot tubs and spas, lakes, rivers, and oceans) have been reported, with almost half resulting in gastrointestinal illness. The findings indicate that *Shigella sonnei* and *Cryptosporidium parvum* infections caused illness in persons exposed at an interactive water fountain and at a beachside park. The Volusia County health department received reports of three children getting an *S. sonnei* infection. Of 86 park visitors interviewed, 38 (44%) came down with a gastrointestinal illness. The most common symptoms were diarrhea, abdominal cramps, fever, vomiting, and bloody diarrhea. All ill persons entered the fountain, and all but two ingested fountain water. The recirculated water passed through a hypochlorite tablet chlorination system before being pumped back to the fountain. Several high-pressure fountain nozzles were used throughout the play area. The fountain was popular with children in diapers and toddlers, and they frequently stood directly over the nozzles. Chlorine levels were not monitored, and the tablets that depleted after 7–10 days of use had not been replaced since the park opened August 7. The chart in Figure 5-18 shows that several clinical cases occurred throughout the period.

The health department of Tarrant County reported to the Texas Department of Health that a group of teenagers attending a cheerleading camp June 9–11 became ill with nausea, vomiting, severe abdominal cramps, and diarrhea, some of which was bloody. Two teenagers were hospitalized with hemolytic uremic syndrome (a reduction in red blood cells because of excessive destruction that can lead to jaundice); and two others underwent appendectomies.

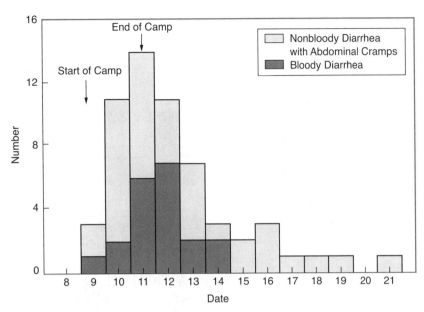

FIGURE 5-18   An example of short-term trends, this chart shows the number of gastroenteritis cases associated with an interactive fountain by date of illness onset—Volusia County, Florida, 1999. Reproduced from Centers for Disease Control and Prevention. Outbreak of gastroenteritis associated with an interactive water fountain at a beachside park—Florida, 1999. *MMWR.* 2000;49(25):565–568.

Stool cultures were taken and sent to the laboratory, which showed the teens were infected with *Escherichia coli* 0111:H8. As the shape of the histogram (Figure 5-19) indicates, the outbreak was confined to the camp and lasted only a short while.

Cyclic patterns represent periodic increases and decreases in the occurrence of health-related states or events. These patterns are often predictable. Some disease cycles are seasonal, whereas cycles of other diseases may be controlled by other cyclic factors such as the school calendar, immigration patterns, migration patterns, duration and course of diseases, placement of military troops, and wars. Other phrases used to describe trends of disease cycles are secular and seasonal cyclical patterns. Cyclic changes refer to recurrent alterations in the occurrence, interval, or frequency of diseases. Some disease outbreaks occur only at certain times but in predictable time frames or intervals over long terms; thus, epidemiologists track cyclic changes over time. The study approach is quite straightforward. Cases of the disease under study are followed and tabulated by time of onset according to a diagnosis or proof of occurrence. Short-term fluctuations should use shorter time elements.

One disease that is very cyclic on a short-term basis is chicken pox (varicella). When outbreaks of chicken pox are viewed over time, major cyclic variations are seen throughout the year. Chicken pox is one of the notifiable diseases and is more easily and accurately tracked than others. The cyclic nature of chicken pox is shown in Figure 5-20.[35] A similarly and dramatically portrayed annual cycle is seen in outbreaks of salmonella food poisoning.

Seasonality is the component that repeats itself in a systematic manner over time. Temporal comparisons may appropriately involve just event data if there is no temporal change in baseline risk factors or in the size of the population of interest. The time scale used will

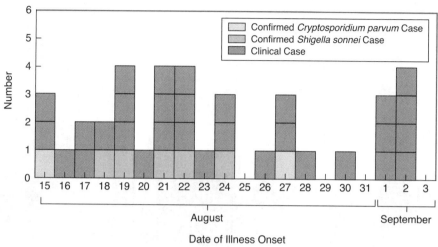

*n = 38.

FIGURE 5-19 An example of short-term trends, this chart shows the number of *Escherichia coli* 0111:H8 cases associated with a foodborne illness at a cheerleading camp, by date of onset in Tarrant County, Texas. Reproduced from Centers for Disease Control and Prevention. Escherichia coli 0111:H8 outbreak among teenage campers—Texas, 1999. *MMWR.* 2000;49(15):321–324.

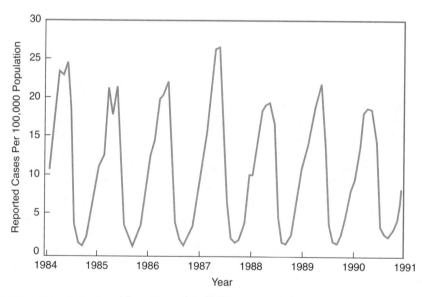

FIGURE 5-20 Example of cyclic trends of disease—cycles of chickenpox (*varicella*) outbreaks over an 8-year period by month. Reproduced from Centers for Disease Control and Prevention. Summary of notifiable diseases, United States—1990. *MMWR.* 1991;39 (53):1–61.

depend on the exposure and the disease, varying from hours to days to weeks to years. The population size, the disease rate, and the time scale will all influence the stability of measures of association between exposure and disease. Shorter time scales require larger population sizes to obtain stable rates.

Several diseases are characterized by seasonal patterns. A **seasonal trend** represents periodic increases and decreases in the occurrence, interval, or frequency of disease. These patterns tend to be predictable. A number of explanations have been given for the occurrence of seasonal patterns. Some disease cycles are seasonal, whereas other disease cycles may be influenced by cyclic factors such as the school calendar, immigration patterns, migration patterns, duration and course of diseases, placement of military troops, wars, famine, and popular tastes in food. Some disease outbreaks occur only at certain times, but in predictable time frames or intervals over long terms. Hence, epidemiologists track cyclic changes over time. Cyclic patterns in disease incidence may implicate an infectious agent; however, temperature, sunlight, behaviors, and environmental factors associated with the season, such as pesticide use for agricultural purposes, may also be considered. The study approach is straightforward; cases of the disease are followed and tabulated by time of onset according to a diagnosis or proof of occurrence.

Certain pathogen-borne diseases have a seasonal pattern that corresponds with changes in the vector populations, which, in turn, are influenced by environments where the vectors live and multiply. For example, in 2005 the nationally reported West Nile virus began late in May, peaked in the third week of August, and then lasted through November (**Figure 5-21**).[36] This cyclic pattern that corresponds with season is consistent with infected mosquitoes being the primary source of spreading the virus to humans.

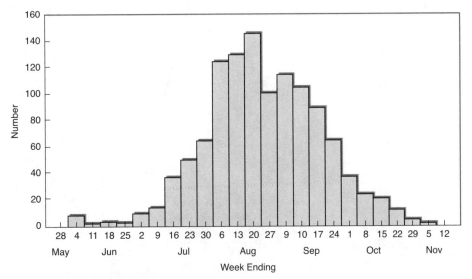

*N = 1,165.
†Meningitis, encephalitis, or acute flaccid paralysis.
§Provisional data as of December 1, 2005.

FIGURE 5-21   Number of reported West Nile virus neuroinvasive disease cases in humans, by week of illness onset—United States, 2005 (1,165 cases). From Centers for Disease Control and Prevention. West Nile Virus activity—United States. *MMWR.* 2005;54(49):1253–1256.

Cyclical disease patterns have also been associated with extreme temperatures, seasonal patterns in diet, physical activity, and environmental factors (e.g., agricultural pesticides). For example, evaluation of daily deaths in England and Wales and in New York has found a relationship between temperature and deaths from myocardial infarction, stroke, and pneumonia. Death rates rise with extreme cold and hot temperatures. The influence of temperature on deaths is much stronger in the elderly.[37]

Seasons show many factors of health interest, such as the fact that children born in the summer achieve higher mean scores on IQ tests than winter-born children. High cholesterol readings in accountants are related to the tax calendar. Suicide rates are tied to seasonal variation and times of year. Mental retardation varies some with season. Births of children with mental retardation peak in February, with the lowest rates seen in the summer. Admission rates to hospitals are cyclic and seasonal. Figure 5-22 is a chart comparing seasonal fluctuations of two different communicable diseases: meningococcal infections and encephalitis. This figure is an example of the observed dramatic seasonal fluctuations of diseases (as is Figure 5-20).

EVALUATION

When a program is initiated to change health behaviors and, ultimately, the risk of developing and dying from disease, the monitoring of behaviors, disease risk, and death rates

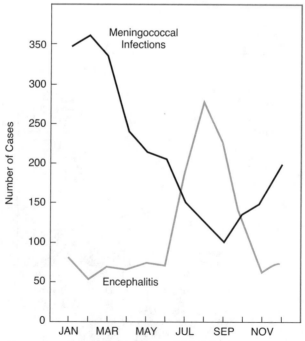

FIGURE 5-22   Example of seasonal variation of different diseases. Meningococcal disease occurs most in the winter months and encephalitis, transmitted by the mosquito, is highest in summer months. From Centers for Disease Control and Prevention. Reported cases of meningococcal infections and of primary encephalitis by month: United States—1968. *MMWR.* 1971;17(32).

between groups and over time is important in order to determine the effectiveness of the program. Health programs can be aimed at improving prevention behaviors (e.g., increasing vaccination levels, reducing smoking, increasing fruit and vegetable consumption, increasing physical activity, decreasing obesity, increasing screening) and subsequent disease risk. On the national level, the Centers for Disease Control and Prevention provides an extensive monitoring system and statistical databases for evaluating the nation's health in terms of prevention and health outcomes.[38] Monitoring efforts have identified considerable progress in reducing smoking prevalence in the United States (Figure 5-14). Consequently, declining rates of heart disease and lung cancer have been observed across racial groups (Figure 5-23).

State public health officials monitor vaccine-preventable disease rates in order to assess whether vaccination programs are effectively reaching the appropriate people. If a vaccine-preventable disease rate begins to rise, this may signal that the vaccination program is not reaching specific at-risk populations. Monitoring these disease rates by racial/ethnic groups, for example, may show that the increasing rate only exists among a given minority group. The public health official should then investigate whether barriers related to culture, language, and access to care is present. The vaccination program should then be altered to address and overcome these barriers.

PUBLIC HEALTH SURVEILLANCE

Surveillance has been around a long time. Surveillance has historically focused on close observation of individuals exposed to a communicable disease such that early manifestations of the disease could be detected and prompt isolation and control measures imposed. This

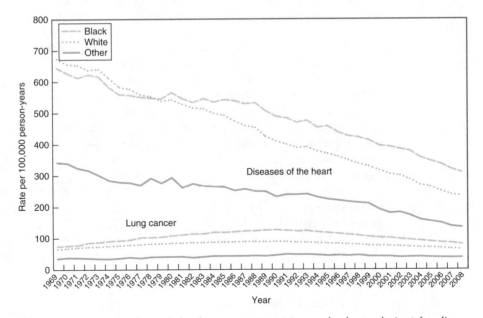

FIGURE 5-23   Age-adjusted death rates (2000 U.S. standard population) for disease of the heart and lung cancer among males by year. Data source: Surveillance Research Program, National Cancer Institute. SEER*Stat software version 6.4.4. Available at: http://www.seer.cancer.gov/seerstat. Accessed January 10, 2012.

form of surveillance is referred to as **medical surveillance**. A more recent form of **surveillance** involves continuous monitoring of health-related states or events within a population. **Public health surveillance** is the systematic ongoing collection, analysis, interpretation, and dissemination of health data. It provides a means for identifying outbreaks of health-related states or events and yields a basis for implementing control measures.

Public health surveillance originally focused on communicable diseases, but now includes the monitoring of injuries, birth defects, chronic diseases, and health behaviors. Public health surveillance is also used to monitor changes in environmental risk factors (physical, biological, chemical, or psychosocial), evaluate prevention and control programs, monitor long-term trends, plan future resource needs for prevention, and suggest topics for future research.

Epidemiologic monitoring occurs for several reasons, such as to identify sudden changes in occurrence and distribution of health-related states or events, to follow long-term trends and patterns in health-related states or events, and to identify changes in risk factors. This is done by first having knowledge of what is usual based on the distribution of occurrences in the same location at an earlier time period or in other similar locations at the same time period. Surveillance provides a means for determining whether health problems exist and, if so, whether they are increasing or decreasing over time and by place. For example, surveillance data may identify a higher than expected number of birth defects, a greater prevalence of low birth weight, a decrease in fertility rates, or a smaller proportion of births attended by skilled health personnel within a specified population.

What is usual may also be determined from local health officials. These officials often know whether more disease is occurring than is expected based on ongoing disease surveillance data through local surveys or health data registries. Many sources of data are available for use in surveillance. Some key sources of surveillance data include mortality reports, morbidity reports, epidemic reports, reports of laboratory utilization (including laboratory test results), reports of individual case investigations, reports of epidemic investigations, special surveys (e.g., hospital admissions, disease registers, and serial surveys), information on animal reservoirs and vectors, demographic data, and environmental data.

Public health surveillance requires a clear definition of person, place, and time elements. In order to set policy and plan programs effectively and efficiently, public health surveillance must represent the health of the population or community it serves. The person element of surveillance is the collection of individuals that share one or more observable characteristics from which data may be collected and evaluated. Person can refer to all people inhabiting a given area or the total number of people of a particular social class, race/ethnicity, or group. Surveillance that aims to obtain representative information from a group or community is referred to as population based.

If all persons in a defined population are not being considered, it is important to avoid bias in the selection of cases. In surveillance systems, it is critical that a case definition be consistently applied in order to avoid changes in frequency and patterns of cases simply because of inconsistent application of the case definition. Some explanations for observed changes in the frequency and pattern of cases in a surveillance system, which are not due to changes in risk exposures, include:

■ Inconsistent interpretation and application of the case definition

■ Change in the case definition

■ Change in surveillance system/policy of reporting

■ Improved diagnosis (e.g., new laboratory test, increased physician awareness, a new physician in town)

- Change in diagnostic criteria
- Change in reporting requirements
- Change in the population
- Change in the level and emphasis on active case detection
- Random events
- Increased public awareness

If change in an outcome variable is not attributed to these alternative explanations, we can then be more confident that it is due to the introduction or increased level of exposure to a given risk factor.

In assessing frequency, it is often more informative to consider the counts in relation to the population from which the health-related states or events occurred. By dividing counts by population values, proportions and rates are obtained. Proportions and rates are more informative than counts alone because they take into account the population size and allow for more meaningful comparisons over time and among different groups. When differences over time or among groups exist in terms of an extrinsic factor such as age or gender, these factors may be adjusted for in order to minimize their potential confounding effect.

Several measures for assessing and monitoring health-related states or events over time are available. Some of these are presented in the next chapter. For rare health-related states or events, a surveillance program should collect data from a large enough population to make it possible to monitor changes/differences in proportions or rates; however, the population needs to be defined so that detailed information that results in unusual occurrences can be detected. If the area or country is very large, this may be a problem. Some population-based registries trying to identify and register all birth defects in large populations may jeopardize accuracy. Although a population-based registry covering a smaller, well-defined geographic area may have high accuracy, it may not be appropriate to generalize the results of the surveillance data to the overall country.

Surveillance is a means to evaluate whether changes occur regularly and can be predicted, or if they are unusual events that are unexpected. Monitoring rates according to month allows us to detect seasonality. Monitoring rates according to year allow us to identify long-term (secular) trends.

Surveillance programs tend to concentrate on health-related states or events that can be obtained with relative ease. Surveillance programs are generally more effective at providing clues as to the causes of an adverse health outcome when the time between the exposure and outcome variables is short. State regulations typically specify the health-related states or events that must be reported, who should submit reports, how and to whom the case reports are to be sent, and what information should be provided. Some statutes and regulations specify control measures and penalties to be imposed on those not reporting.

As a practical matter, we often analyze health problems by time and place simultaneously. This allows us to answer the where and when questions in epidemiology. It is also often informative for organizing data into tables, maps, or both, as well as by potential sites of exposure. By so doing, information can be more effectively communicated and clues as to the causes of the health problems more easily recognized.

Case information is generally ascertained by abstracting information from hospital logs, which includes labor and delivery reports, neonatal intensive care units, pathology reports, and surgery logs. States vary in the extent to which prenatally diagnosed birth defects are collected by the surveillance system.

Sometimes surveillance outcome and exposure data are linked to provide clues as to the causes of the health problem. For example, in one study, researchers linked population-based medical birth data in Norway and Sweden with cancer registry data.[39] The linkage allowed the researchers to identify subsequent cancer risk in children with birth defects. The results found that there was an increased risk of cancer among individuals with birth defects. The highest risks were observed in those with malformations of the nervous system, Down syndrome, and multiple defects. Parents and siblings of individuals with birth defects showed no increased risk of cancer. In another study, linked data allowed researchers to identify that Down syndrome was associated with increased risk of leukemia but was not associated with increased risk of brain tumors.[40] Mental retardation, excluding Down syndrome, was associated with increased risk of acute nonlymphoblastic leukemia, and cleft palate-lip cases developed acute lymphoblastic leukemia more often.

Many surveillance systems employ **secondary data**, which are data collected for other purposes (e.g., vital records, healthcare utilization records, national and local surveys, and environmental data). **Vital records** refer to data on birth, death, marriage, and divorce. This information is available at the local and state levels. Coroners and medical examiners can be a source of information on sudden or unexpected deaths. This information is available at the local and state levels. Notifiable disease reports, laboratory data, hospital data, and outpatient healthcare data are other sources of morbidity data.

Effective surveillance requires fast action. Timeliness is the availability of data in a time frame that is appropriate for action; however, because multiple sources of information are often desired in order to obtain sufficient detail, time of data collection may be delayed. Delays can prevent public health authorities from initiating prompt intervention or feedback. Delays may occur at any phase of the surveillance process (i.e., data collection, management, analysis, interpretation, or dissemination). To avoid delays, specific guidelines are needed on routing, transferring, and storing data; appropriate methods for analysis that can be readily interpreted and communicated; and details of the target audience. A well-planned surveillance system will minimize error and disseminate information in a timely manner.

Those who have a responsibility to report data (e.g., physicians, nurses, and laboratory staff) need to be aware of when and how this is to be done. A list of reportable diseases and mechanisms by which to report a case need to be communicated by the health department to those who need to know. A simple reporting process where only relevant information is requested will improve reporting. Timely, informative, interesting, and relevant feedback will reinforce the importance of participating in the surveillance process.

Preliminary tabulations should be constructed and reviewed to identify obvious errors or highly unusual cases. Computer algorithms and statistical analyses are often useful for identifying inaccurate data and assisting to quickly manage, summarize, and describe the data. Accuracy in registration is critical. Finally, confidentiality is necessary to protect individual privacy.

Assessment of the data typically begins by generating tables and graphs. The best medium for presenting data that can be quickly visualized is a graph. Graphs can emphasize main points and clarify relationships that may otherwise be elusive. Many types of graphs were presented in the previous chapter. The type of graph chosen depends on the type of data being displayed. Presenting too many graphs or graphs that fail to demonstrate anything of interest should be avoided; nevertheless, graphs that depict specific relationships or trends inherent in the data may be particularly useful.

Some surveillance programs include **survival analysis**, which is used for estimating survival (prognosis) in a population under study. It is the probability a case will survive to time t. Its primary purpose is to identify the effects of patient care, treatments, prognostic factors, exposures, or other covariates on survival over time. There are several types of survival measures. We will briefly discuss survival time and survival rate.

Survival time is the average (mean) or median survival time for a group of patients. The median survival time has the advantage of being less sensitive to extreme values. Survival rate is observed survival that measures the proportion of persons surviving regardless of cause of death. This can be calculated using the Kaplan Meier method, the direct method, or the actuarial method.

Survival results are then presented using graphs and in reports. Mean and median survival time can be presented in a bar graph. Survival rates in a single period can also be presented by bars; however, if the emphasis is on pattern of change over time, it is better to use a line graph. Furthermore, the survival report should include the survival rate (or time) and also a complete description of the patients, their health problems, and their treatment.

A very important component of surveillance is disseminating information to those who need to know. Surveillance information should be shared with healthcare providers, laboratory directors, and those who can use the information for administrative, program planning, and decision-making purposes. Surveillance reports targeted at medical and public health communities are intended to inform and to motivate. Summary information on health-related states or events by person, place, and time informs the public as to overall risk and helps the physician anticipate the probability of encountering specific health problems among their patients. Tabular and graphical presentations of the data often make the information more interpretable.

Surveillance reports may demonstrate that the health department is aware of and is acting on the public health problem. Some reports may thank those who submitted case report information, thereby maintaining a spirit of collaboration that actually improves the surveillance system. Surveillance reports may also include information on selected prevention and control efforts and summarize completed epidemiologic investigations.

Finally, the usefulness of a surveillance system is determined, at least in part, by

■ Whether appropriate actions have been taken to date as a result of information from the surveillance system

■ Whether the information has been used to make decisions and to take action

■ Whether monitored prevalence of the outcome variable relates to the level and distribution of services available

■ Whether the information may be used in the future

CAUSAL INSIGHTS

Plotting health-related states or events over time can give the epidemiologist insights into possible causal factors. For example, if a disease occurs only in the summer, then that is when the epidemiologist searches for causal factors. Some of the questions an epidemiologist might ask are:

■ Is the increase a result of exposure to new water sources, for example, drinking from a stream in the mountains?

■ Is it from summertime swimming in a contaminated public swimming pool or a lake?

■ What vectors are available for disease transmission in the given time period and are missing at other times of the year (or in other seasons)?

■ Are vehicles of transmission present during some but not other time periods?

■ Are the cases exposed to certain environmental elements, situations, places, or circumstances during this time period that are not available at other times of the year or in other seasons?

■ Are those affected hiking or camping in the woods in the summer when insects are present that have been implicated in vector-borne diseases?

■ Have food-borne diseases from summertime camping, hiking, fishing, hunting trips or picnics been considered?

■ Are certain fomites used during certain time periods that might not be used during other seasons, such as shared drinking glasses or containers?

Studies involving geographic comparisons of disease frequency between groups, states, and countries, along with migration studies and twin studies, have further yielded important insights into the respective roles genetic and environmental forces have on disease. Some of the questions an epidemiologist might ask include:

■ What are the geographic areas of highest and lowest disease incidence/mortality?

■ What is the relative risk of disease incidence/mortality among selected migrant groups compared with a reference population?

■ What are the unique environmental and behavioral characteristics of these areas?

■ How does time among migrant groups influence change in risk of disease incidence/mortality?

■ What is the time of separation and unique environmental and behavior characteristics among twins?

NEWS FILE

The Lifetime Probability of Developing Cancer in the United States

The lifetime probability (%) of developing invasive cancer is higher in males (44%) than in females (38%). The lifetime probability of developing invasive breast cancer in females is 12% (1 in 8), and the lifetime probability of developing invasive prostate cancer in males is 16% (1 in 6). Other common cancers and their corresponding lifetime probabilities of development are lung and bronchial (8% [1 in 13] in males and 6% [1 in 16] in females), colon and rectal (5% [1 in 19] in males and 5% [1 in 20] in females), and bladder (4% [1 in 26] in males and 1% [1 in 87] in females). The probability of developing invasive cancer is strongly related to age. For example, the probability of developing any invasive cancer from birth to age 39 is 1% (1 in 69) in males and 2% (1 in 47) in females and from age 70 to older ages is 38% (1 in 3) in males and 26% (1 in 4) in females. These estimates are based on the average experience in the population. Hence, for any given individual the risk may be overestimated or underestimated.

From Siegel R, Ward E, Brawley O, Jemal A. Cancer Statistics, 2011. CA Cancer J Clin 2011;61(4);212–236.

Although analytic epidemiologic studies are better suited for establishing valid statistical associations between variables and for providing support for cause-effect relationships, descriptive studies are a good first step in the search for causes of health-related states or events.

CONCLUSION

Describing health-related states or events by person, place, and time allows the epidemiologist to better understand the nature and extent of the health problem. Consideration of person, place, and time elements in descriptive epidemiology is critical in accomplishing the important functions of epidemiology, as described in the outset of the chapter. Descriptive epidemiology through surveillance may identify sudden outbreaks that show up when the observed and expected numbers significantly differ during a given surveillance period. Unexpected health outcomes may also manifest themselves by evaluating fluctuations over the long run. Public health surveillance is used to assess sudden unexpected outbreaks and fluctuations in long-term trends. Survival analyses are also used to assess the lethality of the health problem. Finally, an important role of descriptive epidemiology is to provide causal insights. Identification and descriptions of health problems according to person, place, and time may provide clues as to whether a physical, chemical, biological, or psychosocial factor is contributing to the problem. The rationale for selected hypotheses and the justification for analytic epidemiologic investigation are provided. In later chapters, analytic epidemiology is presented, and approaches for drawing conclusions about causal associations will be explored.

EXERCISES

Key Terms

Define the following terms.

Age effect	Point source
Cohort effect	Population pyramid
Continuous source	Public health surveillance
Constrictive pyramid	Secondary data
Cyclical patterns	Secular trend
Decennial census	Seasonal trend
Dependency ratio	Short-term trend
Epidemic curve	Stationary pyramid
Expanding pyramid	Surveillance
Healthy worker effect	Survival analysis
Longitudinal data	Temporal
Medical surveillance	Time-series design
Period effect	Vital records

STUDY QUESTIONS

1. Refer to the cause-specific death rates in Table 5-1, and discuss possible reasons for the differences between males and females.

2. Refer to Table 5-3, and discuss possible reasons for the observed differences in death rates between those of Hispanic origin and those not of Hispanic origin.

3. Go to the U.S. Census Bureau's site on international demographic data, http://www.census.gov/ipc/www/idb/pyramids.html. Once at this site, select the tab "Data" and then "International Data Base." Submit your job and then choose the tab "Population Pyramid." To access the data choose the Excel tab. Calculate the dependency ratio for Afghanistan and for the United States using 2012 data. Discuss potential reasons for differences in the results.

4. Refer to the population pyramids generated in the previous problem for Afghanistan and the United States. How does the age distribution compare between these two populations?

5. Refer to Figure 5-11. What are some possible explanations for the observed birth cohort effect among those who died at ages 20–24?

6. What do the data in Figure 5-14 tell you about the latency period between smoking and lung cancer?

7. Refer to Table 5-5, and discuss why higher education is associated with cost being less inhibiting with respect to access to care and prescription drugs.

8. Discuss how descriptive epidemiology by person, place, and time may assist in (1) providing information about a disease or condition, (2) providing clues to identify a new disease or adverse health effect, (3) identifying the extent of the public health problem, (4) obtaining a description of the public health problem that can be easily communicated, (5) identifying the population at greatest risk, (6) assisting in planning and resource allocation, and (7) identifying avenues for future research that can provide insights about an etiologic relationship between an exposure and health outcome.

REFERENCES

1. Surveillance, Epidemiology, and End Results (SEER) Program (http://www.seer.cancer.gov). SEER*Stat Database: Mortality—All COD, Aggregated with State, Total U.S. (1969–2008) <Katrina/Rita Population Adjustment>, National Cancer Institute, DCCPS, Surveillance Research Program, Cancer Statistics Branch, released September 2011. Underlying mortality data provided by NCHS (http://www.cdc.gov/nchs).

2. Ries LAG, Kosary CI, Hankey BF, Miller BA, Edwards BK, eds. *SEER Cancer Statistics Review, 1973–1996*. Bethesda, MD: National Cancer Institute; 1999.

3. Central Intelligence Agency. The World Factbook. Life expectancy at birth. https://www.cia.gov/library/publications/the-world-factbook/rankorder/2102rank.html. Accessed January 6, 2012.

4. Mausner JS, Kramer S. *Epidemiology: An Introductory Text*. Philadelphia: PA: Saunders; 1985.

5. Weeks JR. *Population*, 2nd ed. Belmont, CA: Wadsworth; 1981.

6. Hartley SF. *Community Populations*. Belmont, CA: Wadsworth; 1982.

7. Central Intelligence Agency. The World Factbook. Field listing—sex ratio. https://www.cia.gov/library/publications/the-world-factbook/fields/2018.html. Accessed April 20, 2012.

8. Williams DR, Lavizzo-Mourey R, Warren RC. The concept of race and health status in America. *Public Health Rep*. 1994;109:26–41.

9. Senior PA, Bhopal R. Ethnicity as a variable in epidemiologic research. *BMJ*. 1994;309:327–330.

10. Lewontin RC, Rose S, Kamin LJ. *Not in Our Genes: Biology, Ideology, and Human Nature*. New York, NY: Pantheon Books; 1984.

11. Krieger N. The making of public health data: Paradigms, politics and policy. *J Public Health Policy*. 1992;13:412–427.

12. LaVeist TA. Beyond dummy variables and sample selection: What health services researchers ought to know about race as a variable. *Health Serv Res*. 1994;29:1–16.

13. Schulman K, Berlin J, Harless W. The effect of race and sex on physicians' recommendations for cardiac catheterization. *N Engl J Med*. 1999;340:619–626.

14. Committee on Pediatric Research. Race/ethnicity, gender, socioeconomic status—research exploring their effects on child health: a subject review. *Pediatrics*. 2000;105(6):1349–1351.

15. Berkman J. Mortality and marital status. Reflections on the derivations of etiology from statistics. *Am J Public Health*. 1962;52(8):1318–1329.

16. Verbrugge LM. Marital status and health. *J Marriage and Fam*. 1979;41(2):267–285.

17. Schoenborn CA. Marital status and health: United States, 1999–2002 Advance data from vital and health statistics; no 351. Hyattsville, MD: National Center for Health Statistics. 2004.

18. MacMahon B, Pugh TF. *Epidemiology: Principles and Methods*. Boston, MA: Little, Brown and Company; 1970.

19. Monson RR. *Occupational Epidemiology*, 2nd ed. Boca Raton, FL: CRC Press; 1990.

20. National Center for Health Statistics. *Health, United States, 2010 with Chartbook on Trends in the Health of Americans*. Hyattsville, MD: National Center for Health Statistics; 2010, Table 59.

21. National Center for Health Statistics. *Health, United States, 2010 with Chartbook on Trends in the Health of Americans*. Hyattsville, MD: National Center for Health Statistics; 2010, Table 86.

22. National Center for Health Statistics. *Health, United States, 2010 with Chartbook on Trends in the Health of Americans*. Hyattsville, MD: National Center for Health Statistics, 2010; Table 70.

23. Daniels M, Merrill RM, Lyon JL, Standford JB, White GL Jr. Associations between breast cancer risk factors and religious practices in Utah. *Prev Med*. 2004;38:28–38.

24. Merrill RM, Folsom JA. Female breast cancer incidence and survival in Utah according to religious preference, 1985–1999. *BMC Cancer*. 2005;5:49.

25. Maskarinec G, Noh JJ. The effect of migration on cancer incidence among Japanese in Hawaii. *Ethn Dis*. 2004;14(3):431–439.

26. Wachsmuth RC, Turner F, Barrett JH, et al. The effect of sun exposure in determining nevus density in UK adolescent twins. *J Invest Dermatol*. 2005;124(1):56–62.

27. McKiernan JM, Goluboff ET, Liberson GL, Golden R, Fisch H. Rising risk of testicular cancer by birth cohort in the United States from 1973 to 1995. *J Urol*. 1999;162(2):361–363.

28. Liu S, Wen SW, Mao Y, Mery L, Rouleau J. Birth cohort effects underlying the increasing testicular cancer incidence in Canada. *Can J Pub Health*. 1999;90(3):176–180.

29. Snowdon J, Hunt GE. Age, period and cohort effects on suicide rates in Australia, 1919–1999. *Acta Psychiatr Scand*. 2002;105(4):265. http://onlinelibrary.wiley.com/doi/10.1034/j.1600-0447.2002.1193.x/pdf. Accessed April 20, 2012.

30. American Cancer Society. *Cancer Facts & Figures 2011*. Atlanta, GA: American Cancer Society; 2011.

31. Centers for Disease Control and Prevention. Table 3. Estimated numbers and rates (per 100,000 population) of new HIV infections in adults and adolescents, 2006—50 states and the District of Columbia. http://www.cdc.gov/hiv/surveillance/resources/reports/2007report/table3.htm. Accessed April 20, 2012.

32. Merrill RM, Potosky AL, Feuer EJ. Changing trends in US prostate cancer incidence rates. *J Natl Cancer Inst*. 1996;88(22):1683–1685.

33. Merrill RM, Feuer EJ, Warren JL, Schussler N, Stephenson RA. Role of transurethral resection of the prostate in population-based prostate cancer incidence rates. *Am J Epidemiol*. 1999;150(8):848–860.

34. Feuer EJ, Merrill RM, Hankey BF. Cancer surveillance series: interpreting trends in prostate cancer—part II: cause of death misclassification and the recent rise and fall in prostate cancer mortality. *J Natl Cancer Inst.* 1999;91(12):1025–1032.

35. Centers for Disease Control and Prevention. Summary of notifiable diseases, United States—1990. *MMWR.* 1990;39:53.

36. Centers for Disease Control and Prevention. West Nile Virus activity—United States. *http://www.cdc.gov/mmwr/preview/mmwrhtml/mm5449a1.htm* Accessed April 20, 2012.

37. Bull GM, Morton J. Environment, temperature and death rates. *Age and Aging.* 1978;7(4):210–224.

38. Centers for Disease Control and Prevention. Data and Statistics. http://www.cdc.gov/DataStatistics/. Accessed April 20, 2012.

39. Bjørge T, Cnattingius S, Lie RT, Tretli S, Engeland A. Cancer risk in children with birth defects and in their families: a population based cohort study of 5.2 million children from Norway and Sweden. *Cancer Epidemiol Biomarkers Prev.* 2008 Mar;17(3):500–506.

40. Nishi M, Miyake H, Takeda T, Hatae Y. Congenital malformations and childhood cancer. *Med Pediatr Oncol.* 2000;34(4):250–254.

6

General Health and Population Indicators

OBJECTIVES

After completing this chapter, you will be able to:

- Identify common indices used in identifying the health status of populations.
- Calculate, interpret, and apply selected health status measures.
- Understand the vital statistics registration system in the United States.

In 1900, the entire world population was under 2 billion people. The United States Census Bureau estimated that the world population exceeded 7 billion on March 12, 2012.[1] On July 1, 2012, the estimated world population was 7,023,324,899, representing a net increase to the world's population of 77,280,910 (6,440,076 per month, 211,729 per day, 8,822 per hour, and 147 per minute) over the previous year.[1] In this year the birth-to-death ratio was 2.4,[2] and the population density (population per square kilometer) was 51 (24.3 in more developed countries and 71.4 in less developed countries).[3]

Total population estimates and annual growth rates according to less developed and more developed areas in the world are presented in Figure 6-1. The growth rates are much greater for less developed countries than more developed countries. In 2010, the annual growth rate was about 1.3% in less developed countries and 0.4% in more developed countries. Certain indicators of population dynamics, such as crude birth and mortality rates, influence population growth.

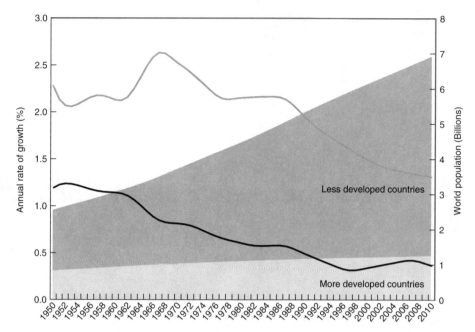

FIGURE 6-1   World population and annual growth rate: 1950–2010. Data source: United Nations Populaton Division, World Population Prospects, the 2010 Revision.

Descriptive epidemiology makes use of several indicators to identify the health status of populations. These indicators are typically related to births and deaths because such data have been more readily available than morbidity data. Health indicators are also often expressed as rates. A rate is the frequency of an event, disease, or condition, in relation to a unit of population, with a time specification. This chapter presents many of the common indicators used in epidemiology for measuring health status.

HEALTH INDICATOR

A **health indicator** is a marker of health status (physical or mental disease, impairments or disability, and social well-being), service provision, or resource availability. It is designed to enable the monitoring of health status, service performance, or program goals. Monitoring is a process in which changes in health status over time or among populations are identified in order to assess progress toward health goals or objectives.

No single health indicator can be expected to reflect all dimensions of health. Therefore, there are several indicators that are commonly used to reflect various dimensions of health. In addition, to fully understand health, it should be studied in the context of economic circumstances, education and employment status, living conditions, social support, sexual relationships, and cultural norms and legal structures. Hence, several categories of indicators are in use today, including the following:

- Health and well-being (e.g., physical fulfillment, psychosocial comfort, and closeness)
- Health resources (e.g., family planning, opportunities for choice, satisfaction with and perceived quality of services)

- Collective justice (e.g., level of disparity in individual health indicators)
- Social capital (e.g., community involvement, trust in others, perceived enabling factors)
- Collective capacity (e.g., community participation)
- Resiliency (e.g., a community's ability to cope with natural disasters that may adversely affect reproduction)
- Functionality (e.g., peace, safety, and factors associated with poor reproductive health such as abuse, exploitation, unwanted pregnancy, disease, and death)

In short, health indicators should be complimentary and in combination reflect the broad scope of health.

As social health issues are in a constant state of change, an array of health indicators are needed to reflect the prevailing health issues or challenges of greatest concern where an intervention is sought. Reporting a health indicator such as the maternal mortality rate helps epidemiologists to understand the problem and create ways to intervene and improve the situation. As a given health problem is improved, new indicators reflecting other major health concerns may surface as priorities. For example, as infant mortality rates fall and population growth ensues, economic and social implications must be considered, and new indicators are needed.

Health indicators tend to involve data that are required by law (e.g., death certificates, hospital discharge information, and notifiable disease). The advantage of using this data is that it typically involves standards for data quality and specified collection methods. Hence, summary statistics of these data tend to be complete and reliable. On the other hand, health indicators may be misleading if the data on which they are based involves small sample size, nonrepresentative sample, poor response rate, changes in reporting over time, differential nonresponse, changes in procedures for data collection, revisions in definitions and values related to health, changes in the socioeconomic characteristics of the population, long-term instability of aggregate levels of health statistics, lack of data to control for confounding factors, and changes in the organization and delivery of health care.[4]

Health indicators for global monitoring are usually presented in the form of a ratio, proportion, percentage, or rate.

In the remainder of this chapter, selected health indicators are defined and discussed.

BIRTH

The birth rate in a given area may be influenced by governmental policies, social beliefs, religious beliefs, abortion rates, poverty or economic prosperity, literacy, infant death rates, conflict (e.g., war, security, safety), and urbanization. **Birth rate** is the ratio of total live births to total population in a given area over a specified time period. It is calculated as follows:

$$Birth\ Rate = \frac{Number\ of\ live\ births\ during\ a\ specified\ time\ period}{Population\ from\ which\ the\ births\ occurred} \times 1{,}000$$

The denominator is the estimated total population at the midpoint of the specified time period. Birth rates are expressed as the number of live births per 1,000 members of the population. The denominator in the rate calculation is measured at the midpoint of the specified time period. The birth rate may be expressed according to factors such as the mother's age, race/ethnicity, or marital status (specific rate), or it may represent the entire population.

A related measure is the **fertility rate**, which represents the number of live births per 1,000 females of childbearing age (15–49 years). It is calculated as follows:

$$Fertility\ Rate = \frac{Number\ of\ live\ births\ during\ a\ specified\ time\ period}{Population\ of\ women\ 15\text{–}49} \times 1{,}000$$

The denominator is the midpoint of the specified time period. Monitoring trends in birth and fertility rates is important for effective planning because changes in the population composition can then be accommodated. For example, high birth and fertility rates result in a large population of dependent children who will require schools and affordable child care. On the other hand, low birth and fertility rates may result in an inadequate number of younger workers supporting a dependent older population.

The **total fertility rate** (TFR) is the total number of children a woman would have by the end of her reproductive period if she experienced the currently prevailing age-specific fertility rates throughout her childbearing life (ages 15–49 years); in other words, it is the average number of births per woman. The age-specific fertility rate (ASFR) is the fertility rate within selected age groups and is calculated as

$$ASFR = \frac{Births\ in\ a\ given\ year\ to\ women\ aged\ X}{Number\ of\ women\ aged\ X\ at\ mid\text{-}year} \times 1{,}000\ women$$

$$X = 15\text{–}19,\ 20\text{–}24,\ 25\text{–}29,\ 30\text{–}34,\ 35\text{–}39,\ 40\text{–}44,\ 45\text{–}49\ years$$

The TFR per woman is then calculated as

$$TFR = \frac{\Sigma ASFRs \times 5}{1{,}000}$$

The TFR is a commonly used indicator of reproductive health and population momentum, and is a proxy for the effectiveness of family planning services. The primary strength of this summary measure is that it is independent of the age structure, unlike the crude birth rate. Hence, it is useful for monitoring trends over time and for international comparisons.

The TFR ranges considerably throughout the world. In 2011, the estimated TFR was highest in Niger (7.3), Uganda (6.7), Mali (6.4), Somalia (6.4), and Burundi (6.2). The lowest TFRs in the world were in Japan (1.2), Taiwan (1.2), Singapore (1.1), Hong Kong (1.1), and Macau (0.9). The rate was 2.1 in the United States and 1.9 in the United Kingdom.[5]

Contraceptive Prevalence

Contraceptive prevalence (CP) is the proportion of women of reproductive age (i.e., 15–49 years) who are using (or whose partner is using) a contraceptive method at a given point in time. The methods of contraception include sterilization, intrauterine devices, hormonal methods, condoms and vaginal barrier methods, rhythm, withdrawal, abstinence, and lactational amenorrhea (lack of menstruation during breastfeeding). The following equation measures utilization of contraceptive methods.

$$CP = \frac{\begin{array}{c}Number\ of\ women\ of\ reproductive\ age\ at\ risk\ of\ pregnancy\ who\ are\ using\\ (or\ whose\ partner\ is\ using)\ a\ contraceptive\ method\ at\ a\ point\ in\ time\end{array}}{Number\ of\ women\ of\ reproductive\ age\ at\ the\ same\ point\ in\ time} \times 100$$

Contraceptive prevalence is useful for measuring progress toward child and maternity health goals. Population-based sample surveys are typically used to estimate contraceptive practice. Smaller scale or more focused group surveys and records kept by organized family planning programs are other sources of information about contraceptive practices.

In 2009, for women aged 15–49, married or in union, the prevalence of any method of contraception was 62.7% (61.2% in less developed regions and 72.4% in more developed regions).[6] Sterilization is used in 20.6% of females and 1.9% of males in less developed countries and in 8.2% of females and 5.5% of males in more developed countries.[6] Other interesting comparisons in the use of birth control exist between less developed (the pill 7.3%, condom 5.9%, rhythm 2.8%, and withdrawal 2.5%) and more developed countries (the pill 18.4%, condom 17.8%, rhythm 3.8%, and withdrawal 6.7%).[6]

MORTALITY

John Graunt (1620–1674) developed a system of tracking and understanding causes of death in London that involved data called "The Bills of Mortality." A couple hundred years later, William Farr (1807–1883) was appointed registrar general in England and built on the ideas of Graunt. Farr's registration system for vital statistics laid the foundation for data collection and the use of vital statistics in epidemiology. The foundations of the work of both Graunt and Farr were death-related statistics.

Mortality is the epidemiologic and vital statistics term for death. In our society, there are generally three things that cause death: (1) degeneration of vital organs and related conditions, (2) disease states, and (3) society or the environment (homicide, accidents, disasters, etc.).[7]

In many countries, laws require the registration of vital events: births, deaths, marriages, divorces, and fetal deaths. All deaths have to be certified by a physician or a coroner. If any foul play is involved in a death, an autopsy is often required, and the results of the autopsy are recorded. An autopsy provides objective data that accurately certify the cause of death. Some physician diagnoses of cause of death are not completely correct because of the difficulty of making such a diagnosis without an autopsy. The physician signing the death certificate may not be the attending physician. Thus, he or she might not have complete information on the cause of death and may record only what he or she knows about the death.

In the United States, all deaths are recorded and reported to local health departments and to the state office of vital statistics. Reports of vital event statistics, including deaths, are reported to the National Center for Health Statistics at the Centers for Disease Control and Prevention (CDC). Legal authority for the registration of births, deaths, marriages, divorces, and fetal deaths resides individually with the 50 states, including Washington, D.C. as well as the five territories (Puerto Rico, the Virgin Islands, Guam, American Samoa, and the Commonwealth of the Northern Mariana Islands). Each of these jurisdictions is responsible for maintaining registries of vital events and for issuing copies of birth, death, marriage, and divorce certificates. The laws of each area provide for a continuous and permanent vital registration system. Each system depends on the conscientious efforts of physicians, hospital personnel, funeral directors, coroners, and medical examiners in preparing or certifying information needed to complete the original death records (Figure 6-2).

Responsible Person or Agency	Birth Certificate	Death Certificate	Fetal Death Report
1. Hospital authority	1. Completes entire certificate using mother and facility worksheets. 2. Files certificate with local office or state office per state law.	When death occurs in hospital, may initiate preparation of certificate: completes information on name, date, and place of death; obtains certification of cause of death from physician; and gives certificate to funeral director. Note: If the attending physician is unavailable to certify to the cause of death, some states allow a hospital physician to certify to only the fact and time of death. With legal pronouncement of the death and permission of the attending physician, the body can then be released to the funeral director. The attending physician still must complete the cause-of-death section prior to final disposition of the body.	1. Completes entire report using patient and facility worksheets. 2. Obtains cause of fetal death from physician. 3. Obtains authorization for final disposition of fetus. 4. Files report with local office or state office per state law.
Funeral director		1. Obtains personal facts about decedent and completes certificate. 2. Obtains certification of cause of death from attending physician or medical examiner or coroner. 3. Obtains authorization for final disposition per state law. 4. Files certificate with local office or state office per state law.	If fetus is to be buried, the funeral director is responsible for obtaining authorization for final disposition. Note: In some states, the funeral director, or person acting as such, is responsible for all duties shown under hospital authority.

FIGURE 6-2   Vital statistics registration system in the United States. From the U.S. Department of Health and Human Services. *Medical Examiners' and Coroners' Handbook on Death Registration and Fetal Death Reporting.* Hyattsville, MD: U.S. Department of Health and Human Services, Public Health Service, National Center for Health Statistics; October 1987. DHHS Publication No. (PHS) 87-1110.

(continues)

Responsible Person or Agency	Birth Certificate	Death Certificate	Fetal Death Report
Physician or other professional attendant	For in-hospital birth, verifies accuracy of medical information and signs certificate. For out-of-hospital birth, duties are same as those for hospital authority, shown above.	Completes certification of cause of death and signs certificate.	Provides cause of fetal death and information not available from the medical records.
Local office* (may be local registrar or city or county health department)	1. Verifies completeness and accuracy of certificate and queries incomplete or inconsistent certificates. 2. If authorized by state law, makes copy or index for local use. 3. Sends certificates to state registrar.	1. Verifies completeness and accuracy of certificate and queries incomplete or inconsistent certificates. 2. If authorized by state law, makes copy or index for local use. 3. If authorized by state law, issues authorization for final disposition on receipt of completed certificate. 4. Sends certificates to state registrar.	If state law requires routing of fetal death reports through local office, performs the same functions as shown for the birth and death certificate.
City and county health departments	1. Use data derived from these records in allocating medical and nursing services. 2. Follow up on infectious diseases. 3. Plan programs. 4. Measure effectiveness of services. 5. Conduct research studies.		
State registrar, office of vital statistics	1. Queries incomplete or inconsistent information. 2. Maintains files for permanent reference and is the source of certified copies. 3. Develops vital statistics for use in planning, evaluating, and administering state and local health activities and for research studies. 4. Compiles health-related statistics for state and civil divisions of state for use of the health department and other agencies and groups interested in the fields of medical science, public health, demography, and social welfare. 5. Sends data for all events filed to the National Center for Health Statistics.		
Centers for Disease Control and Prevention, National Center for Health Statistics	1. Evaluates quality of state vital statistics data and works with states to assure quality. 2. Compiles health-related statistical data files and runs edits to fully process data. 3. Prepares and publishes national statistics of births, deaths, and fetal deaths; constructs the official U.S. life tables and related actuarial tables. 4. Conducts health and social research studies based on vital records and on sampling surveys linked to records. 5. Conducts research and methodological studies in vital statistics methods, including the technical, administrative, and legal aspects of vital records registration and administration.		

FIGURE 6-2   Vital statistics registration system in the United States. *(continued)*

(continues)

Responsible Person or Agency	Birth Certificate	Death Certificate	Fetal Death Report
	6. Maintains a continuing technical assistance program to improve the quality and usefulness of vital statistics. 7. Provides leadership and coordination in the development of standard certificates and report and model laws.		

*Some states do not have local vital registration offices. In these states, the certificates or reports are transmitted directly to the state office of vital statistics.

FIGURE 6-2   Vital statistics registration system in the United States. *(continued)*

Causes of Death

The National Center for Health Statistics developed the standard certificate of death and recommends its use. Each state is expected to include at least the minimum information required as set forth on the U.S. standard certificate of death. Some states include additional information that they deem important. Death statistics are of great importance to epidemiologic activities. **Death certificates** not only provide information on the total numbers of deaths, but they also provide demographic information and other important facts about each person who dies, such as date of birth (for cohort studies), date of death (for accurate age), stated age, place of death, place of residence, occupation, gender, cause of death, and marital status. Other information may include type of injury, place and time of injury, and so forth. See the sample certificate of death for the state of California (Figure 6-3). A separate certificate is used for fetal deaths (Figure 6-4).

Causes of Death on the Death Certificate

The International Classification of Diseases (ICD) is the standard diagnostic classification for mortality statistics. ICD-10 is the latest classification in a series that dates back to the 1850s. It was endorsed by the Forty-third World Health Assembly in May 1990. ICD is designed to promote consistency among countries in the way they collect, process, classify, and present mortality statistics, including a format for reporting causes of death on the death certificate.

The causes of death entered on the death certificate are those diseases, injuries, and morbid conditions that resulted in or contributed to the death. Circumstances of any accident or violent act that produced death are also recorded. The reported conditions are then translated into medical codes according to the classification structure and the selection and modification rules of the current ICD, published by the World Health Organization.[8] The coding rules established by the applicable revision of the ICD give preference to certain categories, consolidate conditions, and systematically select a single cause of death from a sequence of reported conditions. The selected single cause is called the underlying cause of death. The other reported causes are called the nonunderlying causes of death.

Underlying Cause of Death

Found on the death certificate is a space for the underlying cause of death. This is stated on a death certificate directly after the main cause of death. The underlying cause is any disease

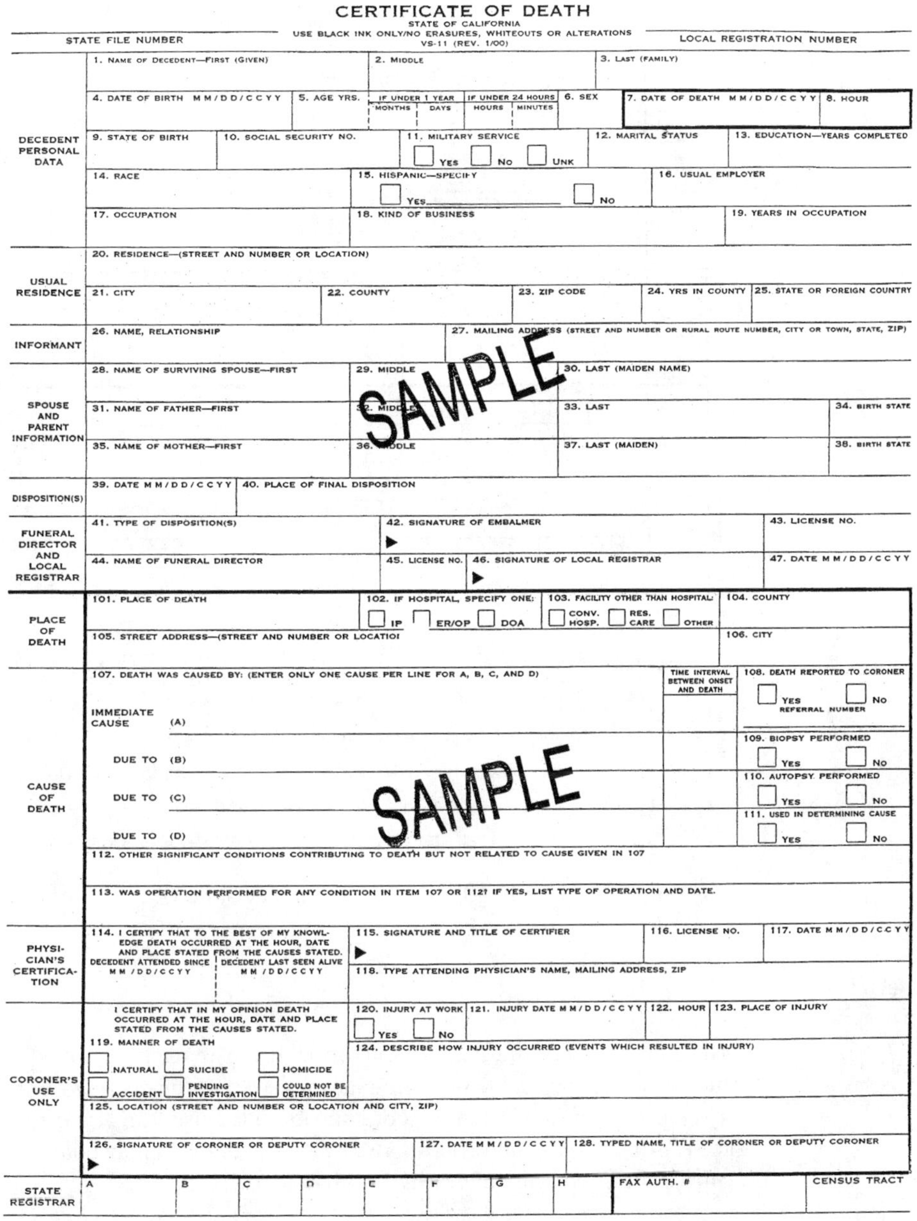
CERTIFICATE OF DEATH
STATE OF CALIFORNIA
USE BLACK INK ONLY/NO ERASURES, WHITEOUTS OR ALTERATIONS
VS-11 (REV. 1/00)
STATE FILE NUMBER
LOCAL REGISTRATION NUMBER

DECEDENT PERSONAL DATA
1. NAME OF DECEDENT—FIRST (GIVEN)
2. MIDDLE
3. LAST (FAMILY)
4. DATE OF BIRTH MM/DD/CCYY
5. AGE YRS.
IF UNDER 1 YEAR MONTHS DAYS
IF UNDER 24 HOURS HOURS MINUTES
6. SEX
7. DATE OF DEATH MM/DD/CCYY
8. HOUR
9. STATE OF BIRTH
10. SOCIAL SECURITY NO.
11. MILITARY SERVICE YES NO UNK
12. MARITAL STATUS
13. EDUCATION—YEARS COMPLETED
14. RACE
15. HISPANIC—SPECIFY YES NO
16. USUAL EMPLOYER
17. OCCUPATION
18. KIND OF BUSINESS
19. YEARS IN OCCUPATION

USUAL RESIDENCE
20. RESIDENCE—(STREET AND NUMBER OR LOCATION)
21. CITY
22. COUNTY
23. ZIP CODE
24. YRS IN COUNTY
25. STATE OR FOREIGN COUNTRY

INFORMANT
26. NAME, RELATIONSHIP
27. MAILING ADDRESS (STREET AND NUMBER OR RURAL ROUTE NUMBER, CITY OR TOWN, STATE, ZIP)

SPOUSE AND PARENT INFORMATION
28. NAME OF SURVIVING SPOUSE—FIRST
29. MIDDLE
30. LAST (MAIDEN NAME)
31. NAME OF FATHER—FIRST
32. MIDDLE
33. LAST
34. BIRTH STATE
35. NAME OF MOTHER—FIRST
36. MIDDLE
37. LAST (MAIDEN)
38. BIRTH STATE

DISPOSITION(S)
39. DATE MM/DD/CCYY
40. PLACE OF FINAL DISPOSITION

FUNERAL DIRECTOR AND LOCAL REGISTRAR
41. TYPE OF DISPOSITION(S)
42. SIGNATURE OF EMBALMER
43. LICENSE NO.
44. NAME OF FUNERAL DIRECTOR
45. LICENSE NO.
46. SIGNATURE OF LOCAL REGISTRAR
47. DATE MM/DD/CCYY

PLACE OF DEATH
101. PLACE OF DEATH
102. IF HOSPITAL, SPECIFY ONE: IP ER/OP DOA
103. FACILITY OTHER THAN HOSPITAL: CONV. HOSP. RES. CARE OTHER
104. COUNTY
105. STREET ADDRESS—(STREET AND NUMBER OR LOCATION)
106. CITY

CAUSE OF DEATH
107. DEATH WAS CAUSED BY: (ENTER ONLY ONE CAUSE PER LINE FOR A, B, C, AND D)
TIME INTERVAL BETWEEN ONSET AND DEATH
IMMEDIATE CAUSE (A)
DUE TO (B)
DUE TO (C)
DUE TO (D)
108. DEATH REPORTED TO CORONER YES NO REFERRAL NUMBER
109. BIOPSY PERFORMED YES NO
110. AUTOPSY PERFORMED YES NO
111. USED IN DETERMINING CAUSE YES NO
112. OTHER SIGNIFICANT CONDITIONS CONTRIBUTING TO DEATH BUT NOT RELATED TO CAUSE GIVEN IN 107
113. WAS OPERATION PERFORMED FOR ANY CONDITION IN ITEM 107 OR 112? IF YES, LIST TYPE OF OPERATION AND DATE.

PHYSICIAN'S CERTIFICATION
114. I CERTIFY THAT TO THE BEST OF MY KNOWLEDGE DEATH OCCURRED AT THE HOUR, DATE AND PLACE STATED FROM THE CAUSES STATED.
DECEDENT ATTENDED SINCE MM/DD/CCYY
DECEDENT LAST SEEN ALIVE MM/DD/CCYY
115. SIGNATURE AND TITLE OF CERTIFIER
116. LICENSE NO.
117. DATE MM/DD/CCYY
118. TYPE ATTENDING PHYSICIAN'S NAME, MAILING ADDRESS, ZIP

CORONER'S USE ONLY
I CERTIFY THAT IN MY OPINION DEATH OCCURRED AT THE HOUR, DATE AND PLACE STATED FROM THE CAUSES STATED.
119. MANNER OF DEATH
NATURAL SUICIDE HOMICIDE
ACCIDENT PENDING INVESTIGATION COULD NOT BE DETERMINED
120. INJURY AT WORK YES NO
121. INJURY DATE MM/DD/CCYY
122. HOUR
123. PLACE OF INJURY
124. DESCRIBE HOW INJURY OCCURRED (EVENTS WHICH RESULTED IN INJURY)
125. LOCATION (STREET AND NUMBER OR LOCATION AND CITY, ZIP)
126. SIGNATURE OF CORONER OR DEPUTY CORONER
127. DATE MM/DD/CCYY
128. TYPED NAME, TITLE OF CORONER OR DEPUTY CORONER

STATE REGISTRAR
A B C D E F G H
FAX AUTH. #
CENSUS TRACT

SAMPLE
SAMPLE

FIGURE 6-3 Sample death certificate. State of California, Revision January 2000.

or injury that initiated the set of events leading to the death. Any violent act or accident that produced the death would be stated on this section of the death certificate. For example, a tumor, such as malignant melanoma, is often the underlying cause of death because cancer cells can spread to distant parts of the body and disrupt the normal functioning of vital organs (e.g., the brain, liver, and lungs).

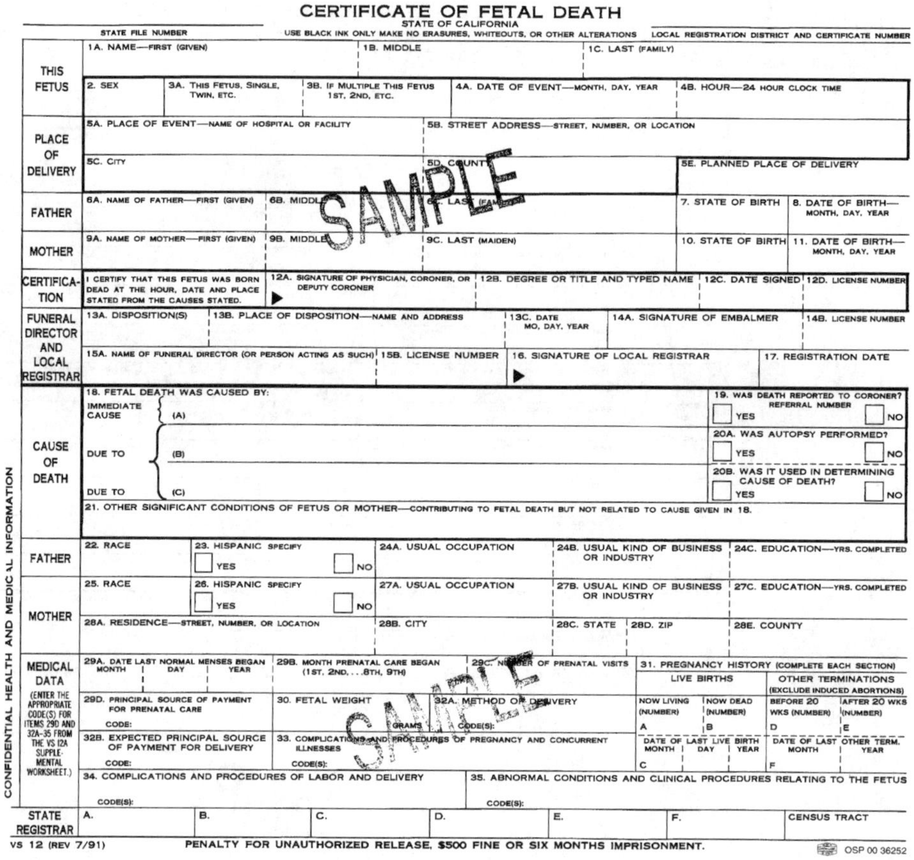
CERTIFICATE OF FETAL DEATH
STATE OF CALIFORNIA
STATE FILE NUMBER
USE BLACK INK ONLY MAKE NO ERASURES, WHITEOUTS, OR OTHER ALTERATIONS
LOCAL REGISTRATION DISTRICT AND CERTIFICATE NUMBER
THIS FETUS
1A. NAME—FIRST (GIVEN) | 1B. MIDDLE | 1C. LAST (FAMILY)
2. SEX | 3A. THIS FETUS, SINGLE, TWIN, ETC. | 3B. IF MULTIPLE THIS FETUS 1ST, 2ND, ETC. | 4A. DATE OF EVENT—MONTH, DAY, YEAR | 4B. HOUR—24 HOUR CLOCK TIME
PLACE OF DELIVERY
5A. PLACE OF EVENT—NAME OF HOSPITAL OR FACILITY | 5B. STREET ADDRESS—STREET, NUMBER, OR LOCATION
5C. CITY | 5D. COUNTY | 5E. PLANNED PLACE OF DELIVERY
FATHER
6A. NAME OF FATHER—FIRST (GIVEN) | 6B. MIDDLE | 6C. LAST (FAMILY) | 7. STATE OF BIRTH | 8. DATE OF BIRTH—MONTH, DAY, YEAR
MOTHER
9A. NAME OF MOTHER—FIRST (GIVEN) | 9B. MIDDLE | 9C. LAST (MAIDEN) | 10. STATE OF BIRTH | 11. DATE OF BIRTH—MONTH, DAY, YEAR
CERTIFICATION
I CERTIFY THAT THIS FETUS WAS BORN DEAD AT THE HOUR, DATE AND PLACE STATED FROM THE CAUSES STATED. | 12A. SIGNATURE OF PHYSICIAN, CORONER, OR DEPUTY CORONER | 12B. DEGREE OR TITLE AND TYPED NAME | 12C. DATE SIGNED | 12D. LICENSE NUMBER
FUNERAL DIRECTOR AND LOCAL REGISTRAR
13A. DISPOSITION(S) | 13B. PLACE OF DISPOSITION—NAME AND ADDRESS | 13C. DATE MO, DAY, YEAR | 14A. SIGNATURE OF EMBALMER | 14B. LICENSE NUMBER
15A. NAME OF FUNERAL DIRECTOR (OR PERSON ACTING AS SUCH) | 15B. LICENSE NUMBER | 16. SIGNATURE OF LOCAL REGISTRAR | 17. REGISTRATION DATE
CAUSE OF DEATH
18. FETAL DEATH WAS CAUSED BY:
IMMEDIATE CAUSE (A)
DUE TO (B)
DUE TO (C)
19. WAS DEATH REPORTED TO CORONER? REFERRAL NUMBER YES NO
20A. WAS AUTOPSY PERFORMED? YES NO
20B. WAS IT USED IN DETERMINING CAUSE OF DEATH? YES NO
21. OTHER SIGNIFICANT CONDITIONS OF FETUS OR MOTHER—CONTRIBUTING TO FETAL DEATH BUT NOT RELATED TO CAUSE GIVEN IN 18.
CONFIDENTIAL HEALTH AND MEDICAL INFORMATION
FATHER
22. RACE | 23. HISPANIC SPECIFY YES NO | 24A. USUAL OCCUPATION | 24B. USUAL KIND OF BUSINESS OR INDUSTRY | 24C. EDUCATION—YRS. COMPLETED
MOTHER
25. RACE | 26. HISPANIC SPECIFY YES NO | 27A. USUAL OCCUPATION | 27B. USUAL KIND OF BUSINESS OR INDUSTRY | 27C. EDUCATION—YRS. COMPLETED
28A. RESIDENCE—STREET, NUMBER, OR LOCATION | 28B. CITY | 28C. STATE | 28D. ZIP | 28E. COUNTY
MEDICAL DATA (ENTER THE APPROPRIATE CODE(S) FOR ITEMS 29D AND 32A-35 FROM THE VS 12A SUPPLEMENTAL WORKSHEET.)
29A. DATE LAST NORMAL MENSES BEGAN MONTH DAY YEAR | 29B. MONTH PRENATAL CARE BEGAN (1ST, 2ND, . . .8TH, 9TH) | 29C. NUMBER OF PRENATAL VISITS | 31. PREGNANCY HISTORY (COMPLETE EACH SECTION)
LIVE BIRTHS | OTHER TERMINATIONS (EXCLUDE INDUCED ABORTIONS)
29D. PRINCIPAL SOURCE OF PAYMENT FOR PRENATAL CARE CODE: | 30. FETAL WEIGHT GRAMS | 32A. METHOD OF DELIVERY CODE(S): | NOW LIVING (NUMBER) A | NOW DEAD (NUMBER) B | BEFORE 20 WKS (NUMBER) D | AFTER 20 WKS (NUMBER) E
32B. EXPECTED PRINCIPAL SOURCE OF PAYMENT FOR DELIVERY CODE: | 33. COMPLICATIONS AND PROCEDURES OF PREGNANCY AND CONCURRENT ILLNESSES CODE(S): | DATE OF LAST LIVE BIRTH MONTH DAY YEAR C | DATE OF LAST OTHER TERM. MONTH YEAR F
34. COMPLICATIONS AND PROCEDURES OF LABOR AND DELIVERY CODE(S): | 35. ABNORMAL CONDITIONS AND CLINICAL PROCEDURES RELATING TO THE FETUS CODE(S):
STATE REGISTRAR | A. | B. | C. | D. | E. | F. | CENSUS TRACT
VS 12 (REV 7/91) PENALTY FOR UNAUTHORIZED RELEASE, $500 FINE OR SIX MONTHS IMPRISONMENT. OSP 00 36252
SAMPLE
SAMPLE

FIGURE 6-4 Sample fetal death certificate. State of California, Revision July 1991.

Death Certificate Data

Data from death certificates and the formal death-reporting system provide a database for studying a variety of epidemiologic issues and events. The main cause of death is entered first on a death certificate. Additional or contributing causes can also be listed (see Figure 6-3). The existing diseases and conditions at the time of death may hold as much epidemiologic value as the listed cause of death.

TYPES OF MORTALITY RATES

Many different mortality rates are used in epidemiology. Listed here are definitions of the death rates commonly found in national reports and used in community health assessments.

Mortality Rate

The first and most basic measure of death is the **crude mortality rate**. The crude mortality rate is calculated as follows:

$$Crude\ Mortality\ Rate = \frac{Number\ of\ deaths\ during\ a\ given\ time\ period}{Population\ from\ which\ the\ deaths\ occurred} \times 100,000$$

The denominator is the midpoint of the specified time period. The term crude is used because it does not account for differences of age, gender, or other variables in any aspect of death. When deaths from a specific cause are of interest, the **cause-specific mortality rate** is calculated as follows:

$$Cause\text{-}specific\ Mortality\ Rate = \frac{\begin{array}{c}Number\ of\ deaths\ from\ a\ specific\ cause\\during\ a\ given\ time\ period\end{array}}{Population\ from\ which\ the\ deaths\ occurred} \times 100,000$$

The denominator is the midpoint of the specified time period. When comparisons are made of these rates between populations or across time, age-adjusted rates may be more appropriate because they control for differences in the age distribution.

INFANT MORTALITY

Infant mortality is a major health status indicator of populations and a key measure of the health status of a community or population. Reflected in infant mortality is prenatal and postnatal nutritional care or the lack thereof. If pregnant women have an intake of sufficient calories and nutrients, including appropriate weight gain, this will improve infant birth weight and reduce infant mortality and morbidity. Seeking immediate medical care on becoming pregnant, along with total abstinence from any drugs, chemicals, alcohol, and smoking, can reduce infant mortality. Declining infant mortality in developing countries has been linked primarily with affordable health services, improvements in the status of women, nutrition standards, universal immunization, and the expansion of prenatal and obstetric services.[9] Breastfeeding has been shown to protect against gastroenteritis and respiratory infections in developing countries.[9]

Infant Mortality Rate

Infant (the period from birth to 1 year) mortality rates are often used as an indicator of health in a country. The infant mortality rate is calculated as follows:

$$Infant\ Mortality\ Rate = \frac{\begin{array}{c}Number\ of\ deaths\ among\ infants\ aged\\0\text{--}1\ year\ during\ a\ specified\ time\ period\end{array}}{Number\ of\ live\ births\ in\ the\ same\ time\ period} \times 1,000$$

Infant mortality rates have consistently decreased over the past 60 years for both more developed and less developed regions in the world (Figure 6-5). There was an 89% decrease in rates for more developed regions and 67% decrease for less developed regions. Infant mortality rates by world region and time is shown in Table 6-1. In 1950–1954, infant mortality rates were lowest in Australia/New Zealand, followed by the United States, Canada, and Northern and Western Europe. The highest rates were in Africa and Asia. Yet decreasing rates occurred over the next 60 years in each region. This ranks among the 10 great achievements in public health.[10]

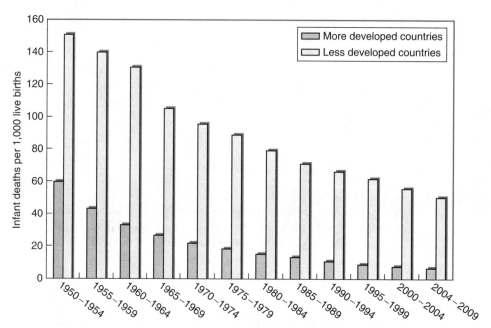

FIGURE 6-5   Infant mortality rates for more developed and less developed countries. Data from United Nations Populaton Division, World Population Prospects, the 2010 Revision.

NEWS FILE

Infant Mortality Rises in the United States for the First Time in Decades

U.S. life expectancy increased from 77.2 in 2001 to 77.4 in 2002; however, during this same time period the infant mortality rate also increased, from 6.8 deaths per 1,000 live births to 7.0 deaths per 1,000. The last time the nation's infant mortality rate increased was in 1958. The increase in this important public health indicator drew the prompt attention of public health officials in the United States. Potential explanations for the increase posed by health officials include a long trend among American women toward delaying motherhood, with the risk of deadly complications greater in older aged women, and increased use of fertility drugs to get pregnant, which is associated with multiple births and other high-risk pregnancies. The primary explanation for increasing U.S. life expectancy despite the infant mortality increase is the steady decreases in deaths associated with heart disease, stroke, and cancer.

After further investigation, the CDC reported that an increase in the birth of very small infants is the major explanation for the increase in U.S. infant mortality in 2002. The number of babies weighing less than 1 pound increased by almost 500 births from 2001 to 2002. The increase primarily occurred in women 20–34 years old. Although most of the increase occurred in babies born in single deliveries, approximately 3% of births were multiple births, which made up approximately 25% of the overall increase in infant mortality.

From MacDorman MF, Martin JA, Matthews TJ, Hoyert DL, Ventura SJ. Explaining the 2001–2002 infant mortality increase: Data from the linked birth/infant death data set. MMWR 2005;53(12):1–24.

TABLE 6-1   Infant Mortality Rates by Time and Region

Region	1950–1955	2005–2010	Decrease (%)
Sub-Saharan Africa	177	85	52
AFRICA	180	79	56
Eastern Africa	177	75	58
Middle Africa	182	110	39
Northern Africa	184	37	80
Southern Africa	104	55	47
Western Africa	193	89	54
ASIA	145	41	72
Eastern Asia	116	20	82
South-Central Asia	171	56	67
Central Asia	127	43	66
Southern Asia	172	56	67
South-Eastern Asia	165	27	83
Western Asia	167	29	83
EUROPE	73	7	91
Eastern Europe	91	10	89
Northern Europe	33	4	86
Southern Europe	77	5	93
Western Europe	45	4	92
LATIN AMERICA AND THE CARIBBEAN	127	22	83
Caribbean	129	35	73
Central America	129	19	85
South America	127	21	83
NORTHERN AMERICA	31	7	79
OCEANIA	60	22	64
Australia/New Zealand	25	5	81
Melanesia	143	46	68
Micronesia	103	25	76
Polynesia	98	17	82

Data from United Nations Populaton Division, World Population Prospects, the 2010 Revision.

Neonatal Mortality Rate

Neonatal (i.e., the period from birth through 27 days of life) mortality rates reflect poor prenatal care, low birth weights, infections, lack of proper medical care, injuries, premature delivery, and congenital defects. A special concern lies in the proper reporting of neonatal deaths. Some deaths in low birth weight (under 2,500 grams) infants may go unreported, and this may be even more so for very low birth weights under 1,000 grams.[11]

The **neonatal mortality rate** is calculated as follows:

$$Neonatal\ Mortality\ Rate = \frac{\begin{array}{c}Number\ of\ deaths\ from\ birth\ through\\ 27\ days\ of\ life\ in\ a\ specified\ time\ period\end{array}}{Number\ of\ live\ births\ in\ the\ same\ time\ period} \times 1,000$$

Neonatal deaths may be subdivided as early (0–7 days) or late (8–27 days).

Postneonatal Mortality Rate

The **postneonatal mortality** rate involves the number of resident newborns dying between 28 and 364 days of age. This is an important measure to track in less developed countries because the rates are influenced primarily by malnutrition and infectious diseases.

The **postneonatal mortality** rate is calculated as follows:

$$Postneonatal\ Mortality\ Rate = \frac{\begin{array}{c}Number\ of\ infant\ deaths\ between\\ 28\ and\ 364\ days\ of\ age\ in\ a\ given\ year\end{array}}{Number\ of\ live\ births\ in\ the\ same\ year} \times 1,000$$

In Figure 6-6, the infant mortality rate is presented according to neonatal and post-neonatal death according to racial groups in the United States. The rates in 1983 are compared with the rates in 2006. The decrease in neonatal mortality rates for Whites, Blacks, American Indian/Alaska Native, and Asian or Pacific Islander were 36%, 29%, 30%, and

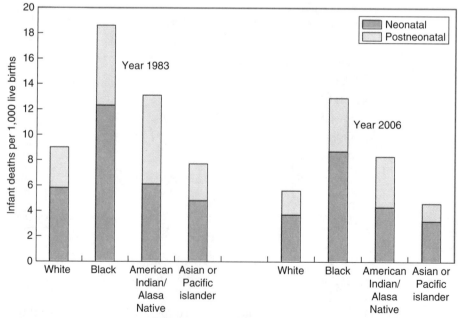

FIGURE 6-6 Neonatal and postneonatal mortality rates by racial groups in the United States, 1983 and 2006. Data from National Center for Health Statistics. *Health, United States, 2010 with Chartbook on Trends in the Health of Americans.* Hyattsville, MD: NCHS;2011, Table 15.

33%, respectively. The decrease in postneonatal mortality rates were 41%, 33%, 43%, and 52%, respectively.

Perinatal Mortality Rates

Perinatal death refers to the death of a fetus or neonate and is used to calculate the perinatal mortality rate per 1,000 births. The numerator of this measure consists of the sum of the number of fetal deaths of 28 or more weeks of gestation plus the number of newborns dying within 7 days of age in a specified geographic area. The denominator of this measure is the sum of the number of live births plus the number of fetal deaths of 28 or more weeks of gestation for the same geographic area. This rate is multiplied by 1,000. The perinatal **mortality rate** is calculated as follows:

$$\text{Perinatal Mortality Rate} = \frac{\text{Number of late fetal deaths and deaths in the first week of life}}{\text{Number of live births plus late fetal deaths}} \times 1,000$$

In the United States, the perinatal mortality rate was 32.5 per 1,000 live births plus late fetal deaths in 1950. By 1980 it dropped to 13.2 and by 2005 it further fell to 6.6.[12]

Fetal Death Rate

The **fetal death rate** is the ratio of fetal deaths divided by the sum of the births (live and still) in that year. The term *fetal death* is used synonymously with stillbirth. This is a good measure of the quality of health care in a country. The fetal death rate is calculated as follows:

$$\text{Fetal Death Rate} = \frac{\text{Number of fetal deaths after 20 weeks of gestation}}{\text{Number of live births plus fetal deaths}} \times 1,000$$

Fetal deaths result from the expulsion or extraction of the fetus from the womb. When the fetus does not breathe or show signs of life on leaving the mother's womb, it is dead. Signs of life are usually determined by breathing, a beating heart, pulsating umbilical cord, or voluntary muscle movement. The fetal death rate was developed as a measure of risk of the stages of gestation.

MATERNAL MORTALITY RATE

The World Health Organization (WHO) defines the **maternal mortality rate** as "the death of a woman while pregnant or within 42 days of termination of pregnancy, irrespective of the duration and site of the pregnancy, from any cause related to or aggravated by the pregnancy or its management but not from accidental or incidental causes."[13] This health indicator is influenced by general socioeconomic conditions; unsatisfactory health conditions related to sanitation, nutrition, and care preceding the pregnancy; incidence of the various complications of pregnancy and childbirth; and availability and utilization of healthcare facilities, including prenatal and obstetric care. Maternal mortality is viewed as a tremendous loss to society because it disrupts the lives of family members, destroys the structure of young families, cuts short the mother's life at an early age, and leaves young children without a mother.

Maternal mortality rate is calculated as follows:

$$Maternal\ Mortality\ Rate = \frac{\begin{array}{c} Number\ of\ deaths\ due\ to\ the \\ pregnancy\ state\ or\ its\ management \\ during\ a\ specified\ time\ period \end{array}}{Number\ of\ live\ births\ in\ the\ same\ time\ period} \times 100{,}000$$

This widely used measure is a general indicator of the overall health of a population. It further represents the status of women in society and the functioning of the health system. Maternal mortality estimates in 2005 were considerably higher in developing regions of the world than they were in developed regions (Table 6-2). The highest maternal mortality rate is in Africa. In sub-Saharan Africa, the lifetime risk of maternal death is 1 in 16. In contrast, in developed regions, the lifetime risk of maternal death is 1 in 2,800.

TABLE 6-2   World Estimates of Maternal Mortality in 2005

	Maternal Mortality Per 100,000 Live Births	Number of Maternal Deaths	Lifetime Risk of Maternal Death: 1 in:
World total	400	536,000	92
Developed regions*	9	960	7,300
Countries of the commonwealth of independent states†		1,800	1,200
Developing regions	450	533,000	75
Africa	820	276,000	26
Northern Africa‡	160	900	5,700
Sub-Saharan Africa	270,000	210	22
Asia	330	241,000	120
Eastern Asia	50	490	300
South central Asia	160	9,200	188,000
Southeast Asia	35,000	8,300	1,200
Western Asia	61	130	170
Latin America and the Caribbean	130	15,000	290
Oceania	430	890	62

*Albania, Australia, Austria, Belgium, Bosnia and Herzegovina, Bulgaria, Canada, Croatia, Czech Republic, Denmark, Estonia, Finland, France, Germany, Greece, Hungary, Iceland, Ireland, Italy, Japan, Latvia, Lithuania, Luxembourg, Malta, Netherlands, New Zealand, Norway, Poland, Portugal, Romania, Serbia and Montenegro, Slovakia, Slovenia, Spain, Sweden, Switzerland, The former Yugoslav Republic of Macedonia, the United Kingdom, and the United States.

†Armenia, Azerbaijan, Belarus, Georgia, Kazakhstan, Kyrgyzstan, Tajikistan, Turkmenistan, Uzbekistan, the Republic of Moldova, the Russian Federation, and Ukraine.

‡Excludes Sudan, which is included in sub-Saharan Africa.

Modified from Maternal mortality in 2005: Estimates developed by WHO, UNICEF, and UNFPA. Available at: http://www.who.int/whosis/mme_2005.pdf. Accessed November 30, 2008.

PROPORTIONAL MORTALITY RATIO

The **proportional mortality ratio** (PMR) is a ratio of the number of deaths attributed to a specific cause to the total number of deaths occurring in the population during the same time period. It indicates the burden of a given cause of death relative to all deaths; that is, the PMR can be useful in determining, within a given subgroup or population, the extent to which a specific cause of death contributes to the overall mortality. The PMR is calculated as follows.

$$PMR = \frac{\text{Number of deaths from a specified cause during a specified time period}}{\text{Number of deaths in the same time period}} \times 100$$

Caution is needed when using the PMR, especially if used to compare differences between different groups or time periods. If different populations have varying causes of disease that lead to death and if mortality rates are compared with the PMR, it can provide distorted findings. The PMR is not a measure of risk or of probability of dying from a specific cause within a group. Comparing percentages is always risky, and this is true for the PMR. Rates are more accurate means of comparison than proportions.[11,14] Here is an example of a PMR.

1. Two cities each had a population of 1,000,000.
2. Death rate from all causes in Metro City was 400 or 40 per 100,000.
3. Death rate from all causes in Suburban City was 900 or 90 per 100,000.
4. Cancer deaths in both cities were 4 per 100,000 or 40 deaths per city. Risk of a cancer-caused death for both cities was the same.
5. Percentage of all deaths from cancer is the proportionate mortality ratio. For each city the PMR was:

$$Metro\ City = \frac{40}{400} \times 100 = 10\%$$

$$Suburban\ City = \frac{40}{900} \times 100 = 4.4\%$$

The PMR fails to reflect the risk of cancer death in these two cities, even though the actual numbers are the same. Deaths from all causes are different.

DEATH-TO-CASE RATIO

The **death-to-case ratio** is the number of deaths attributed to a particular disease during a specified time period divided by the number of new cases of that disease during the same time period. One function of the death-to-case ratio is to measure the various aspects or properties of a disease such as its pathogenicity, severity, or virulence.

In the past, the death-to-case ratio was used more for studying acute infectious diseases. However, it can also be used in poisonings, chemical exposures, or other short-term deaths not caused by disease. This measure has had limited usefulness with chronic diseases because the time of onset may be hard to determine and the time from diagnosis to death is longer. The number of deaths that occur in a current time period may have little relationship to the number of new cases that occur. Prevention and control measures may already be in place for new cases, but long-term and past exposed cases may still die. Whenever the death-to-case ratio is used, it is good to make a statement regarding the time element.

The death-to-case ratio is calculated as follows:

$$Death\text{-}to\text{-}Case\ Ratio = \frac{\begin{array}{c} Number\ of\ deaths\ attributed\ to\ a\ particular \\ disease\ during\ a\ specified\ time\ period \end{array}}{\begin{array}{c} The\ number\ of\ new\ cases\ of\ that\ disease \\ identified\ during\ the\ same\ time\ period \end{array}} \times 100$$

For example, in Connecticut, 2008, the death-to-case ratio of pancreatic cancer was 89% (477/537 × 100).[15]

Do not confuse this measure with the **case-fatality rate**, which is the proportion of persons with a particular condition (cases) who die from that condition. The denominator is the number of incident cases and the numerator is the number of cause-specific deaths among those cases. In a study conducted in April, 2003, the case-fatality rate of severe acute respiratory syndrome (SARS) was 13.2% for patients younger than 60 years and 43.4% for patients 60 years and older. Although patient outcome was strongly associated with age, the time between the onset of symptoms and admission to the hospital did not influence the outcome.[16]

YEARS OF POTENTIAL LIFE LOST

Years of potential life lost (YPLL) is a measure of the relative impact of various health-related states or events on a population. It identifies the loss of expected years of life because of premature death in the population. Death due to causes that tend to affect younger people (e.g., homicide) will result in more years of life lost than deaths that predominately affect older people (e.g., cancer). Improvements in life expectancy can cause an increase in the available work force, which, in turn, benefits society by increasing productivity. A 20-year-old male who dies in an automobile accident caused by drinking and driving could theoretically have lived to average life expectancy of 76 years of age; thus, 56 years of life are lost. When 1,000 deaths like this occur in a given population, 56,000 years of potential life are lost.

Some sources calculate YPLL based on the retirement age of 65 years because this concept can be seen from a strictly economic point of view. However, the social and humane aspects need to be considered. Thus, the average life expectancy rather than age of retirement may be more appropriate. Questions such as, "What is life worth?" are often raised. The losses to society in the cost of training, labor, and tax dollars not paid are often considered. The value of human life is an underlying goal of public health, as are economic factors, because both issues have far-reaching societal implications.[17]

The formula for computation is:

$$YPLL = \sum (endpoint - age\ at\ death\ before\ endpoint)$$

where the endpoint is generally predetermined at the age of 65 years or at the average life expectancy in the population. For example, suppose five workers die because of exposure to a toxic chemical. Further suppose that their ages are 20, 25, 30, 35, and 40 years. Then, the YPLL is

$$YPLL = (65 - 20) + (65 - 25) + (65 - 30) + (65 - 35) + (65 - 40) = 175$$

The average YPLL is 35 (175/5).

For data that is available by age group, the formula is modified, as follows:

$$YPLL = \sum_i (endpoint - midpoint\ of\ age\ group\ before\ endpoint) \times (death\ in\ age\ group)$$

For example, suppose we want to know the YPLL for the age group 0–4 and there were 1,000 deaths in that age group. Then,

$$YPLL = (65 - 2.5) \times 1,000 = 62,500$$

If we wanted to know the YPLL for the age groups 0–4 and 5–9, and the number of deaths in the two age groups were 1,000 and 750, respectively, then

$$YPLL = (65 - 2.5) \times 1,000 + (65 - 7.5) \times 750 = 62,500 + 43,125 = 105,625$$

The total YPLL would involve all age groups prior to age 65. The midpoint for each age group is derived as

$$Age\ Group\ Midpoint = \frac{Minimum\ Age + Maximum\ Age + 1}{2}$$

To illustrate, consider the data in Table 6-3. Use an endpoint age of 65 years. Next, calculate the midpoint age for each age group up to the age group just prior to the age of 65 years. The years to 65 are obtained by subtracting each midpoint age from 65. This represents the years of life lost on average for a person who dies in the specific age group. Then the values in this column are multiplied by the actual number of deaths in that age group to get the age-specific YPLL. The sum of all the age-specific YPLL equals the total YPLL.

If we were to calculate the age-group rates for suicide and self-inflicted injury, we would see that they tend to increase with age. However, because YPLL takes into account the burden of premature death, the greatest YPLL value is in the age group 20–24. The total YPLL because of suicide and self-inflicted injuries is 559,940.

Suppose we were interested in comparing the burden of premature death because of suicide and self-inflicted injury between white and black males in the United States, 2008. YPLL is 489,373 for whites and 47,928 for blacks. However, to make a meaningful comparison of the burden of premature death because of suicide and self-inflicted injury between white and black males, we need to take into account the respective population sizes. The **YPLL rate** is derived by dividing the years of potential life lost by the number in the population upon which the YPLL is derived. The male population through age 64 is 107,135,809 for whites and 18,072,194 for blacks. It follows that the YPLL rates are 457 per 100,000 white males and 265 per 100,000 black males. The ratio of these two rates indicates that the YPPL rate of suicide and self-inflicted injury for white males is 1.72 times (or 72%) greater than for black males.

A concept related to YPLL is that of quality-adjusted life years. This is an indicator of well-being that measures mental, physical, and social functioning. It combines both mortality and morbidity and is sensitive to changes in health among both the well and the ill. By multiplying the measure of well-being by the number of years of life remaining at each age interval, an estimate of the years of healthy life for a population can be determined. The calculation of years of healthy life uses life tables and the average number of years of life remaining at the beginning of each age interval. Age-specific estimates of the well-being of a population compared with the population of the life table are also needed. As life expectancy increases, the tradeoffs between quantity and quality of life become more and more critical. Years of healthy life is an important indicator for populations and must be considered in policy and public health administration activities.[18]

TABLE 6-3   Deaths for Males Attributed to Suicide and Self-Inflicted Injury by Age Group, United States, 2008

Age Group (years)	Midpoint (age)	Years to 65	Number of Deaths	Population	Age-Specific YPLL	Cumulative YPLL
0–4	2.5	62.5	0	10,812,678	0	559,940
5–9	7.5	57.5	0	10,385,399	0	559,940
10–14	12.5	52.5	149	10,291,328	7,823	559,940
15–19	17.5	47.5	1,284	11,099,142	60,990	552,118
20–24	22.5	42.5	2,276	10,991,507	96,730	491,128
25–29	27.5	37.5	2,199	10,968,203	82,463	394,398
30–34	32.5	32.5	2,074	9,909,250	67,405	311,935
35–59	37.5	27.5	2,432	10,499,232	66,880	244,530
40–44	42.5	22.5	2,693	10,685,853	60,593	177,650
45–49	47.5	17.5	3,205	11,273,331	56,088	117,058
50–54	52.5	12.5	3,041	10,508,167	38,013	60,970
55–59	57.5	7.5	2,469	8,992,512	18,518	22,958
60–64	62.5	2.5	1,776	7,222,614	4,440	4,440
65–69	-	-	1,268	5,296,952		
70–74	-	-	1,045	3,980,911		
75–79	-	-	954	3,165,098		
80–84	-	-	862	2,280,721		
85+	-	-	715	1,711,328		

Data are from the National Center for Health Statistics. Available at: www.cdc.gov/nchs.

CONCLUSION

Health indicators are useful in that they describe health status and provide a comparison with health-related policy, program, and service goals. When health indicators are reported according to person, place, and time variables, it is possible to better understand who is at greatest risk and how they have become more susceptible to the health problem. Health indicators are useful for characterizing the health problem, which leads to the research question and formulation of hypotheses. An appropriate analytic study design is then selected for assessing the research hypothesis.

EXERCISES

Key Terms

Define the following terms.

Birth rate	Infant mortality rate
Case-fatality rate	Maternal mortality rate
Cause-specific mortality rate	Mortality
Contraceptive prevalence	Neonatal mortality rate
Crude mortality rate	Perinatal mortality rate
Death certificate	Postneonatal mortality rate
Death-to-case ratio	Proportionate mortality ratio
Fertility rate	Total fertility rate
Fetal death rate	Years of potential life lost (YPLL)
Health indicator	YPLL rate

STUDY QUESTIONS

1. Refer to the following estimated statistics for the United States and Malaysia in 2005.

    United States

   Crude mortality rate = 800 per 100,000

   Crude birth rate = 14 per 1,000

   Life expectancy = 77.7 years

    Malaysia

   Crude mortality rate = 500 per 100,000

   Crude birth rate = 23 per 1,000

   Life expectancy = 72.2 years

    Can the lower crude mortality rate in Malaysia be explained by the fact that the United States has a larger population? What factors could explain differences in birth rates and life expectancy?

2. Table 6-4 gives the mortality statistics for a fictitious county in a rural state for the period from July 1–June 30 (1 year). After reviewing the health status indicators and mortality data, calculate the following mortality rates.

    a. Crude mortality rate

    b. Maternal mortality rate

    c. Infant mortality rate

    d. Neonatal mortality rate

    e. Fetal death rate

  f. Fertility rate

  g. Age-specific mortality rate for persons ages 55 years or older

  h. Cause-specific mortality rate for those who died from heart disease

  i. Cause-specific mortality rate for those who died from stroke

  j. PMR for cancer among persons ages 55 years or older

  k. Postneonatal mortality rate

3. Suppose in a given region in 2012 there were 500 fetal deaths with 28 or more weeks of gestation and 200 newborns dying within the first 7 days of life. The number of live births was 150,000. What is the perinatal mortality rate?

4. Two cities each had a population of 1,000,000. The death rate from all causes in Desert City was 500 or 50 per 100,000. The death rate from all causes in Sun City was 800 or 80 per 100,000. Cancer deaths in both cities were 4 per 100,000 or 40 deaths per city. The risk of cancer-caused death for both cities was the same. Calculate the PMR for cancer in each city.

5. Infant mortality and maternal mortality are two of the most commonly used health status indicators. Why?

For questions 6 through 10 refer to Table 6-5.

TABLE 6-4   Selected Statistics for a Hypothetical Population, July 1 to June 30

Total 1-year population	160,000
Population of women 15–49 years of age	40,000
Population of 55 years of age and older	44,000
Number of live births	3,300
Number of fetal deaths	66
Number of maternal deaths	5
Total deaths	1,444
Number of infant deaths 0-1 years of age	88
Number of deaths under 28 days old	4
Number of deaths between 28 days and 1 year	8
Number of deaths of persons 55 years and older	848
Number one cause of death in the county is heart disease—deaths from heart disease	133
Number two cause of death in the county is from cancer—deaths from cancer	66
Number three cause of death in the county is from cerebrovascular accident (stroke)	56
Number four cause of death in the county is accidents	45
Number of deaths from cancer age 55 years and older	44
Number of persons diagnosed with heart disease	5,600
Number of deaths from other causes	504
Number of persons diagnosed with high blood pressure, arteriosclerosis, and atherosclerosis (precursors for a stroke)	1,200

TABLE 6-5   Deaths Attributed to Suicide and Self-Inflicted Injuries for White and Black Males in the United States, 2008

	Whites		Blacks	
	Deaths	**Population**	**Deaths**	**Population**
0–4	0	8,305,643	0	1,739,648
5–9	0	8,079,129	0	1,618,841
10–14	118	7,992,228	20	1,662,938
15–19	1050	8,603,214	156	1,832,569
20–24	1889	8,640,136	269	1,665,660
25–29	1871	8,647,489	226	1,555,131
30–34	1791	7,844,099	197	1,292,257
35–39	2177	8,400,242	165	1,320,645
40–44	2458	8,679,863	162	1,320,955
45–49	2984	9,313,579	151	1,326,423
50–54	2846	8,784,457	123	1,168,570
55–59	2330	7,608,166	87	924,898
60–64	1683	6,237,564	57	643,659
65–69	1191	4,597,749	43	453,109
70–74	972	3,456,506	44	344,704
75–79	914	2,795,099	27	246,490
80–84	831	2,045,516	18	155,026
85+	691	1,551,927	11	96,135

Data are from the National Center for Health Statistics. Available at: www.cdc.gov/nchs.

6. Calculate the crude mortality rate of suicide and self-inflicted injury for white and black males.

7. Calculate and graph the age-specific mortality rates of suicide and self-inflicted injury for white and black males. Describe.

8. Calculate the age-group specific YPLL for both white and black males. In what age group is the YPLL greatest?

9. Calculate the cumulative YPLL for both white and black males.

10. Calculate the total YPLL rates for white and black males.

11. Graph the age-group specific YPLL rates for white and black males. Describe.

12. Why might the YPLL rate be preferred to the YPLL?

REFERENCES

1. U.S. Census Bureau. International Programs. International Data Base. http://www.census.gov/population/international/data/idb/worldpoptotal.php. Accessed January 12, 2012.

2. U.S. Census Bureau. International Programs. International Data Base. http://www.census.gov/population/international/data/idb/worldvitalevents.php. Accessed January 12, 2012.

3. Population Reference Bureau (World Population Data Sheet) United Nations Population Division. http://www.nationsonline.org/oneworld/world_population.htm. Accessed January 13, 2012.

4. World Health Organization. Reproductive health indicators: guidelines for their generation, interpretation and analysis for global monitoring. Reproductive Health and Research, 2006. http://whqlibdoc.who.int/publications/2006/924156315X_eng.pdf. Accessed January 13, 2012.

5. Central Intelligence Agency. The World Factbook. Total Fertility Rate. https://www.cia.gov/library/publications/the-world-factbook/rankorder/2127rank.html. Accessed January 13, 2012.

6. United Nations. Department of Economic and Social Affairs. Population Division. World Contraceptive Use. http://www.un.org/esa/population/publications/contraceptive2011/wallchart_front.pdf. Accessed January 13, 2012.

7. Weeks JR. Population, 2nd ed. Belmont, CA: Wadsworth; 1981.

8. World Health Organization. International Statistical Classification of Diseases, Tenth Revision, Clinical Modification (ICD-10-CM). http://www.cdc.gov/nchs/icd/icd10cm.htm#10update. Accessed April 21, 2012.

9. Golding J, Emmett PM, Rogers IS. Breast feeding and infant mortality. *Early Hum Dev.* 1997; 49 (Suppl):S143–S155.

10. Centers for Disease Control and Prevention. Ten great public health achievements—United States, 1900–1999. *MMWR.* 1999; 48:1141–1143.

11. Fox JP, Hall CE, Elveback LR. *Epidemiology: Man and Disease.* New York, NY: Macmillan; 1970.

12. National Center for Health Statistics. *Health, United States, 2009: With Special Feature on Medical Technology.* Hyattsville, MD;2010, Table 19.

13. World Health Organization. Maternal mortality ratio (per 100,000 live births). http://www.who.int/healthinfo/statistics/indmaternalmortality/en/index.html. Accessed January 14, 2012.

14. Lilienfeld AM, Lilienfeld DE. *Foundations of Epidemiology.* New York, NY: Oxford University Press; 1980.

15. Surveillance, Epidemiology, and End Results (SEER) Program (http://www.seer.cancer.gov). SEER*Stat Database: Mortality— All COD, Aggregated With State, Total U.S. (1969–2008) <Katrina/Rita Population Adjustment>, National Cancer Institute, DCCPS, Surveillance Research Program, Cancer Statistics Branch, released September 2011. Underlying mortality data provided by NCHS (http://www.cdc.gov/nchs).

16. Donnelly CA, Ghani AC, Leung GM, et al. Epidemiological determinants of spread of causal agent of severe acute respiratory syndrome in Hong Kong. *Lancet.* 2003;361:1761–1766.

17. Pickett G, Hanlon JJ. *Public Health: Administration and Practice.* St. Louis: Times Mirror/Mosby; 1990.

18. U.S. Department of Health and Human Services. *Healthy People 2010: Understanding and Improving Health*, 2nd ed. Washington, DC: US Government Printing Office; 2000.

7

Design Strategies and Statistical Methods in Analytic Epidemiology

OBJECTIVES

After completing this chapter, you will be able to:

- Define analytic epidemiology.
- Distinguish between observational and experimental analytic epidemiologic studies.
- Define case-control and cohort studies, and identify their distinctive features, strengths, and weaknesses.
- Identify appropriate measures of association in case-control and cohort studies.
- Identify common measures used in epidemiology for describing cohort data.
- Identify potential biases in case-control and cohort studies.
- Identify ways to control for biases in case-control and cohort studies at the design and analysis levels.
- Distinguish between effect modification and confounding.

The two general areas of epidemiologic study are descriptive and analytic. Descriptive epidemiologic studies attempt to answer who, what, when, and where questions. We have focused on descriptive epidemiology in the last three chapters. On the other hand, analytic epidemiologic studies attempt to answer questions involving how and why. **Analytic studies** evaluate one or more predetermined hypotheses about associations between exposure and outcome variables. These studies make use of a comparison group. In this chapter the focus is on observational analytic design strategies and statistical methods where the researcher merely observes associations between exposure and outcome variables that have a potential etiologic connection. Observational analytic study designs are important for those exposures that cannot be ethically assigned (e.g., subjecting study participants to cigarette smoking, surgery, or radiation).

OBSERVATIONAL ANALYTIC STUDIES

Four types of analytic studies and their strengths and weaknesses are summarized in Table 7-1. Presentation of each of these study designs is covered in this chapter. These studies can be exploratory (no specific a priori hypothesis) or analytic (specific a priori hypothesis). In an **observational exploratory study** a variety of associations are examined. Such studies are useful for identifying clues as to cause-effect relationships. In an **observational analytic study** evaluation of associations between exposure and outcome variables begins with a specific a priori hypothesis.

CASE-CONTROL STUDY DESIGN

Case-control studies originated in the 1920s, and today are commonly used in epidemiologic research.[1,2] This study design allows researchers to both evaluate diseases with long

TABLE 7-1   Description, Strengths, and Weaknesses of Observational Analytic Study Designs

	Description	Strengths	Weaknesses
Case-control	Presence of risk factor(s) for people with a condition is compared with that for people who do not.	■ Effective for rare outcomes ■ Compared with the cohort study, requires less time, money, and size ■ Yields the odds ratio (when the outcome condition is rare, a good estimate of the relative risk)	■ Limited to one outcome condition ■ Does not provide incidence, relative risk, or natural history ■ Less effective than a cohort study at establishing time sequence of events ■ Potential recall and interviewer bias ■ Potential survival bias ■ Does not yield incidence or prevalence
Case-crossover	Exposure frequency during a window immediately prior to an outcome event is compared with exposure frequencies during a control time or times at an earlier period.	■ Controls for fixed individual characteristics that may otherwise confound the association ■ Effective at studying the effects of short-term exposures on the risk of acute events	■ Does not automatically control for confounding from time-related factors

(continues)

TABLE 7-1   Description, Strengths, and Weaknesses of Observational Analytic Study Designs
(continued)

	Description	Strengths	Weaknesses
Nested case-control	A case-control study conducted within a cohort study. To carry out a nested case-control study, samples or records of interest must be available from before the outcome condition occurred.	■ Has the scientific benefits of a cohort design ■ Less expensive to conduct than cohort studies ■ Smaller sample size required than a cohort study ■ Less prone to recall bias than a case-control study	■ Non-diseased persons from whom the controls are selected may not be representative of the original cohort because of death or loss to follow-up among cases
Cohort	People are followed over time to describe the incidence or the natural history of a condition. Assessment can also be made of risk factors for various conditions.	■ Establishes time sequence of events ■ Avoids bias in measuring exposure from knowing the outcome ■ Avoid Berkson's bias and prevalence–incidence bias ■ Several outcomes can be assessed ■ Number of outcomes grows over time ■ Allows assessment of incidence and the natural history of disease ■ Yield incidence, relative risk, attributable risk	■ Large samples often required ■ May not be feasible in terms of time and money ■ Not feasible with rare outcomes ■ Limited to one risk factor ■ Potential bias caused by loss to follow-up

latency periods and evaluate one or more exposure variables associated with a given outcome. Other names for case-control studies that appear in the literature are case-comparison studies and case-referent studies. A **case-control study** involves grouping people as cases (persons experiencing a health-related state or event) and controls and investigating whether the cases are more or less likely than the controls to have had past experiences, lifestyle behaviors, or exposures. In other words, what is it about their past that made them cases? The outcome is always identified before the exposure. Because a case-control study begins with the outcome and looks back at an antecedent variable or variables, it is retrospective in nature. *Retro spicere* means "to look back." Other epidemiologic studies can also be retrospective in nature, which are discussed later in this chapter.

Selection of Cases

Establishing the diagnostic criteria and definition of disease is the first step in conducting a case-control study. A strict diagnostic criterion for the disease will ensure that cases reflect as homogeneous a disease entity as possible. Hennekens and Buring[3] refer to the situation before the 1940s when the definition of uterine cancer comprised two diseases (of the corpus uteri and uterine cervix) with very different risk factors. Low numbers of sexual partners and high socioeconomic status have been associated with uterine cancer, and a high number of sexual partners and low socioeconomic status have been associated with cervical cancer. Hence, a case-control study attempting to identify the association between number of sexual partners and socioeconomic status with uterine cancer might find no association.

Cases may consist of new cases (incidence) that show selected characteristics during a specific time period in a specified population and a particular area. Cases may also consist of existing cases at a point in time (prevalence). With prevalence data, it may be more difficult to link a specific cause with a disease outcome because it is influenced by both the development and duration of disease. For example, suppose researchers were interested in assessing whether an association existed between exercise and the prevalence of arthritis. It may be that exercise patterns before the development of arthritis are much different than after the onset of symptoms; thus, the timing of when the exposure was evaluated could have a large impact on the association. For this reason, whenever possible, incident cases are preferred to prevalent cases in case-control studies.

Sources for cases can come from records from public health clinics, physician offices, health maintenance organizations, hospitals, and industrial and government sources. Cases should be representative of all persons with the disease. In some situations, all persons with the disease may be included in the study. It is more common, however, that cases come from sampled data. In order for the sampled data to reflect the population of interest, random selection is required. An adequately large random selection of cases from a population of interest ensures that the results of the study can be appropriately generalized. In some situations, researchers may use **restriction**, which involves limiting subjects in a study to those with certain characteristics, such as black males in Atlanta aged 40–59 years in order to reduce potential biases and to increase feasibility. Although restriction may limit generalization, it may be necessary in order to ensure a valid study. Conducting a valid study with definitive results should always be the primary goal of any epidemiologist.

Selection of Controls

To better ensure that a case-control study is valid and reliable, the control subjects should look like the case subjects with the exception of not having the disease. This means that controls need to be selected from the same population from which the cases were drawn. An epidemiologic assumption is that controls are representative of the general population in terms of probability of exposure and that controls have the same possibility of being selected or exposed as the cases. Controls drawn from a population of the same area or populace of the cases should reflect the same gender, age, and other significant factors. Controls from a general population are assumed to be normal and healthy and to reflect the well population from the area.

Sampling of controls from a general population for large studies is an expensive endeavor and thus is not always realistic or possible. Controls are typically drawn from the same hospital or general population as the cases. They may also be drawn from the family, friends, or relatives of the cases. Some advantages and disadvantages of these types of controls are presented in Table 7-2. In some circumstances, it may be useful to select more than one control group to see whether the selection of controls influences the measured association between exposure and outcome variables. It may also be useful to collect more controls than cases when only a limited number of cases are available, which can provide a sufficient sample size to carry out hypothesis testing. The ratio of cases to controls should not exceed 1:4.[4] Controls can be randomly selected from a larger population when the entire population of eligible controls is known. Selection of controls can also be made systematically (i.e., every nth person listed), assuming that the order of potential controls is not related to factors such as age, gender, and education.

Exposure Status

After the cases and controls have been identified, ascertainment of exposure status is performed. Information about exposure status can be obtained through medical records,

TABLE 7-2   Advantages and Disadvantages of Controls from Hospitals, the General Population, and Special Groups

Controls	Advantages	Disadvantages
Hospital	▪ Easily identified, sufficient number, low cost ▪ Subjects more likely aware of antecedent events or exposures ▪ Selection factors that influence decision to come to a particular hospital similar to those for cases ▪ More likely to cooperate, thereby minimizing potential bias from nonresponse	▪ Differ from healthy people such that they do not accurately represent the exposure distribution in the population where cases were obtained
General population	▪ Represent the population from which cases were selected	▪ More costly and time consuming than hospital controls ▪ Population lists might not be available ▪ May be difficult to contact healthy people with busy work and leisure schedules ▪ May have poorer recall than hospital controls ▪ Less motivated to participate than controls from the hospital or special groups
Special groups (e.g., family, relatives, friends)	▪ Healthier than hospital controls ▪ More likely to cooperate than people in the general population ▪ Provide more control over possible confounding factors	▪ If the exposure is similar to the one experienced by cases, an underestimation of the true association would result

Adapted from Hennekens CH, Buring JE. *Epidemiology in Medicine*. Boston: Little, Brown and Company, 1987.

interviews, questionnaires, or surrogates such as spouses, siblings, or employers. Information on exposure status should be collected in a similar manner between cases and controls in order to avoid bias. Blinding interviewers or those assessing medical records as to who the cases are and who the controls are may further minimize bias. It is also preferable to blind those performing the assessment to the hypothesis of the study because such knowledge could influence how they probe or scan records for information.[3]

Because bias can result in studies where the results are based on individual recall, exposure information from medical records is always preferable, when available. For example, researchers interested in assessing the association between chest radiographs during adolescence and female breast cancer should use medical records indicating whether chest radiographs were performed rather than relying on the recall of the study participants, assuming the records exist. It is possible that if the study is based on recall, women with breast cancer would have better recall of having had chest radiographs than women without breast cancer, thereby biasing the results.

The time window on which exposure status in relation to the outcome is determined is critical in case-control studies. This should be influenced by current understanding of the potential causal factors associated with the disease. Is a lifetime duration of smoking (number of years smoked) more important than current smoking for selected disease outcomes? With many forms of smoking-related cancers, the lifetime duration of smoking appears to be more important than current smoking. The level of smoking is also likely to be important. Hence, an exposure variable that captures the duration and intensity of smoking may be much more informative. On the other hand, current smoking has been associated with myocardial infarction.

When limited information of the mechanisms of disease is available, exploring different combinations of the level and duration of exposure is suggested.

ODDS RATIO IN CASE-CONTROL STUDIES

A commonly used measure of the relative probabilities of disease in case-control studies is the **odds ratio** (also called the relative odds). The odds ratio is appropriate for measuring the strength of the association between exposure and disease variables in case-control studies, whereas the risk ratio (also called the relative risk) and the rate ratio are appropriate for measuring the association in cohort studies.

Consider the following 2×2 contingency table. This table is commonly used in epidemiology to summarize the relationship between exposure and health outcome variables (Table 7-3). The letters in the table represent numbers that would actually be present in an epidemiologic study.

The odds ratio (OR) compares the odds of the disease among exposed individuals divided by the odds of disease among unexposed individuals.

TABLE 7-3 2×2 Table

	Cases	Controls	Total
Exposed	a	b	$a + b$
Not Exposed	c	d	$c + d$
Total	$a + c$	$b + d$	$n = a + b + c + d$

$$OR = \frac{a/b}{c/d} = \frac{a \times d}{b \times c}$$

If the odds ratio equals 1, this indicates no association between exposure and disease; if the odds ratio is greater than 1, this indicates a positive association between exposure and disease; and if the odds ratio is less than 1, this indicates a negative association between exposure and disease. The odds ratio can range from 0 to infinity. The odds ratio has nice mathematical properties that make its use attractive to researchers, one of which is the ability to calculate odds ratios with the use of logistic regression.

BIAS IN CASE-CONTROL STUDIES

Bias is defined as systematic error in the collection or interpretation of epidemiologic data. Bias results in inaccurate overestimation or underestimation of the association between exposure and disease. Avoiding bias at the design stage of a study is paramount because of the difficulty of identifying and accounting for it thereafter. Certain potential biases that require consideration as possible explanations for deviations of the results from the truth include selection bias, recall bias, and confounding.

Selection Bias

In case-control studies, **selection bias** refers to the selection of cases and controls for a study that is based in some way on the exposure.[3] With selection bias, the relationship between exposure and disease among participants in the study differs from what the relationship would have been among individuals in the population of interest. Recruiting all cases in a population avoids selection bias.

For example, suppose researchers were interested in assessing the association between postmenopausal hormone use and uterine cancer. What if estrogen use was associated with uterine bleeding such that women taking estrogen were more likely to undergo a physician examination? Refer to Table 7-3, the 2 × 2 table, and let uterine cancer cases and hormone use represent those exposed. In this example, c would be too small, and d would be too big, given the lower examination levels for nonhormone-replacement users. This would cause the odds ratio to be biased upward. The literature does indicate that some, but not all, of the strong positive association observed between hormone use and uterine cancer in case-control studies in the 1970s was explained by selection bias.[5–8]

Hospital-based case-control studies are prone to selection bias. Consider a hospital-based case-control study assessing the strength of the association between smoking and respiratory diseases. Selecting controls from the hospital will likely underestimate the association between smoking and respiratory diseases because patients with nonrespiratory diseases in the hospital are more likely to be smokers than the general population. Considering the formula for the odds ratio, b would be too big and d would be too small, making the odds ratio biased downward. Hospital-patient selection bias has also been called **Berkson's bias**,[9] named after Dr. Joseph Berkson who described it in the 1940s. Randomization minimizes this potential bias in experimental studies.

Prevalence-incidence bias, also called **Neyman's bias**, is a form of selection bias in case-control studies attributed to selective survival among the prevalent cases (i.e., mild, clinically resolved, or fatal cases being excluded from the case group).[10,11] This is not a common form of bias in cohort or experimental studies, but it is common in case-control studies based on prevalence data. For example, if cases with coronary artery disease die rapidly, persons available for study are not the more severe cases. The association between serum cholesterol (high vs. low) and coronary artery disease will be underestimated.

Observation Bias

Observation bias can result from differential accuracy of recall between cases and controls (**recall bias**) or because of differential accuracy of exposure information because an interviewer probes cases differently than he or she does controls (**interviewer bias**). Recall that bias can occur because cases have spent more time pondering why they became cases and consequently have better recall of their exposure status than do individuals who are controls (recall bias). For example, a woman with a child that has neurologic problems may better recall the flu and high temperature she had during pregnancy than would women who do not have a child with a neurologic problem. Similarly, an interviewer who believes there is an association between the flu during pregnancy and having a child with neurologic problems may probe the cases and the controls differently (interviewer bias). This is an argument for blinding the interviewer as to which subjects are cases and which are controls. It also supports the use of medical records for data, if they exist, instead of self-reported information. The odds ratio in this example would be too large, because although a and c might be accurate, b might be too small and d too large.

Misclassification

Misclassification occurs when either exposure or disease status is inaccurately assigned. Almost all studies experience some level of this type of bias. For example, suppose we are interested in measuring the association between hypertension and stroke in a case-control study. If classification of a history of hypertension is accurate in 90% of cases and 90% of controls, wherein the level of misclassification is the same between cases and controls, this is referred to as **nondifferential** (also called **random**) **misclassification.** On the other hand, if classification of a history of hypertension is accurate in 90% of cases and 100% of controls, this is referred to as **differential** (or also called **nonrandom**) **misclassification.** Selection bias or observation bias in case-control studies result in **nonrandom misclassification.** Nonrandom misclassification may result in overestimation or underestimation of the true association. In the prior example, it depends on how the 10% were misclassified. If they all had a history of hypertension but were classified as not having a history of hypertension, then the odds ratio measuring the association between hypertension and stroke would be underestimated. On the other hand, if the 10% of stroke cases were incorrectly classified as having a history of hypertension, then the odds ratio would be overestimated.

Random misclassification in a case-control study will always result in an underestimated odds ratio. Thus, an observed association influenced by this type of misclassification will not be spurious. However, substantial random misclassification can lead to an incorrect conclusion of no association.

Confounding

Confounding occurs when an extrinsic factor is associated with a disease outcome, and independent of that association is also linked with the exposure. Several variables are routinely considered as potential confounders in epidemiologic research, such as age, gender, educational level, and smoking. Suppose the researcher was interested in the association between exercise and heart disease. Failure to control for age, which is generally lower in those who exercise and higher in those with heart disease, may make exercise appear more protective against heart disease than it really is.

Newman, Browner, and Hulley presented a hypothetical example of confounding involving an assessment of the association between coffee drinking and myocardial infarction.[12] To begin, consider the following data:

	Myocardial Infarction	No Myocardial Infarction
Coffee	90	60
No coffee	60	90

$OR = \dfrac{90 \times 90}{60 \times 60} = 2.25$ for the association between coffee and myocardial infarction. However, if the data are stratified by smoking status, the data appear differently.

	Smokers		Nonsmokers	
	Myocardial Infarction	No Myocardial Infarction	Myocardial Infarction	No Myocardial Infarction
Coffee	80	40	10	20
No coffee	20	10	40	80

$OR = \dfrac{80 \times 10}{20 \times 40} = 1$ among smokers, and $OR = \dfrac{10 \times 80}{40 \times 20} = 1$ among nonsmokers.

The difference between the crude odds ratio and the stratified odds ratio quantifies the magnitude of confounding. With a little rearranging of numbers and combining the data in this table, it appears that smoking is associated with coffee (i.e., $OR = 16$) and that smoking is also associated with myocardial infarction (i.e., $OR = 4$).

CONTROLLING FOR BIAS IN CASE-CONTROL STUDIES

Because the potential for bias is always present in observational epidemiologic studies, researchers should address how they dealt with this in writing up their studies. Selection and observation bias are best controlled for at the design level. Selection bias can be minimized by considering incident cases and general population controls. Observation bias is best controlled for by blinding subjects, interviewers, and persons assessing the data. Confounding can be minimized by restriction and matching. On the analysis level, it can also be controlled for through stratification or multiple-regression analysis.

As mentioned previously, a confounder must be associated with the outcome and, independent of that relation, associated with the exposure. To avoid confounding, the level of the potential confounding variable can be restricted such that there is no longer an association between the exposure and the confounding variable. For example, if age and gender are potential confounders of the association between exercise and heart disease, the assessment could be restricted to include only men in their 50s. Although restriction is a simple and convenient way to control for confounding, it reduces the number of subjects eligible for the study, limits the ability to generalize results, and makes it impossible to evaluate whether an association varies across the levels of the confounding factor.

Matching is a strategy for controlling confounding at the design level of a study. However, the analysis level of a study must take into account matching by applying special measures of assessment. In the example assessing the association between exercise and heart disease, a control of a similar age and gender could be selected for each case in order to control for the potential confounding effects of these factors. As a result, the distribution of the confounding factors is forced to be similar between the cases and controls.

Matching controls to cases for confounding factors causes these two groups to be more alike with respect to the factors than if the cases and controls were not matched. For matched variables on true confounders, the cases and controls will have more similar exposure status than would otherwise be true. Failure to take this into account in the analysis will result in underestimation of the true association. The purpose of the matching is to ensure sufficient statistical power to analyze associations and control for confounding. Specific analysis techniques are then used.[3] For a matched-paired case-control study, the odds ratio is modified as follows:

$$OR = \frac{b}{c}$$

It is possible, if data on the potential confounding factors are collected at the design level of the study, to adjust for confounding at the analysis level of a study. This can be done by stratification and multiple-regression analysis. Stratification eliminates the association between the confounder and exposure within the strata (see the example in the previous subsection). The Mantel–Haenszel method is useful for estimating a pooled odds ratio across i homogeneous strata, as follows:

$$OR_{MH} = \frac{\Sigma(a_i\, d_i / n_i)}{\Sigma(b_i\, c_i / n_i)}$$

Multiple logistic regression is a useful technique for computing odds ratios adjusted for other variables (e.g., potential confounders) included in the model.

STRENGTHS AND WEAKNESSES OF CASE-CONTROL STUDIES

A number of strengths and weaknesses have been identified in the literature of case-control studies (see Table 7-1). A primary strength of case-control studies is that they allow investigation of exposure–disease relationships where the latency period is long. As movement has occurred over the past century from acute, infectious diseases to chronic, noninfectious diseases being the primary killers of people, the case-control study design has played an increasingly important role in epidemiologic research.

CASE-CROSSOVER STUDY DESIGN

The case-crossover design is becoming increasingly common in environmental epidemiology. A **case-crossover study** compares the exposure status of a case immediately before its occurrence with that of the same case at a prior time. The rationale for this design is that if precipitating events exist, they should occur more frequently immediately prior to the onset of disease rather than during a period more distant from the onset of disease. The case-crossover study design is especially appropriate where individual exposures are intermittent, wherein the disease occurs abruptly and the incubation period for detection and the induction period are short.[13,14]

In case-crossover studies individuals serve as their own controls. The analytic unit is time—where the time just before the acute event is the "case" time compared with some other time, referred to as the "control" time. The case-crossover design assumes there are no confounding time-related factors or, if they exist, are adjusted for in the analysis. A time-related factor—accumulation of effects—is also assumed to not be present.[15] The simplest case-crossover design is similar to a matched-pair case-control design. For example, in a case-crossover study, cases or deaths of heart disease occurring in a population may be examined to determine the effect of short-term exposure to air pollution. For each affected person, exposure to air pollution is determined for a period near the time of diagnosis or death (case period) and one or more periods when the event did not occur (control period). The relative odds can then be estimated using standard methods of assessing association for matched case-control data. More specifically, suppose that 200 cardiac events are identified and that you are interested in measuring its association with particulate matter in the air. The "case" period is designated as the 24 hours preceding the cardiac event, and the "control" period is designated as 1 week prior to the case period. Furthermore, let particulate matter be classified as high versus low levels, and assume that the data are as follows:

		Control	
		High	**Low**
Case	**High**	60	40
	Low	20	80

In other words, among the cardiac patients, 60 experienced high-particulate matter during the case and control periods, 40 experienced high-particulate matter during the case period but not the control period, 20 experienced low-particulate matter during the case period but high-particulate matter during the control period, and 80 experienced low-particulate matter during both the case and control periods. An odds ratio can be estimated by taking the ratio of discrepant pairs, yielding 2 (= 40/20).

This hypothetical example indicates that a positive association exists between the level of particulate matter and the occurrence of cardiac events. Logistic regression can be used to obtain an adjusted odds ratio in a case-crossover study.

In one study, an association was found between primary cardiac arrest among persons with prior heart disease and an increase in exposure to fine particulate matter. This study was limited to current smokers and to increases in fine particulate matter 2 days prior to the event.[16] In other words, current smokers with preexisting cardiac disease are particularly susceptible to fine particulate matter in the air. Furthermore, it appears to take a few days rather than immediately for the heart to adversely react to particulate matter absorbed into the lungs.

On the basis of case-crossover designs, Barnett and colleagues (2005) found a significantly positive association between air pollutants (NO_2, particles, and SO_2) and hospital admissions for bronchitis, asthma, and respiratory disease in Australia and New Zealand.[17] Forastiere and colleagues (2005) found a positive association between out-of-hospital deaths for coronary heart disease and several air pollutants,[18] and Peel and colleagues (2007) found an increased risk of adverse cardiovascular events with ambient air pollution exposure among individuals suffering from hypertension, diabetes, and chronic obstructive pulmonary disease.[19] Each of these studies were based on objective measures of exposure to particulate matter. Had it been necessary to rely on a person's recollection of exposure, the threat of recall bias would be present.

NESTED CASE-CONTROL STUDY DESIGN

A **nested case-control study** (also called a case-cohort study) is a case-control study "nested" within a cohort study. A sample of cases and noncases are selected, and their exposure status is compared. For example, a nested case-control study of 362 cases and 1,805 matched controls attempted to examine the association between occupational chemical exposures and prostate cancer incidence. High levels of trichloroethylene exposure were significantly associated with an increased risk of prostate cancer among workers.[20] Another nested case-control study involved French uranium miners, where 100 miners who died of lung cancer and 500 controls matched for age were identified. Information about radon exposure was obtained. Smoking information was obtained retrospectively from a questionnaire and occupational medical records. A significantly increased risk of lung cancer caused by radon exposure was found after adjusting for smoking status.[21] Some of the strengths and weaknesses of nested case-control studies are presented in Table 7-1.

COHORT STUDY DESIGN

Cohort as a general term means a group or body of people. As time passes, the group moves through different and successive time periods of life; as the group ages, changes can be seen in the health and vital statistics of the group. Health factors as well as deaths are tracked in cohorts (**Figure 7-1**). In analytic epidemiology, a cohort study generally involves the study

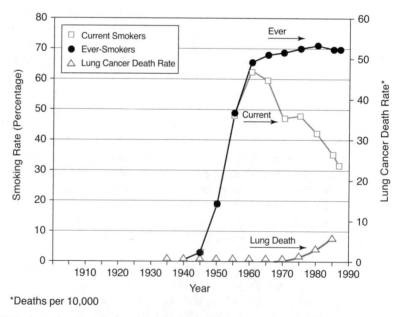

*Deaths per 10,000

FIGURE 7-1   Changes in current smokers, ever-smokers, and lung cancer deaths for white U.S. males born in 1931 to 1940. From National Cancer Institute. Strategies to control tobacco use in the United States: A blueprint for public health action in the 1990s. Bethesda, MD: U.S. Department of Health and Human Services, Public Health Service, National Institutes of Health, 1991; DHHS publication no. (NIH) 92-2789. (http://www.cancer.gov).

of persons who have been exposed and are followed over time with selected health outcomes compared with another group who was not exposed.

Cohorts of persons within a group can be studied as a group, either prospectively or retrospectively. In a **prospective cohort study,** the predictor variable is measured before the outcome has occurred. In a **retrospective cohort study,** a historical cohort is reconstructed with data on the predictor variable (measured in the past) and data on the outcome collected (measured in the past after some follow-up period). The defining distinction between a prospective and retrospective cohort study is the time when the investigator initiates the study, whether before or after the occurrence of the outcome.

Cohort effect, also referred to as generation effect, is the change and variation in the disease or health status of a study population as the study group moves through time. Cohort effects can include any exposure or influence from environmental factors to societal changes. As each group ages, passes through the phases of the life span, and is exposed to the changes of life, such effects will be seen in each person within a cohort, and this will affect the results of the study.

As the cohort advances through time, the incidence rate of the outcome of interest is tracked and compared between exposed and unexposed groups. An advantage of the cohort study over the case-control study is that the incidence rate of several outcome variables can be determined and associated with the exposure variable. As time passes, an increasing number of outcome variables may be considered.

With the Mediterranean diet receiving considerable attention in cardiovascular epidemiology, a group of researchers assessed the association between incidence of hypertension and adherence to the Mediterranean diet. A prospective cohort study was conducted of 9,408 men and women in Spain. Dietary intake was assessed at baseline using a nine-point Mediterranean diet score. Median follow-up was 4.2 years (range, 1.9–9), with 501 cases of hypertension identified. The result of the study was that adhering to a Mediterranean-type diet could aid in preventing age-related changes in blood pressure.[22] In another study, the authors obtained retrospective cohort data by linking records from the Pregnancy Nutrition Surveillance System and the Pediatric Nutrition Surveillance System on 155,411 low-income children born during 1995–2001 in selected areas in the United States. The outcome of interest was childhood obesity based on a body mass index greater than or equal to the 95th percentile for age and gender, determined at age 2–4 years. For non-Hispanic white mothers, smoking duration and quantity were significantly positively associated with obesity, showing a dose–response relationship. For non-Hispanic black mothers, heavy smoking, but not duration, was significantly positively associated with childhood obesity. On the other hand, for Hispanic mothers, there was not a significant association between duration and quantity of smoking during pregnancy and childhood obesity.[23] Further investigation is warranted as to the role bias, and confounding may play in the inconsistent results.

RISK RATIO IN COHORT STUDIES

The **risk ratio** (also called the relative risk) is the measure of association used in cohort studies. This measure reflects the probability of the health-related state or event among those exposed relative to the probability of the health-related state or event among those not exposed. The risk ratio (RR) is calculated as follows, based on Table 7-3.

$$RR = \frac{a/(a + b)}{c/(c + d)}$$

The numerator of the risk ratio is the cumulative incidence rate (or attack rate) of disease among the exposed. The denominator of the risk ratio is the cumulative incidence rate (or attack rate) of disease among the unexposed. These rates are also referred to as measures of risk. A risk ratio equal to 1 indicates no association between the exposure and health-related state or event, a risk ratio greater than 1 indicates a positive association, and a risk ratio less than 1 indicates a negative association. The risk ratio can range from 0 to infinity.

The risk ratio can be interpreted literally. For example, if a risk ratio equals 2.5 in a study examining the association between current smoking and myocardial infarction, then current smokers are 2.5 times more likely to develop a myocardial infarction than are non-smokers. If a risk ratio is equal to 0.5 in a study examining the association between moderate and/or vigorous weekly exercise and myocardial infarction, then moderate and/or vigorous weekly exercisers are 0.5 times as likely as people with lower levels of exercise to develop myocardial infarction. These risk ratios can also be expressed as percent change. The general formulas for expressing risk ratios (or rate ratios, as defined following) as percentages are as follows:

$$\% \text{ Increase Change} = (RR - 1) \times 100 \text{ for } RR > 1$$
$$\% \text{ Decrease Change} = (1 - RR) \times 100 \text{ for } RR < 1$$

Thus, in the first example, it appears that current smokers are 150% more likely to develop myocardial infarction than those who do not currently smoke. In the second example, people who engage in moderate and/or vigorous exercise every week are 50% less likely to develop myocardial infarction than those who do not participate in this level of exercise.

Because we know the total number of exposed and unexposed people in a cohort study, we can calculate relative incidence (risk) and interpret the measure of association more precisely. In contrast, in a case-control study the number of cases and controls is chosen by the investigator. Unless data are considered for the entire population, the total number of exposed or unexposed people will not be known. Hence, the incidence of disease among exposed and the incidence of disease among unexposed people in the population cannot be determined.

Although interpretation of the odds ratio should generally be limited to saying the association is positive, negative, or does not exist, there is an exception. For health-related states or events that are rare (i.e., affecting less than 10% of the population), $a + b$ can be approximated by b, and $c + d$ can be approximated by d. Under such circumstances:

$$RR = \frac{a/(a + b)}{c/(c + d)} \approx \frac{a/b}{c/d} = \frac{a \times d}{b \times c} = OR$$

Hence, it is appropriate to interpret the odds ratio as we would the risk ratio.

RATE RATIO IN COHORT STUDIES

When the total time that exposed and unexposed persons are at risk is available rather than the total number of subjects in the two groups, the presentation of the 2 × 2 contingency table is modified (Table 7-4). Cells a and c still represent the number of exposed and unexposed people who become cases, respectively. If the numbers of person–time units were available rather than the total number of individuals in exposed and unexposed groups, then $a + b$ should be replaced by person–time in the exposed group (PT_e) and $c + d$ replaced by person–time in the unexposed group (PT_o). For acute conditions, person–time may refer to

TABLE 7-4   Cohort Data with Person-Time Denominators

	Cases	Controls	Total
Exposed	a	—	Person Time (PT_e)
Not Exposed	c	—	Person Time (PT_o)
Total	$a + c$	—	Total = $PT^e + PT^o$

Data are from Iso H, Date C, Yamamoto A, et al. Smoking cessation and mortality from cardiovascular disease among Japanese men and women: the JACC study. *Am J Epidemiol* 2005;161(2):170–179.

hours, days, weeks, or months, whereas for chronic conditions, person–time generally refers to years and is estimated using the mid-year population. When the denominator in the calculations shown previously involves person–time, we use the word "rate," rather than the word "risk." The ratio of rates is called a **rate ratio**.

$$Rate\ Ratio = \frac{a/PT_e}{c/PT_o}$$

To illustrate, suppose we were interested in identifying the rate of injury among a group or workers who have a certain job type at Company A versus Company B. Because there are some workers who are part-time, other full time, and others that work overtime, we would like to capture the total hours worked to reflect the time at risk of becoming a case. If the total number of injuries in the past month was 5 in Company A and 8 in Company B, and the corresponding hours employees worked in the last month was 10,000 and 20,000, respectively, then:

$$Rate\ Rate = \frac{5/10,000}{8/20,000} = 1.25.$$

Thus, the rate of injuries in the past month for workers with a given job type was 1.25 times (or 25%) greater in Company A than Company B.

There are several cohort-based measures that are used in epidemiology for communicating health information. Selected measures are presented in Table 7-5. The formulas for these measures are defined in the context of data in the 2 × 2 contingency table (Table 7-2). Note that if the numbers of person–time units were available rather than the total numbers of individuals in exposed and unexposed groups, then $a + b$ should be replaced by PT_e and $c + d$ replaced by PT_o in Table 7-5. To illustrate these measures when person-years are involved, refer to Table 7-6. The incidence rate per 100,000 person-years of cardiovascular disease among current smokers is 399 and among noncurrent smokers is 356; overall the rate is 379. The rate ratio (risk ratio) is 1.122, meaning that male current smokers are 1.122 times (or 12.2%) more likely than nonsmokers to develop cardiovascular disease.

When a causal assumption is made between an exposure and outcome, the difference in risks is called **attributable risk**, which is the absolute risk in the exposed group attributable to the exposure. The attributable risk is calculated as the difference in attack rates (risk difference) or person-time rates (rate difference); $I_e - I_o$.[3] The attributable risk is 43.6 per 100,000—that is, the excess occurrence of cardiovascular disease among male smokers that can be attributed to their smoking is 43.6 per 100,000.

Attributable risk percent can be calculated with the I_e and I_o or the risk ratio. The attributable risk percent equals 10.9% [(1.122 – 1)/1.122 × 100]. This means that if smoking

TABLE 7-5   Commonly Used Epidemiologic Measures for Describing Cohort Data

	Measure	Interpretation
Cumulative incidence rate in the exposed group	$I_e = [a / (a + b)] \times 10^n$	Attack rate (risk) of the health-related state or event for those exposed.
Cumulative incidence rate in the unexposed group	$I_o = [c / (c + d)] \times 10^n$	Attack rate (risk) of the health-related state or event for those exposed.
Cumulative incidence in the total group	$I_t = [(a + c) / n] \times 10^n$	Attack rate (risk) of the health-related state or event.
Risk ratio	$RR = I_e / I_o$	Relative risk.
Attributable risk	$AR = I_e - I_o$	Excess risk of disease among the exposed group attributed to the exposure, typically expressed per 10^n.
Attributable-risk percent	$AR\% = \dfrac{I_e - I_o}{I_e} \times 100$ $= \left[\dfrac{(RR - 1)}{RR} \right] \times 100$	For disease cases that are exposed, this statistic refers to the percentage of disease cases attributed to their exposure.
Population-attributable risk	$PAR = I_t - I_o$	The excess risk of disease in the population attributed to the exposure, typically expressed per 10^n.
Population-attributable risk percent		Percentage of the disease in the population that can be attributed to the exposure.

TABLE 7-6   Total Cardiovascular Disease According to Smoking Status. Study population of 41,782 men aged 40–79 years living in 45 communities across Japan from 1988 to 1990 and followed through the end of 1999

	Cases	Controls	Person-Years
Current smoker	882	—	220,965
Nonsmoker	673	—	189,254
Total	1,555	—	410,219

Data are from Iso H, Date C, Yamamoto A, et al. Smoking cessation and mortality from cardiovascular disease among Japanese men and women: the JACC study. *Am J Epidemiol* 2005;161(2):170–179.

causes cardiovascular disease, nearly 10.9% of cardiovascular disease in males who currently smoke is attributable to their smoking.

Population-attributable risk also assumes a causal association between exposure and disease. The population-attributable risk for the example is 23 per 100,000. To calculate the population-attributable risk, subtract the person-time rate in the unexposed group from the person-time rate in the total population, or $I_t - Io$. This reflects the amount of cardiovascular disease in the population that is attributable to current smoking. This measure says that if current smoking were eliminated from the population, the cardiovascular disease incidence rate could be expected to drop by 23 per 100,000.

The **population-attributable risk** percent is perhaps more easily interpretable. In the example, the population-attributable risk percent is 6.2% $[(379 - 356)/379 \times 100]$. This means that if smoking were eliminated from the population, a 6.2% decrease in the incidence rate of cardiovascular disease could be expected.

DOUBLE-COHORT STUDIES

Double-cohort studies vary from conventional cohort studies in that two distinct populations are involved with different levels of an exposure of interest. To construct a double-cohort study, samples are taken from each of the two populations, unless the populations are small enough such that they are considered in their entirety. The two cohorts are followed up, and the outcome of interest is measured. Double cohorts are employed when the exposure is rare and a relatively small number of people are affected.

For example, suppose a chemical leak occurred at a manufacturing company. The chemical was suspected of causing neurologic problems. The group of workers exposed to the chemical leak was monitored over time for neurologic disorders. Another group of manufacturing workers at a nearby company served as a comparison group of unexposed persons. This group was also followed into the future, and the level of neurologic disorders was compared with that of the exposed group.

SELECTING THE STUDY COHORT

When selecting the study cohort, the population of study should be reviewed to ascertain those people or groups that are likely to become cases. Individuals who already have a disease outcome of interest (prevalent cases) or who are not at risk (e.g., they have had an organ removed such that they cannot become a case) should be excluded from the study. For example, a woman having undergone a total hysterectomy should be excluded from a cohort of women being investigated for uterine cancer. In addition, persons with latent infections or recurring diseases, such as the chronic fatigue immune deficiency syndrome caused by the herpes virus (sometimes implicated in uterine cancer), present a problem because the disease may not be easily diagnosed. It may also be necessary to exclude such individuals. In the interest of saving time and money and avoiding unnecessary testing and effort, appropriate exclusion criteria for a cohort study must be given utmost attention.

Restriction is commonly used in cohort studies. This limits generalization but often improves feasibility and focus. Restriction involves selecting cohorts with limited exposure and a narrow range of behaviors or activities. It can also mean selecting from a limited work environment with restricted exposures or health problems. Heart disease is a health condition often studied among specific working groups, such as mail carriers, longshoremen, and other workers. Cohort studies focusing on respiratory disease may restrict the study to coke workers at steel mills or garment factory workers.

Cohort studies need to come from populations where sampling can be effectively conducted. Adequate sample size is needed to capture the outcome of interest. Hence, researchers may restrict the cohort to high-risk individuals, such as middle-aged men, in the study of heart disease. For some rare outcomes, it might not be feasible to conduct a prospective cohort study. In such cases, a retrospective cohort or case-control study should be employed.

BIAS IN COHORT STUDIES

Biases related to selection and confounding should be considered in cohort studies. Forms of selection bias common in cohort studies are the healthy worker effect, volunteer bias, and loss to follow-up. Misclassification is also a concern in cohort studies. Confounding can occur in cohort studies, but it is more of a concern in double-cohort studies.

Selection Bias

The **healthy worker effect** occurs in cohort studies when workers represent the exposed group, and a sample from the general population represents the unexposed group. This is because workers tend to be healthier, on average, than the general population. In order to work and maintain a job, a certain level of health is required (e.g., some workers must pass a physical examination). On the other hand, the general population includes persons who are not able to get or keep a job because of health problems.

Suppose the researcher was interested in measuring the association between employment at a steel mill and all-cause mortality. Although the workers may be exposed to certain harmful environmental factors, their jobs are often physically demanding, requiring a relatively high level of physical health. These workers may be in better health than an age-, gender-, and racial/ethnic-matched comparison group of people from the same community where the steel workers reside. Consequently, a positive association between working at the steel mill and all-cause mortality is likely to be negatively biased. To avoid this form of bias, a better comparison group would be workers at another manufacturing plant who are not exposed to the same environmental factors as those in the steel mill.

Loss to follow-up is a circumstance in which researchers lose contact with study participants, resulting in unavailable outcome data on those people. This is a common problem in cohort studies, increasingly so in cohorts with longer follow-up times. Loss of participants eligible for follow-up may arise for a number of reasons. Some subjects may refuse to continue their participation and some cannot be located or are unavailable for interview. Participant death is also always a possibility. Loss to follow-up can result in a biased estimate of an association if the extent of loss to follow-up is associated with both exposure and disease. For example, in a study assessing the association between sexual abuse during childhood and psychosocial disorders, sexually abused individuals were more likely lost to follow-up if they developed psychosocial disorders than persons without a history of sexual abuse who developed psychosocial disorders.

As a general rule, the validity of a study requires that loss to follow-up not exceed 20%. Eliminating those not likely to remain in the study, making periodic contact with participants, and providing incentives are approaches frequently used to minimize the problem. The effect of loss to follow-up can be indirectly measured by calculating the risk ratio, assuming that all of those lost would have developed the outcome—then recalculating the risk ratio assuming that none of those lost to follow-up would have developed the outcome. This provides a range wherein the true value lies. In some cases, the range of the risk ratio will not overlap 1, such that loss to follow-up would not change the conclusion of there being an association between exposure and disease variables; however, in some cases, loss to follow-up would cause a positive or negative association to become statistically insignificant.

Confounding

Confounding can influence associations in both case-control and cohort studies. Suppose researchers identified a group of men who were bald and a group of men who were not bald. Men with myocardial infarction were excluded from the study. The two groups were then followed over time in order to see whether bald men were more likely to develop myocardial infarction. Age is a possible confounder because it is associated with myocardial infarction and, independent of that relationship, is associated with baldness. Hence, we may find that bald men are more likely to develop myocardial infarction, but that may be explained by the fact that bald men are more likely to be older. In the calculation of the risk ratio, the numerator would be too large and the denominator too small.

Double-cohort studies are particularly susceptible to confounding. In the previous example involving a chemical leak and suspected neurologic disorders, the control group could be different in ways other than just exposure status such that confounding could produce misleading results.

Misclassification

Misclassifying exposure or outcome status is not a good thing. In a cohort study, if misclassification of the outcome is related to the exposure, then misclassification is differential (nonrandom) and the strength of the measure of association is distorted. If misclassification of the outcome is not related to the exposure, then misclassification is nondifferential (random). To illustrate, suppose a group of women are classified as sexually active and not sexually active, and we follow them into the future to compare their respective risks of cervical cancer. If the sexually active women are more likely to seek medical attention than those who are not, cervical cancer is likely to be more frequently or accurately diagnosed in this group. Hence, the measured association between being sexually active and cervical cancer will be overestimated.

Random misclassification can arise because of inaccuracies in classifying the outcome status of individuals, but these misclassifications occur similarly between exposed and unexposed groups. For example, suppose researchers are interested in assessing the association between the level of physical demands on employees and heart disease. However, some job switching and time-on-the-job can produce misclassification of some of the employees, yet this misclassification is likely to be unrelated to myocardial infarction. The effect of random misclassification is to make the groups more similar, thereby underestimating the association between exposure and disease.

CONTROLLING FOR BIAS IN COHORT STUDIES

Healthy worker bias can be avoided by selecting a comparison group made up of workers not exposed to the exposure of interest. Bias resulting from loss to follow-up can be minimized by restricting the study participants to those likely to remain in the study (e.g., by excluding those with a highly fatal disease or who are likely to move out of the area), collecting personal identifying information (e.g., each participant's telephone number and address as well as those of their employer and a family member), making periodic contact, and providing incentives (e.g., cash or free medical exam). Misclassification can be minimized by refining the definition of the exposed and unexposed groups.

At the study design level, restriction is often used to avoid bias resulting from confounding. In double-cohort studies, confounding can be reduced by choosing comparison groups as similar as possible to the exposed population. Furthermore, collecting data on potential confounders at the beginning of the study makes it possible to adjust for these potential confounders at the analysis level through stratification and multiple-regression techniques.

STRENGTHS AND WEAKNESSES OF COHORT STUDIES

A number of strengths and weaknesses of cohort studies have been identified (Table 7-7).

EFFECT MODIFICATION

When an association between an exposure and disease outcome is modified by the level of an extrinsic risk factor beyond random variation, the extrinsic variable is called an **effect modifier**.[24] An **effect modifier** can influence the relationship between variables in either cohort or case-control data. This means that effect modification can influence associations measured by either odds ratios, risk ratios, or rate ratios. For simplification, this section will focus on odds ratios.

TABLE 7-7   Selected Strengths and Weaknesses of Prospective and Retrospective Cohort and Double-cohort Studies

Study Design	Description	Strengths	Weaknesses
Prospective cohort	The investigator identifies participants, measures exposure status, and follows the cohort over time to monitor outcome events.	More control over selection of participants and exposure and outcome measures than the retrospective cohort	More expensive Longer duration than the retrospective cohort Limited to one exposure variable
Retrospective cohort	The investigator identifies a cohort with already available exposure and outcome data.	Shorter duration Less expensive Fewer numbers required than the prospective cohort More than one exposure can be identified and studied in the same data set	Less control over selection of participants and exposure and outcome measures than the prospective cohort
Double cohort	Two distinct populations with different levels of the exposure are followed.	Useful when distinct cohorts have different or rare exposures	Potential confounding bias from sampling two populations

Adapted from Newman TB, Browner WS, Cummings SR, Hulley SB. Designing a new study: II: cross-sectional and case-control studies. In: Hulley SB, Cummings SR, eds. *Designing Clinical Research: An Epidemiologic Approach.* Baltimore, MD: Williams & Williams, 1988.

In the example that demonstrated confounding in case-control studies, a hypothetical data set showed that the crude odds ratio measuring the association between coffee and heart disease was positive, whereas the stratified odds ratio for smoking showed no association. Confounding was present because the crude odds ratio varied from the stratified odds ratios. When the crude odds ratio is greater than the stratified odds ratios, confounding is positive. When the crude odds ratio is less than the stratified odds ratios, confounding is negative. Had the stratum-specific odds ratios differed beyond random variation and both been higher or lower than the crude odds ratio, then smoking would have been an effect modifier as well as a confounder. In the previous example involving a retrospective cohort design assessing childhood obesity and maternal smoking, race/ethnicity was an effect modifier.[25] This is because the relationship between maternal smoking and childhood obesity varied according to race/ethnicity.

In some cases, a variable can act as both a confounder and an effect modifier (Figure 7-2). For example, positive confounding and the presence of effect modification would exist if the crude odds ratio was greater than the stratified odds ratios and if the stratum-specific odds ratio differed beyond random variation. Negative confounding and the presence of effect modification would exist if the crude odds ratio was smaller than the stratified odds ratios, which differed from each other. If the stratum-specific odds ratios differ greatly to the point that they overlap the crude odds ratio, then effect modification is present and confounding is not relevant.[27]

Confounding and effect modifying variables are treated differently. On one hand, a confounder is a nuisance variable that produces a misleading picture of the association between variables. Ways to control for confounding at the study design and analysis levels have been discussed. On the other hand, an effect-modifying variable influences the association between two other variables in an informative way. That is, if the association between two variables differs across the level of a third variable, this is of interest and should be described rather than controlled for.[3]

CONCLUSION

Analytic epidemiologic studies attempt to answer how and why health-related states or events occur. Analytic studies make use of a comparison group. Case-control, cohort, case-crossover, and nested case-control studies are types of observational analytic study designs. These study designs make use of a comparison group. For example, the analysis of a case-control study is a comparison between cases and controls and is made with respect to the occurrence of an exposure whose potential causal role is being assessed. The analysis of a cohort study is a comparison between exposed and unexposed with respect to the frequency of an outcome whose potential role is being evaluated.

If $OR_c > OR_1 = OR_2$, positive confounding

If $OR_c < OR_1 = OR_2$, negative confounding

$OR_1 \neq OR_2$, effect modification present

Note that small differences in OR_1 and OR_2 are likely explained by random error. Also, the same ideas apply for RR.

FIGURE 7-2   Identifying confounding and effect modification.

The odds ratio is an appropriate measure of association in a case-control study involving data classified as exposed (yes/no) and outcome (yes/no). On the other hand, the risk ratio or rate ratio are appropriate measures of association in cohort studies involving two level classifications of exposure and outcome status. Other useful measures for describing cohort data include attributable-risk, attributable-risk percent, population-attributable risk, and population-attributable risk percent.

Misclassification refers to error in classifying exposure and/or outcome status. Although such error is inevitable in any study, minimizing its influence is imperative. Misclassification may be random or nonrandom, depending on whether the misclassification with respect to the exposure (or the outcome) is independent of the outcome (or the exposure). Random misclassification always underestimates the association between exposure and outcome variables.

Bias is a deviation of the results from the truth. Types of bias unique to case-control and cohort studies were presented and ways to minimize these biases explored. It is imperative to design your studies in order to minimize threats of validity due to bias. Once the data are collected, there is little that can be done to remove the effects of bias, with the exception that if data were collected on a potential confounder, that variable could be adjusted in the analysis by stratification or multiple regression.

An effect modifier is a third variable that modifies the association between two other variables. Unlike a confounder, which is a nuisance, an effect-modifying influence of a third variable on an exposure-outcome relationship may be very informative. The influence of an effect modifier can be measures by comparing the appropriate measure of association across the levels of the third variable.

EXERCISES

Key Terms

Define the following terms.

Analytic studies

Attributable risk

Attributable-risk percent

Berkson's bias

Bias

Case-control study

Case-crossover study

Cohort

Cohort effect

Cohort study

Confounding

Differential (nonrandom)
  misclassification

Effect modifier

Healthy worker effect

Interviewer bias

Loss to follow-up

Matching

Misclassification

Nested case-control study

Nondifferential (random)
  misclassification

Observation bias

Observational analytic study

Observational exploratory study

Odds ratio (relative odds)

Population attributable risk

Population attributable risk percent

Prevalence-incidence bias
  (Neyman's bias)

Prospective cohort study

Rate ratio

Recall bias

Restriction

Retrospective cohort study

Risk ratio (relative risk)

Selection bias

STUDY QUESTIONS

1. What is the primary distinction between observational and experimental analytic epidemiologic studies?

2. What study design may be either retrospective or prospective? Explain.

3. Discuss the general steps you would take to design a case-control study.

4. What are the primary sources of bias in case-control studies?

5. What steps would you take to minimize bias and confounding in a case-control study?

6. Discuss the advantages and disadvantages of hospital, general population, and special population controls in a case-control study.

7. Discuss the strengths and weaknesses of case-control studies.

8. Discuss the general steps you would take to design a cohort study.

9. What are the primary sources of bias in cohort studies?

10. Compare and contrast effect modification with confounding.

11. As the hospital epidemiologist, you have been requested by the hospital administration to study the effects of administering antibiotics to patients at different time frames (2-hour intervals up to 24 hours) before they have surgery that involves opening the chest cavity. The study is aimed at reducing infections caused by surgery as well as reducing deaths. The study is to take place over the next 15 years. Design an appropriate study. Explain and justify the study design chosen.

12. You have been asked to study the effects of stress across the life span of people who have a close family member with HIV/AIDS. The study is to be from the time of diagnosis until the death of the family member. Design an appropriate study. Explain and justify the study design chosen.

13. In the coffee–myocardial infarction example, in which smoking was shown to be a confounder (see the section on confounding under case-control studies), show that there is an association between smoking and coffee and also an association between smoking and myocardial infarction.

14. Suppose 45 traffic accidents occur on a given road and you are interested in measuring whether the accidents are associated with rain showers. The "case" period is designated as the 24 hours preceding the accident and the "control" period is designated as 1 week prior to the case period. Among the accident cases, 7 experienced rain showers during the case and control periods; 16 experienced rain during the case period but not during the control period; 4 experienced no rain during the case period but rain during the control period; and 18 experienced no rain during either the case or control periods. Use an appropriate measure and describe whether an association exists between rain showers and traffic accidents.

15. Match the types of ratio in the left column with the types of study in the right column.

Ratio	Study
__ Rate ratio	a. Case-crossover
__ Risk ratio	b. Case control
__ Odds ratio (paired data)	c. Cohort involving attack rates
__ Odds ratio (unpaired data)	d. Cohort involving person-time rates

REFERENCES

1. Last JM, ed. *A Dictionary of Epidemiology.* New York, NY: Oxford University Press; 1995.
2. Schlesselman JJ. *Case-Control Studies: Design, Conduct, Analysis.* New York, NY: Oxford University Press; 1982.
3. Hennekens CH, Buring JE. *Epidemiology in Medicine.* Boston, MA: Little, Brown and Company; 1987.
4. Gail M, Williams R, Byar DP, et al. How many controls? *J Chron Dis.* 1976;29:723.
5. Smith DC, Prentice R, Thompson DJ, et al. Association of exogenous estrogens and endometrial cancer. *N Engl J Med.* 1975;293:1164.
6. Ziel HK, Finkle WD. Increased risk of endometrial cancer among users of conjugated estrogens. *N Engl J Med.* 1975;293:1167.
7. Horwitz RI, Feinstein AR. Alternative analytic methods for case-control studies of estrogens and endometrial cancer. *N Engl J Med.* 1978;299:1089.
8. Hutchison GB, Rothman KJ. Correcting a bias? *N Engl J Med.* 1978;299:1129.
9. Berkson J. Limitations of the application of fourfold table analysis to hospital data. *Biometrics.* 1946;2:47–53.
10. Reid MC, Lachs MS, Feinstein AR. Use of methodological standards in diagnostic test research: getting better but still not good. *JAMA.* 1995;274:645–651.
11. Choi BC, Noseworthy AL. Classification, direction, and prevention of bias in epidemiologic research. *J Occup Med.* 1992;34(3):265–271.
12. Newman TB, Browner WS, Hulley SB. Enhancing causal inference in observational studies. In: Hulley SB, Cummings SR, eds. *Designing Clinical Research: An Epidemiologic Approach.* Baltimore, MD: Williams & Williams; 1988.
13. Maclure M, Mittleman MA. Should we use a case-crossover design? *Annu Rev Public Health.* 2000;21:193–221.
14. Jaakkola JJK. Case-crossover design in air pollution epidemiology. *Eur Respir J.* 2003;21:81S–85S.
15. Szklo M, Nieto JM. *Epidemiology Beyond the Basics.* Sudbury, MA: Jones and Bartlett Publishers; 2007.
16. Sullivan J, Ishikawa N, Sheppard L, Siscovick D, Checkoway H, Kaufman J. Exposure to ambient fine particulate matter and primary cardiac arrest among persons with and without clinically recognized heart disease. *Am J Epidemiol.* 2003;157(6):501–509.
17. Barnett AG, Williams GM, Schwartz J, et al. Air pollution and child respiratory health: a case-crossover study in Australia and New Zealand. *Am J Respir Crit Care Med.* 2005;171:1272–1278.
18. Forastiere F, Stafoggia M, Picciotto S, et al. A case-crossover analysis of out-of-hospital coronary deaths and air pollution in Rome, Italy. *Am J Respir Crit Care Med.* 2005;172:1549–1555.
19. Peel JL, Metzger KB, Klein M, Flanders WD, Mulholland JA, Tolbert PE. Ambient air pollution and cardiovascular emergency department visits in potentially sensitive groups. *Am J Epidemiol.* 2007;165(6):625–633.
20. Krishnadasan A, Kennedy N, Zhao Y, Morgenstern H, Ritz B. Nested case-control study of occupational chemical exposures and prostate cancer in aerospace and radiation workers. *Am J Ind Med.* 2007;50(5):383–390.
21. Klervi L, Solenne B, Dominique B. Lung cancer risk associated to exposure to radon and smoking in a case-control study of French uranium minors. *Health Physics.* 2007;92(4):371–378.
22. Núñez-Córdoba JM, Valencia-Serrano F, Toledo E, Alonso A, Martínez-González MA. The Mediterranean diet and incidence of hypertension: the Seguimiento Universidad de Navarra (SUN) Study. *Am J Epidemiol.* 2008;169(3):339-346.
23. Sharma AJ, Cogswell ME, Li R. Dose-response associations between maternal smoking during pregnancy and subsequent childhood obesity: effect modification by maternal race/ethnicity in a low-income US cohort. *Am J Epidemiol.* 2008;168(9):995–1007.
24. Miettinen OS. Confounding and effect modification. *Am J Epidemiol.* 1974;100:350–353.
25. Kleinbaum DG, Kupper LL, Morgenstern H. *Epidemiologic Research: Principles and Quantitative Methods.* Belmont, CA: Lifetime Learning Publications; 1982.

Experimental Studies in Epidemiology

OBJECTIVES

After completing this chapter, you will be able to:

- Discuss the role of randomization in experimental studies.
- Discuss the role of blinding in experimental studies.
- Identify the general strengths and weaknesses of controlled trials.
- Identify the advantages to using a run-in design, a factorial design, a randomized matched pair design, or a group-randomized design.
- Discuss some of the ethical issues associated with experimental studies.

An experiment is an operation that is repeatable under stable conditions and that results in any one of a set of outcomes. In an **experimental study**, researchers evaluate the effects of an assigned intervention on an outcome; the investigators intervene in the study by influencing the exposure of the study participants. As such, experimental studies are commonly called intervention studies. In contrast to the experimental study design, all other study designs are observational.

There are various types of experimental study designs, each with their strengths and weaknesses. The experimental study is an epidemiologic design that has the potential to produce high quality data and resemble the controlled experiments performed by basic science researchers. The experimental study is the most useful for supporting cause-effect relationships and for evaluating the efficacy of prevention and therapeutic interventions. The purpose of this chapter is to introduce general principles and methods of designing and carrying out experimental studies.

EXPERIMENTAL STUDY DESIGNS

In 1747, James Lind conducted an experimental study by identifying a group of 12 sailors with similar symptoms of scurvy.[1] He divided them into six groups of two and supplemented their regular diet with a specific dietary intervention. The intervention that produced a noticeable improvement in the sailors was citrus fruit. In the mid-1800s, Louis Pasteur used an experimental design to demonstrate the effectiveness of his new vaccine against anthrax.[2] Since the days of Lind and Pasteur, there have been many advances in experimental study designs.

The experimental study makes use of a comparison group, which allows for the testing of specific research hypotheses. The study design also allows the researcher to have more control over the level of exposure, establish a time sequence of events, and control for confounding through random assignment and bias through blinding. Hence, the experimental study is considered to be the "gold standard" in epidemiology for basing conclusions about causal relationships, particularly when random assignment and blinding are feasible.

Each replication (repetition) of an experiment that can be repeated is called a trial. One or more outcomes can result from each trial. A **clinical trial** is used to evaluate the efficacy and safety of a new drug or a new medical procedure; a **prophylactic trial** is used to evaluate preventive measures; and a **therapeutic trial** is used to assess new treatment methods. Some trials are used to identifying the efficacy of screening tests and diagnostic procedures, while others focus on evaluating ways to help those with chronic and incurable diseases. The unit of measurement in each of these trials is the individual.

The unit of measurement in a community trial is a community or group (e.g., a school, classroom, or city). A **community trial** tests a group intervention designed for the purpose of educational and behavioral changes at the population level. Community interventions generally use quasi-experimental designs (i.e., the investigators manipulate the study factors but do not assign individual subjects the intervention through random assignment. However, to minimize the threat of confounding factors, a sufficiently large number of groups may be assigned randomly.

The strongest methodological design is a **between-group design** where outcomes are compared between two or more groups of people receiving different levels of the intervention. A **within-group design** may also be used where the outcome in a single group is compared before and after the assigned intervention. An important strength of this design is that individual characteristics that might confound an association (e.g., gender, race, genetic susceptibility) are controlled. However, the within-group design is susceptible to confounding from time-related factors such as the media or economic conditions.

In some rare situations in nature, unplanned events produce a natural experiment. A **natural experiment** is an unplanned type of experimental study where the levels of exposure to a presumed cause differ among a population in a way that is relatively unaffected by extraneous factors so that the situation resembles a planned experiment.[2] For example, screening and treatment for prostate cancer in the Seattle–Puget Sound area differed considerably from screening and treatment in Connecticut during the period from 1987 to 1990. Specifically, prostate-specific antigen testing was 5.4 (95% confidence interval, 4.7 to 6.1) times higher in Seattle than in Connecticut, and the prostate biopsy rate was 2.2 (1.8 to 2.7) times higher. The researchers noted that the 10-year cumulative incidences of radical prostatectomy and external beam radiation up to 1996 were, respectively, 2.7% and 3.9% for those in Seattle compared with 0.5% and 3.1% for those in Connecticut. On this basis, they wanted to assess whether mortality from prostate cancer from 1987 to 1997 differed between Seattle and Connecticut. The adjusted rate ratio of prostate cancer mortality during the study period for Seattle and Connecticut was 1.03 (0.95 to 1.11). In other words, the 11-year follow-up data showed no difference in prostate cancer mortality between the two areas, despite much more intensive screening and treatment in Seattle.[3]

RANDOMIZATION

When the study group is determined, in an ideal situation the participants are then assigned to the intervention and control groups by random assignment. Random assignment makes intervention and control groups look as similar as possible, thereby minimizing the potential influence of confounding factors. With **random assignment**, chance is the only factor that determines group assignment, thus allowing the application of inferential statistical tests of probability and determination of the levels of significance. Randomized controlled trials are the most common type of trial conducted in clinical settings.

Participants can be randomly assigned to more than just two study groups when the efficacy of various levels of a treatment or combinations of treatments is being investigated. As with the other research designs, inferential statistical tests of probability are applied and levels of significance determined. An important feature of randomization is that it balances out the effect of confounding. Assuming that smoking is a confounding factor, randomization of a sufficiently large number of participants will produce a similar distribution of smokers (in terms of age started, duration, and intensity of smoking) between the intervention and control groups.

Although it is possible to adjust for confounding factors at the analysis phase of a study, this assumes that data on the suspected confounders were collected at the outset of the study. Nevertheless, although our best thinking might identify many possible confounding factors, there may be some not considered. Randomization has the advantage of controlling for both known and unknown confounders. Thus, randomization of a sufficiently large number of participants produces groups that are alike on average. In some situations, a physician may strongly believe in an intervention and place patients with more severe health problems in that group. Similarly, patients with more serious health problems may self-select the intervention. Randomization has the advantage of eliminating bias resulting from physician or patient selection.

BLINDING

Blinding is used in experimental studies to minimize potential bias from the placebo effect. A **placebo** is a substance containing no medication or treatment given to satisfy a patient's expectation to get well.[4] In some experimental studies that involve drug treatments, the placebos given to the control group are virtually indistinguishable (to blind the patients and providers, when possible) from the true intervention, providing a comparative basis for determining the effect of the treatment being investigated. The **placebo effect** is the effect on patient outcomes (improved or worsened) that may occur because of the expectation by a patient (or provider) that a particular intervention will have an effect. The placebo effect is independent of the true effect (pharmacologic, surgical, etc.) of a particular intervention. Just as a patient may respond to the intervention itself and not the specific therapeutic benefit of the intervention, an assessing investigator, albeit honest, may believe in a certain intervention, and unconscious bias may arise in the way the researcher evaluates those participants who receive the intervention.

Blinding patients in controlled clinical trials in order to minimize the placebo effect dates back about 100 years. In 1907, a double-blind placebo-controlled trial was conducted by W. H. R. Rivers to explore the association between alcohol and other substances and fatigue. Harry Gold advanced the double-blind placebo-controlled design in the 1940s and 1950s in several lectures and publications. In the 1950s, Henry Beecher estimated that in over two dozen studies that he assessed the placebo effect was responsible for about one third of those who showed improvement. The contributions of these and other researchers led the Food and Drug Administration to recommend (in the 1970s) but not require that new drug trials be double blinded.[5,6]

In a **single-blinded** placebo-controlled study, the participants are blinded, but investigators are aware of who is receiving the active treatment. In a **double-blinded** study, neither the participants nor the investigators know who is receiving the active treatment. In a **triple-blinded** study, not only are the treatment and research approaches kept a secret from the participants and investigators, but the analyses are completed in a way that is removed from the investigators.[7–11]

In drug studies, a placebo is a pill of the same size, color, and shape as the treatment; however, for nondrug studies, such as those involving behavior changes or surgery, it may be impossible or unethical to blind. It may also be problematic to blind in drug studies where a treatment has characteristic side effects. Building side effects into a placebo, which has no potential therapeutic advantages, may be unethical.

The need for blinding is related to whether the outcome is subjectively determined. For example, if the outcome measure is pain relief, a placebo would be highly desirable, whereas if the outcome measure was based on a urine sample or blood test, blinding the patient would be unnecessary. In drug studies where placebos are used, compliance and retention in the study may be much better because patients will think they are benefiting from a given medication.

NONRANDOMIZATION

Several reasons exist for not using random assignment. First, large research populations are not always available, especially in clinical settings. Research is expensive, and funds may not be adequate for the research procedures, follow-up treatments, and testing of large study and control groups. Another restraint is the lack of participants with the disease or condition or a desire to participate. If a large population is to be treated with a preventive measure such as immunization, the epidemiologist would not purposely have half the population assigned at random to a control group and leave them at risk of getting the disease because they were not immunized.

Randomization cannot be applied if an entire population is to be affected or subjected to the treatment. If fluoride is added to the water supply of a city, there is no way to include or exclude certain individuals. If seat belt laws are implemented, control groups are not selected, and randomization is not used in the enforcement of the law. If randomly selected control groups are available, a comparison group may be selected from individuals with traits similar to those of the participants in the treatment group. A pre-test/post-test approach will allow the treatment group to serve as its own control. The changes from the pre-test results to the post-test results often show a statistically significant cause-effect relationship.[7–11]

When randomization is not feasible, a concurrent comparison group in a nonrandom process (convenience sample) may be chosen. If one city has fluoridated water, another city without fluoridated water could serve as a control, and dental outcomes from both groups could be used to evaluate the efficacy of fluoridation. Another example involves seat belt use. If one state requires seat belt use and another does not, the death rate from motor vehicle accidents or some other seat belt-related outcome measure between the two states could be compared in order to determine the efficacy of seat belt use. Although convenience samples are common in the literature, they are susceptible to unmeasured confounding factors.

DESIGNING A RANDOMIZED CONTROLLED TRIAL

A **protocol** is a detailed written plan of the study. The protocol helps the investigator to organize, clarify, and refine various aspects of the study, thereby enhancing the scientific rigor and the efficacy of the project. The elements of a protocol are the research questions, background and significance, design, subjects, variables, and statistical issues. This section focuses on the design portion of the protocol. There are six steps involved with designing a randomized controlled trial: (1) selecting the intervention, (2) assembling the study cohort, (3) measuring baseline variables, (4) choosing a comparison group, (5) ensuring compliance, and (6) selecting the outcome (also called the **end point**).[12,13]

Selecting the Intervention

Selecting the intervention begins with the research objective, whether it is to treat or prevent disease. In trials aimed at evaluating the efficacy of a treatment, the investigator must establish that the therapy is safe and active against the disease, provide evidence that the therapy is potentially better than another, and provide evidence that the therapy is likely to be implementable in the field.

There are different stages for testing new therapies that must occur before a drug is granted a license. When laboratory testing and animal studies show that a new drug has potential to benefit patients, it is first evaluated as a phase I trial. A **phase I trial** is an unblinded, uncontrolled study with typically less than 30 patients. The purpose of phase I trials is to determine the safety of a test in humans. Patients in phase I trials often have advanced disease and have already tried other options. They often undergo intense monitoring. Drugs that show promise advance to phase II trials. **Phase II trials** are relatively small (up to 50 people), randomized blinded trials that test tolerability, safe dosage, side effects, and how the body copes with the drug. If there is good evidence that the new treatment is at least as good as existing treatments, further testing in a phase III trial is warranted. Phase II trials also evaluate which types of disease a treatment is effective against, further assess side effects and how they can be managed, and reveal the most effective dosage level. **Phase III trials** are typically much larger and may involve thousands of patients (see Exhibit, News File). **Phase IV trials** are large studies (may or may not involve random assignment) conducted after the therapy has been approved by the Food and Drug Administration (FDA) to assess the rate of serious side effects and explore further therapeutic uses. These trials typically involve random assignment and are used to evaluate the efficacy of a new treatment. Different dosages or methods of administration of the treatment are often part of the evaluation.

Behavioral interventions usually begin with an identified problem. When a problem, such as relatively high levels of sexually transmitted diseases, is observed in a population through descriptive epidemiologic methods, tailored programs can be developed. Identifying high-risk behaviors for disease, where these risk behaviors are most common, and understanding why these behaviors are more readily adopted by this group and not others are important in designing the intervention. Behavioral interventions are often developed from behavior theory and refined with focus groups. New interventions are often developed from existing interventions shown to be efficacious in other settings. Evaluation of behavioral interventions often requires pilot testing in order to provide evidence that a larger scale assessment is worth doing.

Assembling the Study Cohort

Before assembling the study cohort, inclusion and exclusion criteria must be established and an appropriate sample size determined. Inclusion and exclusion criteria influence the extent to which the results can be generalized. There is often a compromise between the population most efficient for answering the research question and the population best for generalizing the study findings. If the outcome of interest is rare, it may be necessary to include in the cohort only those at high risk for developing the outcome. For example, a coronary heart disease cohort study may restrict participants to males who are at least 40 years of age. Hence, generalization of the study results would be limited to a narrower group than the entire population. In a therapeutic trial, only persons with certain clinical criteria may be included. In a prevention trial, only persons at risk of developing an outcome of interest should be included.

Exclusion criteria are employed to help control error. Loss to follow-up is a primary concern in randomized controlled trials. Persons may be excluded from a study if they are likely to be lost to follow-up (e.g., alcoholics, psychotic patients, homeless persons, and persons planning on moving out of the country). Those with rapidly fatal conditions who are unlikely to be alive at the end of the follow-up period may also be excluded.

Sample size calculations are employed to ensure that the number of participants is adequate to test the specific hypothesis or hypotheses motivating the study. Sample size calculation is based on (1) formulation of the null and one- or two-tailed research hypothesis, (2) the search for the appropriate statistical test, (3) effect size (and in some cases, variability), (4) the desired level of statistical significance for a one- or two-tailed test and the desired probability of failing to reject the null hypothesis when it is actually false, and (5) use of the appropriate table or formula for estimating the sample size. These tables and formulas are available in most introductory biostatistics books.

Measuring Baseline Variables

Measuring baseline variables such as identifying information (name, address, telephone number), demographic information (age, gender, race/ethnicity, marital status, education, income), variables that might be associated with the outcome (e.g., cigarette smoking), and clinical features (e.g., serum cholesterol, blood pressure, glucose level) allow the researcher to accomplish certain objectives.

Identifying information is necessary for maintaining contact with the study participants and for minimizing loss to follow-up. Demographic information is useful for characterizing the study cohort. The first table of reports and papers describing results from randomized controlled trials typically compares baseline characteristics, including demographics, in the study groups. This allows assessment of how well the randomization balances out the effects of these potential confounding factors. In nonrandomized studies, collecting demographic information is particularly important so that potential confounding effects can be adjusted for in the analysis. Measuring variables that might be associated with the outcome, such as smoking habits, allows for statistical adjustment of the potential confounding influence in nonrandomized controlled trials and evaluation of change in risk behaviors between baseline and follow-up. Finally, collecting clinical information serves three purposes: it can influence inclusion in or exclusion from the study, it indicates whether randomization balances out clinical features between intervention and control groups, and it provides baseline measures for comparison in within-group designs.

Choice of a Comparison Group

When the efficacy of a new drug for treating a given illness is under investigation and existing drugs are currently available, the new drug is compared with the current treatment. Comparing a new drug with nothing is rarely done, unless there is no efficacious treatment available for the disease. The aim is to identify whether improvements can be made over the status quo. Similarly, in a study assessing the efficacy of a dietary program for recovering heart attack patients, it would be unethical to not allow those who are not randomly assigned the program to assume special diets designed for heart attack patients.

Ensuring Compliance

The power of the study is directly influenced by compliance with the protocol. If study follow-up involves visiting a clinic for medical assessment, adherence can be improved by contacting patients by telephone or mail shortly before their appointments and providing reimbursement for time and travel. If the study involves adhering to the intervention protocol, the investigator should select a drug or behavioral intervention that is well tolerated. Drugs that require several dosages or have severe side effects and behavior interventions that require dramatic lifestyle changes and involve considerable time and effort on the part of the patient will have lower levels of compliance than less complex and intense programs.

Measuring compliance throughout the study will allow the investigators to make changes if needed. Low compliance will require changes to bolster compliance (e.g., more regular contact with patients and higher incentives). Compliance can be monitored in drug studies by self-report, pill counts, and urine and blood tests. Compliance in the area of behavioral interventions can be monitored by self-report and direct evaluation.

Selecting the Outcome (End Point)

It is not always clear what outcome variable is best. In order to minimize cost and increase feasibility, surrogate markers of the actual phenomenon of interest are often used. For example, instead of considering the effect of an HIV/AIDS drug on death, investigators might select a major AIDS-defining event as a surrogate end point for death (e.g., parasitic infections, fungal infections, viral infections, HIV dementia, HIV wasting syndrome, a neoplasm). A colon cancer prevention program could use polyps as an end point instead of diagnosis of or death resulting from colon cancer. Surrogate end points become particularly useful in randomized controlled trials when the outcome phenomenon of interest is rare.

The power of a study is greater when the outcome variable is continuous rather than dichotomous (e.g., CD_4 count [or T-cell count as it is sometimes called] versus the presence or absence of a bacterial infection in HIV/AIDS patients). For dichotomous outcome variables, power is influenced more by the number of occurrences of the outcome than by the number of participants in the study[14]; however, the decision on an outcome variable should be driven by whichever variable or variables are best for satisfying the research objective.

It is often desirable to consider more than one outcome variable. For example, an intense diet and physical activity-modification program, designed to ultimately reduce the risk of chronic health problems, measured change in several health indicators between baseline and 6 weeks. Variables with improved scores included health knowledge, percent body fat, total steps per week, and most nutrition variables were measured. Clinical improvements were seen in resting heart rate, total cholesterol, low-density lipoprotein cholesterol, and systolic and diastolic blood pressure.[15]

PILOT STUDY

A **pilot study** is a standard scientific approach that involves a preliminary analysis that can greatly improve the chance of funding for major studies. Information from pilot studies can also markedly improve the chance that the study will be successfully conducted. These studies require careful planning, with clear objectives and correct applications of methods. Some of the uses of pilot studies include: determining the feasibility, required time, and cost of recruitment and randomization; determine the feasibility and efficacy of planned measurements, data collection instruments, and data management systems; and obtain information on the effect of the intervention on the main outcome and statistical variability allows for more accurate sample size estimation.

SELECTED SPECIAL TYPES OF RANDOMIZED STUDY DESIGNS

Under certain conditions, variations of the randomized controlled trial may have some advantages. Four of these study designs are presented in this section. They include run-in design, factorial design, randomized matched pairs, and group randomization.

Run-In Design

For placebo-controlled studies, the run-in design can be useful for minimizing bias associated with loss to follow-up. In the **run-in design**, all participants in the cohort are placed on a placebo and followed for some period of time (usually a week or two). Those who remain in the study are then randomly assigned to either the treatment or placebo arm of the study. A limitation of this design is that the participants in the cohort at the time of randomization may no longer reflect the population of interest.

In a behavioral intervention, it might be useful to place all participants on the intervention and then, after a short time period, randomly assign those compliant with the program to the different levels of the intervention. For example, recovering heart attack patients in a selected cohort could all be placed on a new dietary intervention, and then, after a run-in period, those who are compliant would be randomly assigned to remain on the program or change to a standard dietary program used for recovering heart attack patients. The efficacy of the new dietary intervention can be assessed, but depending on the extent of initial dropout, it may have limited generalization to the population of heart attack patients as a whole.

Factorial Design

A **factorial design** is an experimental design in which two or more series of treatments are tried in all combinations. This design allows investigators to address the efficacy of two interventions in a single cohort of participants. In a factorial design, participants are randomly assigned to one of four groups. The groups represent the different combinations of the two interventions. In a placebo-controlled drug study, the groups could be (1) drug A and drug B, (2) drug A and placebo B, (3) placebo A and drug B, and (4) placebo A and placebo B. Comparing the outcomes for groups 1 and 2 with groups 3 and 4 allows evaluation of the efficacy of drug A. Comparing the outcomes for groups 1 and 3 with groups 2 and 4 allows evaluation of the efficacy of drug B. Factorial designs also offer an efficient approach for studying combination effects of treatments on an outcome. For example, researchers recently assessed the efficacy of the addition of levamisole or interferon-a to adjuvant chemotherapy with 5-fluorouracil in patients with stage III colon cancer. In one arm of the study, patients received 5-fluorouracil weekly for one year; in arm 2, patients received 5-fluorouracil plus levamisole; in arm 3, patients received 5-fluorouracil plus interferon; and in arm 4, patients received both 5-fluorouracil and both levamisole and interferon. The study found that adding levamisole, interferon, or both levamisole and interferon to the 5-fluorouracil, provided no significant benefit over 5-fluorouracil alone.[16]

The factorial design is also useful in primary prevention programs. In one study, investigators used the factorial design to evaluate low-dose aspirin (100 mg/day) and vitamin E (300 mg/day) as tools in the prevention of cardiovascular events (cardiovascular death, stroke, or myocardial infarction) in type 2 diabetic patients having at least one cardiovascular risk factor. Although low-dose aspirin was shown to lower the risk of cardiovascular events, no significant reduction in any of the endpoints occurred because of Vitamin E.[17]

Randomization of Matched Pairs

Matching is a procedure that aims to make study and comparison groups similar with respect to extraneous (or confounding) factors. Randomization of matched pairs improves covariate balance on potential confounding variables. Matched randomization provides more accurate estimates than unmatched randomization and may involve matching on several potential confounders.[18] In a **randomized matched pairs** design of an experiment for paired comparison, the assignment of participants to treatment or control is not completely at random, but the randomization is restricted to occur separately within each pair. One participant is randomly assigned the study group (e.g., a dietary program, a drug) in each matched pair, and the other is assigned to the comparison control group.

Group Randomization

In **group randomization**, instead of individuals being randomly assigned the intervention, groups or naturally forming clusters are randomly assigned the intervention. There are many examples of group randomization where groups may involve practices, schools, hospitals, or communities. Individuals or patients within a cluster are likely to be more similar to each other compared with those in other clusters according to selected variables. For example, the World Health Organization randomly assigned 66 factories in the United Kingdom, Belgium, Italy, and Poland to intervention and control groups. The primary outcome variable was death from coronary heart disease. The intervention significantly reduced coronary heart disease and total deaths.[19]

Randomization by group is less efficient statistically than randomization by individual. Sample size calculations and interpretation of the results are more difficult with randomized groups than they are with randomized individuals, and the sample size required for adequate statistical power is larger than with individual level randomization.[20, 21] Some reasons for conducting a group-randomized study include it being more feasible to deliver the intervention on the group level, political and administrative considerations may warrant it, it is a means to avoid contamination between individuals allocated to competing interventions, and the very nature of the intervention may justify it.[22]

STRENGTHS AND WEAKNESSES OF DOUBLE-BLIND RANDOMIZED CLINICAL TRIALS

The best study design for establishing cause–effect relationships is the double-blind randomized clinical trial. This is because blinding minimizes bias and randomization minimizes confounding. In addition, control over exposure status allows investigators to evaluate the influence of precise dosages and amounts on the outcome of interest; however, ethical and practical considerations often make this study design impossible to administer. Beyond drug studies, blinding is often impossible. In addition, many exposures (such as smoking) would be unethical to randomly assign. Some of the strengths and weaknesses of blinded randomized controlled trials are shown in Table 8-1.

ETHICS IN EXPERIMENTAL RESEARCH

In the United States, the Public Health Service Act of 1985 ratified the establishment of institutional review boards (IRBs). These boards are assigned at the institution level to review plans for research involving human subjects. IRBs are specifically charged with protecting the rights and welfare of people involved in research. The establishment of IRBs in this country was, in part, a result of the moral problems associated with the **Tuskegee syphilis study**, which assessed the natural course of syphilis in untreated black males from Macon County, Alabama.

In the early 1900s, poverty-stricken blacks in the southern United States were referred to as a "syphilis-soaked race." Macon County was one of the worst. This eastern county in Alabama was economically depressed, even though the rich soil made it one of the best agricultural areas in the south, with cotton as its most common crop. In this rural setting, much of the agriculture activity was tied to poor black sharecroppers. Medical facilities were meager, and access to physicians and medical care was almost nonexistent. Physicians expected

TABLE 8-1   Selected Strengths and Weaknesses of Blinded Randomized Controlled Studies

Strengths	Weaknesses
Can demonstrate cause–effect relationships with a high level of confidence because of the tightly controlled conditions not possible in observational studies	Only appropriate approach for some research questions
	Allow investigators to control the exposure levels as needed
Sometimes produce a faster and cheaper answer to the research question than observational studies	Many research questions are not suitable for experimental designs because of ethical barriers and because of rare outcomes
	Many research questions are not suitable for blinding
	Standardized interventions may be different from common practice (reducing generalizability)
	May have limited external validity because of use of volunteers, eligibility criteria, and loss to follow-up

Oleckno WA. *Essential Epidemiology: Principles and Applications*. Prospect Heights, IL: Waveland Press, 2002; Hulley SB, Feigal D, Martin M, Cummings SR. Designing a new study: IV: experiments. In: Hulley SB, Cummings SR, eds. *Designing Clinical Research: An Epidemiologic Approach*. Baltimore, MD: Williams & Williams, 1988.

full payment in cash for their services. Blacks used physicians only in extreme emergencies, and conditions like Syphilis were simply endured.[23]

Under these conditions, in 1928, the Julius Rosenwald Fund, in collaboration with the Public Health Service, endeavored to identify the prevalence of Syphilis in southern rural blacks with the intention of providing treatment to cases; however, the 1929 stock market crash and the Great Depression financially devastated the Rosenwald Fund. Consequently, the treatment phase of the study was not pursued. At this time, the Public Health Service decided to conduct a prospective study to evaluate the natural history of syphilis in untreated black men, with the end point being death. Cases and controls were then followed into the future, with the cases falsely led to believe that they were receiving free treatment. The study began in the fall of 1932 and lasted until 1977, when Peter Buxton, an employee with the Public Health Service, alerted the public of the moral concerns associated with the study.[24]

The Tuskegee study had nothing to do with medical experiments, and no treatment was offered for Syphilis. No new drugs were tested, nor were there efforts made to establish the efficacy of older chemical treatments, such as Salvarsan (an arsenic derivative), which was used to treat syphilis for years. The three stages of Syphilis were clearly understood, as were the incubation periods of each. The mode of transmission of the Syphilis Spirochete pathogen was also well understood. Still, the Public Health Service never established a formal protocol for this study and withheld treatment. The Wassermann test for Syphilis was developed in 1907. The synthetic drug Salvarsan was available and moderately successful in treating syphilis. Penicillin was made readily available in 1945, yet no treatment with this antibiotic was attempted (Figure 8-1).[24] There were several ethical problems associated with this study, including:

1. There was no informed consent. Patients were not informed that they were participants in an experiment or that they had a contagious disease.

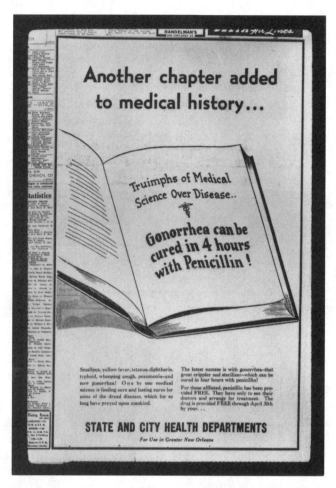

FIGURE 8-1   Penicillin was made widely available in 1945. This antibiotic became known as the "miracle drug," with promises of rapid cures of many infectious diseases, including Gonorrhea. Picture courtesy of Centers for Disease Control and Prevention, Atlanta, Georgia.

2. Diagnostic spinal taps (called "back shots") for Neurosyphilis were misrepresented as special free treatment when, in actuality, treatment was withheld.

3. The contagious nature of the disease was never made known to families of infected cases, such that transmission to wives and children occurred.

4. Because treatment would eliminate a case from the study, cases were actively prevented from receiving treatment (e.g., physicians were told not to treat them, and they were not allowed to be drafted because the preinduction physical could reveal the condition).

5. Published statistics from the study (e.g., that life expectancy was reduced by 20% in patients) were intended to promote fear of the disease in order to provide further support for the study.[24]

Three principles should guide research involving human participants: respect for persons, beneficence, and justice (Table 8-2).[24]

TABLE 8-2 Principles for Guiding Research Involving Human Participants

Respect for persons	■ Obtain informed consent from participants.
	■ Maintain confidentiality.
	■ Avoid stigma and discrimination.
	■ Compensate participants for their time and any adverse consequences from participation.
Beneficence (Action taken for the benefit of others)	■ Research design and methods must be scientifically sound.
	■ Risks associated with research participation must be acceptable in relation to the potential benefits.
Justice (Moral rightness in action or attitude)	■ The benefits and burdens of research are distributed fairly.
	■ Equitable access to benefits of research is ensured.
	■ Avoid targeting vulnerable populations who are incapable of making informed and free choices about participation when other populations are suitable for research.

Data from Fischbach RL. The Tuskegee legacy. *Harv Med Alumni Bull* 1992;93:24–28.

Investigators using experimental designs must show respect and do no harm. It is morally required that informed consent be obtained, that participants be informed that they may or may not be randomly assigned to the treatment group, that participants be compensated for injury, that vulnerable populations (e.g., mentally handicapped, financially destitute) are not taken advantage of, and that controlled clinical trials be stopped when definitive results are available. Participants should also be protected against poorly designed studies that waste time and resources and that might produce misleading results. For experimental research to be of value, sound scientific methodology and research control methods must be used. Honest reporting and delineation of potential biases are expected.

CONCLUSION

A study design is a formal approach of scientific or scholarly investigation. It is the program that directs the researcher along the path of systematically collecting, analyzing, and interpreting observations. Analytic study designs utilize a comparison group that has been explicitly collected. With the exception of the experimental study, all study designs are observational. An experimental study involves evaluating the effects of an assigned intervention on an outcome. An experimental study may have a between-group design, a within-group design, or a combination of both.

Random assignment involves assigning participants to levels of the intervention by a chance mechanism. The value of random assignment is that it makes the groups look alike in all important aspects and only differ in the program or treatment each receives. Randomization eliminates the source of bias in treatment assignment, assuming the sample size is sufficiently large. However, random assignment interferes with the doctor-patient relationship and may not be ethical or feasible.

An experimental study may involve blinding. Blinding has the advantage of controlling for bias. In a single-blinded study the participants are blinded to whether they are receiving the active treatment, in a double-blind study the participants and the investigators at the time of assessment are blinded as to who is receiving the active treatment, and in a triple-blinded study the participants and researchers are blinded and the analyses are conducted by a third party. However, blinding may not be ethical or feasible for certain types of experimental studies.

The steps for designing a randomized controlled trial were presented. These steps involve selecting the intervention, inclusion and exclusion criteria, measuring baseline variables, choosing a comparison group, ensuring compliance, and selecting the outcome. In designing an experimental study, consideration should always be given to the ethical principles involving respect for persons, beneficence, and justice.

Selected special types of randomized study designs were presented. The run-in design is useful for minimizing bias in placebo-controlled studies; the factorial design is an efficient

NEWS FILE

Aspirin and Colorectal Cancer

Low-dose aspirin has been shown in several experimental studies to reduce the risk for a second heart attack and certain types of stroke—mainly by preventing blood clots from forming. Aspirin has also been shown to reduce the risk of colon cancer. A study completed in 1991 by American Cancer Society researchers and reported in the *New England Journal of Medicine* was the first large prospective study to show a link between aspirin use and a reduced risk of colon cancer. The study showed the death rate from colon cancer to be approximately 40% lower in men and women who used aspirin regularly compared with those who did not. A larger study involving nurses and published in the *New England Journal of Medicine* in 1995 involved 121,701 U.S. nurses between 30 and 55 years of age. The study found that subjects who took four to six aspirin tablets a week for 20 years were less likely to develop colon cancer, compared with subjects who took less aspirin; however, in a more recent study, researchers at Brigham and Women's Hospital found that men who took one regular aspirin tablet (325 milligrams) every other day for 5 years in a randomized clinical trial gained no extra protection against colorectal cancer. The findings were reported in the May 1 issue of *Annals of Internal Medicine* and were based on a nationwide study of 22,000 healthy male physicians between the ages of 40 and 84 years. The researchers indicated that these results may possibly be explained by the fact that these men made healthy lifestyle choices beyond using aspirin that could have lowered their risk for colorectal cancer. The relatively short duration of time the study participants took aspirin may also explain why there was no reduction in colon cancer risk in those who took aspirin. Dr. Charles Fuchs, Chief of Ambulatory Services at the Dana-Farber Cancer Institute in Boston, said, "The longer you take [the aspirin] the more you reduce the risk." Fuchs further said, "It takes about 10 years for epithelial cells in the intestines to turn cancerous, so aspirin use for a decade or more is probably necessary to gain a benefit."

Data from American Cancer Society News Center. http://www.cancer.org/docroot/NWS/content/ NWS_1_1x_Aspirin_and_Colorectal_Cancer.asp?sitearea=NWS&viewmode=print&; 1998.

design that allows us to test two or more hypotheses for the price of one; the randomization of matched pairs improves covariate balance on potential confounding variables; and the group randomization design carries certain advantages such as randomization (i.e., avoids bias and achieves balance on average) and being more feasible to deliver the intervention on the group level, but is less efficient statistically than randomization by individuals.

EXERCISES

Key Terms

Define the following terms.

Between-group design	Phase IV trial
Clinical trial	Pilot study
Community trial	Placebo
Diagnostic and screening studies	Placebo effect
Double-blinded study	Prophylactic trial
End point	Protocol
Experimental study	Random assignment
Factorial design	Randomized matched pairs
Group randomization	Run-in design
Institutional review board	Single-blinded study
Natural experiment	Therapeutic trial
Observational study	Triple-blinded study
Phase I trial	Tuskegee syphilis study
Phase II trial	Within-group design
Phase III trial	

STUDY QUESTIONS

1. Which of the answer sets below best matches the strengths/weaknesses listed in the left column with the study designs in the right column?

    ___ More susceptible to individual characteristics that might confound an association (e.g., age, gender, genetic susceptibility).

    A. Between-group design

    B. Within-group design

    ___ More susceptible to confounding from time-related factors (e.g., learning effects, external factors).

    ___ Outcome of interest is compared before and after the intervention in a single cohort.

2. What type of study would you choose if it was unethical to assign a concurrent comparison group using randomization?

3. List some reasons why randomization may not be preferred to a convenience sample.

4. List some reasons why randomization might be preferred to a convenience sample.

5. What are the primary benefits of randomization?

6. Which of the answer sets below best matches the definitions in the left column with the phases of trials listed in the right column?

____ Studies involving animals or cell cultures	A. Preclinical
____ Conducted to determine the safety of a treatment in humans. Patients go through intense monitoring	B. Phase I
____ Large studies (may or may not be a randomized trial) conducted after the therapy has been approved by the FDA to assess the rate of serious side effects and explore further therapeutic uses	C. Phase II D. Phase III E. Phase IV
____ Relatively large randomized blinded trials used to evaluate the efficacy of an intervention	
____ Investigator explores test tolerability, safe dosage, side effects, and how the body copes with the drug	

7. Experimental studies can involve therapeutic or preventive trials. Provide an example for each of these types of trials.

8. What study design allows for testing a less mature hypothesis along with a more mature hypothesis?

9. What study design allows for answering two or more questions in a single study?

10. What study design minimizes bias resulting from loss to follow-up?

11. List five ethical problems that occurred in the Tuskegee syphilis study.

12. Which of the answer sets below best matches the considerations listed in the left column with the ethical principles in the right column?

____ Risks associated with research participation are acceptable in relation to the potential benefits	A. Respect for persons
____ The benefits and burdens of research are distributed fairly	B. Beneficence
____ Confidentiality	C. Justice
____ Informed consent	
____ Research methods are scientifically sound	

13. Design your own randomized controlled trial using the steps given in the chapter.

REFERENCES

1. Lilienfeld AM, Lilienfeld DE. *Foundations of Epidemiology*, 2nd ed. New York, NY: Oxford University Press; 1980, pp. 30–31.

2. Garrison FH. *History of Medicine*. Philadelphia, PA: Saunders; 1926.

3. Lu-Yao G, Albertsen PC, Stanford JL, Stukel TA, Walker-Corkery ES, Barry MJ. Natural experiment examining impact of aggressive screening and treatment on prostate cancer mortality in two fixed cohorts from Seattle area and Connecticut. *BMJ*. 2002;325:740.

4. *Stedman's Medical Dictionary for the Health Professions and Nursing*, 5th ed. Baltimore, MD: Lippincott Williams & Wilkins; 2005.

5. Shapiro AK, Shapiro E. *The Powerful Placebo: From Ancient Priest to Modern Physician*. Baltimore, MD: Johns Hopkins University Press; 1997, p. 272.

6. Beecher HK. The powerful placebo. *JAMA*. 1955;159(17):1602–1606.

7. Alreck RL, Settle RB. *The Survey Research Handbook*. Homewood, IL: Irwin; 1985.

8. Kerlinger FN. *Foundations of Behavioral Research*, 3rd ed. New York, NY: Holt, Rinehart and Winston; 1986.

9. Neale JM, Liebert RM. *Science and Behavior*, 3rd ed. Englewood Cliffs, NJ: Prentice Hall; 1986.

10. Timmreck TC, Braza G, Mitchell J. Growing older: a study of stress and transition periods. *Occup Health Saf*. 1984;53(9):39–48.

11. Rothman KJ. *Modern Epidemiology*. Boston, MA: Little, Brown and Company; 1986.

12. Hulley SB, Feigal D, Martin M, Cummings SR. Designing a new study: IV: experiments. In: Hulley SB, Cummings SR, eds. *Designing Clinical Research: An Epidemiologic Approach*. Baltimore, MD: Williams & Williams; 1988.

13. CancerHelp UK. Phase 1, 2, 3, and 4 trials. http://cancerhelp.cancerresearchuk.org/trials/types-of-trials/phase-1-2-3-and-4-trials. Accessed April 21, 2012.

14. Yusuf S, Collins R, Peto R. Why do we need some large, simple randomized trials? *Stat Med*. 1984;3:409–420.

15. Aldana SG, Greenlaw RL, Diehl HA, et al. Effects of an intensive diet and physical activity modification program on the health risks of adults. *J Am Diet Assoc*. 2005;105(3):371–381.

16. Lu M, Krams M, Zhang L, Zhang ZG, Chopp M. Assessing combination treatments in acute stroke: preclinical experiences. *Behav Brain Res*. 2005;162(2):165–172.

17. Sacco M, Pellegrini F, Roncaglioni MC, Avanzini F, Tognoni G, Nicolucci A, PPP Collaborative Group. Primary prevention of cardiovascular events with low-dose aspirin and vitamin E in type 2 diabetic patients: Results of the Primary Prevention Project (PPP) trial. *Diabetes Care*. 2003;26(12):3264–3272.

18. Greevy R, Lu B, Silber JH, Rosenbaum P. Optimal multivariate matching before randomization. *Biostatistics*. 2004;5(2):263–275.

19. Kornitzer M, Rose G. WHO European collaborative trial of multifactorial prevention of coronary heart disease. *Prev Med*. 1985;14(3):272–278.

20. Cosby RH, Howard M, Kaczorowski J, Willan AR, Sellors JW. Randomizing patients by family practice: sample size estimation, intracluster correlation and data analysis. *FamPract*. 2003;20(1):77–82.

21. Underwood M, Barnett A, Hajioff S. Cluster randomization: a trap for the unwary. *Br J Gen Pract*. 1998;48(428):1089–1090.

22. Green SB. The advantages of community-randomized trials for evaluating lifestyle modification. *Control ClinTrials*. 1997;506-513.

23. Jones JH. *Bad Blood: The Tuskegee Syphilis Experiment*. New York, NY: The Free Press; 1993.

24. Fischbach RL. The Tuskegee legacy. *Harv Med Alumni Bull*. 1992;93:24–28.

9

Causality

OBJECTIVES

After completing this chapter, you will be able to:

- Understand the distinction between statistical inference and causal inference.
- Understand basic concepts of hypothesis formulation and testing.
- Understand the potential influences of chance, bias, and confounding on measures of association.
- Be familiar with selected criteria for establishing causal associations.
- Understand how webs of causation can be used as tools in epidemiology.

Over the centuries, it has been observed that certain environmental exposures, conditions, or behaviors were associated with disease and recovery. For example, Hippocrates (460–377 BC) observed that malaria and yellow fever most commonly occurred in swampy areas; Thomas Sydenham (1624–1689) found that useful treatments and remedies for disease included exercise, fresh air, and diet; Ignaz Semmelweis (1818–1865) discovered that puerperal fever could be drastically cut by the use of hand-washing standards in obstetrical clinics; John Snow (1813–1858) identified fecal-contaminated water as a source of cholera; Bernardino Ramazzini (1633–1714) observed that exposure to certain materials and violent and irregular motions and unnatural postures imposed on the body while working was linked with various diseases and conditions; the Framingham study (1948–1998) identified poor diet and lack of exercise as increasing the risk of heart disease; and many more recent studies have identified poor diet, sedentary lifestyle, obesity, tobacco and alcohol, infectious agents, reproductive factors, and occupational exposures as explaining most cancer.[1–6]

Modern epidemiology continues to study associations between certain environmental exposures, conditions, or behaviors and health-related states or events. However, beyond establishing valid statistical associations, at the heart of epidemiology is uncovering the causes of health problems. The idea is that when a causal association is established, a protection and control attitude can occur rather than a mere reaction to the public health crisis.

A causal association requires a statistical association that is not explained by chance, bias, or confounding. For this reason, this chapter begins with the approach for identifying a valid statistical association. However, conclusions about causality require consideration of other factors as well, such as biologic plausibility and temporality.

In this chapter we introduce statistical inference, present the steps of hypothesis testing, identify potential exposure-outcome bias due to chance, bias, and confounding, introduce causal inference, discuss selected criteria for establishing causal associations, and introduce webs of causation.

STATISTICAL INFERENCE

Epidemiologic studies often utilize sample data from a population of interest. A **sample** is a subset of items that have been taken from the population. Some reasons why samples are often studied instead of populations are as follows:

1. Samples can be studied more quickly than large populations.
2. Studying a sample is often less expensive than studying an entire population.
3. Studying the entire population may be impossible.
4. Sample results can be more accurate than results based on populations since for samples, more time and resources can be spent on training the people who observe and collect the data and on procedures that improve accuracy.
5. Samples of the population that reflect specific characteristics may be more appropriate for studying a certain health-related state or event than the entire population.[7]

Conclusions about the population based on sampled data are most likely to be reliable and valid if each person in the population has an equal probability of being selected for the study. **Statistical inference** refers to a conclusion about a population based on sampled data. With sampled data we can make probability statements about observations in a study, such as that we are 95% confident that the true rate is between a lower and upper limit. A **confidence interval** is a range of reasonable values in which a population parameter lies, based on a random sample from the population. Confidence intervals can be calculated for any statistical measure from a sample.

HYPOTHESIS DEVELOPMENT AND TESTING

The epidemiologic research process starts with a statement of the health problem. The problem involves a given health outcome, which is a consequence or end result. Once the health problem is established it is followed by a research question that asks about why and how the problem exists. A research hypothesis is then formulated, data is collected, and an appropriate statistical test used to evaluate the hypothesis.

Hypothesis Formulation

A **hypothesis** is a suggested explanation for an observed phenomenon or a reasoned proposal predicting a possible association among multiple phenomena.[8] It is based on learned and scientific observation from which theories or predictions are made. Statistical evaluation supports or refutes the presence of an observed phenomenon or association.

Fundamental to the development of hypothesis testing is inductive reasoning. This is the process leading from a set of specific facts to general statements that explain those facts. **Inductive reasoning** relies on[9]:

1. Exact and correct observation

2. Accurate and correct interpretation of the facts in order to understand findings and their relationship to each other and to causality

3. Clear, accurate, and rational explanations of findings, information, and facts in reference to causality

4. Development based on scientific approaches, using facts in the analysis and in a manner that makes sense based on rational scientific knowledge

Hypothesis Testing

Hypothesis testing begins with a statement about what is commonly believed (the status quo), which is called the null hypothesis (H_0). We then make a statement that contradicts the null hypothesis, called the alternative (research) hypothesis (H_1). In descriptive epidemiology, we often employ statistical hypothesis tests to assess whether a set of data for a single variable came from a hypothesized distribution. Analytic epidemiology focuses on testing hypotheses about the relationship between exposure and outcome variables. Our null and research hypotheses serve as the framework for identifying statistical significance.

Six steps are useful for evaluating whether an association between exposure and outcome variables is statistically significant.

Step 1. Formulate the null hypothesis (H_0) in statistical terms. The null hypothesis is typically set at no association (e.g., $H_0: OR = 1$).

Step 2. Formulate the alternative (or research) hypothesis (H_1) in statistical terms. The investigator may wish to test whether there is an association (e.g., $H_1: OR \neq 1$). The null hypothesis is assumed correct unless there is sufficient evidence from the sample data to indicate otherwise. The research hypothesis is a tentative suggestion that a certain phenomenon exists.

Step 3. Select the level of significance for the statistical test and the sample size. The level of significance is generally 0.05, but if a more conservative test is desired, 0.01 might be used. In exploratory studies, the level of significance may be 0.1 or higher. Selecting an appropriate sample size is necessary to assure sufficient power to evaluate the hypotheses. There are various cookbook approaches to estimating sample size. Interested readers should refer to a biostatistics or clinical research book for assistance.

Step 4.   Select the appropriate test statistic and identify the degrees of freedom and the critical value.

Step 5.   Collect the data and estimate the measure of association and the test statistic.

Step 6.   If the observed measure exceeds the critical value, reject H_0 in favor of H_1; otherwise, do not reject H_0.

For data appearing in the 2×2 contingency tables, the chi-square (χ^2) test is appropriate. There are different forms of this test, which depend on the study design being used (see "Common Study Designs with Selected Measures of Association and Test Statistics"**Appendix II**). For example, in an unmatched case-control study, the following equation is appropriate:

$$\chi^2 = \frac{\left(|ad-bc| - \frac{n}{2}\right)^2 n}{(a + b)(c + d)(a + c)(b + d)}$$

To identify the critical value that we compare our calculated χ^2 value to, we first must determine the degrees of freedom (DF). We do this for a table with r rows and c columns as DF $=$ $(r - 1) \times (c - 1)$. For the 2×2 contingency table, the DF $= (2 - 1) \times (2 - 1) = 1$. Now refer to the first line of the χ^2 distribution giving the values of the χ^2 for 1 DF that cut off specified proportions of the upper tail of the distribution (Table 9-1). The critical value from the χ^2 table that separates the upper 5% of the χ^2 distribution from the remaining 95% is 3.84. A significance level of 0.01 would have given a critical value of 6.63 and so on.

When no cell in the 2×2 contingency table has an expected count less than 1 and no more than 20% of the cells have an expected count less than 5, the χ^2 test may be used.[10] The expected value in each cell is obtained by multiplying the row total by the column total that corresponds with a given cell and dividing by n. However, when the sample size is small, the Fisher exact test (see a general biostatistics book for details of the test) is more appropriate for evaluating the association between dichotomous variables.[11] This test is computationally demanding, but is available in computer statistical software.

Now let's consider the disease Sarcoidosis. This is a systematic granulomatous disease of unknown cause that mostly involves the lungs. It causes fibrosis there, but it also involves the lymph nodes, skin, liver, spleen, eyes, phalangeal bones, and parotid glands.[12] Researchers were interested in exploring the hypothesis that behaviors associated with rural living play some role in the development of Sarcoidosis.[13] One of the exposures considered was the use of a coal stove. The 2×2 contingency table of data on coal stove use and Sarcoidosis is presented in Table 9-2. Application of the six steps of hypothesis testing gives the following:

TABLE 9-1   Partial Chi Square (χ^2) Table

	Area in Upper Tail			
Degrees of Freedom	0.10	0.05	0.01	0.001
1	2.71	3.84	6.63	10.83

This table only shows the values of χ^2 for 1 degree of freedom that cut off specified portions of the upper tail of the distribution.

TABLE 9-2   Association between Sarcoidosis and Use of Coal Stoves

| | Sarcoidosis | | |
Use of a coal stove	Yes	No	Total
Yes	10	4	14
No	34	84	118
Total	44	88	132

Step 1. Sarcoidosis is not associated with use of a coal stove, expressed in statistical terms as $H_0{:}OR = 1$.

Step 2. Sarcoidosis is associated with use of a coal stove, expressed in statistical terms as $H_1{:}OR \neq 1$.

Step 3. For this test $\alpha = 0.05$. The sample size was based on an appropriate sample size calculation.

Step 4. The χ^2 test is appropriate for this research question because the observations are nominal data. There is 1 degree of freedom. The critical value for one degree of freedom and $\alpha = 0.05$ is 3.84.

Step 5. The odds of Sarcoidosis in the group that used a coal stove compared with the group that did not use a coal stove is estimated as:

$$Odds\ Ratio = \frac{10 \times 84}{4 \times 34} = 6.18$$

The calculated chi-square value is:

$$\chi^2 = \frac{\left(|10 \times 84 - 4 \times 34| - \frac{132}{2}\right)^2 \times 132}{(10 + 4)(34 + 84)(10 + 34)(4 + 84)} = 8.40$$

Step 6. The estimated $OR = 6.18$ is statistically significant; that is, the null hypothesis is rejected because the observed value of $\chi^2 = 8.40$ is greater than the critical value of 3.84.

Another way to assess statistical significance is to compare the predetermined significance level ($\alpha = 0.05$) with the P value. The **P value** equals the probability that an effect at least as extreme as that observed in a particular study could have occurred by chance alone, given that there is truly no relationship between the exposure and disease. The P value is based on the test statistic. To obtain the P value for the example, go to the row of Table 9-1 that corresponds with 1 DF and then go across the row to 8.40. The observed value does not actually appear on the table but is between two values that do appear (i.e., 6.63 and 10.83). To obtain the corresponding P value for 8.40, move up a row. The P value is between 0.01 and 0.001. Thus, there is sufficient evidence to reject the null hypothesis since $P < 0.05$. The exact P value, which in this example is 0.0038, can be determined with the use of a computer statistical package.

The confidence interval is another way to evaluate statistical significance of association between exposure and outcome variables. A confidence interval for an estimated odds ratio, risk ratio, or rate ratio indicates statistical significance if it does not overlap 1, since 1 means no association. Otherwise there is a significant association. We generally prefer confidence intervals to P values for evaluating statistical significance because they yield more information. Equations for confidence intervals involving the odds ratio, risk ratio, rate ratio, or prevalence proportion ratio are presented later in this volume (see "Summary of Confidence Intervals for Evaluating Selected Hypotheses" Appendix III). These equations are more complex than the confidence interval equations for attack and person-time rates shown in Chapter 4, "Design Strategies and Statistical Methods in Descriptive Epidemiology". Hence, we typically obtain these confidence intervals using a computer statistical software package.

Chance

Because statistical inference involves drawing a conclusion about some characteristic of the population based on sample data, we may find a result merely by **chance** (i.e., the "luck of the draw"). Sample size is directly related to chance. As the sample size increases, the probability that the results are due to chance decreases. The P value provides a means for evaluating the role of chance. The P value ranges from 0 to 1. A small P value indicates that the result is unlikely to be a product of chance. By convention, a P value less than or equal to 0.05 indicates that the role of chance is sufficiently small that the investigators are willing to reject a null hypothesis in favor of the alternative.

Applying a hypothesis test can lead to a wrong conclusion. Two kinds of mistaken conclusions are called Type I and Type II errors. A **Type I error** occurs when H_0 is rejected, but H_0 is true. A **Type II error** occurs when H_0 is not rejected, but H_0 is false. The probability of committing a Type I error is determined by the significance level of the test, represented by the Greek letter α; that is, $\alpha = P(\text{Type I error})$. The probability of committing a Type II error is denoted by β, where $\beta = P(\text{Type II error})$. The **power** of a test of hypothesis is $1 - \beta$, or the probability of rejecting H_0 when H_0 is false. Power can also be thought of as the chance that a given study will detect a deviation from the null hypothesis when one really exists.

An estimated measure of association such as the odds ratio contains no information about the sample size. Although the P value is directly influenced by the sample size, it is also influenced by effect size. Consequently, a small P value may result when there is a strong association between the exposure and outcome, but the sample size is moderate or small. On the other hand, a confidence interval reveals more about the sample size because the width of the interval is directly related to the sample size. A **confidence interval** is a range of reasonable values in which a population parameter lies, based on a random sample from the population. A significance level of 0.05 corresponds with a 95% confidence interval. For the odds ratio computed under step five in the hypothesis testing example above, the 95% confidence interval is 1.81 to 21.05. If each cell is multiplied by 100, the same odds ratio is obtained, but the 95% confidence interval is 2.37 to 2.59.

If a 95% confidence interval overlaps 1, the P value will be greater than 0.05. On the other hand, if the 95% confidence interval does not overlap 1, the P value will be less than 0.05. From the previous example, $P = 0.0014$ is not statistically significant for $\alpha = 0.001$. Consequently, the 99.9% confidence interval of 0.79 to 48.3 does overlap one.

Bias

Bias involves the deviation of the results from the truth and can explain all or part of an observed association between exposure and outcome variables. There is usually very little that can be done to correct for bias once it is present in a study. Bias is minimized by properly designing and conducting the research investigation. It is important for a researcher to identify likely sources of bias, their direction, and magnitude of effect in order to design and conduct their research to minimize threats of bias.

Confounding

Confounding occurs when the relationship between an exposure and a disease outcome is influenced by a third factor, which is related to the exposure and, independent of this relationship, is also related to the health outcome. Confounding should always be considered as a possible explanation for an observed association, particularly in descriptive epidemiologic studies (i.e., ecologic studies and cross-sectional studies) and nonrandomized analytic epidemiologic studies (i.e., observational case-control and cohort studies). For example, suppose that ice cream consumption and murder have a strong statistically significant correlation. Does eating ice cream make people want to kill or does killing result in a desire for ice cream? The explanation may be that because hot temperatures are related to both ice cream consumption and murder, heat is confounding this relationship and is the true explanation for the association.

Only the randomized experimental study allows us to balance out confounding among groups. For example, if smoking was a potential confounder and a large number of people were randomly assigned to either a treatment or control group, it would be expected that the distribution of smokers would be similar between the two groups. Not only should the distribution of smokers to nonsmokers be similar, but the duration of smoking and the amount of smoking should be similarly distributed between groups. When randomization is not possible, approaches such as matching and restriction may be used at the design level of a study, and stratification and multiple regression may be used at the analysis level of a study to control for confounding.

Causality

A conceptual framework for causality was presented in the outset of this book. Some causal models were presented, which are simplifications of often complex causal associations. The epidemiologic triangle is a traditional model that characterizes infectious disease causation. The model shows the interaction and interdependence of the agent, host, environment, and time. This model, however does not adequately describe certain noninfectious diseases. Thus, other models have been proposed such as the causal pie model, which shows that a "sufficient" cause almost always comprises a range of component causes, especially with chronic diseases, which tend to have a **multifactorial etiology**.[14]

Different sufficient causes may have certain component causes in common. If all sufficient causes have a common component cause it is a "necessary" cause. Necessary causes that are also sufficient often relate to the definition of the disease (e.g., lead exposure is a necessary cause of lead poisoning and high doses of radiation is necessary for radiation sickness). On the other hand, exposure to rubella virus (Rubivirus) is necessary for rubella to develop, but not sufficient, because not everyone infected develops the disease. The host must be susceptible and other host factors necessary to cause disease.

A related term to causal component is **risk factor**, which is a factor that is associated with the increased probability of a human health problem. Although a risk factor is not necessarily sufficient to cause disease, its presence does increase the chance of developing the disease. Risk factors are also referred to as at-risk behaviors or predisposing factors. An

at-risk behavior is an activity performed by persons who are healthy, but are at greater risk of developing a health-related state or event because of the behavior. **Predisposing factors** are those existing factors or conditions that produce a susceptibility or disposition in a host to a disease or condition without actually causing it. Predisposing factors precede the direct cause. More will be said about predisposing factors shortly.

CAUSAL INFERENCE

Causal inference is a conclusion about the presence of a health-related state or event and reasons for its existence. The connection between human health and physical, chemical, biological, social, and psychosocial factors in the environment is based on causal inference. To understand this term better, consider that in our daily lives each of us infers that something is true or highly probable based on our expectations and experiences. We may exercise on a regular basis in hopes that it will improve our physical and emotional health, and we may choose to run rather than walk because we expect that this form of exercise is better for cardiovascular health. Inference in epidemiology is similar to inference in daily life in that it is also based on expectations and experience. However in science, expectations are referred to as hypotheses, theories, or predictions and experiences are called results, observations, or data. Inference in everyday life serves as a basis for action.[15] Similarly, causal inferences provide a scientific basis for medical and public health action.

Inferences that we make on a daily basis differ from the manner in which scientists make inferences. The inferences we make are informal and based on expectations about a given event, reasons for its existence, and experience with similar situations. On the other hand, scientists typically base their inferences on the application of formal methods. Causal inferences are made with methods comprising lists of criteria or conditions applied to the results of scientific studies—one of these criteria being a valid statistical association. Inferences are then made based on "judgment" and "logic" that generally follow an acceptable mode of scientific reasoning.[15]

A statistical association may be "judged" to be causally associated based on the totality of evidence. This evidence should include an understanding of the nature of disease transmission. A **direct causal association** has no intermediate factor and is more obvious. For example, a trauma to the skin results in a bruise or infection while Salmonella results in Enteritis. Eliminating the exposure will eliminate the adverse health outcome. On the other hand, an **indirect causal association** involves one or more intervening factors and is often much more complicated. For example, Leptospirosis leads to Hemolysis by hemolysing red blood cells, which then leads to Hemoglobinuria. A clinician may say that Leptospirosis causes Hemoglobinuria, but a pathologist may attribute Hemoglobinuria to Leptospirosis. Similarly, poor diet and stress may cause high blood pressure, which in turn causes heart disease. In this example, diet and stress indirectly influence heart disease.

In paraplegics confined to wheelchairs, the rate for cancer of the bladder is higher than in the nonconfined population. Some urologists suggest that bladder cancer is a result of the person with paraplegia having to hold the urine for long periods of time, causing the urine to become concentrated. The indirect cause of bladder cancer might be the paraplegia handicap and being confined to a wheelchair. It might also be a combination of excessive coffee drinking and not being able to drain the bladder frequently, the coffee being made too strong, or the simple strong concentration of the substance sitting in the bladder for prolonged time periods. The epidemiologist must be careful to assess all variables in the causality of disease, considering both direct and indirect causes.[16–20]

It is also possible for there to be both direct and indirect causal associations. For example, a person may directly contract rabies by inhalation as they enter a cave, where rabies-infected bats roost. They may also contract the disease by an infected skunk or fox living in the bat-infested cave.

A causal mechanism that requires the joint influence of multiple components (also called component causes) includes factors that are predisposing, enabling, precipitating, and reinforcing.[21,22]

1. **Predisposing factors.** These are the factors or conditions already present in a host that produce a susceptibility or disposition to a disease or condition without actually causing it (e.g., age, immune status). If the host is immunized against the disease or if the host has a natural resistance to the disease, he or she will respond by not getting the disease. If not protected, the host will respond by getting the disease because of exposure to the pathogen or agent. If sensitized to a condition, the host will respond accordingly. For example, if the host has an allergic sensitization to a substance and then is exposed to the substance, an allergic reaction will follow. In cancer research, an inherent condition called the Li-Fraumeni syndrome predisposes the person to a greater susceptibility of sarcomas, brain cancer, breast cancer, and leukemia.

2. **Reinforcing factors.** Reinforcing factors have the ability to support the production and transmission of disease or conditions, support and improve a population's health status, and help control diseases and conditions. The factors that help aggravate and perpetuate disease, conditions, disability, or death are negative reinforcing factors. Negative reinforcing factors are repetitive patterns of behavior that recur and perpetuate and support a disease that is spreading and running its course in a population. Positive reinforcing factors are those that support, enhance, and improve the control and prevention of the causation of disease.

3. **Enabling factors.** Enabling factors affect health through an environmental factor in either a positive or negative way. These factors include services, living conditions, programs, societal support, skills, and resources that facilitate a health outcome's occurrence. Some of the factors that enable a disease to spread can be the lack of public health and medical care services. Conversely, the availability of and access to public health and medical care services can prevent, control, intervene, treat, and facilitate recovery from diseases and conditions while improving the health status of the population. The obvious disease causation concern and epidemiologic approach is to enable health services and halt the promotion and production of disease. Consider that when coal miners smoke and are exposed to coal dust, they are more likely to develop lung cancer than coal miners who do not smoke. Coal dust alone is a cause of black lung but has been inconsistently linked with lung cancer.[23] Hence, working in a coal mine appears to enable the progression of lung cancer.

4. **Precipitating factors.** Precipitating factors are essential to the development of diseases, conditions, injuries, disabilities, and death. An example of a precipitating factor is an infectious agent, which is associated with the definitive onset of the disease. Lack of seat belt use in cars, drinking and driving, and lack of helmet use by motorcycle riders all precipitate a higher level of traffic deaths. The cause of a disease, condition, or injury may be fairly obvious, while in other cases it may not be so obvious. Several causal components may be present in the cause, especially in chronic diseases or those caused by lifestyle and behavior.

CAUSAL CRITERIA

In 1856, philosopher John Stuart Mill formed three methods of hypothesis formulation in disease etiology: the method of difference, the method of agreement, and the method of concomitant variation.[24]

1. **Method of difference.** The frequency of disease occurrence is extremely different under different situations or conditions. If a risk factor can be identified in one condition and not in a second, it may be that factor, or the absence of it, that causes the disease. For example, Valley Fever (coccidioidomycosis) occurs only in the deserts of the southwestern United States.

2. **Method of agreement.** If risk factors are common to a variety of different circumstances and the risk factors have been positively associated with a disease, then the probability of that factor being the cause is extremely high. For example, increasing trends in cigarette smoking is directly associated with increasing trends in lung cancer in many different places throughout the world.

3. **Method of concomitant variation.** The frequency or strength of a risk factor varies with the frequency of the disease or condition. For example, increased numbers of children who are not immunized against Measles causes the incidence rate for Measles to go up.

Sir Austin Bradford Hill built on Mill's postulates about causality in 1965 when he outlined nine criteria that could be used to determine whether statistical associations were causal associations.[25]

1. **Strength of association.** When the research problem is established, a research hypothesis is formulated about an expected association between variables. A study design is then selected and an appropriate statistical test applied to the data. The statistical association is then deemed to be significant or not. The question then arises whether a measured association, or lack thereof, is real—that is, does the measured association represent the "truth"? This question comes from the fact that the results are due to chance, bias, or confounding. A chance finding may result because of nonrandom sampling or small numbers; bias may influence the results if data are not correctly representative because of selection or observation, and confounding may cause a spurious result because it is not properly controlled for in the study design or analysis. In general, a strong statistical association between an exposure and health outcome provides greater evidence of there being a causal association because it is more likely to be real (valid). A weakness of this criterion is that it is possible for a weak statistical association and to still be a causal association, such as in the case of smoking and coronary heart disease.[26]

2. **Consistency of association.** This occurs when associations are replicated by different investigators, in different settings, with different methods. For example, the 1964 report of the U.S. Surgeon General identifying a causal association between cigarette smoking and lung cancer was based on 29 case-control studies and seven prospective cohort studies.[27]

3. **Specificity.** Specificity of association means an exposure is associated with only one disease or the disease is associated with only one exposure. Specificity was an important part of **Koch's postulates** (or Henle-Koch postulates) that were published in 1880.[28] Koch applied these postulates to establish the etiology of Anthrax and Tuberculosis, although they can be generalized to other diseases. The postulates state:

   a. The parasite occurs in every case of the disease in question and under circumstances that can account for the pathologic changes and clinical courses of the disease.

   b. It occurs in no other disease as a fortuitous and nonpathogenic parasite.

c. After being fully isolated from the body and repeatedly grown in pure culture, it can induce the disease anew.

These postulates remain important in judging whether a causal relationship exists between an organism and disease; however, they are inadequate for most diseases, especially noninfectious chronic diseases.[29]

Although this criterion may support a causal hypothesis, failure to satisfy it cannot rule out a causal hypothesis because many exposures may be related to a given disease or many diseases may be related to a given exposure. For example, increased risk of lung cancer is associated with cigarette smoking, diet, radon gas, and asbestos. On the other hand, cigarette smoking has been associated with several cancers, heart disease, and stroke. When diseases are grouped together or misclassified, specificity diminishes.

4. **Temporality.** In order for an exposure to cause a disease, the exposure must precede the disease. For example, it has been established that mosquito bites precede malaria. The strength of cohort studies is that they allow researchers to establish a time sequence of events. However, temporality is often difficult or impossible to establish with other study designs.

5. **Biologic gradient.** An increasing amount of exposure increases the risk of disease. Studies have identified direct association between duration of smoking and age-related macular degeneration. This provides evidence that smoking may be causally related to blindness.[30–32] However, a threshold may exist such that above that point, the risk does not change. In addition, the gradient may not be linear.

6. **Biological plausibility.** Is the association biologically supported? Biological assessment often involves experiments in controlled laboratory environments. For example, tobacco smoke is known to contain over 60 carcinogens, including formaldehyde and benzopyrene.

7. **Coherence.** Causal inference is consistent with known epidemiologic patterns of disease. Yet this criterion appears to be redundant with other criteria, such as consistency or biologic plausibility.[26]

8. **Analogy.** Analogous situations with previously demonstrated causal associations provide support of there being a causal association; however, analogies abound.[26]

9. **Experimental evidence.** The randomized, double-blind experimental study design is the best for establishing cause–effect relationships. This is because randomization is effective in balancing out the effect of known and unknown confounders, and blinding is effective at controlling for bias; nevertheless, ethics and feasibility greatly limit application of this criterion in human populations. The order in which epidemiologic study designs are effective at establishing causal associations is as follows:

Rank	Study Design
1	Randomized, double-blind experimental study
2	Community trial
3	Prospective cohort study
4	Retrospective cohort study
5	Case-control study
6	Cross-sectional study
7	Ecologic study
8	Case report or case series

In addition to controlling for bias and confounding, the ranking is based on an ability to measure a temporal sequence of events, the strength of an association, and the dose–response relationship.

WEB OF CAUSATION

Epidemiologic investigation of causal associations in disease began historically with communicable disease epidemics. However, one microbe cannot be singled out as the cause of a disease in behaviorally, occupationally, or environmentally caused chronic conditions or disorders. In lifestyle, work-related, and behaviorally induced disease states, individuals are subject to risk factors in small doses, sometimes in many doses and from many sources, all resulting in a chain of causation. The many risk factors and their various sources make a complex web of causation for a chronic disease that may involve several organ systems and possibly several sites in a single organ system. A **web of causation** is a graphic, pictorial, or paradigm representation of complex sets of events or conditions caused by an array of activities connected to a common core, common experience, or event. A single-line chain of events can be found in parts of or within phases of a web of causation. A single chain of events can be seen in some chronic, behavioral, or environmentally caused diseases or conditions. The complexity of behaviorally or lifestyle-caused conditions or environmentally-caused diseases requires that all facets, risk factors, exposures, or contributing causes be understood and shown so that understanding is complete and the investigation is thorough. Cardiovascular disease and heart disease are good examples.

Some behaviorally founded chronic diseases develop from multiple exposures to a single source and a single agent. Cancer of the lip, gums, mouth, and throat from chewing tobacco is a good example. The chewing tobacco is the single agent and the single source to which the user has multiple exposures. The person, place, and time elements are quite limited yet identifiable because smokeless tobacco use is growing in some areas of the population; especially among younger males in certain places in the United States, such as rural areas with the "cowboy" images, trends, and social influences. A web of causation for cancer of the mouth with smokeless tobacco would be fairly simple and would include factors such as free samples given to teens from tobacco companies in hopes of hooking the youth—social influences, gender, age, place, parental influences, physiological factors, addiction factors, and so forth.[33]

When obvious cause-effect associations are seen, as in smokeless tobacco and cancer of the mouth, then investigations are easy to accomplish. However, when a group of the population comes down with a single disease or several related diseases with a single clear and obviously identifiable source lacking, a web of causation can be of value. Sometimes multiple exposures from multiple sources cause diseases and adverse conditions. For example, if a high rate of pancreatic cancer occurs in a group of children within a limited geographical area, the search for the source and the actual cause is not a simple task. If cancer of the pancreas, kidneys, and liver are seen in the same population group, the investigation becomes even more complicated. Even though all three organs are located within the abdominal cavity, the functions and chance of exposure for each vary as each has a totally different physiologic process.

Questions about causation are not easily answered. As for pancreatic cancer, the epidemiologist might ask several questions. What are the sources or types of carcinogen (e.g., radiation or chemical)? Is there some genetic predisposition in the population group? When lacking a common and clear source of disease, citizens have looked at all kinds of possibilities. For example, the presence of high-tension power lines in the area, such as in a case in Denver, Colorado, has been suspected in certain types of cancer and genetic diseases. When the cause of disease is not clear, other factors must be considered, such as the possible presence of hazardous waste dumps under the homes; problems with food, water, and the surface soil; the use of pesticides and herbicides, air pollution, and gases; the close proximity to chemical plants or other industries; and others. Thus, a web of causation could be constructed to help solve the mystery of sources and causation.

Webs of causation are graphic, pictorial, or paradigm representations of complex sets of events or conditions caused by an array of activities connected to a common core, experience, or event. In webs of causation, the core or final outcome is the disease or condition. Webs have many arms, branches, sources, inputs, and causes that are somehow interconnected or interrelated to the core. Webs can also have a chain of events in which some events must occur before others can take place.

Identifying and ascertaining the specific details of the various factors leading to disease, disability, injury, or death enhance webs of causation. Two approaches to enhancing webs of causation are the use of decision trees and fish bone cause–effect analysis diagrams. The **decision tree** is a flow chart that visually presents a process through which lines and symbols lead to proper decisions and understanding of the role of certain risk factors in webs of causation. Fish bone diagrams provide a visual display of all possible causes that could potentially contribute to the disease, disorder, or condition under study.

The complexity of webs of causation is presented for coronary heart disease (Figure 9-1), asthma (Figure 9-2), and lead poisoning (Figure 9-3). Consider this latter example in which lead poisoning may result from a multitude of events and sources. Children are particularly

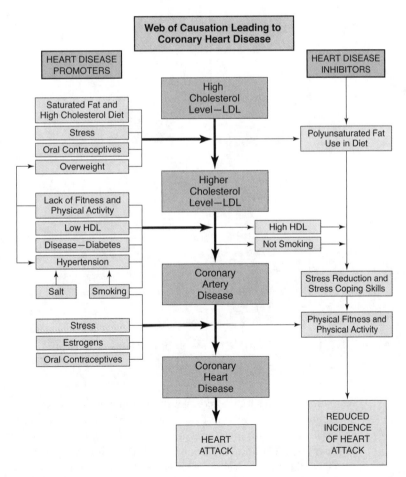

FIGURE 9-1 Example of a web of causation for coronary heart disease. Adapted from R Sherwin, in Mausner JS, Kramer S. *Epidemiology: An Introductory Text*. Philadelphia, PA: WB Saunders; 1985.

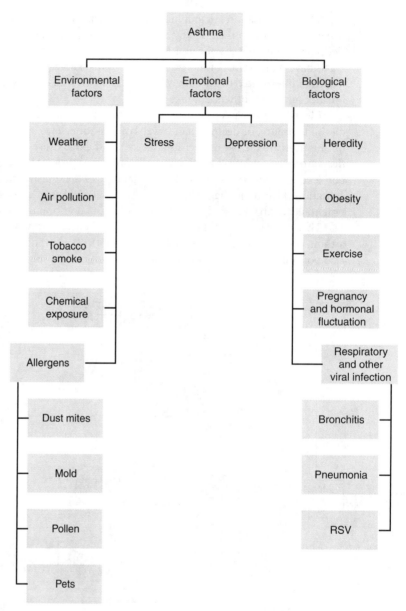

FIGURE 9-2   Example of a web of causation for asthma.

susceptible to lead's toxic effects. Lead poisoning, unlike other childhood diseases, produces no symptoms early in the disease. The child has no reaction to the exposure and does not appear ill at first, thus most cases go undiagnosed and untreated. Over the years, the Centers for Disease Control and Prevention have set the safe lead exposure levels lower and lower. Scientific studies and clinical observation in children continue to show that even the smallest amount of lead exposure in children can have detrimental effects. In screenings of children to determine levels of lead in the body, the test of choice is now blood lead measurements. The primary control of lead poisoning is prevention measures, especially if these are targeted to

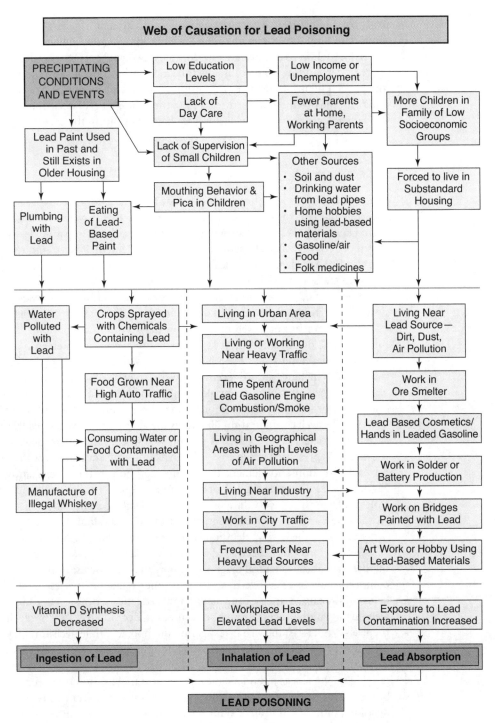

FIGURE 9-3   Example of a web of causality for lead poisoning.

high-risk populations. Screening and medical treatment of lead-poisoned children remain important until the sources of lead in the environment are eliminated.

Although webs of causation are complex, two concepts universally apply. First, a complete understanding of the causal factors and mechanisms is not required or necessary for the development of effective prevention and control measures. Second, it is possible to interrupt the production of a disease by cutting the chains of occurrences of the various factors at strategic points that will stop the chain of events in the causation of the disease.

DECISION TREES

Webs of causation have limitations in that they may not directly lead the epidemiologic investigator right to the cause. Decision trees, used with webs of causation, are the suggested approach. When constructing a web of causation, a separate decision tree would be developed for each aspect, factor, and causation element. The yes–no response of decision trees leads the epidemiologist closer to discovering the cause than a web of causation alone. Decision trees, as used in disease diagnosis, can ask leading questions that are answered either yes or no, thus eliminating possibilities of causation while leading the investigator down the correct path toward discovery, assuming the questions are answered correctly.

Some branches of a web of causation may require second level assessments, as secondary levels of causation or risk factors may have to be taken into account. This may require the development of a second level set of webs. In some cases, a third level of assessment, which includes a third level set of webs, may be required. The second and third levels of webs feed into the appropriate branches of the main web, accounting for all possible risk factors or factors that contribute to the disease, directly and indirectly.

A spider web configuration illustrates the elements of a web of causation with the disease as the focus (Figure 9-4).[34] A second web of causation that focuses on the causes of the disease is presented in Figure 9-5.[34] An example of a decision tree that must be adapted for each situation and element under consideration in the investigation is presented in Figure 9-6.[34] In summary, a web of causation is a quasi-flow chart that identifies every possible risk factor from every dimension of living, leading eventually to the diagnosed disease. At each step and for each element, a decision tree is established and worked through in order to assure the correct decision is being made leading to causation of the disease.

Decision trees have been used as decision-making tools with regard to administration of pharmaceuticals, medical diagnoses, emergency care decision-making, health screening, communicable disease investigation, and other related activities. In chronic disease and behaviorally caused diseases and disorder investigations, decision trees are supportive to the web investigation process. In webs of causation, decision trees are not techniques in and of themselves but assist the web investigation method. Multiple decisions may be used in complex disorders with multiple risk factors and multiple exposures and agents, such as found in heart disease, stroke, and cancer.

Figure 9-6 assists in understanding just how the decision trees work. Diamond-shaped boxes represent decision points. Rectangular boxes represent activities. "Yes" and "No" decision points are indicated. While arrows show the direction to the next activity or decision point, decision trees can reroute activities back toward the beginning if certain criteria are not met or the decision falls short of meeting expectations. Decision trees are followed until the final step is met; in Figure 9-6, "no further action" is the final result.[33]

Using the decision-tree technique within the web of causation may be less complex in some cases and may not require extensive decision trees for all risk factors. On the other

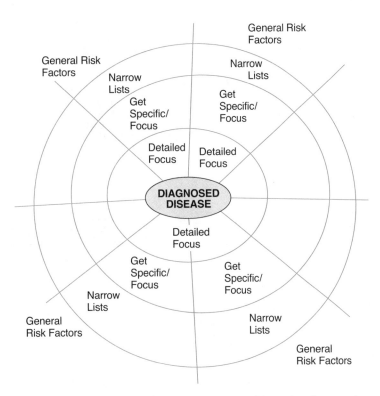

FIGURE 9-4   Basic concept in the construction of a web of causation with the disease as the focus.

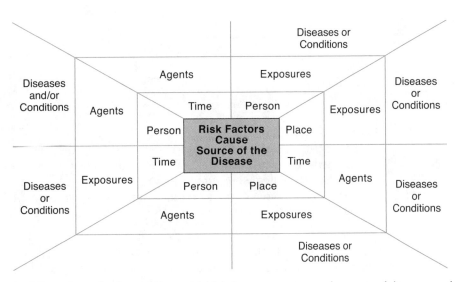

FIGURE 9-5   Web of causation with risk factors, cause, and source of disease as the focus of the investigation.

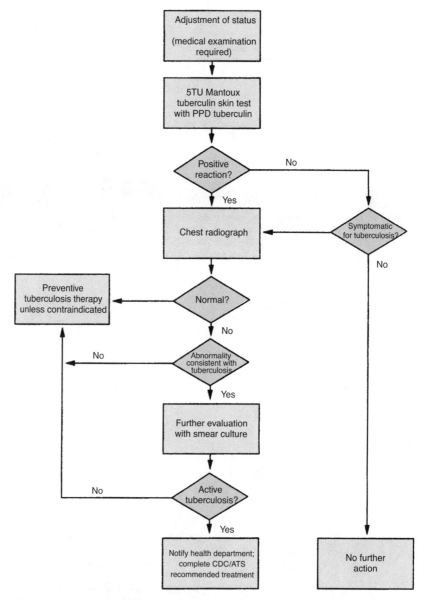

FIGURE 9-6 Example of a decision tree used in epidemiological decision making, showing the decision making activities for tuberculosis screening for non-immigrants in the United States who request permanent residence. From Centers for Disease Control and Prevention. Tuberculosis among foreign-born persons entering the United States. *MMWR.* 1990;39(RR-18):1–13, 18–21.

hand, certain risk factors may be quite complex, and as a result, the decision trees must also be complex. For example, in a hypothetical case of an outbreak of increased heart attacks in air traffic controllers, all risk factors would be listed. Risk factors considered might be stress, smoking or tobacco use, drug use, illicit drug use, alcohol use, age, hours worked, years in profession, emotional stability, personal problems, social problems, sleep habits, physical fitness, and diet/nutrition.

Decision trees would then be developed for each risk factor or subelement of the risk factor. Using diet and nutrition as an example, a decision tree could be constructed on eating habits and food selection, vitamin and nutrient intake, fat consumption and cholesterol levels, salt intake, and sugar and caffeine consumption.

Construction of a Web of Causation and Decision Trees

Steps for constructing webs of causation and decision trees are as follows:

1. Identify the problem, affirm the condition, and obtain an accurate diagnosis of the disease.
2. Place the diagnosis at the center or bottom of the web.
3. Brainstorm and list all possible sources for the disease.
4. Brainstorm and list all risk factors and predisposing factors of the disease.
5. Develop subwebs and tertiary level subwebs for the various branches of webs if needed.
6. Organize and arrange lists of sources and risk factors from general and most distant from the disease, in steps, being more specific and focused as the steps move closer toward the diagnosis of the disease.
7. Develop and work through causation decision trees for each element under consideration on the way toward the diagnosed disease.

FISH BONE DIAGRAM (CAUSE-EFFECT DIAGRAM)

A **fish bone diagram** (Figure 9-7) is also referred to as cause–effect diagram and isdeveloped to provide a visual presentation of all possible factors that could contribute to a disease,

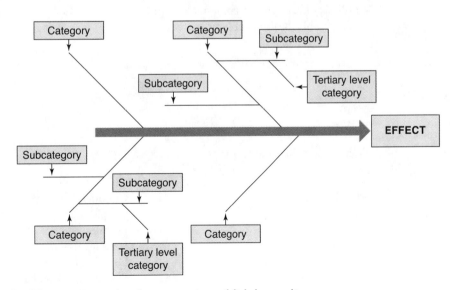

FIGURE 9-7   Example of construction of fish bone diagram.

disability, or death. This type of diagram can assist the epidemiologist in defining, determining, uncovering, or eliminating possible causes.

The first step in the fish bone diagram activity is to brainstorm lists of all potential causes or contributing risk factors. The fish bone diagram is then constructed by placing the categories of causes on the "bones" of the diagrams, making it a visual display for easy study and analysis. The second step is to develop subcategories of all specific causes for each of the major category areas. Each branch of the fish bone is given a label or becomes a category, and subcategories are placed on the lines that make up the bones. It is also possible to add a third (tertiary) level of cause to the bones of the diagram. The head of the fish bone is assigned a box that contains the effect or outcome, which is the disease, disability, condition, injury, or death.

The diagram is complete when all possible risk factors or causes have been properly placed within the categories and subcategories of the diagram, on the lines that create the fish bone effect. An outline of the categories, subcategories, and tertiary levels can be developed and presented as well. An assessment of the facts at the tertiary, subcategory, and category levels should be made for each statement. The statements are answered yes or no or are answered true or not true.

CONCLUSION

This chapter introduced statistical inference as a conclusion about some characteristic of the population based on sample data. The fundamentals of hypothesis development and testing were presented, as they relate to evaluating the association between two level exposure and outcome variables. We emphasized that a valid statistical association is one that is not explained by chance, bias, or confounding. The process of causal inference often involves consideration of selected criteria. The totality of evidence is then used to draw conclusions about causality. Webs of causation were also introduced as means to assessing complex factors of causation, as more commonly seen with chronic diseases and conditions. The emphasis of causality in epidemiology provides a scientific basis for preventing and controlling public health problems.

EXERCISES

Key Terms

Define the following terms.

Analogy	Coherence
At-risk behavior	Confidence interval
Bias	Consistency of association
Chance	Decision tree
Confounding	Direct causal association
Biological plausibility	Enabling factors
Biologic gradient	Experimental evidence
Causal inference	Fish bone diagram

Hypothesis
Indirect causal association
Method of concomitant variation
Inductive reasoning
Koch's postulates
Method of agreement
Method of difference
Multifactorial etiology
Predisposing factors
Power
Precipitating factors

P value
Reinforcing factors
Risk factor
Sample
Specificity
Statistical inference
Strength of association
Temporality
Type I error
Type II error
Web of causation

STUDY QUESTIONS

1. For each of the following statements, indicate whether the statistical association is likely the result of chance, bias, or confounding.

   a. A case-control study showed that a strong association exists between birth order and Down syndrome.

   b. A case-control study found a positive association between self-reported chest radiographs during pregnancy and breast cancer.

   c. A randomized clinical trial found that drug A versus placebo did not significantly improve 10-year survival ($RR = 0.35$; 95% confidence interval, 0.14–55.01).

   d. A cohort study found no statistical association between smoking and pancreatic cancer ($RR = 1$; P value $= 0.85$).

   e. A hospital-based case-control study identified a strong association between oral contraceptives and thromboembolism. Many doctors suspected the association and hospitalized some women who used oral contraceptives for evaluation.

2. Match the following methods for minimizing chance, bias, and confounding in an experimental study.

   __ Chance   a. Randomization

   __ Bias   b. Blind

   __ Confounding   c. Increase sample size

3. Recall the causal criteria presented by Sir Austin Bradford Hill in 1965. Discuss these criteria in the context of smoking and lung cancer.

4. Suppose you suspect, based on descriptive epidemiology, that college students who perform better academically are more likely to have an office job and be obese 10 years after graduation. You decide to select 500 graduating seniors randomly, and classify them accord-

ing to grade point average as high versus low (where the cut point is at the median of the GPAs for these students). The resulting 2×2 contingency table is as follows:

Obese at 10 Years

GPA	Yes	No	Total
High	60	190	250
Low	40	210	250
Total	100	400	500

Apply this data to the six steps of hypothesis.

5. Match the following

    ___ Predisposing factors   a. Facilitate manifestation of a disease (e.g., housing)

    ___ Enabling factors   b. Associated with definitive onset of disease (e.g., toxin)

    ___ Precipitating factors   c. Increase level of susceptibility in a host (e.g., age)

    ___ Reinforcing factors   d. Aggravate presence of disease (e.g., repeated exposure)

6. Compare a direct causal association with an indirect causal association. Use specific examples.

7. Define and compare the difference between statistical inference and causal inference.

8. Why might studying a sample be preferred to a population?

9. A component cause is also called which of the following?

    a. Risk factor

    b. Web of causation

    c. Epidemiologic triangle

    d. Each of the above are component causes

10. Webs of causation play a more useful role when one is trying to describe disease etiology for which type of disease?

    a. Acute

    b. Infectious

    c. Chronic

    d. Two of the above

REFERENCES

1. Hippocrates. Airs, waters, places. In: Buck C, Llopis A, Najera E, Terris M, eds. *The Challenge of Epidemiology: Issues and Selected Readings*. Washington, DC: World Health Organization; 1988, pp. 18–19.

2. Dorland WA, ed. *Dorland's Illustrated Medical Dictionary*, 25th ed. Philadelphia, PA: Saunders; 1974.

3. Cumston CG. *An Introduction to the History of Medicine*. New York, NY: Alfred A. Knopf; 1926.

4. Garrison FH. *History of Medicine*. Philadelphia, PA: Saunders; 1926.

5. Dawber TR, Kannel WB, Lyell LP. An approach to longitudinal studies in a community: the Framingham study. *Ann NY Acad Sci*. 1963;107:539–556.

6. Agency for Toxic Substances & Disease Registry. Cancer Fact Sheet. http://www.atsdr.cdc.gov/com/cancer-fs.html. Accessed January 21, 2012.

7. Dawson B, Trapp RG. *Basic & Clinical Biostatistics*, 4th ed. New York, NY: Lange Medical Books/McGraw-Hill; 2004.

8. Merriam-Webster. Hypothesis. http://www.merriam-webster.com/dictionary/hypothesis. Accessed April 21, 2012.

9. Shindell S, Salloway JC, Oberembt CM. *A Coursebook in Health Care Delivery*. New York, NY: Appleton-Century-Crofts; 1976.

10. Cochran WE. Some methods for strengthening the common $x^{2\text{-test}}$. *Biometrics*. 1954;10:417–451.

11. Rosner B. *Fundamentals of Biostatistics*, 4th ed. Belmont, CA: Wadsworth Publishing Company; 1995.

12. *Stedman's Medical Dictionary for the Health Professions and Nursing*, 5th ed. Baltimore, MD: Lippincott Williams & Wilkins; 2005.

13. Kajdasz DK, Lackland DT, Mohr LC, Judson MA. A current assessment of rurally linked exposures as potential risk factors for sarcoidosis. *Ann Epidemiol*. 2001;11:111–117.

14. Fox JP, Hall CE, Elveback LR. *Epidemiology: Man and Disease*. New York, NY: Macmillan Company; 1970.

15. Weed DL. Causal and preventive inference. In: Greenwald P, Kramer BS, Weed DG, eds. *Cancer Prevention and Control*. New York, NY: Marcel Dekker, Inc.; 1995.

16. MacMahon B, Pugh TF. *Epidemiology: Principles and Methods*. Boston, MA: Little, Brown and Company; 1970.

17. Mausner JS, Kramer S. *Epidemiology: An Introductory Text*. Philadelphia, PA: WB Saunders; 1985.

18. Lilienfeld AM, Lilienfeld DE. *Foundations of Epidemiology*. New York, NY: Oxford University Press; 1980.

19. Friedman GD. *Primer of Epidemiology*. New York, NY: McGraw-Hill; 1974.

20. Kelsey JL, Thompson WD, Evans AS. *Methods in Observational Epidemiology*. New York, NY, Oxford University Press; 1986.

21. Evans AS. Causation and disease: the Henle-Koch postulates revisited. *Yale J Biol Med*. 1976;49: 175–195.

22. Green L, Krueter M. *Health Promotion Planning*, 2nd ed. Mountain View, CA: Mayfield Publishing Company; 1991.

23. International Agency for Research on Cancer. Coal dust. http://www.inchem.org/documents/iarc/vol68/coal.html. Accessed December 16, 2008.

24. Mill JS. A System of Logic, *Ratiocinative and Inductive*, 5th ed. London, UK: Parker, Son and Bowin; 1862.

25. Hill AB. The environment and disease: association or causation? *Proc R Soc Med*. 1965;58:295–300.

26. Rothman KJ. *Epidemiology: An introduction*. New York, NY: Oxford University Press; 2002.

27. U.S. DHEW. Smoking and health: Report of the advisory committee to the Surgeon General of the Public Health Service. PHS Publication No. 1103. Washington, DC: U.S. Government Printing Office; 1964.

28. Koch R. Überdieätiologie der tuberkulose. In: *Verhandlungen des KongressesfürInnereMedizin.* ErsterKongress, Wiesbaden; 1882.

29. Evans AS. Causation and disease: a chronological journey. *Am J Epidemiol.* 1978;108:249–258.

30. Delcourt C, Diaz JL, Ponton Sanchez A, Papoz L. Smoking and age-related macular degeneration: the POLA study. *Arch Ophthalmol.* 1998;116:1031–1035.

31. Hankinson SE, Willett WC, Colditz GA, et al. A prospective study of cigarette smoking and risk of cataract surgery in women. *JAMA.* 1992;268:994–998.

32. Christen WG, Manson JE, Seddon JM, et al. A prospective study of cigarette smoking and risk of cataract in men. *JAMA.* 1992;268:989–993.

33. National Cancer Institute. *Strategies to Control Tobacco Use in the United States.* Hyattsville, MD: Public Health Services, U.S. Department of Health and Human Services; 1992.

34. Centers for Disease Control and Prevention. Tuberculosis among foreign-born persons entering the United States. *MMWR.* 1990;39(RR-18):1–13, 18–21.

10

Field Epidemiology

OBJECTIVES

After completing this chapter, you will be able to:

- Define field epidemiology.
- Discuss the role of the epidemiologist in planning and establishing an epidemiologic study for assessing epidemics.
- Be familiar with the steps of a field investigation.
- Be familiar with epidemiologic questions that may be helpful in a field investigation.
- Define cluster and cluster investigation and discuss the process for investigating clusters.
- Identify the primary challenges in detecting reported clusters.
- Describe methods for assessing reported clusters.

An interesting, exciting, and challenging part of epidemiology is working in the field conducting epidemiologic investigations of epidemics. Epidemiologists have been called disease detectives.[1] Epidemiologic field investigations typically involve disease outbreaks. **Outbreak** carries the same definition as epidemic, but is typically used when the event is confined to a geographic area that is more limited in scope. The purpose of this chapter is to provide a definition of field epidemiology and discuss the specific activities conducted by field epidemiologists.

Field epidemiology has been defined as the application of epidemiology under a set of general conditions:

- The problem is unexpected.
- A timely response may be demanded.
- The intervention of epidemiologists and their presence in the field are required to solve the problem.
- The investigation time is likely to be limited because of the need for a timely intervention.[2]

Field investigations involving acute problems may differ from conventional epidemiologic studies in three important ways. First, field investigations often do not start with a clear hypothesis. Gathering descriptive data on person, place, and time may be required before the hypothesis can be formulated and tested. Second, acute problems involve an immediate need to protect the public and resolve the concern; hence, in addition to data collection and analyses, public health action often occurs. Third, field epidemiologists must decide when the available information is sufficient to take appropriate action.[2]

Field investigations involve several activities. These activities can include abstracting information from a variety of sources, collecting specimens for laboratory tests, conducting clinical exams to confirm cases, identifying the natural course of the disease, and producing reports and graphs.[3,4] However, field investigation may pose unique challenges beyond the scientific ideal. For example, abstracted information can vary considerably in completeness and accuracy, small numbers may greatly restrict statistical power, collecting biological specimens "after the fact" may be impossible, and cooperation may be at a low level.[2] Nevertheless, the highest scientific quality possible should be sought under such limitations.

CONDUCTING A FIELD INVESTIGATION

Epidemiologic field investigations generally involve disease outbreaks that are confined to localized areas and have been traced to a common source, outbreaks that have spread from person to person, or a combination of the two. Disease outbreaks investigated in the field are typically limited to a specific time period. Disease outbreak is a term used synonymously with epidemic and is technically more correct if the epidemic is confined to a localized area.[5] Several steps in the field investigation process are listed in order (Table 10-1), although some of these steps may be applied simultaneously.

Prepare for Fieldwork

The success of an epidemiologic field investigation begins with making sure the research team has the appropriate scientific knowledge, supplies, and equipment; appropriate administrative arrangements are made; and consultation roles established.

It may be necessary to conduct a literature review to better understand the purported health problem and to communicate with experts on the topic. The investigative team often consists of a group with differing expertise and experience. The epidemiologist is critical to these groups because of their ability to describe aspects of the health problem by person, place, and time factors, as well as assists in formulating the study hypotheses, conducting the analyses, and in communicating the findings. Other members of the team may include,

TABLE 10-1   Steps for Conducting a Field Investigation

1. Prepare for field work.
2. Establish the existence of an epidemic or outbreak.
3. Confirm the diagnosis.
4. Establish criteria for case identification.
5. Search for missing cases.
6. Count cases.
7. Orient the data according to person, place, and time.
8. Classify the epidemic.
9. Determine who is at risk of becoming a case.
10. Formulate hypotheses.
11. Test hypotheses.
12. Develop reports and inform those who need to know.
13. Maintain surveillance to monitor trends and execute control and prevention measures.
14. Carry out administration and planning activities.

for example, a sanitarian if the health problem involves environmental aspects, or a public health nurse if the problem is connected with a child-care setting or school.

Prior to embarking to the field, it is important that the process of decision making be established and the team member's respective roles understood. Making travel and financial arrangements is also important. Finally, identifying and making contact with persons or groups in the field, on both state and local levels, should occur prior to departure.

Establish the Existence of an Epidemic or Outbreak

First, the epidemiologist must verify that a disease outbreak exists. Local health officials will likely know if disease rates are above those that are normally expected; however, the presence of a disease outbreak can be difficult to detect. On the other hand, some perceived outbreaks may not be real. Incorrect positive diagnoses by physicians, for example, can give the false impression of an outbreak.

The **attack rate** is an appropriate statistic for investigating disease outbreaks because it describes rapidly occurring, new cases of disease in a well-defined population over a limited time period. The attack rate is a cumulative incidence rate expressed as a percentage (see Chapter 4 "Design Strategies and Statistical Methods in Descriptive Epidemiology"). Attack rates are usually calculated with person characteristics (e.g., age, gender, race/ethnicity, and occupation) in order to identify high-risk groups.

Confirm the Diagnosis

Laboratory techniques employed by trained professionals are required to confirm clinical diagnosis of cases. Assessment of the clinical findings should be done to ensure the correctness and reliability of the findings; however, in some settings, it might not be possible to confirm all cases. If a swift public health response is needed and several people are confirmed cases, it may be sufficient to identify others as cases if they display the same signs and symptoms; nevertheless, this should only be done by an appropriately trained individual.

False-positive test results can cause considerable concern and give inaccurate information in a disease investigation. Some conditions, injuries, or behaviorally caused occurrences cannot be confirmed with laboratory tests. It is easier to diagnose a bacteria-caused disease than an occupational or environmental disorder or condition, but these too must be verified. On the other hand, some diseases or conditions are only verifiable with laboratory findings, and some exotic or unique diseases can be verified only through a limited number of specialized labs, including the Centers for Disease Control and Prevention (CDC).

Establish Criteria for Case Identification

A case definition involves standard clinical criteria that are used to establish whether a person has a particular disease. Applying a standard case definition will guarantee that every case is consistently diagnosed, no matter when and/or where the diagnosis occurs. For certain rare but very lethal (e.g., plague) communicable diseases that require a quick response, a loose case definition may be appropriate. On the other hand, in many epidemiologic studies where a quick response is less critical and identifying causal associations is important, it may be more essential to be sure that people in the study have the disease. In this situation, a stricter set of criteria for establishing the presence of a disease might be in order. The identifying features (e.g., signs, symptoms, disease progression, place and type of exposure, lab findings) will depend on the condition and disease under investigation.

Search for Missing Cases

The epidemiologist should search for cases that have not been recognized or reported. Physicians, clinics, health maintenance organizations, hospital emergency departments, public health clinics, migrant health clinics, and related facilities should be canvassed to ascertain whether other people might have the disease or condition under investigation. Asymptomatic persons or mild cases and their contacts should be evaluated. Individuals are placed into appropriate categories, initially separating the suspected cases from probable cases.

Count Cases

Disease frequency must be determined. This involves quantifying the occurrence of disease in the population being investigated. Identifying the size of the at-risk population from which the cases derive is necessary to calculate attack rates.

Orient the Data According to Person, Place, and Time

Person.   The epidemiologist should quickly become acquainted with the person-related issues and characteristics associated with the disease under investigation. Line listings should include information that characterizes the population and that can be adjusted for in the analysis, including inherent characteristics of people (age, race/ethnicity, gender), acquired characteristics (immunity or marital status), activities (occupation, leisure, use of medications), and conditions (socioeconomic status, access to health care). The interactions of family, friends, fellow workers, and relatives need to be considered. Certain person characteristics will have more relevance to some diseases or conditions than others. For example, if diabetes is discovered to be occurring in epidemic proportions, the epidemiologist should include the characteristic of race in the analysis because certain races have higher rates of some diseases than others. Specifically, Native Americans have higher rates of diabetes, blacks have higher rates of hypertension, and Asians have lower rates of cardiovascular diseases.

Place.   The concentration of cases needs to be determined with regard to residence, birthplace, place of employment, school district, hospital unit, country, state, county, census tract, street address, map coordinates, and so forth. This allows the epidemiologist to understand the geographic extent of disease, gain an understanding of where the agent that causes a disease resides and multiplies, and better understand what may carry or transmit, spread, and cause a disease. A spot map is often an effective way to present this data pictorially. If possible, the epidemiologist might also plot on a map the locations of exposures, the locations of each case at the time of exposure, or when those exposed were identified as a case.

Time.   Presenting each case by time of onset with an epidemic curve can provide important information about the disease outbreak. An **epidemic curve** is a histogram, in which cases are plotted by time of onset that shows the course of an epidemic. It is important to be familiar with the incubation period and how time affects the modes and vehicles of transmission. Chronologic events, step-by-step occurrences, chains of events tied to time, and time distribution of the onset of cases should be determined and plotted on charts and graphs. From the epidemic curve information, the nature of the course of the disease is determined, and the researcher can ascertain whether people were exposed and infected at about the same time or at different times. Look for clustering of disease by both time and place. Determine and fix the time of the index case and the time of onset of the outbreak. Use the information from incubation periods to determine time factors in the course of the disease peaks and valleys in the epidemic curve.

Classify the Epidemic

The mode of transmission is assessed, and a determination is made as to whether the disease outbreak is a **common-source epidemic** (starting at a specific point through intermittent or continuous exposure to a source over days, weeks, or years [See News File]), a **propagated epidemic** (spread gradually from person to person), or a result of a common source of exposure that is then spread secondarily from person to person. A **mixed epidemic** involves a combination of both types of epidemics. Mixed epidemics typically begin with a common source and then are propagated from person to person. For example, in September 1973, diarrhea caused by *Salmonella Typhimurium* developed in 32 individuals in a hospital in Maine. The source of the outbreak was raw egg beaten in milk and then drunk as eggnog. However, 14 additional persons developed the illness who had not drunk the eggnog but presumably acquired the infection through person-to-person spread of *S. typhimurium*.[6] The following questions should be asked when classifying an epidemic:

- Is the outbreak from a single source or a single-point exposure?
- Is disease spread from person-to-person?

High Rates of Respiratory and Mental Health Problems in World Trade Center Rescue and Recovery Workers

Almost half of over 1,000 screened rescue and recovery workers and volunteers who responded to the World Trade Center attacks have new and persistent respiratory problems. More than half of these people also have persistent psychological symptoms. These results are based on preliminary data from a medical screening program funded by the CDC and administered by the Mount Sinai Medical Center, New York City.

The findings reported in the CDC's *Morbidity and Mortality Weekly Report* are based on evaluation of data from 1,138 participants (91% were men and the median age was 41 years) who voluntarily enrolled in the World Trade Center Worker and Volunteer Medical Screening Program. Through August 2004, the screening program has provided free standardized medical assessments, clinical referrals, and occupational health education to nearly 12,000 workers and volunteers exposed to environmental contaminants, psychological stressors, and physical hazards. Besides respiratory and mental health effects, program participants also reported lower back and upper- or lower-extremity pain, heartburn, eye irritation, and frequent headache.

Only 21% of the workers and volunteers participating in the screening program had appropriate respiratory protection September 11–14, 2001. Also, 51% met the predetermined criteria for risk of mental health problems. The responses also indicated that the participants' risk for posttraumatic stress disorder was four times the rate of posttraumatic stress disorder in the general male population.

The CDC's National Institute for Occupational Safety and Health has increased efforts to protect emergency responders from health and safety hazards in responding to terrorist incidents. New criteria were established for testing and certifying respirators used by emergency responders against chemical, biological, radiological, and nuclear exposures. The National Institute for Occupational Safety and Health also is partnering with responders, emergency response agencies, manufacturers, and other federal agencies to improve respirators and other personal protective equipment, improve training and education for responders, and improve safety management at disaster sites.

From Centers for Disease Control and Prevention. Physical health status of World Trade Center rescue and recovery workers and volunteers—New York City, July 2002–August 2004. MMWR 2004;53(35): 807–812; Centers for Disease Control and Prevention. Mental health status of World Trade Center rescue and recovery workers and volunteers—New York City, July 2002–August 2004. MMWR. 2004; 53(35):812–815.

■ Is there continued exposure to a single source?

■ Is the outbreak from multiple sources and/or exposures?

■ Is the outbreak airborne? Behaviorally or chemically caused? Does the outbreak involve multiple events or exposures?

■ Are the sources of infection from unapparent sources?

■ Is there a vector involved in the transmission?

■ Is there an animal reservoir of infection?

The shape of the epidemic curve for a point-source epidemic typically rapidly increases, peaks, and then gradually decreases. With a continuous common-source epidemic, the increase may be more gradual and the curve more symmetric, covering a longer period of time. The curve typically contains one primary peak. With a propagated epidemic, the epidemic curve is usually a series of successively larger peaks.

Determine Who Is at Risk of Becoming a Case

The epidemiologist must determine who is ill and who is well in the exposed group. The people in the group can be classified by their individual disease and exposure histories. Clinical, medical, and laboratory findings need to be confirmed, evaluated, and analyzed in order for all cases to substantiate the diagnosis. Asymptomatic individuals or mildly ill persons should be medically evaluated. Searches should be made for human and animal sources of infection in those at risk. The people exposed are separated from those not exposed. The ill are separated from the well. The status of the health of each case must be determined by exposure. The 2×2 contingency table is useful for classifying cases by exposure status.

Formulate Hypotheses

Firmly establish the source and type of epidemic. Is the outbreak from a common source or is it propagated? Identify the most probable source for the epidemic—the event, infection, or exposure source. Establish the mode of transmission. Use and analyze the information acquired earlier in the investigation, including but not limited to: case counts; assessing those at risk; the sources of the epidemic; time, place, or person factors; and attack rates. For example, if it is a foodborne epidemic, in addition to investigating those ill from the exposure, the source of food must be investigated along with the food handling, preparation, production, and preservation. If the outbreak is environmentally caused, the conditions of the environment in which the individuals spent time must be investigated (e.g., the air at a worksite or skin exposure to chemicals). Consider all possible sources from which the disease could be contracted: milk supplies, water supplies, seafood sources, food-packing houses, imported foods, and so on.

Animal sources of infection, as well as human sources, should be considered. Researchers should study attack rates for the well/unexposed and the ill/exposed. They should also evaluate all suspected vehicles of transmission and assess frequency and levels of exposure. Variations in prevalence and incidence should be evaluated. As information comes in, it should also be evaluated and the data assembled. Pertinent grouping of data based on time, place, person characteristics, and attack rates must be completed. Findings of collateral investigators and personnel, such as physicians, laboratory personnel, and hospital healthcare providers, should be gathered and assessed. Overall, the epidemiologist should develop hypotheses concerning the source of the outbreak as well as the mode of transmission (if an infectious disease).

Hypotheses should be developed for all aspects of the investigation. For example, in a foodborne outbreak, hypotheses should be developed for:

- The source of infection
- The vehicle of infection
- The suspect foods

- The mode of transmission
- The type of pathogen (based on clinical symptoms, incubation periods)
- The time factors in the outbreak and course of the disease
- The place factors in the outbreak
- The person characteristics and factors in the outbreak
- The outside sources of the infection
- The transmission of the disease outside of the study population
- The exposed, unexposed, well, and ill cases/individuals

Test the Hypotheses

As data and information are acquired, the various hypotheses should be evaluated. The hypotheses need to be tested and established and shown to be consistent or inconsistent with facts. If established facts or information cannot substantiate a hypothesis, either more information should be gathered, or the research hypothesis should be rejected.

Develop Reports and Inform Those Who Need to Know

The report typically presents a narrative of the investigation and a review of the course of the epidemic in the form of a case study. Tables, graphs, charts, or any useful and helpful illustrations are presented, as well as any pertinent epidemiologic data, tests, laboratory reports, information, and characteristics. A good epidemiologic report compares the hypotheses with the established facts.

Communicable diseases bring with them a more urgent need to inform the public than do noncommunicable diseases. When a disease poses a risk or danger to the public, those who are in a position to intervene and control the epidemic need to be informed first. Public health officials, related government agencies, physicians, hospitals, health maintenance organizations, medical clinics, schools, universities, and any group of people at risk should be informed. Unfortunately, many times public health officials know of a health concern but fail to inform those who need to know most—the population at risk. Public health officials have a responsibility to warn the public and the population at risk and should not hesitate to do so. Sometimes officials are fearful that such information will create a panic, but this is not a reason to withhold information from the public or at least those who are at risk.

Execute Control and Prevention Measures

The main purpose of epidemiology and its investigations is to understand disease epidemics so that basic public health morbidity and mortality prevention and control measures can be employed. An epidemiologic investigation not only identifies the mode of transmission, but it also identifies the source of the outbreak. When the links to the continuance of the disease are understood, then intervention can occur, the links can be broken, and the course of the disease outbreak can be stopped. The aim of public health disease-control programs and of epidemiology is to stop the spread of disease and to stop epidemics and prevent them from starting. Immunization programs are the first line of defense in prevention and control of some communicable diseases. Risk-factor prevention and health protection programs are the first line of defense in behaviorally caused or environmentally founded chronic diseases. Epidemiologic investigations are conducted if prevention and control measures have failed or were never adequately implemented.

Administration and Planning Activities

Public health goals are accomplished only through an organized effort carried out with government assistance and under government administration. For epidemiologic activities to occur and be successful, organization, coordination, communication, planning, and funding assistance are all necessary. Immunization clinics and programs must be established and implemented. In the case of an epidemic, administrative plans and measures to provide treatment and care for the victims of the epidemic must be considered. Unbiased investigations are best handled by an agency without vested interests. Government agencies often have the experts and professionals to carry out appropriate investigations of diseases, conditions, and disorders. Specialized investigations often require assistance from special laboratory facilities, cooperation with private physicians, hospitals, health maintenance organizations and clinics, and individuals, all of whom are more likely to cooperate with the administration of a public health department. Financial support to protect the public health is provided through the administrative activities of government agencies and entities.[3,4,7]

INVESTIGATION OF A FOODBORNE ILLNESS

Food poisoning, foodborne illness, and food-caused epidemics are quite common, but most are not serious—and people rarely see their physicians unless it is serious. Thus, little public health attention is paid to such occurrences. However, the 1993 Jack-in-the-Box epidemic caused by *Escherichia coli*, which received national media attention, brought concern for food protection and preparation into the living rooms of families across America, because hamburger meat contaminated in meat processing plants was identified as the possible source of infection.

Even if an epidemic of staphylococcal food poisoning is occurring (e.g., acquired from a fast-food restaurant), most people simply take care of the matter at home: have a bout of diarrhea, take some over-the-counter antidiarrheal drugs, and feel better the next day. Hundreds of persons could be involved, but the family doctor and the medical community—let alone the public health department—never know because the outbreak is short and individuals recover quickly. In more serious foodborne and waterborne illnesses, such as Amebic Dysentery and those caused by Salmonella, Giardia, and shigella, people do not recover so quickly; the symptoms are stronger and last longer, and medical intervention is usually needed. These diseases are serious and sometimes cause death; this makes them more likely to be reported.

Illnesses arising from consumption of contaminated or spoiled foods and liquids, that is, solid foods, liquid foods, milk, water, and beverages, are classified as **foodborne illnesses**. Foodborne illnesses are usually classified three ways: (1) food infections, (2) food poisoning, and (3) chemical poisoning.

Food infection is a result of the ingestion of disease-causing organisms (pathogens) such as bacteria and microscopic plants and animals. Examples of food infections are Salomonellosis, Giardiasis, Amebiasis, Shigellosis, Brucellosis, Diphtheria, Typhoid fever, and Tularemia.

Food poisoning is the result of preformed toxins that are present in foods prior to consumption; these toxins are often the waste products of bacteria. The two most common forms are Staphylococcus infection and Botulism. Staphylococcal food poisoning produces cramps and a short bout of diarrhea about six hours after consumption and is a milder form of food poisoning. The most serious and deadly form of food poisoning is botulism. The amount of botulinum toxin that will fit on the head of a pin will cause death in humans. Obviously, this toxin is extremely poisonous.

Chemical foodborne illness is called **chemical poisoning**. Some chemical agents that are beneficial and are essential nutrients in the diet can cause foodborne illness if consumed in large enough dosages (e.g., Zinc, Vitamin A, Niacin). Chemical agents that preserve food, improve eating quality (Nitrite, Monosodium Glutamate), or assure a clean and sanitary food handling environment (pesticides, cleaners) can likewise cause foodborne illness if consumed in large enough amounts.

Public health and medical personnel, as in any disease investigation, must work together as a team. Personnel involved in a major disease investigation could possibly include epidemiologists, sanitarians, physicians, nurses, and laboratory personnel such as microbiologists, medical technologists, medical laboratory technicians, and chemists.

The epidemiology team interviews, if possible, all persons who were present at the time of the ingestion of suspect foods. When large groups or populations are involved in an outbreak, it may not be feasible to interview all suspected cases. It has been suggested that in groups of more than 50 people, 50% should be interviewed, and in groups over 100 people, 25% should be interviewed. Standardized interviewing procedures should be used. Random sampling techniques can help determine who should be interviewed and tested. All interviewers should use questions that are standardized, the information of which is collected on a standard form.

Any good epidemiologic investigation should interview both ill and well persons. Half of the study population should come from each category. Tabulation and analysis of the data should be completed as well. In foodborne disease outbreaks, certain rates should always be included in the analysis and reports. Those factors necessary to a good investigation will identify and include:

■ Who ate the food
■ Who did not eat the food
■ Calculation of attack rates for each food
■ For each food, calculation of the attack rates among those who ate it
■ For each food, calculation of the attack rates among those who did not eat it
■ Computation of the relative risk (the ratio of the attack rate of those eating the food to those who did not eat the food)

Table 10-2 presents selected steps for investigating a foodborne disease epidemic.

Examples of How Field Epidemiology Influenced Public Health

Example 1: *E. coli* O157:H7 Outbreak Associated with Contaminated Alfalfa Sprouts. In the final week of June 1997, the Michigan Department of Community Health observed an increase in laboratory reports of *E. coli* O157:H7 infection. Greater than two times the typical number of infected cases were reported, as compared with the previous month.

TABLE 10-2   Investigating a Foodborne Disease Epidemic

Obtain a diagnosis and make a disease determination.

Establish that an outbreak has taken or is taking place.

Determine which foods are contaminated and which are suspect.

Determine whether toxigenic organisms, infectious organisms, or chemical toxins are involved.

Ascertain the source of contamination. How did the foodstuff become contaminated? Who contaminated it? Where was it contaminated? Was it contaminated by direct or indirect sources?

After determining the source of poison and contamination, ascertain the extent of contamination that could occur.

Identify foods and people implicated in the contamination and intervene to stop further spread of the disease.

Ensure medical treatment.

Exercise intervention, prevention, and control measures.

Inform those who need to know—private citizens, appropriate leaders, and public officials.

Develop and distribute reports.

The increase in cases continued through the first two weeks of July. Thirty-eight cases of confirmed O157:H7 infections meeting the case definition from 10 counties in the lower-peninsula of Michigan are presented in Figure 10-1. The field investigation identified consumption of contaminated alfalfa sprouts as the source of the outbreak.[8]

Consequently, the implicated seed lot discontinued distribution to sprouting companies. About 6,000 pounds of seed were removed from the marketplace. The Division of

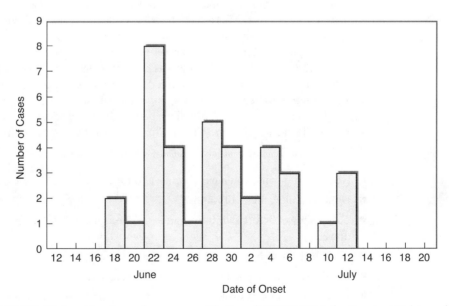

FIGURE 10-1   Number of persons with *E. coli* O157:H7 infection in Michigan by date, June 15–July 15, 1977. From CDC. Available at http://www.2a.cdc.gov/epicase studies/graphics/ecolii.pdf. Accessed December 29, 2008.

Food and Drugs in the state where the contaminated seeds originated conducted meetings with the seed growers to explain the necessity of protecting alfalfa and other seeds used in sprouting from possible contamination. The media was used to inform the public about the risk of contaminated sprouting seeds. Additionally, the Center for Food Safety and Quality Enhancement worked closely with the sprout industry to improve the safety of sprout consumption.[8]

Example 2: *E. coli* O157:H7 Outbreak Associated with Contaminated Spinach.   More recently (Fall of 2006), an extensive field investigation of an *E. coli* O157:H7 outbreak involving 205 confirmed cases and three deaths was conducted. The investigation identified contaminated Dole brand baby spinach grown in California as the cause of the outbreak. The source of the outbreak appeared to be contamination near the presence of wild pigs and surface waterways exposed to feces from cattle and wildlife. This and other outbreaks led the U.S. Food and Drug Administration (FDA) to announce an initiative called "Leafy Greens," which focused on produce, contamination agents, and corresponding public health concerns.[9] The FDA also provided recommendations in a publication entitled "Guide to Minimize Microbial Food Safety Hazards of Fresh-cut Fruits and Vegetables," which discussed ways to prevent microbial contamination while processing fresh-cut produce, and emphasized washing all produce thoroughly before eating. Although aggressive hand washing would not have prevented the *E. coli* outbreak involving spinach, the risk of contamination from several other sources could have been reduced.

Example 3: Outbreak of Cryptosporidium.   Cryptosporidiosis is an infectious diarrheal disease caused by *cryptosporidium* parasite. Clinical manifestations include frequent, watery diarrhea, nausea, vomiting, abdominal cramps, and low-grade fever. For immuno-compromised persons the illness may be more severe, causing weight loss, anorexia, malaise, severe abdominal cramps, and debilitating diarrhea. The illness is transmitted from fecally contaminated food and water, from animal-to-person contact, and from person-to-person contact. There have been several outbreaks of Cryptosporidiosis in the United States. One very large outbreak occurred in Milwaukee in 1993, affecting over 400,000 people.[10] In 2007, over 500 cases were reported during July and August throughout Utah. In a normal year, about 30 cases are reported. The Utah Department of Health and local health departments took immediate action, asking public pool managers to take aggressive action to help stop the ongoing outbreak of the infection. Steps taken included super-chlorinating the pools, installing better filtering devices, and limiting pool use to adults ages 18 years and older. The CDC provides a list of six guidelines people may follow to stay safe:

- Do not swim when you have diarrhea and for two weeks after the disease has cleared.
- Do not swallow the pool water.
- Take a shower before swimming, and wash your hands after using the toilet or changing diapers.
- Take the kids on bathroom breaks and check diapers often.
- Change diapers in a bathroom and not at pool-side.
- Wash your child thoroughly (especially the rear end) with soap and water before swimming.[11]

BASIC EPIDEMIOLOGIC QUESTIONS

Although practicing epidemiologists often ask a set of common questions, they are rarely ever written out, let alone published. This may be because each case or each epidemic poses a new and different set of questions. However, some commonality does exist among the many epidemiologic questions that can be asked. Table 10-3 presents some epidemiologic questions that the beginning epidemiologist can refer to, if for no other reason than to stimulate thought and possibly new and different questions about the investigation.

If a disease occurs only in the summer, the epidemiologist searches for the causative factors that would be available only in that time period. Is the increase of the disease a result

TABLE 10-3   Some Investigative Epidemiologic Questions to Consider

In whom (which groups) is the disease present?

In whom (which groups) is the disease absent?

What are the sick people doing that the healthy people are not?

What are the healthy people doing that the sick people are not?

What are the healthy people not doing that the sick people are?

What are the sick people not doing that the healthy people are?

Can you determine whether certain cause–effect relationships are present in individuals with the condition, disease, or characteristics of interest?

Can you determine whether certain cause–effect relationships are blocked or not present in individuals with the condition, disease, or characteristics of interest?

What are the common experiences among all of the ill persons? Common food? Common water? Common exposure to the disease? Common housing? Common clothing? Common use of fomites? Common exposure to animals/vectors? Frequenting the same places? Common behavior? Common lifestyle?

What are the common experiences among the well persons? Common food? Common water? Common immunity to the disease? Common housing? Common use of sanitation? Common control of animals/vectors? Frequenting the same places? Common behavior? Common lifestyle?

Does the disease cluster by time and place?

What risk factors are present in persons with the condition?

Are risk factors present in persons without the condition?

What risk factors are absent in persons who do not have the condition (healthy people)?

What risk factors are absent in persons with the condition?

What exposures to the disease exist in the sick population?

What exposures to the disease are lacking in the healthy population?

What vectors can be implicated in the disease exposure and outbreak?

How have the cases been exposed to the vectors?

What fomites can be implicated in the disease exposure and outbreak?

What waterborne activities and exposures are implicated in the disease outbreak?

What foodborne activities and exposures are implicated in the disease outbreak?

What airborne activities and exposures are implicated in the disease outbreak?

What risk factor activities and exposures are implicated in the disease outbreak?

of exposure to new water sources, for example, drinking from a stream in the mountains or swimming in a contaminated public swimming pool or a lake? Is it a vector-borne disease? What vectors are available for disease transmission in the given time period and are missing at other times of the year or seasons? Are vehicles of transmission present during the time period that are not present during other time periods? Are the cases/subjects exposing themselves during this time period to environments, situations, places, or circumstances not available at other times of the year or in other seasons (e.g., hiking or camping in the woods in the summer when insects are present that are implicated in vector-borne diseases)? Are certain fomites used during a certain time period that might not be used during other seasons, such as shared drinking glasses or containers? Are risk factors only seen in certain locations or places? Do they occur only at work, only at home, or at the site of recreation (mountains, beaches, public swimming pool, etc.)?

DISEASE CLUSTERS

A **disease cluster** is an unusual aggregation, real or perceived, of health events that are grouped together in time and space and that are reported to a health agency.[12] It generally occurs in response to the sudden introduction into the human environment of a physical stress, chemical or biological agent, or psychosocial condition. Examples of clusters can involve injury or death related to accidents (e.g., plane crashes, fires, worksite conditions), natural disasters (e.g., flooding, tropical cyclones, tornadoes, volcanic eruptions, earthquakes, drought), political and social upheaval (e.g., unavailable health care, wars, racial discrimination), food poisoning caused by improper food handling introducing bacterial contaminants, and cluster of birth defects or cancer associated with biological and chemical contaminants.

A **cluster investigation** involves reviewing unusual numbers of health-related states or events, real or perceived, grouped together in time and location.[13] Cluster investigations are conducted to confirm reported disease cases, identify whether the number of cases is above what is expected and, if possible, identify causal relationships. For example, among 50 cluster investigations of childhood Leukemia and Lymphoma in the United States during 1961 through 1977, where the cases were confirmed and higher than normal levels of the disease established, chemicals were implicated in all but eight.[14]

Investigations of noninfectious disease clusters have also been useful in identifying potential biological and environmental causes such as clusters of Angiosarcoma found in vinyl chloride workers,[15] neurotoxicity and infertility found in kepone workers,[16] Dermatitis and skin cancer found in individuals wearing contaminated gold rings,[17] and Adenocarcinoma of the vagina found for women who consumed Diethylstilbestrol during pregnancy.[18] In each of these studies there were definable health outcomes, confirmation of an elevation of the problem through statistical methods, a suspected environmental agent, and a short-term public health impact that was immediate and self-evident.[12]

Some selected health outcomes and their associated environmental risk factors are presented in Table 10-4.

The contrast between disease clusters and sentinel events should be emphasized. Although a disease cluster involves the occurrences of seemingly unexpected events where no clearly recognized cause exists, **sentinel events** are occurrences of unexpected health-related states or events that occur from specific, recognized causes; the adverse health outcome has a known cause.[18] To illustrate, nine individuals were diagnosed with elevated

TABLE 10-4   Selected Organ/System Events and their Toxic Exposure Risks

Organ/System	Exposure Risks
Respiratory	Asbestos, radon, cigarette smoke, glues
Dermatologic	Dioxin, nickel, arsenic, mercury, cement (chromium), polychlorinated biphenyls, glues, rubber cement
Liver	Carbon tetrachloride, methylene chloride, vinyl chloride
Kidney	Cadmium, lead, mercury, chlorinated hydrocarbon solvents
Cardiovascular	Carbon monoxide, noise, tobacco smoke, physical stress, carbon disulfide, nitrates, methylene chloride
Reproductive	Methylmercury, carbon monoxide, lead, ethylene oxide
Hematologic	Arsenic, benzene, nitrates, radiation
Neuropsychologic	Tetrachloroethylene, mercury, arsenic, toluene, lead, methanol, noise, vinyl chloride

From the Centers for Disease Control and Prevention. Disease clusters: An overview evaluating a disease cluster. Available at: http://www.atsdr.cdc.gov/HEC/CSEM/cluster/evaluating.html. Accessed December 7, 2008.

blood lead levels at local hospitals in Alabama from March through October 1991.[19] A cluster investigation showed that all had recently drunk illicit distilled alcohol (Moonshine) made in two automobile radiators containing lead-soldered parts. The framework for investigating sentinel events in occupational settings was established in the early 1980s by David Rustein and colleagues at the National Institute for Occupational Safety and Health. The concept of a Sentinel Health Event (Occupational), SHE(O), was defined as an unnecessary disease, disability, or untimely death that is occupationally related, with its occurrence yielding evidence of a failure in prevention.[20] An epidemiologist's role in the investigation of sentinel health may be described as assisting in recognition of the event; participating in evaluation, often with the aid of an industrial hygienist; arranging for appropriate interventions; and summarizing and disseminating relevant information from the investigation to prevent similar cases elsewhere and in the future.[21]

Guidelines for Investigating Clusters

A four-stage process to cluster investigation has been proposed by the CDC: (1) initial response, (2) assessment, (3) major feasibility study, and (4) etiologic investigation (CDC, 1990). These stages incorporate many of the steps for conducting a field investigation. They are to be tailored according to the specific setting where the cluster is under investigation. An advisory committee may also be selected to provide consultation at critical decision points of the investigation. A brief description of these stages is presented here.

Stage I: Initial Contact and Response.   Each year in the United States there are over 1,000 calls placed to public health officials about suspected disease clusters.[22] Although the vast majority of cluster investigations of the putative cluster turn out not to be real, the local health department takes each of these calls very seriously. The purpose of this stage is to collect relevant information from those reporting the possible cluster. The recommended procedures are as follows:

- Obtain identifying information on the caller
- Obtain initial data on the suspected cluster, including proposed health events, suspected exposure(s), number of cases, geographic area, and time period of concern
- Obtain identifying information on those affected
- Discuss initial impressions
- Obtain additional information on cases such as a follow-up time for contact, if necessary
- Assure that a written response to their concern will be received
- Keep a log of initial and follow-up contacts
- Notify the public affairs office in the local health agency about the contact

Some alternative explanations for a reported disease cluster are presented in Table 10-5.

Although new environmental data may be required early in the cluster investigation, existing data, if available, may also be useful. If the cluster investigation shows the presence of a single and rare disease and identifies a plausible exposure or a plausible clustering, then we proceed to Stage II.

Stage II: Assessment.   This stage has three phases: (1) preliminary evaluation to determine whether an excess of the health problem has occurred, (2) case evaluation to assure that a biological basis is present, and (3) a further evaluation of some or all of the suspected cases to describe the epidemiologic characteristics. These phases may be performed sequentially or concurrently.

Preliminary Evaluation.   The primary aim of the preliminary evaluation is to determine quickly whether an excess of the health-related state or event has occurred and to describe the characteristics of the cluster. This process involves (1) determining the geographic area and

TABLE 10-5   Issues Frequently Associated with Reported Clusters

An assortment of unrelated diseases and disease processes means a common origin is unlikely.

If only women or older persons are affected, for example, this might indicate that an environmental pollutant is an unlikely cause.

For neoplasm, an implicated environmental carcinogen is only plausible if the affected residents have lived in the area for a sufficiently long period of time because of the long latency period that typically accompanies cancer.

Deceased cases may not provide useful information for linking exposure and disease because exposure may not be available and confounding factors may be present.

A rare disease cluster may be a result of chance and not related to a given exposure.

New diagnostic procedures may explain a cluster.

Changes in reporting practices may explain a cluster.

Misdiagnoses by physicians may explain a suspected cluster.

Migration patterns (e.g., existence of a new military base, housing area, or retirement area) may explain a cluster.

Increased awareness in certain diseases may explain a cluster.

time period for study, (2) ascertaining those cases within the established time and space boundaries, (3) identifying an appropriate reference population, (4) determining whether there is a sufficient number of cases for assessment and whether a denominator is available for calculating rates and other statistics, and (5) if small numbers prevent obtaining meaningful rates or if the denominator is not available, assessing space, time, or space-time clustering. Geographic information systems software is now available for conducting surveillance of putative clusters according to spatial or space-time clustering and to evaluate statistical significance.

To identify unusual aggregations of adverse health outcomes requires knowledge of what is usual based on the distribution of cases in the same location during an earlier time period or in other similar locations during the same time period.[23] What is usual may be obtained from local health officials who often know whether more disease is occurring than is expected based on ongoing disease surveillance data through local surveys or health data registries. Although laboratory confirmations are ideal, they may not be initially available for some acute conditions. However, there still may be sufficient evidence available to warrant an investigation.

Unreported or unrecognized cases can sometimes be identified through physicians, clinics, health maintenance organizations, hospital emergency departments, public health clinics, migrant health clinics, and related facilities and should be canvassed to ascertain whether other people might have the disease or condition under investigation. Case identification should be restricted according to a specific time period, geographic region, and diagnostic group. Applying a standard case definition guarantees that every case is consistently diagnosed regardless of where and when the diagnosis occurs. In general, case definitions work best when information is also available about a probable exposure (e.g., lead, radiation, cigarettes).

Rates are useful for determining whether the putative cluster is actually unusual. Rates are preferred to counts because they take into account the population size and can be effectively compared with rates in other time periods or places. However, to avoid misleading rates, the population value in the rate calculation needs to be appropriately selected. Attack rates are typically used in cluster investigations; however, the person-time rate may be appropriate in some situations because it allows each person's contribution to the denominator of the rate calculation to be only as much time as observation in the at-risk population. Consideration of adjusting the rates for potential confounders may also make comparisons between/among rates more meaningful.

The probability that there is an excess of the health-related state or event being considered is obtained through statistical methods; this probability is the P value. The interpretation of the conventional P value is dependent, however, on whether the hypothesis is a priori or not, which will be discussed more fully. If an excess of the health problem is supported from the preliminary evaluation, the next step is to do a case evaluation.

Case Evaluation.   The purpose here is to verify the diagnosis. False-positive results are a concern in that they may cause considerable alarm and present the impression that a suspected cluster is real. Diagnosis verification often requires obtaining a referral to the responsible physician and permission to examine the patient's record, access to pathology and medical examiner's reports if possible, and sometimes histological re-evaluation. In reality, though, obtaining confirmation and re-evaluation may not be possible. Laboratory tests are not applicable with certain conditions, injuries, or behaviorally caused occurrences. Furthermore, occupational or environmental disorders or conditions are often difficult to diagnose.

If an excess of the health problem is supported by case confirmation, then proceed to occurrence evaluation. If not confirmed, the investigators may still proceed if biologic plausibility persists.

Occurrence Evaluation.   In this step, the characteristics of the cluster are defined, which typically requires a field investigation. The procedure is as follows: (1) identify the appropriate geographic and temporal boundaries, (2) ascertain all potential cases according to the specified time and space boundaries, (3) identify numerator and denominator data and their availability, (4) identify appropriate epidemiologic and statistical methods for describing and analyzing the data, (5) review the literature and consider biologic plausibility, (6) assess whether an exposure-event relationship can be established, (7) identify the public pulse (perceptions, reactions, needs), and (8) complete the descriptive investigation.

It is critical here to select appropriate geographic and temporal boundaries. As a rule, the boundaries should correspond to the entire area that could have been exposed to the suspected cause. If the selected boundary is too small, the rate calculation will be overestimated. On the other hand, if the selected boundary is too big, the rate calculation will be underestimated.

The epidemiologist should consider whether the disease cluster is associated with a common source or propagated from person to person. We are able to narrow the potential cause of the cluster by classifying it by type of outbreak. For example, diseases that are spread from person to person are biologically based, whereas adverse health outcomes that are not communicable arise from physical or psychosocial stressors or chemical contaminants.

Clusters should be determined with regard to residence, birthplace, place of employment, school district, hospital unit, census tract, street address, map coordinates, and so on. By so doing, the epidemiologist can understand the geographic extent of disease and possibly a better idea of the cause. A map may be an effective way to present this data pictorially, especially if the map includes the locations of exposures, the locations of each case at the time of exposure, or when those exposed were identified as being a case.

Epidemic curves are commonly used to present each case by time of onset. Chronologic events, step-by-step occurrences, chains of events tied to time, and time distribution of the onset of cases should be determined and plotted on charts and graphs. The epidemiologists should determine the nature of the course of the disease and ascertain whether people were exposed and infected at about the same time or at different times, look for clustering of disease by both time and place, and use the information from incubation or latency periods to determine time factors in the course of the disease peaks and valleys in the epidemic curve.

If an excess of cases is confirmed, along with compelling epidemiologic and biologic evidence, then we proceed to the final stage.

Stage III: Major Feasibility Study.   The purpose of this stage is to associate the excess number of cases with the putative exposure. The steps are as follows:

- Review the literature for putative exposures of the health event under consideration.
- Select the appropriate study design and consider the attendant cost, sample size, use of previously identified cases, area and time dimensions, and selection of a control group.
- Determine the required case and control data needed, which should include laboratory and physical measurements.
- Consider the appropriate methods for assessment.
- Outline the logistics for collecting and processing the data.
- Determine the analysis plan (e.g., hypotheses to be tested, power to detect differences).
- Consider the current social and political climate and the potential impact of decisions and outcomes.
- Consider the resource requirements of the study.

When the exposure assessment is complete, the question arises of whether sufficient information is available to formulate a plausible hypothesis. The research hypothesis is formulated by first identifying the most probable source for the cluster. If it is thought to be biologically caused, consideration should be given to known or potential pathways by which the contaminants might impact the population at risk (e.g., air, water, soil, food). If the cluster is environmentally caused, the conditions of the environment in which the individuals spent time must be investigated (e.g., the air at a worksite or skin exposure to chemicals).

Evaluating dose-response relationships within clusters requires accurate measurement of exposure according to appropriate time and place factors. Personal measurement of exposure on a continuous scale is best for assessing dose-response relationships. The next best type of exposure information is the direct measure of a concentration of toxic contaminants in a specific environment (air, water, soil, and food). If direct measures of exposure are not available, then indirect proxy measures of exposure may be the best option (e.g., use of drinking water, distance from a contamination site, duration of residence, and residence of employment).

Hypotheses should be developed for all aspects of the investigation. Hypotheses are supported by the study design, data, methods, logistics, and context. With sufficient resources and justification for an etiologic investigation we can then proceed to Stage IV.

Stage IV: Etiologic Investigation.   The etiologic investigation involves a standard epidemiologic study approach, with specific criteria for establishing a cause and effect relationship. When the results of the investigation are obtained, a report should follow, presenting a narrative of the investigation. The report should contain any pertinent epidemiologic data, tests, laboratory reports, information, and characteristics. A good epidemiologic report compares the research hypotheses with the established facts. When the links to the health problem are understood, then intervention can occur, the links can be broken, the course of the health problem can be stopped, and, if necessary, environmental cleanup can begin. It is often where prevention and control measures have failed or were never adequately implemented that disease clusters arise.

Data Challenges in Cluster Investigations.   Cluster investigations require accurate diagnostic information; case information according to person, place, and time; length of time cases lived in the area in question; potential changes in diagnostic or reporting procedures; migration patterns; and increased public awareness of the disease in question. In addition, a sufficient number of cases are needed in order to rule out chance as an explanation for the cluster finding. Unavailable data limit all levels of a cluster investigation. Lack of availability to quality health tracking data may:

- Cause long delays in cluster investigations
- Prevent public health officials from identifying disease trends
- Inhibit the identification of true disease clusters
- Reduce the number of cluster investigations carried out by states, meaning that some clusters go uninvestigated
- Deter communities from getting the information and help they need when a suspected cluster arises[22]

Statistical Challenges in Cluster Investigations.   The primary statistical challenge with cluster investigations involves the fact that most cluster analyses involve post hoc (also called posteriori) rather than a priori hypotheses. **Post hoc hypotheses** refer to a formulation of the hypotheses after observation of an event such as an excess of cancer. Hypotheses of this type are problematic because the conventional *P* value is only interpretable with **a priori hypotheses**—that is, those hypotheses established without prior knowledge of the level of the health events in a specified population. Selectively choosing a suspected cluster for statistical testing is equivalent to multiple testing because the probability of finding a significant result increases as we become highly selective in testing only a given area out of many. Suppose that there is a cluster reported in a region that has 20 subareas, and we conclude that the disease rate in the area is statistically significant at the 5% level. By selectively choosing this area out of 20, we have essentially simultaneously conducted 20 tests. If the null hypothesis is true, we would expect one in 20 independent tests to be significant by chance alone at the 5% level of significance. Therefore, the chance of occurrence in the random variation of disease may be the sole explanation for the unusual events.

A second challenge is that rates have the danger of being overestimated because of "**boundary shrinkage**" of the population where the cluster is presumed to exist. Consider a putative cluster of childhood Leukemia in the United Kingdom around a nuclear processing site at Windscale (later called Sellafield) reported in 1983.[24] A journalist purported that an excess of Leukemia could be due to radiation discharged from the nuclear processing site. The journalist initially focused on the health among employees at the plant. During the investigation, however, he was informed about a number of childhood Leukemia cases in Seascale, a village close to the plant. An investigation found that the rate of childhood Leukemia in the area containing the village was significantly higher than the national rate. However, multiple comparisons and boundary shrinkage because of post hoc testing of hypotheses made the study findings potentially misleading.[25] The first problem was that the journalist may have followed several leads before focusing on Leukemia cases. Hence, multiple comparisons had been made (regardless of whether significance tests were made), making interpretation of the P value invalid. Second, after the identification of the group of cases, the underlying population corresponding to the suspected cluster was selected. The narrower this underlying population is defined, the greater the estimated rate of the health problem and the more pronounced the statistical significance. This situation has been compared by Kenneth Rothman to the Texas sharpshooter who first fires his gun and then draws a target around the bullet hole.[26]

With post hoc hypotheses where significance tests are inappropriate, alternative methods of assessment include the following:

▪ Performing the study in a different location, but with a similar exposure

▪ Excluding the cases in the original cluster and using new cases in the test of significance, assuming further case ascertainment occurred

▪ Looking for factors that distinguish the cases from others in the cluster, other than their residence

▪ Evaluating a dose-response relationship between the exposure and health event[27]

CONCLUSION

Epidemiology provides the scientific basis, the systematic approach, and the population and prevention perspective that are needed in field investigations of public health problems. The main purpose of conducting a field investigation is to understand disease epidemics or outbreaks so that basic public health morbidity and mortality prevention and control measures can be taken. Field epidemiology is the application of epidemiology under a set of general conditions: the problem is unexpected, a timely response may be demanded, travel to and work in the field is required, and the investigation time is likely to be limited. Selected steps were described for conducting field investigations of outbreaks of adverse health-related states or events. Common questions to consider in this process were also presented.

A disease cluster is an unusual aggregation, real or perceived, of health events that are grouped together in time and space and that are reported to a health agency. A cluster investigation involves reviewing unusual numbers of health-related states or events. Cluster investigations are conducted to confirm reported cases, identify whether the number of cases is above what is expected and, if possible, identify causal relationships. A disease cluster involves the occurrence of an unexpected health-related state or event where no clearly recognized cause exists. On the other hand, a sentinel event is the occurrence of an unexpected health-related state or event that has a specific, recognized cause. The CDC's four stages for conducting a cluster investigation were developed. Unavailable data, poor quality data, and post hoc hypotheses (resulting in multiple comparisons and boundary shrinkage) limit cluster investigations. However, with post hoc hypotheses where significance tests are inappropriate, alternative methods of assessment are available.

EXERCISES

Key Terms

Define the following terms.

A priori hypotheses	Foodborne illnesses
Attack rate	Food infection
Boundary shrinkage	Food poisoning
Chemical poisoning	Mixed epidemic
Cluster investigation	Outbreak
Common-source epidemic	Post hoc hypotheses
Epidemic curve	Propagated epidemic
Field epidemiology	Sentinel events

STUDY QUESTIONS

1. Each of the following tend to characterize an epidemiology field investigation EXCEPT:

    a. The problem is unexpected.

    b. A timely response may be demanded.

    c. The epidemiologist's presence in the field is required to solve the problem.

    d. When several people are confirmed cases, it may be sufficient to identify others as cases if they display the same signs and symptoms.

    e. All of the above are true.

2. Match the definitions in the left column with the terms in the right column.

    ___ Often synonymous with epidemic; sometimes the preferred word, as it may escape sensationalism associated with the word epidemic. It also applies when the scope of the disease is limited.

    ___ The occurrence of a disease within a specific community or region that is clearly in excess of the expected level for a given time period.

    ___ An aggregation of cases of a disease or other health-related condition, particularly cancer and birth defects, that are closely grouped in time and place.

A. Epidemic

B. Outbreak

C. Cluster

3. What is the most common statistic to use for investigating an outbreak?

4. How would you classify an epidemic if the epidemic curve showed a rapid rise, peak, and gradual decrease?

5. List at least three things that should be done in preparing for fieldwork.

6. Where might the epidemiologist search for cases that have not been identified?

7. What information should be combined with disease frequency data?

8. What is the primary purpose of providing a final report in a field investigation?

9. A "good" final report in a field investigation should include all of the following EXCEPT:

    a. A description of the intervention and its effects.

    b. A review of the course of the epidemic in the form of a case study.

    c. A comparison of the hypotheses with the established facts.

    d. Tables, graphs, and charts.

    e. A "good" final report should include all of these things.

10. List and describe the four-stage process of cluster investigation as described by the Centers for Disease Control and Prevention.

11. In which stage of the four-stage process are attack rates calculated?

12. What should a good epidemiologic report include?

13. What are two statistical challenges in cluster investigation?

14. What is the primary distinction between a cluster and a sentinel health-related state or event?

15. Which of the answer sets below best matches the activities listed in the left column with the stages of the field epidemiologic process in the right column?

___New diagnostic procedures may explain a cluster.

___ Consider the resource requirements of the study.

___ Determine the required case and control data needed, which should include laboratory and physical measurements.

___ Preliminary evaluation to determine whether an excess of the health problem exists.

___ Assure that a written response to their concern will be received.

___ Consider criteria for establishing a cause-effect relationship.

A. Initial response

B. Assessment

C. Major feasibility study

D. Etiologic investigation

REFERENCES

1. Jaret P. Stalking the world's epidemics: the disease detectives. *Natl Geogr Mag.* 1991;179(1):114–140.
2. Goodman RA, Buehler JW. Field epidemiology defined. In: Gregg MB, ed. *Field Epidemiology*, 2nd ed. New York, NY: Oxford University Press; 2008. 3–15
3. Mausner JS, Kramer S. *Epidemiology: An Introductory Text.* Philadelphia, PA: W.B. Saunders; 1985.
4. Friedman GD. *Primer of Epidemiology.* New York, NY: McGraw-Hill; 1978.
5. Last JM, ed. A *Dictionary of Epidemiology*, 3rd ed. New York, NY: Oxford University Press; 1995.
6. Steere AC, Hall WJ III, Wells JG, et al. Person-to-person spread of Salmonella typhimurium after a hospital common-source outbreak. *Lancet.* 1975;1(7902):319–322.
7. Lilienfeld AM, Lilienfeld DE. *Foundations of Epidemiology.* New York, NY: Oxford University Press; 1980.
8. Centers for Disease Control and Prevention Case Study. A multistate outbreak of E. coli 157:H7 infection. http://www2a.cdc.gov/epicasestudies/graphics/ecolii.pdf. Accessed April 21, 2012.
9. Investigation of an Escherichia coli O157:H7 Outbreak Associated with Dole Pre-Packaged Spinach. http://www.dhs.ca.gov/ps/fdb/local/PDF/2006%20Spinach%20Report%20Final%20redacted%20no%20photosfigures.PDF. Accessed April 4, 2007.
10. Juranek DD. Cryptosporidiosis: sources of infection and guidelines for prevention. *Clin Infect Dis.* 1995;21(Suppl 1):S57–S61.
11. Centers for Disease Control and Prevention. Healthy Swimming. http://www.cdc.gov/healthyswimming/.Accessed December 4, 2008.
12. Centers for Disease Control and Prevention. Guidelines for investigating clusters of health events. *MMWR.* 1990;39(RR-11):1–23.
13. Centers for Disease Control and Prevention. Glossary of Terms. http://www.atsdr.cdc.gov/glossary.html#G-A-. Accessed December 7, 2008.
14. Heath CW Jr. Community clusters of childhood leukemia and lymphoma: evidence of infection? *Am J Epidemiol.* 2005;162(9):817–822.
15. Waxweiler RJ, Stringer W, Wagoner JK, et al. Neoplastic risk among workers exposed to vinyl chloride. *Ann NY Acad Sci.* 1976;271:40–48.
16. Cannon SB, Veazey JM Jr, Jackson RS, et al. Epidemic kepone poisoning in chemical workers. *Am J Epidemiol.* 1978;107:529–537.

17. Centers for Disease Control and Prevention. Disease Clusters: An Overview Evaluating a Disease Cluster. http://www.atsdr.cdc.gov/HEC/CSEM/cluster/evaluating.html. Accessed December 7, 2008.

18. Joint Commission on Accreditation of Healthcare Organizations. Setting the standards for quality in health care. Sentinel event. http://www.jointcommission.org/SentinelEvents/. Accessed December 7, 2008.

19. Centers for Disease Control and Prevention. Elevated blood lead levels associated with illicitly distilled alcohol—Alabama, 1990–1991. *MMWR.* 1992;41(17):294–295.

20. Rutstein D, Mullan R, Frazier T, et al. The sentinel health event (occupational): a framework for occupational health surveillance and education. *J Am Public Health Assoc.* 1983;73:1054–1062.

21. Halperin WE, Trout D. Field investigations of occupational disease and injury. In: Gregg MB, ed. *Field Epidemiology,* 2nd ed. New York, NY: Oxford University Press: 2008. 376-396.

22. Dutzik T, Baumann J. *Health Tracking and Disease Clusters: The Lack of Data on Chronic Disease Incidence and Its Impact on Cluster Investigations.* Washington, DC: U.S. PIRG Education Fund, 2002.

23. Hertz-Picciotto I. *Environmental Epidemiology.* Philadelphia, PA: Lippincott-Raven Publishers; 1998.

24. Gardner JM. Review of reported increases of childhood cancer rates in the vicinity of nuclear installations in the UK. *J Royal Stat Soc Ser A.* 1989;152:307–325.

25. Olsen SF, Martuzzi M, Elliott P. Cluster analysis and disease mapping—why, when, and how? A step by step guide. *BMJ.* 1996;313:863–866.

26. Rothman KJ. A sobering start for the cluster busters' conference. *Am J Epidemiol.* 1990; 132(Suppl):S6–S13.

27. Wilkinson P, ed. *Environmental Epidemiology.* New York, NY: Open University Press; 2006.

11

Chronic Disease Epidemiology

OBJECTIVES

After completing this chapter, you will be able to:

- Compare and contrast chronic versus acute diseases and conditions.
- Define latency period, risk factor, and other terms frequently used in chronic disease epidemiology.
- Identify multiple risk factors associated with common chronic diseases and conditions in the United States.
- Discuss primary prevention and control in chronic-disease epidemiology.
- Understand the components and applications of the health belief model.

During the first half of the 1900s, epidemiology focused on disease-causing infectious agents or pathogens and factors such as water quality and supply systems, waste control, and housing and food quality. In its infancy, epidemiology focused on a single pathogen, a single cause of disease, with the challenge of isolating the causal agent in order to prevent and stop the spread of disease. As improvements were made in supplying safe water, appropriate disposal of waste, clean housing, and regulation of food handling, morbidity and mortality levels from infectious agents have been greatly reduced in many developed parts of the world. Antibiotics and immunization programs have further reduced the threat of infectious disease. As these public health efforts have taken hold, life expectancy has increased.

In the United States, for example, life expectancy has been generally increasing since the 1940s, and was 78.7 years (76.2 for males and 81.1 for females) in 2010.[1] As life expectancy increases, particularly in more developed countries, a greater proportion of people are encountering diseases more common in older age, such as heart disease or cancer. Chronic diseases include cardiovascular diseases, mainly heart disease and stroke; cancer; chronic respiratory diseases; diabetes; and others such as mental disorders, bone and joint disorders, and vision and hearing impairments. In the United States, of the 2,465,932 total deaths that occurred in 2010, 24% were from diseases of the heart, 23% from cancer, 6% from chronic lower respiratory diseases, 5% from cerebrovascular diseases, 5% from accidents (unintentional injuries), 4% from Alzheimer's disease, 3% from diabetes mellitus, and 2% from pneumonia and influenza.[1] In contrast, in 1900 pneumonia and influenza led the way accounting for 11.8% of all deaths, followed by tuberculosis, with 11.3% of all deaths.[2]

With the shift from infectious to noninfectious conditions explaining most illness and death in the United States and many other places throughout the world, the scope of epidemiology has changed. New study designs and statistical methods have been developed to better study chronic diseases and noninfectious conditions. The purpose of this chapter is to present the epidemiology of chronic disease. Emphasis is given to environmental and behavioral aspects of chronic disease epidemiology.

CHRONIC DISEASE EPIDEMIOLOGY

Chronic disease epidemiology involves the study of the distribution and determinants of chronic diseases and conditions in human populations and the application of that study to prevent and control these diseases and conditions. In contrast to acute diseases that are characterized as severe and of short duration, a chronic disease tends to be less severe but of long and continuous duration. The pathologic changes that occur before clinical manifestation of a chronic disease is relatively long. This time is referred to as the **latency period**. The idea that many chronic diseases have several interrelated causes has been confirmed through epidemiologic studies in modern times. Many of the diseases of today are influenced by more than just infectious agents but also by socioeconomic, cultural, political, and other environmental factors. These factors may affect chronic disease directly or indirectly by affecting diet, physical activity, tobacco use, and intermediate risk factors (e.g., raised blood pressure, raised blood glucose, abnormal blood lipids, and excessive body weight).

Today seven out of 10 deaths among Americans are from chronic diseases.[1] About one in four people with chronic disease experience daily activity limitations.[3] In the United States, the percentage of chronic disease for Medicare fee-for-service beneficiaries was high and varied by age (Figure 11-1).[4] Beneficiaries less than 65 years of age (who are primarily disabled) were 56% more likely to have depression and 43% less likely to have asthma, compared to older beneficiaries. The percentage of chronic disease for Medicare fee-for-service beneficiaries varied according to sex (Figure 11-2). Women were 24% less likely to have ischemic heart disease, 7% less likely to have diabetes, 14% less likely to have chronic kidney disease, and 38% less likely to have cancer. However, they were 13% more likely to have hypertension, 73% more likely to have arthritis, 78% more likely to have depression, 44% more likely to have Alzheimer's disease, and 100% more likely to have asthma.

The most frequently mentioned chronic conditions were arthritis or other musculoskeletal conditions. For ages 18–44 years, mental illness was the second leading mentioned chronic condition, and for ages 45–54 and 55–64 years, heart or other circulatory disorders were the second leading mentioned chronic condition. For the older population, arthritis

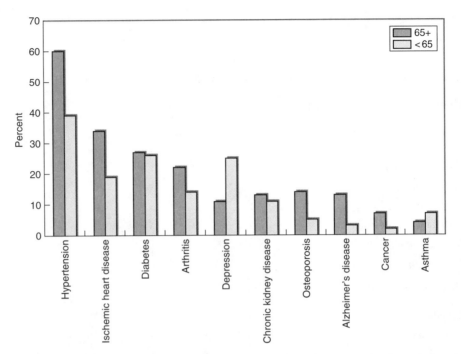

FIGURE 11-1   Percentage of Medicare fee-for-service beneficiaries with selected chronic diseases by age group, 2008. Data from Centers for Medicare & Medicaid Services. Chronic Conditions among Medicare Beneficiaries, Chart Book. Baltimore, MD. 2011.

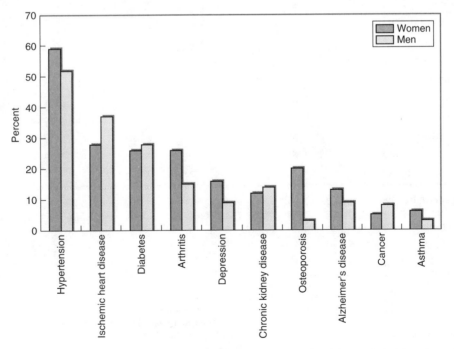

FIGURE 11-2   Percentage of Medicare fee-for-service beneficiaries with selected chronic diseases by sex, 2008. Data from Centers for Medicare & Medicaid Services. Chronic Conditions among Medicare Beneficiaries, Chart Book. Baltimore, MD. 2011.

TABLE 11-1   Top Eight Leading Causes of Death in the United States According to Selected Risk Factors

Risk Factors	Heart Disease	Cancer	Stroke	Accidents	Diabetes	Cirrhosis	Suicide	Homicide
Physical, Chemical, and Biological Environments								
Worksite risks/exposures		X		X				
Environmental hazards		X		X				
Vehicular hazards				X				
Household hazards				X				
Medical care risks		X	X	X	X	X	X	
Radiation exposures		X		X				
Infectious pathogens	X	X						
Engineering/design hazards				X				
Social Environment								
Poverty	X	X	X	X	X	X	X	X
Low educational level	X	X	X	X	X	X	X	X
Lack of work skills	X	X	X	X	X	X	X	X
Disrupted families	X	X	X	X	X	X	X	X
Behaviorally Related								
Smoking/tobacco use	X	X	X	X				
Alcohol use/abuse	X	X	X	X		X	X	X
Nutrition/diet	X	X	X		X	X		
Lack of exercise/fitness	X	X	X		X			
High blood pressure	X		X					
Cholesterol levels	X		X					
Overweight/obesity	X	X			X			
Stress	X		X	X			X	X
Drug use/abuse	X		X	X			X	X
Lack of seat belt use				X				
Genetic Related								
Chromosome/genetic defects	X	X	X		X	X	X	
Congenital anomalies	X	X	X		X	X	X	
Developmental defects	X	X	X		X	X	X	

Data are from the Centers for Disease Control and Prevention. *Chronic Disease and Health Promotion Reprints from MMWR*, 1985–1989. Hyattsville, MD: Public Health Services, U.S. Department of Health and Human Services, 1992; National Center for Health Statistics. *Health in the United States—1990.* Hyattsville, MD: Public Health Services, U.S. Department of Health and Human Services, 1991; National Cancer Institute. *Strategies to Control Tobacco Use in the United States.* Hyattsville, MD: Public Health Services, U.S. Department of Health and Human Services, 1992; and Green LW, Krueter MW. *Health Promotion Planning: An Educational and Environmental Approach.* Mountain View, CA: Mayfield Publishing, 1991.

and musculoskeletal conditions were again the most commonly mentioned chronic condition, followed by heart or other circulatory problems (Figure 11-2).

As discussed already in this book, a **risk factor** is a characteristic, condition, or behavior, such as smoking, that increases the possibility of disease or injury. Risk factors include certain behaviors, environmental exposures, or inherent human characteristics that increase the chance of a specific health condition.[5] On the basis of epidemiologic research, risk factors have been identified for several leading chronic diseases and conditions (Table 11-1). As shown, social forces are most consistently related to the selected chronic diseases and conditions listed in Table 11-1. In addition, many of the behavioral, environmental, and biological risk factors are associated with multiple diseases and conditions. Heart disease, cancer, and stroke are strongly influenced by behavioral risk factors, whereas accidents are more strongly associated with environmental risk factors. Biological factors also play an important role in the development of both diseases and adverse health conditions.

THE ENVIRONMENT AND CHRONIC HEALTH PROBLEMS

From a medical perspective, the **environment** reflects the aggregate of those external conditions and influences affecting the life and development of an organism; it is all that is external to the human host.[5,6] Hence, the environment may be thought of as physical, chemical, biological, and social factors that can influence the health status of people. Some of the physical, chemical, and biological risk factors for selected diseases and conditions are presented in Table 11-2.

TABLE 11-2   Selected Chronic Conditions and their Environmental Risk Factors

Respiratory	Asbestos, radon, cigarette smoke, glues, carbon monoxide, lead, nitrogen dioxide, ozone, PM_{10}, sulfur dioxide.
Dermatologic	Dioxin, nickel, arsenic, mercury, cement (chromium), polychlorinated biphenyls (PCBs), glues, rubber cement
Liver	Carbon tetrachloride, methylene chloride, vinyl chloride
Kidney	Cadmium, lead, mercury, chlorinated hydrocarbon solvents
Cancer	Chemicals, viruses, bacteria, radiation
Cardiovascular	Carbon monoxide, noise, tobacco smoke, physical stress, carbon disulfide, nitrates, methylene chloride
Reproductive	Methylmercury, carbon monoxide, lead, ethylene oxide
Hematologic	Arsenic, benzene, nitrates, radiation
Methemoglobinemia	Benzocaine, dapsone, nitrates
Neuropsychologic	Tetrachloroethylene, mercury, arsenic, toluene, lead, methanol, noise, vinyl chloride
Noise-induced hearing loss	Extreme and prolonged noise events

Adapted from Centers for Disease Control and Prevention. Disease clusters: An overview evaluating a disease cluster. Available at http://www.atsdr.cdc.gov/csem/csem.asp?csem=20&po=5. Accessed January 28, 2012.

Physical Stresses and Health

Physical stresses that influence health and health-related behaviors include excessive heat, cold, and noise; radiation (electromagnetic, ultrasound, microwave, x-irradiation); vehicular collisions; workplace injuries; climate change; ozone depletion; housing; and so on (**Exhibit 11-1: "News File"**). These physical stresses may result in both acute and chronic conditions. For example, radiation exposure can cause severe, intense results such as radiation burn, nausea, fatigue, vomiting, and diarrhea. On the other hand, several chronic conditions may result from radiation exposure such as damage to the central nervous system and cancer.

To illustrate, consider the case of radiation and health. All humans are regularly exposed to natural and manmade sources of radiation; it is present in the air, water, soil, and food. Radiation exposure comes from the earth's crust (e.g., uranium, radium, plutonium) and from outer space and the sun. Radiation increases with altitude and increased radioactive materials in the earth. Radiation exposure may also occur because of human activities, such as industrial processes, medical procedures (diagnostic nuclear medicine, mammography, medical X-rays, radiation therapy), luminous clocks and watches, glazed and tinted products, tobacco products, treatment of spent fuel, and misuse of radioactive substances.

In the United States, radon gas accounts for the majority of annual radiation exposure and cosmic, terrestrial, internal radiation, and manmade sources account for the remaining exposure (**Figure 11-3**).

The three basic pathways through which people are exposed to radiation are inhalation (breathing radioactive materials into the lungs), ingestion (swallowing radioactive material), and direct (external) exposure. Radiation exposure may be external or internal to the body and the consequences of exposure will depend on total dose, dose rate, and percentage and region of the body exposed. Greater potential for human harm is associated with increases in a combination of these factors. The probability of an adverse health effect is dependent on the size of the dose.

The effects of chronic radiation exposure occur sometime after the initial exposure. High levels of radiation exposure over a shorter duration or lower levels of radiation exposure over a longer duration have been associated with benign tumors, precancerous lesions, cancer (leukemia, breast, bladder, colon, liver, lung, esophagus, ovarian, multiple myeloma, and stomach), cataracts, skin changes, and chromosomal aberrations. Chronic health effects associated with radiation exposure before conception include childhood cancer and chromosomal and other congenital anomalies.[7]

Ionizing radiation is high-energy radiation capable of breaking chemical bonds in atoms and molecules. As such, ionizing radiation is capable of causing cancer. Cancer occurs when genes that regulate cell duplication, apoptosis (cell suicide), or DNA repair are injured or damaged. Ultraviolet radiation from the sun is the most common cause of cancer, primarily in the form of skin cancer. Consider that our skin consists of two main layers and several types of cells within these layers. The top layer, the epidermis, contains three types of cells: squamous, basal, and melanocytes (the cells which give skin its color). The bottom layer is called the dermis. Over 1 million new cases of basal cell and squamous cell carcinomas and less than 1,000 deaths from these carcinomas occurred in the United States in 2010.[8] On the other hand, 68,130 new cases of malignant melanoma and 8,700 deaths from the disease were estimated to have occurred the same year in the United States.[9]

Melanoma skin cancer starts in the melanocytes. Although melanoma skin cancer is much less common than basal cell or squamous cell skin cancers, it is much more serious. This is because melanoma cells developing in the skin can enter the circulatory system and

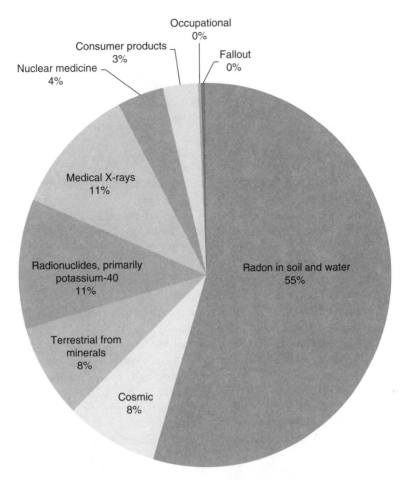

FIGURE 11-3 Sources of radiation exposure in the United States. Data source: National Council on Radiation Protection and Measurements. Ionizing radiation exposure of the population of the United States, NCRP Report No. 93. Washington DC: National Council on Radiation and Protection and Measurements; 1987.

spread to distant organs, such as the liver or brain. Cancer cells in the liver, for example, originating in the melanocytes of the skin, are referred to as "metastatic melanoma" rather than "liver cancer." Because of the potential for melanoma cells to disrupt the normal operation of distant vital organs and become life threatening, melanoma is more serious than squamous or basal cell skin cancers. Basal and squamous cell skin cancers are more likely to occur in individuals with chronic exposure to the sun (lifeguards, sailors, construction workers, farmers, etc.). On the other hand, melanoma skin cancer is more likely to occur in individuals with acute exposure to the sun, particularly during adolescence. Skin cancer occurs most frequently in individuals with fair skin. It can appear in many different forms (a change on the skin, a small lump, or a flat, red spot that is rough or scaly) and is typically treated using surgery, chemotherapy, and radiation therapy.

Ionizing radiation can directly harm the developing fetus and result in birth malformations. Ionizing radiation exposure has been associated with reduced head or brain size, slowed growth, blindness, spina bifida, cleft palate, and mental retardation.[10] Maternal thyroid exposure to diagnostic radiation is associated with a slight reduction in birth weight.[11] However, exposure of the embryo to radio frequency—an extremely low frequency—and intermediate frequency electromagnetic fields has not shown an adverse affect on childhood development.[12] In addition, an estimated 4 per 1,000 fetuses between 8 and 15 weeks gestation exposed to 1 REM (a measure of ionizing radiation) will become mentally retarded.[13]

Chemicals and Health

Several chemicals (e.g., drugs, acids, alkali, heavy metals, poisons, and some enzymes) in the environment are capable of causing chronic disease and adverse health conditions (see Table 11-2). Lead is a metal found in manufactured products and in the environment that has been associated with serious health effects. As leaded gasoline has been phased out in the United States, the level of lead in the air has decreased by 89% (Figure 11-4). Elevated blood lead levels (> 10 μg/dL) in children 1 to 5 years of age have decreased from 88% during 1976 to 1980 to 8.6 during 1988 to 1991 and to 2.2% in about 2000.[14] Smelters and battery plants are the major sources of lead pollution in the air. A person's exposure to lead occurs through breathing and ingesting it in food, water, soil, or dust.[15]

Lead can accumulate in various parts of the body (i.e., in the blood, bones, muscles, and fat). Infants and children are most sensitive to lead—even low levels, especially before 72 months of life. Lead exposure may damage organs including kidneys, liver, brain and nerves, and other organs; lead to osteoporosis; affect the brain and nerves, which can cause seizures, mental retardation, behavioral disorders, memory problems, and mood changes; affect the heart and blood, such as causing high blood pressure and increased heart disease or anemia; affect animals and plants with the same effects as in humans; and affect reproductive and neurological function in fish.[16]

There are various social forces that influence environment lead intake. In developed countries, individuals with low education levels or low income living in poor areas are often

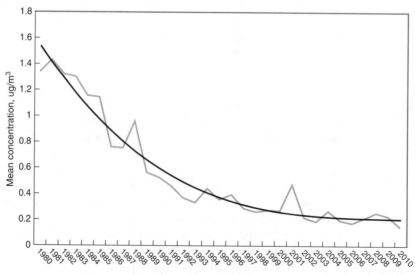

FIGURE 11-4   Lead air quality in the United States, 1980–2010 (based on annual 3-month averages of 31 sites). Data source: http://www.epa.gov/air/airtrends/lead.html

forced to live in older houses that may contain lead plumbing or lead-based paint.[17–19] In turn, these poor housing conditions precipitate the ingestion of lead by individuals through drinking water or accidental eating of lead paint or lead-containing dust.

Regulations throughout the developed world since the 1970s have been effective at greatly lowering exposure to lead.[17] Banning leaded gasoline has caused average blood lead levels to fall sharply.[20] Unfortunately, in many developing countries, leaded gasoline is still allowed, and is a major source of lead exposure.[21,22] Poor children in developing countries are at greatest risk for lead exposure and subsequent poisoning.[22] About 7% of children in North America have blood levels above 10 µg/dL, but the percentage is about 34% in Central and South American children.[21]

Toxicokinetics

The area of study on how a chemical substance enters the body and the course it takes while in the body is called **toxicokinetics**. The name originates from kinetics, which means movement, and the study of movement of toxic substances. The processes of toxicokinetics are absorption (entrance of the substance into the body), distribution (movement of the substance from where it enters the body to other sites in the body such as liver, blood and lymph circulation, kidney, and lungs), **biotransformation** (transformation produced by the body of the substance into new chemicals), and excretion (ejection of the substance or metabolites from the body). When a substance is ingested or inhaled, it is still considered outside the body until it crosses cellular barriers in the gastrointestinal tract or lungs. Absorption can also be through the skin, implants, conjunctal instillations (eye drops), and suppositories. Although cell membranes (cell walls) are designed to prevent foreign invaders or substances from entering into bodily tissue, some substances are able to enter cells of local tissue, blood capillaries and the body's blood circulatory system, or the lymphatic system. Once in the circulatory system, a chemical can be excreted, stored, biotransformed into metabolites, its metabolites can be excreted or stored, or its metabolites can interact or bind with cellular components. Metabolites are new chemicals that are produced through transformations produced by the body; they are produced by metabolism and are necessary for taking part in particular metabolic processes. Biotransformation is essential to survival. It is the process by which absorbed nutrients (food, oxygen, etc.) are transformed into substances required by the body to function normally. Most chemicals undergo biotransformation. The body is efficient at biotransforming body wastes or chemicals that are not normally produced or expected into water-soluble metabolites excreted into bile and excreted from the body. Detoxification occurs when biotransformation metabolites a substance to lower toxicity; however, metabolites may become more toxic, interact with cellular macromolecules such as DNA, and cause serious health effects (cancer, birth defects).

Factors that influence the severity of toxicity of a substance that enters the body include: route of exposure; duration of exposure; concentration of exposure; rate and amount absorbed; distribution and concentrations within the body; efficiency by which the body changes the substance and the metabolites produced; substance or metabolites ability to pass through cell membranes and affect cell components; duration and amount of a substance or metabolites in body tissues; and rate, amount, and site of departure of the substance or metabolites from the body.[23]

The International Agency for Research on Cancer (IARC) has classified several agents as carcinogenic to humans. A summary and update of some of IARC Monographs are presented elsewhere.[24] In 2003, the National Institute for Occupational Safety and Health produced a list

TABLE 11-3   Selected Carcinogens in the Workplace

Carcinogen	Occupation	Type of Cancer
Aromatic amines, solvents	Rubber industry	Bladder, leukemia, stomach, lung, skin, colon, lymphoma
Asbestos	Construction workers	Lung, larynx, gastrointestinal tract
Benzene	Boot and shoe manufacture and repair	Leukemia, lymphoma
Nickel	Nickel refining	Lung, nasal sinuses
Radon	Underground mining	Lung
Soot, tars, oils	Coal, gas, petroleum workers	Skin, lung, bladder
Vinyl chloride	Rubber workers, polyvinyl chloride manufacturing	Liver
Wood dust	Furniture manufacturing	Nasal cavity

From National Institute for Occupational Safety and Health—Occupational Cancer. (2003). Available at: http://www.cdc.gov/niosh/topics/cancer/. Accessed December 13, 2008.

of 133 substances considered to be potential occupational carcinogens. Some of these workplace carcinogens are presented in Table 11-3. The National Institute for Occupational Safety and Health estimated 40,000 new cases of cancer and 20,000 cancer deaths each year in the United States caused by occupational exposures.[25] Compared to the estimated number of new cancer cases and cancer deaths in the United States in 2010,[9] this means that about 3% of cancer cases and 4% of cancer deaths are related to occupational exposures.

Biologic Agents and Health

When we think about biologic agents capable of causing disease such as some viruses and bacteria, we typically think of acute, infectious diseases like malaria, schistosomiasis, typhoid and paratyphoid fevers, diarrhea, and so on; however, as discussed (see Chapter 3 "Practical Disease Concepts in Epidemiology"), infectious agents can also cause chronic conditions such as tuberculosis, syphilis, polio, leprosy, and even cancer. To illustrate, consider the role of viruses in cancer.

Viruses are infectious agents that enter living cells, where they make duplicates of the infected cell. The genetic instructions of the virus are stored in large molecules called nucleic acids. The virus is able to trigger the development of diseases, including cancer, as the nucleic acids are inserted into the chromosomes of the infected cell. A list of some viruses associated with human cancer is presented in Table 11-4.

Human antiviral vaccines are currently available for Hepatitis A and HPV. Hepatitis A is an acute liver disease caused by the Hepatitis A virus. It may last a few weeks to several months, but does not cause chronic infection. On the other hand, it is a risk factor for liver cancer. It is transmitted by ingestion of fecal matter, close person-to-person contact, or ingestion of contaminated food or drinks. The Centers for Disease Control and Prevention recommends the hepatitis A vaccination for all children at least one year of age, for travelers to selected countries, and for others who may be at risk of the disease.

There are almost 40 types of HPV that can infect genital areas of both men and women. It is a common virus that is transmitted through genital contact, typically during sexual

TABLE 11-4   Viruses and Cancer

Virus	Type of Cancer
Epstein-Barr virus	Burkitt's lymphoma
Human Papillomavirus (HPV)	Cancers of the cervix, anus, vagina, vulva, penis, orophayrnx
Hepatitis B and C viruses	Liver cancer
Human T-cell lymphotrophic virus	Adult T-cell leukemia
Kaposi's sarcoma-associated Herpes virus	Kaposi's sarcoma

From National Cancer Institute. Understanding and Preventing Cancer, 2000.

intercourse. Most sexually active people will become infected with HPV over their lifetime. Although most HPV types do not cause serious health problems and go away on their own, some types are associated with cancers of the genital system. Unlike most vaccine-related diseases, there is now a vaccine available that prevents the types of genital HPV that cause most cervical cancer and genital warts. The vaccine Gardasil is administered in three shots over a 6-month period. It is routinely recommended for 11- to 12-year old girls, but is also recommended for women ages 13 to 26 years who have not been vaccinated.

In addition to some viruses, bacteria have also been associated with chronic health problems. For example, **Helicobacter pylori** is a bacterium that can cause chronic conditions such as dyspepsia (heartburn, bloating, and nausea), gastritis (stomach inflammation), and ulcers in the stomach and duodenum, as well as stomach cancer and lymphoma.[26,27] *Helicobacter pylori* infection is caused by swallowing the bacteria in food or liquid or through contaminated utensils. The rate of infection increases with age and is more common in developing countries and places with poor sanitation. Antibiotic drugs are used to treat the infection. Various antibiotics are used together to prevent the bacteria from developing a resistance to any given antibiotic. Researchers are currently studying ways to treat this infection more effectively.

The Social Environment and Health

Several social forces have been associated with leading chronic diseases (see Table 11-1). For example, in the United States, the percent of persons and families below the poverty level was 13.2% in 2008.[1] "Poverty level" is based on family income and family size using U.S. Census Bureau poverty thresholds.[28] The percentage of adults experiencing different types of chronic pain (Figure 11-5) or chronic disease (Figure 11-6) decreases with greater income. A challenge with income and health, however, is that not only does low income relate to more reports of serious health conditions but poor health leads to lower income.

We also see in children that health problems such as asthma, attention deficit hyperactivity disorder, and ear infections also tend to decrease with greater income (Figure 11-7). However, respiratory and food allergies tend to increase with greater income. This has been observed previously, and may be partially explained by disparities in food allergy diagnosis.[29]

Not only are factors such as income, education, work skills, and family disruptions associated with several chronic diseases, but social disruptions such as ethnic violence, war,

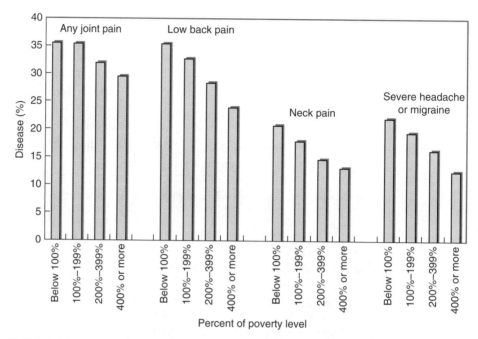

FIGURE 11-5   Prevalence of selected types of chronic pain by percent of poverty level, ages 18 years and older in the United States 2009. Data from National Center for Health Statistics. *Health, United States, 2010 with Chartbook on Trends in the Health of Americans.* Hyattsville, MD: NCHS; 2011, Table 52.

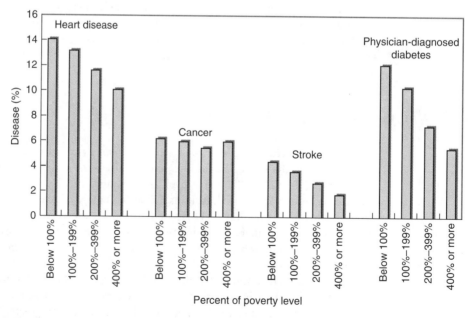

FIGURE 11-6   Prevalence of selected chronic diseases by percent of poverty level, ages 18 years and older in the United States 2008–2009. Data source: National Center for Health Statistics. *Health, United States, 2010 with Chartbook on Trends in the Health of Americans.* Hyattsville, MD: NCHS; 2011, Tables 49, 50.

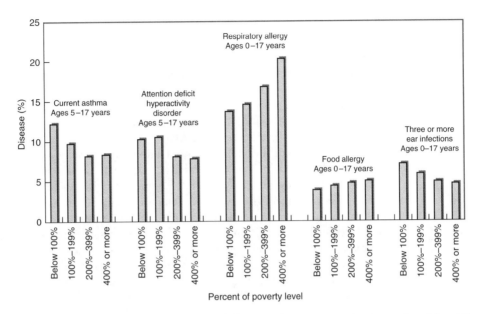

FIGURE 11-7   Prevalence of selected diseases by percent of poverty level in children in the United States 2007–2009. Data source: National Center for Health Statistics. *Health, United States, 2010 with Chartbook on Trends in the Health of Americans.* Hyattsville, MD: NCHS; 2011, Table 46.

acts of terrorism, and natural disasters are as well. For example, war is associated with mental and physical disabilities; families and households may promote certain dietary behaviors that can increase or decrease the risk of selected chronic diseases; social networks and social supports may have implications on a persons' ability to deal with and survive chronic health problems; neighborhoods and communities may include environments that facilitate physical activity (e.g., parks and recreational centers, bike paths, and safe walking areas), which in turn reduces the risk of certain chronic conditions; and public health policy (e.g., non-smoking in public places) may reduce exposure of risk factors to individuals for certain chronic diseases.

BEHAVIOR AND CHRONIC HEALTH PROBLEMS

Many of the diseases and conditions today are influenced by lifestyles of modern populations: career pressures, sedentary lifestyles, high density population living, poor diet, crime, drugs, gangs, poverty, pollution, fear, stress, and economic struggles.[30,31] The primary objectives set forth by *Healthy People 2020* are to reduce coronary heart disease deaths, cancer deaths (especially lung cancer), mental disorders, work-related injuries, and diabetes.[32] Motivating behavior change is fundamental to achieving these primary objectives.

In contrast to environmental exposures over which persons typically have little or no control, many risk factors for chronic disease and conditions are modifiable through behavior change. For example, cancer is a disease that is largely lifestyle related. Doll and Peto (1981) estimated that smoking explained roughly 30% of all cancer deaths, diet explained another 35%, and the remainder was due to viruses, bacteria, radiation, industrial carcinogens, family predisposition, and so on.[33]

Smoking and Chronic Disease

In the United States, annual per capita cigarette consumption was near zero in 1900, peaked in 1963, and declined thereafter, although at a much smaller rate after 1993.[34] The peak coincides with the first Surgeon General's report and subsequent media coverage of the potentially harmful effects of tobacco.[35,36] Some major social influences followed to promote declines in the demand for tobacco (e.g., the nonsmokers' rights movement, increased federal excise tax, and health warning labels).[37]

In 1955, 57% of the adult male population (ages 18 years and older) and 28% of the adult female population smoked cigarettes. In 2010, these percentages for adult males and females have decreased to 18.4 and 15.6, respectively.[38] The 2006 National Health Interview Survey identified the highest adult smoking prevalence in American Indian/Alaska Natives; in those with less than a high school degree; in the age range 18–24 years; and in those below the federal poverty level.[39] Almost a quarter of high school students in the United States smoke cigarettes.[40] This is a particular concern because those who start smoking before 21 years of age have the hardest time quitting. About 30% of youth smokers continue smoking and go on to die prematurely from smoking-related disease. In addition, teen smokers are more likely to use alcohol and illegal drugs and experience panic attacks, anxiety disorders, and depression.[40]

Canadian researchers reported several chronic diseases and conditions associated with cigarette smoking[41,42] based on three prior reviews and meta-analyses.[43–45] These chronic diseases and conditions included several cancers (lip and oropharyngeal cancer, esophageal cancer, stomach cancer, anal cancer, pancreatic cancer, laryngeal cancer, lung cancer, cervical cancer, vulvar cancer, penile cancer, bladder cancer, renal cancer), ischemic heart disease, pulmonary circulatory disease, cardiac dysrhythmias, heart failure, stroke, arterial disease, pneumonia and influenza, chronic obstructive pulmonary disease, ulcers, Crohn's disease, ulcerative colitis, pregnancy complications, stillbirths, neonatal conditions, sudden infant death syndrome, and accidents by fire and flames.

Current age-adjusted smoking prevalence is 37% for persons with a smoking-related chronic disease (29% for coronary heart disease, 30% for stroke, 49% for emphysema, and 41% for bronchitis) compared with 19% for those with no chronic disease; former age-adjusted smoking prevalence was 26% for persons with a smoking-related chronic disease (61% for lung cancer, 33% for other cancer, 32% for coronary heart disease, 23% for stroke, 29% for emphysema, 20% for chronic bronchitis, and 24% for other chronic diseases) compared with 16% for those with no chronic disease, and never age-adjusted smoking was 64% for those with no chronic disease.[39]

Along with decreasing levels of cigarette smoking in this country, we would expect decreasing rates of smoking-related diseases. Age-adjusted mortality rates (2000 U.S. standard population) decreased from 1970 through 2008 by 63% for heart disease (502.6 to 188.1 per 100,000), 91% for atherosclerosis (27 to 2.4 per 100,000), and 73% for cerebrovascular diseases (151.9 to 41 per 100,000).[46] For all causes of death, the age-adjusted mortality rates decreased by 39% (1,242.2 per 100,000 to 762.8 per 100,000).[46]

Diet and Chronic Disease

The association between diet and heart disease, cancer, stroke, and diabetes is well established. Although social forces such as family and income influence diet, behavior also plays an important role. Earlier we mentioned that as much as 35% of all cancer is attributed to diet. Modifying one's diet to consume low amounts of fat can reduce the risk of cancers of the colon/rectum, breast, and prostate, and diets rich in whole grains, vegetables, and fruits are protective against cancers of the lung, colon/rectum, bladder, breast, oral cavity, stomach, cervix, and esophagus.[47] Also, consuming dietary fiber is important for reducing the risk of cancers of the breast and colon/rectum.[48]

To further illustrate, in a study comparing daily per capita consumption of dietary fat and age-adjusted mortality from breast cancer among 21 countries, a 5.5-fold increase in breast cancer incidence was observed in countries having the highest fat intake.[49] Studies of populations migrating from areas with low breast cancer rates to regions with high rates show that these populations eventually stay within the high rates of their new country.[50] The type of fat consumed is also important in the development of breast cancer. Studies have indicated that it is the polyunsaturated fats (high in omega-6 fatty acids, principally linoleic acid) that are strongly associated with breast cancer.[51] On the other hand, in countries such as Greece, where monounsaturated fatty acids (like olive oil) are frequently consumed, breast cancer risk is comparatively low.[52] In an article reviewing seven studies on the association between dietary fiber and risk of breast cancer, an inverse association was found in six of the seven studies.[53]

Poor nutrition is an important risk factor for osteoporosis. Other risk factors include aging, heredity, medications, and other illnesses. Impaired bone mineralization leads to bone softening diseases and loss of bone mass that is characteristic of the progressive systemic skeletal disease known as osteoporosis. In 2004, the Surgeon General of the United States described osteoporosis and other bone diseases as affecting more than 10 million individuals and causing about 1.5 million fractures annually in the United States.[54] Women are at a greater risk of osteoporosis than men because of their smaller bone structure, hormonal changes, and pattern of bone loss.[55,56] One out of every two women over the age of 50 years will have an osteoporosis-related fracture.[56] Dietary risk factors for osteoporosis include eating disorders, drug use, low calcium and dairy intake, excess soda consumption, and chronic alcoholism.[57] Family history, physical inactivity, medications, aging, other illnesses, low body mass, and tobacco smoking are other important risk factors for osteoporosis.

Body Weight and Chronic Disease

Although a person's weight has a genetic component, the increasing proportion of obese people in the United States and elsewhere indicates that it is primarily behavior related. Overweight and obesity trends in the United States and elsewhere in the world are of primary concern because of several associated health complications, including high blood pressure, stroke, heart disease, diabetes mellitus, osteoarthritis, impaired functioning of the heart and lungs, gallbladder disease, hyperlipidemia, osteoarthritis, obstructive sleep apnea, injuries, and cancer (e.g., colon, rectum, breast, uterus, cervix, and prostate).

Sexual Practices and Chronic Disease

Sexual behaviors have been associated with increased risk for certain chronic diseases. For example, early sexual activity among adolescents renders the immature cervical epithelium vulnerable to carcinogens (e.g., HPV) and increases the risk of cervical cancer.[58] A review of Figure 5-3, "Age-specific rates of carcinoma in situ of the uterine cervix, 1991–1995" showed that the pattern in rates of cervical carcinoma in situ across the age span was consistent with an infectious agent being the primary cause of this disease. In addition, pregnancy and delivery, particularly at a younger age, may cause cervical erosions that increase exposure to potential carcinogens.

Sexually transmitted infections can endanger the fetus and newborn. For example, if syphilis is untreated, it can cause stillbirth, newborn death, or chronic bone defects. Sexually transmitted infections affect 1 in 2,000 babies.[59] Being sexually active (as opposed to abstaining from or postponing sexual activity), having many sexual partners (either serially or concurrently), and practicing unprotected sex (which includes the irregular or incorrect use of condoms) with an infected partner are the primary ways that venereal diseases are transmitted. HIV/AIDS is typically transmitted through sexual practices. AIDS is the total breakdown of the body's immune system. When this occurs, the body is open to infection from any type of virus. Syphilis can also result in a slow breakdown of the immune system. Chronic conditions associated with HIV/AIDS include depression, fatigue, and weight loss, as well as Kaposi's sarcoma, a malignant tumor of blood vessels in the skin; individuals with HIV develop an immune deficiency that makes them more susceptible to Kaposi's sarcoma.[60] Untreated syphilis can damage the heart, aorta, brain, eyes, and bones.[61]

Behavior Changes for Better Health

An important part of epidemiology is applying risk factor information on preventing and controlling health problems. As risk factors for disease are identified and the extent of these risk factors made known through epidemiologic investigations, the potential for effective prevention and control efforts grows. Current knowledge tells us that many chronic conditions could be avoided by:

- Maintaining a healthy weight
- Eating no more than two or three servings of red meat per week
- Taking a multivitamin with folate every day
- Drinking less than one alcoholic drink a day
- Eating five or more servings of fruits and vegetables per day
- Eating more high fiber foods such as whole grains, wheat cereals, bread, and pasta
- Including cruciferous vegetables in your diet (such as broccoli, cabbage, etc.)
- Not smoking
- Getting adequate sleep
- Protecting oneself from the sun
- Avoiding certain workplace exposures
- Protecting oneself and partner(s) from sexually transmitted infections
- Exercising regularly

The Centers for Disease Control and Prevention puts considerable resources into annually collecting and disseminating health risk factor information. The Behavior Risk Factor Surveillance System is a state-level prevalence survey in the United States that monitors actual behavioral risks, rather than information on attitudes or knowledge, associated with premature morbidity and mortality.[38] This information is particularly useful for planning, initiating, supporting, and evaluating prevention programs.

Health Belief Model

Many behavior change models are based on the belief that knowledge itself is not a sufficient motivating factor for changing problem behaviors. This is a widely accepted premise in health behavior change theory.[62] According to the **Health Belief Model**, a widely used conceptual framework for understanding health behavior, behavior change requires a rational decision-making process that considers perceived susceptibility to illness, perceived consequences or seriousness of the illness, belief that recommended action is appropriate or efficacious to reduce risk, and belief that the benefits of action outweigh the costs.[63–65] For example, an individual may be aware of potential adverse health outcomes associated with smoking, cardiovascular disease, and cancer, but unless these health outcomes are perceived to be personally threatening and serious, the potential benefits from not smoking may not outweigh the perceived costs of this behavior.

The health belief model is an attempt to identify factors that influence behavior change. The health belief model originally involved four concepts representing perceived susceptibility, perceived severity, perceived benefits, and perceived barriers. Two extensions of these concepts in more recent years include cues to action and self-efficacy. The following table in *Theory at a Glance: A Guide for Health Promotion Practice* presents the concepts, along with definitions and applications, of the health belief model (Table 11-5).[66]

TABLE 11-5   Concepts, Definitions, and Applications of the Health Belief Model

Concept	Definition	Application
Perceived susceptibility	One's opinion of chances of getting a condition	Define population(s) at risk, risk levels; personalize risk based on a person's features or behavior; heighten perceived susceptibility if too low
Perceived severity	One's opinion of how serious a condition and its consequences are	Specify consequences of the risk and the condition
Perceived benefits	One's belief in the efficacy of the advised action to reduce risk or seriousness of impact	Define action to take; how, where, when; clarify the positive effects to be expected
Perceived barriers	One's opinion of the tangible and psychological costs of the advised action	Identify and reduce barriers through reassurance, incentives, assistance
Cues to action	Strategies to activate "readiness"	Provide how-to information, promote awareness, reminders
Self-efficacy	Confidence in one's ability to take action	Provide training, guidance in performing action

From Glanz K, Marcus Lewis F, Rimer BK. *Theory at a Glance: A Guide for Health Promotion Practice.* Bethesda, MD: National Institutes of Health, 1997.

HEREDITY AND CHRONIC HEALTH PROBLEMS

Many health problems have an inherent component. For example, although most cancer occurs in individuals with no family history of the disease, cancer susceptibility genes that increase the chance of developing the disease are present in some families.[67] For example, about 5–10% of breast cancer patients and 9% of prostate cancer patients are believed to have an inherited susceptibility gene.[68–70] Some hereditary conditions associated with cancer are: hereditary retinoblastoma, which is a risk factor for retinoblastoma; xeroderma pigmentosum, which is a risk factor for skin cancer; Wilms' tumor, which is associated with renal cancer; Li-Fraumeni syndrome, which is a risk factor for sarcomas, brain cancer, breast cancer, and leukemia; familial adenomatous polyposis, which is a risk factor for colon and rectal cancers; Paget's disease of the bone, which is a risk factor for bone cancer; and Fanconi's anaplastic anemia, which is a risk factor for leukemia, liver, and skin cancer.

Another example involves epilepsy. There is strong evidence linking epilepsy to a genetic influence, and two epilepsy genes have been identified. Epilepsy can be defined as unprovoked seizures. Clinically, epilepsy is subclassified according to seizure type.

Partial seizures include:

- Partial seizures with elementary symptomatology (generally without impairment of consciousness)
- Partial seizures with complex symptomatology (generally with impairment of consciousness)
- Partial seizures secondarily generalized

Generalized seizures (involves entire brain) include:

- Petit mal
- Bilateral massive epileptic myoclonus
- Infantile spasms
- Clonic seizures
- Tonic seizures
- Tonic-clonic seizures (grand mal)
- Atonic seizures
- Akinetic seizures

Two additional classifications used are idiopathic, which have genetic origins, and cryptogenic, which have nongenetic origins, such as head trauma. Epilepsy is the most common neurological disorder, with about 4% of the U.S. population suffering from this condition. The risk of unprovoked seizures in offspring of mothers and fathers with epilepsy is shown in **Figure 11-8**.[71] Other causes of epilepsy include head trauma, stroke, or brain infection, with 25% of cases resulting from these factors.

Osteoporosis is a disease that tends to run in families. Having a parent or sibling with the disease puts one at greater risk, especially if there is a family history of fractures. Yet, the disease may be offset by proper diet and other lifestyle-related behaviors, as discussed previously. On the other hand, poor diet and lifestyle-related activities may result in osteoporosis, even when there is not a genetic predisposition for the disease. For example, in nursing home populations it was found that supplemental calcium and vitamin D, plus

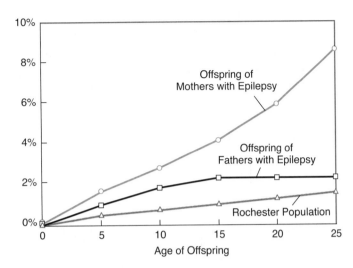

FIGURE 11-8   Risk of unprovoked seizures in offspring of mothers and fathers with epilepsy for the general population of Rochester, Minnesota, 1935–1979. From Ottman R. Genetic epidemiology of epilepsy. *Epidemiol Rev.* 1997;19(1):120–127.

external hip protectors, can reduce hip fractures by 50%.[72] Research has also shown that replacement estrogen therapy prevents or greatly reduces loss of bone mass in both women who have had their ovaries removed and in women with intact ovaries. Women who had taken estrogen for 7 years before reaching age 75 had a higher bone mass. Women who go through menopause later in life have a reduced risk of hip fracture.

MULTIFACTORIAL ETIOLOGY IN CHRONIC DISEASE EPIDEMIOLOGY

In this chapter, we have presented physical, chemical, biological, and social environments; personal behavior and social factors; and heredity as important components of chronic disease. As many have observed previously, including William Farr (1807–1883), combinations of these components may be required before the chronic disease or condition occurs.[73] The previous example illustrates that multiple components influence osteoporosis. In addition, more than one combination of components may be sufficient to cause a chronic disease or condition (see "Rothman's causal pies" in Chapter 1). Thus, we see the complexity of causation in chronic disease epidemiology. The webs of causation presented in Chapter 9, "Causality," illustrate attempts to better understand complex relationships.

Brain tumors provide an example of a disease where both environmental and genetic factors have been implicated; that is, both factors appear to be required prior to brain cancer. Brain tumors are among the most lethal cancers. A person with a brain tumor has a 52% chance of surviving 1 year. The list of environmental agents includes physical (radiation), chemical, and biological agents. Exposures to organic solvents, vinyl chloride, pesticides, and polycyclic aromatic hydrocarbons have been implicated as occupational risks. In addition, it has been well established that some persons inherit a predisposition to develop brain tumors.

The most common type of brain tumor in adults is gliomas, with the main type of glioma being astrocytes (star-shaped). It is not uncommon for patients with a glioma to have multiple tumors. It is highly unusual for brain tumors to metastasize outside the central nervous system (CNS); however, there is some seeding within the CNS. The brain is a common place for metastasis from cancers in the lung, breast, rectum, kidney, and stomach. There is a predominance of glioma in men and predominance of meningioma in females. Figure 11-9 shows graphs of the incidence for various types of brain tumors.[74]

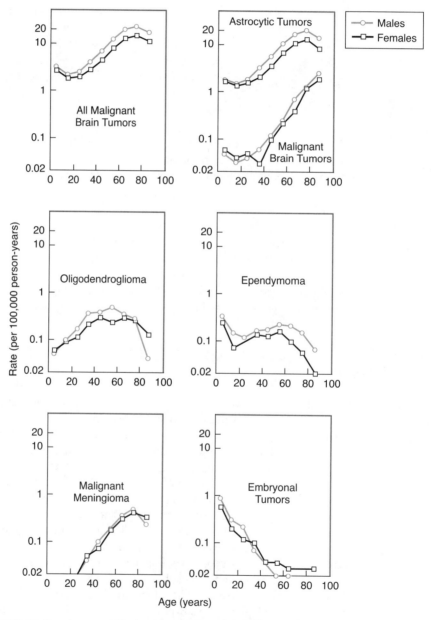

FIGURE 11-9   Age-specific incidence rates for malignant brain tumors. The blue line represents males and the black line represents females. From Inskip PD, Linet MS, Heinemann EF. Etiology of brain tumors in adults. *Epidemiol Rev.* 1995; 17(2):382–404.

PRIORITIES IN DISEASE PREVENTION AND CONTROL

Prevention is hard to measure and cannot always be demonstrated by empirical research, but like quality, it is observable. Common sense dictates that prevention works and must be made the main focus of all health care and public health activity in order to maintain and improve the health status of populations. Fear and pain can be powerful motivational forces in changing behavior; however, to avoid chronic diseases, one must embrace healthy behaviors and lifestyles long before pain or fear occurs. Prevention and control of diseases, disorders, injuries, disabilities, and death in populations remains the primary purpose for the existence of epidemiology.

The interaction between physical, chemical, biological, psychosocial, environmental, personal behaviors, and inherent risk factors often makes prevention efforts complex and sometimes infeasible. It also emphasizes why prevention programs need to be specifically tailored to given societies and cultures; however, despite the complexities of primary prevention, it provides the greatest potential for minimizing public suffering and healthcare costs.

The following questions can be useful in establishing priorities in disease prevention and health promotion:

1. Which disease, disorder, or condition has the greatest impact on illness, disability, injury, lost work time or school time, unnecessarily using up health resources, rehabilitation costs, causing family disruption, economic impact, and costs?

2. Are special populations or groups of people suffering from exposures to diseases, agents, risk factors, or hazards?

3. Which susceptible populations are most likely to respond to prevention, intervention, and control measures?

4. Which risk factors, diseases, agents, or hazards are most likely to respond to control measures?

5. Are there diseases, disabilities, injuries, disorders, or conditions that need to be investigated, that are being overlooked, or that are not being responded to by other organizations or agencies?

6. Of the many risk factors, diseases, agents, or hazards, which would yield the greatest improved health status, social impact, and economic benefit to the target population?

7. Of the many risk factors, diseases, agents, or hazards, which are of national, regional, state, or local concern and of major priority for an epidemiological investigation?

CONCLUSION

This chapter focused on chronic disease epidemiology. A chronic disease is a health-related state or event that is long-lasting or recurrent; it is a persistent medical condition. Chronic diseases are characterized by long latency periods and complex causal mechanisms. Chronic disease epidemiology involves the study of the distribution and determinants of chronic disease in human populations and the application of this study for taking appropriate prevention and control measures.

Climate Conditions Affect Physical Activity among Adults in the United States

A recent study, reported in the *American Journal of Health Behavior*, 2005, quantified the effects of climate on physical activity. The study matched data from 255 weather stations with results from a physical activity survey of people in 355 U.S. counties. Weather measurements—taken four times a day at each weather station—included daily air temperature, dew point temperature, wind speed direction, sea level pressure, and total cloud cover. To gauge physical activity, the researchers took data from an ongoing national telephone survey of adults 18 years and older, a project between Centers for Disease Control and Prevention and U.S. states and territories. Meeting the recommendation for physical activity was defined as 30 minutes of moderate physical activity 5–7 days a week or 20 minutes of vigorous physical activity 3–7 days a week. Moderate activity included brisk walking, biking, vacuuming, and gardening; vigorous activity included running, aerobics, and heavy yardwork.

The study found that the highest physical activity was linked to moist moderate conditions in winter, dry polar air in spring, dry tropical air in summer, and moist polar air in fall. Moist tropical air is warm and very humid, the researchers say, with cloud cover in winter and partial cloud cover in summer. Muggy conditions "are consistently associated with lowest mean percentages meeting recommendations for physical activity," the researchers found. Dry tropical air is warm and sunny. Polar air, which leads to coldest conditions, can be either dry with little cloud cover or moist with cloud cover and often precipitation. Counties that ranked in the top quarter for physical activity had the highest percentage of dry, moderate days, followed by moist polar days and then dry polar days. Counties in the bottom quarter had the highest percentage of days with moist tropical conditions.

After Montana, with 60.9%, the states with highest percentages of respondents meeting recommended physical activity levels were Utah with 59.2%, Wisconsin with 57.9%, and New Hampshire with 55.9%. On the other hand, after Puerto Rico, at 30.9%, the states with the lowest percentages were Hawaii with 36.4%, North Carolina with 37.4%, and Kentucky with 37.6%. Physical activity also varied significantly among seasons, with activity highest in summer at 48.4%, 46.2% in spring, 45.8% in fall, and 44.6% in winter.

From Merrill RM, Shields EC, White GL Jr, Druce D. Climate conditions and physical activity among adults in the United States. Am J Health Behav. 2005;29(4):371–381.

Public health and individual decision making rely on epidemiologic information for making informed choices. Through epidemiologic research, risk factors for many chronic diseases are known. Physical, chemical, biological, and psychosocial environments, behaviors, and inherent risk factors have all been identified to affect health-related states or events, with a combination of these risk factors often involved. Because of the multifactorial etiology of many chronic diseases, prevention and control efforts are typically much more complicated than that of infectious diseases, where a single pathogen is identified as the causal agent.

The health belief model attempts to identify the combination of factors that influence a person to change their behavior. These factors include perceived susceptibility, perceived severity, perceived benefits, perceived barriers, cues to action, and self-efficacy. Health educators often find that effective prevention and control programs require more than just educating people about risk factors for disease. For example, a health education program aimed at reducing risk behaviors associated with heart disease may be ineffective if poverty levels are high such that a nutritious diet is not affordable and the economy promotes feelings of hopelessness.

EXERCISES

Key Terms

Define the following terms.

Biotransformation
Chronic disease epidemiology
Environment
Health belief model
Helicobacter pylori

Latency period
Physical stresses
Ionizing radiation
Risk factor
Toxicokinetics

STUDY QUESTIONS

1. A chronic disease may be which of the following:

    a. Infectious, communicable

    b. Noninfectious, noncommunicable

    c. Neither (a) or (b)

    d. Both (a) and (b)

2. Chronic diseases are mainly caused by what general factors?

3. Why are primary prevention measures more complex for chronic diseases such as heart disease or cancer than infectious acute conditions like cholera or Lyme disease?

4. Select a chronic disease example and apply it to the six concepts presented for the health belief model.

5. Describe how osteoporosis is influenced by multiple risk factors.

6. Name the three common pathways in which people are exposed to radiation.

7. What are the general causes of cancer? What are the relative contributions of these causes in the United States?

8. List and describe the four processes of toxicokinetics.

9. Describe some of the health effects associated with lead exposure.

10. Fill in the right side of the table.

Virus/Bacteria	Type of Cancer
Human Papillomavirus (HPV)	
Helicobacter pylori bacterium	
Kaposi's sarcoma-associated Herpes virus	
Hepatitis B and C viruses	
Epstein-Barr virus	
Human T-cell lymphotrophic virus	

REFERENCES

1. Murphy SL, Xu JQ, Kochanek KD. Deaths: Preliminary Data for 2010. National Vital Statistics Reports; vol 60 no 4. Hyattsville, MD: National Center for Health Statistics; 2012.

2. Centers for Disease Control and Prevention. Achievements in Public Health, 1900–1999: Control of Infectious Diseases. *MMWR.* 1999;48(29):621–629.

3. Anderson G. *Chronic Conditions: Making the Case for Ongoing Care.* Baltimore, MD: John Hopkins University; 2004.

4. Centers for Medicare & Medicaid Services. *Chronic Conditions among Medicare Beneficiaries, Chart Book.* Baltimore, MD; 2011.

5. Last JM, ed. *A Dictionary of Epidemiology*, 4th ed. New York, NY: Oxford University Press; 2001.

6. *Stedman's Medical Dictionary for the Health Professions and Nursing*, 5th ed. New York, NY: Lippincott Williams & Wilkins; 2005.

7. Wilkinson P, ed. *Environmental Epidemiology.* New York, NY: Open University Press; 2006.

8. National Cancer Institute. Skin cancer. http://www.cancer.gov/cancertopics/types/skin. Accessed January 28, 2012.

9. Jemal A, Siegel R, Xu, J, Ward E. Cancer statistics, 2010. CA: *A Cancer J Clin.* 2010;60(5):277–300.

10. Gilbert Barness E. Teratogenic causes of malformations. *Ann Clin Lab Sci.* 40(2):99-114.

11. De Santis M, Di Gianantonio E, Straface G, et al. Ionizing radiations in pregnancy and teratogenesis: a review of literature. *Reprod Toxicol.* 2005;20(3):323–329.

12. Juutilainen J. Developmental effects of electromagnetic fields. *Bioelectromagnetics.* 2005;7:S107–S115.

13. Environmental Protection Agency. Health effects. http://www.epa.gov/radiation/understand/index.html. Accessed January 28, 2012.

14. Meyer PA, Pivetz T, Dignam TA, Homa DM, Schoonover J, Brody D. Surveillance for elevated blood lead levels among children—United States 1997–2001. *MMWR.* 2003;52(SS10):1–21.

15. Environmental Protection Agency. Six common air pollutants: Lead: How lead affects the way we live and breathe. http://www.epa.gov/air/lead/. Accessed January 28, 2012.

16. Lidsky TI, Schneider JS. Lead neurotoxicity in children: basic mechanisms and clinical correlates. *Brain.* 2003;126:5–19.

17. Pokras, MA, Kneeland, MR. Lead poisoning: using transdisciplinary approaches to solve an ancient problem. *EcoHealth.* 2008;5(3):379–85.

18. Cleveland, LM, Minter, ML, Cobb, KA, Scott, AA, German, VF. Lead hazards for pregnant women and children: part 1: immigrants and the poor shoulder most of the burden of lead exposure in this country. Part 1 of a two-part article details how exposure happens, whom it affects, and the harm it can do. *AJN. 2008*; 108(10):40–9; quiz 50.

19. Jones, RL, Homa, DM, Meyer, PA, Brody, DJ, Caldwell, KL, Pirkle, JL, Brown, MJ. Trends in blood lead levels and blood lead testing among US children aged 1 to 5 years, 1988–2004. *Pediatrics*. 2009;123(3):e376–85.

20. Meyer, PA, Brown, MJ, Falk, H. Global approach to reducing lead exposure and poisoning. *Muta Res*. 2008; 659(1-2):166–75.

21. Payne, M. Lead in drinking water. *CMAJ*. 2008; 179(3):253–4.

22. Meyer, PA, McGeehin, MA; Falk, H. A global approach to childhood lead poisoning prevention. *Int J Hyg Envir Heal*. 2003;206(4-5)(4–5):363–9.

23. National Library of Science. Toxicology tutor II: Toxicokinetics. http://sis.nlm.nih.gov/enviro/toxtutor/Tox2/amenu.htm. Accessed January 28, 2012.

24. Cogliano VJ, Baan R, Straif K, Grosse Y, Lauby-Secretan B, El Ghissassi F, Bouvard V, Benbrahim-Tallaa L, Guha N, Freeman C, Galichet L, Wild CP. Preventable exposures associated with human cancers. *J Natl Cancer Inst*. 2011; 21;103(24):1827–39.

25. National Institute for Occupational Safety and Health—Occupational Cancer, 2003. http://www.cdc.gov/niosh/topics/cancer/. Accessed December 13, 2008.

26. Munoz N. Helicobacter and stomach cancer. *Cancer Epidemiol Biomarkers Prev*. 1994;3:445–451.

27. Koehler CI, Mues MB, Dienes HP, Kriegsmann J, Schirmacher P, Odenthal M. Helicobacter pylori genotyping in gastric adenocarcinoma and MALT lymphoma by multiplex PCR analyses of paraffin wax embedded tissues. *Mol Pathol*. 2003;56:36–42.

28. DeNavas-Walt C, Proctor BD, Smith JC. Income, poverty, and health insurance coverage in the United States: 2008. U.S. Census Bureau Current Population Report, P60–236.Washington, DC: U.S. Government Printing Office; 2009. http://www.census.gov/prod/2009pubs/p60-236.pdf.

29. Gupta RS, Springston EE, Warrier MR, Smith B, Kumar R, Pongracic J, Holl JL.The prevalence, severity, and distribution of childhood food allergy in the United States. *Pediatrics*. 2011;128(1):e9–17.

30. Program Resources Department. American Association of Retired Persons and the Administration on Aging. A Profile of Older Americans—1989.

31. Porterfield JD, St. Pierre R. *Healthful Aging*. Guilford, CT: Dushkin Publishing; 1992.

32. U.S. Department of Health and Human Services. Office of Disease Prevention and Health Promotion. *Healthy People 2020*. Washington, DC. http://www.healthypeople.gov/2020/topicsobjectives2020/default.aspx. Accessed January 30, 2012.

33. Doll R, Peto R. Quantitative estimates of avoidable risk of cancer in the United States today. *J Nat Cancer Inst*. 1981;66:1191–1308.

34. Shopland DR. Effect of smoking on the incidence and mortality of lung cancer. In: Johnson BE, Johnson DH, eds. *Lung Cancer*. New York, NY: John Wiley and Sons; 1995: 1–14.

35. Schottenfield D. Epidemiology of cancer of the esophagus. *Semin Oncol*. 1984;11:92–100.

36. U.S. Public Health Service. Smoking and Health. Report of the Advisory Committee to the Surgeon General of the Public Health Service. Washington, DC: U.S. Department of Health, Education, and Welfare, Public Health Service, Center for Disease Control, 1964. PHS Publication No. 1103.

37. National Cancer Institute. Strategies to Control Tobacco Use in the United States: A Blueprint for Public Health Action in the 1990s. Smoking and Tobacco Control Monograph No. 1. Bethesda, MD: National Institutes of Health, 1991. NIH Publication No. 92–3316.

38. Centers for Disease Control and Prevention. About the BRFSS. National Center for Chronic Disease Prevention and Health Promotion. Behavior Risk Factor Surveillance System. http://apps.nccd.cdc.gov/BRFSS/index.asp. Accessed January 29, 2012.

39. Rock VJ, Malarcher A, Kahende JW, Asman K, Husten C, Caraballo R. Cigarette smoking among adults—United States, 2006. *MMWR*. 200756(44):1157–1161.

40. MedlinePlus. Smoking and youth. Available at: http://www.nlm.nih.gov/medlineplus/smoking-andyouth.html. Accessed January 29, 2012.

41. Single E, Rehm J, Robson L, et al. The relative risks and etiologic fractions of different causes of death and disease attributable to alcohol, tobacco, and illicit drug use in Canada. *CMAJ*. 2000;162(12):1669–1675.

42. Single E, Robson L, Rehm J, et al. Morbidity and mortality attributable to alcohol, tobacco, and illicit drug use in Canada. *Am J Public Health.* 1999;89:385–390.

43. English DR, Homan CDJ, Milne E, et al. *The Quantification of Drug Caused Morbidity and Mortality in Australia,* 1995 edition. Canberra: Commonwealth Department of Human Services and Health, 1995.

44. Fox K, Merrill J, Chang H, Califano J. Estimating the costs of substance abuse to the Medicaid hospital care program. *Am J Public Health.* 1995;85:48–54.

45. Shultz J, Novotny T, Rice D. Quantifying the disease impact of cigarette smoking with SAMMEC II software. *Public Health Rep.* 1991;106:326–333.

46. Surveillance, Epidemiology, and End Results (SEER) Program (http://www.seer.cancer.gov). SEER*Stat Database: Mortality— All COD, Aggregated With State, Total U.S. (1969–2008) <Katrina/Rita Population Adjustment>, National Cancer Institute, DCCPS, Surveillance Research Program, Cancer Statistics Branch, released September 2011. Underlying mortality data provided by NCHS (http://www.cdc.gov/nchs).

47. Weinstein IB. Cancer prevention: recent progress and future opportunities. *Cancer Res.* 1991;51(Suppl):5080S–585S.

48. Willet WC. Epidemiologic studies of diet and cancer. *Med Oncol Tumor Pharmacother.* 1990;7:93–97.

49. Prentice RL, Kakar F, Hursting S, Sheppard L, Klein R, Kushi LH. Aspects of the rationale for the Womens' Health Trial. *J Nat Cancer Inst.* 1988;80:802–814.

50. Schatzkin A, Greenwald P, Byar DP, Clifford CK. The dietary fat-breast cancer hypothesis is alive. *JAMA.* 1989;261:3284–3287.

51. Cohen LA, Kendall ME, Zang E, Meschter C, Rose DP. Modulation of N-nitrosomethylurea-induced mammary tumor promotion by dietary fiber and fat. *J Nat Cancer Inst.* 1991;83:496–501.

52. Rose DP, Boyar AP, Wynder EL. International comparisons of mortality rates for cancer of the breast, ovary, prostate, and colon and per capita food consumption. *Cancer.* 1986;58:2363–2371.

53. Shankar S, Lanza E. Dietary fiber and cancer prevention. *Hematol Oncol Clin North Am.* 1991;5:25–41.

54. U.S. Department of Health and Human Services. Bone Health and Osteoporosis: A Report of the Surgeon General. Rockville, MD: U.S. Department of Health and Human Services Office of the Surgeon General, 2004.

55. Martin JT, Coviak CP, Gendler P, Kim KK, Cooper K, Rodrigues-Fisher L. Female adolescents' knowledge of bone health promotion behaviors and osteoporosis risk factors. *Ortho Nursing.* 2004;23:235–244.

56. Vondracek S, Hansen L. Current approaches to management of osteoporosis in men. *Am J Soc Health Syst Pharm.* 2004;61:1801–1811.

57. Mayo Clinic. Osteoporosis. http://www.mayoclinic.com/health/osteoporosis/DS00128/DSECTION=risk-factors. Accessed April 11, 2012.

58. Lorincz AT, Reid R, Jenson AB, Greenberg MD, Lancaster W, Kurman RJ. Human Papillomavirus infection of the cervix: relative risk associations of 15 common anogenital types. *Obstet Gynecol.* 1992;79:328–337.

59. Birth defects fact sheet. http://health.state.ga.us/pdfs/epi/mch/gbdris/birthdefects.fs.04.pdf. Accessed December 13, 2008.

60. National Cancer Institute. Treatment statement for health professionals. Kaposi sarcoma treatment PDQ. http://www.meb.uni-bonn.de/cancer.gov/CDR0000062914.html. Accessed December 13, 2008.

61. MERCK. Syphilis. http://www.merck.com/mmhe/sec17/ch200/ch200b.html. Accessed December 13, 2008.

62. Prochaska JO, DiClemente CC. Stages of change in the modification of problem behaviors. *Prog Behav Modif.* 1992;28:184–218.

63. Rosenstock IM. Why people use health services. *Milbank Mem Fund Q.* 1966;44:94–127.

64. Rosenstock IM. Historical origins of the health belief model. *Health Educ Q.* 1974;2:328–335.

65. Janz NK, Becker MH. The health belief model: a decade later. *Health Educ Q.* 1984;11:1–47.

66. Glanz K, Marcus Lewis F, Rimer BK. *Theory at a Glance: a Guide for Health Promotion Practice.* Bethesda, MD: National Institutes of Health, 1997.

67. Brose MS, Smyrk TC, Weber B, Lynch HT. Genetic Predisposition to Cancer. In: *Cancer Medicine* e.5: Section 3: Cancer Etiology, Holland-Frei Cancer Medicine, 6th edition. London: B.C. Decker; 2003, Chapter 16.

68. Ford D, Easton DF, Stratton M, et al. Genetic heterogeneity and penetrance analysis of the BRCA1 and BRCA2 genes in breast cancer families. *Am J Hum Genet.* 1998;62:676–689.

69. Couch JF, Farid LM, DeShano ML, et al. BRCA2 germline mutation in male breast cancer cases and breast cancer families. *Nat Genet.* 1996;13:123–125.

70. Carter BS, Beaty TH, Steinberg GD, Childs B, Walsh PC. Mendelian inheritance of familial prostate cancer. *Proc National Acad Sci USA.* 1992;89:3367–3371.

71. Ottman R. Genetic epidemiology of epilepsy. *Epidemiol Rev.* 1997;19(1):120–127.

72. Cumming RG, Nevitt MC, Cummings SR. Epidemiology of hip fractures. *Epidemiol Rev.* 1997;19(2):244–253.

73. Fox JP, Hall CE, Elveback LR. *Epidemiology: Man and Disease.* New York, NY: Macmillan Company; 1970.

74. Inskip PD, Linet MS, Heineman EF. Etiology of brain tumors in adults. *Epidemiol Rev.* 1995;17(2):382–404.

12

Clinical Epidemiology

OBJECTIVES

After completing this chapter, you will be able to:

- Define clinical epidemiology.
- Understand various aspects of screening and diagnostic tests.
- Describe selected measures for evaluating prognosis.
- Describe how these measures of prognosis can be biased and how bias can be avoided.

In the past few decades, the application of epidemiologic methods has moved in several physiological and methodological directions. The definition of epidemiology presented in the outset of this book uses the term "health-related states or events," in order to capture the broad application of this discipline. With the wide scope of epidemiology comes an expanded illumination of information for improving public health planning and decision making, as well as individual decision making.

To clarify the application areas of epidemiology by physiology or disease, or by methodological approach, several extensions to the word epidemiology have been added. Some of the specialty areas include cancer epidemiology, infectious disease epidemiology, social epidemiology, and environmental epidemiology. A list of the specialty areas of epidemiology is presented in "Classification and Specialty Journals in Epidemiology" (Appendix IV). The specialty area that involves the application of epidemiology to screening and diagnosis, prognosis, and treatment is called clinical epidemiology. The primary aim of clinical epidemiology is to promote the quality of clinical and patient-oriented health care. This chapter presents the basics of clinical epidemiology.

CLINICAL EPIDEMIOLOGY

Clinical epidemiology focuses specifically on patients and the application of epidemiologic methods to assess the efficacy of screening, diagnosis, and treatment in clinical settings. The primary aim of clinical epidemiology is to identify the health consequences of employing a test or administering a treatment. Questions relevant to clinical epidemiology include the following:

1. Who is most likely to participate in screening and diagnostic testing?
2. How accurate is the screening or diagnostic test?
3. If a treatment is efficacious, what proportion of patients benefit from the treatment?
4. What characterizes those who benefit and those who do not benefit from the treatment?
5. How much do patients benefit from a treatment?
6. What are the risks associated with screening, diagnostic testing, and treatment?

SCREENING AND DIAGNOSIS

Medical **screening** is used to suggest or detect disease among individuals in a population without signs or symptoms of the health problem. Screen detection of disease is intended to identify asymptomatic individuals with a disease as early as possible in order to reduce morbidity and mortality from the disease. Some examples of screening include a skin test called the tuberculin, or PPD test, for detecting tuberculosis; the Beck Depression Inventory for detecting depression; the Pap test (or Pap smear) for identifying the possible presence of cervical cancer; the fecal occult blood test for identifying possible signs of severe disorders such as colon cancer; the mammogram for identifying the possible presence of breast cancer; and the prostate-specific antigen (PSA) test for identifying the possible presence of prostate cancer. Diagnosing disease may involve multiple stages of assessment. For example, to diagnose the presence of cancer, a doctor must look at a sample of the affected tissue under the microscope. Thus, when a Pap test, a fecal occult blood test, a mammogram, or a PSA test indicate the possible presence of cancer, a biopsy is taken, which is a surgically removed small piece of tissue for examination. Microscopic examination indicates whether a tumor is present and if so whether it is malignant. If malignant, the tumor is referred to as cancer.

To illustrate why a screening test alone may not be sufficient, consider that a number of factors may cause an elevated PSA score, such as infection, benign prostatic hyperplasia, recent physical activity, or ejaculation. If a man is suffering from an infection, for example, the physician may have him get another PSA test after the infection has subsided. If the PSA score remains elevated, then a biopsy may be recommended. If the biopsy is negative, then other explanations for the elevated score may be investigated.

A diagnosis is applied to a patient on a one-on-one basis by a physician or other qualified healthcare provider in a medical setting. In general, diagnosis involves the evaluation of signs and symptoms, screening results, and biopsies (for cancer), and may involve subjective judgment based on the experience of the physician. Diagnosis is a prerogative of the physician.

Screening Program Considerations

Screening for disease involves a number of policy-related issues, such as who should be screened, for what diseases should we screen, what is the appropriate age when screening should occur, and how should risk status influence screening. **Mass screening** is not selective, but involves application of screening tests to the total population. On the other hand, **selective screening** involves applying a screening test to a high-risk group. Selective screening is more likely than mass screening to result in a greater yield of true cases and be the most economical.

In 1968, the World Health Organization published a set of guidelines for planning and implementing screening programs.[1] The **screening guidelines** that follow remain applicable today:

1. The disease or condition being screened for should be a major medical problem.
2. Acceptable treatment should be available for individuals with diseases discovered in the screening process.
3. Access to healthcare facilities and services for follow-up diagnosis and treatment for the discovered disease should be available.
4. The disease should have a recognizable course, with identifiable early and latent stages.
5. A suitable and effective test or examination for the disease(s) should be available.
6. The test and the testing process should be acceptable to the general population.
7. The natural history of the disease or condition should be adequately understood, including the regular phases and course of the disease, with an early period identifiable through testing.
8. Policies, procedures, and threshold levels on tests should be determined in advance to establish who should be referred for further testing, diagnostics, and possible treatment.
9. The process should be simple enough to encourage large groups of persons to participate.

Screening should not be an occasional activity but should be done as a regular and ongoing process.

Underlying each of these guidelines is a desire to maximize the public's health and to minimize any adverse effects of the screening process. Epidemiologic methods provide a means of evaluating each of these guidelines. For example, descriptive epidemiologic methods are useful for establishing and understanding the extent of the public health problem, the efficacy of treatment, access to health care, the natural course of disease, and the efficacy of a screening or diagnostic test.

Validity, Reliability, and Yield

Screening activities are only as effective as the tests and examinations used; therefore, each screening test needs to have strong validity and reliability. The **validity** of a test is shown by how well the test actually measures what it is supposed to measure. If it is a cholesterol screening test, the question is: Can it give accurate enough readings so that the individual actually knows how high or low his or her cholesterol really is? Validity is determined by the sensitivity and specificity of the test. The state of the disease, the severity of it, the level and amount of exposure, nutritional health, physical fitness, and other factors influencing the health status of the individual also influence and affect test responses and findings.[2–7] **Reliability** is based on how well the test performs in use over time—its repeatability. Can the test produce reliable results each time it is used and in different locations or populations? The difference between validity and reliability is illustrated in Figure 12-1. Yield is another term sometimes used in reference to screening tests. **Yield of a screening test** is the amount of screening the test can accomplish in a time period—that is, how much disease it can detect in the screening process.

Good validity	Poor validity	Poor validity
Good reliability	Good reliability	Poor reliability

FIGURE 12-1   Difference between validity (a type of accuracy) and reliability (repeatability).

EVALUATING THE SCREENING TEST

Screening tests are not perfect. It is possible for a test to be positive when, in fact, the person does not have the disease. The test may also be negative when the person does have the disease. An incorrect screening result for cancer, for example, has implications for whether a biopsy is recommended. A false positive test may cause unnecessary stress, anxiety, and treatment. A false negative test may cause a false sense of security and failure to benefit from treatment. Hence, there are problems associated with incorrect screening results. For this reason, screening tests should be properly evaluated.

When evaluating a screening or diagnostic test, consider the possible situations shown in Table 12-1. The top of the table shows the true disease status. The test results may be:

True positive (TP)—Indicating a person has the disease when, in fact, they do. This can lead to needed care and treatment.

False positive (FP)—Indicating a person has the disease when, in fact, they do not. This can cause unnecessary stress, anxiety, and treatment.

False negative (FN)—Indicating a person does not have the disease when, in fact, they do. This can cause a false sense of security and a lack of needed care and treatment.

True negative (TN)—Indicating a person does not have the disease when, in fact, they do not. Of course, this is the preferred situation.

TABLE 12-1   True Disease Status According to Possible Test Results

Test Result	True Disease Status	
	Present	**Not Present**
Positive	TP	FP
Negative	FN	TN
	TP + FN	FP + TN

Sensitivity and Specificity

The validity of a test was determined by its sensitivity and specificity. These measures of validity capture the extent of FPs and FNs. **Sensitivity of a screening test** is the proportion of subjects with the disease who have a positive test [TP / (TP + FN)]; that is, sensitivity is the ability of the test to correctly identify those with the disease.[8] **Specificity of a screening test** is the proportion of subjects without the disease who have a negative test [TN / (FP + TN)].[8] Specificity is the ability to correctly identify those without the disease.

The proportion of FNs is the complement of sensitivity. Conversely, the proportion of FPs is the complement of specificity.

The **overall accuracy** of a test is another measure of a screening test's validity. It is measured as follows:

$$Overall \ accuracy = (TP + TN) / (TP + FN + FP + TN)$$

This measure of a screening test's validity is less useful than sensitivity and specificity.

Predictive Value Positive and Predictive Value Negative

The ability of a test to predict the presence or absence of a disease indicates the test's worth. The predictive value of a screening test is influenced by the sensitivity and specificity of the test as well as the prevalence of disease in the population undergoing testing. The higher the prevalence of a disease in a population, the more likely a positive test will represent a TP. The lower the prevalence of a disease in a population, the more likely a positive test will represent a FP. Rare diseases require a more specific test in order to be clinically useful.[8]

The prevalence of disease in a specified group of individuals is referred to as the **prior probability**. It is the probability of having a disease prior to the diagnostic test. It is influenced by factors such as age, gender, and clinical characteristics. For example, the prior probability of prostate cancer may be near zero in an Asian man younger than 40 years of age but above 50% in an African American man over 70 years of age.

Predictive value positive (PV+) is equal to the probability that an individual with a positive test actually has the disease. It can be expressed as:

$$PV+ = \frac{Sensitivity \times Prior \ probability}{[Sensitivity \times Prior \ probability] + [(1 - Specificity) \times (1 - Prior \ probability)]}$$

On the other hand, the predictive value of a negative test (PV−) is the probability that a person who has a negative test does not have the disease. It can be expressed as:

$$PV- = \frac{Specificity \times (1 - Prior \ probability)}{[Specificity \times (1 - Prior \ probability] + [(1 - Sensitivity) \times Prior \ probability)]}$$

Posterior probability is the name sometimes given to predictive value positive or predictive value negative because they are probabilities determined after the test results.

To illustrate, consider a screening test for tuberculosis in a small private college. Hypothetical findings of the screening test are as follows:

Diseased and positive on the test   = 50

Diseased and negative on the test   = 15

No disease and positive on the test   = 75

No disease and negative on the test   = 1,710

Sensitivity is 50 / (50 + 15) = 0.77, and specificity is 1,710 / (75 + 1,710) = 0.96. The overall accuracy of the test is 0.95. If the prior probability of tuberculosis was 3.5%, then the probability that a person with a positive test will have tuberculosis (PV+) is 0.41. On the other hand, the probability that a person with a negative test does not have tuberculosis (PV−) is 0.99. If, however, the prior probability of tuberculosis was 20%, then PV+ becomes 0.82 and PV− becomes 0.94.

In the event that the prior probability is not known, the following simplified equations may be used:

$$PV+ = TP / (TP + FP)$$
$$PV- = TN / (FN + TN)$$

For this example, PV+ = 50 / (50 + 75) = 0.40 and PV− = 1710 / (15 + 1,710) = 0.99.

Positive and Negative Likelihood Ratio Tests

Two additional measures for appraising screening and diagnostic evidence are the positive and negative likelihood ratios (LR+ and LR−, respectively). Sensitivity and specificity are susceptible to levels of the base rate of the health-related state or event in the sample being considered. The base rate is the percentage of people in a sample with the health-related state or event of interest. A base rate of 50% means that prior to administering a diagnostic test, the probability of a person having the health problem is 50%. A lower base rate in a sample means there are fewer people who have the health problem. Specificity will thus be higher than in a sample with a 50% base rate. This is because of a greater probability that a correct diagnosis is "normal," even before the diagnostic test is administered. On the other hand, sensitivity will be lower if the base rate in a sample is less than 50%, as there are fewer affected people with the health problem. Thus, there is a lower probability that the correct diagnosis is "abnormal" even before the diagnostic test is administered. Likelihood ratios are less sensitive to variations in the base rate than are sensitivity and specificity. When the base rate of a sample is 50%, sensitivity, specificity, LR+, and LR− will yield the same conclusions about the accuracy of a screening or diagnostic test; however, if the base rate is high or low, the likelihood ratios are the preferred diagnostic measures.

Positive likelihood ratio reflects the level of confidence we can have that a person who obtains a score in the affected range truly does have the health problem. The formula for calculating this measure is:

$$LR+ = \frac{Sensitivity}{(1 - Specificity)} = \frac{TP/(TP + FN)}{FP/(FP + TN)}$$

In other words, this measure is the proportion of TPs among cases divided by the proportion of FPs among noncases. The range of this measure is 1 (neutral) to infinity (very positive). Conversely, **negative likelihood ratio** is the confidence that a score in the unaffected range comes from a person who truly does not have the health problem. The formula for calculating this measure is:

$$LR- = \frac{(1 - Sensitivity)}{Specificity} = \frac{FN/(TP + FN)}{TN/(FP + TN)}$$

This is a measure of the proportion of FNs to the proportion of TNs. The lower the LR− for a diagnostic test, the greater the confidence we have that a person who obtains a score in the unaffected range truly does not have the health problem. The range of this measure is 0 (extremely negative) to 1 (neutral). Values, descriptors, and interpretations of positive and negative likelihood ratios have been presented by Sackett and colleagues[9,10] and are presented in Table 12-2.

Consider again the previous hypothetical data involving a screening test for tuberculosis. On the basis of that data, the LR+ = 0.77 / (1 − 0.96) = 19.25 (very positive) and the LR− = (1 − 0.77) / 0.96 = 0.24 (moderately negative). Thus, it is very likely that a positive test comes from a person with tuberculosis. On the other hand, a negative test score is insufficient to rule out tuberculosis.

PROGNOSIS

Nineteenth-century physicians, particularly those in France, aimed at correctly diagnosing and providing an accurate prognosis for their patients. The focus was less on curing disease

TABLE 12-2   Interpreting Positive and Negative Likelihood Ratios

	Positive Likelihood Ratio (LR+)			Negative Likelihood Ratio (LR−)	
Value	Descriptor	Interpretation	Value	Descriptor	Interpretation
≥ 10	Very positive	Positive test score very likely to have come from a person with the health problem	≤ 0.10	Very negative	Negative test score very unlikely to have come from a person with the health problem
3	Moderately positive	Positive test score suggestive but insufficient to diagnose health problem	≤ 0.30	Moderately negative	Negative test score suggestive but insufficient to rule out health problem
1	Neutral	Positive test score uninformative for diagnosing health problem	1	Neutral	Negative test score uninformative for ruling out disorder

Data from Sackett DL, Hanes RB, Guyatt GH, Tugwell P. *Clinical Epidemiology: A Basic Science for Clinical Medicine.* Boston: Little, Brown and Company, 1991; and Sackett DL, Straus SE, Richardson WS, Rosenberg W, Haynes RB. *Evidence-Based Medicine: How to Practice and Teach,* 2nd ed. Edinburgh: Churchill Livingston, 2000.

and more on achieving an accurate prognosis for the patient. Several decades later, the focus shifted in Western medicine to curing disease, which is the primary aim today.

The word **prognosis** comes from the Greek prognostikos. The word combines pro (before) with gnosis (a knowing).[11] Hippocrates used the word just as we do today, as a prediction or forecast of the course of a disease for a given patient. It is based on anticipation from the usual natural history of the disease or peculiarities unique to the case.

A prognosis of the likely outcome of a disease is generally based on the presence of signs, symptoms, and circumstances. A **prognostic indicator** is a factor (e.g., a tumor characteristic) that helps forecast the likely outcome of a disease or the effectiveness of a treatment. Clinical and laboratory findings provide prognostic information. For example, a cancer workup involves assigning a grade and a stage. Based on microscopic appearance, doctors assign a numerical grade to most cancers. A low number refers to cancers with fewer cell abnormalities than those with higher numbers. Doctors also ask certain questions in order to assign a stage of the disease. These questions are as follows: How large is the tumor, and how far has it invaded into surrounding tissues? Have cancer cells spread to regional lymph nodes? Has the cancer spread (metastasized) to other regions of the body? Answers to these questions are prognostic indicators that tell the doctor the likely behavior of the cancer and its probable responsiveness to treatment. A patient's likely responsiveness to treatment and their chance of survival are better with low grade and stage disease. Hence, several screening methods are available to check for cancer in people with no clinical symptoms, some of which were mentioned at the beginning of this chapter.

Lists of prognostic indicators for selected health problems have been developed. For example, traditional prognostic indicators for heart failure include symptoms; ejection fraction (left and right ventricle); exercise capacity (peak VO2, 6 minute walking distance); central haemodynamic; doppler echo; left ventricular size, volumes, shape, and mass; arrhythmias; serum sodium; and thyroid function.[12] These prognostic indicators provide information about the patient's overall heart health, response to therapy, and when the treatment should begin. The International Prognostic Index is a tool developed by oncologists to achieve a prognosis for patients with aggressive non-Hodgkin's lymphoma. The index combines prognostic information by assigning one point for each of the following prognostic factors:

- Age greater than 60 years
- Stage III or stage IV disease
- Elevated serum lactate dehydrogenase
- ECOG/Zubrod performance status of 2, 3, or 4
- More than 1 extranodal site
- The index is then evaluated as follows:
    - Low risk (0 to 1 points)—5-year survival of 73%
    - Low-intermediate risk (2 points)—5-year survival of 51%
    - High-intermediate risk (3 points)—5-year survival of 43%
    - High risk (4 to 5 points)—5-year survival of 26%

The International Prognostic Index has been found to be a useful clinical tool. It is commonly used by oncologists. It is also used as a guide for risk stratification in clinical trials for lymphoma.[13]

A simple epidemiologic measure of prognosis is the **case-fatality rate**. This measure is the proportion of newly diagnosed cases that die from a given disease or condition in a specified time period. It is most useful for measuring prognoses of acute infectious diseases and conditions. The problem in using this measure with chronic diseases and conditions is that it is difficult to associate the death with the diagnosis. When the clinical course of an illness is relatively long, prognosis is often measured using survival analysis. Two approaches used in survival analysis are:

1. **Survival time**—the average or median survival time for a group of patients. Survival time provides a good idea of how long patients tend to live after diagnosis with a disease or condition. The average survival time measures the "typical" time of survival; however, this measure is sensitive to extreme values, and a patient who survives much longer or shorter than others will greatly affect the average survival time. This limitation may be overcome by using the median survival time.

2. **Survival rate**—proportion of persons surviving regardless of cause of death. The survival rate is a measure of survival of a patient group for a specific period after diagnosis or treatment. It is interpreted as the proportion (or percentage) of patients surviving a specified amount of time after diagnosis or treatment. A commonly used measure is the 5-year survival rate. The 5-year survival rate has been considered by some as the cure rate; however, this is not an appropriate time to reflect cure for some diseases, such as breast cancer, where 10 or more years would be more effective. For more lethal cancers, such as that of the pancreas, survival of 1 or 2 years might better reflect cure.

The survival rate is typically calculated using the life table method (also called the Actuarial method) and the product limit method (also called the Kaplan-Meier method).

Proportional hazards models are a subclass of survival models that are also used in evaluating prognoses. A popular form of the proportional hazards model is the Cox model.[14,15] The Cox model, also called the proportional hazards model, is also useful for analyzing survival data. The model indicates the probability that a person will experience an event (e.g., death) in the next interval of time, given that they have survived until the beginning of the interval.

Survival time provides a good idea of how long patients tend to live after diagnosis with a disease or condition. The average survival time measures the "typical" time surviving. However, this measure is sensitive to extreme values, and a patient who survives much longer or shorter than others will greatly affect the average survival time. This limitation may be overcome by using the median survival time.

The survival rate is a measure of survival of a patient group for a specific period of time after diagnosis or treatment. It is interpreted as the proportion (or percentage) of patients surviving a specified amount of time after diagnosis or treatment. A commonly used measure is the 5-year survival rate. The 5-year survival rate has been considered by some as the cure rate; however, this is not an appropriate time to reflect the cure for some cancers, such as breast cancer, where 10 or more years would be more effective. For more lethal cancers such as that of the pancreas, survival of 1 or 2 years might better reflect the cure. A description of how to calculate observed survival rates using the Actuarial method or the Kaplan-Meier method is presented elsewhere.[16]

Lead-Time Bias

Screening is intended to improve the prognosis of diagnosed cases. Screening is particularly important for chronic disease in which there is a high prevalence of individuals in the presymptomatic phase of the disease. However, because screening advances the time of diagnosis, it may be difficult to evaluate the benefit of early treatment. In other words, the difference in time between the date of diagnosis with screening and the date of diagnosis without screening is called **lead time**. If lead time is counted in the survival time of patients, it will give a misleading picture of the benefit of treatment. This inflation of survival is called **lead-time bias**.[17]

Length Bias

The idea of **length bias** sampling is that slow-progressing cases of disease with a better prognosis are more likely to be identified than faster-progressing cases of disease with a poorer prognosis. For example, a person with a slower growing tumor has a better prognosis than a person with a faster growing tumor. Because a slower growing tumor has a longer preclinical phase than a faster, more lethal tumor, it is more likely to be detected through screening. Hence, screening more often identifies cancer that would not have killed the patient or even been detected before death from other causes occur. Thus, cases identified through screening tend to have a better prognosis than the average of all cases because of length bias sampling.[17]

Selection Bias

Selection bias is a type of bias that is caused by choosing nonrandom, nonrepresentative data for analysis. Selection bias may make a test look better or worse than it really is in terms of survival. For example, a test would look better than it actually is if younger, healthier people are more likely to get the test. This may occur because of differential advertising or long distances to the screening facility. Hence, fewer people in the screening population will develop the illness, and the test will appear to have a positive effect. On the other hand, if high-risk individuals (e.g., those with a family history of the disease) are more likely to pursue screening, then there will be a greater chance of people dying of the illness among those screened in the screening group than on average.

Overdiagnosis Bias

Overdiagnosis bias occurs when screening identifies an illness that would not have shown clinical signs before a person's death from other causes. Overdiagnosis bias tends to make screening efforts look good because of increased identification of abnormalities; however, if the abnormalities are harmless, then the individual may undergo unnecessary treatment, with its accompanying risk. In the past decade, there has been considerable debate over the efficacy of widespread prostate cancer screening, as autopsy studies have shown that the majority of men with prostate cancer die of other causes before clinical symptoms of the disease manifest themselves.

Avoiding Bias

The best way to avoid these biases when evaluating the efficacy of a screening test or a treatment is to use the randomized controlled trial.[17,18] Through randomization, different prognostic factors are balanced out between groups, and the "true" screening or treatment effect can be determined. For example, the rationale for the National Cancer Institute's

Prostate, Lung, Colorectal, and Ovarian Cancer Screening Trial (or PLCO) is to identify the efficacy of selected screening tests without the biases described in this section.

The PLCO trial aims to determine if selected cancer screening tests reduce deaths from prostate, lung, colorectal, and ovarian cancer. The trial enrolled 155,000 men and women ages 55 through 74 years between 1992 and 2001. Initially, participants were randomly assigned to one of two groups. One group received routine health care from their healthcare provider. The other group received screening tests for prostate, lung, colorectal, and ovarian cancers. The screening ended in late 2006. Follow-up will continue for up to 10 more years in order to determine the efficacy of selected screenings.

HEALTH OUTCOMES RESEARCH

Closely related to clinical epidemiology is a relatively new field called outcomes research. **Outcomes research** seeks to understand the end results of clinical practices and interventions. By combining information about the care people are getting in terms of screening and diagnosis, prognosis, and treatment with the outcomes they experience, outcomes research has become important in developing better ways to monitor and improve clinical care.

Implicit in outcomes research is the principle that every clinical intervention produces a change in a patient's health status and this change can be measured.[19] It is believed that evidence about the benefits, risks, and results associated with clinical care can improve the quality and value of care. For example, outcomes research in prostate cancer has provided information that is useful for patients in making choices about their care. In particular, one study identified that for men treated with radiation for prostate cancer, 7% needed to wear pads for wetness, 23% had problems with impotence since treatment (for ages 70 years or younger only), 10% had bowel dysfunction, and 17% worried about still having cancer. Corresponding percentages for surgery were 32, 56, 3, and 10, respectively.[20]

The best treatment approach for prostate cancer depends on the outcomes that matter most to the patient.

Historically, outcome measures used for determining the necessity of an intervention and its success have included symptoms (e.g., difficulty breathing), biometric measures (e.g., blood cholesterol, glucose, PSA), clinical events (e.g., stroke), or death (e.g., infant mortality rate); nevertheless, other outcomes that matter to patients should not be overlooked, such as how they function and their experiences with care. In recent years, instruments have been developed (e.g., the SF-36, Medicare Health Outcomes Survey) for assessing patients' overall level of functioning. Instruments assessing patients' experiences with care have also been developed (e.g., Consumer Assessment of Health Care).[21]

Although outcomes research has identified many useful strategies for improving the quality and value of care, it must be kept in mind that such strategies are only as good as their translation into practice.

CONCLUSION

Clinical epidemiology involves the application of epidemiologic methods to improve the quality and value of patient care. Clinical epidemiology involves assessment of the efficacy of screening, diagnosis, and treatment strategies in clinical settings. Screening activities were described as being only as effective as the tests and examinations used. The importance of strong test validity and reliability was emphasized.

A valid test represents what it is intended to represent. A reliable test is reproducible, with nearly the same value each time it is measured. Various measures for evaluating diagnostic tests were introduced. Sensitivity is the proportion of persons with the disease who test positive; specificity is the proportion of persons without the disease who test negative; predictive value positive is the proportion of persons who test positive who have the disease; and predictive value negative is the proportion of persons who test negative who do not have the disease. Two related measures are positive and negative likelihood ratio tests. Positive likelihood ratio indicates the level of confidence we can have that a person with a score in the affected range actually has the health problem. Negative likelihood ratio is the confidence that a score in the unaffected range comes from a person who does not have the health problem.

Prognosis refers to the likely outcome of a patient and is influenced by prognostic indicators (e.g., signs, symptoms, circumstances). Two common measures of prognosis are the case-fatality rate and the survival rate. These measures of prognosis are susceptible to lead time bias, length bias, selection bias, and overdiagnosis bias. The best way to avoid these biases in studies evaluating the efficacy of a screening test or of a treatment is the randomized, blinded controlled trial.

Health outcomes research is an attempt to combine information about the care people are getting with the outcomes they experience. Outcomes research assumes that evidence about the benefits, risks, and results associated with clinical care can improve the quality and value of care. The effectiveness of health outcomes research depends on the level that strategies for improving the quality and value of patient care are translated into practice.

EXERCISES

Key Terms

Define the following terms.

Case-fatality rate
Clinical epidemiology
False negative
False positive
Lead time
Lead-time bias
Length bias
Mass screening
Outcomes research
Overall accuracy
Overdiagnosis bias
Posterior probability
Positive likelihood ratio (LR+)
Negative likelihood ratio (LR−)
Predictive value positive (PV+)
Predictive value negative (PV−)

Prior probability
Prognosis
Prognostic indicator
Reliability
Screening
Screening guidelines
Selection bias
Selective screening
Sensitivity of a screening test
Specificity of a screening test
Survival rate
Survival time
True negative
True positive
Validity
Yield of a screening test

STUDY QUESTIONS

1. Why is random assignment in a clinical trial an effective way to avoid confounding?

2. A screening test for a newly discovered disease is being evaluated. In order to determine the effectiveness of the new test, it was administered to 880 workers, and 120 of the individuals diagnosed with the disease tested positive. A negative test finding occurred in 50 people who had the disease. A total of 40 persons not diseased tested positive for it. Construct a 2 × 2 table, similar to the one in Table 12-1, and calculate the following:

    a. Prevalence of the disease

    b. Sensitivity

    c. Specificity

    d. Predictive value positive

    e. Predictive value negative

    f. Likelihood ratio positive

    g. Likelihood ratio negative

    h. Overall accuracy

3. Screening has been associated with certain types of measurement bias. Match the descriptions of bias resulting from screening in the left column with the names of these types of bias in the right column.

    ___ The screening test looks better than it actually is, because younger, healthier people are more likely to get the test.

    ___ Screening identifies an illness that would not have shown clinical signs before death from other causes.

    ___ Slow-progressing cases of disease with a better prognosis are more likely to be identified than faster-progressing cases of disease with a poorer prognosis. Thus, cases diagnosed through screening tend to have a better prognosis than the average of all cases.

    ___ Difference in the time between the date of diagnosis with screening and the date of diagnosis without screening, which, if counted in the survival time of patients, will give a misleading picture of the benefits of treatment.

    A. Lead-time bias

    B. Length bias

    C. Selection bias

    D. Overdiagnosis bias

4. As an occupational health epidemiologist, you are required to measure the effect of stress on the workers in your manufacturing plant. Two different tests previously developed to

measure stress in industrial workers are selected: stress test alpha and stress test delta. The sensitivity and specificity of each test are shown here.

Stress Test Alpha	Stress Test Delta
Sensitivity = 60%	75%
Specificity = 95%	90%

a. Which test generates the greatest proportion of FNs?

b. Which test generates the greatest proportion of FPs?

c. Which test would you prefer?

5. Everyone eventually dies; thus, why isn't the case-fatality rate for a given disease 100%?

REFERENCES

1. Wilson JMG, Jungner F. Principles and Practice of Screening for Disease, Paper No. 34. Geneva, Switzerland: World Health Organization; 1968.
2. MacMahon B, Pugh TF. *Epidemiology: Principles and Methods.* Boston, MA: Little, Brown and Company; 1970.
3. Mausner JS, Kramer S. *Epidemiology: An Introductory Text.* Philadelphia, PA: WB Saunders; 1985.
4. Lilienfeld AM, Lilienfeld DE. *Foundations of Epidemiology.* New York, NY: Oxford University Press; 1980.
5. Friedman GD. *Primer of Epidemiology.* New York, NY: McGraw-Hill; 1974.
6. Kelsey JL, Thompson WD, Evans AS. *Methods in Observational Epidemiology.* New York, NY: Oxford University Press; 1986.
7. Fox JP, Hall CE, Elveback LR. *Epidemiology: Man and Disease.* New York, NY: Macmillan; 1970.
8. Browner WS, Newman TB, Cummings SR. Designing a new study: III: diagnostic tests. In: Hulley SB, Cummings SR, eds. *Designing Clinical Research: An Epidemiologic Approach.* Baltimore, MD: Williams & Williams; 1988.
9. Sackett DL, Hanes RB, Guyatt GH, Tugwell P. *Clinical Epidemiology: A Basic Science for Clinical Medicine.* Boston, MA: Little, Brown and Company; 1991.
10. Sackett DL, Straus SE, Richardson WS, Rosenberg W, Haynes RB. *Evidence-Based Medicine: How to Practice and Teach,* 2nd ed. Edinburgh, Scotland: Churchill Livingston; 2000.
11. *Stedman's Medical Dictionary for the Health Professions and Nursing,* 5th ed. Baltimore, MD: Lippincott Williams & Wilkins; 2005.
12. Piepoli M. Diagnostic and prognostic indicators in chronic heart failure. *European Heart Journal.* 1999;20:1367–1369.
13. Sehn LH, Mukesh C, Fitzgerald C, Gill K, Hoskins P, Klasa R, Savage KJ, Shenkier T, Sutherland J, Gascoyne RD, Connors JM. The revised International Prognostic Index (R-IPI) is a better predictor of outcome than the standard IPI for patients with diffuse large B-cell lymphoma treated with R-CHOP. *Blood.* 2007;109:1857–1861.
14. Cox DR. Regression models and life-tables (with discussion). *J R Stat Soc Ser B.* 1972;34:187–220.
15. Cox DR, Oaks D. *Analysis of Survival Data.* London, England: Chapman and Hall; 1984.
16. SEER Program. Self-Instructional Manual for Cancer Registrars. Book 7—Statistics and Epidemiology for Cancer Registrars. Department of Health and Human Services. National Institutes of Health. NIH Publication no. 94-3766.
17. Rothman KJ. *Epidemiology: An Introduction.* New York, NY: Oxford University Press; 2002.
18. Gates TJ. Screening for cancer: evaluating the evidence. *Am Fam Physician.* 2001;63(3):513–523.

19. *Webster's New World Medical Dictionary.* Definition of health outcomes research. http://www.medterms.com/script/main/art.asp?articlekey=3667. Accessed December 20, 2008.

20. Fowler FJ Jr, Barry MJ, Lu-Yao G, et al. Outcomes of external-beam radiation therapy for prostate cancer: a study of Medicare beneficiaries in three Surveillance, Epidemiology, and End Results areas. *J Clin Oncol.* 1996;14(8):2258–2265.

21. Clancy CM, Eisenberg JM. Outcomes research: Measure the end results of health care. *Science.* 1998;282:245–246.

Glossary

A priori hypothesis: a hypothesis that is established without prior knowledge of the level of the health-related state or event in a specified population; involving deductive reasoning from a general principle to a necessary effect—prior to the facts that come from data analysis.

Abortion: termination of pregnancy by removal of a fetus from the uterus before it is mature enough to live on its own. An abortion may be induced (deliberate termination of pregnancy) or spontaneous (unexpected, the same as a miscarriage).

Abortion rate: calculated by dividing the number of abortions performed during a specified time period by the number of women ages 15–44 during the same time period.

Absorption rate: the rate at which a substance is absorbed into the body.

Accuracy of a variable: the degree to which a variable actually represents what it is intended to represent. Accuracy is a function of systematic error (bias). The variable becomes less accurate as the error increases.

Active carriers: individuals who have been exposed to and harbor a disease-causing organism (pathogen) and who have done so for some time, even though they may have recovered from the disease.

Active immunity: the body produces its own antibodies against a specific invading substance, called an antigen, thereby providing very selective protection.

Active primary prevention: behavior change on the part of the individual that prevents a disease or disorder before it happens (e.g., exercising, not smoking, reducing dietary fat intake).

Activity limitations: difficulties an individual may have in executing activities.

Acute: relatively severe with sudden onset and short duration of symptoms.

Age effect: the primary change in risk for a given health-related state or event is age.

Agent: something capable of producing an effect; the cause of the disease.

Age-adjusted rate: a weighted average of the age-specific rates, where the weights are the proportions of persons in the corresponding age groups of a standard population.

Airborne transmission: transfer of bacteria or viruses on dust particles or on small respiratory droplets that may become aerosolized when individuals sneeze, cough, laugh, or exhale. Transmission allows organisms that are capable of surviving for long periods of time outside the body and are resistant to drying to enter the upper and lower respiratory tract. Diseases capable of airborne transmission include influenza, polio, whooping cough, pneumonia, and tuberculosis.

Allergies and inflammatory diseases: invasion of or injury by a foreign object or substance that causes an inflammatory reaction in the body.

Alternative hypothesis: See *research hypothesis*.

Alpha (α): probability of committing a Type I error; level of significance, usually selected to be 0.05.

Analogy: a criterion in causal inference stating that analogous situations with previously demonstrated causal associations provide support for there being a causal association.

Analytic epidemiology: addresses the why and how questions; applies statistical inferences about health-related states or events in the population based on sampled data.

Analytic studies: a type of epidemiologic study that tests one or more predetermined hypotheses about associations between exposure and outcome variables. These studies make use of a comparison group.

Antibodies: proteins generally found in the blood that detect and destroy invaders such as bacteria, viruses, and fungi.

Antibiotics: medicines that kill bacteria.

Antigen: a substance that when introduced in the body prompts the immune system to produce antibodies.

Antigenicity: the capacity to stimulate the production of antibodies or the capacity to react with an antibody.

Anthrax: a serious bacterial infection caused by *Bacillus anthracis* that occurs primarily in animals.

Area map: the number or rate of a health-related state or event by place, using different colors or shadings to represent the various levels of the disease, event, or behavior.

Arithmetic mean: the measure of central location one is likely most familiar with because it has many desirable statistical properties; it is the arithmetic average of a distribution of data.

Atomic theory: the belief that everything is made of tiny particles.

At-risk behavior: an activity performed by a person that puts them at greater risk of developing a health-related state or event.

Attack rate: calculated by dividing the number of cases by the number of persons followed. It involves a specific population during a limited time period, such as during a disease outbreak. It is also referred to as a cumulative incidence rate or risk.

Attributable risk: the amount of absolute risk of a health-related state or event among the exposed group that can be attributed to the exposure. It is assumed that the exposure is a cause of the outcome.

Attributable risk percent: among cases that are exposed, it is the percentage of those cases attributed to the exposure. It is assumed that the exposure is a cause of the outcome.

Bar charts: commonly used for graphically displaying a frequency distribution that involves nominal or ordinal data.

Beta (β): probability of committing a Type II error. Common values of beta are 0.1 or 0.2.

Berkson's bias: hospital-patient selection bias, named after Dr. Joseph Berkson, who described it in the 1940s. In a case-control study where both cases and controls are selected from the hospital, the controls tend to be more likely exposed to the exposure under consideration than the general population from which the cases came from. This tends to cause the odds ratio to be underestimated.

Between-group design: outcomes are compared between two or more groups of people receiving different levels of the intervention.

Bias: the deviation of the results from the truth; it can explain an observed association between exposure and outcome variables that is not real.

Biologic gradient: a criterion in causal inference wherein an increasing risk of disease occurs with greater exposure.

Biological plausibility: a criterion in causal inference in which a causal association is consistent with existing medical knowledge.

Biological transmission: transfer of a pathogen to a susceptible host by a vector, with the pathogen undergoing reproduction, developmental changes, or both while in the vector.

Biotransformation: a substance is changed from one chemical to another (transformed) by a chemical reaction within the body.

Birth rate: calculated by dividing the number of live births during a specified time period by the population from which the births occurred, typically expressed as the number of live births per 1,000 people.

Boundary shrinkage: the boundary where a possible disease cluster exists is ill-defined, accentuating the apparent risk by focusing the investigation tightly on the cases making up the cluster.

Box plots: have a single axis and present a summary of data.

Cancer: a collective name that refers to a group of many diseases with one common characteristic—uncontrolled cell growth or the loss of the cell's ability to perform apoptosis (cell suicide).

Carrier: contains, spreads, or harbors an infectious organism.

Case: a person who has been diagnosed with a health-related state or event.

Case definition: a standard set of criteria applied in a specific situation to ensure that cases are consistently diagnosed, regardless of where or when they were identified and who diagnosed the case.

Case-fatality rate: the proportion of people with a given disease who die from the disease within a specified time period. This measure is an indicator of the seriousness of the disease and the prognosis for those with the disease.

Case report: a profile of a single individual.

Case series: a small group of patients with a similar diagnosis.

Case severity: the severity of the illness.

Case-control study: grouping people as cases (persons experiencing a health-related state or event) and controls and investigating whether the cases are more or less likely than the controls to have had past experiences, lifestyle behaviors, or exposures.

Case-crossover study: compares the exposure status of a case immediately before its occurrence with that of the same case at a prior time.

Categorical variables: phenomenon not suitable for quantification but can be measured by classifying them into categories; nominal and ordinal data.

Causal inference: a conclusion about the presence of a health-related state or event and the reasons for its existence.

Cause: something that produces an effect, result, or consequence in another factor.

Cause-specific mortality rate: number of deaths assigned to a specific cause during a given time interval divided by the estimated mid-interval population.

Chance: a factor to consider when establishing the validity of a statistical association. Chance may explain a relationship between an exposure and disease outcome when the measured association is based on a sample of the population of interest. If everyone in the population is considered, then chance does not play a role. An association may appear to exist merely because of the luck of the draw—chance. As the sample size increases, the sample becomes more like the population and the role of chance decreases. The degree to which chance variability occurs may be monitored by the P value.

Chebychev's inequality: allows us to say that for any number k that is greater than or equal to 1, at least $[1 - (1 / k)^2]$ of the measurements in the set of data lie with k standard deviations of the mean.

Chemical poisoning: food-borne illness that results from chemical contamination of food or drink.

Childbed fever: a uterine infection, usually of the placental site, secondary to childbirth; puerperal fever; septicaemia.

Cholera: an acute infectious disease characterized by watery diarrhea, loss of fluid and electrolytes, dehydration, and collapse.

Chronic: less severe but of a continuous duration, lasting over a long period of time (3 or more months) if not a lifetime; not acute.

Chronic disease: a health-related state or event that is long lasting or recurrent; persistent or lasting medical condition.

Chronic disease epidemiology: the study of the distribution and determinants of chronic diseases and conditions in human populations and the application of that study to prevent and control these diseases and conditions.

Clinical epidemiology: focuses specifically on patients and the application of epidemiologic methods to assess the efficacy of screening, diagnosis, and treatment in clinical settings.

Clinical trial: a new drug or a new medical device is administered among humans in order to evaluate its efficacy and safety. Usually participants are selected based on inclusion and exclusion criteria.

Cluster investigation: reviewing unusual numbers of health-related states or events, real or perceived, grouped together in time and location.

Coefficient of determination: the correlation coefficient squared; it represents the proportion of the total variation in the dependent variable that is determined by the independent variable.

Coefficient of variation: a measure of relative spread in the data; the standard deviation for a set of values is divided by the mean of those values. This measure allows for comparing the variability among two or more sets of data representing different scales.

Coherence: a criterion in causal inference wherein there is consistency with known epidemiologic patterns of disease.

Cohort: a group or body of people, often defined by experiencing a common event (e.g., birth, training, or enrollment) in a given time span.

Cohort effect: the change and variation in the health-related state or event of a study population as the study group moves through time.

Common-source epidemic: an epidemic that arises from a specific source.

Communicability: ability to spread from infected to susceptible hosts.

Communicable disease: an infectious disease that is contagious, or capable of being transmitted to susceptible hosts.

Community trial: the assignment of an intervention on the community level and examination of its effects. The community level may involve schools, cities, city blocks, counties, and so on.

Confidence interval: a range of reasonable values in which a population parameter lies, based on a random sample from the population.

Confounder: lurking variable; an extrinsic factor that is associated with a disease outcome and, independent of that association, is also associated with the exposure. Failure to control for a confounder can cause the measured association between exposure and outcome variables to be misleading.

Confounding: to cause to become confused or perplexed; when the internal validity of a study is compromised because the research failed to control or eliminate a confounder.

Congenital and hereditary diseases: genetic and familial tendencies toward certain inborn abnormalities; injury to the embryo or fetus by environmental factors, chemicals, or agents such as drugs, alcohol, or smoking; or innate developmental problems possibly caused by chemicals or agents.

Consistency of association: a criterion in causal inference wherein the relationship between an exposure and outcome variable is replicated by different investigators in different settings with different methods.

Constrictive pyramid: a population pyramid showing a lower number or percentage of younger people; low birth rate.

Construct validity: a measurement that conforms to a theoretical construct; a test or scale that measures what it claims to measure.

Content validity: involves how well the assessment represents all aspects of the phenomena being studied.

Contingency table: where all entries are classified by each of the variables in the table.

Continuous data: measurable quantities not restricted to taking on integer values (e.g., age, weight, temperature).

Continuous source: an epidemic where exposure is constant over time, but at relatively low levels. The epidemic curve tends to increase and decrease more gradually than for a point source exposure.

Continuous variable: quantified on an infinite scale.

Contraceptive prevalence: the proportion of women of reproductive age (i.e., 15–49 years) who are using (or whose partner is using) a contraceptive method at a given point in time.

Convalescence: the recovery period after illness.

Convalescent carriers: individuals that harbor a pathogen and who, although in the recovery phase of the course of the disease, are still infectious.

Correlation coefficient: measures the strength of the linear association between two numerical variables (also called the Pearson correlation coefficient).

Cross-sectional survey: a survey conducted at a point in time, also called prevalence surveys.

Crude mortality rate: total number of deaths reported during a given time interval divided by the estimated mid-interval population.

Crude rate: the rate of an outcome that is calculated without any restrictions such as age, sex, or weighted adjustment of group-specific rates.

Cumulative incidence rate: a measure of the risk of a health-related state or event in a defined population during a specified time period. Typically calculated by dividing the number of new events in a population by those at risk of the event at the beginning of the specified time period and multiplied by a rate base of 100. See *attack rate*.

Cyclic patterns: periodic increases and decreases in the occurrence of health-related states or events.

Data: numerical information from selected variables; observations or measurements of a phenomenon of interest.

Death certificates: provide information on the total number of deaths and also provide demographic information and other important facts about each person who dies, such as date of birth (for cohort studies) and of death (for accurate age), stated age, place of death, place of residence, occupation, gender, cause of death, and marital status.

Death-to-case ratio: the number of deaths attributed to a particular disease during a specified time period divided by the number of new cases of that disease during the same time period.

Decennial census: census of the population taken by the Census Bureau in years ending in zero.

Decision tree: a decision tool that uses a graph or model of decisions and their possible consequences.

Defection: the period during which the pathogen is killed off or brought into remission by the immune system.

Defervescence: the period when the symptoms of an illness are declining.

Degenerative diseases: progressive deterioration over time in the function or structure of the affected tissues or organs, whether due to normal bodily wear or lifestyle choices.

Dependency ratio: calculated by dividing the population under age 15 and over age 64 by the population aged 15 through 64; when multiplied by 100, it represents the number of dependents for every 100 people of working age.

Descriptive epidemiology: provides a description of the who (person), what (clinical characteristics), when (time), and where (place) aspects of health-related states or events in a population.

Descriptive study designs: the most common types of descriptive study designs are case reports and case series, cross-sectional surveys, and ecologic designs.

Differential (nonrandom) misclassification: see *misclassification*.

Direct causal association: has no intermediate factor and is more easily understood.

Direct transmission: the direct and immediate transfer of an agent from a host/reservoir to a susceptible host.

Disability: the diminished capacity to perform within a prescribed range.

Disease: an interruption, cessation, or disorder of body functions, systems, or organs.

Discrete data: integers or counts that differ by fixed amounts, with no intermediate values possible (e.g., number of new cases of lung cancer reported in the United States in a given year, number of children, and number of sick days taken in a month).

Discrete variable: its scale is limited to integers.

Disease cluster: an unusual aggregation, real or perceived, of health events that are grouped together in time and space and that are reported to a health agency.

Distribution: movement of the substance from where it enters the body to other sites in the body (e.g., liver, blood and lymph circulation, kidney, lung).

Double-blinded study: neither the participants nor the assessing investigator(s) know who is receiving the active treatment.

Ecologic fallacy: an error that occurs if one mistakenly assumes that because the majority of a group has a characteristic, the characteristic is associated with those experiencing the outcome.

Ecologic study: an epidemiologic study where specific individuals are not studied, but instead groups of people are compared, such as comparing injury rates from one occupation to another.

Effect modifier: an extrinsic factor that modifies the association between two other variables.

Effectiveness: the ability of a program to produce benefits among those who are offered the program.

Efficacy: the ability of a program to produce a desired effect among those who participate in the program compared with those who do not.

Empirical rule: states that approximately 68% of the observations are within one standard deviation of the mean, 95% of the observations are within two standard deviations of the mean, and almost all the observations are within three standard deviations of the mean.

Enabling factors: factors or conditions that allow or assist the health-related state or event to begin and run its course.

End point: a study outcome in a randomized controlled trial.

Endemic: the ongoing, usual, or constant presence of a disease in a community or among a group of people.

Environment: physical, biological, chemical, social, and cultural factors, and so on, any or all of which can influence the health status of populations.

Epidemic: a condition where an increase in the number of cases of disease occurs above what is normally expected for a given time and place.

Epidemic curve: a histogram that shows the course of an epidemic by plotting the number of cases by time of onset.

Epidemiology: the study of the distribution and determinants of health-related states or events in human populations and the application of this study to the prevention and control of health problems.

Etiology: the science and study of the causes of disease and their modes of operation.

Excretion: ejection of the substance or metabolites from the body.

Experimental evidence: a criterion in causal inference wherein an experimental study design has the greatest potential for supporting cause-effect relationships because of control over measurements and monitoring, the ability to establish a time sequence of events, and the ability to control for bias by employing an appropriate sample, random assignment, and blinding.

Expansive pyramid: a pyramid showing a broad base and has a tall, pointed shape, which represents a rapid rate of population growth and a low proportion of older people.

Experimental study: an epidemiologic study where the participants in the study are deliberately manipulated for the purpose of studying an intervention effect. An intervention is assigned to selected participants to determine its effect on a given outcome. Two common types of planned experimental studies in epidemiology are randomized controlled trials and community trials. With the exception of the experimental study, all study designs are observational.

Exploratory observational studies: no specific a priori hypothesis is specified; a variety of associations are examined.

External validity: the degree that the results of a study may be generalized to other populations.

Factorial design: an experimental design in which two or more series of treatments are tried in all combinations.

False negative (FN): a diagnostic test that indicates that someone does not have a disease when in fact they do.

False positive (FP): a diagnostic test that indicates that someone has a disease when in fact they do not.

Fastigium: the period maximum severity or intensity of a disease or fever.

Fetal death rate: calculated by dividing the number of fetal deaths after at least 20 weeks of gestation by the number of live births plus fetal deaths.

Field epidemiology: application of epidemiology under the following set of general conditions: the timing of the problem is unexpected; a timely response is demanded; public health epidemiologists must travel to and work in the field to solve the problem; and the extent of the investigation is likely to be limited because of the imperative for timely intervention and by other situational constraints on study designs or methods.

Fish bone diagram: provides a visual display of all possible causes that could potentially contribute to the disease, disorder, or condition under study.

Fomite: an object such as clothing, towels, and utensils that can harbor a disease agent and are capable of transmitting it.

Food infection: a result of the ingestion of disease-causing organisms (pathogens) such as bacteria and microscopic plants and animals.

Food poisoning: the result of preformed toxins that are present in foods prior to consumption; these toxins are often the waste products of bacteria.

Foodborne illnesses: illnesses arising from consumption of contaminated or spoiled foodstuffs and liquids.

Frequency distribution: a complete summary of the frequencies of the values or categories of a measurement made on a group of people.

Frequency polygon: a graphical display of a frequency table.

Geometric mean: calculated as the nth root of the product of n observations. It is used when the logarithms of the observations are normally distributed.

Group randomization: groups or naturally forming clusters are randomly assigned the intervention, as opposed to individuals randomly being assigned the intervention.

Health belief model: a conceptual framework that describes a person's health behavior as an expression of health beliefs.

Health indicator: a marker of health status (physical or mental disease, impairments or disability, and social well-being), service provision, or resource availability.

Healthy carrier: an individual who has been exposed to and harbors a pathogen but has not become ill or shown any of the symptoms of the disease.

Healthy worker effect: occurs in cohort studies when workers represent the exposed group and a sample from the general population represents the unexposed group.

Helicobacter pylori: a bacterium that can cause chronic conditions such as dyspepsia (heartburn, bloating, and nausea), gastritis (stomach inflammation), and ulcers in the stomach and duodenum, as well as stomach cancer and lymphoma.

Herd immunity: based on the notion that if the herd (a population or group) is mostly protected from a disease by immunization then the chance that a major epidemic will occur is limited.

Histogram: a frequency distribution for discrete or continuous data.

Horizontal transmission: transmission of infectious agents from an infected individual to a susceptible contemporary.

Host: an organism, usually a human or an animal, that harbors the disease.

Hypothesis: a suggested explanation for an observed phenomenon or a reasoned proposal predicting a possible causal association among multiple phenomena.

Immunization: the introduction of a substance that can cause the immune system to respond and develop antibodies against a disease.

Impairment: any loss or abnormality of psychological, physiologic, or of the anatomic structure or function.

Incidence rate: Number of new cases of a specified health-related state or event reported during a given time period divided by the estimated population at mid-interval.

Incidence density rate: accounts for varying time periods of follow-up. See also *person-time rate.*

Incubation period: the stage of presymptomatic disease that begins with exposure and ends with the onset of symptoms; used in the context of acute infectious disease.

Incubatory carrier: an individual exposed to and harbors a pathogen, is in the beginning stages of the disease, is showing symptoms, and has the ability to transmit the disease.

Index case: the first disease case brought to the attention of the epidemiologist.

Indirect causal association: involves one or more intervening factors and is often much more complicated and difficult to understand than a direct causal association.

Indirect transmission: disease that results when an agent is transferred or carried by some intermediate item, organism, means, or process to a susceptible host.

Inductive reasoning: moving from specific observations to broader generalizations and theories.

Infant mortality rate: number of deaths among infants ages 0–1 year during a specified time period divided by the number of live births in the same time period.

Institutional Review Board (IRB): a group assigned at the institution level to review plans for research involving human subjects; the group is charged with protecting the rights and welfare of people involved in research.

Instrument bias: the result of faulty function of a mechanical instrument, such as a scale that produces consistently low body weight measures because it has not been properly calibrated.

Intermittent carrier: an individual who has been exposed to and harbors a pathogen and who can spread the disease at different places or intervals.

Internal validity: the extent to which the results of a study are true for the target population.

Interquartile range: the middle 50% of the data; the difference between the third quartile (75th percentile) and first quartile (25th percentile).

Interviewer bias: differential accuracy of exposure information between cases and controls because the interviewer probes cases differently than controls.

Invasiveness: the ability to get into a susceptible host and cause disease.

Ionizing radiation: high energy radiation capable of producing ionization in substances in which it passes; radiation with enough energy so that during an interaction with an atom, it can remove tightly bound electrons from the orbit of an atom, causing the atom to become charged or ionized.

Isolation: the separation of persons who have a specific infectious illness from those who are healthy and the restriction of their movement to stop the spread of that illness.

Koch's postulates: four criteria formulated by Robert Koch and Friedrich Loeffler in 1884 and refined and published by Koch in 1890 to establish a causal relationship between a causative microbe and a disease.

Latency period: the time from exposure to clinical symptoms; the presymptomatic phase of disease; used in the context of chronic disease.

Lead time: difference in time between the date of diagnosis with screening and the date of diagnosis without screening.

Lead-time bias: the survival time is improved because screening led to the discovery of the disease earlier, not because the time of death was extended.

Length-bias: screening is more likely to detect slower growing tumors that are less lethal; identifying disease that is less deadly or likely to be detected prior to death from other causes can result in making a screening program appear better than it really is.

Likelihood ratio: incorporates both sensitivity and specificity of the test and provides a direct estimate of how much a test result will change the odds of having a disease.

Line graph: a graph with an x-axis (horizontal) and a y-axis (vertical). The x-axis has numbers for the time period, and the y-axis has numbers or rates for what is being measured. Line graphs are useful for displaying information that changes over time, such as cancer rates, injury rates, and air quality.

Line listing: a table of data where each row represents a case and each column represents variable information on the case, such as personal characteristics, clinical information, and so on.

Logistic regression: a form of statistical modeling that is often appropriate for categorical outcome variables. It describes the relationship between a categorical response variable and a set of explanatory variables. The response variable is usually dichotomous, but may be polytomous.

Longitudinal data: the same sample of respondents is observed in a subsequent time period.

Loss to follow-up: circumstance in which researchers lose contact with study participants, resulting in unavailable outcome data on those people. This is a potential source of selection bias in cohort studies.

Malnutrition: a condition that arises when the body does not get the right amount of vitamins, minerals, or other nutrients to maintain healthy tissues and proper organ function.

Mass screening: not selective, but involves application of screening tests to the total population.

Matched-paired analysis: used to analyze matched case-control studies. The odds ratio in a matched-paired study is interpreted the same as in an unmatched case-control study but is calculated as b/c.

Matching: a method used to ensure that two study groups are similar with regard to an extrinsic study or factors that might distort or confound a relationship between an exposure and outcome being studied. Matching may be employed in both case-control and cohort studies. There are two types of matching, frequency matching and pair (individual) matching. Pair matching links each member of the case group to a member of the control group with similar characteristics (e.g., age, sex, and smoking status). Frequency matching is more commonly used. The control subjects are chosen to ensure that the frequency of the matching factors is the same as found in the case group; that is, the distribution of a potential confounder is determined for the case group and controls are selected to match this frequency distribution. Individual matching involves selecting a control to match a case with respect to the potential confounding factor.

Maternal mortality rate: calculated by dividing the number of deaths due to childbirth during a specified time period by the number of live births in the same time period; measure of the proportion of pregnant women who die from causes related to or aggravated by the childbirth process: labor and delivery, poor obstetric care, pregnancy complications, puerperium problems, and poor management.

Measures of central tendency: ways of designating the center of the data. The most common measures are the mean, median, and mode.

Measures of dispersion: measures that describe the spread of the data or its variation around a central value. The most common measures of dispersion are the range, interquartile range, average deviation, variance, and standard deviation.

Mechanical transmission: vector-borne disease transmission processes that occur when the pathogen, in order to spread, uses a host (e.g., a fly, flea, louse, or rat) as a mechanism for a ride, for nourishment, or as part of a physical transfer process.

Median: the number or value that divides a list of numbers in half; it is the middle observation in the data set.

Medical surveillance: close observation of individuals exposed to a communicable disease such that early manifestations of the disease could be detected and prompt isolation and control measures imposed.

Metabolic diseases: inherent errors of metabolism that comprise a large class of genetic diseases that involves disorders of metabolism, which is the collection of chemical changes that occur within cells during normal functioning.

Method of agreement: a single factor is common to a number of circumstances where the disease occurs at a high frequency.

Method of concomitant variation: the frequency or strength of a risk factor varies in proportion to the frequency of the disease or condition.

Method of difference: involves recognizing that if the frequency of a disease differs between two locations, it may be because a particular factor varies between those two places. For example, vastly different levels of colon cancer between Japan and the United States suggest that differences in diet may be the explanation.

Misclassification: when the exposure or the status of the health-related state or event is inaccurately assigned. In a case-control study, misclassification results if the exposure status is incorrectly assigned. The level of misclassification may be similar between cases and controls (random, nondifferential) or differ between cases and controls (nonrandom, differential). In a cohort study, misclassification results if the outcome status is incorrectly assigned. The level of misclassification may be similar between exposed and unexposed groups (random, nondifferential) or differ between exposed and unexposed groups (nonrandom, differential).

Mixed epidemic: when victims of a common-source epidemic have person-to-person contact with others and spread the disease, further propagating the health problem.

Mode: the number or value that occurs most often; the number with the highest frequency.

Modes of disease transmission: different ways in which disease is transferred.

Monitor: to observe something over time or among populations (e.g., health status, physical conditions, or substances) in order to assess progress toward health goals or objectives.

Mortality: the epidemiologic and vital statistics term for death.

Mortality rate: Total number of deaths reported during a given time interval divided by the estimated mid-interval population.

Multifactorial etiology: of or arising from many factors.

Multiple logistic regression: an extension of logistic regression in which two or more independent variables are included in the model.

Multiple regression: an extension of simple regression analysis in which there are two or more independent variables.

Natural experiment: an unplanned type of experimental study where the levels of exposure to a presumed cause differ among a population in a way that is relatively unaffected by extraneous factors so that the situation resembles a planned experiment.

Negative likelihood ratio (LR−): how much the odds of the disease decrease when a test is negative.

Neonatal mortality rate: calculated by dividing the number of deaths among infants less than 28 days old during a specified time period by the number of live births in the same time period; reflects poor prenatal care, low birth weights, infections, lack of proper medical care, inquiries, premature delivery, and congenital defects.

Nested case-control study: a case-control study nested within a cohort study (also called a case-cohort study).

Neyman's bias: see *prevalence-incidence bias*.

Nominal data: unordered categories or classes (e.g., gender, race/ethnicity, marital status, occupation).

Nondifferential (random) misclassification: see *misclassification*.

Null hypothesis: a statement that there is no association between the predictor and outcome variables in the population.

Observation bias: systematic error that arises from inaccurate measurements or misclassification of subjects according to exposure and outcome status (also called measurement bias).

Observational study: researchers observe events for individuals in the study without altering them.

Observer bias: a distortion, conscious or unconscious, in the reporting of the measurement by the observer.

Odds ratio: a commonly used measure of the relative probabilities of disease in case-control studies.

Ordinal data: the order among categories provides additional information (e.g., stage or grade of cancer).

Outbreak: carries the same definition as epidemic but is typically used when the event is confined to a more limited geographic area.

Outcomes research: describes research (usually medical) that seeks to understand the end results of clinical healthcare practices and interventions.

Overall accuracy: a measure of a screening test's validity, calculated as (TP + TN) / (TP + FN + FP + TN)

Overdiagnosis bias: occurs when screening identifies an illness that would not have shown clinical signs before a person's death from other causes.

Overnutrition: the consumption of too much food, eating too many of the wrong things, too little physical activity and exercise, or taking too many vitamins or dietary supplements.

Pandemic: an epidemic affecting or attacking the population of an extensive region, country, or continent.

Participation restriction: any problem an individual may experience in their involvement in life situations.

Passive immunity: involves the transfer of antibodies to one person produced by another person.

Passive primary prevention: does not require behavior change on the part of the individual in order to prevent a disease or disorder from occurring (e.g., eating vitamin-enriched foods, drinking fluoridated water).

Pathogens: organisms or substances such as bacteria, viruses, fungi, or parasites capable of producing disease.

Perinatal mortality rate: calculated by dividing the number of stillbirths and deaths in infants 6 days of age or younger by the number of births (live and still).

Period effect: a change in the rate of a condition affecting an entire population at a given point in time.

Person-time rate: the rate that new health-related states or events occur in a population. It is calculated by dividing the number of new cases during a specified time period by the total person-time units at risk of the event.

Person-time units: total person-time units are the sum of each individual's time at risk in a population and comprise the denominators used in calculating person-time rates.

Personal hygiene: process of maintaining high standards of personal body maintenance and cleanliness.

Phase I trials: unblinded and uncontrolled studies involving a few volunteers to test the safety of an intervention.

Phase II trials: relatively small randomized blinded trials that test tolerability and different intensity or dose of the intervention on surrogate or clinical outcomes.

Phase III trials: relatively large randomized blinded trials that test the effect of the therapy on clinical outcomes.

Phase IV trials: large trials or observational studies conducted after the therapy has been FDA approved. These trials assess the rate of serious side effects and explore additional therapeutic uses.

Physical stresses: of or relating to the body, such as excessive heat, cold, and noise; radiation (electromagnetic, ultrasound, microwave, x-irradiation); vehicular collisions; workplace injuries; climate change; ozone depletion; housing; and so on.

Pilot study: a standard scientific approach that involves preliminary analysis that can greatly improve the chance of obtaining funding for major clinical trials; a small-scale experiment or set of observations undertaken to decide how and whether to launch a full-scale project.

Placebo: an inactive substance or treatment given to satisfy a patient's expectation of treatment.

Placebo effect: the effect on patient outcomes (improved or worsened) that may occur because of the expectation by a patient (or provider) that a particular intervention will have an effect.

Point source: epidemic in which persons are exposed to the same exposure over a limited time period.

Population pyramid: a graphical illustration that shows the distribution of age groups in a population (also called an age-sex pyramid). It received its name because it often forms the shape of a pyramid.

Population-attributable risk: amount of absolute risk of a health-related state or event in a population that can be attributed to the exposure. This measure assumes that the exposure causes the outcome.

Population-attributable risk percent: the percent of the absolute risk of a health-related state or event in a population that can be attributed to the exposure. This measure assumes that the exposure causes the disease.

Portal of entry: the entryway through which the pathogen or disease-causing agent enters the body.

Portal of exit: disease transmission that occurs when the pathogen leaves the reservoir through a portal.

Positive likelihood ratio (LR+): how much the odds of the disease increase when a test is positive.

Post hoc hypotheses: derived from observed facts; the formulation of hypotheses after observation of an event such as an excess of cancer.

Posterior probability: the name sometimes given to predictive value positive or predictive value negative because they are probabilities determined after the test results.

Postneonatal mortality rate: calculated by dividing the number of infant deaths between 28 days of age and 1 year by the number of live births in the same year; this measure is influenced primarily by malnutrition and infectious diseases.

Power: the power of a statistical test measures the test's ability to reject the null hypothesis when it is actually false; power is directly associated with sample size. It is equal to $1 - \text{beta}$.

Precipitating factors: the factors essential for the development of diseases, conditions, injuries, disability, and death.

Precision: the reproducibility of repeated measurements such as made by the same person over time (within-observer reproducibility) or between different people (between-observer reproducibility). Also called reproducibility, reliability, and consistency.

Predictive value positive (PV+): the probability that an individual with a positive test actually has the disease.

Predictive value negative (PV−): the probability that an individual with a negative test does not have the disease.

Predisposing factors: those existing factors or conditions that produce a susceptibility or disposition in a host to a disease or condition without actually causing it. Predisposing factors precede the direct cause.

Prevalence-incidence bias: a form of selection bias in case-control studies attributed to selective survival among the prevalent cases (i.e., mild, clinically resolved, or fatal cases being excluded from the case group); also called Neyman's bias.

Primary case: the first disease case in the population.

Primary prevention: effort to prevent a disease or disorder before it happens.

Prior probability: prevalence proportion of disease that is used in the calculation of PV+ and PV−.

Prodromal period: the second stage of illness and the period in which signs and symptoms of disease first appear.

Prognosis: the prospect of recovery as anticipated from the usual course of disease; a prediction of the probable course and outcome of a disease.

Prognostic indicator: information (e.g., clinical, laboratory) that helps forecast the likely outcome of a disease; factors such as staging, tumor characteristics, and laboratory information that may indicate treatment effectiveness and outcome.

Propagated epidemic: an epidemic that arises from an infectious agent transmitted from one infected person to another.

Prophylactic trial: an experimental study that helps to determine how to prevent disease or conditions from occurring in healthy people. See also *clinical trial*.

Prophylaxis: any medical or public health effort intended to prevent, rather than treat or cure a disease; guarding or preventing beforehand.

Prophylactic trial: tests preventive measures. Participants are typically healthy volunteers with a range of exposures and possible outcomes.

Proportion: a ratio in which the numerator is included in the denominator.

Proportional mortality ratio: a ratio of the number of deaths attributed to a specific cause to the total number of deaths occurring in the population during a specified time period.

Prospective cohort study: an analytic epidemiologic study that classifies participants according to exposure status and then follows them over time to determine if the rate of developing a given health-related state or event is significantly different between the exposed and the unexposed groups.

Protocol: the detailed written plan of the study; the outline of the study protocol may include the research questions, background and significance, design (time frame, epidemiologic approach), subjects (selection criteria, sampling), variables (predictor variables, confounding variables, outcome variables, and statistical issues (hypotheses, sample size, and analytic approach).

Public health surveillance: the systematic ongoing collection, analysis, interpretation, and dissemination of health data.

***P* value:** is a probability that ranges from 0 to 1 and provides a means of evaluating the role of chance.

Quarantine: the separation and restriction of the movement of persons who, although not yet ill, have been exposed to an infectious agent and may become infectious themselves.

Random assignment: the random allocation of participants to one or another of the study groups. Participants have an equal probability of being assigned to any of the groups. This process minimizes any confounding effects by balancing out the potential confounding factors among the groups.

Random error: chance variability; the greater the error, the less precise the measurement.

Randomized matched pairs: the design of an experiment for paired comparison in which the assignment of participants to treatment or control is not completely at random, but the randomization is restricted to occur separately within each pair.

Range: the difference between the largest (maximum) and smallest (minimum) values of a frequency distribution.

Rate: a proportion with the added dimension of time. The numerator consists of health-related states or events during a given time period and the denominator consists of persons at risk during the same time period.

Rate base: a unit of measure commonly used in expressing rates. It is multiplied by the rate to avoid fractional rates and allows the rate to be expressed per 10^n, where n is typically between 2 and 5.

Rate ratio: a measure of the strength of association between dichotomous exposure and outcome variables that involves the ratio of person-time rates.

Ratio: a relationship between two quantities, normally expressed as the quotient of one divided by the other.

Recall bias: a type of observation bias (or measurement bias) that can occur in case-control and cross-sectional studies because of differential recall about past exposure status between those who have the disease compared with those who do not. In general, cases tend to have better recall.

Regression: a statistical analysis for assessing the association between two variables; the regression equation is used to estimate the change in the dependent variable (y) per unit change in the independent variable (x). The investigator determines which variable is dependent and which variable is independent based on observation and experience.

Rehabilitation: any attempt to restore an afflicted person to a useful, productive, and satisfying lifestyle and to provide the highest quality of life possible, given the extent of the disease and disability; a component of tertiary prevention.

Reinforcing factors: have the ability to support the production and transmission of disease or conditions, or they have the ability to support and improve a population's health status and help control diseases and conditions.

Relative frequency: derived by dividing the number of people in a group by the total number of people; that is, a part of the group is expressed relative to the whole group.

Relative odds: see *odds ratio*.

Reliability: how well the test performs in use over time—its repeatability.

Research hypothesis: a specific version of the research question that summarizes the main element of the study; the basis for tests of statistical significance.

Reservoir: the habitat (living or nonliving) in or on which an infectious agent lives, grows, and multiplies and where it depends for its survival in nature.

Restriction: limiting subjects in a study to those with certain characteristics, such as those at high risk for developing a health-related state or event or those in the age range 40–49. Restriction may improve the feasibility of a study and limit confounding.

Retrospective cohort study: an analytic epidemiologic study where the cohort represents a historical cohort assembled using available data sources.

Risk factor: a characteristic, condition, or behavior, such as obesity, that increases the possibility of disease or injury; something that contributes to the production of an adverse health outcome.

Risk ratio: a measure of the strength of association between dichotomous exposure and outcome variables that involves the ratio of attack rates (also called relative risk).

Run-in design: an experimental study in which all subjects in the cohort are placed on placebo and followed up for some period of time (usually a week or two) prior to random assignment.

Sample: a subset of items that have been selected from the population.

Screening: used to suggest whether an individual is likely to have a disease and if they should undergo diagnostic testing to confirm the presence of the disease. Screening is a type of secondary prevention.

Screening guidelines: any guideline made known by an authoritative organization such as the National Cancer Institute for early detection of a malignancy common in a particular population, in which an early diagnosis may result in a complete cure or improved survival.

Scurvy: a disease caused by deficiency of vitamin C, characterized by spongy and bleeding gums, bleeding under the skin, and extreme weakness

Seasonal trend: periodic increases and decreases in the occurrence, interval, or frequency of disease.

Secondary attack rate: the rate of new cases occurring among contacts of known cases.

Secondary case: a person who becomes infected from contact with a primary case after the disease has been introduced into the population.

Secondary data: data that comes from previous research studies, medical records, healthcare billing files, death certificates, vital records, national and local surveys, environmental data, and other sources.

Secondary prevention: activities aimed at health screening and early detection in order to improve the likelihood of a cure and reduce the chance of disability or death.

Secular trend: the long-term change in morbidity or mortality rates for a given health-related state or event in a specified population.

Selection bias: systematic error that occurs from the way the participants are selected or retained in a study (e.g., Berkson's bias in case-control studies and loss to follow-up in cohort studies).

Selective screening: testing for a disease or condition in a population using screening criteria, as opposed to universal screening; targeted testing for a disease or condition on a high-risk group.

Sensitivity of a screening test: the proportion of positive tests among those who actually have the disease.

Sentinel events: occurrences of unexpected health-related states or events that result from specific, recognized causes.

Serial survey: a cross-sectional survey that is routinely conducted.

Short-term trends or fluctuations: unexpected increases in health-related states or events, usually brief.

Single-blinded study: a placebo-controlled study in which the subjects are blinded, but the investigators are aware of who is receiving the active treatment.

Smallpox: an acute, highly infectious disease caused by the variola virus, characterized by high fever and aches with subsequent eruption of pimples that blister and form pockmarks.

Spearman's rank correlation coefficient: obtained by ranking two sets of outcomes x and y separately and calculating a coefficient of rank correlation; a measure of association that is robust to outlying values; an alternative to the Pearson correlation coefficient when outlying data exists such that one or both of the distributions are skewed.

Specificity: an exposure is associated with only one disease or the disease is associated with only one exposure.

Specificity of a screening test: the proportion of subjects who have a negative test result who do not actually have the disease.

Spot map: a pictorial display of the geographic location of each health-related state or event that occurs in a defined area.

Standard deviation: the square root of the variance.

Stationary pyramid: more block shaped, with low fertility and low mortality.

Statistical inference: an inference or conclusion made about a population based on sampled data.

Stem-and-leaf plot: a display that organizes data to show its distribution. Each data value is split into a "stem" and a "leaf."

Strength of association: a critical criterion in causal inference wherein a statistical association should not be due to chance, bias, or confounding.

Study design: the plan that directs the researcher along the path of systematically collecting, analyzing, and interpreting data.

Subject bias: distortion of the measurement by the study subject such as inaccurate exposure status because of poor recall or the influence of an inadequately trained interviewer.

Surrogate: to put in place of another or a substitute for something else.

Surveillance: observation or monitoring.

Survival analysis: a collection of statistical procedures for data analysis in which the outcome variable of interest is time until an event occurs.

Survival rate: proportion of persons in a study or treatment group surviving for a given time after diagnosis.

Survival time: the percent of people who survive a disease for a specific amount of time.

Suspect case: an individual (or a group of individuals) who has all the signs and symptoms of a disease or condition but has not been diagnosed as having the disease, or had the cause of the symptoms connected to a suspected pathogen.

Temporal: time or time-related elements or issues.

Temporality: a criterion in causal inference involving a linear process of past, present, and future.

Tertiary prevention: efforts to limit disability by providing rehabilitation where disease, injury, or a disorder has already occurred and caused damage.

Therapeutic trial: a trial used to test new treatment methods. See also *clinical trial*.

Time-series design: a sequence of measurements of some numerical quantity made at or during two or more successive periods of time.

Total fertility rate: the total number of children a woman would have by the end of her reproductive period if she experienced the currently prevailing age-specific fertility rates throughout her childbearing life (ages 15–49 years).

Toxicokinetics: an area of study of how a substance enters the body and the course it takes while in the body; the description of the rate a chemical will enter the body and what happens to it.

Toxin: a poisonous substance produced by living cells or organisms and capable of causing harm to the body.

Triple-blinded study: blinding the participants and those doing the outcome assessment, but also the analyses are completed separate from the primary investigators.

True negative (TN): a negative test result for someone without the disease.

True positive (TP): a positive test result for someone with the disease.

Tuskegee syphilis study: a cohort study that assessed the natural course of syphilis in untreated black males from Macon County, Alabama.

Two-way (or bivariate) scatter plot: used to depict the relationship between two distinct discrete or continuous variables.

Type I error: when the null hypothesis (H_0) is rejected but H_0 is true.

Type II error: when H_0 is not rejected but H_0 is false.

Typhoid fever: an infectious disease characterized by a continued fever, physical and mental depression, rose-colored spots on the chest and abdomen, diarrhea, and sometimes intestinal hemorrhage or perforation of the bowel.

Typhus: any of several forms of infectious disease caused by rickettsia, especially those transmitted by fleas, lice, or mites and characterized by severe headache, sustained fever, depression, delirium, and the eruption of red rashes on the skin.

Undernutrition: a consequence of consuming too little essential vitamins, minerals, and other nutrients or excreting them faster than they can be replenished.

Validity: see *internal validity* and *external validity*.

Validity of a test: how well the test actually measures what it is supposed to measure.

Validity of a variable: The degree to which a variable represents what it is intended to represent; how well the measurement represents the phenomenon of interest.

Variable: a characteristic that varies from one observation to the next and can be measured or categorized.

Variance: the average of the squared differences of the observations from the mean.

Variolation: inoculation with a weak strain of smallpox as a method to induce immunity against more virulent strains of the disease; this method of immunizing patients against smallpox is now obsolete.

Vector: an invertebrate animal (e.g., tick, mite, mosquito, bloodsucking fly) that is capable of transmitting an infectious agent to humans.

Vector-borne transmission: transfer of a disease to a human by a vector.

Vehicle-borne transmission: transfer of a disease via a particular vehicle, for example, needle use.

Vertical transmission: transmission from an individual to its offspring through sperm, placenta, milk, or vaginal fluids.

Viability: the capacity of the pathogen or disease-causing agent to survive outside the host and to exist or thrive in the environment.

Virulence: the disease-evoking power of a pathogen.

Vital records: data on birth, death, marriage, and divorce.

Vitamins: organic components in food that are needed in very small amounts for metabolism, growth, and for maintaining good health.

Waterborne: a disease that travels in both surface and groundwater supplies.

Waterborne transmission: spread of disease that occurs when a pathogen such as cholera or shigellosis is carried in drinking water, swimming pools, streams, or lakes used for swimming.

Web of causation: graphic, pictorial, or paradigmatic representation of complex sets of events or conditions caused by an array of activities connected to a common core or common experience or event.

Within-group design: the outcome of interest is compared before and after an intervention. This design is more susceptible to confounding from time-related factors (e.g., learning effects where participants do better on follow-up cognitive tests because they learned from the baseline test, influences from the media, or other external factors).

Years of potential life lost (YPLL): a measure of the relative impact of various health-related states or events on a population; it identifies the loss of expected years of life because of premature death in the population.

Yield of a screening test: the amount of screening the test can accomplish in a time period—that is, how much disease it can detect in the screening process.

YPLL rate: the years of potential life lost divided by the number in the population upon which the YPLL is derived.

Zoonoses: those diseases and infections that are transmitted between vertebrate animals and humans.

Zoonosis: an infectious organism in vertebrate animals (e.g., rabies or anthrax) that can be transmitted to humans through direct contact, a fomite, or a vector.

Case Studies

CASE STUDY I: SNOW ON CHOLERA

Snow J. *On the Mode of Communication of Cholera.* **(Excerpted and adapted from the original 1855 edition as found in** *Snow on Cholera* **by John Snow, Commonwealth Fund: New York, 1936)**

ABOUT DR. JOHN SNOW

John Snow was born in 1813 and died in 1858. Dr. Snow was alive at the beginning of the golden era of bacteriology and infectious disease discovery and was actively involved in his professional pursuits at the time of Ignaz Semmelweis, MD, Louis Pasteur (1822–1895) of France, and John Koch, MD (1843–1910), of Germany. At the time, these scientists led the world in the discovery of microbes, vaccines, and advanced scientific and biomedical knowledge about communicable diseases. Dr. Snow was a distinguished anesthesiologist in England who, among other accomplishments, administered chloroform to Queen Victoria at the birth of two of her children. Dr. Snow is most famous for his cholera investigations, including the epidemic in the Soho District of London, where he removed the handle from the Broad Street pump as a move to halt the cholera epidemic.

A. OBSERVATIONS ON CHOLERA

Communication of Cholera

There are certain circumstances connected with the progress of cholera, which may be stated in a general way. Cholera travels along the great tracks more slowly. In extending to fresh inland or continent, it always appears first at a sea-port. It never attacks the crews of ships going from a country free from cholera to one where the disease is prevailing, until they have entered a port or had intercourse with the shore. Its exact progress from town to town cannot always be traced; but it has only appeared where there has been ample opportunity for it to be conveyed by human intercourse.

There are also innumerable instances which prove the communication of cholera, by individual cases of the disease, in the most convincing manner. Instances such as the following seem free from every source of fallacy. . . . I called lately to inquire respecting the death of Mrs. Gore, the wife of a labourer, from cholera, at New Leigham Road, Streatham. I found that a son of the deceased had been living and working at Chelsea. He came home ill with a bowel complaint, of which he died in a day or two. His death took place on August 18th. His mother, who attended on him, was taken ill on the next day and died the day following (August 20th). There were no other deaths from cholera registered in any of the metropolitan districts, down to the 26th of August, within two or three miles of the above place; the nearest being at Brixton, Norwood, or Lower Tooting. . . .

John Barnes, aged 39, an agricultural labourer, became severely indisposed on the 28th of December, 1832. He had been suffering from diarrhoea and cramps for two days previously. He was visited by Mr. George Hopps, a respectable surgeon at Redhouse, who, finding him sinking into collapse, requested an interview with his brother, Mr. J. Hopps, of York. This experienced practitioner at once recognized the case as one of Asiatic cholera; immediately inquired for some probable source of contagion, but in vain: no such source could be discovered. When he repeated his visit on the day following, the patient was dead; but Mrs. Barnes (the wife), Matthew Metcalfe, and Benjamin Muscroft, two persons who had visited Barnes on the preceding day, were all labouring under the disease, but recovered. John Foster, Ann Dunn, and widow Creyke, all of whom had communicated with the patients above named, were attacked by premonitory indisposition, which was however arrested. Whilst the surgeons were vainly endeavouring to discover whence the disease could possibly have arisen, the mystery was all at once, and most unexpectedly, unravelled by the arrival in the village of the son of the deceased John Barnes. This young man was apprentice to his uncle, a shoemaker, living in Leeds. He informed the surgeons that his uncle's wife (his father's sister) had died of cholera a fortnight (2 weeks/14 days) before that time, and that, as she had no children, her wearing apparel had been sent to Monkton by a common carrier. The clothes had not been washed. Barnes had opened the box in the evening; on the next day he had fallen sick of the disease.

During the illness of Mrs. Barnes, her mother, who was living in Tockwith, a healthy village five miles distant from Moor Monkton, was requested to attend her. She went to Monkton accordingly, remained with her daughter for two days, washed her daughter's linen, and set out on her return home, apparently in good health. Whilst in the act of walking home she was seized with the malady, and fell down and collapsed on the road. She was conveyed home to her cottage, and placed by the side of her bedridden husband. He, and also the daughter who resided with them, took the malady. All the three died within two days. Only one other case occurred in the village of Tockwith, and it was not a fatal case.

A man came from Hull (where cholera was prevailing), a painter by trade. His name and age are unknown. He lodged at the house of Samuel Wride, at Pocklingto. He was attacked on his arrival on the 8th of September, and died on the 9th. Samuel Wride himself was attacked on the 11th of September, and died shortly afterwards. . . .

Liverpool. (Mr. Henry Taylor, reporter.) A nurse attended a patient in Great Howard Street (at the lower part of the town), and on her return home, near Everton (the higher part of the town), was seized and died. The nurse who attended her was also seized, and died. No other case had occurred previously in that neighbourhood, and none followed for about a fortnight. . . .

It would be easy, by going through the medical journal and works which have been published on cholera, to quote as many cases similar to the above as would fill a large volume. But the above instances are quite sufficient to show that cholera can be communicated from the sick to the healthy; for it is quite impossible that even a tenth part of these cases of consecutive illness could have followed each other by coincidence, without being connected as cause and effect.

Besides the facts above mentioned, which prove that cholera is communicated from person to person, there are other factors as well. First, being present in the same room with a patient, and attending to him, does not necessarily expose a person to the morbid poison. Second, it is not always requisite that a person should be very near to a cholera patient in order to take the disease, as the morbid matter producing it may be transmitted to a distance. It used to be generally assumed, that if cholera were a catching or communicable disease it must spread by Effluvia given off from the patient into the surrounding air, and inhaled by others into the lungs. This assumption led to very conflicting opinions respecting the disease. A little reflection shows, however, that we have no right thus to limit the way in which a disease may be propagated, for the communicable diseases of which we have a correct knowledge may spread in very different manners. The itch, and certain other diseases of the skin, are propagated in one way; Syphilis, in another way; and intestinal worms in a third way, quite distinct from either of the others. . . .

Cholera Propagated by Morbid Material Entering the Alimentary Canal

Diseases which are communicated from person-to-person are caused by some material which passes from the sick to the healthy, and which has the property of increasing and multiplying in the systems of the persons it attacks. In syphilis, smallpox, and vaccinia, we have physical proof of the increase of the morbid material, and in other communicable diseases the evidence of this increase, derived from the fact of their extension, is equally conclusive. As cholera commences with an affection of the alimentary canal, and as we have seen that the blood is not under the influence of any poison in the early stages of this disease, it follows that the morbid material producing cholera must be introduced into the alimentary canal. In fact, it must be swallowed accidentally, for persons would not take it intentionally; and the increase of the morbid material or cholera poison, must take place in the interior of the stomach and bowels. It would seem that the cholera poison, when reproduced in sufficient quantity, acts as an irritant on the surface of the stomach and intestines, or what is still more probable, it withdraws fluid from the blood circulating in the capillaries, by a power analogous to that by which the epithelial cells of the various organs abstract the different secretions in the healthy body. For the morbid matter of cholera having the property of reproducing its own kind, must necessarily have some sort of structure, most likely that of a cell. It is no objection to this view that the structure of the cholera poison cannot be recognized by the microscope, for the matter of smallpox and chancre can only be recognized by their effects, and not by their physical properties.

The period which intervenes between the time when a morbid poison enters the system, and the commencement of the illness which follows, is called the period of incubation. It is, in reality, a period of reproduction, with regards to the morbid matter, and the disease is due to the crop of progeny resulting from the small quantity of poison first introduced. In cholera, this period of incubation or reproduction is much shorter than in most other epidemic or communicable diseases. From the cases previously detailed, it is shown to be in general from 24 to 48 hours. It is owing to this shortness of the period of incubation, and to the quantity of the morbid poison thrown off in the evacuations, that cholera sometimes spreads with a rapidity unknown in other diseases. . . .

The instances in which minute quantities of the ejections and dejections of cholera patients must be swallowed are sufficiently numerous to account for the spread of the disease. Nothing has been found to favour the extension of cholera more than want of personal cleanliness whether arising from habit or scarcity of water. The bed linen nearly always becomes wetted by the cholera evacuations, and as these are devoid of the usual colour and odour, the hands of persons waiting on the patient become soiled without their knowing it. Unless these person are scrupulously clean in their habits and wash their hands before taking food, they must accidentally swallow some of the excretion, and leave some on the food they handle or prepare, which has to be eaten by the rest of the family. The post-mortem inspection of bodies of cholera patients has hardly ever been followed by the disease that I am aware, this being a duty that is necessarily followed by careful washing of the hands. It is not the habit of medical men to be taking food on such occasion. On the other hand, the duties performed about the body, such as laying it out, when done by women of the working class, who make the occasion one of eating and drinking, are often followed by an attack of cholera. Persons who merely attend the funeral, and have no connexion with body frequently contract the disease, in consequence, apparently of partaking of food which has been prepared or handled by those having duties about the cholera patient, or his linen and bedding.

The involuntary passage of the evacuations in most bad cases of cholera, must also aid in spreading the disease. Mr. Baker, of Staines, who attended to 260 cases of cholera and diarrhoea in 1849, chiefly among the poor, informed me in a letter with which he favoured me in December of that year, that "when the patients passed their stools involuntarily the disease evidently spread." It is amongst the poor, where a whole family lives, sleeps, cooks, eats and washes in a single room, that cholera has been found to spread once introduced. Still more in those places termed common lodging amongst the vagrant class, who lived in a crowded state, that cholera was most fatal in 1832. The Act of Parliament for the regulation of common lodging houses, has caused the disease to be much less fatal amongst these people in the late epidemics. When, on the other hand, cholera is introduced into the better kind of houses, as it often is by means that will be afterwards pointed out, it hardly ever spreads from one member of the family to another. The constant use of the hand-basin and towel, and the fact of the apartments for cooking and eating being distinct from the sick room, are the cause for this.

If the cholera had no other means of communication than those we have been considering, it would be constrained to confine itself chiefly to the crowded dwellings of the poor, and would be continually liable to die out accidentally in a place, for want of the opportunity to reach fresh victims; but there is often a way open for it to extend itself more widely and reach well-to-do classes of the community. I allude to the mixture of the cholera evacuations with the water used for drinking and culinary purposes, either by permeating the ground, and getting into the wells, or by running along channels and sewers into the rivers from which entire towns are sometimes supplied with water.

In 1849 there were in Thomas Street, Horsleydown, two courts close together, consisting of a number of small houses or cottages, inhabited by poor people. The houses occupied one side of each court or alley—the south side of Trusscott's Court, and the north side of the other, which was called Surrey Buildings. They were divided into small back areas in which situated the privies of both courts, communicating with the same drain, and there was an open sewer which passed the further end of both courts. In Surrey Buildings the cholera committed fearful devastation, whilst in the adjoining court there was but one fatal case, and another case that ended in recovery. In the former court, the slops of dirty water, poured down by the inhabitants into a channel in front of the houses, got into the well from which they obtained their water; this being the only difference that Mr. Grant, the Assistant Surveyor for the Commissioners of Sewers, could find between the circumstances of the two courts.

In Manchester, a sudden and violent outbreak of cholera occurred in Hope Street, Salford. The inhabitants used water from a particular pump/well. This well had been repaired, and a sewer which passes within nine inches of the edge of it became accidentally stopped up, and leaked into the well. The inhabitants of 30 houses used the water from this well; among these there occurred 19 cases of diarrhoea, 26 cases of cholera, and 25 deaths. The inhabitants of 60 houses in the same immediate neighbourhood used other water; among these there occurred eleven cases of diarrhoea, but not a single case of cholera, nor one death. It is remarkable, that, in this instance, out of the 26 persons attacked with cholera, the whole perished except one.

Dr. Thomas King Chambers informed me, that at Ilford, in Essex, in the summer of 1849, the cholera prevailed very severely in a row of houses a little way from the main part of town. It had visited every house in the row but one. The refuse which overflowed from the privies and a pigsty could be seen running into the well over the surface of the ground, and the water was very fetid; yet it was used by the people in all the houses except that which had escaped cholera. That house was inhabited by a woman who took linen to wash, and she, finding that the water gave the linen an offensive smell, paid a person to fetch water for her from the pump in the town, and this water she used for culinary purposes as well as for washing.

The following circumstance was related to me, at the time it occurred, by a gentleman well acquainted with all the particulars. The drainage from the cesspools found its way into the well attached to some houses at Locksbrook, near Bath, and the cholera making its appearance there in the autumn of 1849, became very fatal. The people complained of the water to the gentleman belonging to the property, who lived at Weston, in Bath, and he sent a surveyor, who reported that nothing was the matter. The tenants still complaining, the owner went himself, and in looking at the water and smelling it, he said that he could perceive nothing the matter with it. He was asked if he would taste it, and drank a glass of it. This occurred on a Wednesday; he went home, was taken ill with the cholera, and died on the Saturday following, there being no cholera in his own neighbourhood at the time.

CASE STUDY QUESTIONS

1. Concerning John Barnes, what are the modes of disease transmission and what are the epidemiologic terms by which they are identified?

2. How long is a fortnight?

3. In the examples or circumstances presented, what were the various modes of transmission stated or at least alluded to? Which were correct? Which were incorrect and why? What role did personal hygiene and sanitation (including food preparation and hand washing) play in the transmission of the disease and continuation of an outbreak?

4. Several instances of causal association were presented or alluded to in the examples presented in the case. List the various instances of association that can be identified from the examples or situations presented in the case. What role did social class, poverty, and housing arrangements play in association? What role did water play?

5. Describe the disease, cholera, as presented by John Snow and also describe cholera as it is known today.

6. What hypotheses were developed by John Snow about the cause (etiology), signs and symptoms, spread, and course of the cholera disease? How do the observations and hypotheses of Snow conform to modern understanding and knowledge of cholera?

7. What is different about those who develop cholera compared with those who do not?

8. What epidemiological phenomenon can be observed in the Locksbrook, near Bath, example?

B. CHOLERA AND THE BROAD STREET OUTBREAK

The most terrible outbreak of cholera which ever occurred in this kingdom, is probably that which took place in Broad Street, Golden Square, and the adjoining streets, a few weeks ago. Within 250 yards of the spot where Cambridge Street joins Broad Street, there were upwards of 500 fatal attacks of cholera in 10 days. The mortality in this limited area probably equals any that was ever caused in this country, even by the plague; and it was much more sudden, as the greater number of cases terminated in a few hours. The mortality would undoubtedly have been much greater had it not been for the flight of the population. Persons in furnished lodgings left first; then other lodgers went away, leaving their furniture to be sent for when they could meet with a place to put it in. Many houses were closed altogether, owing to the death of the proprietors, and in a great number of instances, the tradesmen who remained had sent away their families: so that in less than six days from the commencement of the outbreak, the most afflicted streets were deserted by more than three-quarters of their inhabitants.

There were a few cases of cholera in the neighbourhood of Broad Street, Golden Square, in the latter part of August and the so-called outbreak, which commenced in the night between the 31st of August and the 1st of September, was, as in similar instances, only a violent increase of the malady. As soon as I became acquainted with the situation and extent of this irruption of cholera, I suspected some contamination of the water of the much frequented street-pump in Broad Street, near the end of Cambridge Street. But on examining the water, on the evening of the 3rd of September, I found so little impurity in it of an organic nature, that I hesitated to come to a conclusion. Further inquiry, however, showed me that there was no other circumstance or agent common to the circumscribed locality in which this sudden increase of cholera occurred, and not extending beyond it, except the water of the above mentioned pump. I found, moreover, that the water varied, during the next two days, in the amount of organic impurity, visible to the naked eye, on close inspection, in the form of small white flocculent particles. I concluded that, at the commencement of the outbreak, it might possibly have been still more impure. I requested permission, therefore, to take a list, at the General Register Office, of the deaths from cholera, registered during the week ending 2nd of September, in the subdistricts of Golden Square, Berwick Street, and St. Ann's Soho, which was kindly granted. Eighty-nine deaths from cholera were registered during the week in the three subdistricts (see Figure I-1). Of these, only six occurred in the four first days of the week. Four occurred on Thursday, the 31st of August, and the remaining 79 on Friday and Saturday. I considered, therefore, that the outbreak commenced on the Thursday; and I made inquiry, in detail, respecting the 83 deaths registered as having taken place during the last 3 days of the week.

On proceeding to the spot, I found that nearly all the deaths had taken place within a short distance of the pump. There were only 10 deaths in houses situated decidedly nearer to another street pump. In five of these cases the families of the deceased persons informed me that they always went to the pump in Broad Street, as they preferred the water to that of the pump which was nearer. In three other cases, the deceased were children who went to school near the pump in Broad Street. Two of them were known to drink the water; and the parents of the third think it probable that their child did as well. The other two deaths, beyond the district which this pump supplies, represent only the amount of mortality from cholera that was occurring before the eruption took place (see Figure I-1, map of the Broad Street and Golden Square area of London).

With regard to the deaths occurring in the locality belonging to the pump, there were 61 instances in which I was informed that the deceased persons used to drink the pump-water from Broad Street, either constantly or occasionally. In six instances I could get no information, owing to the death or departure of everyone connected with the deceased individuals; and in six cases I was informed that the deceased persons did not drink the pump-water before their illness" (see Figure I-1, map of the Broad Street and Golden Square area of London).

The result of the inquiry then was that there had been no particular outbreak or increase of cholera, in this part of London, except among the persons who were in the habit of drinking water of the above mentioned pump-well.

I had an interview with the Board of Guardians of St. James's parish, on the evening of Thursday, 7th of September, and represented the above circumstances to them. In consequence of what I said, the handle of the pump was removed on the following day.

The additional facts that I have been able to ascertain are in accordance with those above related; and as regards the small number of those attacked, who were believed not to have drank the water from the Broad Street pump. It must be obvious that there are various ways in which the deceased persons may have taken it without the knowledge of their friends. The water was used for mixing with spirits in all the public houses around. It was used likewise at dining rooms and coffee shops. The keeper of a coffee shop in the neighbourhood which was frequented by mechanics, and where the pump water was supplied at dinner time, informed me (on 6th of September) that she was already aware of nine of her customers who were dead. The pump-water was also sold in various little shops, with a teaspoonful of effervescing powder in it, under the name of sherbet; and it may have been distributed in various other ways with which I am unacquainted. The pump was frequented much more than is usual, even for a London pump in a populous neighbourhood.

There are certain circumstances bearing on the subject of this outbreak of cholera which required to be mentioned. The workhouse in Poland Street is more than three-fourths surrounded by houses in which deaths from cholera occurred, yet out of 535 inmates only 5 died of cholera, the other deaths which took place being those of persons admitted after they were attacked. The workhouse has a pump-well on the premises, in addition to the supply from the Grand Junction Water Works, and the inmates never sent to the Broad Street pump for water. If the mortality in the workhouse had been equal to that in the streets immediately surrounding it on three sides, upwards of 100 persons would have died.

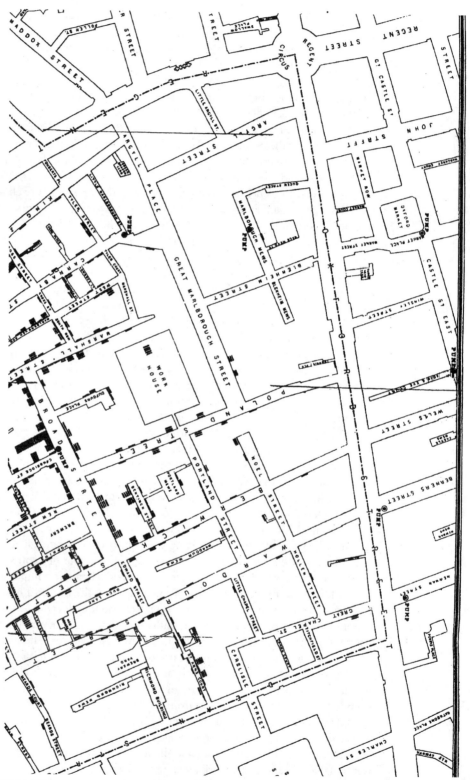

FIGURE I-1   Snow's dot map of the Broad Street and Golden Square area of London.

(continues)

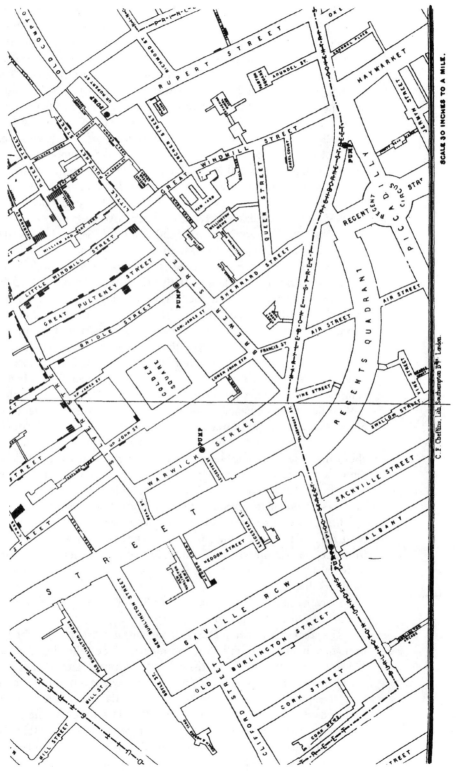

FIGURE I-1   Snow's dot map of the Broad Street and Golden Square area of London.
(continued)

There is a brewery in Broad Street, near to the pump, and on perceiving that no brewer's men were registered as having died of cholera, I called on Mr. Huggins, the proprietor. He informed me that there were above 70 workmen employed in the brewery, and that none of them had suffered from cholera, at least in a severe form, only two having been indisposed, and not that seriously, at the time the disease prevailed. The men are allowed a certain quantity of malt liquor, and Mr. Huggins believes they do not drink water at all; and he is quite certain that the workmen never obtained water from the pump in the street. There is a deep well in the brewery, in addition to the New River water.

A 28-year-old mother in the eighth month of pregnancy, went herself (although they were not usually water drinkers), on Sunday, 3rd September, to Broad Street pump for water. The family removed to Gravesend on the following day; and she was attacked with cholera on Tuesday morning at seven o'clock, and died of consecutive fever on 15th September, having been delivered. Two of her children drank also of the water, and were attacked on the same day as the mother, but recovered.

In the "Weekly Return of Births and Deaths" of September 9th, the following death is recorded as occurring in Hampstead district: At West End, on 2nd September, the widow of a percussion-cap maker, aged 59 years, diarrhoea two hours, cholera epidemic, 16 hours.

I was informed by this lady's son that she had not been in the neighbourhood of Broad Street for many months. A cart went from Broad Street to West End every day, and it was the custom to take out a large bottle of the water from the pump in Broad Street, as she preferred it. The water was taken on Thursday, 31st August, and she drank of it in the evening, and also on Friday. She was seized with cholera on the evening of the latter day, and died on Saturday, as the above quotation from the register shows. A niece, who was on a visit to this lady, also drank of the water; she returned to her residence, in a high and healthy part of Islington, was attacked with cholera, and died also. There was no cholera at the time, either at West End or in the neighborhood where the niece died. Besides these two persons, only one servant partook of the water at Hampstead West End, and she did not suffer, or at least not severely. There were many persons who drank the water from the Broad Street pump about the time of the outbreak, without being attacked with cholera; but this does not diminish the evidence respecting the influence of the water, for reasons that will be fully stated in another part of this work. (These activities are shown in Figure I-2, which presents the dates/chronological events of the Broad Street pump cholera epidemic.)

It is pretty certain that very few of the 56 attacks placed in the table to 31st August occurred till late in the evening of that day. The irruption was extremely sudden, as I learned from the medical men living in the midst of the district, and commenced in the night between the 31st August and 1st September (see Figure I-2). There was hardly any premonitory diarrhoea in the cases which occurred during the first three days of the outbreak; and I have been informed by several medical men, that very few of the cases which they attended on those days ended in recovery.

The greatest number of attacks in any one day occurred on the 1st day of September, immediately after the outbreak commenced. The following day the attacks fell from 143 to 116 and the day afterwards to 54. A glance at Figure I-2 and Figure I-3 shows that the fresh attacks and deaths continued to become less numerous every day after 1st and 2nd of September. On September 8th—the day when the handle of the pump was removed—there were 12 attacks; on the 9th, 11 attacks; on the 10th and 11th 5 attacks and on the 12th only 1; after this time, there were never more than 4 attacks on one day. During the decline of the epidemic the deaths were more numerous than the attacks (compare Figure I-2 with Figure I-3), owing to the decease of many persons who had lingered for several days in consecutive fever.

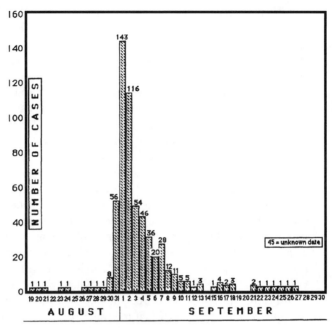

FIGURE I-2   The dates and numbers of attacks of cholera in the Broad Street pump cholera epidemic, London.

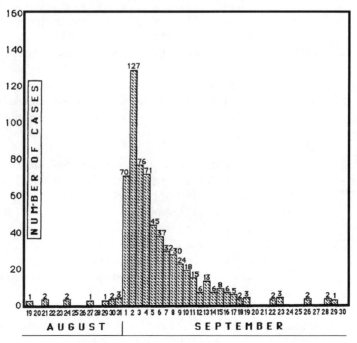

FIGURE I-3   The dates and numbers of deaths from cholera in the Broad Street pump cholera epidemic, London.

There is no doubt the mortality was much diminished by the flight of the population which commenced soon after the outbreak; but the attacks had so far diminished before the use of the water was stopped, that it is impossible to decide whether the well still contained the cholera poison in an active state or whether, from some cause, the water had become free from it. The pump-well has been opened, and I was informed by Mr. Farrell, the superintendent of the works, that there was no hole or crevice in the brickwork of the well, by which any impurity might entered. Consequently in this respect, the contamination of the water is not made out of the kind of physical evidence detailed in some of the instances previously related. I understand that the well is from 28 to 30 feet in depth, and goes through the gravel to the surface of the clay beneath. The sewer, which passes within a few yards of the well, is 22 feet below the surface. The water at the time of the cholera contained impurities of an organic nature, in the form of minute whitish flocculi visible on close inspection to the naked eye. Dr. Hassall, who was good enough to examine some of this water with a microscope, informed me that these particles had no organised structure, and he thought they probably resulted from decomposition of other matter. He found a great number of very minute oval animalcules in the water, which are of no importance except as an additional proof that the water contained organic matter on which they lived. The water also contained a large quantity of chlorides, indicating no doubt, the impure sources from which the spring is supplied. Mr. Eley, the percussion-cap manufacturer of 37 Broad Street, informed me that he had long noticed that the water became offensive, both to the smell and taste, after it had been kept about two days. This, as I noticed before, is the character of water contaminated with sewage. Another person had noticed for months that a film formed on the surface of the water when it had been kept a few hours.

I inquired of many persons whether they had observed any change in the character of the water, about the time of the outbreak of cholera, and was answered in the negative. I afterwards, however, met with the following important information on this point. Mr. Gould, the eminent ornithologist, lives near the pump in Broad Street, and was in the habit of drinking the water. He was out of town at the commencement of the outbreak of cholera, but came home on Saturday morning, the 2nd of September, and sent for some of the water almost immediately, when he was much surprised to find that it had an offensive smell, although perfectly transparent and fresh from the pump. He did not drink any of it. Mr. Gould's assistant, Mr. Prince, had his attention drawn to the water and perceived its offensive smell. A servant of Mr. Gould who drank the pump water daily, and drank a good deal of it on August 31st, was seized with cholera at an early hour on September 1st. She ultimately recovered.

Whether the impurities of the water were derived from the sewers, the drains, or the cesspools, of which latter there are a number in the neighbourhood, I cannot tell. I have been informed by an eminent engineer, that whilst a cesspool in a clay soil requires to be emptied every six or eight months, one sunk in the gravel will often go for 20 years without being emptied, owing to the soluble matters passing away into the land-springs by percolation. As there had been deaths from cholera just before the great outbreak not far from this pump-well, and in a situation elevated a few feet above it, the evacuations from the patients might, as a matter of course, be amongst the impurities finding their way into the water, and judging the matter by the light derived from other facts and considerations previously detailed, we must conclude that such was the case. A very important point in respect to this pump-well is that the water passed with almost everybody as being perfectly pure, and it did in fact contain a less quantity of impurity than the water of some other pumps in the same parish, which had no share in the propagation of cholera. We must conclude from this outbreak that the quantity of morbid matter which is sufficient to produce cholera is inconceivably small, and that the shallow pump-wells in a town cannot be looked on with too much suspicion, whatever their local reputation may be.

Whilst the presumed contamination of the water of the Broad Street pump with evacuations of cholera patients affords an exact explanation of the fearful outbreak of cholera in St. James's parish, there is no other circumstance which offers any explanation at all, whatever hypothesis of the nature and cause of the malady be adopted.

CASE STUDY QUESTIONS

1. What are the time factors and implications for this case? Explain the time lag from attacks in Figure I-2 to deaths in Figure I-3.

2. What are the place factors and implications for this case? Compare the workhouse with the brewery and the pub. Discuss migration and its effect on the epidemic. What place issues are important to this case?

3. What did the persons who got the disease do differently than those who did not get the disease (e.g., the inmates in the workhouse)?

4. From Figure I-2, what is the index case? What date is the beginning of the epidemic? What other time factors are discerned from this chart? How did Snow establish the time of onset?

5. What accurate observations were made about wells, cesspools, and ground water, the purity of the water, and its contamination? What inaccurate and misunderstood observations were made about the water, its flow, and its contamination?

6. What evidence did Snow use to establish the fact that a cholera epidemic was occurring? Did Snow clearly demonstrate the cause and source of the outbreak of cholera in the Golden Square area? Explain.

7. What were Snow's initial and basic hypotheses concerning the epidemic? What processes and procedures did Snow use to establish his hypotheses about the outbreak?

8. The obvious control measure applied was the removal of the handle from the Broad Street pump. What role did the removal of the pump handle play in the decline of the epidemic? Did the removal of the pump handle have an effect on the control of the epidemic? What other social and political roles did removing the handle from the pump play?

C. CHOLERA EPIDEMIC OF 1853 AND TWO LONDON WATER COMPANIES

London was without cholera from the latter part of 1849 to August 1853. During this interval an important change had taken place in the water supply of several of the south districts of London. The Lambeth Company removed their water works, in 1852, from opposite of Hungerford Market to Thames Ditton: thus, obtaining a supply of water quite free from the sewage of London. The districts supplied by the Lambeth Company are, however, also supplied, to a certain extent, by the Southwark and Vauxhall Company, the pipes of both companies going down every street, in the places where the supply is mixed (different houses getting water from one or the other water companies). Due to this intermixing of the sources of water, the effect of the alteration made by the Lambeth Co. on the progress of cholera was not so evident, to a cursory observer, as it would otherwise have been. It attracted the attention, however, of the Registrar-General, who published a table in the "Weekly Return of Births and Deaths," for the 26th of November 1853, of which the following is an abstract, containing as much as applies to the south districts of London.

It thus appears that the districts partially supplied with the improved water suffered much less than the others, although, in 1849, when the Lambeth Company obtained their new supply, these same districts suffered quite as much as those supplied entirely by the Southwark and Vauxhall Company. The Lambeth water extends to only a small portion of some of the districts necessarily included in the groups supplied by the companies and when the division is made in a little more detail, by taking subdistricts, the effect of the new water supply is shown to be greater than appears in Table I-1.

As the Registrar-General published a list of all the deaths from cholera which occurred in London in 1853, from the commencement of the epidemic in August to its conclusion in January, 1854, I have been able to add up the numbers which occurred in the various subdistricts on the south side of the Thames, to which the water supply of the Southwark and Vauxhall Company. and the Lambeth Companies, extends.

Although the facts shown in Table I-2 afford very strong evidence of the powerful influence which the drinking of water containing the sewage of the town exerts over the spread of cholera, when that disease is present, yet the question does not end here. For the intermixing of the water supply of the Southwark and Vauxhall Company with that of the Lambeth Company, over an extensive part of London, admitted of the subject being sifted in such a

TABLE I-1

Water Companies	Source of Supply	Population	Deaths by Cholera in 13 Weeks, Ending November 19	Deaths in 100,000 Inhabitants
Lambeth, Southwark & Vauxhall	Thames, at Thames Ditton and at Battersea	346,363	211	61
Southwark & Vauxhall	Thames, at Battersea	118,267	111	94
Southwark & Vauxhall, Kent	Thames, at Battersea; the Ravensbourne, in Kent, & ditches and wells	17,805	19	107

TABLE I-2

Subdistricts	Population in 1851	Deaths from Cholera—1853	Deaths by Cholera in Each 100,000 Living	Water Supply
First 12 subdistricts	167,654	192	114	Southwark & Vauxhall
Next 16 subdistricts	301,149	182	60	Both
Last 3 subdistricts	14,632	0	0	Lambeth Company

way as to yield the most incontrovertible proof on one side or the other. In the subdistricts enumerated in the above table as being supplied by both companies, the mixing of the supply is of the most intimate kind. The pipes of each company go down all the streets, and into nearly all the courts and alleys. A few houses are supplied by one company and a few by the other, according to the decision of the owner or occupier at that time when the water companies were in active competition. In many cases, a single house has a supply different from that on either side. Each company supplies both rich and poor, both large houses and small; there is no difference either in the condition or occupation of the persons receiving the waters of the different companies. Now, it must be evident that if the diminution of cholera, in the districts partly supplied with improved water, depended on this supply, the houses receiving it would be the houses enjoying the whole benefit of the diminution of the malady. The houses supplied with the water from Battersea Fields would suffer the same mortality as they would if the improved supply did not exist at all. As there is no difference whatever, either in the houses or the people receiving the supply of the two water companies, or in any of the physical conditions with which they are surrounded. It is obvious that no experiment could have been devised which would more thoroughly test the effect of water supply on the progress of cholera than this, which circumstances placed ready made before the observer.

The experiment, too, was on the grandest scale. No fewer than 300,000 people of both sexes, of every age and occupation, and of every rank and station, from gentlefolks down to the very poor, were divided into two groups without their choice, and in most cases, without their knowledge, one group being supplied with water containing the sewage of London, and amongst it, whatever might have come from the cholera patients, the other group having water quite free from such impurity.

To turn this grand experiment to account, all that was required was to learn the supply of water to each individual house where a fatal attack of cholera might occur. I regret that in the short days at the latter part of last year, I could not spare the time to make the inquiry; and indeed, I was not fully aware at that time, of the intimate mixture of the supply of the two water companies, and the consequently important nature of the desired inquiry.

Cholera Epidemic of 1854

When the cholera returned to London in July of the present year, however, I resolved to spare no exertion which might be necessary to ascertain the exact effect of the water supply on the progress of the epidemic, in the places where all the circumstances were so happily adapted for the inquiry. I was desirous of making the investigation myself, in order that I might have the most satisfactory proof of the truth or fallacy of the doctrine which I had been advocating for five years. I had no reason to doubt the correctness of the conclusions I had drawn from the great number of facts already in my possession, but I felt that the circumstance of the cholera poison passing down the sewers into a great river, and being distributed through miles of pipes. Yet producing its specific effects, was a fact of so startling a nature, and so vast importance to the community, that it could not be too rigidly examined, or established on too firm a basis.

I accordingly asked permission at the General Register Office to be supplied with the addresses of persons dying of cholera, in those districts where the supply of the two companies is intermingled in the manner I have stated above. Some of these addresses were published in the "Weekly Returns," and I was kindly permitted to take a copy of others. I commenced my inquiry about the middle of August with two subdistricts of Lambeth, called Kennington, first part and Kennington, second part. There were 44 deaths in these subdistricts down to the 12th of August, and I found that 38 of the houses in which these deaths occurred were supplied by the Southwark and Vauxhall Company, four houses were supplied by the Lambeth Company, and two had pump-wells on the premises and no supply from either of the companies.

As soon as I had ascertained these particulars, I communicated them to Dr. Farr, who was much struck with the result, and at his suggestion the registrars of all the South districts of London were requested to make a return of the water supply of the house in which the attack took place, in all cases of death from cholera. This order was to take place after the 26th August, and I resolved to carry my inquiry down to that date, so that the facts might be ascertained for the whole course of the epidemic.

The inquiry was necessarily attended with a good deal of trouble. There were very few instances in which I could at once get information I required. Even when the water rates are paid by the residents, they can seldom remember the name of the water company until they have looked for the receipt. In the case of working people who pay weekly rents, the rates are invariably paid by the landlord or his agent, who often live at a distance. The residents know nothing of the matter. It would, indeed, have been almost impossible for me to complete the inquiry, if I had not found that I could distinguish the water of the two companies with perfect certainty by a chemical test. The test I employed was founded on the great difference in the quantity of chloride of sodium (salt) contained in the two kinds of water, at the time I made the inquiry. On adding solution of nitrate of silver to a gallon of the water of the Lambeth Company, obtained at Thames Ditton, beyond the reach of the sewage of London, only 2.28 grains of chloride of silver were obtained, indicating the presence of .95 grains of chloride of sodium in the water. On treating the water of the Southwark and Vauxhall Company in the same manner, 91 grains of chloride silver were obtained, showing the presence of 37.9 grains of common salt per gallon. Indeed, the difference in appearance on adding nitrate of silver to the two kinds of water was so great, that they could be at once distinguished without any further trouble. Therefore when the resident could not find clear and conclusive evidence about the water company, I obtained some of the water in a small phial, wrote the address on the cover, when I could examine it after coming home. The mere appearance of the water generally afforded a very good indication of its source, especially if it was observed as it came in before it had entered the water-butt or cistern; and the time of its coming in also afforded some evidence of the kind of water, after I had ascertained the hours when the turn-cocks of both companies visited any street. These points were, however, not relied on, except as corroborating more decisive proof, such as the chemical test, or the company's receipt for the rates.

According to a return which was made to Parliament, the Southwark and Vauxhall Company supplied 40,046 houses from January 1st to December 31st 1853, and the Lambeth Company supplied 26,107 houses during the same period. Consequently, as 286 fatal attacks of cholera took place, in the first 4 weeks of the epidemic, in houses supplied by the former company, and only 14 in houses supplied by the latter, the proportion of fatal attacks to each 10,000 houses was as follows: Southwark and Vauxhall 71, Lambeth 5. The cholera was therefore 14 times as fatal at this period, amongst persons having the impure water of the Southwark and Vauxhall Company, as amongst those having the purer water from Thames Ditton.

As the epidemic advanced, the disproportion between the number of cases in houses supplied by the Southwark and Vauxhall Company and those supplied by the Lambeth Company, became not quite so great, although it continued very striking. Table I-3 is the proportion of deaths to 10,000 houses, during the first seven weeks of the epidemic, in the population supplied by the Southwark and Vauxhall Company, the Lambeth Company, and in the rest of London (see Figure I-4, map of River Thames area).

TABLE I-3

	Number of Houses	Deaths from Cholera	Deaths in Each 10,000 Houses
Southwark and Vauxhall Company	40,046	1,263	315
Lambeth Company	26,107	98	37
Rest of London	256,423	1,422	59

The mortality in the houses supplied by the Southwark and Vauxhall Company was therefore between eight and nine times as great as in the houses supplied by the Lambeth Company.

CASE STUDY QUESTIONS

1. Compare the person characteristics of the households that received their water from the different water suppliers.

2. Concerning the water supply system and structure from the two different water companies, explain the soundness of the research approach. Is this a descriptive or analytic epidemiologic research design?

3. What were some of the practical problems and barriers that Snow faced that slowed his inquiry of the cholera epidemic of 1854? How might this relate to modern-day epidemiological investigations?

4. "As the epidemic advanced, the disproportion between the number of cases in houses supplied by the Southwark and Vauxhall Company, and those supplied by the Lambeth Company, became not quite so great. . . ." From an epidemiological point of view, why was this so? Give detailed epidemiological reasoning and discussion addressing person, place, and time issues.

D. EPIDEMIOLOGIC ISSUES

John Snow's Answers to Objections

All the evidence proving the communication of cholera through the medium of water confirms that with which I set out, of its communication in the crowded habitations of the poor, in coal-mines and other places, by the hands getting soiled with evacuations of the patients, and by small quantities of these evacuations being swallowed with the food, as paint is swallowed by house painters of uncleanly habits, who contact lead-colic in this way.

There are one or two objections to the mode of communications of cholera that I am endeavouring to establish, which deserve to be noticed. Messrs. Pearse and Marston state, in their account of the cases of cholera treated at the Newcastle Dispensary in 1853, one of the dispensers drank by mistake rice water evacuation without any effect whatsoever. In rejoinder to this negative incident, it may be remarked, that several conditions may be requisite to the communication of cholera with which we are as yet unacquainted.

FIGURE I-4   Thames area of London (shaded parts are the areas served by two different water companies).

(continues)

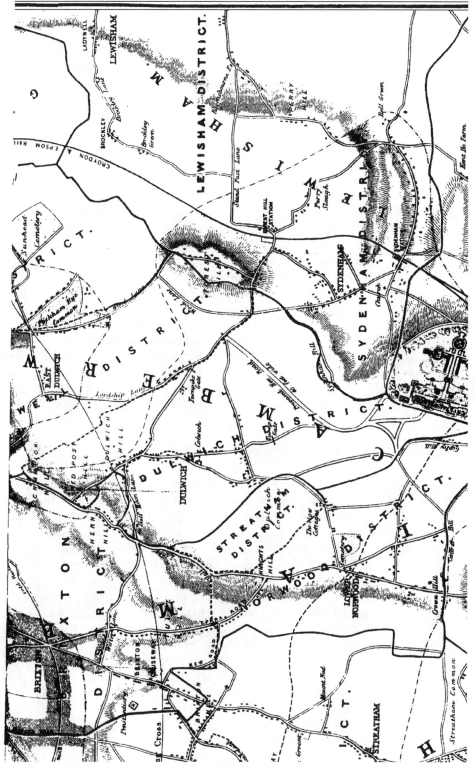

FIGURE I-4 Thames area of London (shaded parts are the areas served by two different water companies). *(continued)*

Certain conditions we know to be requisite to the communication of other diseases. Syphilis we know is only communicable in its primary state, and vaccine lymph must be removed at a particular time to produce its proper effects. In the incident above mentioned, the large quantity of the evacuation taken might even prevent its action. It must be remembered that the effects of a morbid poison are never due to what first enters the system, but to the crop of progeny produced from this during a period of reproduction, termed the period of incubation. If a whole sack of grain, or seed of any kind, were put into a hole in the ground, it is very doubtful whether any crop whatever would be produced.

An objection that has repeatedly been made to the propagation of cholera through the medium of water is that every person who drinks of the water ought to have the disease at once. This objection arises from mistaking the Department of Science to which the communication of cholera belongs, and looking on it as a question of chemistry, instead of one of natural history, as it undoubtedly is. It cannot be supposed that a morbid poison, which has the property, under suitable circumstances of reproducing its kind, should be capable of being diluted indefinitely in water, like a chemical salt. Therefore, it is not to be presumed that the cholera poison would be equally diffused through every particle of water. The eggs of the tapeworm must undoubtedly pass down the sewers into the Thames, but it by no means follows that everybody who drinks a glass of water should swallow one of the eggs. As regards to the morbid matter of cholera, many other circumstances, besides the quantity that is present in a river at different periods of the epidemic must influence the chances of it being swallowed, such as its remaining in a butt or other vessel till it is decomposed or devoured by animalcules, or it's merely settling to the bottom and remaining there. In the case of the pump-well in Broad Street, Golden Square, if the cholera poison was contained in the minute whitish flocculi visible on close inspection to the naked eye, some persons might drink of the water without taking any, as they soon settled to the bottom of the vessel.

Duration of Epidemic and Size of Population

There are certain circumstances connected with the history of cholera which admit of a satisfactory explanation according to the principles explained above, and consequently tend to confirm those principles. The first point I shall notice, the period of duration of the epidemic in different places, refers merely to the communicability of the disease, without regard to the mode of communication. The duration of cholera in a place is usually in direct proportion to the number of the population. The disease remains but two or three weeks in a village, and two or three months in a good-sized town. While in a great metropolis it often remains a whole year or longer. I find from an analysis which I made in 1849 of the valuable table of Dr. Wm. Merriman, of the cholera in England in 1832, that 52 places are enumerated in which the disease continued less than 50 days, and the average population of these places is 6,624. Forty-three places are likewise down in which the cholera lasted 50 days, but less than 100; the average population of these is 12,624. And there are, without including London, 33 places in which the epidemic continued 100 days and upwards, the average population of which is 38,123; if London be included, 34 places, with an average of 78,832.

There was a similar relation in 1849 between the duration of the cholera and the population of the places which it visited; a relation which points clearly to the propagation of the disease from patient to patient. For if each case were not connected with a previous one, but depended on some unknown atmospheric or telluric condition, there is no reason why the 20 cases which occur in a village should not be distributed over as long a period of time as twenty hundred cases which occur in a large town.

Effect of Season

Each time cholera has been introduced into England in the autumn, it has made but little progress and has lingered rather than flourished during the winter and spring. It increases gradually during the following summer, reaches its climax at the latter part of the summer, and declines somewhat rapidly as the cool days of autumn set in. On the contrary, in most parts of Scotland, cholera has each time run through its course in the winter immediately following its introduction. I have now to offer what I consider an explanation, to a great extent, of the peculiarities in the progress of cholera. The English people, as a general rule, do not drink much unboiled water, except in warm weather. They generally take tea, coffee, malt liquor, or some other artificial beverage at the meals, and do not require to drink between meals except when the weather is warm. In summer, however, a much greater quantity of drink is required, and it is more usual to drink water at that season than in cold weather. Consequently, whilst the cholera is chiefly confined in winter to the crowded families of the poor, and to the mining population, who . . . eat each other's excrement at all times, it gains access as summer advances to the population of the towns. There is a river which receives the sewers and supplies the drinking water at the same time; and, pump-wells and other limited supplies of water happen to be contaminated with the contents of the drains and cesspools. There is a greater opportunity for the disease to spread at a time when unboiled water is more freely used.

In Scotland, on the other hand, unboiled water is somewhat freely used at all times to mix with spirits; I am told that when two or three people enter a tavern in Scotland and ask for a gill of whiskey, a jug of water and tumbler-glasses are brought with it. Malt liquors are only consumed to a limited extent in Scotland, and when persons drink spirits without water as they often do, it occasions thirst and obliges them to drink water afterwards.

There may be other causes besides the above which tend to assist the propagation of cholera in warm weather, more than in cold weather. It is not unlikely that insects, especially the common house-flies, aid in spreading the disease. An ingenious friend of mine has informed me that, when infusion of quassia has been placed in the room for the purpose of poisoning flies, he has more than once perceived the taste of it on his bread and butter.

Alternative Theories

Dr. Farr discovered a remarkable coincidence between the mortality from cholera in the different districts of London in 1849, and the elevation of the ground. The connection being of an inverse kind, the higher districts suffering least, and the lowest suffering most from this malady. Dr. Farr was inclined to think that the level of the soil had some direct influence over the prevalence of cholera, but the fact of the most elevated towns in this kingdom, as Wolverhampton, Dowlais, Merthyr Tydvil, and Newcastle-upon-Tyne, having suffered excessively from this disease on several occasions, is opposed to this view, as is also the circumstance of Bethlehem Hospital, the Queen's Prison, Horsemonger Lane Gaol, and several other large buildings, which are supplied with water from deep wells on the premises, having nearly or altogether escaped cholera, though situated on a very low level, and surrounded by the disease. The fact of Brixton, at an elevation of 56 feet above Trinity high-water mark, having suffered a mortality of 55 in 10,000 whilst many districts on the north of the Thames, at less than half the elevation, did not suffer one-third as much, also points to the same conclusion.

I expressed the opinion in 1849, that the increased prevalence of cholera in the low-lying districts of London depended entirely on the greater contamination of the water in these districts, and the comparative immunity from this disease of the population receiving the improved water from Thames Ditton. During the epidemics of last year and the present, as shown in the previous pages, entirely confirms this view of the subject; for the great bulk of this population live in the lowest districts of the metropolis.

It is not necessary to oppose any other theories in order to establish the principles I am endeavouring to explain, for the field I have entered on was almost unoccupied. The best attempt at explaining the phenomena of cholera, which previously existed, was probably that which supposed that the disease was communicated by Effluvia given off from the patient into the surrounding air, and inhaled by others into the lungs. But this view required its advocates to draw very largely on what is called predisposition. In order to account for the numbers who approach near to the patient without being affected, whilst others acquire the disease without any near approach. It also failed entirely to account for the sudden and violent outbreaks of the disease, such as that which occurred in the neighbourhood of Golden Square.

Another view having a certain number of advocates is that cholera depends on an unknown something in the atmosphere which becomes localized, and has its effects increased by the gases given off from decomposing animal and vegetable matters. This hypothesis is, however, rendered impossible by the motion of the atmosphere, and even in the absence of wind, by the laws which govern the diffusion of aeriform bodies. Moreover, the connection between cholera and offensive Effluvia is by no means such as to indicate cause and effect. Even in London, as was before mentioned, many places where offensive effluvia are very abundant have been visited very lightly by cholera, whilst the comparatively open and clean districts of Kennington and Clapham have suffered severely. If inquiry were made, a far closer connection would be found to exist between offensive effluvia and the itch, than between these effluvia and cholera. Yet as the cause of itch is well-known, we are quite aware that this connection is not one of cause and effect.

Mr. John Lea of Cincinnati, has advanced what he calls a geological theory of cholera. He supposes that the cholera poison, which he believes to exist in the air about the sick, requires the existence of calcareous or magnesian salts in the drinking water to give it effect. This view is not consistent with what we know of cholera, but there are certain circumstances related by Mr. Lea which deserve attention. He says that in the western districts of the United States, the cholera passed round the arenacious, and spent its fury on the calcareous regions; and that it attacked with deadly effect those who used the calcareous water, while it passed by those who used sandstone or soft water. He gives many instances of towns suffering severely when river water was used, whilst others, having only soft spring water or rain water, escaped almost entirely. He states that there has been scarcely one case of cholera in families who used only rain water. The rivers, it is evident, might be contaminated with the evacuations, whilst it is equally evident that the rain water could not be so polluted. As regards sand and all sandstone formations, they are well known to have the effects of oxidizing and thus destroying organic matters; whilst the limestone might not have that effect, although I have no experience on that point. The connection which Mr. Lea has observed between cholera and the water is highly interesting, although it probably admits of a very different explanation from the one he has given.

CASE STUDY QUESTIONS

1. What did Snow observe regarding the association between city size and length of epidemic?

2. Snow suggested several reasons for the failure of contaminated water to produce disease in all who consume it. Why is it that not everyone became sick or died when they consumed the cholera causing bacterium *Vibrio cholerae*?

3. Which of Snow's observations about time and seasons and their effects on epidemics were correct and which were incorrect? Why?

4.   Several different theories and hypotheses have been presented. Which of these are consistent with known scientific and biomedical knowledge and common sense? Which of these are not? Why?

CASE STUDY II: WORKING THROUGH AN INFECTIOUS DISEASE OUTBREAK

Adapted from "A Multistate Outbreak of Cyclosporiasis." The investigators of this study were Barbara L. Herwaldt, MD, MPH; Marta-Louise Ackers, MD; Michael J. Beach, PhD; and the Cyclospora Working Group from the Centers for Disease Control and Prevention. The case study was prepared by Jeanette K. Stehr-Green, MD and reviewed by Charles Haddad; Robert Tauxe, MD, MPH; and Roderick C. Jones, MPH

This case study is based on investigations undertaken in 1996 and 1997 in the United States and abroad that were published in the *Morbidity and Mortality Weekly Report*, the *New England Journal of Medicine*, and the *Annals of Internal Medicine*.

PART I: BACKGROUND

On May 20, 1996, the following article appeared on the front page of the *Toronto Sun*:

Exotic Parasite Sickens Canadian Businessmen by Xavier Onnasis

TORONTO – Public health officials today confirmed that three Canadian businessmen, two from Toronto and one from Ottawa, were diagnosed with cyclosporiasis, a parasitic disease seen only in tropical countries and overseas travelers. The three men, who had recently traveled to the United States, became seriously ill with diarrhea over the weekend (May 16–18). One of the men was hospitalized at Princess Margaret Hospital when he collapsed due to severe dehydration.

NEWS FILE

CDC Cyclosporiasis Fact Sheet

Cyclospora cayetanensis (SIGH-clo-SPORE-uh KYE-uh-tuh-NEN-sis) is a parasite composed of one cell, too small to be seen without a microscope. The first known human cases of illness caused by *Cyclospora* infection (i.e., cyclosporiasis) were reported in 1979. Cases began being reported more often in the mid-1980s. In the last several years, outbreaks of cyclosporiasis have been reported in the United States and Canada.

How is *Cyclospora* spread?

Cyclospora is spread by people ingesting something, for example, water or food that was contaminated with infected stool. For example, outbreaks of cyclosporiasis have been linked to various types of fresh produce. *Cyclospora* needs time (days or weeks) after being passed in a bowel movement to become infectious. Therefore, it is unlikely that *Cyclospora* is passed directly from one person to another. It is unknown whether animals can be infected and pass infection to people.

(continues)

CDC Cyclosporiasis Fact Sheet (continued)

Who is at risk for infection?

People of all ages are at risk for infection. In the past, *Cyclospora* infection was usually found in people who lived or traveled in developing countries. However, people can be infected worldwide, including the United States.

What are the symptoms of infection?

Cyclospora infects the small intestine (bowel) and usually causes watery diarrhea, with frequent, sometimes explosive, bowel movements. Other symptoms can include loss of appetite, substantial loss of weight, bloating, increased gas, stomach cramps, nausea, vomiting, muscle aches, low-grade fever, and fatigue. Some people who are infected with *Cyclospora* do not have any symptoms.

How soon after infection will symptoms begin?

The time between becoming infected and becoming sick is usually about 1 week.

How long will symptoms last?

If not treated, the illness may last from a few days to a month or longer. Symptoms may seem to go away and then return one or more times (relapse).

What should I do if I think I may be infected?

See your healthcare provider.

How is *Cyclospora* infection diagnosed?

Your healthcare provider will ask you to submit stool specimens to see if you are infected. Because testing for *Cyclospora* infection can be difficult, you may be asked to submit several stool specimens over several days. Identification of this parasite in stool requires special laboratory tests that are not routinely done. Therefore, your healthcare provider should specifically request testing for *Cyclospora*. Your healthcare provider may have your stool checked for other organisms that can cause similar symptoms.

How is infection treated?

The recommended treatment for infection with *Cyclospora* is a combination of two antibiotics, trimethoprim-sulfamethoxazole, also known as Bactrim*, Septra*, or Cotrim*. People who have diarrhea should rest and drink plenty of fluids.

I am allergic to sulfa drugs; is there another drug I can take?

No alternative drugs have been identified yet for people who are unable to take sulfa drugs. See your healthcare provider for other treatment recommendations.

How is infection prevented?

Avoiding water or food that may be contaminated with stool may help prevent *Cyclospora* infection. People who have previously been infected with *Cyclospora* can become infected again.

Dr. Richard Schabas, Ontario's Chief Medical Officer, reported that cyclosporiasis was exceedingly rare in North America and that much was still unknown about this disease. Cyclosporiasis is caused by the microorganism *Cyclospora cayetanensis*. *Cyclospora* infects the small bowel and usually causes watery diarrhea, with frequent, sometimes explosive, bowel movements. Symptoms can include bloating, increased gas, stomach cramps, nausea, loss of appetite, and profound weight loss. The illness is diagnosed by examining stool specimens in the laboratory.

Dr. Schabas declined to identify a source of infection for the three businessmen but indicated that the parasite is transmitted through contaminated food or water but not by direct person-to-person spread. The time between exposure to the parasite and becoming sick is usually about 7 days.

Dr. Schabas reported that all three men had attended a meeting in Texas on May 9–10. He said Ontario Health Department staff would be investigating leads locally and in Texas.

CASE STUDY QUESTIONS

1. What is the incubation period for cyclosporiasis?

2. How will it be used in the investigation?

3. On what sources of infection should public health officials focus for the three cases of cyclosporiasis?

4. Is it possible that one of the men was the source of infection for the others?

5. Do you think that it is likely that the businessmen became infected with cyclosporiasis in Texas?

PART II: OUTBREAKS IN TEXAS

The chief medical officer of the Ontario Health Department notified the Texas Department of Health (TDH) about the *Cyclospora* infections in the three Canadian businessmen. The businessmen had attended a meeting at a private club in Houston, Texas on May 9–10.

A total of 28 people had attended the Houston business meeting. Participants came from three U.S. states and Canada. Meals served during the meeting were prepared at the restaurant operated by the private club. Rumors among restaurant staff suggested that other attendees at the meeting had also become ill.

TDH, the Houston Health & Human Services Department, and the Centers of Disease Control and Prevention (CDC) initiated an epidemiologic investigation to identify the source of the cyclosporiasis outbreak.

Because the outbreak appeared to affect a small, well-defined group of individuals (i.e., meeting attendees), investigators undertook a retrospective cohort study to investigate the source of the cyclosporiasis.

Investigators first surveyed people who attended the meeting to characterize the illness associated with the outbreak. (Twenty-seven of the 28 meeting attendees were interviewed.) All ill people experienced severe diarrhea and weight loss. In addition, 87% reported loss of appetite; 87% reported fatigue; 75% reported nausea; 75% reported stomach cramps; and 25% reported fever. Five ill people had stool specimens positive for *Cyclospora*.

Based on this information, investigators defined a case of cyclosporiasis for the cohort study as diarrhea of at least 3 days duration in someone who had attended the business meeting. Laboratory confirmation of *Cyclospora* infection was not required.

Of the 27 meeting attendees who were interviewed, 16 (59%) met the case definition for cyclosporiasis. Onsets of illness occurred from May 14 through May 19 (Figure I-5).

Investigators questioned both ill and well meeting attendees about travel history and food and water exposures during the meeting.

Restaurant management at the private club refused to take calls from investigators or cooperate with the investigation. As a result, a list of foods served at meals during the meeting was obtained from the meeting organizer. No menu items were confirmed by restaurant staff.

Twenty-four meeting attendees provided information on foods eaten during the meeting. (Four attendees, including three cases, did not provide the information.) Investigators examined the occurrence of illness among people who ate different food items.

Twelve (92%) of 13 attendees who ate the berry dessert became ill. Only one (9%) of 11 attendees who did not eat the berry dessert became ill. The relative risk for eating berries was 10.2 (p-value < 0.0001). No other exposures were associated with illness.

Case-patients reported that the berry dessert contained strawberries.

On June 4, before the first investigation had been completed, TDH was notified of another outbreak of cyclosporiasis involving physicians who attended a dinner on May 22 at a Houston, Texas restaurant. A second cohort study was undertaken. Nineteen attendees were interviewed, of which 10 met the case definition for cyclosporiasis (i.e., diarrhea of at least 3 days duration).

Attendees who ate dessert at the dinner were more likely to become ill than attendees who did not. Illness, however, was not associated with eating a particular type of dessert. No other exposures were associated with illness.

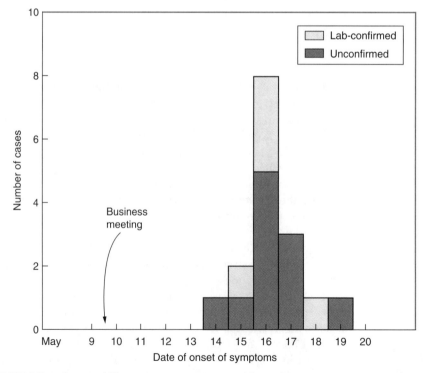

FIGURE I-5   Onset of illness among patients with cyclo-sporiasis, Houston business meeting, May 1996.

All desserts were garnished with either one fresh strawberry (for regular patrons) or with a strawberry, blackberry, and raspberry (for VIPs). Of the seven attendees who reported eating a strawberry, all seven became ill. Of the eight attendees who reported not eating a strawberry, only one became ill (relative risk = 8.0, p-value = 0.001). (Note: four attendees, including two cases, could not recall whether they had eaten a strawberry and were excluded from this analysis.)

Based on the results of the two cohort studies, investigators hypothesized that strawberries were the source of the cyclosporiasis outbreaks in Houston.

TDH staff examined invoices and other records from the two restaurants involved in the Texas cyclosporiasis outbreaks. The strawberries consumed at both the May 9–10 business meeting and the May 22 physician dinner were grown in California. The individual producers/distributors of the strawberries, however, were not determined.

On May 31, TDH released a public health advisory about the presumed link between the consumption of California strawberries and the cyclosporiasis outbreak. The State Health Officer advised consumers to wash strawberries "very carefully" before eating them, and recommended that people with compromised immune systems (e.g., people with HIV infection, patients on cancer chemotherapy) avoid them entirely.

A few days later, Ontario's chief medical officer reported on an outbreak of cyclosporiasis in the Metro Toronto area affecting 40 people. Ontario public health officials believed California strawberries were also the source of the Toronto outbreak. A public health advisory, similar to the one from Texas, was issued.

Concurrent with the announcements from Texas and Ontario, CDC encouraged physicians from across the United States to report cases of cyclosporiasis to their local or state health department so that the source of the *Cyclospora* could be investigated further.

CASE STUDY QUESTIONS

1. What are the two most common types of epidemiologic studies used to investigate the source of an outbreak (or other public health problem)?

2. Which would you use to investigate the source of the cyclosporiasis outbreak in Texas? Why?

3. Why would you question people who did not become ill about possible sources of infection with *Cyclospora*?

4. In your own words, interpret the results of the cohort study.

5. What problems in study design or execution, should you consider when reviewing the results of this study (or any epidemiologic study)?

6. What additional studies might confirm (or refute) the hypothesis that strawberries were the source of the cyclosporiasis outbreaks?

7. You are writing a newspaper article about the cyclosporiasis outbreaks in Texas and Ontario. It is thought that the cyclosporiasis problem is ongoing. Four people are available for interview: the CDC expert on cyclosporiasis, one of the Canadian businessmen who became ill following the meeting in Houston, the owner of the private club in Houston where the first outbreak occurred, and the attorney for the California Strawberry Grower's Association. Your deadline is looming. You have time to ask each of these people only three questions. What would you ask them?

PART III: OUTBREAKS IN OTHER STATES

Despite recommendations by health departments in Texas and Ontario to wash strawberries carefully before eating them, cases of cyclosporiasis continued to occur nationwide. By the end of June, over 800 laboratory-confirmed *Cyclospora* infections were reported to CDC from 20 states, the District of Columbia, and two Canadian provinces (Figure I-6).

Discrepancies began to appear in the link between California strawberries and the *Cyclospora* infections. Investigations undertaken by the New York City Health Department and South Carolina Department of Health and Environmental Control pointed toward raspberries as the source of the cyclosporiasis outbreaks in their jurisdictions.

In late June, the New Jersey Department of Health and Senior Services (NJDHSS) initiated an epidemiologic investigation to identify the source of infection among cyclosporiasis cases in New Jersey residents. The cases to be included in the New Jersey study were not linked together by a common event and did not occur in a well-defined group of people.

To assess possible risk factors for infection among the cases of cyclosporiasis in New Jersey, NJDHSS conducted a case-control study. In contrast to the Texas investigation, a case of cyclosporiasis for this study was defined as a patient with laboratory-confirmed *Cyclospora* infection and a history of diarrhea.

For the New Jersey case-control study, cases were identified by reviewing laboratory records from all clinical laboratories in the state. Forty-two cases were identified. Two controls were identified for each case through telephone calls to randomly selected households in the community. To be eligible for the study, controls could not have had loose stools during the previous 30 days.

Investigators interviewed 30 case-patients and 60 controls by telephone using a standardized questionnaire that asked about possible exposures (including consumption of 17 fruits and 15 vegetables, water and soil exposures, and animal contact) during the period of interest.

FIGURE I-6   States with laboratory-confirmed Cyclospora infections (shaded), May and June, 1996.

TABLE I-4

Ate Raspberries	Case	Control	TOTAL
Yes	21	4	25
No	9	56	65
Total	30	60	90

Case-patients and controls were similar with respect to age, sex, and level of education. Twenty-one (70%) of 30 case-patients and four (7%) of 60 controls had eaten raspberries. The odds ratio for eating raspberries was 32.7 (p-value < 0.000001). No other exposures (including strawberries) were associated with illness.

Studies from other states and Canada supported the results from New Jersey, New York City, and South Carolina. A total of 725 cases of cyclosporiasis associated with 55 different events (e.g., wedding receptions, parties, buffets) were investigated. The only exposure consistently associated with cyclosporiasis was the consumption of raspberries.

Raspberries were served at 54 of the 55 events and were the only berries served at 11 events. (Reexamination of the events associated with the initial outbreaks in Texas and Ontario indicated that raspberries were included among the implicated berry items served at those events.) The median attack rate for cyclosporiasis among persons who ate items that contained raspberries at the different events was 93%. Furthermore, for 27 of the 41 events for which adequate data were available, the associations between the consumption of raspberries and cyclosporiasis were statistically significant (p-value < 0.05).

The origin (i.e., producer) and mode of contamination of the raspberries served at the events were unknown. Due to the large number of raspberry producers at the time of the outbreaks (both domestic and international), public health officials could not recall the implicated raspberries or remove them from the marketplace. Traceback investigations were planned.

CASE STUDY QUESTIONS

1. Would you undertake a case-control or a cohort study to investigate the source of the cyclosporiasis cases in New Jersey? Why?

2. How might you identify cases of cyclosporiasis for the case-control study? Who would you use as controls?

3. In your own words, interpret the results of the New Jersey case-control study.

4. Would you alert the public of this possible public health threat? Defend your answer.

PART IV: TRACEBACK AND ENVIRONMENTAL INVESTIGATIONS

To identify the sources of raspberries served at the 54 events linked to outbreaks of cyclosporiasis, CDC, the U.S. Food and Drug Administration (FDA), and health departments from the affected states obtained information on the place and dates of purchase of the implicated raspberries. Distributors and importers of the raspberries were identified through invoices and shipping documents. Airway bill numbers and importation documents (e.g., Custom's forms), supplied by importers, were used to identify overseas shipments and exporters.

By the third week of July, investigators had documented the source of the raspberries for 29 of the 54 cyclosporiasis-associated events. For 21 of these events, the raspberries definitely came from Guatemala. For 8 events, the raspberries could have originated there. No commonalities were found in the U.S. ports of entry for the implicated raspberries.

During the outbreak period, raspberries had been imported from a number of countries. Based on monthly data from the U.S. Department of Agriculture, Guatemalan raspberries represented 4–20% of fresh raspberries (domestic and imported) shipped within the United States in April–June of 1996.

At the time of the investigation, seven Guatemalan exporters, of which A and B were the largest, shipped raspberries to the United States. The raspberries for 25 of the 29 events were traced to only one Guatemalan exporter per event:

- 18 of 25 (72%) to Exporter A
- 5 (20%) to Exporter B
- 1 (4%) to Exporter C
- 1 (4%) to Exporter D

Using exporter records, the raspberries were traced back to the farm where they were grown. Because exporters typically combined raspberries from multiple farms in a shipment, investigators could identify only a group of contributing farms (an average of 10 farms with a range of 2–30) rather than one source farm per event. More than 50 farms could have contributed to implicated shipments of raspberries.

To investigate how raspberries were grown and handled in Guatemala, CDC and FDA investigators visited Exporters A, B, C, and D and the seven most commonly implicated raspberry producing farms (six supplying Exporter A and one supplying Exporter B).

The six most commonly implicated farms supplying Exporter A were in the same region of Guatemala. All six began harvesting for the first time in 1996 and often had raspberries in the same shipment. Five of the farms obtained agricultural water from wells. These wells varied in construction, depth, and quality. Two of the five farms also stored well water in reservoirs constructed of concrete blocks and covered with concrete. The sixth farm used river water. The farm that supplied raspberries to Exporter B was 25 km from the closest of the six farms that sold raspberries to Exporter A. That farm used well water, which was stored in a mesh-covered, plastic-lined, man-made reservoir.

At all seven farms, ground-level drip irrigation was used (primarily during the dry season) to avoid direct contact between raspberries and water. Agricultural water was also used to mix insecticides and fungicides that were sprayed directly onto raspberries, sometimes as late as the day they were harvested. At all farms, the raspberries were picked and sorted by hand, packed in plastic containers, and flown to the United States within 36 hours of picking.

Agricultural water at the seven farms (and on Guatemalan raspberry farms, in general) was filtered to remove debris but not microbes. Testing of agricultural water samples from the seven farms indicated at least intermittent contamination with bacteria commonly found in sewage and human waste (i.e., "coliforms" such as *Escherichia coli*). No *Cyclospora* were found.

No *Cyclospora* were found in samples of Guatemalan raspberries obtained from the farms during the traceback investigation.

Investigators hypothesized that the raspberries became contaminated through spraying with insecticides and fungicides that had been mixed with contaminated water from improperly constructed or maintained wells near deep pit latrines or seepage pits. The wells may have been particularly vulnerable to contamination during the rainy season (e.g., from surface-water runoff), when the 1996 outbreak occurred. Once contaminated, the raspberries remained contaminated until eaten because they were too fragile and covered with crevices to be washed thoroughly.

By July 18, 1996, CDC and FDA declared that raspberries from Guatemala were the likely source of the *Cyclospora* outbreak.

CASE STUDY QUESTIONS

1. Does the traceback information support raspberries as the source of the cyclosporiasis outbreak?

2. Given what you know about the transmission of Cyclosporiasis, on what cultivation or harvesting practices would you focus in the investigation of the raspberry producing farms?

3. Cyclospora were not found in any Guatemalan raspberries or water samples. If the Guatemalan raspberries were the source of the cyclosporiasis outbreaks, list plausible explanations for this finding.

PART V: CONTROL AND PREVENTION MEASURES

Although the government of Guatemala was skeptical of study findings and suspicious of potential trade barriers, Guatemalan raspberry growers and exporters and the Guatemalan Berries Commission (a growers' organization) collaborated with CDC and FDA to decrease the risk of contamination of Guatemalan raspberries during growth, harvest, and packaging.

The Guatemalan raspberry growers voluntarily improved employee hygiene, sanitation, and water quality. They implemented systems to monitor the production of the raspberries so that potential points of contamination could be identified and addressed (i.e., *Hazard Analysis and Critical Control Point* systems). The Guatemalan Berries Commission established a farm classification system (with only farms in the best class permitted to export) in an attempt to minimize the exportation of *Cyclospora*-contaminated raspberries to the United States.

During the fall and winter of 1996, no outbreaks of cyclosporiasis in the United States were linked to Guatemalan raspberries. In the spring of 1997, however, another multistate outbreak occurred. By the end of May, more than a thousand new cases of cyclosporiasis had been reported from 18 states and two provinces in Canada. Consumption of raspberries was strongly associated with the outbreaks and the preponderance of the traceback data implicated Guatemala as the source of the raspberries, suggesting either some farms did not fully implement the control measures or the contamination was associated with a source against which these measures were not directed.

In the face of warnings by U.S. public health authorities on the danger of eating Guatemalan raspberries, the government of Guatemala and the Guatemalan Berries Commission voluntarily suspended exports of fresh raspberries to the United States on May 30, 1997. The interruption of exportation caused large economic loss for the producers, especially small and medium-sized producers.

CDC and FDA continued to work with the government of Guatemala and the Berries Commission to determine when the safety of Guatemalan raspberries could be assured and exports could resume. The exportation of raspberries resumed in mid-June; however, U.S. public health authorities continued to warn of the dangers of eating Guatemalan raspberries.

In December 1997, amid objections from the Guatemalan government, the FDA announced that it was blocking imports of raspberries from Guatemala for 1998. Before this time, the FDA rarely denied imports without physical evidence, and this ban was based only on epidemiological evidence about past outbreaks and FDA observations on current raspberry production practices. Congressional representatives and supporters of free trade railed about protectionism and questioned the science behind the decision since *Cyclospora* had not been identified on any raspberries from Guatemala.

The U.S. ban on importation of Guatemalan raspberries became effective on March 15, 1998 and continued through August 15, the normal Guatemalan raspberry exporting season. With the ban in place, outbreaks of cyclosporiasis did not occur in 1998 in the United States.

Canadian officials decided not to block the importation of Guatemalan raspberries in 1998. In May and June, a multicluster outbreak of cyclosporiasis occurred in Ontario involving over 300 people. Investigations linked the outbreak to raspberries from Guatemala.

Beginning in the spring of 1999, the United States allowed entry of raspberries from farms that complied with a detailed program of food safety practices and successfully passed Guatemalan government inspections and FDA audits. That spring, there were several cyclosporiasis outbreaks in the United States and Canada; however, Guatemalan raspberries were not implicated as a source for any. In 2000, two outbreaks of cyclosporiasis were linked to raspberries traced to one Guatemalan farm. That farm discontinued exportation of raspberries.

As of June 2004, no further outbreaks of cyclosporiasis have been associated with Guatemalan raspberries. However, only three of the original 85 Guatemalan raspberry growers continue to export raspberries.

CASE STUDY QUESTIONS

1. What specific measures would you suggest to decrease the likelihood of contamination of raspberries from the Guatemalan farms?

2. Do you believe that the raspberries were the source of the multistate outbreaks of cyclosporiasis? Which of the criteria for causality (i.e., strength of association, biological plausibility, consistency with other studies, exposure precedes disease, and dose-response effect) have been satisfied in the linkage between raspberries and cyclosporiasis? How would you convince others on the validity of these findings?

CASE STUDY III: COMMON-SOURCE OUTBREAK OF WATERBORNE SHIGELLOSIS AT A PUBLIC SCHOOL

Adapted from Baine WB, Herron CA, Bridson K, et al. Waterborne shigellosis at a public school. *Am J Epidemiol.* 1975;101(4). By permission of Oxford University Press.

Shigellosis is an intestinal tract infection that is caused by *shigella* organisms. It has four major subgroups of pathogens. The source of infection is excreta of infected individuals or carriers. Shigellosis is usually spread by ingesting food or water contaminated by fecal matter. In addition, flies are a vehicle/vector of contamination, and fomites have also been implicated in the spread of the disease. Epidemics are often found in crowded populations living with poor sanitation and are a source of bacillary dysentery found in children living in endemic areas.

The incubation period is 1–4 days. In younger children, the onset can be sudden. Symptoms include fever, irritability, drowsiness, anorexia, nausea or vomiting, diarrhea, and abdominal cramps. Within 3 days, blood, pus, and mucus appear in the stools. The number of stools increases rapidly to about 20 or more a day—severe diarrhea. In the laboratory findings of sample specimens, the *shigella* bacteria are found in the stools. The white blood count is often reduced at the onset and goes up to 13,000. Plasma carbon dioxide is usually low, showing a response from the diarrhea-induced metabolic acidosis. Prevention and control are performed by preventing the spread of contaminated food, water, and flies through sanitation, which may include hand washing before food handling, soaking contaminated clothes in soap and water until boiled, isolating patients and carriers, and stools (source: Berkow R. [Editor-in-Chief]. *The Merck Manual*, 14th ed. Rahway, NJ: Merck and Co.; 1982).

CASE OF COMMON-SOURCE OUTBREAK OF WATERBORNE SHIGELLOSIS AT A PUBLIC SCHOOL

In November 1972, a public school in Stockport, Iowa (population 334) experienced an outbreak of gastrointestinal illness. Of the 269 pupils who attended the public school, 194 (72%) were affected, and 14 of the 23 faculty and staff (61%) were also affected. Laboratory and clinical exams showed that the etiological agent was *Shigella sonnei*. Of the 698 student contacts with members of infected households, 97 (14%) also developed diarrhea. Secondary cases also occurred in 3 of the 32 people living in households owned by members of the school's staff.

Shigellosis is most often spread from person to person; common-source outbreaks also occur and must be considered in any epidemiological investigation. Water and food should both be considered as modes of transmission.

In the second week of November 1972, a physician in Fairfield, Iowa contacted the Iowa State Department of Health by telephone to report a case of shigellosis infection in a young woman who was from Stockport, Iowa. The young woman/patient lived in an apartment across the street from a county middle school. The young woman shared a common water supply with the school. Several guests who attended a gathering at her apartment on November 4th had experienced gastrointestinal illness.

It was discovered that there were high levels of absenteeism at the school because of gastrointestinal illnesses. Similar illnesses were also reported among members of the local high school boys basketball team. A high school boys basketball team from the neighboring town also reported gastrointestinal illnesses. The two teams had played a scrimmage at the middle school's gym on November 15th.

Van Buren County, with a population of 8,643 according to the 1970 census, is a small county located in southeastern Iowa near the Missouri border. This is a rural county, with 37% of the mostly white residents living on farms. Almost 22% of the residents lived below the federal poverty level, and 755, or 22%, of the 3,399 households in the county lacked in some or all standard plumbing facilities. All sixth, seventh, and eighth grade students in the Van Buren School District attended the middle school in Stockport. In November of 1972, the enrollment at the middle school was 289 and 25 teachers and staff.

The layout of the school is an important epidemiological consideration in this case of a common-source outbreak. The school included a main building and an annex that housed the gym and several classrooms. The gym was used for physical education classes, and high school teams in the region used it for practice games. Included in the buildings of the school was an old garage, across the street from the school and east of the main building. The building was used as a shop for industrial arts classes. The eastern-most third of the shop building was the private residence/apartment of the young woman mentioned previously here, who also developed shigellosis (see building map in Figure I-7).

The water supplies for the middle school, the gym, the shop, and the private apartment all came from wells on the school grounds (see Figure I-7). Environmental studies were conducted to test the school's water supply. Microbiological testing of the wells was done. The wells' construction was studied. Water flow and cross connection tests were carried out on the water supply and the sewage system of the middle school and nearby buildings, with fluorescent dye studies.

The family and guests at the gathering in the young woman's apartment on November 4th were questioned about gastrointestinal illness. The students and faculty and staff of Van Buren on November 30th were interviewed and surveyed. Interviews included questions addressing customary daily consumption of the water at the school, including the fountain in

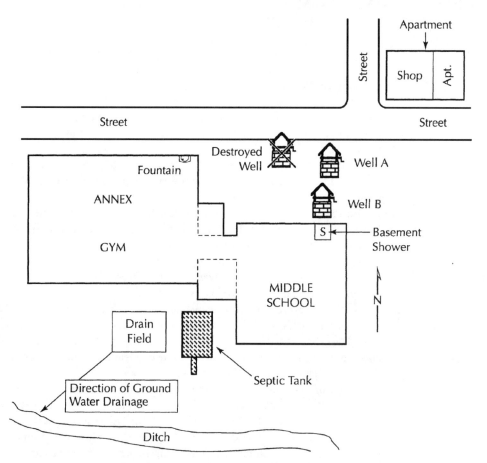

FIGURE I-7　Van Buren County Middle School building map.

TABLE I-5   Shigellosis Secondary Attack Rates

General Secondary Attack Rates

Questionnaires Returned by	Total Number	Number Returned	Attack Rate %
Families of students	245	169	—
Household contacts	698	97	—
Asymptomatic students	37	5	—

the gym, illnesses, date of onset, symptoms, school absenteeism, physician visits, and hospitalizations. The two basketball teams were also surveyed and asked for an estimated amount of water they consumed at the scrimmage on November 15th. Most symptomatic and some asymptomatic cases submitted rectal swabs for bacteriological culture using standard laboratory procedures.

To investigate secondary transmission of the disease, questionnaires were distributed to families of students, faculty and staff, and all of the basketball players in order to determine incidence (see Table I-5). A secondary case was defined as diarrhea beginning between November 10th and December 4th, among household members (or contacts) of students, faculty and staff, and ball players. Rectal swabs for culture were obtained from available family members of the groups. Those groups consisted of 10 families chosen at random from the first 40 families to report an apparent secondary infection, three families out of five of the students in which there were apparent secondary cases without illness in the pupil and three families of faculty and staff with apparent secondary infection. Cultures were obtained from the index case, an eighth grader and two of the participants in the apartment gathering; all were positive. In the questionnaire, gastrointestinal illness was defined by symptoms of the disease: nausea, vomiting, bowel movements that were loose, frequent, or bloody, cramps, or tenesmus. Questionnaires were retrieved from 93% of the students and 92% of the faculty and staff; 194 students and 14 faculty and staff reported gastrointestinal illness in November.

Of the families of the middle school faculty and staff, three returned questionnaires on secondary attacks at 88% or 22 out of 25. Three of 32 household contacts had diarrhea, for a secondary attack rate of 9%.

Rectal swabs were positive for *Shigella sonnei* for 96 out of 123 symptomatic staff members and three of six faculty and staff. Rectal swabs from 13 of 23 asymptomatic students were positive for *Shigella sonnei*, as shown by cultures.

Eleven of 12 of those at the apartment gathering developed gastrointestinal illness within 4 days of November 4th. Several students and faculty and staff reported illness in the first week of November (see Tables I-6 and I-7). The first peak in the epidemiology curve occurred on Friday, November 10th, with an average of 12 cases a day for the next 5 days. Forty-five cases occurred on Thursday, November 16th. The outbreak then tapered off rapidly. Male and female attack rates were about the same and grade level showed no difference in attack rates. No clear trends in water consumption and illness attack rates were seen (see Table I-8). From November 16th to 19th, 7 of 18 high school basketball players on the visiting team and 10 local high school ball players developed diarrhea. Four of 25 rectal swabs were positive; all four were symptomatic. Diarrhea attack rates among basketball players were directly correlated to water consumption at the school's fountain in the gym.

The main water sources for the school complex were from the water wells in the schoolyard north of the school house. When the shigellosis outbreak occurred, water well A was

TABLE I-6   Date of Onset of Gastrointestinal Illness, Van Buren Middle School, Stockport, Iowa, 1972

Date of Illness Onset	Number of Cases	Date of Illness Onset	Number of Cases
November		November	
2	1	16	45
3	1	17	30
4	2	18	7
5	2	19	1
6	1	20	6
7	2	21	3
8	2	22	0
9	3	23	1
10	19	24	3
11	11	25	0
12	12	26	0
13	9	27	2
14	6	28	2
15	14	29	0
		30	1

TABLE I-7   Date of Onset of Secondary Attack Rates of Gastrointestinal Illness in Faculty and Staff, Van Buren Middle School, Stockport, Iowa, 1972

Date of Illness Onset	Number of Cases	Date of Illness Onset	Number of Cases
November		November	
7	1	22	8
8	0	23	2
9	0	24	3
10	1	25	13
11	3	26	4
12	1	27	4
13	4	28	2
14	0	29	9
15	0	30	8
16	5	December	
17	2	1	3
18	5	2	0
19	3	3	5
20	7	4	0
21	3	5	0

TABLE I-8   Attack Rates of Gastrointestinal Illness by Usual Amount of Water Consumed Daily at the Middle School

Estimated Amount of Water Drunk	Students		Faculty	
	No. Ill/Total	Attack Rate (%)	No. Ill/Total	Attack Rate (%)
0 glasses	4/11		3/3	
1 glass	14/19		2/5	
2 glasses	24/36		1/2	
3 glasses	38/57		1/3	
4 glasses	43/56		2/2	
5 glasses	28/38		0/1	
6+ glasses	43/50		3/3	

in use. Well A supplied water to the shop and to the apartment. Even though shigellosis is rarely transmitted by water, at the time of the outbreak, the water supply for the school was suspected. The suspect well was not chlorinated at the time of the outbreak, and because it was suspected, it was super-chlorinated on November 17th. The Stockport municipal water company had a water system under construction, and special priority was given to connecting the school to the new water supply. The water was connected on November 21st. One of the three wells was destroyed in the process of hooking up the municipal water system. Investigation of the two remaining wells showed that they were shallow bored well cases with ceramic pipe segments, having joints that were not watertight. The outflow pipes of the submersible pump pierced the lining of the well below ground level. The hole allowed seepage of ground water into the well. Well B, which was closer to the school, was not in use at the time of the shigellosis epidemic; however, when the pump in one well was turned on, it lowered the water table in both wells. Well B was located in a slight depression on the surface of the earth and could be contaminated by surface water as well as ground water sources. Indeed, debris was found floating in well B. On the opposite side of the school from the wells was a septic tank that fed a drain field that emptied into a ditch southeast of the school. Attempts with dye were made to show cross-contamination. All efforts failed to reveal any cross-contamination by the appearance of the dye in the school well-water supply. Other attempts to show cross-contamination involved using fluorescent dye in the toilet in the apartment located in the shop building across the street from the school, as well as the school yard storm drains; all failed, with one exception, to show cross-contamination of the well water.

Showers for the students were adjacent to the gym, but visiting teams used the shower located in the utility room on the basement floor of the school. The shower was installed only shortly before the shigellosis outbreak. The shower drained down into a bed of gravel under the basement floor. Hooking the shower to the sewer system had been considered unnecessary, as it drained well. Dye studies flushed down the drain of the shower, located only a few feet from the wells, showed up in the well water within 3 hours. This same shower was used by three faculty members during the time period of the outbreak. Two of the three faculty members were among those documented with shigellosis on November 13th, and the other was identified with the disease on November 15th and had febrile diarrhea. On November 16th, water samples were taken from the tap in the boys restroom. They revealed a total coliform count of 125 per 100 ml. A second water sample was obtained from the school on November 17th before the super-chlorination of the supply. The second water sample revealed a coliform (a number of 16+), and *Shigella sonnei* was recovered from a 1600-mL sample.

CASE STUDY QUESTIONS

1. The common-source and first cases of the outbreak were from the well water. Explain how the secondary cases of shigellosis probably occurred. Identify the probable mode(s) of transmission in the secondary cases.

2. Was the basketball team from the neighboring community a primary transmission case or secondary? Why? What role did the neighboring basketball team play in secondary cases?

3. In this instance, a secondary case was defined as diarrhea beginning between November 10th and December 4th. Why are these dates chosen for this purpose and how do they help determine what a secondary case is in this investigation?

4. Much concern was given to whether a case was symptomatic or asymptomatic. What is the significance of these two states of illness, and why is this important in this particular disease?

5. Calculate the secondary attack rates for Table I-5.

6. What problems or shortcomings did you see in this study? What would be necessary to overcome such shortcomings?

7. What type of sewage system in the school complex was used and how effective was it? What role did it play in disease transmission?

8. What was the attack rate for the students in November?

9. What caused the epidemic to taper off after November 16th?

10. What was the attack rate for the faculty and staff in November?

11. What is the sensitivity for the symptomatic students, faculty, and staff using the rectal swab test?

12. What is the specificity for the asymptomatic students, faculty, and staff using the rectal swab test?

13. Develop and construct a bar chart of the epidemiological curve for the shigellosis outbreak using the data in Table I-7. Identify the index case and date, and explain who the index case was. What date was the water chlorinated? What did chlorinating the water do to the epidemic curve?

14. Develop a bar graph of the secondary attack rate for the shigellosis epidemic using the data from Table I-7. Explain why the secondary epidemic curve is different than that of the primary epidemic curve.

15. Calculate the attack rates for the various amounts of water consumption as it relates to illness onset, found in Table I-8.

16. What are your observations as to the source of the contamination of the well water with *Shigella sonnei* that caused the outbreak? Give two possible sources for the pathogen getting into the water supply: (1) direct and (2) indirect.

17. What are the control and prevention measures needed for this case and shigellosis?

CASE STUDY IV: RETROSPECTIVE ANALYSIS OF OCCUPATION AND ALCOHOL-RELATED MORTALITY

Adapted from Brooks SD, Harford TC. Occupation and alcohol-related causes of death. *Drug and Alcohol Dependence.* **1992;29(3):245–251.**

The liver is the organ that is most often seriously damaged by heavy drinking. Even moderate drinking damages body tissues, which are quickly mended. The more and the longer a person drinks, the more lasting and serious the effects are on the body. The connection between heavy drinking of alcohol and heart disease has been known for over 100 years. For years, malnutrition was pointed to as the cause of the physiological damage. Malnutrition is still a major factor, but now it is known that alcohol does damage the body tissues and organs directly. One area of the heart affected is the mitochondria (energy-producing cells in the cardiac muscle), which results in alcoholic cardiomyopathy (heart muscle degeneration). Without energy, the heart's pumping action fails over time. Arrhythmia of the heart is also seen in heavy drinkers because alcohol disrupts the natural heart rhythms. High blood pressure and cancer are also caused by heavy drinking. Cancer of the liver, larynx, nasopharynx, and esophagus are seen more frequently in heavy drinkers. Ulcerative lesions are seen in the small intestine. The pancreas is vulnerable to alcohol abuse, resulting in pancreatitis. Alcoholic myopathy or muscle weakness is also seen at serious clinical levels in heavy drinkers (source: Schlaadt RG. *Wellness: Alcohol Use and Abuse. Guilford*, CT: Dushkin Publishing Group; 1992).

CASE OF OCCUPATION AND ALCOHOL-RELATED CAUSES OF DEATH, CALIFORNIA

Are alcohol-related causes of death associated with similar occupational groups? Is heavy drinking associated with different occupations? Most studies have focused on cirrhosis of the liver deaths related to alcohol drinking. Several research studies found that cirrhosis mortality is associated with the following occupations: bartenders, waiters, cooks, longshoremen, seamen, salesmen, wholesale and retail trades, entertainment and recreation workers, truck drivers, garage proprietors, and personal service workers. The studies also found that cirrhosis is highest in lower status jobs—blue collar workers. Also, jobs with high exposure to alcohol use and/or consumption have high drinking levels. Only 8–12% of heavy drinkers die from cirrhosis.

Many other alcohol- and occupation-associated conditions occur but do not get as much focus as cirrhosis of the liver. The more common conditions in which alcohol is implicated as a cause of death include digestive tract cancers, pancreatic disorders, certain cardiovascular diseases, and accidents and injuries.

WHICH ALCOHOL-RELATED CAUSES OF DEATH ARE ASSOCIATED WITH WHICH OCCUPATIONS?

The California Occupational Mortality Study (COMS) data set was employed to assess mortality data for the years 1979–1981. A 2% sample of employed persons from the 1980 census of California was used. The COMS contains the occupation of each decedent (person who died).

This study, like any occupation-based study, is restricted to the work life span as far as age of subjects is concerned. This study used ages 16–64 years. Certain persons, because of their source of work, were excluded as subjects: homemakers, retired persons, students, disabled, military personnel, etc. Only mainstream-type employment was used in this study to establish occupations at risk for heavy alcohol drinking. Military/nonworkers/unknowns were also analyzed. Underlying causes of death was used from the ICD-9-CM (see Chapter 2, "Historic Developments in Epidemiology") for cirrhosis, digestive organ cancers, injuries, suicides, and homicides (see Table I-9).

Thirteen occupational groups were identified, using the Census Bureau's 1980 Alphabetical Index of Industries and Occupations. Age-adjusted mortality rates per 100,000 were calculated for each of the 13 occupational groups (see Table I-10). The numerator used was the number of occupation-specific deaths in each category of underlying cause of death in California from 1979 to 1981. The denominator for each occupational group was from the 20% sample of the 1980 Census of California used in the COMS, which was 173,438 deaths in California from 1979 to 1981.

Males and whites had the highest percent for each of the causes of death. Older age groups had the largest percentage of deaths for cirrhosis and digestive organ cancers. Younger age groups had higher percentages in injuries, suicides, and homicides. Military/nonworkers/unknowns had a pattern similar to that of workers, except for females, who had higher death rates related to alcohol than the female workers. The age-adjusted mortality rate for all other causes of death per 100,000 for the State of California was 238.77.

Research findings show that individuals in certain occupations drink alcohol more heavily than persons in other occupations. Factors that contribute to heavy alcohol consumption include opportunity to drink, time, location, availability of alcohol, work group or social group that has drinking as a custom, job stress, time pressures, and work rotations. Additionally, heavy drinking may occur in jobs that have low job visibility, high turnover, little supervision, and minimal job qualifications. High stress on the job, low accountability, and easy access to alcohol are factors that may contribute to heavy and destructive use of alcohol. From an epidemiologic research point of view, all of these factors may serve as confounding variables to occupation and alcohol abuse research.

Certain occupations may allow drinking on the job, as supervisors know little about it. Some people work in the field independently, away from the work site, and other jobs may actually encourage drinking on the job or at lunch. Many studies fail to differentiate between drinking on the job, job-related alcohol consumption, and nonjob-related drinking. It is suspected that workplace drinking risks are low as compared with after-hours or lunchtime drinking. Other factors that may contribute to heavy drinking regardless of the work setting are the biological/physiological, psychological, familial, social class, religious influences, peer pressure, and other nonwork-related factors and variables.

TABLE I-9   Alcohol Related Deaths in California, 1979–1981

Cirrhosis	5.5%
Digestive organ cancers	5.7%
Injuries	13.7%
Suicide and homicide	
All other causes	64.9%

TABLE I-10   Age-Adjusted Mortality Rates for Occupational Groups and Cause of Death Per 100,000

Occupational Group	Cirrhosis Mortality Rate	Digestive Cancer Mortality Rate	Injury Mortality Rate	Suicide Mortality Rate	Homicide Mortality Rate
Executive, administrative, and managerial	13.6	25.1	32.47	13.72	10.02
Professional specialty	15.24	23.76	35.79	20.39	7.97
Technicians and related support areas	19.82	26.47	54.86	22.99	8.83
Sales	16.72	26.17	35.58	17.43	12.62
Administrative support, including clerical	13.5	20.07	23.97	12.15	7.58
Private household service	15.07	22.46	16.79	7.14	17.14
Protective service	36.17	40.46	61.02	33.95	38.13
Other service	29.66	26.46	47.97	18.28	25.6
Farming, forestry, and fishing	41.23	28.56	158.87	23.75	56.68
Precision production, craft and repair	33.98	34.69	91.29	32.78	30.51
Machine operators and assemblers	25.67	27.76	55.66	19.23	26.49
Transportation and material moving	39.58	38.45	112.84	28.41	34.64
Handlers, equipment, cleaners, and laborers	75.97	52.26	129.14	39.33	77.11
State of California	20.07	21.01	50.44	18.71	18.64

CASE STUDY QUESTIONS

1. What occupations are most vulnerable to acquiring cirrhosis of the liver from heavy drinking? List several of the occupations identified by research studies that are more vulnerable to alcohol-induced, cirrhosis-related deaths and that have the highest mortality rates.

2. Other than cirrhosis, what major diseases have causation implications of heavy alcohol use? List several.

3. Discuss why this study was restricted to ages 16–64 years. Discuss the research design implications of the age span restrictions in occupational studies.

4. In this study, which occupations had the highest digestive organ cancer mortality rate?

5. In this study, which occupations had the highest injury mortality rate?

6. In this study, which occupations had the highest suicide mortality rate?

7. In this study, which occupations had the highest homicide mortality rate?

8. Two occupational groups repeatedly exceeded the state average for alcohol-related deaths. Which two were they? Why? Provide an explanation.

9. What figures were used for the numerator of this study? What figures were used for the denominator? Was the use of the numerator and denominator appropriate for age-adjusted rates?

10. Develop and show the formula for the age-adjusted digestive cancer mortality rates for the top four at-risk occupations for this disease found in Table I-10.

11. What are the possible confounding variables for research in occupations and heavy drinking that lead to fatal diseases? Identify and explain which factors are confounding variables and how they serve as confounding variables.

12. Develop and construct a web of causation along with appropriate decision trees for occupational group-related alcohol deaths.

CASE STUDY V: RETROSPECTIVE COHORT STUDY OF THE ASSOCIATION OF CONGENITAL MALFORMATIONS AND HAZARDOUS WASTE

Adapted from Geschwind SA, Stolwijk JAJ, Bracken M, et al. Risk of congenital malformations associated with proximity to hazardous waste sites. *Am J Epidemiol.* **1992;135(11):1197–1207.**

Congenital anomalies or malformations are difficult to pinpoint as to cause. Some congenital malformation causes are understood, many are not. Causes may be single isolated cases, whereas others are multiple and varied. Some malformations at birth are inherited, and some are sporadic in their manifestation. Congenital defects are sometimes apparent and sometimes hidden, taking years to become obvious. About 10% of neonatal deaths are caused by congenital malformations. A major malformation is apparent at birth in 3–4% of newborns. By the fifth year, up to 7.5% of all children manifest a congenital malformation. The incidence of certain congenital malformations varies with the defect (cleft lip occurs at the rate of 1 per 1,000 births in the United States) and the geographic area (spina bifida is about 4 per 1,000 births in Ireland and 2 per 1,000 in the United States). Interfamily marriage and culture practices can contribute to congenital malformations, as can perinatal problems and environmental exposures. Genetic factors are responsible for many congenital anomalies and syndromes. On the other hand, multiple factors are often involved in causing congenital malformations. Drugs taken while pregnant, infectious agents, and irradiation are known to cause birth defects. Chemicals in the environment as well as exposure to hazardous materials and waste in the environment, and exposure to radiation in the worksite or environment have also been implicated (source: Berkow R, ed. *The Merck Manual*, 14th ed. Rahway, NJ: Merck and Company; 1982).

CASE ON CONGENITAL MALFORMATIONS ASSOCIATED WITH PROXIMITY TO HAZARDOUS WASTE SITES

Much concern has been expressed by the general public and public health scientists alike over the effects of exposure to environmental pollutants and how they have increased in modern society. It remains unclear whether chronic exposure to toxic chemicals in the environment is present in sufficiently high doses to produce adverse medical effects in humans. Inadvertent exposure to hazardous waste such as Love Canal (a neighborhood in Niagara Falls, New York, located in the white collar LaSalle section of the city) has increased concern about any adverse effects the exposure might have on reproductive health. It also remains unclear whether individuals who live near toxic chemical waste sites receive doses in sufficient amounts to pose a health hazard, especially to reproductive functions. One concern is that many toxic chemicals present in toxic waste landfills and hazardous waste sites are cytotoxic. That is, they affect cells, tissues, and organs at specific stages of development and inhibit or interfere with normal growth, especially in embryo and fetus growth, as well as developmental stages.

High rates of birth defects have been reported in children exposed to mercury, solvents, and certain toxic chemicals. Community-based studies have been conducted based on reports of clustering of disease around hazardous waste sites. Rarely have congenital defects in infants born to exposed parents been well documented.

This study uses a four-tiered hypothesis approach in order to evaluate the relationship between birth defects and the potential exposure to toxic waste sites: (1) Does residential proximity to a waste site when pregnant increase risk of bearing a child with a defect? (2) Do defects of specific organ systems correlate with proximity to a toxic waste site? (3) Were defects associated with off-site migration of chemicals? How does the epidemiologist clarify whether this increases potential health risks? (4) Have chemical types associated with certain organ system defects been evaluated?

Pesticides have been associated with oral cleft (lips or palate), or musculoskeletal defects, heavy metals with nervous system defects, solvents with nervous system defects or digestive system defects, and plastics with chromosomal anomalies. Do the later phases corroborate the initial findings? Finally, this study's aim was to test the association of environmental and health data bases and geographic mapping methods for ascertaining environmental exposures.

Databases of the New York State Department of Health were used: Congenital Malformation Registry (CMR) and the Hazardous Waste Site Inspection Program. The two programs were linked together for analysis of the four tiers of hypotheses. The Congenital Malformation Registry includes reports of all congenital malformations for the state's hospitals, medical facilities, and private physicians diagnosed in children up to 2 years of age. In the state of New York, 917 waste sites in 62 counties were available. New York City sites as well as several other sites were eliminated due to inadequate information. For final study, 590 waste sites in 20 counties were used. Epidemiological map study approaches included each site being assigned a longitude and latitude using EPA and New York Department of Environmental Conservation records (see Figure I-8, Map of New York State with Waste Sites Identified as Small Black Triangles).

A total of 34,411 cases of malformations were recorded in the CMR for the years 1983–1985 and 1984–1986 birth cohorts. Any cases that were unusual were eliminated: multiple births, redundant cases, CDC exclusions list to avoid misclassification of malformations, census mapping coordinates missing, addresses incomplete, and locations without a census tract. The study was based on 12,442 congenital malformations and 9,313 cases. One case could have more than one defect.

Eight categories of malformations were used from ICD-9-CM (see "Historic Developments in Epidemiology" in Chapter 2) that have been reported by research studies in the literature as being associated with exposures to chemicals or toxic substances (see Table I-11). Each individual exposure was unknown, and each could have had multiple exposures to a complex mix of chemicals. All cases were put under one general analysis. Each case was then placed in one of the eight categories and analyzed. More than one defect was found present in each case.

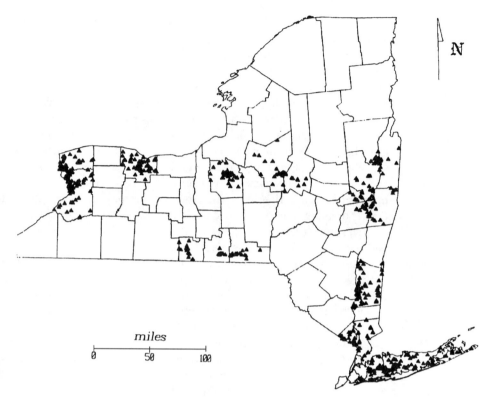

FIGURE I-8 Map of New York state with waste sites identified.

Controls were selected from birth certificate records: 17,802 or 12% of the 506,183 live births for 1983–1984 in the State of New York. Cross-checks were made to assure no congenital malformations were included in the control. Confounding variables were excluded from both cases and controls, and the information included the following:

- Maternal age
- Parity
- Race
- Birth weight of the child
- Education
- Length of gestation
- Address and county of residence
- Gender of the child
- Any pregnancy complications

Addresses for cases and controls were each assigned a latitude and longitude. Coordinates were taken from census blocks based on Standard Metropolitan Statistical Areas, and Postal Carrier Route centroids (a centroid is the center point of the Postal Carrier Route boundary); zip code centroids were used. A sample of 500 addresses was taken at random as a test of the mapping methods. The mapping procedure was accurate within 200 feet, 80% of the time.

TABLE I-11   Eight Categories of Malformations ICD-9-CM

Oral cleft defects

Musculoskeletal defects

Nervous system defects

Integument defects

Digestive system defects

Chromosomal anomalies

Syndromes

Remaining defects without category

Data from ICD-9, *International Classification of Diseases*, 9th revision

Hazardous waste sites were assessed using the Hazardous Waste Site Inspection Program (HWSIP), which estimates the likelihood of human exposure. Possible exposure routes into humans include inhalation, ingestion, and dermal contact, which occur by environmental exposure transmission from air, groundwater, surface, water, or soil. This study included all residents within a 1-mile radius of the waste site edge. Still, absolute risk of exposure was uncertain. Assessment was based on a set of scores of a variety of factors: chemical exposure, a probability score chance of contaminant transport from the site, a target factor score that accounts for the population and distance from the waste site, and a weighting factor score giving each exposure a level of relative importance. The assessment excluded the total population portion of the target factor score to give greater weight to the residents surrounding the waste sites.

Five general categories of chemicals grouped by chemical properties were developed. The five categories were as follows:

1. Pesticides
2. Metals
3. Solvents
4. Plastics
5. Unknown

An exposure risk index was completed for each case. The index accounted for distance and hazard ranking score within a 1-mile radius of the birth residence. Waste sites based on evidence of off-site migration of contaminants were separated from nonmigration sites.

All case and control coordinates were matched to hazardous waste sites by a matching program. Distance and direction from the hazardous waste site for the residence of each case or control living within a 1-mile radius of the edge of the site were considered potentially exposed. Risk was determined by association between mothers' (maternal) proximity to waste sites and presence of congenital anomalies (birth defects).

A 12% increased risk for birth defects associated with maternal proximity to toxic waste sites was found. Odds ratios were used to assess the association between proximity to toxic sites and maternal residence. An odds ratio score above 1.01 shows a positive association, and the higher the score the stronger the association. Table I-12 presents the odds ratios for

TABLE I-12   Odds Ratios for All Congenital Malformations and for Specific Malformations in Infants with Residential Proximity to Selected Hazardous Waste Sites, New York State, 1983–1984

Number of Cases[‡]	Congenital Malformation(s)	Odds Ratio[†§]
9,313	All malformations combined	1.12**
421	Nervous system	1.29*
2,730	Musculoskeletal system	1.16**
1,370	Integument system	1.32**
232	Oral clefts	1.15
429	Digestive system	0.89
245	Chromosomal anomalies	1.18
575	Syndromes[‖]	1.15
4,003	Other (data too limited to infer associations with chemical exposure)	1.01

* $p < 0.05$; ** $p < 0.01$.
[†] Data from ICD-9, *International Classification of Diseases*, 9th revision
[‡] The numbers of cases for the individual organ systems do not add up to the total number of cases for all defects combined because individuals may have had more than one defect.
[§] Adjusted for maternal age, race, education, complications during pregnancy, parity, population density for county of residence, and gender of the child, by logistic regression.
[‖] Syndromes include all defects coded as "syndrome" in the New York State Congenital Malformations Registry, or any child with four or more defects.

congenital malformations with residential proximity to selected hazardous waste sites. Table I-13 presents odds ratios and exposure risk index for all congenital malformations and for three specific body systems affected by documented chemical leaks at hazardous waste sites. Table I-14 presents odds ratios for congenital malformations for all infants with specific malformations and residential proximity to selected toxic waste sites and chemical groups.

CASE STUDY QUESTIONS

1. What are controls in a research study and how are they used? How are controls used in this study?

2. What are confounding variables? How might they affect a research study? What are the problems and limitations of confounding variables in this study?

3. From Table I-12, which malformations had the highest odds ratio? Which malformations had the lowest odds ratio? What is the significance of each?

4. From Table I-13, which body systems were at the most risk of exposure to chemical leaks? What is the significance of such a determination?

5. From Table I-14, which three combinations of "chemicals associated with congenital malformation" were the highest? Which chemicals were linked to and associated with malformations according to the odds ratio? Explain the assessment and the meaning of Table I-14.

TABLE I-13   Odds Ratios and Exposure Risk Index for All Congenital Malformations and for Three Specific Body Systems Affected by Documented Chemical Leaks at Hazardous Waste Sites

Exposure	All Malformations Combined (740–759)	Nervous System (740–742)	Musculoskeletal System (754–756)	Integument System (757)
Exposure Risk Index				
No exposure risk	1.00	1.00	1.00	1.00
Low exposure risk	1.09** (1.04–1.15)§	1.27* (1.03–1.57)	1.09 (1.00–1.18)	1.22** (1.08–1.38)
High exposure risk	1.63** (1.34–1.99)	1.48 (0.69–3.16)	1.75** (1.31–2.34)	2.63** (1.90–3.67)
Chemical Leaks				
Not exposed	1.00	1.00	1.00	1.00
Exposed, but no leaks found at site	1.08* (1.02–1.15)	1.35* (1.06–1.72)	1.08 (0.98–1.20)	1.22* (1.06–1.40)
Exposed, and leaks found at site	1.17** (1.08–1.27)	1.16 (0.87–1.55)	1.16* (1.03–1.31)	1.38** (1.17–1.62)

* $p < 0.05$; ** $p < 0.01$.
† Adjusted for maternal age, race, education, complications during pregnancy, parity, population density for county of residence, and gender of the child, by logistic regression.
‡ Data from ICD-9, *International Classification of Diseases*, 9th revision
§ Numbers in parentheses, 95% confidence interval.

TABLE I-14   Odds Ratios for Congenital Malformations for All Infants with Specific Malformation Codes† and Residential Proximity to Selected Toxic Waste Sites Containing Associated Chemical Groups: New York State, 1983–1984

Chemical and Associated Malformation (Reference)	OR‡§	CI‡§
Pesticides/oral clefts (13–15)	1.27	0.84–1.92
Pesticides/musculoskeletal system (16, 17)	1.20*	1.05–1.38
Metals/nervous system (18–20)	1.34*	1.07–1.67
Solvents/nervous system (21–23)	1.24*	1.01–1.54
Solvents/digestive system (24, 25)	0.91	0.73–1.13
Plastics/chromosomal anomalies (26–29)	1.46*	1.01–2.11

* $p < 0.05$.
† Previously related to chemical exposures in the literature.
‡ Data from ICD-9, *International Classification of Diseases*, 9th revision; OR = odds ratio; CI = confidence interval.
§ Adjusted for maternal age, race, education, complications during pregnancy, parity, population density for county of residence, and gender of the child, by logistic regression.

6. From the three tables and the final assessments, what are the findings of this study with regards to exposure and proximity to hazardous waste sites and congenital malformation? Explain your answer.

7. What prevention and control programs can be implemented to reduce congenital malformations from environmental exposure?

8. (Optional) Pick one form of congenital malformation, develop and construct a web of causation for the disorder.

CASE STUDY VI: HISTORY AND EPIDEMIOLOGY OF POLIO EPIDEMICS

Infantile paralysis, as it was first known, was a most difficult disease to understand. For centuries, people became crippled and no one seemed to know why, for the paralysis was not associated with a disease. It was observed that mostly young people were paralyzed, and often the legs, back, and the arms were affected. Historically, this crippling disease was called infantile paralysis, anterior infantile, or a variety of other names. The term infantile paralysis became popular because this disease was thought to be confined to children, although it had been observed in almost all ages.

Infantile paralysis was studied by physicians/epidemiologists, and the disease was eventually called poliomyelitis. The real breakthrough came when the infection was finally discovered to be a biphasic disease. The first phase of the disease has symptoms that are similar to those of the flu or a bad cold. It is the second phase in which the crippling occurs, as the virus moves from the blood into the central nervous system (CNS), where nerve cells in the spinal cord and/or brain are destroyed and replaced with fatty deposits. The devastating result is the irreversible loss of control of the lungs, limbs, or other musculoskeletal structures. Atrophy of muscles is caused by loss of neuromotor control of the affected muscles. The sensory nerves are mostly unaffected and feelings remained. The part of the spinal cord affected by the virus is the anterior horn of the gray matter of the spinal cord.

When the two levels of the disease were finally discovered, the door was opened for more effective epidemiological investigations. The disease, when running its course, did not always progress into the second phase in all people, and those fortunate enough to experience only the first phase usually escaped paralysis.

The virus, when finally discovered, was thought to be harbored only in the upper respiratory tract, but was later found throughout the body, with its highest concentrations in the gastrointestinal tract.

The Salk killed-virus vaccine, injected intramuscularly, has a moderate level of effectiveness. Albert Sabin developed a more effective vaccine in the form of a weakened live vaccine taken orally in sugar cubes, thus targeting the higher concentration of the virus in the gastrointestinal tract with the Sabin vaccine being the more effective of the two. From the use of these vaccines, millions of people have escaped the crippling paralysis caused by the poliovirus.

BRIEF REVIEW OF POLIOMYELITIS AS IT IS KNOWN TODAY

The virus responsible for polio is very small compared with many other viruses, such as the smallpox and chickenpox viruses. The poliovirus falls in the Enterovirus class of the Picornavirus group. It exists in three immunological virus types: Type I is the most likely to cause paralysis and lead to identifiable epidemics due to the observed paralysis. The infection is highly contagious and is spread via fecal–oral and pharyngeal–oropharyngeal (mouth–throat) routes.

The main source of spread is from the lesser types, labeled as inapparent infections, which occur widely in unimmunized populations. The risk of direct person-to-person transmission comes from the fact that inapparent cases are mistaken for colds or influenza. The apparent or overt outbreak is rare except during epidemics, and even then the ratio of inapparent infections to clinical cases exceeds 100:1. Epidemics are most likely to occur when basic public health measures such as hand washing are neglected and when food sanitation is poor, and through interpersonal transmission by those who think the infection is only the flu. Where sanitation and hygiene are poor, virus circulation can be extensive. When the infection and immunity are acquired in the first few years of life, cases are sporadic and confined largely to children less than 5 years old, and epidemics do not occur. Polio is a seasonal disease occurring in the summer and fall in temperate climates. Tropical climates and underdeveloped countries experience epidemics year round. Unvaccinated populations are at high risk of epidemics.[1]

The virus multiplies in the pharynx and intestinal tract and is present in the blood, throat, and feces during the incubation period. After onset, it can be recovered from the throat for about 1–2 weeks and from the feces for 3–6 weeks or longer. CNS involvement lasts several days, disappearing as antibodies develop. Factors predisposing patients to serious neurologic involvement include increasing age, recent inoculations (recent DTP is commonly found connected to the onset of poliomyelitis), recent tonsillectomy, pregnancy, and physical exertion concurrent with onset of the CNS phase. In older cases, the first phase might not be accounted for, or the minor illness might go unobserved.[1]

Rotary International has been working toward a goal of eradicating poliomyelitis from the earth by eventually vaccinating every person in all countries, especially those countries that are underdeveloped. There is also much effort being put forth to eliminate the polio vaccination in the United States, much as was done with smallpox. The eventuality is that all people are to be protected by vaccination, and the source of the pathogen will be eliminated. Some segments of the public health community are warning that to halt polio immunizations is a bad move and have issued similar warnings about smallpox vaccinations being stopped. In regard to smallpox, the world now has a massive population of susceptibles who could become infected with smallpox—all of those born after 1978. Much media attention has been focused on the few rare cases of children acquiring polio from the immunization process. However, the media fails to point out the millions of persons who could be crippled today from paralytic polio if it were not for the polio vaccine.

CASE STUDY QUESTIONS

1. Identify the pathogenic agent and the group to which infantile paralysis belongs.

2. Identify locations in the body where this pathogen is harbored.

3. Identify the mode of disease transmission and related epidemiological implications.

FIRST POLIO EPIDEMIOLOGIC STUDIES

Some early observations of Dr. Ivar Wickman in several cities in Sweden (Umea, Goteborg, Stockholm, and Tingsryd [population 3,000, 200 miles southwest of Stockholm] in the summer of 1905) follow.

A minor case of the illness, with its outward symptoms (as opposed to the inward progress of the disease as it occurs when it has moved into the CNS) is what Swedish epidemiologist Ivar Wickman observed in the early part of the 20th century. These observations were crucial to detecting and understanding the total picture and scope of the disease and its two-phase process.[2]

Names of Polio

Wickman referred to this child-crippling disease as Heine-Medin Disease in 1907. Jacob Von Heine (1799–1878) was a German orthopedist and Wickman's teacher. Oskar Medin (1847–1927) was a Swedish pediatrician. Wickman named polio after Heine and Medin because they had both conducted the earliest adequate study of the disease.[2]

Other names of polio included "debility of the lower extremities," a term used in the late 1700s, "morning paralysis," used in the mid 1800s, and "Heine-Medin Disease," used in the late 1800s and early 1900s. "Infantile paralysis" was the most commonly used term in the early 1900s, and "anterior poliomyelites" was later derived from the work of Dr. John Shaw. With the discovery of the virus, it was called "poliomyelites" and shortened to "polio."[2–5]

The mid-1800s through the early 1900s was an amazing era for advances in microbiology, epidemiology, medicine, and science, all of which in some way contributed to the understanding of polio and the discovery of the poliovirus.[2] Wickman and Medin believed that Bergenholtz deserved credit for observing the first polio epidemic, a minor outbreak of 13 cases in the small village of Umea in northern Sweden in 1881.[2–5]

Age Issues: Not Just a Child's Disease

As early as 1858, Q. Vogt described the first case of poliomyelitis in an adult (Switzerland). Polio was previously thought to occur only in children. In the 1905 epidemic, it was reported by Wickman that 45% of those stricken with the disease were over the age of 10 years, and 21% were over the age of 15 years. Wickman observed that poliomyelitis was not limited to children and that, as epidemics recurred, they included older age groups. The concept of the disease as "infantile paralysis" became obscured.[2]

In 1884, the first accurate account of the encephalitic form or cerebral type of polio was documented by Adolf von Strümpell in Vienna. He suggested that the causative agent could be localized in the brain and the spinal cord.[2]

Epidemiologists struggled for a long time, trying to understand the disease and identify true outbreaks, as the disease goes through a two-phase process before getting to the paralytic phase. At first, only the paralytic phase was clearly recognized and identified as infantile paralysis because the first phase was so easily confused with other diseases such as the flu, common colds, and related conditions. This was the case with an outbreak of polio in Oslo, Norway, which was thought to be spinal meningitis. Epidemics of influenza have also been confused with the first phase of poliomyelitis because the symptoms are quite similar. Such a mistaken occurrence took place in Los Angeles in the mid 1930s, causing a panic among healthcare professionals. Mild cases of the disease that did not reach the paralytic stage were thought to constitute 5–25% of all cases.[2]

Disease investigators of the day were a frustrated lot because of the lack of clear understanding and diagnosis of the disease. Numerous field workers, such as nurses, who were hired to trudge through communities during polio outbreaks in an attempt to trace relationships between multiple paralytic cases, often found only dead ends. Countless case questionnaires and forms were completed with the assistance of families in an effort to trace the disease and its transmission. The data from these questionnaires were analyzed in order to trace the spread of the disease.[2–5]

Even though clustering of polio cases was observed in rural communities in Norway and France, it was Sweden's epidemiologists/physicians who further connected polio outbreaks to rural areas and provided the most advances in poliomyelitis in the years 1890–1914.[2]

Karl Oskar Medin

Many of the advances in the knowledge of polio are attributed to Karl Oskar Medin. Medin is given a great deal of credit for detecting and assembling a comprehensive set of clinical features of the disease—the best effort done to this point in history. The greatest recognition of his work came when he, as a reliable, articulate, and experienced pediatrician, presented his observations to the 10th International Medical Congress in Berlin in 1890. Medin was also concerned about community care (public health aspects) of children. He was chairman of the Stockholm Board of Health from 1906–1915. He was also known for his role as an excellent teacher and had many pupils.[2]

Medin was born in 1847 in a small town near Stockholm and attended college at Uppsala, obtaining his medical licentiate at Stockholm in 1875. He was a prominent pediatrician in Sweden, a professor of pediatrics at the Karolinska Institute, and head physician at the General Orphan Sylum in Stockholm, giving him 30 years' experience in pediatric medicine in an all-child setting. Medin clarified the picture of poliomyelitis but gained for Sweden the unfortunate reputation of being the country where the worst outbreaks had occurred at the time.[2]

In 1887, Medin investigated an outbreak of 44 cases. Before that, he had stated that the cases of polio showing up at Polyclinic Hospital in Stockholm were infrequent. Attending to such an epidemic gave Medin considerable experience in dealing with polio in a great number of children.[2]

Medin divided the cases into two groups: (1) the spinal type that consisted of 27 cases of the paralytic type and (2) those with less common signs based on unusual location of the lesions. Medin was able to establish clearly the clinical course of the disease. The site of the pathological lesion had been previously established as being in the spinal cord, but it was Medin who established that there is first a phase that affects the body's total systems and then later a paralytic phase. He established that early minor symptoms and signs, such as fever, headache, and malaise, were symptoms of the early phase and later could (or may not) be followed by serious damage to the CNS. In certain areas of the spinal cord, the lesions could cause paralysis of various muscle groups or organs when the motor neurons were destroyed. Any disease involvement with the CNS always led to complications and some form of paralysis, even if it was minor. Medin followed the patients in the outbreak closely, making astute observations, documenting the early features of the disease, and observing that the disease subsided for a brief interim afebrile period, thus giving the course of the disease a biphasic pattern, with a major bout of fever experienced in both the first and last acute phases of the illness. The minor illness and its accompanying symptoms represented the first phase, and the second phase was more complicated and serious, resulting in paralysis to some parts of the body (see Figure I-9). These observations were followed and advanced by Kling and his colleagues, including Ivar Wickman.[2]

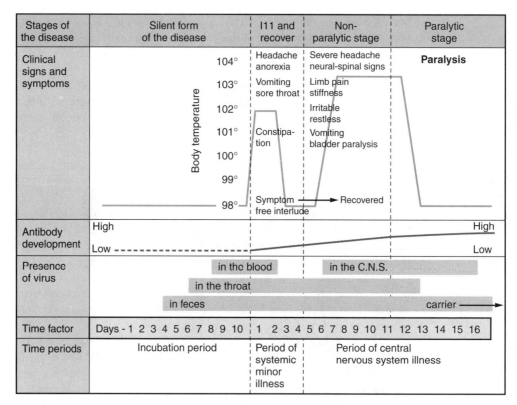

FIGURE I-9 Graphic representation of time factors in the course of the disease poliomyelitis. Adapted from Reagan H. Schematic Representation of Major Findings in the Typical Course of Clinically Biphasic Poliomyelitis. Unpublished handout.

Why the Scandinavian region experienced the first wave of the extensive polio epidemic is not clear. The epidemic of 1905 was the worst, with over 1,000 cases. It is known that polio seems to occur in rural areas as much as, if not more than, in large cities, and Scandinavia was quite rural at the time. Less exposure to a disease led to the population's having less immunity to the disease. There seemed to be higher immunity in city dwellers and lower immunity in rural populations.[2]

Ivar Wickman

Ivar Wickman, Medin's pupil, was thoroughly educated about poliomyelitis by his mentor. Wickman experienced two epidemics while working at the Medical Clinic in Stockholm—one in Stockholm and the other in Goteborg in 1903. Wickman was born in Lund in the southern tip of Sweden in 1872. He studied in Lund and Stockholm and, later in his career, on the European continent. He passed the medical board exams in 1895, at which time he became Medin's assistant in the Stockholm Pediatric Clinic. He wrote a 300-page monograph on polio in 1905, making him one of the leading experts in the field. Wickman, a man with well-known publications and advanced training, including the advanced medical degree of "Doctor of Medicine," applied for the directorship of the now prestigious Stockholm Pediatric Clinic, feeling sure that he would be accepted for the position. He was not and consequently committed suicide in 1914 at the age of 42.[2]

Epidemiological Questions

Among the clinical pathological observations made by Wickman was concern with how the agent (of which he was not sure) traveled through the community and how it entered the human host. How did it spread throughout the body, and how was it eliminated? Did it travel within the body along the nerves, in the lymphatic system, or in the blood? From the 1905 epidemic of 1,031 cases, he wanted to know what the nature of the disease was. Was it actually contagious? How did it spread? Was it spread by direct contact with infected sick people? Did healthy people carry the agent? Was it waterborne or foodborne? Was it spread like typhoid? (We now know the answer is yes—both are feces-borne.[2])

Key Epidemiological Points

The number of cases was no doubt increased by Wickman's inclusion of cases of both the paralytic type and the abortive or nonparalytic type. Whether to include nonparalytic cases was always a subject of debate among epidemiologists and statisticians. Wickman's astute observation that the nonparalytic cases were as important to the transmission of the disease, if not more so than the paralytic cases, was a major epidemiological contribution. The abortive type, or nonparalytic cases, and paralytic cases are two ends of a continuum. Nonparalytic or abortive cases were lucky and escaped having a serious outcome from such a crippling disease, with no more than what might seem to be a bad case of the common cold. The course of the disease ends either because of a high immune response by the body or because the person gets only a mild dose of the pathogen and/or a mild case of the disease, develops immunity, and is therefore no longer susceptible. Paralytic cases might die, but most often, they are crippled and devastated for life. These advanced cases suffered major or minor deformation of limbs, a total loss of use of limbs, or confinement to an iron lung for the rest of their lives.

Mild cases (abortive/nonparalytic cases) were found to be just as contagious as paralytic cases and could not be ignored. A relationship between main roads and railway routes and the spread of the epidemic of 1905 was established. An association with disease spread was developed based on busy traffic centers, which allowed frequent communication between rural and urban dwellers. Wickman followed many rural outbreaks, pursuing epidemiological investigations with tireless energy.[2]

It was observed by W. Wernstedt in the 1911 epidemic that, if an outbreak visited a certain locale, in the next few years that area would be spared an epidemic. Wernstedt observed and reported that the areas hardest hit by the 1905 and 1908 epidemics had little activity during the major epidemic of 1911. He attributed this to a natural immunization process caused by past outbreaks. He also observed a reduced incidence of the disease in the following years because of this general natural immunization. Wernstedt is given credit for his observation about acquired immunity to the disease from unapparent infections.[2]

The abortive and nonparalytic cases were of major concern to public health officials and epidemiologists because of their ability to spread the disease and continue to transmit it. The paralytic phase confined a person to bed so that the person was no longer out and about spreading the disease. To the family and more so to the individual, the paralytic form of the disease was of major concern as it changed the lives and structure of families and in many cases ruined lives. Even though to Wickman both forms were equally infectious, the focus of the medical community seemed to be limited to the paralytic form of the disease. Attack rates of paralytic polio in rural areas were about 3.0 to 3.7 per 1,000. Wickman established not only that polio was a disease of the CNS but also that the disease was highly contagious, spread mainly through its subclinical infectious state, and biphasic in its course. All clinical studies done later in monkeys verified not only the clinical but also the public health and epidemiological observations of Wickman.

In 1911, Kling and his team of virologists proved Wickman's observations to be correct; that is, that the mild or inapparent cases of the infection were indeed very contagious and thus of great concern in the spread of the disease. Kling and his colleagues, by isolating the pathogen in the mucous membranes, were able to show that the agent propagated itself in the mucous membranes and then penetrated them to cause the infection. The infection was spread both by the oral route and the fecal route, with the feces/gastrointestinal route being more significant. Kling's virology studies confirmed the two phases of the disease and that the abortive stage was as contagious as the paralytic phase. They also demonstrated that healthy carriers do exist during an epidemic. Studies showed that the virus persists in the throat for about 2 weeks in most cases but that it could be there for as long as 180 days (6 months) and 200 days (7 months). The pathogen's ability to produce inflammation was reduced after the 14-day period, which showed that the virus weakens after its acute stage.[2]

Rural Observations

Many investigators observed that rural areas often had more serious epidemics than urban areas. In Sweden, there was a tendency for polio to attack rural areas, especially remote villages in Sweden's sparsely settled countryside. Wickman was able to trace the movements of people during the epidemic. Ruralness seemed to contribute to the disease, due to the fact that lack of travel, remoteness of villages, and infrequent contact with outside people did not allow even a mild form of the disease to be experienced by rural folk, which would have produced immunity. Thus, outbreaks occurred often in rural areas, with the inevitable result of crippled children, partly due to a lack of immunity in infants and youth.[2]

Epidemic Curve

Wickman developed an epidemic curve of the cases. The epidemic curve for this Swedish outbreak was much like other disease outbreaks, a significant epidemiological point. For epidemic curves to occur, a population of susceptibles must be available, as well as a disease that has an identifiable course and time duration. The disease enters the population with a few cases, and as the pathogen is transmitted through the population, more and more cases occur (see "Herd Immunity" in Chapter 3, Figures 3-5 and 3-6). Depending on the disease's incubation period and the usual course and duration of a case of the disease, the shorter the incubation and duration, the more pronounced the epidemic curve. What allows an epidemic to continue is the number of susceptibles in the population at risk. In a totally susceptible population, like that in the late 1800s and early 1900s in Sweden, the disease spreads like wildfire, and the epidemic curve is extreme and pronounced. What causes the epidemic to subside and diminish is the number of susceptibles left. Who is left to get the disease? The epidemic curve diminishes when susceptibles have become diseased or have died. The diseased recover and are now immune, or the still-healthy have fled and can no longer be exposed. The epidemic curve diminishes because of the recovery/immunity of the previously ill or the death of the diseased cases. Immunization/vaccination and mild cases of the disease reduce the susceptibles and stop an epidemic by herd immunity. Numbers of nonparalytic cases compared with paralytic cases vary from epidemic to epidemic. The ratio of paralytic to nonparalytic cases varies because of the circumstances of the outbreaks.[2]

Not only did Wickman recognize that the pathogens often missed the CNS, but he realized that the abortive/nonparalytic cases actually outnumbered the paralytic cases. He learned quickly that paralysis was the dramatic side of the disease, but that if the infected cases were lucky enough to escape paralysis, they were no less contagious. Wickman observed that, in one village in the middle of the epidemic, more than half were of the nonparalytic type. He observed that the infection was spread mostly by the nonparalytic cases.[2]

Observed symptoms in nonparalytic types could be stiff neck, pain, stiffness in the back, or merely a fever. Wickman's colleagues viewed a diagnosis of infantile paralysis in the absence of paralysis as ridiculous. The skepticism would remain for many years to come.[2]

Wickman demanded that poliomyelitis be considered a highly contagious disease. Mild cases (abortive/nonparalytic cases) must also be taken seriously and considered just as contagious as paralytic cases because of their infectious nature. Wickman was as concerned with slightly ill cases and healthy carriers or inapparent cases as he was with full-blown paralytic cases. Clinical and laboratory evidence eventually proved this epidemiological observation to be true.[2]

In the summer of 1905, Wickman investigated an outbreak in a school near Tingsryd, a village of 3,000, with 18 cases occurring between August and October. The school was the primary site from which the infection spread. Twelve of the 18 infected people attended the school, and the remaining 6 lived at the school. Six children from only four houses, who had no contact with any of the other 52 attending the school, also came down with the disease and were considered both abortive and paralytic cases.[2]

Wickman held that the incubation period was 3–4 days to onset of the minor illness phase, with the time period to onset of fever in the paralytic phase being 8 to 10 days. Later, when studies were done with the live attenuated poliovirus vaccine, it was demonstrated that the incubation period to first onset was 3–4 days.[2]

Poliovirus Discovered

The poliovirus was discovered in 1908 in Vienna by Karl Landsteiner and E. Popper. In 1911, one of the worst polio epidemics (3,840 cases) of all time hit Sweden. Scandinavia was labeled as the source and breeding ground of the polio disease because much of the reported research occurred there. The 1911 epidemic further emphasized this negative image.[2]

The Swedish medical community, particularly the clinical virologists, tried their best to understand and study the new findings about polio, especially because they now knew the agent was a poliovirus. In the 1911 epidemic, this presented an opportunity for a team from the State Bacteriological Institute in Stockholm to study the clinical and virological aspects of polio. The team was headed by Carl Kling.[2]

Carl Kling went to the Pasteur Institute after the 1911 epidemic subsided and became known as the world's leading authority on poliomyelitis. He was associated with the Pasteur Institute for 25 years and in 1919 was made director of the State Bacteriological Institute in Stockholm. He also made radio broadcasts about polio. He never married and died in 1967 at the age of 80 years, after 50 years of work on poliomyelitis.[2] He claimed that poliomyelitis was waterborne.

Kling and his team obtained tissue samples from victims who had died. Most importantly, they were able to recover poliovirus samples from various anatomical sites throughout the body, showing that the disease invaded more than just the CNS. The team also recovered samples of the poliovirus from living patients, proving that the abortive phase of the disease was just as communicable as the paralytic phase. They also were able to acquire samples of the virus in "healthy carriers."[2]

Kling and his colleagues knew the virus was filterable and therefore could be separated from other material and used experimentally. They also knew that the virus caused lesions in the spinal cord and brain of monkeys and humans. The virus had been shown to be in the mucous membranes of the throat and nasal passages of monkeys as well as the lymph nodes next to the small intestine (mesenteric lymph nodes). The agent was also found in the tonsils, pharyngeal mucous membranes, and salivary glands of humans and monkeys, oropharynx, trachea, and, especially important, in the blood, the walls, and contents of the small intestine. Fourteen fatal human cases of polio confirmed all of the sites. Then 11 acutely ill patients provided specimens, and the poliovirus was recovered from basically all the same body sites in the live acute cases of the disease. Thus, monkey experiments, fatal/dead cases, and live acute cases all produced basically the same findings—that is, the pathogen was found in all the same sites throughout the body.[2]

Doubts by American researchers, physicians, and scientists and some Europeans concerning the presence of the pathogen in the gastrointestinal tract and rectum, as well as doubts concerning the virus's weakening over time, caused delays and setbacks in developing a vaccine well into the 1930s.[2]

CASE STUDY QUESTIONS

1. Using the data below and a computer spreadsheet, create an epidemic curve bar graph.

   Person/Disease: Cases of poliomyelitis recorded in Sweden

   Place: Sweden

   Time: Monthly reporting for the years of 1905, 1906, 1907; from January 1905 through July 1907

   Frequency: For the y-axis of the graph: 50-case increments up to 400 cases

1905 Cases			1906 Cases			1907 Cases		
Jan.	=	1	Jan.	=	48	Jan.	=	9
Feb.	=	5	Feb.	=	33	Feb.	=	9
Mar.	=	4	Mar.	=	36	Mar.	=	11
Apr.	=	4	Apr.	=	24	Apr.	=	6
May	=	8	May	=	41	May	=	5
Jun.	=	20	Jun.	=	15	Jun.	=	13
Jul.	=	138	Jul.	=	21	Jul.	=	51
Aug.	=	367	Aug.	=	32			
Sept.	=	242	Sept.	=	49			
Oct.	=	140	Oct.	=	22			
Nov.	=	69	Nov.	=	31			
Dec.	=	38	Dec.	=	24			

2.   From the epidemic curve created in study question 1, what have you learned from this case thus far? Discuss the implications and observations of all time aspects of this disease. Discuss seasonal variation, cyclic trends, implication for duration of the disease, and incubation periods.

3.   List the various names by which polio has been known.

4.   Discuss and explain the issues of age and its implications for the epidemiology of polio and infantile paralysis.

5.   Why did physicians and epidemiologists have such a difficult time identifying outbreaks and the spread of polio? Explain and discuss in detail.

6.   From your reading and study thus far and from studying "Age-group specific number of females for every 100 males in the United States, 1978 and 2008" (see Figure 5-8), explain and discuss polio as a biphasic (two-phase) disease and the problems this two-phase process posed in investigating polio epidemics.

7.   List the many epidemiological observations made by Wickman about infantile paralysis and its spread. Who later confirmed these observations, and how did he verify them?

8.   What were the epidemiologist observations of Wernstedt?

9.   Explain and discuss the terms, abortive case and anterior case. What are other terms used for each of these two terms? Explain the role of these two terms in polio epidemics. What observations did Kling make about the abortive cases or phase?

10.   When was the poliovirus discovered? Explain its characteristics and the locations in the body where it was originally discovered.

FIRST MAJOR EPIDEMIC OF POLIOMYELITIS IN AMERICA: RUTLAND, VERMONT

It was in the summer of 1894 in Vermont that the first major U.S. poliomyelitis epidemic occurred. Charles S. Caverly, MD, a practicing doctor, member of the state board of health, and public health officer for the state of Vermont, presented a report on the epidemic. Caverly, though a very successful practicing physician, was excited about public health and epidemiology. He came from a rural area of a rural state, born in Troy, New Hampshire in 1856. He attended New Hampshire schools and Dartmouth College, graduating in 1878. He received his medical degree from the University of Vermont in 1881. He also did postgraduate work at the College of Physicians and Surgeons in New York City and was professor of hygiene and preventive medicine at the University of Vermont, from which he later received an honorary science doctorate degree.

Caverly reported that in Rutland County there was an outbreak of an acute nervous disease that invariably was attended with some paralysis. The first cases occurred in Rutland and Wallingford about mid-June. The epidemic progressed through July into surrounding towns.

This first U.S. epidemic was the largest reported in the world thus far, with 132 documented cases. Six of the cases had no paralysis, but all had distinct nervous symptoms. Caverly was one of the first to recognize the abortive nonparalytic cases, even though he probably overlooked hundreds of them. This epidemic was also the first to be studied by a public health officer. From the advantage of his political position, Caverly was able to call meetings and coordinate the exchange of information.

Caverly was most diligent in his effort to identify each case. The previous summer, a small epidemic had occurred 125 miles away in Boston, making the outbreak in some nearby cities somewhat predictable. Public health officials have observed that poliomyelitis epidemics usually terminate when cold weather sets in and show up again in a neighboring city the next summer, much as they did in Scandinavia. (This makes epidemiological sense, as the new city is where susceptibles are now available. Those in the city of the recent outbreak had naturally acquired immunity yet interacted on a close personal basis for the disease to be communicated.) Caverly was able to show that the age distribution was much greater than previously reported (Dr. Mary Jacobi in 1886 had suggested that infantile paralysis was limited to children 18 months to 4 years of age). Caverly reported 20 cases (probably only paralytic cases) in the 9- to 12-year age range and 12 cases over the age of 15 years. The shift in age to include older age groups, including adults (Franklin D. Roosevelt, the 32nd president of the United States, who served from 1933 to 1945, contracted poliomyelitis at the age of 39), was observed more frequently from this point on. Adults were not excluded from the Rutland epidemic, even though most cases occurred in children. Caverly attempted to classify cases according to sites of paralysis. The death rate from this epidemic was quite high at 13.5%. This figure held with later observations that the older the patient was who contracted poliomyelitis, the greater the death rate. Caverly reported a curious observation—that the paralytic disease also affected domestic animals, with horses, dogs, and fowl dying with various types and degrees of paralysis. Dr. Charles Dana, professor of nervous diseases at Cornell University Medical College, verified that one of the fowls with paralysis of its legs had an acute poliomyelitis of the lower portion of the spinal cord, yet Landsteiner in Vienna and Flexner could not produce cases of poliomyelitis in other animals. Finally, they turned to primates to produce experimental polio, yet this paralytic disease has been reported throughout this era as occurring in domestic animals.

Caverly made gross mistakes beyond the animal paralysis issue. He suggested that infantile paralysis was not contagious. He seemed to try to define the disease by the old Hippocratic theory of medicine—because heating is mentioned in 24 cases and chilling of the body in only 4 cases, he determined that there was a general absence of infectious disease as a causative factor in the epidemic.

Despite his errors, Caverly made major contributions for his time; he was the first health officer and physician to do a major systematic study of an infantile paralysis epidemic, and he was the first to recognize and confirm the occurrence of nonparalytic cases.

CASE STUDY QUESTIONS

1. What unique epidemiological observations and contributions about the epidemic of infantile paralysis were made by Dr. Caverly from his experience in rural Vermont?

2. What epidemiological observations did Dr. Caverly make regarding age of infantile paralysis victims and polio epidemics?

3. What were some critical thinking and observational errors regarding epidemiology that were made by Dr. Caverly?

SIMON FLEXNER, MD AND WADE HAMILTON FROST, MD: AMERICAN EPIDEMIOLOGISTS WHO INVESTIGATED POLIOMYELITIS

Flexner

When the news of Landsteiner's discovery of the poliovirus reached the United States, Simon Flexner, MD, the new director of the Rockefeller Institute of Medical Research in New York City, took advantage of the opportunity the new discovery presented. The Rockefeller Institute was well funded, had just had much success in an attack on meningococcal meningitis, and had a well-equipped institute including facilities to handle primates, which was supported by a staff of qualified researchers.

New York had recently suffered through a poliomyelitis epidemic of about 750–1,200 cases in 1907. Flexner was appointed as one of the 12 members of a committee appointed by the New York Neurological Society to study the polio epidemic. A report was finally produced by the committee in 1910, which included the findings of Landsteiner. Flexner also described in his work, supported by Dr. Martha Wollstein, that they had obtained samples of the pathogen from two fatal cases, one in New Jersey and one in New York in 1909. They inoculated monkeys and were able to pass the two strains from monkey to monkey in serial fashion. Most of their work was on monkeys, yet they claimed that what occurred in primates was also true for humans, a statement the medical community questioned. Flexner himself noted that in different species of monkeys the poliovirus behaved differently, making animal model research a bit unpredictable and making it hard to develop a protocol applicable to humans.

Simon Flexner, who was considered a laboratory doctor and one of the foremost experts on poliomyelitis at the time, did not have the answers for many practical questions of practicing doctors: How long was a case of poliomyelitis contagious? Why is poliomyelitis contagious to some and not to others? The key question at the time was this: "How do you best treat poliomyelitis?" The fact that the disease was known to be caused by a virus provided the general practice doctor with no cure or solution to treatment. Viruses are small, difficult to see, and mysterious. Much laboratory work was done by Flexner and his colleagues at the Rockefeller Institute and published in the Journal of the American Medical Association from 1909 to 1913 as news updates on poliomyelitis, again establishing Flexner as the expert on the disease.

In 1910, Flexner and his colleagues in the United States, and Landsteiner and his colleagues in Vienna, were able to demonstrate that the serum of monkeys that had recovered from experimental poliomyelitis contained antibodies (which Flexner called germicidal substances) that, when mixed with a small amount of active poliovirus, would actually neutralize or inactivate the poliovirus and render it inert. Later, A. Netter and C. Levaditi, in Paris, found the same antibodies in humans recovering from the disease. This was a landmark discovery that would benefit later vaccine research. For Flexner, this was the last major breakthrough, and his polio research started to subside, as did that of Landsteiner and his colleagues in Europe.

Stubbornly clinging to lines of thinking that are not accurate has plagued medicine from the very beginning—so it was with Flexner. He refused to accept certain clinical facts, which led him away from important discoveries, including virology as a method of clinical investigation. Flexner retired in 1935 from the Rockefeller Institute and died in 1946 before the polio vaccine was discovered and before the discovery that the poliovirus was indeed a family of viruses instead of being a single virus. Flexner was also faced with the separation at that time between practicing physicians and researchers. MDs were to practice medicine and not dabble in anything remotely resembling experimental research. During the 1911 epidemic in New York, Flexner worked at the Rockefeller Hospital instead of at the institute, rigidly clinging to the idea that physicians should practice their art at the bedside in the hospital, not in the laboratory. Thus, as a physician, he was not allowed to do testing in virology. Contention existed between the hospital medical director and Flexner because of the opposition to collaborative work among the physicians and the researchers. Meanwhile, the physicians wished to stretch their efforts beyond mundane medicine into the areas of research. The Rockefeller Hospital study, even though it included 200 cases, offered little insight beyond what was provided by the Swedes.

Treatment offered by the Rockefeller groups was similar to that offered elsewhere: mild sedative, bed rest, and medication to control pain. From a public health perspective, cases should be treated like any other communicable disease—they should be made aware of their contagious conditions, be quarantined, and have disinfection carried out. In the wards with poliomyelitis cases, caps and long gowns were worn by those working with patients. Hands were thoroughly scrubbed with soap and a nail brush, and soaked in a corrosive substance.

In 1912, two physicians, Rosenau and Brues, set forth the theory that poliomyelitis was spread by the stable fly. W. H. Frost and a colleague (J. F. Anderson) were able to show experimentally that this was untrue. Frost relied on a clinical laboratory for his work, much as Flexner did, but also traveled the countryside, much like Wickman did in Sweden, going door to door investigating poliomyelitis outbreaks. He gathered serum specimens for laboratory tests, which in turn, allowed statistical analysis. The use of statistics in epidemiology was greatly advanced by Frost in this era.[2]

Frost

Frost contributed much to the epidemiology of polio from 1910 to 1930. He quickly grasped the importance of knowing how polio was spread and is credited with establishing a strong foundation of statistics as a basis for epidemiological study. He was considered one of America's leading epidemiologists in the 1920s and 1930s.

In 1908 Frost was assigned to the Hygienic Laboratory. Two years later, after investigating pellagra, tetanus, typhoid, and water pollution, he was assigned to field investigations of poliomyelitis epidemics, even though he had limited knowledge of the disease. He and J. F. Anderson, the new director of the Hygienic Laboratory, learned quickly, and their involvement with this new disease led to the composition of a 50-page monograph on poliomyelitis, which they called a précis. This document contained subject matter not included in Wickman's 300-page monograph and not covered by the Rockefeller Institute of Medical Science. Frost would eventually become dean of the School of Hygiene and Public Health at Johns Hopkins University.[2]

Frost and Anderson addressed and recorded age of the onset of cases in various epidemics in different environmental conditions. Frost, like Wickman, observed that the disease was more contagious than medical science believed at the time and was quick to point out that direct contact was probably one of the main means of disease transmission. Frost observed in the 1910 epidemic that the disease was transmissible from person-to-person, probably by direct contact, and appeared to be highly contagious under some circumstances, affecting a considerable proportion of the population of a limited area.[2]

For a short time, the stable fly and other biting insects were implicated as possible vectors of the poliovirus. Anderson and Frost in 1912–1913 tested the stable fly and showed that vectors were not generally involved in the disease's transmission. Frost had worked on poliomyelitis epidemics in Mason City, Iowa, in 1910; Cincinnati, Ohio, in 1911; and

Buffalo and Batavia, New York, in 1912. He knew from experience and firsthand observation that vectors were not implicated in disease transmission, but that direct person-to-person contact was. Frost was able to observe the disease in different environments and settings, including large cities, small towns, and rural areas. Not since Wickman in Sweden, had any other epidemiologist so painstakingly completed statistical studies on epidemics. No other epidemiologist had been afforded the opportunity to make scientific observations and draw learned conclusions on the three dimensions of investigation: close clinical observation, laboratory experiments, and statistical analysis. Frost, like Wickman, had used spot maps to mark the location of the residences of paralytic, abortive, and suspicious cases.[2]

Frost's Epidemiological Methods

Frost was able to observe increases and decreases in incidence and prevalence in rural versus city settings. He made seasonal and meteorological charts surrounding the times of epidemics. Included in his investigations were other observations of epidemics, such as sanitary conditions of individual cases, milk supply, food supply, observation of paralytic cases in humans and domestic animals, and the presence and absence of flies, mosquitoes, and other insects. His knowledge base was founded on house-to-house surveys, countless clinical observations, statistical analysis of the findings, and years of community-based experience, all confirming that poliomyelitis was spread by direct contact.[2]

Frost came to a most fundamental epidemiological conclusion: that an accurate diagnosis must be made before an investigation can proceed. In the case of poliomyelitis, the abortive case (those without paralytic symptoms) must be identified, as they are so numerous as to be of great epidemiological significance. Thus, Frost was able to use the laboratory to achieve a more accurate diagnosis of the poliomyelitis in all types of cases. He was able to collect serum samples from nine cases in the Iowa epidemic and with the help of Anderson analyzed them. Thus, proving Flexner, as well as Netter and Levaditi of France, incorrect in their assumptions based on monkey experiments: that the blood of victims recovered from the disease (in monkeys at least) did not contain poliovirus. Frost showed that abortive or unapparent infections of poliomyelitis did indeed contain the antibodies.

Frost and Anderson were always extremely cautious in their claims and reports, which often weakened their position and respect. They were hesitant to make any strong affirmative stance on their discoveries for fear they would not be accepted. The investigators at the hospital of the Rockefeller Institute heard of the findings on Frost's work and went on to show that human sera from recovered adults, did have high amounts of polio antibodies, much as paralytic patients did.

Frost was the first to use such a combination of methods and such a sophisticated arsenal against poliomyelitis, yet he was overly cautious. He observed that during epidemics, the incidence of the disease was affected by susceptibility to the infection. Age was one of the key observations about poliomyelitis, with susceptibility being limited to the first half decade of life and the risk diminishing thereafter. (Naturally acquired immunity probably accounted for this factor; either the victim had a mild case and was no longer susceptible, had a bad case and died, or was paralyzed. After an epidemic had passed through a community, the disease was no longer contagious until a new crop of susceptibles in the form of new children came along.) Early on, the lack of understanding of the role of the abortive, mild, or inapparent cases in a population caused Frost to conclude that widespread immunization of the population against the disease was unjustifiably radical. Frost was able to share his vast experience of poliomyelitis investigation in the 1916 epidemic.

CASE STUDY QUESTIONS

1. What were the epidemiological limitations of Flexner's work on polio? List and discuss several of these limitations.

2. Who was Dr. Frost, and what were his contributions to epidemiological investigations of infantile paralysis/polio?

3. How did Dr. Frost contribute in the way of understanding modes of disease transmission in poliomyelitis?

4. Which specific methods and approaches was Dr. Frost able to use and establish as solid epidemiological methodology?

POLIOMYELITIS EPIDEMIC IN LOS ANGELES, 1934

By the spring of 1934, a great deal was known about poliomyelitis. The mode of transmission was known to be person to person. The two-phase process of the disease was well understood, and mild nonparalytic infections or anterior poliomyelitis as well as paralytic infections were all understood to be major means of contagion. Animals and most insects were eliminated as vectors. It was known that some victims would die in a few days, some would have crippling paralysis, and others would recover without a sign. The poliovirus had been isolated and identified from most parts of the body—most importantly, the CNS; blood; saliva; gastrointestinal tract, especially the small intestine; mesenteric lymph nodes; and nasopharynx. The damage caused by the poliovirus was known to be done in the spinal cord's anterior horn of the gray matter and in brain tissue.[2]

When the poliomyelitis epidemic hit Los Angeles, many horror stories from past epidemics had been deeply implanted in the minds of medical and nursing professionals. It appears that the medical professionals at the time were well informed about the facts of poliomyelitis, yet most ignored them and, moreover, failed to inform the public. The Contagious Unit of the Los Angeles County General Hospital was responsible for most of the activities of the epidemic, and fear of the disease seemed to dominate its efforts, in spite of evidence that much of the sickness that occurred in June of 1934 was not poliomyelitis.[2]

Physicians and nurses were strained, worried, and terrified of contracting the disease themselves. By June 15, 1934, 50 cases a day were being admitted to most hospitals, yet by June 29, only 1 fatal case of poliomyelitis had occurred, producing a sample of the poliovirus. A second case produced another sample on July 4.[2]

When the Poliomyelitis Commission arrived in Los Angeles from Yale University School of Medicine, headed by Dr. Leslie T. Webster of the Rockefeller Institute of Medical Science of New York City, a public meeting was held to review the situation of the epidemic. The meeting digressed to physicians and nurses discussing their risk of getting poliomyelitis and whether they might receive disability pensions if paralyzed by the disease and were disabled in the line of duty.[2]

New interns in training at the Los Angeles County Hospital were deprived of teaching and proper guidance because the attending physicians were afraid of getting the disease and stayed away. Instead they consulted by phone as opposed to going to the hospital. Doctors who worked at the County Hospital in the communicable disease wards, were not welcome on house calls because their patients viewed the hospital as a pest house.[2]

No one knew how much of the disease outbreak that year was really polio. Nearly all adults, especially the nurses and doctors, were afraid of getting paralytic polio. In those who got the serious form of the disease, healthcare providers observed much pain and weakness, but very few deaths occurred. The number of cases of paralysis was much lower than one would expect. The question was this: Could it be another virus or a different strain of the virus? Dr. Webster believed that 90% of the cases were actually not poliomyelitis.[2]

Researchers had little success in searching for the poliovirus in the nasal passages of suspected victims through nasal washings. The disease could not be produced in monkeys or lab animals. Webster believed that the problem was complex and that the infantile part of infantile paralysis was missing because most cases were in adults. The paralysis phase of the disease was also missing, as no paralysis occurred in most cases.[2]

Oral washings with ropy (an adhesive, stringy-type thread that was soaked in a special solution and swirled around in the throat in order to capture samples of mucous tissue) were done routinely. Ropy washes were able to gather a few flakes of mucus and the debris in the mucus. The ropy washes used a special solution that helped save samplings of potential poliovirus evidence and preserved the specimens for months (101 days) for later study. Even after such a long time, the specimens could be spun in a centrifuge and yield the virus. Thus, in future outbreaks, disease investigators would not need to take an army of public health workers along to gather specimens.[2]

Hysteria raged on in the main populace. Not only was the general public afraid of getting the disease, but a major part of the medical and nursing profession was also participating in the fear. Yet officials were not daring enough to tell the public that the disease was not polio. It was disclosed that half of the 1,301 suspected cases were not poliomyelitis. The actual attack rate was estimated to be from 4.4% to 10.7%.[2]

There was no doubt that Los Angeles was visited by an epidemic of poliomyelitis in the summer of 1934, but it was a mild one. Most of the people who were sick that summer were sick either from another disease (encephalitis, meningitis, or influenza) or from a mild form or a different strain of the poliovirus. Patients had atypical symptoms for polio (rheumatoidal or influenzal with striking emotional tones of fear that they might get polio). It was observed by U.S. Public Health Service officer Dr. A. G. Gilliam, of the Los Angeles County Hospital's personnel, "Irrespective of actual mechanisms of spread and identity of the disease, this outbreak has no parallel in the history of poliomyelitis or any other CNS infections."[2]

As an unfortunate outcome of this epidemic and its resulting hysteria, patients who exhibited even a slight degree of weakness were immobilized in plaster casts. This was a common practice in the 1930s, and many were subjected unnecessarily to this treatment.

CASE STUDY QUESTIONS

1. By 1934, a great deal was known about poliomyelitis. Summarize all that was known about the epidemiology of polio.

2. How serious was the polio epidemic of 1934? What were the social, psychological, and political implications and their effects on the epidemiology of polio surrounding this case?

3. What were the final conclusions about the polio epidemic of 1934 in Los Angeles, and what were the implications for the future?

EPILOGUE

Polio epidemics continued across America. The last national poliomyelitis epidemic was in the early 1950s. In 1954, Dr. Jonas E. Salk began immunizing with killed (formalin-inactivated poliomyelitis viruses) vaccine, called the poliovirus vaccine. Later, Albert B. Sabin developed the live vaccine, called the oral poliovirus vaccine, usually taken orally in sugar cubes. In the late 1980s, post-polio syndrome was discovered, and investigations of this late phase of poliomyelitis have continued.

REFERENCES

1. Berkow R, ed. *The Merck Manual of Diagnosis and Therapy*, 14th ed. Rahway, NJ: Merck, Sharp and Dohme; 1982.
2. Paul JR. *A History of Poliomyelitis.* New Haven, CT: Yale University Press; 1971.
3. Millard FP. *Poliomyelitis (Infantile Paralysis).* Kirksville, MO: Journal Printing Company; 1918.
4. Smith JS. *Patenting the Sun.* New York, NY: William Morrow and Company; 1990.
5. Rogers N. *Dirt and Disease.* New Brunswick, NJ: Rutgers University Press; 1990.

II

Common Study Designs with Selected Measures of Association and Test Statistics

Study Design	Measure of Association	Tests of Significance
Case-control Unmatched	$Odds\ Ratio\ (OR) = \dfrac{a \times d}{c \times b}$	$\chi^2 = \dfrac{(|\,ad - bc\,| - n/2)^2 n}{(a+b)(c+d)(a+c)(b+d)}$
Summary odds ratio	$OR_{MH} = \dfrac{\Sigma(a_i d_i/n_i)}{\Sigma(b_i c_i/n_i)}$	$\chi^2_{MH} = \dfrac{\{\Sigma a_i - \Sigma[(a_i + c_i)(a_i + b_i)/n_i]\}^2}{\Sigma(a_i + b_i)(c_i + d_i)(a_i + c_i)(b_i + d_i)/(n_i^2(n_i - 1))}$
Matched	$OR = \dfrac{b}{c}$	$\chi^2 = \dfrac{(|b - c| - 1)^2}{(b + c)}$
Cohort Cumulative incidence	$Risk\ Ratio\ (RR) = \dfrac{a/(a + b)}{c/(c + d)}$	$\chi^2 = \dfrac{(|ad - bc| - n/2)^2 n}{(a+b)(c+d)(a+c)(b+d)}$
Summary risk ratio	$RR_{MH} = \dfrac{\Sigma[a_i(c_i + d_i)/n_i]}{\Sigma[c_i(a_i + b_i)/n_i]}$	$\chi^2_{MH} = \dfrac{\{\Sigma a_i - \Sigma[(a_i + c_i)(a_i + b_i)/n_i]\}^2}{\Sigma(a_i + b_i)(c_i + d_i)(a_i + c_i)(b_i + d_i)/(n_i^2(n_i - 1))}$
Incidence density	$Rate\ Ratio = \dfrac{a/T_e}{c/T_o}$	$\chi^2 = \dfrac{\{a - [T_e(a + c)]/T\}^2}{T_e[T_o(a + c)]/T^2}$
Cross-sectional	$Prevalence\ Ratio = \dfrac{a/(a + b)}{c/(c + d)}$	$\chi^2 = \dfrac{(|ad - bc| - n/2)^2 n}{(a+b)(c+d)(a+c)(b+d)}$

MH = Mantel-Haenszel.
a = number of exposed individuals with the outcome
b = number of exposed individuals without the outcome
c = number of unexposed individuals with the outcome
d = number of unexposed individuals without the outcome
n = total number of individuals in the sample
i = level of stratification
T = total time a cohort of exposed (e) and unexposed (o) people are followed

Summary of Confidence Intervals for Evaluating Selected Hypotheses

For testing $H_0: OR = 1$ in an unmatched case-control study

$$95\% \text{ CI}(OR) = \exp\left[\ln OR \pm \left(1.96 \times \sqrt{\frac{1}{a} + \frac{1}{b} + \frac{1}{c} + \frac{1}{d}}\right)\right]$$

For testing $H_0: OR = 1$ in a matched case-control study

$$95\% \text{ CI}(OR) = \exp\left[\ln OR \pm \left(1.96 \times \sqrt{\frac{1}{b} + \frac{1}{c}}\right)\right]$$

For testing $H_0: OR = 1$ in a stratified case-control study

$$95\% \text{ CI}(OR_{MH}) = OR_{MH}\left(1 \pm 1.96/\sqrt{\chi^2_{MH}}\right)$$

For testing $H_0: risk\ ratio = 1$

$$95\% \text{ CI}(RR) = \exp\left[\ln RR \pm \left(1.96 \times \sqrt{\frac{b/a}{a + b} + \frac{d/c}{c + d}}\right)\right]$$

For testing $H_0: RR = 1$ in a stratified cohort study

$$95\% \text{ CI}(RR_{MH}) = RR_{MH}\left(1 \pm 1.96/\sqrt{\chi^2_{MH}}\right)$$

For testing H_0 : *rate ratio = 1*

$$95\% \text{ CI(Rate Ratio)} = \exp\left[\ln(\text{Rate Ratio}) \pm 1.96\sqrt{\frac{1}{a} + \frac{1}{c}}\right]$$

For testing H_0 : *Prevalence Ratio = 1* in a cross-sectional study

$$95\% \text{ CI(PR)} = \exp\left[\ln\text{PR} \pm \left(1.96 \times \sqrt{\frac{b/a}{a+b} + \frac{d/c}{c+d}}\right)\right]$$

REFERENCES

1. Katz D, Baptista J, Azen SP, Pike MC. Obtaining confidence intervals for the risk ratio in cohort studies. *Biometrics.* 1978;34:469–474.
2. Ederer F, Mantel N. Confidence limits on the ratio for two Poisson variables. *Am J Epidemiol.* 1974;100:165–167.
3. Ahlbom A. *Biostatistics for Epidemiologists.* Boca Raton, FL: Lewis Publishers; 1993.
4. Woolf B. On estimating the relation between blood group and disease. *Ann Hum Genet.* 1955;19:251–253.
5. Schlesselman JJ. *Case-Control Studies: Design, Conduct, Analysis.* New York, NY: Oxford University Press; 1982.

IV

Classification and Specialty Journals in Epidemiology

As the scope of epidemiology has expanded, several extensions of the word epidemiology have been developed. Physiology or disease classifications of epidemiology involving the study of the frequency, distribution, and determinants of selected health problems in human populations include:

- Cancer epidemiology
- Cardiovascular disease epidemiology
- Diabetes epidemiology
- Epidemiology of aging
- Epidemiology of zooneses
- Infectious disease epidemiology
- Injury epidemiology
- Neurological disease epidemiology
- Obesity epidemiology
- Oral health epidemiology
- Psychiatric epidemiology
- Renal disease epidemiology
- Reproductive epidemiology
- Respiratory epidemiology

Thus, these word extensions are used to describe specific areas of epidemiologic application. In addition, the use of epidemiology in these focus areas may also involve the development and evaluation of prevention and control efforts.

There are a number of methodological approaches used in epidemiology, which are often peculiar to their area of application. As such, extensions to the word epidemiology have also been developed to clarify these areas of methodological use.

- Biomarker epidemiology
- Clinical epidemiology
- Conflict epidemiology
- Economic epidemiology
- Environmental epidemiology
- Field epidemiology
- Genetic epidemiology
- Infection control and hospital epidemiology
- Lifecourse epidemiology
- Molecular epidemiology
- Nutritional epidemiology
- Pharmacoepidemiology
- Primary care epidemiology
- Public health practice epidemiology
- Social epidemiology
- Spatial epidemiology
- Surveillance epidemiology (clinical surveillance)
- Tele-epidemiology

Some of the major journals that are general to the field of epidemiology, in the order of impact factor (IF, which reflects the likelihood that papers in the journal will be cited), are as follows:

- Epidemiologic Reviews – 2010 IF 8.238
- Epidemiology – 2010 IF 5.866
- International Journal of Epidemiology – 2010 IF 5.759
- American Journal of Epidemiology – 2010 IF 5.745
- European Journal of Epidemiology – 2010 IF 4.535
- Journal of Clinical Epidemiology – 2011 IF 3.753
- Annals of Epidemiology – 2010 IF 3.238
- Journal of Epidemiology and Community Health – 2011: 3.04
- Epidemiologic Perspectives and Innovations – 2011 IF 1.58
- The Open Epidemiology Journal – 2010 IF 1.182

Journals also exist to reflect some of the specialty areas of epidemiology. Some of these journals, in the order of their IF, are listed here:

- Cancer – 2010 IF 4.926
- Genetic Epidemiology – 2010 IF 3.988
- Cancer Epidemiology Biomarkers and Prevention – 2010 IF 3.919
- Pharmacoepidemiology and Drug Safety – 2010 IF 2.342
- Epidemiology and Infection – 2010 IF 2.257
- Pediatric and Perinatal Epidemiology – 2010 IF 1.928
- Cancer Epidemiology – 2010 IF 1.182

Epidemiologic Associations and Societies

American College of Epidemiology (ACE)
Peter Kralka, Executive Director
1500 Sunday Drive, Suite 102
Raleigh, NC 27607
Ph: (919) 861-5573 Fax: (919) 787-4916
E-mail: info@acepidemiology.org
Founded: 1979

American Public Health Association (APHA)
800 I Street
NW Washington, DC 20001-3710
Ph: (202) 777-APHA Fax: (202) 777-2534
E-mail: comments@apha.org
Founded: 1872

American Society for Microbiology
1752 N Street, NW
Washington, DC 20036-2904
Ph: (202) 737-3600
E-mail: webmaster@asmusa.org
Founded: 1883

The Association for Professionals in Infection Control and Epidemiology (APIC)
1275 K St., NW, Suite 1000
Washington, DC 20005-4006
Ph: (202) 789-1890 Fax: (202) 789-1899
E-mail: info@apic.org

Council of State and Territorial Epidemiologists (CSTE)
2872 Woodcock Boulevard, Suite 303
Atlanta, GA 30341
Ph: (770) 458-3811 Fax: (770) 458-8516
E-mail: pmcconnon@cste.org
Founded: 1992

International Epidemiological Association (IEA)
1500 Sunday Drive, Suite 102
Raleigh, NC 27607
E-mail: nshore@firstpointresources.com
Founded: 1954

International Society for Environmental Epidemiology
44 Farnsworth Street
Boston, MA 02210
Ph: (617) 482-9485 Fax: (617) 482-0617
E-mail: peters@helmholtz-muenchen.de
Founded: 1987

National Foundation for Infectious Diseases (NFID)
4733 Bethesda Avenue, Suite 750
Bethesda, Maryland 20814
Ph: (301) 656-0003 Fax: (301) 907-0878
E-mail: info@nfid.org
Founded: 1950

Society for Epidemiological Research (SER)
PO Box 990
Clearfield, UT 84098
Ph: (801) 525-0231 Fax: (801) 774-9211
E-mail: membership@epiresearch.org
Founded: 1967

Society for Healthcare Epidemiology of America (SHEA)
1300 Wilson Boulevard, Suite 300
Arlington, VA 22209
Ph: (703) 684-1006 Fax: (703) 684-1009
E-mail: info@shea-online.org
Founded: 1980

VI

Selected Answers to Chapter Questions

CHAPTER 1

2. As many infectious diseases have been controlled in modern times, life expectancy has increased, and noninfectious diseases and conditions have become the primary causes of death in the United States (see Table 1-2). The study of epidemiology includes communicable diseases, noncommunicable diseases, injuries, trauma, mental disorders, birth defects, maternal-child health, occupational health, environmental health, and behaviors related to health (e.g., nutrition, exercise, and seat belt use).

4. Refer to Table 1-1.

6. Persons aged less than four years and more than 80 years are the most vulnerable to falls. Persons more than 60 years of age accounted for 44% of the total emergency calls caused by nonindustrial falls. Susceptibility to falls is related to development in young children and general health and strength.

8. The epidemiologic triangle is based on the communicable disease model. It shows the interaction and interdependence of the agent, host, environment, and time. The advanced epidemiologic triangle expands the agent to more than just biologic agents to include physical stressors, chemicals, and psychosocial influences. The host is expanded to groups or populations and their characteristics. The environment refers to behaviors, cultures, ecologic elements, and psychological factors. With chronic disease, the time element associating the dimensions of the triangle may involve several years.

10. By identifying high-risk behaviors, who in a community participates in such behaviors, where these people are located, and whether existing programs are available or need to be developed to reach these people, effective public health prevention and control efforts can be made. Dissemination of risk factor information to the public provides a basis for informed individual decision making.

CHAPTER 2

1. F, G, H, O, J, V, A, P, T, S, N, D, U, I, E, B, C, M, L, Q, R, K
3. John Graunt, William Farr
5. Case-control and cohort

CHAPTER 3

2. Congenital and hereditary diseases, allergies and inflammatory diseases, degenerative diseases, metabolic diseases, and cancer. Refer to the section entitled "Classification of Diseases."
4. Microbe sources (Table 3-4), animal sources (Table 3-5), and inanimate sources (Table 3-6).
6. Refer to Table 3-7.
8. If a sufficient proportion of a group of people are immune from contracting an illness, then there is almost no chance of a major epidemic occurring.
10. Except for asthma, breathing problems, and speech problems, the chronic conditions listed in the figure increase with age. Asthma and breathing problems are most common in children under five years of age. Speech problems are greatest in children ages five to 11 years, followed by children under five years of age. Attention deficit/hyperactive disorder and learning disabilities are the leading problems in children 12 to 17 years of age.

CHAPTER 4

1. Nominal
3. Yes. Some of the difference in rates described for the previous problem may be due to differences in the age distribution among racial groups in the different areas.
5. Breast cancer is more common in older ages. When we adjust for differences in the age distribution, the rates continue to be highest in white women and lowest among women in the other racial group. The age-adjusted rate is 4% greater in whites than blacks and 34% greater in whites than women in the other racial group.
7. White women with breast cancer tend to have the disease diagnosed at an older age.

Age	White		Black		Other	
	Cases	Relative Frequency	Cases	Relative Frequency	Cases	Relative Frequency
< 50	7,420,076	0.6646	3,344,874	0.7559	1,586,388	0.7206
50–54	830,549	0.0744	293,626	0.0664	148,548	0.0675
55–59	736,737	0.0660	244,829	0.0553	131,258	0.0596
60–64	567,178	0.0508	162,834	0.0368	89,008	0.0404
65–69	400,785	0.0359	111,761	0.0253	69,068	0.0314
70+	1,210,138	0.1084	266,941	0.0603	177,188	0.0805
		1.0000		1.0000		1.0000

The largest percentage of cases is in the 70 and older group for whites but in the less than 50-year-old group for black and other racial groups. This may be because white women have a higher life expectancy such that they are more likely to live to age 70 years and older.

9. Whites: 146.8 (95% CI = 144.6−149.1); Blacks: 109.5 (95% CI = 106.4−112.5); Other: 94.0 (95% CI 90.0−98.1).

11. The *SMR* is 0.98 for blacks. Hence, 2% fewer first primary female malignant breast cancer cases in blacks were observed than expected had they experienced the same age-specific rates as white females.

13. The incidence rate is a measure of risk, whereas the point prevalence proportion is a measure of burden. Incidence reflects the occurrence of new cases over a specified time period whereas point prevalence proportion reflects the magnitude of a public health problem at a point in time. Prevalence is often used when it is difficult to identify when someone became a case, such as for arthritis or type II diabetes.

15. Disease A has better survival (lower mortality).

17. $70/390 \times 100 = 17.9$

19. The correlation coefficient indicates the strength of the linear association between exercise and pulse. As exercise goes up, pulse goes down. Nine percent of the variation in pulse (per minute) is explained by exercise (in hours per week).

21. Perform the analysis in stratified age groups or simply add age to a multiple regression model or a multiple logistic regression model.

CHAPTER 5

1. For example, diseases of the heart are 1.5 times higher in men. Estrogen in women has been shown to be protective against heart disease. Differences between sexes may also be influenced by differences in risk factors such as smoking, blood cholesterol, blood pressure, and physical activity.

3. Afghanistan is 84; the United States is 50.

5. The decline in deaths for those in later birth cohorts may be because of decreasing involvement in crime among these black males. Alternatively, police interaction with these individuals may have changed because of police training and behaviors.

7. Higher education is associated with higher income and medical insurance.

CHAPTER 6

2. a. 903 per 100,000
   b. 152 per 100,000
   c. 27 per 1,000
   d. 1 per 1,000
   e. 20 per 1,000
   f. 83 per 1,000
   g. 1,927 per 100,000

   h. 83 per 100,000

   i. 35 per 100,000

   j. 5.2%

   k. 2.4 per 1,000

4. Desert City is 8%; Sun City is 5%.

6. 21.2 per 100,000 for whites and 9.1 per 100,000 for blacks.

8. Age group 20–24 for both white and black males.

	White		Black	
0–4	0	489,373	0	47,928
5–9	0	489,373	0	47,928
10–14	6,195	489,373	1,050	47,928
15–19	49,875	483,178	7,410	46,878
20–24	80,283	433,303	11,433	39,468
25–29	70,163	353,020	8,475	28,035
30–34	58,208	282,858	6,403	19,560
35–39	59,868	224,650	4,538	13,158
40–44	55,305	164,783	3,645	8,620
45–49	52,220	109,478	2,643	4,975
50–54	35,575	57,258	1,538	2,333
55–59	17,475	21,683	653	795
60–64	4,208	4,208	143	143

10. For all ages through 64 years, the YPLL rate was 457 for white males and 265 for black males, per 100,000.

12. The YPLL rate allows us to make more meaningful comparisons because the size of the population is taken into account.

CHAPTER 7

1. Researchers do not manipulate the exposure in an observational analytic study. Examples of observational analytic studies designs are case-control, cohort, and case-crossover. In these studies the investigator merely observes and evaluates associations between exposure and outcome variables. On the other hand, in an experimental study, the researchers assign or influence the level of exposure.

3. Establish the diagnostic criteria and definition of disease, select cases, and controls, and ascertain exposure status while controlling for bias.

5. At the design level, selection bias can be minimized by considering incident rather than prevalent cases, and general population controls can be selected. Observation bias can be controlled by blinding subjects, interviewers, and persons assessing the data. Confounding can be minimized by restriction and matching. Also, confounding can be controlled for at the analysis level through stratification or multiple regression analysis.

7. General population controls represent the population from which cases were selected. However, they are more costly and involve more time to collect than hospital controls. In addition, population lists may not be available, and it may be difficult for healthy people to participate with their busy schedules. Controls from the general population may also have poorer recall and less motivation to participate than controls from the hospital.

Special groups are healthier than hospital controls, more likely to cooperate than general population controls, and provide more control of possible confounding factors. However, if the exposure is similar to that experienced by the cases, an underestimation of the true association would result.

Case-control studies can be relatively small and inexpensive, require relatively little time, and are useful for studying rare outcomes. They yield an odds ratio, which has nice statistical properties. They may, however, be problematic in establishing a sequence of events. There is also potential for bias in measuring risk factors. They are limited to a single outcome variable. They do not yield prevalence, incidence, or excess risk and are prone to selection and observation bias.

9. Selection bias caused by healthy worker effect or loss to follow-up; confounding.

11. Prospective cohort study. A retrospective cohort study may also be possible, depending on available hospital records.

13.

	Coffee	No Coffee
Smoking	120	30
No Smoking	30	120

$$OR = \frac{120 \times 120}{30 \times 30} = 16$$

	MI	No MI
Smoking	100	50
No Smoking	50	100

$$OR = \frac{100 \times 100}{50 \times 50} = 4$$

15. D, C, A, B

CHAPTER 8

2. Convenience sample.

4. Eliminates conscious bias caused by physician or patient selection, averages out unconscious bias caused by unknown factors, and makes groups alike on average.

6. A, B, E, D, C

8. Factorial design

10. Run-in design

12. B, C, A, A, B

CHAPTER 9

2. C, B, A

4. Step 1: Academic performance in college is not associated with obesity 10 years after graduation. This is expressed in statistical terms as $H_0 : RR = 1$.

   Step 2: Academic performance in college is associated with obesity 10 years after graduation. This is expressed in statistical terms as $H_1 : RR \neq 1$.

   Step 3: For this test, we use $\alpha = 0.05$. The sample size is large enough that chance is not likely to be a problem.

   Step 4: $DF = 1$. The critical value for 1 degree of freedom and α of 0.05 is 3.84.

   Step 5: Chi-square = 4.51 and the corresponding P value is 0.0336. $RR = 1.50$.

   Step 6: Reject the null hypothesis because the observed value of χ^2 is greater than the critical value of 3.84. Interpretation: those performing better academically in college are 1.5 times (or 50%) more likely to be obese 10 years after graduation.

6. Direct causal association involves a causal pathway with no intervening factors (e.g., an automobile accident and paralysis). Indirect causal association involves a causal pathway with intervening factors (e.g., poor diet resulting in high cholesterol and high cholesterol resulting in arteriosclerosis).

8. ■ Samples can be studied more quickly than large populations.

   ■ Studying a sample is often less expensive than studying an entire population.

   ■ Studying the entire population may be impossible.

   ■ Sample results can be more accurate than results based on populations since for samples, more time and resources can be spent on training the people who observe and collect the data and on procedures that improve accuracy.

   ■ Samples of the population with specific characteristics may be more appropriate for studying a certain health-related state or event than the entire population.

10. C

CHAPTER 10

1. E

3. Attack rate

5. Conduct a literature review to better understand the public health problem; communicate with experts on the topic; organize the appropriate investigative team; identify the specific roles of the team members; make travel and financial arrangements; contact appropriate people in the field prior to departure.

7. Disease frequency data should be combined with the at-risk population from which the cases derived in order to calculate attack rates.

9. A

11. Stage II

13. Post hoc hypotheses and boundary shrinkage.

15. A, C, C, B, A, D

CHAPTER 11

2. Physical, chemical, biological, and psychosocial environments, as well as behavioral and inherent risk factors are involved in chronic disease epidemiology.

4. Most adverse health conditions associated with smoking occur later in life. Hence, a young person may begin smoking because they do not feel susceptible to a disease that may only occur in the distant future. The perceived severity is likewise difficult to comprehend, whereas perceived benefits may be clear (e.g., feel more accepted among selected peer groups, feel greater independence, and more like an adult). Barriers may exist, however, in the form of high cost and accessibility to tobacco products. A school health counselor may try to discourage a student from smoking by providing steps on how to stop smoking, support mechanisms, and encouragement. Counsel and education may influence the person's confidence (self-efficacy) in being able to stop smoking.

6. The three basic pathways people may be exposed to radiation are: inhalation (breathing radioactive materials into the lungs), ingestion (swallowing radioactive material), and direct (external) exposure.

8. Absorption involves entrance of the substance into the body. An ingested or inhaled substance is considered outside the body until it crosses cellular barriers in the gastrointestinal tract or lungs. Absorption can also be through the skin, implants, conjuctival instillations (eye drops), and suppositories. Hence, there is a distinction between the exposure dose (outside dose) and the absorbed dose (internal dose). For a substance to enter the body, cell membranes (cell walls) must be penetrated. Cell membranes are designed to prevent foreign invaders or substances from entering into bodily tissue.

Distribution involves movement of the substance from where it enters the body to other sites in the body (e.g., liver, blood and lymph circulation, kidney, lung). After a substance passes the lining of the skin, lung, or gastrointestinal tract, it enters the fluid surrounding the cells of that organ (interstitial fluid) versus fluid inside the cells (intracellular fluid). Interstitial fluid represents about 15% of body weight and intracellular fluid about 40% of body weight. A toxicant can leave the interstitial fluid in three ways: entering cells of local tissue, entering blood capillaries and the body's blood circulatory system, and entering the lymphatic system. Once in the circulatory system, a chemical can be excreted, stored, biotransformed into metabolites, its metabolites excreted or stored, or its metabolites interact or bind with cellular components.

Biotransformation involves transformation produced by the body of the substance into new chemicals (metabolites). Biotransformation is essential to survival. It is the process by which absorbed nutrients (food, oxygen, etc.) are transformed into substances required by the body to function normally. The body is efficient at biotransforming body wastes or chemicals that are not normally produced or expected into water-soluble metabolites excreted into bile and excreted from the body. Biotransformation may result in detoxification or make a substance more toxic (bioactiviation).

Excretion involves ejection of the substance or metabolites from the body. Toxicants or their metabolites may be passed from the body through feces, urine, or expired air.

10.

Virus/Bacteria	Type of Cancer
Human Papillomavirus (HPV)	Cancers of the cervix, anus, vagina, vulva, penis, orophyrnx
Helicobacter pylori bacterium	Stomach cancer
Kaposi's sarcoma-associated Herpes virus	Kaposi's sarcoma
Hepatitis B and C viruses	Liver cancer
Epstein-Barr virus	Burkitt's lymphoma
Human T-cell lymphotrophic virus	Adult T-cell leukemia

CHAPTER 12

1. It tends to balance out the effect of potential confounding factors between intervention and control groups, assuming the sample size is sufficiently large.

3. C, D, B, A

5. The case fatality rate should be measured over a fixed, specified time period. Historically, this measure has been used with acute infectious illnesses that progress toward recovery or death over a short time period; that is, this is an appropriate measure of the deaths that result if they occur in a short time period from disease onset and the deaths are a result of the disease.

Index